Land

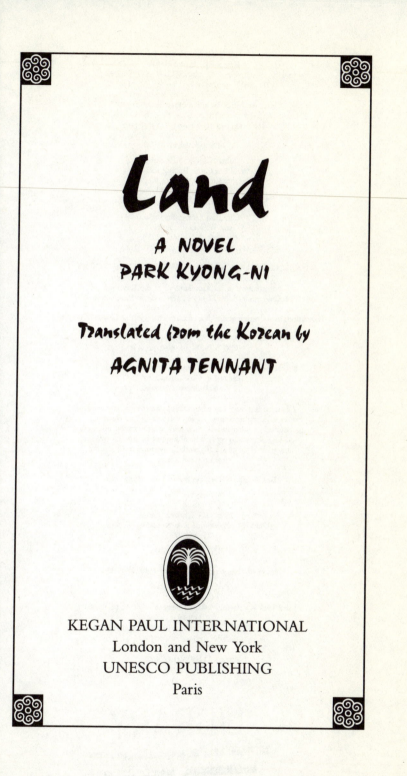

Land

A NOVEL
PARK KYONG-NI

Translated from the Korean by

AGNITA TENNANT

KEGAN PAUL INTERNATIONAL
London and New York
UNESCO PUBLISHING
Paris

First published in 1996 by
Kegan Paul International
UK: P.O. Box 256, London WC1B 3SW, England
Tel: (0171) 580 5511 Fax: (0171) 436 0899
E-mail: books@keganpau.demon.co.uk
Internet: http:/www.demon.co.uk/keganpaul/
USA: 562 West 113th Street, New York, NY 10025, USA
Tel: (212) 666 1000 Fax: (212) 316 3100

Distributed by

John Wiley & Sons Ltd
Southern Cross Trading Estate
1 Oldlands Way, Bognor Regis
West Sussex PO22 9SA, England
Tel: (01243) 779 777 Fax: (01243) 820 250

Columbia University Press
562 West 113th Street
New York, NY 10025, USA
Tel: (212) 666 1000 Fax: (212) 316 3100

UNESCO COLLECTION OF REPRESENTATIVE WORKS
The publication of this work was assisted by a
contribution of the Government of the Republic
of Korea under UNESCO's Funds-in-Trust Programme

Translation, introduction and index of main characters © UNESCO, 1996

KEGAN PAUL INTERNATIONAL ISBN 0–7103–0508–7
UNESCO ISBN 92–3–103251–8

Phototypeset in 11 on 13 pt Bembo by Intype London Ltd
Printed in Great Britain by
TJ Press, Padstow, Cornwall

British Library Cataloguing in Publication Data

Kyong-Ni, Park
Land
I. Title   II. Tennant, Agnita
(Unesco Collection of Representative Works)
895.734 [F]

ISBN 0–7103–0508–7

Library of Congress Cataloging-in-Publication Data

Pak, Kyŏng-ni, 1926–
[T'ogi. English]
Land/Park Kyong-ni; translated from the Korean by Agnita
Tennant.
p.   cm. UNESCO Collection of representative works
ISBN 0–7103–0508–7
I. Title.
PL992.62.K9T6313   1995
895.7'34–dc20   95–15879
                                      CIP

LAND

Acclaimed as the most powerful and important piece of modern Korean writing, the epic sweep of *Land* is breathtaking in its conception and execution. Set against the background of the struggle between conservative and modernizing forces at the turn of the century, it follows the fortunes of several generations of Korean villagers during a time of unsurpassed turbulence and change. To Korean readers, upon whose imagination *Land* has an unparalleled hold, and for whom the characters and village itself have a palpable reality, it is the great national novel – the work that embodies the many elements that make up the Korea and the Koreans of today. Carrying on over forty years, the saga evokes the nation's past, with all its unresolved conflicts, hereditary sorrows and regrets, and is a unique study of the interaction of character, heredity, environment, and history.

Beginning with the celebration of the Harvest Moon Festival in the village in 1897, the plot revolves around the household of Choi Chisoo, a rich landowner, who, though envied by many for his wealth, is embittered by the fact that his wife has not borne him a son. Characters emerge upon whom the rest of the story devolves, and who will remain in the reader's memory – the magnificent Lady Yoon with her prophetic wisdom; the willful Sohi, daughter of Choi Chisoo; the tender-hearted Wolsun, accepting as her due the ignominy of life as a shaman's daughter; and many others, displaying every aspect of the human capacity for virtue or vice, treachery or truth. In the theatre of history that is modern Korea, the author Park Kyong-ni has examined every element that has shaped national events and the consciousness of the people to produce a magnificent work that is a monumental achievement in the literature of Korea, and of the world at large. Here, in one book, is the heart and soul of Korea.

THE AUTHOR

Park Kyong-ni, one of Korea's most important authors, was born in 1926 in Chungmoo, on the southern coast, and educated at Jinjoo Girls' High School. She started writing in the 1950s as her country struggled to recover from the devastation of the Korean War. Since then she has published many short stories and essays and a number of novels. Her major works include *A Floating Island* (1959), *The Daughters of the Apothecary Kim* (1962), and *The Marketplace and the Battlefield* (1964). This is the early part of her greatest achievement, the novel *Land*, completed in 1994, on which she spent some twenty-five years. In this work, Park brought to a culmination the themes that she had been exploring in her earlier books, such as women's sorrows, love, human dignity and the conflict between traditional values and those of the new age.

Index of Main Characters

Kuchon	(Hwani) Half-brother of Choi Chisoo
Lady Yoon	Mother of Choi Chisoo and of Kuchon, grandmother of Sohi, runs the Choi household
Magdal *ne*	Villager, widow
Pyongsan	Villager, declined aristocrat, husband of Haman *dek*
Samsoo	Servant of the Choi household
Samwol	Maidservant of the Choi household
Sohi	Daughter of Choi Chisoo and the lady of the *byoldang*
Soodong	Servant of Choi Chisoo
Wolsun	Daughter of a shaman, runs a tavern in the town, lover of Yongi
Yi Pongi	Villager, father of Dooman
Yimi	Daughter of Chilsung
Yongi	Villager, husband of Kangchon *dek*, lover of Wolsun
Yongpari	Villager
Yoon Bo	Village carpenter, friend of Kang *posoo*

Chapter One

1897 *Chusok*, the festival of the harvest moon. Even before the magpies had come to the persimmon tree in the garden to give their morning greeting, the children in their colourful clothes, with ribbons in their plaits were scurrying through the alleys of the village, pine cakes in their mouths, and jumping with glee. For the grown-ups, it would already be mid-morning before they had offered the ancestral sacrifices and visited the family graves, and by the time they had shared food with their neighbours the day would be half over. From then on they would gather in the threshing yard and the excitement would grow.

The women folk were bound to fall behind the men and the old people in getting themselves ready, for they had to wait on the family and deal with the food before they could begin to think about their own embellishment. Meanwhile, out in the fields where the heavy heads of grain made golden waves, the flocks of birds, feeling unrestrained, were having themselves a banquet.

'Shoo! You wicked birds!'

The old crone who had been frantically scaring them away, having changed into crisply starched clothes, would now be watching the scene in the threshing yard.

Chusok seemed to be a day of festivity and gluttony not only for the people of the village, men and women, young and old, but also for the dogs, the pigs, the horses, the oxen and even for the rats that popped in and out of the drains.

In the *sarang* of the Choi *champan* house, the sound of the brass gongs from the distant threshing yard – the quick rhythm of the *kwangari* and the slow heavy beat of the *jing* – came mournfully, like the sound of sobbing. The peasant farmers stood shaking hats decked with flowers, their spirits rising as, absorbed in the dance, they forgot the pain and sadness of daily life.

I

Money and grain had been distributed generously from the Choi *champan* house, for although it was not a bumper harvest, it was well up to average. For once whole families could loosen their belts, pat stomachs that were full of white rice, and for a while forget their worries. Today, even if the children broke stalks of millet they would not be punished. Old people, satisfying their hunger after months of craving for meat, now trudged to and from the privy.

The strong young men of the neighbourhood had already deserted the village for the town, gone off in a crowd to the wrestling competition, with hopes of returning with the top prize of an ox. The house appeared deserted. The sun shone brightly in the yard. But where were the people? The newly pasted paper on the doors made everything look unfamiliar. In the threshing yard, for a time, the festivity seemed to have ceased until suddenly, as if seized with convulsions, the gongs rang out. Faster, higher, led by the *kwangari*, the sound of the *jing* quickened also.

'*Gai-geng, gai-ai-geng, Dumm-mm-mn Gai-geng, gai-ai-geng, Dum-mm-mn*' rang the gongs and threading between them came the sound of the drums. The stirring sounds of percussion seemed to set the blue sky revolving, and the trees in their autumn colours started to dance animatedly.

With eyes like the crescent moon, even when he was not smiling, Suh Keum Dol would be out in front, leading the players. Despite the lines on his face of a man approaching fifty, he seemed to have regained the youthfulness of sixteen. His body had aged, but not his elegant voice, which soared above the undulations of the melody, and with all the performer's inborn ability to make his audience laugh or weep, he could still capture their hearts. Even now, widows, spellbound by his plaintive song, cast amorous glances.

'When I think that that wonderful voice will some day rot in the ground.'

'When he's gone, how we'll miss those funeral songs!'

'Hush, his wife might hear you. She'd have a fit if she did.'

'How is it that with all he has to offer, he thinks of no one but his own wife – isn't it strange?'

'Why would anyone take that much care of an ancestral tablet? I suppose it must be a bond ordained by heaven.'

'For a man, never to have known any other woman cannot be normal. There must be something wrong with him, don't you think?'

So the women of the village would talk.

Yoon Bo, known as 'widower' (though never actually married, maybe because of his pockmarked face), carpenter by profession and fisherman on the Sumjin River, interrupted them: 'Listen to me all of you! Don't they say that even with love you have to give to receive?'

'What did you say? Talking in your sleep . . .'.

'It's not right to be doing this ritual only on the threshing floor. Let's go to the river and perform it there as well.'

'Whatever for?'

'Don't you think we'd better warm up the heart of the Dragon King? That's the way to make the fish plentiful.'

'Fresh-water fish that can't be used as an offering – what good are they? Let's go to Dangsan Hill!'

While others argued noisily for or against, Dooman's father just continued steadily to beat the large gong.

Bong-gi as he shook his pointed hat would grin broadly, embarrassed at being watched by the crowd of women. These were men in their mid-thirties, in their working prime, and established with families.

Of a slightly younger set was Yongi, smiling gently as he struck a drum slung over his shoulder with a piece of white hemp, holding his tall body gracefully as he circled. Whoever you like to mention, he was the one with the finest build and the best looks and as he beat the long drum his smile melted the lump in your heart.

While Chilsung struck his drum, '*Du-dong! Du-dong!*'

Yongpari, slim and graceful, danced with a measured surge of energy. The wives peering between the old people and the children, sniffed with a mixture of embarrassment and pride at the antics of their husbands. When they had run through the whole repertoire on the threshing floor, the farmers, feeling a little hungry, would not go to the river or to Dangsan, but weave through the village alleys until they were pushing into the yard of a house with a big gate, where they would make an offering to the god of the site and

3

then wiping their sweat with rake-like hands, set about the food and drink.

The Harvest Moon Festival of the eighth lunar month – doesn't it have something of the translucent and frosty pathos of the finest hemp? How can a festival associated with the moon, which crosses the river of darkness like a shadow of death, be regarded as a symbol of abundance? As it hangs coolly over the ridge of the mountain the twigs of trees cast lacy shadows and a young widow clad in white silk walks the night road alone. Isn't the harvest moon of the eighth month perhaps a festival that celebrates the closing of a sorrowful life, that resembles the pathos of hemp, revealing the art of renunciation to all living things, and especially to the poor? Over the autumn landscape rolls the dead fruit that has ripened and fallen, leaving its seed scattered here, there and everywhere. The cool wind, after circling as if to examine the solemn and desolate carcasses, is soon catching people's hearts and touching the strings of plaintive memories.

This is when they reflect on their many separations: elderly parents who perished in years of bad harvest, unable to keep alive on grass roots and bark; children in epidemics, left to die without medication, rolled up in a straw mat and buried in the nearby hills; a husband during the uprising dragged into the governor's house and beaten to a resentful death; and those many neighbours now asleep underneath the earth. The breeze plays gently on the strings of these sorrowful memories.

'Perhaps they are better off in the other world?'

There are those who take comfort from the ripening grain, but there are other hearts into which these ripening fields hammer nails, because of those who perished through poverty and hunger.

'If only it had been like this, we could have managed to eat . . .'.

After this festival, bountiful and boisterous, yet desolate and sad, like fine hemp, the great empty fields that stretch from the hills to the far distant horizon will lie bare under the glow of the sky. The thickets on the mound behind the village and on the peak that stands out lonely above it will turn yellowish and wither. Over the memorials set up for this, that, or the other reason, over the mossy monument in honour of a virtuous widow, over the one or two

4

zinnias by the spirit post, the cold dry wind will blow. After that one will hear the sounds of the approaching winter's long nights.

When the sun had disappeared behind the western hills the gongs, heard from the far end of the village, sounded even more like sobbing. It looked as though they were set to go all through the night. Indeed, only now with the rising of the moon, were the village maidens about to begin their celebrations as they gathered by the sandy shore of the river and listened to the lapping of the water.

The maidservant Guinyo stood outside the room and asked, 'Shall I bring in your supper, sir?'

It was the second time she had called. There was no reply.

'Allow me to light the lamp, sir.'

She opened the door and went in. Choi Chisoo, present master of the Choi *champan* house, did not raise his eyes from his book. An evening glow like the colour of aged paper flowed into the room. The light of the lamp flickered and brightened. Had he really been reading in that dusky gloom? A golden thread of light slid down the ridge of his nose, sharp on his downturned face. Seen from the side, it seemed to be filled with all the nervous tension and distress of the world, and the whole room was charged with a dangerous atmosphere, as if at any moment he might suddenly spring up with glaring eyes and scream.

'Just spread the bedding.'

'Yes, sir.'

He did not give her even a glance, but Guinyo smiled with her eyes and pursed her full lips. A man of delicate health, it seemed that he had been exhausted by the irksome household events connected with the festival.

'Aren't you going to eat anything, sir?'

After spreading out the bedding at the warm end of the room, she waited for an answer to her inquiry, but had to leave without one. She crossed the wooden-floored hall and walked through the room on the opposite side into a small backroom, where she took from her bosom a tiny mirror and studied her face, just as she had before going in to see her master. When she had patted her hair, and once more looked into her own very dark eyes, she put the mirror back. Faint light still penetrated the paper-covered door that gave on to the backyard. She opened it, and was about to slip her feet into the shoes left on the shoe-stone, when she paused to stare across to the other side. The backyard of the *sarang* was surrounded by a low hedge of hardy orange trees, and beyond it was a bamboo grove which backed on to the tiled house occupied by Kim *subang* and his wife, who were responsible for all the affairs of the estate, both house and land. Between the hedge and the tiled house was a vegetable patch across which she spotted Kuchon passing. Her cold eyes followed his profile and as she turned her gaze away, it was with a faint smile like the slither of a whip snake's tail. Slipping her feet into the shoes, and hitching up her long skirt, she went round the corner of the *sarang* towards the inner part of the house.

The field of vegetables had begun to blur in the enveloping dusk and Mrs Kim, sloppily dressed, bustled in and out of the kitchen. It was time for the hens to be in their coop but they were still pecking at the cabbages. Walking slowly, his eyes fixed on the ground, Kuchon went on as far as the pavilion on Dangsan Hill. He stood in front of it for a long time and then after slowly mounting the steps he sat sideways on the rail. Was he waiting for the moon to rise? No lights showed yet in the village but the hexagonal lamp hung on a column of the Choi house gave out a milky glow.

Soon the moon would rise. It would shine on the lily pond, covered with fallen leaves, in the *byoldang*, the young mistress' quarters, on the softness of thatched roofs where lay globular gourds, on the lonely path through the pine woods, white like the parting in a girl's hair. All earthly creatures dream of, chase after, and seek to embrace the pale heavenly beauty of the moon, but she is a stone maiden devoid of the warmth of life, a sad and solitary traveller through the vale of death, crossing the river of darkness.

Kuchon half-closed his eyes and looked down on the village. At the last full moon of the first month, the people had built on Dangsan a moon house.

'Yoo – hoo – the moon is out!'

The children had yelled looking up at it, and the dogs had followed suit by barking. Each cherishing a wish in his heart, they had gathered round the moon house, and set fire to it. As the flames flared upwards, the women, palms together had bowed again and again. The men's faces had glowed red in the light of the fire, and their eyes flashed, as dark as charcoal. When this simple-hearted and devout expression of their wishes was ended, the village people began to chatter like a market-day crowd. The men took out their pipes, while the women blew noses made shiny by the fire and wiped them with the hem of their skirts, greeting each other again. They exchanged news of relatives, told how a cow had been mated, how the steaming of rice-cakes had gone wrong, or of worries about a shroud for an elderly parent. At last the moon house collapsed in the flames and then, where it had fallen, even the flames died, until only a curtain of silvery light stretched endlessly in all directions and, like shadows playing within it, they had scattered and gone their ways. The moon rose. Its face shone down from the ridge around which the curve of the river wound away. The dark outlines of trembling leaves could be seen more clearly, and the smooth bark of the branches showed up as grey, and then brown. The sobbing of *kwangari* and *jing* could be heard from far away, and, a little nearer, the singing of the girls by the riverside.

The moon lifted itself off the mountain ridge. It was still red, but would soon grow pale. The Sumjin River flashed white, with the Province of Cholla on the far side, and that of Kyong Sang on this, the gentle curves of the ridge line being clearly visible. As Kuchon sat sideways on the rail of the pavilion watching the spectacle of the rising moon, his eyes flashed and sparkled. Was it moonlight, or tears, or if not, some tragic yearning?

Chapter Two

KIM *SUBANG* was arguing loudly: 'Every year it is exactly the same, the same people causing all the trouble!'

'Would anyone choose to cause trouble?'

'Shut up! The ox died. . . I couldn't work because I broke my leg . . . My daughter's wedding got me into debt. What's the next excuse going to be?'

Knowing him to be quite harmless, the other mumbled, 'If I am just making up excuses, may I be struck by lightning. I wish you wouldn't talk about things you know nothing about.'

'We can't go on like this. We can't. Like a tree between two walls – what am I supposed to do?'

It seemed that after dealing with these tenants, each with a different reason for demanding sympathy, even the mild Kim *subang* was growing irritable. For several days now the Choi household, inside and out, had been bustling with activity. Into the line of storerooms went an endless succession of sacks of rice and the work of transporting them into town·had exhausted the servants. Even the strong horses from the stables and the plump oxen from the barns were almost worn out. The servants' quarters, in their own way, were just as busy, swarming with tenants and stewards assembled from near and far. And to keep them all fed, great iron pots had to be constantly boiling rice and giving it out.

'Look here! Now just listen to me.'

'Whether I listen or not, it's quite plain, isn't it? It's obviously not enough – there is no doubt about that.'

'Isn't that just what I was going to explain?'

'Say it a thousand times, and it's the same thing.'

'This is hopeless! To make sure that not one bit of gravel got in there we opened our eyes as wide as owls.'

'What's the use of opening them wide, if you can't see with them?'

'So you mean to say that we put chaff in? There's no earthly reason why it should be short.'

The arguments going on outside the wall were in voices blurred by a few bowls of rice wine.

'Bongsoon. Ha-ha-ha. Here I am!'

A small girl creeping on tip-toe behind the legs of Kuchon, busy carrying in sacks of rice, put out her face. She had a tiny, charming face and was five years old. Whatever might come in the future, for the present she was the one and only heir of Choi Chisoo. Her name was Sohi. It was said that she resembled her mother, the mistress of the *byoldang*, but she also took after her grandmother. Her inability to be quiet was put down to her age, and her high spirits to her grandmother. Bongsoon, who had been searching everywhere, was about to cross over to her but she twisted round and ran in front of Kuchon, squealing with laughter.

'I told you, Miss, you'll be in trouble if you fall over.'

Bongsoon looked ready to cry, but like a fledgling that has begun to stretch its wings, Sohi ran here and there, and was not to be caught. Her feet, in tiny green shoes with maroon trimmings were very agile.

'Please, Miss!'

Using Kuchon's legs as a shield she once again hid behind them, just to tease Bongsoon, who was in a flutter lest her charge might be knocked over by the workers' feet and fearful that they might be found in this state by her ladyship. Then Kuchon stopped what he was doing.

'You must stop this, Miss.'

'I'm not going to fall over.'

She jumped up and tugged spitefully at the tail of his sweat-soaked shirt.

'Please stop it.'

Rebuking her quietly, he turned, still with the sack of rice on his back, and said,

'Bongsoon, take her to the *byoldang* . . .'. He paused and then completed the sentence, 'To the *byoldang* and play there.'

Sohi, pulling at the tail of his skirt, hindered him from going one way or the other.

'Miss, let's go and play with the doll's tea-set,' coaxed Bongsoon, taking her hand, but she shook it off.

'I want to play here!'

'If you get in the way you'll be knocked over.'

Kuchon's voice was still quiet.

'Don't want to. I won't go.'

'If her ladyship sees you, you'll be scolded.'

'I'm not scared of granny!'

She had let go of Kuchon's shirt tail and looked straight at him, insistent. But then, as if she really did fear her grandmother, she ran off, calling him names: 'Kuchon's a fool – an idiot – an ugly monk!'

Bongsoon ran after her. The red ribbons in their hair dangling below the hems of their jackets flapped as they ran, and then they disappeared from sight. Beneath the sack of rice, Kuchon stared vacantly at their backs and moved towards the storeroom.

With a grunt from the effort, he dropped the sack to the floor. Samsoo, who with Dori was grabbing the bags and stacking them, thrust his hook into it and said, 'A big man like you knocked out by the weight of one sack – what's the matter?'

'Wipe your face,' added Dori, pityingly.

Kuchon lifted the sleeve of his shirt, matted with straw, and mopped his brow. His face was pale and his eyes sunk deep. Samsoo had already put the hook in the sack but as Dori was only staring in bewilderment at Kuchon wiping himself, he blew his nose loudly, and rubbing his snot-smeared hand on his clothes, he said, 'If you go on like this, you'll make yourself ill.'

Still wiping himself, Kuchon stared blankly at him as he continued, 'Whatever it is you are up to, we'd like to know about it.'

Kuchon stood with a vague expression as if hearing some far off sound, and then his eyes flashed wildly. Samsoo said nothing further. Dori did not speak either. They raised the bag of rice. After that they talked about the weather, about how the wen on the face of Pak *subang* who brought rice from Boochon had this year grown even bigger, and so on, Dori trying even harder than his companion to put on an air of indifference. Watching Kuchon's expression out of the corner of his eye, Samsoo said, 'Hurry up and get some more. Nothing's going to stop the sun from going down.'

Kuchon picked up the sacking that he used to protect his back, flung it over his shoulder, and with his long arms dangling, turned to go.

'No, I don't like him. I don't like my father.'

Sohi stamped her feet repeatedly while the seamstress, Bongsoon *ne* (Bongsoon's mother) coaxing her, re-tied the ribbon on the front of her jacket. Kuchon lowered his gaze as he passed.

'But her ladyship said so. You must go and offer greetings to the Master.'

Approaching middle age, Bongsoon *ne* had a pale complexion, and was on the plump side. Sohi caught hold of her skirt and said, 'I want to go to Dooman's house to see the puppy.'

'If her ladyship knows, there will be trouble. You will be scolded. Bongsoon, take the young lady to the Master's room at once.'

She patted her on the back as she spoke to her daughter.

'I told you, I hate my father. He keeps going "A-hem! A-hem!" '

She stretched her neck and imitated her father's cough. Repressing a smile, Bongsoon's mother said, 'That's an awful thing to say. Bongsoon, off you go!'

'Let's go then, Miss.'

Bongsoon spoke resignedly, as if she also disliked going.

'All right, then, I'll go with you right up to the yard of the *sarang*.'

Bongsoon *ne* urged them from behind as if they were chickens. Very slowly and reluctantly Sohi moved forward.

'You will go now, Miss?'

As she nodded her head and looked up, her eyes were filled with fear. In the front yard of the *sarang* the sun was shining splendidly. The plum tree as high as the ridge tiles on the garden wall, the magnolia spreading its smooth grey branches, the pomegranate and the cape jasmine all looked as if they were resting languidly in the sunshine of a spring day, but the sap had already stopped circulating and not many withered leaves were left. The plantain also, though it had been trimmed, seemed to be yellowing. The two children, who had been nervously looking at each other and holding sweating hands, finally made up their minds and walked up to the door of Chisoo's room. Bongsoon cleared her throat and called, 'Master, the young lady has come to inquire after your health. Her ladyship told her to offer you greetings.'

She must have rolled the words round inside her mouth many times, for they flowed out like a recital. From within came the sound of shallow coughing. When it ceased, a gloomy voice resounded, 'Come on in.'

Leaving her little shoes side by side on the shoe stone, Sohi stepped up on to the floor of the verandah. Her face was pale. When she went in through the door that Bongsoon opened for her, Chisoo, as if he had just got up, was sitting in front of his small desk. The bedding at the warm end of the room was half turned over, and there was white dust on the ink stone, the water container, the brushes and the scroll. It also covered the porcelain incense burner on top of the bureau, and the books stacked around at random.

'Is it cold outside?'

He looked at her intently with his long narrow eyes. As if these words had never reached her ears, she spread out her red skirt and bowed lightly to the floor.

'I respectfully inquire whether there has been any recent improvement in your health, father?'

Just as Bongsoon had done, she cleared her throat and spoke in the loud monotone.

'I am all right. I hope you are eating well, and not catching cold?'

His voice sounded as dreary as before, like the scratching of metal shreds. It seemed as though he was well aware of her fear, but there was no effort to lessen it in the cool and pitiless way that he stared at her. As though afraid that if she avoided his eyes thunder and lightning might strike, she continued to look straight at him as she shook her head. He smiled, but it was a smile that served only to freeze her heart. Moving his eyes away from her, he turned the pages of a book left open on his desk. For a man with a weak constitution, his bones were on the heavy side, but it was a pitiably white and emaciated hand that pressed the page as his eyes moved down the column of letters. Not only his hands, but his whole being was like the gaunt branches of the dried up magnolia in the court, yet rather than arousing sympathy, he generated a powerful atmosphere of fear, so unbearable that one could hardly breathe. It was not only that his eyes, impervious to any emotion, expressed an extreme self-negation, but the whole of his bony frame was like the crystallization of an atmosphere that inflicted pain on others through the power of this self-denial. Once in his room, Sohi knew that she could not stand up to go until the word of dismissal was uttered. Holding her breath while her faint heart beat faster, she could move only her shoulders. For a small child, how agonizing to be unable to move! From time to time there came the sound of a turning page.

'Kilsang!'

At this sudden, ear-splitting cry, she jumped from her place like a coiled spring.

'Kilsang!'

'Yes, sir!'

With the reply came the sound of running feet. From below the verandah rang the voice of a small boy.

'Did you call, master?'

'Why is the room so cold?'

'I'll make up the fire at once, sir.'

'What I asked was, why is the room so cold?'

Blue veins stood out on his forehead. Sohi's face turned white.

'Yes, sir. I'll make up the fire at once, at once.'

'Fool! I asked a question. "Why is the room so cold?" Stupid boy!'

'I am very sorry, master.'

The boy sounded as if he was frightened but, perhaps because he was accustomed to it, he ran like a well-trained hunting dog to the back and returned with an armful of firewood.

The nervous excitement set off a severe bout of coughing. Chisoo pulled out a handkerchief and stuffed it in his mouth, but the coughing did not lessen. As his eyes widened, his eye balls reddened and bulged. It did not allow him the briefest respite. With his

13

mouth blocked, the whole of his upper body shook. It was a desolate sight. After he had almost choked, the coughing lessened and in a voice all but inaudible with the gurgling of phlegm, he just managed to say, 'You . . . you . . . may go.'

As she opened the door and stepped out on to the verandah Sohi was retching as if about to vomit.

'Oh Miss!'

Bongsoon, who had been waiting on the verandah, took her in her arms. The retching changed into hiccups. Tear-drops stood out in her eyes.

'Miss!'

Gathering the hem of her skirt, Bongsoon wiped away the tears.

Chapter Three

THE sun was going down on a day so busy there had been no time to breathe. Perhaps the climax had now passed. Most of the visitors staying in the servants' quarters had left, on their donkeys, before sunset. The kitchen of the Choi household, as large as that of a monastery, fell quiet. Like the seashore at ebbtide, the whole house felt spacious and empty. Only last night the kitchen and servants' quarters had been swarming until late. Because of the Master's temperament, and his family being quiet and few in number, the many servants had been trained to behave quietly, but things had been so hectic that, even now after the visitors had gone, they were still working late.

At last the doors of the storerooms were shut, the padlocks put on, the bunch of keys taken to the *anbang* in the inner quarters, and so the day's work came to an end. In the kitchen things had been a bit slow. The over-tired cook had gone to her room early, so Yoni clattered the pots alone in the final washing up, and it was some time before the clinking ceased and the the kitchen light went out. Then the lights went out in the maids' rooms, and finally in the *anbang*, where her ladyship slept and, almost at the same time, in the room of Bongsoon *ne*. The whole household became as quiet as 'a sudden halt to the scurrying of mice.' The moon, in the middle of its tenth month, hung circular, but with a little gone from one side. In the angles of the walls where the shadows were dark, there lurked an eerie chill. From a room in the corner of the servants' quarters came now and again the ailing sound of the elderly retainer Bawoo, awaiting the day of his death, accompanied by the murmurs of Gannan *halmum*, bent with age, as she sat grieving at her husband's side. In one of the male servants' rooms that had long since been dark, a light came on.

'What do you need a light for?'

Dori, lying down, spoke angrily as he raised his head.

15

'I want a smoke,' said Samsoo.

'Has he gone out again?'

'Yes, he's gone.'

He had said that he wanted to smoke, but he just sat there awkwardly. 'Dori.'

'What?'

'Shall we follow Kuchon for once and see where he goes?'

'It's obvious that he has got a girl and goes out to see her — what's the use of chasing after him like a couple of clowns?'

'That's not all there is to it. I think that, like he says, he really does go into the hills. But why? – that's what I want to know. Just for once, let's follow him.'

'What if we meet a tiger?'

'If you are born to be tiger-meat, you won't avoid it by sitting in a corner of the room.'

'When the time comes for me to be eaten, I'll be eaten, but I don't fancy walking out to it on my own two feet.'

'All right, don't. You don't have to if you don't want to. I'll go by myself.'

'It's too late. Even if you do, it'll be no use.'

Samsoo had opened the door and was putting his feet into the straw shoes under the wooden step. Dori suddenly got up.

'If you're told not to go, you want to go that's human nature. If he has gone, he'll be a long way off by now. It's useless anyway.'

Dori, who had not wanted to go, was now hurriedly following.

'If you're coming, put out the light.'

He leant against the wooden step and stretched into the room to blow out the lamp. For once his short plump body seemed to lengthen.

'That damned old man ought to be choked with pebbles. What has he got to live for?' mumbled Samsoo as he spat at the ailing sounds from Bawoo.

'Can we decide our own lifespan? Do you think you are going to live for ever?'

Dori spoke sharply.

They followed the high wall of the *byoldang*, mindful of the sound of their steps. The side entrance was firmly closed. The iron

16

scrollwork on the wooden door stood out darkly. They passed the front of the storerooms and came out through the backyard of the Master's quarters. The small gate between two posts in the hardy orange hedge had been left open. Lately, for some reason or other, Kuchon had taken to going off in the middle of the night to wander in the woods of Dangsan. There were times when, passing the distant Goso fort, he crossed the Sinsong peak and went deep into the hills before returning. In these rough valleys, where wild animals that had crept down from Chiri mountain shook the forest with their roaring, he would wander like a madman, until at dawn he returned exhausted. But no one in the servants' rooms guessed where he had been – there was no reason why anyone in their senses should wander hills that were full of wild animals in the middle of the night. The servants of the Choi household thought that it was an affair. They guessed that if it wasn't a disreputable widow from a nearby village, he must have fallen for some servant girl from the house of a gentleman near the town. If they asked, 'Where were you last night?' he would say briefly, 'In the hills'. It didn't seem likely, but if they said, 'You'll be eaten by tigers', there was no response.

'Kuchon, are you sure you've not been bewitched by a lady fox? You are in trouble – real trouble. There won't even be any of your bones left.'

The talk floated around at this level – no one could ask him directly if he went to see a woman. The night before, when the servants had given up their rooms to the visitors and slept huddled together like shrimps, he had seemed to be trying hard not to go out, until in the end he sat up and muttered to himself, 'I can't sleep . . .' He seemed to be suffering like an animal shut up in a cage.

'What passion is burning in your heart to keep you awake?' asked Soodong, who had seemed to be asleep.

'Passion? What do you mean "passion"?'

In contrast to his former muttering, he spoke coolly.

'Useless thoughts they are, quite useless.'

' . . . .'

17

'For people like us, it's get up, wear yourself out with work, fill your stomach, and sleep – what else is there?'

'. . . .'

'Don't think about vain things. A man's got to live according to his lot. Otherwise, he won't live out his days – no chance – how could he? Just go to sleep.'

The elderly Soodong offered his advice as if he had some inkling of the affair. Kuchon had become very emaciated, but as his body weakened his spirit seemed to grow stronger, for his attitude was calmer than before, his stride more steady, and his eyes, once bloodshot, had cleared. Even so, when he was in a lonely place by himself, behind the storerooms or by the well, something like a convulsive smile would appear on his face.

A couple of years ago – more precisely, on a bitterly cold day in the winter before last – a shabbily dressed young man with a bundle in his hand had turned up at the house. Appearing to be about twenty-one or twenty-two, he looked poor and hungry, but his distinguished face and well-proportioned figure carried a certain air of intelligence. When he was given some supper, even though he was shaking with cold and hunger, he ate slowly as if deep in thought. When the small food table had been taken away, he sat for a while in silence and then, instead of just requesting a place to sleep for the night, he unexpectedly asked to be taken on as a labourer. Kim *subang* shook his head in a sympathetic way.

'You don't look as though you are used to hard work – how can you ask to be a labourer?'

He said briefly, 'I have a strong body.'

Kim *subang* had been going to refuse, for apart from the fact that the mistress did not like taking on people from other areas, there was no need of more labour, but his mind was strangely drawn to him. Moved by some feeling stronger than mere pity towards this young man, who seemed to have some bright spiritual flame within his depths, he had mentioned him to Lady Yoon, and, instead of the anticipated brief dismissal he was unexpectedly ordered to let her see him. After regarding his face attentively, she closed her eyes, without saying a word, and the young man, holding his head straight, simply lowered his gaze. At last, whatever her thoughts

18

may have been, she told him that if he wished, he would be given a trial, and asked no questions about his record or his origins. That was how he came to be there. He was not a registered serf, but a free man who could come and go as he wished.

Four years before, in the thirty-first year of King Kojong, public and private serfdom had been abolished, so that the people had long been freed from its yoke. But the system was deep-rooted, and its practice did not disappear overnight, particularly in rural areas far from the capital, where there was really no change. He knew how to read and write. He may not have wanted anyone to know but it had come out with the discovery that, unknown to the others, he had been teaching Kilsang, the boy who attended Choi Chisoo in the *sarang*. Even if they did not know the extent of his learning, all the servants, with the exception of Samsoo, regarded him as an educated man, and from that point of view he came to be treated with respect. He was a man of few words. Though not very strong, he used his head when he worked and did not fall behind the others, and fully aware of his position as a servant, he always kept strictly within the boundaries of his duties. On rare occasions he would smile gently, as if that was the limit to his expression of emotion, but it was a warm and friendly smile and sometimes it seemed as though something of the innocence of childhood hung about him. Because of this, not only the girls but even his male colleagues felt for him a strange kind of affection. No doubt they were proud that someone who had the same menial status as themselves should have a distinguished appearance, character and learning. Whatever the source of the gossip about him, most of it was guesswork, and the one fact with some foundation – the only word from the man himself – was that he came from a village called Ku Chon in Muju, this being the origin of his name. There was no lack of rumours, such as that he had been a servant at a monastery and had studied at a hermitage in the Ku Chon Valley, and so on, but he denied that he had worked at a monastery or done any studying. Apart from the one statement that his surname was 'Kim', he had never said anything about his personal history or his parents or family. When the wife of Kim *subang*, indiscreet, brazen, insensitive and with ten times the curiosity of anyone else, asked him, 'Where do you come from?' he only smiled, and gave no answer. Moving close and nudging him as if to dig it out, she said again, 'I mean, where were you born?' He continued only to smile.

'If you had a human birth, there must be some place where your natal cord was thrown away, mustn't there? You don't even know that?'

'. . . .'

'Well, that's really strange. I can't believe that you're a murderer, so why hide your birth place? There must be something you daren't speak about, eh?'

The smile dropped from his face. In his eyes something flashed like a blade. It would have been well if she could have left it there, but she went on.

'Even crows and magpies have a birthplace. They say that in a strange part you're glad to see even a magpie from your home ground – so where is it?'

'Why should I answer that?'

There was murder in his eyes. He turned away as she looked at him open-mouthed. He went to the well and splashed water on his face. The back of his neck had gone red up to his ears.

Dori and Samsoo crossed the vegetable patch and came out on the path to the pavilion.

'No trace of him – where's he gone?' said Dori as he hitched up his trousers,

'Let's go back.'

The sun had been warm during the day but the night breeze was chilly on the backs of their necks. Withered briars, shaken by the wind, made a noise as if some man or animal was hidden beneath them.

'Seeing we've come this far against the cold wind, let's go on up Dangsan.'

Samsoo walked in front, a long shadow going before him.

'It's cold. It must be the end of autumn,' mumbled Dori as he followed.

'Autumn's gone long since.'

'How quickly time passes.'

20

'Look! there he goes!' called Samsoo in a low voice.

Wherever he may been wandering, Kuchon, with the edges of his white cotton clothes flapping, was now on the path up to the pavilion.

'Ha! So he really does go to the hills! What on earth for? I'm so cold my jaws are rattling.'

Ignoring Dori's mumbling, Samsoo quickly began to run after Kuchon. Dori, following him, ran also. Kuchon, who had gone up to the pavilion, was looking down towards a place to one side of it, a little lower down, connected to the flat ground in front of the pavilion by three flights of stone steps. Although it did not show up clearly, because of the bright moonlight, a faint light could be seen in the thatched garden house that stood there.

'Let's get into the shadow – we might be seen.'

As he followed Samsoo into hiding in a shady spot Dori said, 'It looks as though the master is there.'

'Certainly the light's burning.'

'He's not fit yet – why on earth should he go up to the garden house?'

'Have you ever known him not to do just what he wanted to do?' mumbled Samsoo half-heartedly, as he carefully watched Kuchon's movements.

Kuchon showed his profile as he stood looking down at the house. The edges of his garments flapped in the wind but his body was as motionless as if it had been turned into a stone Buddha.

'What is he standing there for? – it beats me.'

'Don't speak so loudly.'

Samsoo jabbed him with his elbow. Kuchon turned in their direction.

'Has he seen us?'

'Keep your trap shut!'

Slowly moving back, Kuchon went to the front of the pavilion and stood in the middle of the steps, his face turned towards them. The direct light of the moon showed him clearly, despite the distance, rigid, as if he were wearing a silver mask. With his back to the name-plate of the pavilion and the outlines of the eaves rising each side of him, his stationary figure could have been mistaken for

21

one of the columns that bore the weight of the structure. The next moment he was flying away.

'Let's follow him – he's off!' said Samsoo.

The white garments flickered off towards the woods of Dangsan. Perhaps because of an uncanny feeling, added to the chill of the wind, Dori was trembling. Once in the woods, Kuchon's pace quickened. The pine needles, lifted on the wind, sighed as if possessed. Light and shade flickered sharply. Between the sounds of the agitated woods came the intermittent cries of an owl. Struggling for breath, Dori asked, 'Running on blindly like this, where are we going to end up?'

Samsoo's chasing steps halted at a point where the trees were sparse. Jumping over a stream, Kuchon climbed up on to a rock. The murmur of water could be heard. Samsoo led Dori into hiding behind a thick-trunked oak tree. Dried briars waved in front of their eyes, through which they could see him sitting on the rock. As before, at the pavilion, he was facing in the direction of the two men hidden behind the tree. Even though they were nearer than before, they were less likely to be spotted because of the many kinds of cover provided by the woods, and they could see his face more clearly. It seemed as though they could even look into the depths of his eyes set deep under thick eyebrows. Amidst the eerie solitude, the owl's calls continued ceaselessly. Although the wind had not died down, the bird sounded as if it was much nearer. Kuchon's head fell forward and, stretching out his arms, he pressed himself against the rock. Then a truly amazing thing happened.

The two men were astonished to hear the sound of weeping like someone's heart being torn apart. Could any man on earth cry like that? It was not loud, but Kuchon's wailing drove the two men hidden behind the oak tree into utter confusion. They felt frightened.

They heard it again. On all sides of them stood the black peaks of mountains. The moon hanging in mid-heaven looked as cold as a fragment of ice.

How much time had passed? Only when the weeping suddenly stopped, and the ends of white clothing flickered before their eyes and passed, did the two men regain their wits. Like a madman,

22

Kuchon had begun to run towards the mountain path. Automatically Samsoo and Dori darted after him.

'Haven't we been seduced by a ghost? Aren't I dreaming?'

These thoughts flashed through Dori's mind as, unthinkingly, he ran. Kuchon flew ahead. The mountain trail ended but running on trackless paths, snapping off the branches that got in his way, he seemed to have so much strength left that he could still have jumped across a precipice of a thousand yards. He was like a man possessed.

'My goodness. I'll choke to death,' whispered Dori.

The figure of Kuchon had already disappeared from their sight. Though they rushed about here and there, they could not discover which direction he had taken.

'Damn it! This is just impossible. It must be magic. He must have flown. He couldn't have just used his legs.'

Sunk to the ground, gasping for breath, Dori was lost in wonder.

'It's because of you we lost him, you stupid idiot!' Samsoo burst out angrily, clicking his tongue.

'All the way you've been messing about.'

'He's superhuman, superhuman – where else does he get such strength? He looks so delicate, you wouldn't think he could be so strong.'

Regardless of Samsoo's anger, Dori was so moved he went on muttering like this. The call of a fox came from afar.

'There's nothing more we can do. Let's go down.'

'Let me get my breath back.'

'It's all your fault we lost him! With you getting in the way of my feet, I couldn't run. You're as fat as a pig. Why don't you get your weight down a bit, damn you!'

Turning abruptly, Samsoo started to walk back quickly the way they had come.

'Look at him – having a fit! Do you want to go by yourself? Let's stay together.'

Dusting off his behind, Dori stood up and trotted after him. When they had reached the pavilion, Samsoo shook his head as he said, 'Whatever you say . . . whatever you say . . .'.

'He must have some great sorrow.'

'Sorrow?' repeated Samsoo contemptuously.

'How could anyone weep like that if he didn't have some great sorrow eating up his bones?'

'Well, crying is one thing – but that rascal Kuchon, whatever you say, he must be one of the Dong Hak rebels.'

'Don't accuse an innocent man.' Dori raised his voice.

'How could anyone run up and down the hills like that if he hadn't lived the life of a fugitive?'

'They say he was a servant at a monastery, so naturally he'd be good at climbing hills. "With no feet, a word can travel a thousand miles." An idle word like that can ruin a man.'

'Even if he did belong to the Dong Hak, what does it matter? Yoon Bo was one too. I have a certain idea and I'm pretty sure of it.'

'Pretty sure? What proof have you got?'

'Don't you think it's strange? Why does he never say anything about where he comes from?'

Chapter Four

HEARING that the illness of Jang-am *sonseng*, who had turned his back on the world to live in the village of Hwa Sim Li, not far from the town, had become very serious, Choi Chisoo left soon after midday, taking Soodong with him. It was his first outing for nearly six months. It could not be said that he himself was fully recovered, but as Jang-am *sonseng* was the one man whom he really respected as a mentor, he could not be over-concerned with the possible effect on his own health. It was quite a cold day. The wind blowing across the Sumjin River ruffled the scrub as it passed. Along the main road from Pyong Sa Ri to the town, which followed the river for more than seven miles, went ox-carts and men with loads of firewood on their backs. As they heard the sound of hooves behind them the wood cutters and farmers looked round and quickly moved over, awkwardly avoiding the piercing stare of his eyes as they bowed to the Master on his horse.

The figure of Choi Chisoo, swaying on his horse, with the hem of his long coat and the ribbon of his wide-brimmed hat flapping in the wind, had gone perhaps half a mile from the village, when Lady Yoon called the seamstress, Bongsoon *ne*. Placing her needle in the front edge of her *jogori*, she bowed before the door.

'Did you call, madam?'

'Where is Sohi?'

'I think she is with her mother.'

There was a short silence.

'I would like her to be taken out somewhere.'

'Yes, ma'am?'

'I want her kept away from the *byoldang*.'

As she stood bent at the waist, the colour changed on the seamstress' face.

'It's rather windy, ma'am.'

'Windy?'

'Yes. It's chilly, too. I wouldn't like her to catch a cold . . .'

As she took the needle from the edge of her *jogori* and stuck it into her piled up hair, Bongsoon *ne*'s hand was trembling violently.

'Cold, is it? Then call Bongsoon and tell her to take her to the *sarang*. Don't on any account let her go into the *byoldang*.'

'Yes, ma'am.'

As Bongsoon *ne* withdrew, instead of going to look for her daughter, she wavered as if unable to put one foot in front of the other. She again took the needle from her hair and put it back on the front of her *jogori*, and then hitched up the waist of her skirt, which had slipped slightly. Flustered, she left the house to call her daughter and then came in again.

'What trouble! It had to come sooner or later, but what a disgrace for a great family! As they say, "You can cheat on the horoscope but you can't cheat fate!" It's Buddha standing on his head, it's all topsy-turvy. How awful, at her age!'

Samwol, carrying a bowl of rice gruel between her hands, noticed Bongsoon *ne* muttering.

'What are you talking to yourself for?'

'Talking to myself?'

'You were mumbling something on your own.'

'How's Gannan *halmum*?'

'She looks better, but its Bawoo who is really bad. He doesn't recognize anyone and even if you put gruel in his mouth, he spills it out again.'

'That's old age. Have you seen Bongsoon anywhere?'

'I haven't. What's wrong? Your face looks terrible.'

'Nothing really.'

She stopped and, without another word, turned towards the barn and disappeared. Bogi was chopping firewood.

'Have you seen Bongsoon?'

Only after he had brought down his axe on the wood after letting forth a cry did he say briefly, 'No.'

'Where has Kuchon gone to?'

Bogi stopped as he was about to throw down the split wood and turned to look at her with a tense expression. Dori, who had been

26

moving about inside the shed, started, and put out his face to stare at her. A long silence passed between the three of them. While it lasted, the same look of sympathy and helpless resignation passed over their faces.

'I've no idea where he's gone.'

Bogi spat on his palm and changing his grip, picked up the axe.

'Hell! Why does that flock of crows have to make such a row?' spat out Dori, and he drew his face back inside the shed.

'Bad weather's coming,' said Bogi.

As ashy clouds built up in the sky crows gathered and flew around. From the barn the sound of oxen chewing the cud suddenly became audible.

Bongsoon *ne* set off towards the *byoldang*.

'Where's that child gone to?'

'Mummy!'

With a patter of feet, Bongsoon came running from behind her.

'What do you want me for, eh? Bogi told me to come because you were looking for me.'

'Where have you been?'

'At the house behind. Mrs Kim asked me.'

'Bongsoon, come here.'

She grabbed the child's arm and took her into a corner.

'What's wrong?'

Frightened at the sight of her mother's tense face, she pulled her arm away.

'I won't go there again. I promise.'

She blindly begged forgiveness.

'Where's the young Miss? Is she in the *byoldang*?'

Bongsoon was baffled by these words, which seemed to bear no relation to her mother's expression.

'She was with her mother just now.'

'Go and fetch her.'

'Why?' she asked, relaxed.

'She's to go and play in the *sarang*.'

'What if the Master comes?'

'He's not in. Go and take her there quickly.'

'Not in?'

'Go to the back room of the *sarang* and play with the doll's tea-set. Not only that, but you mustn't come out until I tell you. Do you understand?'

'Why?'

'Just do as you're told, that's enough.'

'What if she wants to go back, and starts crying?'

'Well . . . even so, you mustn't. In the *byoldang* . . . in the *byoldang*, there is a big snake and they are going to try and catch it.'

In the middle of making up a story she suddenly became angry.

'Do you hear what I say?'

Back in her room she sat with folded arms.

'I just can't get on with my work . . .'

Unfolding them again, she stirred the charcoal in the brazier. In the yard Samwol was calling Kim *subang*. After stirring the brazier and smoothing it with the poker she laid it down and listened for any further sound from outside.

A memory returned to her. It was an incident that had occurred when she was a child, at Unbong. Even now, at more than forty, she remembered it vividly. It must have been at the time when the barley was swelling. Seeing a crowd of people going up the hill behind the village, she had followed them. The attraction was the corpse of one of the servants of Yom *jinsa*'s house. Although it was hidden under a straw mat, the matting was soaked with blood, and on the ground as well there was a congealed pool. Pushing through the grown-ups and sticking out her head she saw one of the dead man's feet protruding from a corner of the mat. It was a big foot in a straw shoe. On the blood-stained matting blowflies were buzzing. For whatever crime he had committed, he had, they said, been beaten to death. Even now, when she remembered that big bluish foot, she lost her appetite.

Listening out for sounds from outside, she shook her head in an effort to erase the vision of that great foot. The voice of Kim *subang* was heard: 'Did you call, my lady?'

Lady Yoon's voice was not audible, only that of the steward saying from time to time, 'Yes, Ma'am, yes, Ma'am.'

After a while rapid footsteps passed her room. There was the sound of bustle in the servants' quarters. It went on for a long time.

Then came the sound of the storeroom being shut and locked. After that the whole of the great wide household with its walls beyond the walls, and walls yet again, was enveloped in a dreadful silence. Sohi had been coaxed as far as the outside wall of the *byoldang*, but, unlike at other times, she was sulky and insisted on going back there to play housekeeping.

'The Master's not in. Didn't I just tell you that he wasn't?'

'It's a lie.'

'It's not. Mummy told me.'

Sohi and Bongsoon, holding the basket of playthings, were wrangling like this when they heard, 'Bongsoon, what are you doing here?'

They both looked round. Lady Yoon's calm, deep-set eyes were fixed on Sohi. She was very tall. The upper half of her body was straight and her shoulders seemed to stand out in her lined cotton *jogori*. She looked more than her fifty-five years, but her long eyes were beautiful. The impression she gave was not so much feminine as scholarly.

'Go and play in the *sarang*. At once.'

They said, 'Yes, Ma'am,' and without another word joined hands and ran off. They crossed the rear courtyard and went into the back room.

Kilsang's voice came from outside, 'Bongsoon, is the room nice and warm?'

'Yes, it's lovely,' she shouted back.

Choi Chisoo had said that he would stay the night at Hwa Sim Ri, but one never knew how things might turn out, so Kilsang had been lighting an extra fire, and had seen the children going into the back room with the toy basket. While they were taking out the table set that he had carved from pieces of paulownia and arranging it, he brought in some food for the doll's tea-party. It was obvious that something very serious was going on but he seemed to be quite unaware of it. As always, his face looked happy.

'Roast some chestnuts and bring them in.'

Bongsoon gave the order in the dignified style of her ladyship.

'Right-oh.'

He took a wooden bowl of chestnuts, and went towards the

29

outside fireplace. Taking pine nuts, dates and dried persimmons from a gourd bowl, Bongsoon was chopping them into pieces and laying them out on plates while Sohi, looking wretched, was merely a spectator. Of the children, she was the only one who seemed to be uneasy.

'Bongsoon, let's go back to mummy,' she urged.

'We can't. In the pond there's a snake as big as this . . .'.

Stopping her work, Bongsoon spread out her arms to show how big it was. Sohi quietened down. She disliked and feared her father and while she did not dislike her grandmother, she was frightened of her. But it looked as if snakes were what she feared most of all. With the bowl on his knee, Kilsang was squatting down in front of the fire in the outside fireplace, cutting off the tops of the chestnuts with a pocket knife.

'Let me start by chasing away the wandering spirits. You lie down and groan as if you were ill.'

After making Sohi lie down on her side, Bongsoon lifted the gourd and brandishing an ornamental knife, she chanted: 'You are not the god of the house, nor the guardian of the ancestral spirits, but the spirit of a wanderer who starved to death! If you have set your eyes on the five-year-old daughter of Choi, now receive some rice in the big gourd and some salt water in the small one and be gone! Hey! At once! If you don't clear off, I'll float you off on the Daedong River with a cast-iron cauldron over your head so that you won't have as much as the smell of soy sauce or bean paste . . .'.

From somewhere outside, probably by the left hand wall of the back room, a quiet voice could be heard, though naturally, with Bongsoon babbling, it did not reach the ears of the children: 'It's all come out!'

It was the low soft voice of Guinyo, who never betrayed her excitement.

'What's come out?' said Samwol in a petulant tone.

'They've locked up Kuchon.'

'. . . .'

'And how do you feel about that, Samwol? Are you happy, or does your heart ache?'

'How can you talk like that? Is it something to rejoice about?'

'I didn't say it was. I'm just curious to know how you feel about it, that's all.'

'Oh, thank you very much. I've heard people say "A fly can fasten on a horse's tail and go a hundred miles", but really you ought to check your scheming mind.'

'I'm not deaf, but I can't quite make out what you're saying. What do you mean?'

'I know it isn't something to be praised, but now, when someone's life is in danger, you seem to be pleased. Why? With your mouth grinning like a gourd you'd better mind it doesn't split.'

'Huh!'

Bongsoon was now picking up the pine nuts and dates that she had scattered over the floor in chasing out the wandering spirit.

'Miss, your headache is better, isn't it? The evil spirit has run away.'

With a yawn of boredom, Sohi again pleaded to go back to the *byoldang*. Bongsoon had to bring out the story of the snake once more.

'Make other people weep and one day it will be your turn! I know all about it. You lured Kuchon into meeting the mistress, pretending you cared about her.'

'May I be struck by lightning!'

'Shut up. Then you went to her ladyship to inform on them. Such wickedness!'

'You are trying to trap me. There was nothing to tell. She knew all about it and it was as clear as daylight. Not only that, but Samsoo knew already, and he'd been spreading rumours all round the village. What more was there for me to say?'

At the fireplace, Kilsang was turning the chestnuts over in the embers with a wooden poker.

'Samwol, haven't you got any guts?'

'Don't worry I won't ask you to lend me any.'

'Haven't you got any more spirit than a dead tree? Because of Kuchon you couldn't sleep, and you were burning your heart out. Are you going to take their side now?'

'I tell you, don't worry about me. If someone else is burning

31

their heart out, why should your back be itching? 'Give the disease and give the medicine.' Do you think I don't know you, you bitch?'

'I don't know anything about it. "Just a bystander eating a piece of cake" . . . by nature I'm a sound sleeper. Once the sun's gone down, I wouldn't even know if somebody carried me off.'

'I'm sure! Those big owl's eyes — they say they can only see in the dark.'

This conversation outside the back room might seem fantastic, but so was the spectacle inside:

> Sprit of the one who starved to death!
> Spirit of the one killed by smallpox!
> Spirit of the one killed by typhus!
> Spirit of the one killed by fever!
> Spirit of the one stabbed to death!
> Spirit of the one strangled to death!
> Spirit of the one that died wandering to and fro!

Bongsoon, doing what she called a 'street exorcism', had laid out food and was summoning countless spirits, as if she really was possessed. With a ringing voice, with eyes that sparkled with frenzy, and gestures of hands and body that could not be regarded as innocent child's play, it was so realistic and intense that an uncanny air of sadness hung about her.

These games of hers were a great worry to her mother. Not only could she play the shaman, but also the clown, with a skill that made you gasp. Two years older than Sohi, she was seven. She was slim and quiet by nature but as if prompted by some inner voice, in the role of clown or shaman, anything once heard she could reproduce exactly and in a beautiful voice. It seemed that it was some kind of innate talent and the indication of a sad future.

If Bongsoon *ne* thumped her on the head or the back saying, 'You wicked imp! Do you want to become an actress or a witch?' Kim *subang*'s wife would always stand up for her, saying 'Why do you do that? It's a kind of talent — why punish her?'

Further, if she was bored, she would encourage her saying, 'Come

32

on, Bongsoon, aren't you going to give us a song? Let's hear that famous voice.'

Then the child's eyes would sparkle and she would start to sing:

> *A wretched woman's fate,*
> *In the springtime of sixteen*
> *To be parted from her lover.*

At such times, if her mother heard it, she would be thrashed or scolded.

'A woman growing old and a child – you make a well-matched pair of idiots! Can't you stop that epileptic fit?'

On this occasion, ignoring Sohi, who kept on yawning in the background, Bongsoon was carried away in rapture: 'Ogunima, let's be like you. Ogunima, let's take a bow. Baby Ogunima, let me think of your origin . . .'.

'Having a fit again? Carrying on like that you really will become a witch,' chided Kilsang as he brought in the roast chestnuts.

She stopped abruptly.

'If you tell my mum, I'll kill you.'

'Of course I'll tell her. Why not?'

Bongsoon looked into the bowl.

'What did you shell them for?'

'To make them easier to eat.'

As if at last she had found an outlet for her irritation, Sohi screamed, 'I don't like them like that!'

Puzzled, Kilsang said, 'Why not, Miss?'

'Why did you take off the shells?'

'So that you wouldn't get your hands dirty.'

'You soiled them. I don't like them. I won't eat them.'

'I kept them clean.'

'I mean your hands are dirty.'

'You can see they're not.'

He spread them out and looked up at her with sad and embarrassed eyes.

'If you carry on like this, I won't give you a piggy-back any more, Miss.'

'Then I'll thrash you. I'll say, "Here rascal, bare your leg!" '

She glared at him with eyes that showed both sleepiness and irritation.

'I'm sorry, Miss. I'll go and get some more and bring them when they're ready.'

Meanwhile the children had fallen asleep on the warmest spot on the *ondol* floor. Outside, it grew dark. Kilsang, who had said he would bring more chestnuts, did not come, and no one sought them.

In the middle of the night, Bongsoon *ne* came in and quietly, so as not to wake them, covered the children with a quilt and squatted down beside them.

Just after the third watch of the night there was a death in the house, the death of the old man Bawoo.

'Hell! By the time daylight comes there will be a pile of dead bodies!' spat out Samsoo.

But when lights were being kindled all through the house because of Bawoo's death, in the mountain valley of the Goso Fortress a lantern was seen passing by.

Chapter Five

ON this night when thick darkness, closely packed on all sides, and the wind from the direction of the Sumjin River, screaming and hurling itself along, seemed to clash in a fierce battle, Kuchon and the lady of the *byoldang*, cleaving the scrub, ankle deep in leaves, disappeared without trace. Three days later, at the house, with no chief mourner, the funeral of old Bawoo took place. For a few days afterwards, as the hours came for an offering at the makeshift shrine in the backyard, Gannan *halmum* keened in a creaky voice, like a pair of bellows, but when she was no longer able to move, though someone saw to the regular offering, there was no one else to weep sadly in her place. Clamped down under leaden silence, the household servants went quietly about their tasks like a swarm of fish swimming under water. Who had opened the door of the cell that night? It remained an insoluble riddle. There was no way of getting at what might be in the mind of the expressionless Lady Yoon, or of Chisoo, crouched in his quarters. Mysterious also was their motive for passing over, against all expectation, the investigation and punishment of whoever it was who had opened it. Whether there had been some overall plan agreed between the Master, Chisoo, and the one pillar and authority of the household, Lady Yoon, this was a secret of which they could gain no inkling. It was whispered among the servants that her ladyship had sent people out in all directions to search for this immoral couple who had gone, throwing dirty water on the family reputation, but whether even that was true, there was no way of knowing.

In contrast to the death-like quiet that prevailed over the rest of the house, the *byoldang* was, day and night, in a state of turmoil. Bongsoon and her mother, and Kilsang and Samwol faced daily affliction.

'Bring back my mother! Bring back my mother!'

35

It was truly hard to bear the ceaseless rampaging of Sohi who went into fits and screamed and fainted and threw around anything she could lay her hands on. Bongsoon *ne* looked distraught and her once plump form was almost wearing thin.

'If only she could understand, I could talk to her . . . What have I done to deserve this?'

Then she would turn to brush away tears of pity. Almost every day, repeating exactly the same words, she would ask, 'Where has my mother gone?'

'She has gone to Seoul.'

'Why?'

'To see your grandfather.'

'Where's my grandfather?'

'He's in Seoul.'

'Then why didn't she take me?'

'It's so far, you wouldn't be able to walk.'

'Couldn't I go in a palanquin?'

'It's too far. You have to go over the mountain and across the river, and over another mountain and across another river, and then . . .'.

'Couldn't Kilsang take me on his back?'

'Well, maybe he could, . . . but there are tigers in the hills, fierce tigers with fire in their eyes like a brazier, and if they saw a child, Grrrh! – they would gobble you up.'

'Well, when will she come back?'

'. . . .'

'After I've slept how many nights?'

After pinching her knee, Sohi closed her fists and pummelled Bongsoon *ne*'s breast.

'When you are grown up. She will come when you are grown up.'

After a short silence, 'How many nights before I'm grown up?'

If there was still no answer, then on Sohi's well-shaped forehead, as smooth as a gourd, the veins would stand out and she would start throwing herself about.

In this southern region, in the early winter before it begins to freeze, if there is no wind, it only needs the sun to shine and it is

36

as warm as spring. All day long the sun had poured down generously on the courtyard of the *byoldang* so that even after it had set and night had come, it was still warm. On the surface of the pond where during the day the sunshine had drawn up the carp to play, there was now the occasional sound of a falling leaf. Afflicted by Sohi, and exhausted, Bongsoon lay deep in sleep with Samwol in the second room of the *byoldang* while her mother, with her arm offered to Sohi as a pillow, was gazing blankly at the fluttering oil lamp. Under the light which, even without any draught, flickered from the burning of its own wick, Sohi, also exhausted, slept like a dove with low even breathing.

'I ought to get up and get on with some work.'

But with her body heavy and her mind half-conscious with tiredness, Bongsoon *ne* was unable to raise herself. Even if she tried to sleep, it did not come. In her mind, slackened by weariness, all sorts of things turned dizzily and moved around and, shaken off, only formed new patterns like spiders' webs. What had happened on that night would seem like a dream, a fiction, and then come very vividly, as if it had happened just the day before, and it seemed as though the dusty wind that had been blowing as Bawoo's lonely bier had gone over the hill was now filling the room and making things look hazy, an illusion caused by the flickering light of the lamp and the shadows.

'I ought to go and see Gannan *halmum*. I wonder if she's still breathing.'

But still she could not raise herself. She felt that the old man Bawoo, leaning on his stick, was about to appear from somewhere, gazing at her with his good and wise old eyes.

'Bongsoon's mother, I am grateful. Why did you bother with grave clothes for a useless old creature like me? I'm not worthy.'

She could almost hear his voice.

'Bawoo, poor old man! – how sad his eyes looked! With the house in this state, I can't ask the mistress, and as a servant, I can't call Dr Mun myself, so what can I do for Gannan *halmum*? It looks as Dooman *ne* is bringing her some medicine, but she's got her own sick mother-in-law to look after, and hardly enough for herself . . .'.

Suddenly in Bongsoon *ne*'s mind the smirking face of Guinyo

37

sprang up. She reflected vaguely on a trivial incident that had happened during the day, associated with that smile. It was a feeling of relief, like the passing away of indigestion, yet also it left an unpleasant after-taste, a sense of disquiet, as when there is a snake above the ceiling.

'An evil and malicious girl she always wants to harm someone – that's the trouble with her.'

However hard she tried to think well of her face when smiling, it was frightening, and however much she tried to sympathize when her face was angry, it was equally alarming.

The servants, though unable to be more than silent spectators of a situation whose outcome they could not guess, could not hide the fact that they experienced an intricate sense of conflict. Loyalty to their master required them to feel hate and anger for this immoral couple who had gone after bringing disgrace on the long and illustrious history of the house, and it could not be said that they did not feel hate and anger, yet their emotions could not be pinned down to this one area of hatred or rage, for some indescribable pain or anxiety still remained in their minds. Why was this so? That the couple were obvious sinners and unforgivable destroyers of morality no one could deny and they could not understand why they felt such extreme concern about their future. Could it be some kind of ever-flowing love or protective instinct of which they themselves were unaware? A gracious and beautiful woman by her mere existence makes men happy, while being an object of women's yearning, and this applies also to a man. The feelings of the servants might be summed up as a conflict between gloom on behalf of their master's house and despair for the couple.

Guinyo was the only one to be completely different. Her elated manner, as if fanning the flames of a house already on fire, was disagreeable to them, so that she was openly ostracized. But the more she became an outsider and was hated, the more provocative and contemptous became her manner towards the others. She was like a ball that bounces back as hard as it is hit. It was by no means a nervous reaction, but rather a tenacious counter-attack that held on grimly, so much so that those who had been given to gossiping about her were forced by this hostile pressure to keep quiet when in her presence. Only Soodong continued mercilessly to pour out insults directed at the back of her head.

'Once started, that creature goes from bad to worse like an adder lifting its head back higher and higher.'

At the same time the strange thing was that Samwol, who had herself been in love with Kuchon, was more sympathetic than anyone towards the two who had disappeared. It seemed as though the fact that the man she loved had stolen the beautiful lady from the boudoir made her proud.

'No one could say it was right. Their sin deserves death, everyone knows that, but the way that bitch Guinyo carries on I just wonder how any human heart could be so cold. She goes round the place from one end to the other, giggling away as if it was all just a stage show. Really it turns my stomach, I can't stand it. Whatever the rights and wrongs of it, she was the one who waited on the Young Mistress, wasn't she? You can't find the slightest trace of concern in her face, yet when she appears before the Mistress she puts on an expression as if to say, "How can I bear this mountainous weight of worry?" '

'She's a snake. She's been like that ever since she was child. Full of malice. This time, too, it all came out through her telling tales.'

Listening to this conversation between Samwol and Yoni's mother, the cook, Bongsoon *ne* said, 'Nonsense. It can't be true. Did anyone hear her giving them away?'

'You only say that because you don't know anything about it.'

'Be quiet. It's better not to repeat vague stories like that. I know she's got a nasty nature, but it's not likely that her ladyship would listen to tales.'

Although Bongsoo *ne* had rebuked them, for without clear proof she would not join in, she herself had strong suspicions of Guinyo, and in fact her own feelings were even more bitter. This was because of the way Guinyo had treated her daughter. One day Bongsoon, as if sensing that it was something improper, had said sulkily, 'Mummy, do you know what Guinyo said? She said I ought to go and work in a tavern. What's that?'

'What?'

Once, she would have clouted her on the head, saying, 'Silly girl. It's all because of your antics,' but now, even when she asked 'Why did she tell me to go off to a tavern?' her mother could find no words. When Sohi was screaming, turning white, and rolling her eyes to the point of swooning, Bongsoon *ne*, in a flurry and sweating profusely, crying 'What's to be done! What's to be done!', could not worry about whether or not her daughter played the shaman or the clown. Hoping only to get safely through the day, she was not likely to smack her, but rather to ask for her help. To her, Bongsoon was a precious child miraculously born in later years as if in a dream, born after her father's death and never knowing his face. For her mother, it was pitiful to see the little thing being worn out by day-long attendance on Sohi, but at least she still had her own mother. As the saying goes, 'Lay out a mat for an epileptic and he doesn't have a fit'. Bongsoon, who, when her mother had threatened her had been keen on playing the shaman in secret, now, perhaps tired out by Sohi, no longer enjoyed doing it with her. Threatened by her mother she had only been afraid of the beating and had paid no attention to what was said about her, but now she showed a sensitive reaction to Guinyo's teasing and vaguely understood the mocking intention.

'H'm, completely possessed by the spirit or the god, aren't you? It's your destiny you were born for it. Do a rite for the house-god and will it appease the offended ancestors? Offer up your soul, and will it bring back the departed? Ha, ha, ha! As tiny as a toe, the way you carry on so young, it's extraordinary! How mournfully your chant goes up and down the brows of the twelve hills! At any rate, if you are going to be a famous singer, you'll have to shed some blood over the great mountains and rivers. H'm. Bongsoon's mother has only one daughter, but she'll have plenty of sons-in-law. I've never seen a seamstress or a carpenter living well but thanks to her daughter, Bongsoon's mother will live in luxury.'

Bongsoon *ne* had heard Guinyo's giggling and these mocking words.

'That creature! I'll have to sort things out with her,' she had thought.

So, on one occasion, she had deliberately stopped her: 'Do you have some grievance against me?'

'What did you say?'

'I said, do you have some grievance against me? If you have, you ought to settle it with me instead of taking it out on a kid who's still soft on the top of her head.'

'What on earth are you talking about?'

She looked up at Bongsoon *ne* unblinkingly.

'Do you mean to be like that?'

'Like that or like this, I've no idea what it's all about.'

'Don't be so deceitful. What will become of you, with such a wicked mind? It's not just that I'm standing up for my own child. What does a young child know about these things anyway? How can any decent person say such nasty things about a little one who's still got all her life in front of her?'

'Well, now I've heard everything! I don't have any luck with people. If I sit down, it's talked about, and if I stand up, it's talked about. I don't know why, as soon as they see me, whether it's children or grown ups, they all want to jump on me. You have to speak sometimes, unless you are dumb. If you are going to take up every innocent word and make something out of it, where will it end?'

She spoke with impressive calmness and logic. Bongsoon *ne* felt overpowered by her cold stare.

'What. . . What did you say?' she stammered, with embarrassment.

She felt their roles were being unfairly reversed, but no words would come. The more angry she felt, the more her lips trembled and her speech was blocked. It was unfortunate for a woman like Bongsoon *ne*, with no experience in verbal warfare to come up against someone like Guinyo. At that moment the thoughtless wife of Kim *subang* appeared from nowhere and thrust herself between them saying, 'What a row! People eating rice cooked in the same pot shouldn't fight. As they say, "Splitting one's stomach over children's words." You don't look like it, Bongsoon *ne*, but you must be pretty silly, too.'

'What. . . what did you say?'

'Is there anything wrong with what I'm saying? I'm not taking sides with Guinyo, but it's a matter of principle. Children develop

41

through being told off, or beaten, don't they? She's precious to you, but the more precious she is, the more humbly she should be brought up. That way she'll live long.'

With a sneer, Guinyo took the opportunity to disappear.

Bongsoon *ne*'s status in the house was due to the fact that she was not a serf and was treated with respect by Lady Yoon, but even more she was respected for her good manners and her fair-mindedness. Even the roughest of the male servants were restrained in her presence – only Guinyo had never regarded her very highly while she, without any clear reason, had never thought much of Guinyo, until finally a collision came, in which Bongsoon *ne* had come off worse. And on the same day Guinyo lost out to Sohi.

The children were playing beside the pond. Kilsang sat on the stump of a tree making a small straw basket. Bongsoon *ne*, sitting by the open door of the room across from the *byoldang*, was sewing while she kept an eye on them.

'It's not like winter. It feels as if spring is coming,' said Samwol as she entered the courtyard.

She squatted on the edge of the verandah with a frown.

'It's pretty serious.'

'What is?'

'It's Gannan *halmum*. She refuses to eat even gruel. It looks like we might have a second funeral.'

'No improvement at all?'

'None at all. A childless old woman is the saddest of all.'

> *Oh, must you go? Oh, must you go?*
> *What kind of fate is this? . . .*

Bongsoon sang to herself as one by one she threw pebbles into the pond. Then Sohi scurried in, 'Samwol, give me a piggy back.'

'Of course, Miss.'

She quickly got up from the verandah and offered her back to the little girl. With Sohi on her back she strolled up and down the courtyard while she hummed in tune to Bongsoon's song until suddenly she stopped. Bongsoon was singing, 'Bringing up his child on begged milk' from the songs of Sim Chong:

Baby, baby, do not cry!
Your mother has gone afar
To the pear-blossom village of Nakyang East
Her cherished lover to see.
To mistress Lee in the Yellow Dragon Grave,
To confide her sadness.
Having lost your mother
Do you cry to pour out your sorrow?
Do not cry, do not cry!
What a fate to be born and lose
Your mother after seven days,
To suffer in a swaddling cloth.
Do not cry, do not cry!
Tiger butterfly on the Japonica,
When March comes round again
The blossoms will come back.

'Bongsoon, you make me cry. How sadly you sing!'

Samwol's eyes were brimming with tears, when from behind came cackling laughter. As she swung round, there were daggers in her wet eyes. Swaying from the waist, Guinyo came nearer.

'A child woken up in the middle of sleep will cry, but this one laughs. She must have dreamt that she's been to the Western Paradise and brought back the elixir of life.'

There was a sharp blade in the tone of Samwol's sarcasm.

'Samwol!'

'What do you want with me? I'd better watch out. When you are friendly, it scares me.'

These two, who fought a battle of words every time they collided, were so experienced that their exchanges were at a high level of sophistication.

'Don't they say that a widow's sorrow only a widow can know?'

As she said this Guinyo threw a quick glance at Bongsoon *ne* as if to say that she was not included, though there was a hidden intention to provoke her indirectly.

'That may well be so. I understand that, but I don't want any share in your affairs.'

'Who was asking you to share in my affairs? I don't have anything to be depressed about or yearn over. I have nothing at all to mourn for, but the young Miss, who has lost a mother's love, and you who've lost the one you love, carrying, and being carried, while listening to a song of parting – this is so pitiable, and yet somehow laughable as well. Never mind, Samwol – I know how you feel.'

'I've a good mind to squash your beak, but I won't because there might not be enough water to wash my hands with. You'd better go quickly and offer the Master a basin of water for a wash.'

'I guess you've got pangs of jealousy.'

'That's right. My stomach hurts. Come and stroke it.'

Samwol moved close to Guinyo.

'Tcha!'

'No!' cried Guinyo.

Sohi, on Samwol's back, had spat in her face.

'Miss!' Bongsoon *ne* cried loudly.

Guinyo lifted the hem of her skirt to wipe her face while Samwol laughed loudly. Bongsoon laughed as well. Kilsang, after beginning to laugh, checked himself, and, embarrassed, stood up awkwardly.

'As tasty as crushed sesame seeds! ha! ha! Serves you right. If you make uncalled-for remarks, you get them back.'

Bongsoon kept on laughing excitedly.

'What's so funny?'

Guinyo's face was white with rage.

'What's so funny?'

After clouting Bongsoon on the head, she gave Sohi a stare so filled with resentment and hatred that it would never be forgotten. Then she swept out of the yard.

'Miss!'

As she stuck the needle into the front of her *jogori*, and stepped down into the yard, Bongsoon *ne*'s eyes were stern. Perhaps because she was a little scared by a light in her eyes that she had never seen before, Sohi tightened her grip on Samwol's neck and laying her head sideways gave a shy smile.

'That was a naughty thing to do. You mustn't spit, even at animals. If her ladyship knew, she would call it bad manners and tell me off.'

44

'I won't do it again. But I hate her.'

That had been earlier in the day. Now Sohi slept, her mouth firmly shut, breathing healthily.

'They say that people come in thousands of grades, even tens of thousands, but even so, how could Guinyo be like that?'

In order to put out the oil lamp, Bongsoon *ne* twisted herself to release the arm that had been pillowing Sohi's head, but left it there for a moment while she examined her expression. A tiny hand explored her bosom. The little hand parted her *jogori* and touched her breast. As if she could perceive the different feeling, even in her sleep, she sat up, and looked down at Bongsoon *ne*, rubbing her eyes. As she realized that it was not her mother, she burst into shrieks as if to tear into shreds the silent night.

'Stop crying, Miss!'

Bongsoon *ne* held her and rocked her in her arms, but she still kicked her legs and screamed.

'Bongsoon *ne*!'

A voice came from outside. She started.

'Yes, ma'am?'

Quickly she put Sohi down and opened the door. Standing in the light from the room was Lady Yoon. Her broad forehead looked even broader, as if she were all forehead. Although there was a calm light in her deep-set eyes, she looked like a ghost.

'Your ladyship!'

Bongsoon *ne* abandoned the crying child and going out on to the verandah, stepped down into the courtyard. It was not possible that the sound of crying could have been heard in the main house. Lady Yoon must have been strolling round the *byoldang*.

'Can't you stop it?' rebuked Lady Yoon in a quiet voice.

Sohi, lying face-down on the floor, did not stop crying, despite the presence of her grandmother, whom she greatly feared.

'Can't you stop it?'

'I want my Mummy!'

Lady Yoon turned on her heels. Samwol, also awake, tidied her clothes as she hastened down to the courtyard. Lady Yoon chose a fairly thick switch from the willow tree growing beside the lily pond and broke it off. In the darkness the white sleeve of her *jogori* looked like a heron's wing. The naked trees standing here and there seemed to be solemn witnessess of her action. Bongsoon *ne* and Samwol stood and watched her with their hands clasped before them, their whole bodies trembling. Moving slowly she stepped up on to the verandah, leaving her shoes on the stone and entered the room.

'Are you going to stop or not?' Her face still down on the floor, the child screamed even harder. The switch in Lady Yoon's hand came down on the child's legs.

'Please, Your Ladyship!'

From the courtyard Bongsoon *ne* gave a choking cry. Once, twice, three times. Red lines were instantly drawn on the tender calves. Sohi sprang up, and from the sewing basket left at the far end of the room she snatched what she could, mostly skeins of thread, and flung them around. A look of astonishment sprang into Lady Yoon's ice-cold eyes, and then a kind of convulsive smile ran across her lips.

'What a stubborn creature!' she muttered to herself, as if satisfied, and left the room.

Throwing the switch into a corner of the courtyard, she went out of the *byoldang* without a further word. Rushing into the room, Bongsoon *ne* picked up the child, who had fainted, blue in the face, while Samwol fetched cold water to sprinkle on her.

'Oh, Miss! Oh, Miss!'

Bongsoon *ne* shook her. She opened her eyes. She did not cry, but the little bundle of tenacity gave out one piercing scream: 'Bring back mummy!'

Chapter Six

KANGCHONG *DEK*, who had been vigorously sweeping the yard with a worn-down broom, stamped her foot. 'Damned fowl!'

The hen, which had been pecking the ground in search of feed, stretched out its neck from a fluffy collar of feathers and scuttled away looking as if it were falling backwards. Having run just far enough, it now began to cackle and cluck.

'This damned life – I might as well finish with it, cut off my hair and go into a nunnery . . .'.

Still wielding the broom, she grumbled away as if aiming at some listener. With a small body, swarthy complexion and solid build, she gave the impression of being short-tempered. Whether or not he had heard his wife's complaints, Yongi, filling up the trough in the back yard with steaming cattle food, shook his head to get rid of the straws on the back of his neck. As if it could smell the feed, the hungry ox that had been sitting in the stall with bent knees rose abruptly. The bell round its neck tinkled rhythmically and in tune with it the beast slowly blinked its eyes as it resumed chewing the cud.

In the early morning the village was quiet. Like children in cotton-padded winter clothes, the houses in their newly thatched golden roofs huddled cosily like cockle-shells and the village now settled into the leisurely and peaceful season of winter. Only the roofs of Yoon Bo's fenceless and isolated shack by the river and the three-roomed cottage of Kim Pyongsan, who would run off without even putting his shoes on properly whenever he heard of somewhere to gamble, lay like grey tattered rags, neglected from one year to the next.

Yongi's place comprised of a lower section with store and cow-shed, and, facing it, a house which was slightly tilted. As the sun shone on them, the roofs gave the impression of newness. They were in good order. It was only the thatch on top of the stone and mud outer walls that was shabby. It had not been replaced last autumn, or even the year before, so that the straw crumbled in decay, while the withered gourd vines that grew over it swayed in the wind. It could have been laziness on Yongi's part, or it might have been that having covered the two buildings there had not been enough straw left over to finish it, though it should have been possible to borrow that much from a neighbour to complete the refurbishing of the house. But in view of the way that the maize stalk ribs were showing through the clay wall near the kitchen it looked more like a lack of interest. On the outside wall of the kitchen hung bunches of dried sage and radish leaves which fluttered like the vines on top of the wall thatch.

'Yongi, aren't you going to the market?' A loud voice called from outside the gate.

'Of course I am. Come in.'

Yongi, who had been stirring the cow-feed, lay the wooden spoon on the rim of the iron pot, and lifting the trough, pushed it into the stall.

'What a lot of work you've done,' said Kangchong *dek*, straightening her back as Chilsung came through the gate.

'You must have been up all night.'

'Even when you've done everything there is to do, the nights still seem to stretch on now like toffee in the summer,' he replied unenthusiastically as he put down on top of a wooden mortar a bundle of straw shoes tied together in a circle with a hemp cord.

'Damn it! It's a big bundle of nothing. How many pence will I get for it?'

He clicked his tongue.

'You can dig a hole ten feet deep and not get a penny for it. It is all worth the effort'

Kangchong *dek* silently scrutinized the bundle of shoes. With a sideways glance, Chilsung took out a short pipe from his waist-band. As he strolled across the yard, Yongi said, 'Just hang on a minute.'

'It's already nearly midday. We'd better hurry up or the market will be over.'

'That's right.'

Treading heavily on the wooden verandah, which had loose boards, he opened the bamboo-cane door and bending his tall figure almost in half went inside. The pillars that came through the verandah floor to support the roof were bumpy with knots. On them were pasted texts with characters that had become almost illegible – phrases such as 'May the parents live for a thousand years'; 'May the descendants prosper for countless generations'; 'Peace over all the land'; or 'May all be well in the four quarters'. They had been requested from Kim *hunjang* of the village school and put there when Yongi's mother, then still alive, was doing up the house to welcome her only son's newly wed wife. It had been more than ten years ago. As she swept the yard Kangchong *dek* went on, 'You are so hard working, your wife must be very happy.'

Skilfully concealing the middle finger of his right hand, cut off at the second joint, Chilsung struck the flint to light his filled pipe, and gave it a suck.

'As happy as a dog in summer.'

'When you do everything for her just like the tongue in her mouth, what does she have to worry about? No wonder she's so plump and smooth.'

'Yes, so much so that with her big stomach she can hardly stand up.'

'The fate of a woman, depends on who she marries – even whether she is clever or not depends on the man.'

'The Fertility Gods must have gone blind. Why does she have to produce so many kids?'

They were on different planes.

She finally burst into anger: 'It's because you have too many blessings. You don't think about those with none!'

Chilsung sniggered.

'I wish some one would take away a few of these damned blessings.

'Only where it's sunny, does the sun shine, and only where it's wet is there nothing but rain. Why is the world so unfair?'

She pulled up a withered weed and threw it on to the pile of sweepings.

49

'We need both sunshine and showers. Children should come according to how much wealth you have, but when you have nothing, and every corner of the house is filled with kids, how are you ever going to straighten your back?'

Without commenting on this, Kangchong *dek* took a new line: 'Is there anyone in the world as lazy as the man of this house? There are only two of us in the family, yet he never even notices if the soles of my shoes have worn through.'

'You're paying the price of his good looks, you know. He's as smart as a bowl licked clean by a dog, so you will have to just look on his face and live.'

The smoke from Chilsung's pipe curled up along the straight ridge of his nose.

'I can't feel this is my own life.'

'Well, that's partly your own fault – you don't go about it the right way.'

'Why? Am I a juggler? You can't clap with one hand.'

Wearing a headband and a change of clothes, Yongi came out of the room. He was stooping in the same manner as when he had gone in.

'What a lot of chatter.'

'Why? We've been singing your praises.'

'Well, things are looking up! Praising me! The sun will rise from the west.'

He gave a weak laugh.

'If you've got any eyes, look at this!'

Holding up a worn-out straw shoe, she glared at her husband.

'If you were pretty and clever like Chilsung's wife, I'd not only make you straw shoes, but leather ones too.'

'So I'd be the wife of a leather worker!' She yelled, red in the face.

'No thanks – I don't want to have butchers for my in-laws.'

'You have to have some children to have in-laws.'

'Well, is your life over? Has your backbone hardened with age?'

'If you don't want to be related to a butcher,' said Yongi, further provoking her, 'what about a shaman?'

50

'H'm. I know you have a grievance big enough to reach the sky. I didn't stop you from marrying that shaman.'

She plied her brush so vigorously that clouds of dust flew over Chilsung's cotton socks.

'Oh, take it easy! What crime has the yard committed?'

Chilsung sniggered again as he moved out of the way. Yongi picked up two birds, put them in a string sack and flung the sack over his shoulders.

'Let's go.'

Tucking his pipe into his waistband, Chilsung likewise flung the bundle of straw shoes over his square shoulders.

'This wretched life. I can't go on like this. I can't. Just waste the money you get for the chickens, and I'll show you!'

Taking his wife's shrill voice on the back of his head, Yongi said, 'Well, really! That'd made a cow laugh! When did I ever waste any money?'

As if speaking for her to hear, Chilsung said, 'It's market day that's the enemy – market day!'

Following the embankment through the rice fields, they went towards the river. Running after them, Kangchong *dek* shouted, 'Look here! Buy me a comb with fine teeth, and a shuttle for the loom. And don't forget!'

'I've wandered through the whole eight provinces and never seen a woman as jealous as that,' spat out Chilsung.

Although he had been teasing her himself a few moments before. Yongi did not say anything.

The fields changed to a greyish-brown colour, looked empty and desolate. The sun shone warmly and the puddles in the bottoms of the rice fields remained unfrozen. Stalks of dried grass standing on the banks were reflected in the water. Unable to forget the sweet taste of the fruit, a thieving crow sat at the top of a persimmon tree, rubbing his beak against the bark, while on straw stacked against a farmyard fence, sparrows perched basking in the sun. Urchins played with tops on the threshing floor and the widow Magdal *ne*, was heading towards the village, her arms folded and her shoulders hunched.

As the two men reached the riverside road they saw that the

market-goers had dwindled and realized that they were late. Hastening their steps they heard themselves being hailed from behind. Yoon Bo was walking along the bank towards them.

'Going to the market?' he boomed.

In thickly padded clothes, patched here and there, he spoke in rounded and resonant tones, 'If you're going to the market, get me some *miyok*. I'll give you the money when you bring it.'

Even as he came near to Yongi, who had stopped to wait for him, carrying his fishing rod and basket, he did not lower his voice.

'I don't know whether I've got enough money,' said Yongi, 'and anyway, what do you want *miyok* for?'

'Well, tomorrow marks the day when old "Pock Mark" came into the world.'

His face, chaffed by the river wind, glowed dark and red. His pock marks, whether because the blisters had been big ones or several had merged into one, were the size of peas and broadly engraved, giving him a forbidding appearance. His neck was thick and long. In his youth he had been known as a strong man and the ox awarded in the wrestling ring had always been his. His imposing body was a solid as a birch. Chilsung, who had been standing awkwardly, muttered, 'You couldn't have been born with pock marks.'

Yoon Bo, giving him only a glance, said to Yongi, 'I'd clean forgotten about it. Seeing you on the way to market reminded me. If I was away from home, it would be different.'

'Home or away, all by yourself, what cheer do you get from *miyok* soup?'

Chilsung again broke in with an unkind remark.

'Bastard! Did I say I was having a baby? Did I say I wanted it for myself?'

Shouting loud enough to shatter their eardrums, he waved his arms.

'Listen, you scoundrel! Your birthday is a day to offer devotion to your mother, who suffered for ten months carrying you in her stomach to give you life! A wretch like you, with no respect for his parents, would think of nothing but filling his own guts. Bastard!

52

A man must look to his origins before he stuffs food in his own gob'

If anything more was said, Yoon Bo's fists would be flying. Chilsung was not a weakling. But he turned his face away and left it at that.

'If you're short of money, it doesn't matter.'

Toward Yongi, his voice was soft.

'I can get it. Catch a few fish before I come back.'

Yongi spoke cheerfully and turned to go. Humming to himself. Yoon Bo walked down the embankment to the sandy shore of the river.

'His manners suit his looks. After giving birth to a thing like that, do you think his mother gurgled down *miyok* soup?'

Chilsung spat on the side of the track and wiped his mouth with his sleeve.

'Why speak like that about his dead mother? What he said was absolutely right.

'In that wretched state, he bounds all round the town like a conquering hero – I can't stand it.'

'. . .'.

'When I think about it, I'm sorry for him really, but when a man like him without a penny to his name goes round talking so big – no wonder even at his age he has to put up with a life that's no better than floating duck weed.'

'He's living in his own way – what's wrong with that? If he'd wanted to, he could have built a tiled house and had some land. He's not such an unfortunate man as you seem to think.'

Dissatisfied with Yongi's words, Chilsung kept silent. Sand blown on the wind stuck their faces. The wide expanse of fields came to an end. There were stone steps on the path all the way up through the un-irrigated rice fields on the steeply sloping hill. The curves of the Sumjin River took it sometimes far from the path, sometimes near.

Chilsung mumbled to himself, 'Like lice in the hem of a beggar's trousers, there's Choi *champan* family land in every hill and valley, but who will get it all in the end? Maybe it's because the world spins too fast these days? Or because the common people are too lively? Nowadays the gentry don't seem to be able to keep their place. They're the first to cut their topknots, and they say that in Seoul they even wear tight trousers. I reckon their power is running out.'

'. . .'.

'Isn't it so Yongi?'

'What?'

'Naturally, I'm talking about the nobility (or is it the triviality?) of Choi *champan's* family.'

Yongi shifted his sack. The bluish combs of the cocks that poked their heads through the holes shook also.

'After such a disgrace he should have shut himself up in a corner of the house and kept out of everyone's sight. Why does he have to flutter around on Dangsan? Seeing the way he behaves I can understand how his wife might take to another man.'

'Why do you have such a loud mouth?'

' "You can even run down the King when you are out of sight," as they say.'

'. . .'.

'We low-bred people, who've never been taught from the start, can't be blamed for bad manners.'

'Low-bred people are still human, aren't they? There's the same human standard for high or low.'

'The same? Is it the same for the fellow in a mansion who fusses over his meat and the fellow with barley gruel in a hut like a crab's shell?'

'Why ask me? Do I know any better than you? All I'm saying is, it's not right to run down the Choi *champan* house when you are living by their grace.'

Eyes rolling, Chilsung put his face close to Yongi's.

'Ha! Ha! Don't make me laugh! What grace?'

'Ever since the days of your ancestors you've lived on their land. Is it right to abuse them?'

'Ya! Don't talk like a little saint. All that rice that rots away in their storerooms, whose grace is that? Tell me that!'

'. . .'.

'Well, it's not long to wait. It's getting near. When a servant can take his master's wife, when even the Queen can be dragged away by her hair and killed like a dog, when high-ranking ministers can be drowned in Seoul . . . and more people's uprisings to come . . .'

'Don't talk such rubbish.'

'Rubbish? We all come into the world the same way. Why should we, with four limbs as good as anyone else's, have to spend our lives in tattered shirts and eat barley gruel?'

'If you have such a great grievance, take it to the Fertility Gods. Seeds sown in poor soil have to grow there.'

Yongi turned his eyes towards the river. Chilsung was silent for a while, till he gave a long sigh.

'With all these many pieces of land, if he'd give us just one bit, like pulling out one hair, we'd be able to loosen our belts for good, and have a chance to live.'

'If something's not yours, you have to regard it as dog shit. Having a lot of wealth doesn't give you peace of mind.'

'Don't talk rubbish. With wealth you can buy yourself a place in the government. Don't talk such high-flown stuff! Just think about what a sight we are – two strong full-grown men plodding along to the market on a cold day like this, one with a few straw shoes on his back and the other with a couple of hens!'

Suddenly, Chilsung cried like a mad man and waved his arms to the sky.

'Wait and see! My day will come! Do you think the Choi *champan* family have had great wealth from ancient times? Isn't it just wealth built up by sucking people's blood from the days of their grand-fathers? Isn't it wealth built up by snatching a rice field in return for a measure of barley in a year of famine? They say that in the old days when gentleman scholars passed through this village they used to cover their faces with their fans to avoid the sight of the great whale-like house of Choi *champan*. With money a thief becomes a nobleman and a servant gets to employ a coachman. How can you get wealth without committing crimes? Do lumps of land drop down from the sky? Or pieces of gold rise out of the soil? Loyalty? Human obligation? Do you become a rich man or a squire by keeping human obligations? According to how well you beat up other people, take out their livers and gobble them up, you become rich and gentlemanly. Why, look at Kim Pyongsan – some gentleman! He's one of the gentry isn't he, though he's from a family of "dog-legged gentry", and look at his situation. There's no one in this village, except for the most gutless, who treats him like a gentleman. And why? Because he's got no money.'

As if astonished, Yongi smiled and said, 'Why do you twist the argument like that? Are you trying to say that Pyongsan has failed to become wealthy through keeping human obligations? Or that because he's not rich he's not treated like a gentleman? It's plain enough that it's not because he's poor that he's not treated like a gentleman, but because he's failed in his human obligations.'

'Him, well, he's unlucky . . .' muttered Chilsung, and returned to his theme.

'Now even the house of Choi *champan* shows the signs of ruin. Yes, it's on the way out. I'm not saying this just because I was slapped on the cheek by one of the servants of that damned household. After four generations of one son, they have only a weakling of a daughter, so even if they build a shrine for the Fertility Gods, what good will it do them?'

'You talk as if the Master was already under the earth. Do you know something that I don't?'

'Of course I do. It's the spirits that are against them.'

Chilsung's argument did not fit together. He seemed to be saying that immoral or evil deeds done in order to amass wealth could be excused even while he was accusing them and criticizing these bad deeds.

'Damn it all, what's it got to do with me what becomes of children and children's children? Whichever way up it is, if only I could live for once talking loudly before I die!'

It seemed that what was in his mind could be summed up as a belief that for his own well-being, any means, even if criminal, could be regarded as worthy.

'Damn it all! If only that wretched widow hadn't come to a sudden end . . .'

'. . .'

'That damned widow.'

Before he was twenty Chilsung had turned his back on his native village saying that he didn't want to be a peasant wearing a torn shirt and eating barley gruel. A few years later he had come back to marry, have children, and settle down in the unwanted role of a peasant. Behind his back there was gossip about the fact that he had returned with one of his fingers cut off in the middle. It was whispered that it had been bitten off by a chaste widow he had attempted to rape in one of the villages that he visited as a pedlar. He himself said nothing about the cause of his lost finger, but he often talked about how he had nearly got off with a certain rich widow who had suddenly died and so shattered his dream of getting hold of some capital. Whenever he heard the mixture of disappointment and pride in Chilsung's words, Yoon Bo, rolling his eyes like a plaice, would abuse him.

' "The skate that got away was as big as a cow's blanket" is that it? A youngster not yet dry behind the ears trying to empty a woman's purse – it's clear what your future path will be, you rascal.'

'Your belly aches because you've got nothing to put in it. It's not likely that anyone will offer you anything either'. Chilsung would reply.

Yoon Bo was at peace with all the world, yet for some reason he hated Chilsung so much that if his name was but mentioned, even in the middle of the night, he would come out brandishing a club, and whenever he saw him he would bare his yellow teeth in abuse and raise his fists ready to attack.

The well-proportioned figure of Yongi, with his headband and the sack over his shoulder, and Chilsung, with a hemp cloth tied round his head, padded pantaloons and *jogori*, the string of straw shoes over his shoulder, entered the market at a leisurely pace.

Bong-gi, who had been squatting on the ground in the midst of the teeming market-place eating a bowl of thick soup, saw them coming and smiled.

'What idiots! coming along just as it's closing. Is it to grab the wrist of a loose wench? Or to pick up the dropped coins?'

'We've come now to avoid the sight of you squatting there at dawn shivering like a puppy with the mange – so what?'

Chilsung spat out the words with no sign of respect for a man older than himself, indeed with great contempt.

'Hey, you rascal, is that the way to speak to your uncle? I've never heard such insolence. Say "Good boy to your grandson, and he'll pull your whiskers," as they say. It's because you're not old enough yet, so as a wise uncle I'll put up with it. Aren't you hungry? The soup is nice and tasty.'

A servile smile appeared on his face, which was mottled with dark patches.

'Are you going to buy me some, then?'

The smile quickly disappeared from his eyes, with big areas of white, and they flashed.

'I've not money for that.'

'All right. That's fair enough, if you haven't got it. But let me have what you owe me some time today.'

Saying this, Chilsung stepped close to him.

'Wouldn't I have paid you, if I had it?'

'No one gets a penny out of me. Don't think it's easy to do me out of it, because I've never let a penny go in the whole of my life! Not a chance! Keep on putting it off and the baby in the womb becomes an old man. I'll have to take a chest or a cabinet or whatever I can get.'

Bong-gi put down his bowl and jumped to his feet. Hopping up and down as if to suggest the sky was too low, and waggling his straggly beard.

'D-d-do you think you can? N-n-no chance. Let's see who will die and who will live!'

As if the chest was even now being carried away before his eyes, he shouted and foamed at the mouth. While these two were quarrelling, Yongi, standing apart, exchanged greetings with a middle-aged man from Chong-am who was a relative by marriage.

'Whatever happened, I was going to see her married last autumn, you know, and then what? Her mother falls ill. For smooth family life there shouldn't be any illnesses.'

'Mind out! Mind out! You're not in your own backyard you know.'

A man bent under a huge load of seafood called angrily as he prodded their backs with his stick. Yongi's in-law, red in the face, turned on him: 'Words are enough. You don't need to use a stick.'

Yongi added, 'Look here, a young man like you can't treat your elders like that.'

'Worked to death, how can I tell young from old, in this crowd, with the sun already going down and my guts on fire.'

'What an idiot!'

The carrier had already disappeared into the crowd.

'Buy some *dok! Dok!* You know what happens if you don't have some *Kaepi dok* in the tenth month . . .'

'What's wrong with you? If you don't want it, that's it. "Even the world's worst mother-in-law can't interfere with the inside of your sleeve".'

The cries and chatter mingled with the choruses of beggar groups, while Chilsung, wherever he had gone, was nowhere to be seen. Yongi put down the net with the chickens at his feet and just stood there.

'Leftovers! Leftovers! You've never seen anything so cheap in all your life! Tell me if you have! I'm letting it go dirt cheap as I'm off to Seoul to look for my son. Whoever buys the lot is in luck. Dirt cheap, I say, dirt cheap!'

The gaunt old man jabbered away. In summer he walked barefoot over the hot pebbles and in winter he would survive on a lump of cold rice in a bowl of soup, as he looked up at the sunrise from where he had slept under the eaves of a village inn, shifting from one market to another, one town to another, as he had done last year, the year before, for ten years or more.

'I'm off to look for my son in Seoul. Take the lot and be lucky!'

Until the day when he resigned from the world, ceased to trade and gave up his painful roaming he would spread out his soiled goods and jabber away.

'I'm throwing the lot away dirt cheap and going to Seoul to look for my son.'

A rough-looking man with a red neck was weaving his way amid the traders, his hawk-like eyes flashing, as he collected the market rents. At last there came the subdued bustle of closing time. Near the end Yongi sold off his fowls to a pedlar and bought the piece of *miyok* asked for by Yoon Bo and the fine-toothed comb and shuttle for his wife.

'Finished?'

Chilsung suddenly appeared.

'Yes – what about you?'

'Yes – long since.' He had a sickle and a hoe blade, without handles, tied with straw cord. The pieces of metal, with a bluish tinge, as if new from the foundry, would doubtless be used next summer to make a small arable patch on the slope of a hill. He also carried a couple of salted mackerel.

They left the market and went into the tavern where the road forked.

'Is her ladyship of the *champan* house well?' asked Wolsun, hostess at the wine shop.

Her eyes seemed to be staring at some distant spot beyond Yongi's shoulders. Their blue pupils would flash yellow. Taking off his straw shoes, Yongi replied, 'Very much as usual.'

Withdrawing her gaze, she wiped the table. Her lowered eyes seemed asleep. Sitting before the table, Chilsung smiled awkwardly. Yongi looked angry. A middle-aged man, with the air of a pedlar, who had been sitting drinking cross-legged, glanced at the side-dishes that Wolsun had put for the new arrivals.

'Bongsoon's mother is all right, too?' She asked further.

'You never fail to ask politely every time we come in,' said Chilsung, and Yongi replied, 'She seems to be having a hard time with the young Miss.'

People said that Wolsun should have become a shaman, like her mother, and that, because she had not, there were often times when her soul went out and left her empty. This was because the spirits came over her head to harass her. Perhaps so, for there were frequent occasions when she sat vacantly as if she were an idiot. After emptying the plate clean, the middle-aged man stroked his wine-stained beard, rubbed his nose, and still hesitated, although he did not seem to have anything else to do, until finally he stood up to go and said, 'I'll pay up next market day. I'm sorry about that, but what can I do? . . . heh! heh! heh!'

He opened his mouth to laugh weakly and, unable to leave quickly, made as if to be looking for something fallen on the floor, though there didn't seem to be anything there.

60

'Every time putting it off like that, what are you going to do in the end? You already owe quite a lot . . .'.

Wolsun spoke with an air of resignation. Yongi lowered his cup and stared sharply at the man.

'By the next market day, for sure. If only I could get what they owe me from the inn . . .'.

He stealthily crept out.

'Do you dig the soil somewhere to keep your business going? You have to see that you get what's due to you.'

Yongi spoke sharply.

'What can you do when they've got nothing?'

'That's what they call "Sending an offering without knowing to which temple".'

Seeing that Yongi was unhappy about it, Chilsung also chimed in, 'You look around a room, as they say, before you shit in it. You must tighten your grip.'

'When you are old and sick, who will . . .'.

The words died away in Yongi's mouth. After looking down at the table for a while, he put down a few coins and abruptly stood up.

'Let's go!'

'Why, it's getting dark already!'

As they were about to set off, after putting on their shoes, Wolsun said again, 'How is the Master of the *champan* house?'

'Always about the same.'

Yongi went out without looking back.

At the ferry they boarded a returning market-boat. Turning its back on the estuary, it went up stream. The darkness seemed to flow in from all around them, and then suddenly the round moon was bobbing in the water.

Chapter Seven

THEY had left late, so obviously they would be back late. Kangchong *dek* knew this but rather than think about supper, she was absorbed in looking out for them. As the thin light of early winter faded and all around darkness grew, she still kept vigil at the gate, staring in the direction of the river.

'He is stuck in that woman's wine shop! I won't go on like this, I won't!'

As Chilsung had said, she was a very jealous woman. With a life-long yearning for human affection, it had been her misfortune to marry a man like Yongi, good looking enough to arouse peculiar emotions in the hearts of women buried under heavy work, especially those who were widowed or lacked marital affection. For this woman, jealousy seemed to be an ever-burning fire within her, and having no child as a blood-tie to bind the man's feet continually added fuel to the flame. She thought of other women as little more than potential seducers of Yongi, and because of this pathological enmity she had a lonely existence even in her own village.

'A rootless woman like that . . .'. She blurted out, referring to Wolsun, but it did not ease her mind. She fully appreciated that, short of being birds on the wing, there was no way in which Yongi and Wolsun could indulge in physical love, but she could not tolerate his making even a brief call at the tavern. So market day had to be seen as an enemy. She had heard from the gossip-loving village women, until it made her ears sore, the story of how Yongi and Wolsun had had to part long ago, before she had married him.

'What do you need from the market? It's only an excuse.'

She would fret madly, but it did not prevent him from going there.

'That bitch, with eyes like a dog, what does he see in her?'

Forcing herself to leave the gate, she began to cook the supper in the light of pine resin.

'My liver's on fire! I can't bear the waiting!'

Putting on to the small table a bowl of boiled barley, some soya-bean soup left over from breakfast, and *kimchi* that tasted only of salt and hot pepper, she carried it into the room. As if Yongi was sitting at the top end waiting for it, she banged it down.

'My liver's burning with a thousand flames. I can't bear it. I don't care whether he's coming to eat it or not! I'll smash up this life! I'll shave my head and become a nun!'

She left the house and walked across the bare vegetable patches towards Dooman *ne*'s.

'Men, they're all black inside. If it was somebody else's wife, even a mortar with a skirt round it would send them mad.'

She thought of Yongi's words, 'If you were pretty and clever like Chilsung's wife, I'd not only make you straw shoes, but leather ones too.'

'Men they are all . . .'.

Perhaps it was a puddle – as one foot slipped in, the other one kicked the air and sent one of her worn out shoes flying some distance.

'Men, they all have the stomachs of thieves.'

She recovered her lost shoe, put it on, and resumed her hurried, magpie-like steps.

'Huh! What's the good of having someone clever and pretty? Will a flirtatious bitch like that see to the offerings for his dead parents?'

In the bright moonlight a hardy orange tree suddenly rose up in front of her. She picked up a stone, placed it on the pile of stones that surrounded the tree, and putting her palms together made countless bows: 'Great and wise tree-god, please fulfil my desire. Please bestow upon me the blessing of a son.'

She prayed with reverence, but as soon as she turned away her mind resumed its normal state. As she entered Dooman *ne*'s gate the pigs in the sty grunted and the dog ran out barking.

'Boksil, it's me, it's only me.'

Brushing the dog out of the way and putting one hand on the verandah to help herself up, she said, 'I just wondered how the work was getting on, *songnim*.'

With a click the door opened from within. In the light of a small oil lamp a number of women sat close together on the floor. Dooman *ne* stretched forward her head,

'Come in, *dongseng*.'

'I've been busy doing nothing . . . Have you finished?'

Entering the room, she closed the door. As the light of the lamp flickered, so did the women's faces.

'You're a bit early!'

'What a struggle you must have had to get here by dawn!'

'Aren't you a bit early to see the moon at dawn?'

Everyone had a sarcastic remark to throw at her. It was the day they were making a shroud for Dooman *ne*'s mother-in-law, in readiness for her death. The work seemed to be finished and they had all been gossiping, except Yamu *ne* who, perhaps because she had eaten too much, reclined against the wall and stroked her stomach just below her breasts. Scratching her side, Kangchong *dek* squeezed herself in to sit amongst them.

'The room's nice and warm.'

'I've cooked lunch and supper, so the room is boiling, isn't it?'

Dooman *ne* was not unwelcoming.

'I knew you were busy, but even so, I couldn't manage it. I don't know why I've been so busy doing nothing . . .'.

The widow Magdal *ne* said teasingly, 'I know what's on your mind, Kangchong *dek*. It's market day, isn't it? All day long your heart has been burning. How many gourd bowls have you smashed up?'

'That rootless wench? – why should I be jealous of a shaman bitch like her?'

Inwardly she cursed Magdal *ne*.

(That cow, with a face like a cymbal that's been beaten all night, and no man of her own, and when there's a chance she runs out with both her legs down one side of her pants.)

'Her mother was a shaman, but Wolsun isn't.'

'If the mother's a shaman, the daughter is too. Where do ducklings go but to the water?'

The corners of Kangchong *dek*'s eyes tilted upwards. Dooman *ne* quietened them.

'Listen, all of you. There's going to be trouble. Stop it now. Kangchong *dek* wouldn't you like some noodles?'

'Yes, please if you have some. So you've been having a late snack?'

Chilsung's wife, Yimi *ne*, cornered her with, 'How shameless, she doesn't even know where the needle and thread have gone to and she's going to have some noodles!'

Because of the words 'clever and pretty', Kangchong *dek* had kept her face away from Yimi *ne* ever since she had entered the room.

'Yimi *ne*, what's making your belly ache?'

Though there may have been a little bad feeling, Yimi *ne* had not spoken in anything but her usual tone, but Kangchong *dek* took up her words and pounced fiercely.

'Is it because you've stored up your own provisions in this house that you're worried? Is it because Dooman *ne* owes you some grain?'

'What on earth? Have I said something bad enough for my tongue to be pulled out? As they say "Thrashed in the market place so he comes home and beats his wife!"'

In place of Dooman *ne*, who had gone out to the kitchen, Haman *dek*, the eldest of them, intervened, 'It's wrong to quarrel at the end of doing a good work.'

Exchanging glances, Yimi *ne* and Magdal *ne* screwed up their lips. Yamu *ne* burping, continued to rub her stomach. To the degree that Kangchong *dek* disliked her, Yimi *ne* was never friendly towards Kangchong *dek*. This could be seen from the way that although at twenty-eight she was three years younger, she did not use respectful forms when she spoke to her. Yimi *ne* was extremely healthy and good-looking. Her stomach was noticeably swollen but perhaps because of the winter her skin was white and glowing and she did not look like a pregnant woman. Needless to say, she was proud of her appearance and among the people of the village there was no one to disagree with the opinion that she was the best-looking.

Kangchong *dek* looked rather pitiful as with a sucking noise she tucked into the noodle soup brought in by Dooman *ne*.

'You must have fixed up the loom, *songnim*, haven't you. . .'. Dooman *ne* stopped short. She had intended to ask Magdal *ne* but, confused by the quarrel, she had made a mistake. Perplexed, Haman *dek* replied, 'I keep my loom in use twelve months of the year. As for our own cotton, I haven't got round to carding it yet.'

'Of course. Have you had a good crop?'

'Not too good.'

Yamu *ne* who had been rubbing her stomach all the time joined in, 'Honestly, I think I'd rather wear hemp even in the coldest month than put up with the noise of the carding tool.'

'Who wouldn't?' Yimi *ne* readily agreed.

Tonight, as any other night, after she had returned home, Haman *dek*, would be weaving until the cock crew at dawn, and, except for some miracle, it was unlikely that she would ever escape her fate of earning a wage by weaving. Kim Pyongsan, the fallen gentleman referred to by Chilsung as one of the 'dog-legged', was Haman *dek*'s husband, and was now reduced to a level no better than that of the market traders. His wife, who, with her worn out clothes carefully mended, presented a better appearance than any one else in the room, came from the middle class. Kim Pyongsan had married beneath him and she had endured frightening poverty and the outrageous behaviour of her husband with a strength that came perhaps from a determination to uphold and cherish the prestige of the so-called 'gentry'. She looked older than her years and there was always a feverish flush on her narrow heart-shaped face. Wiping the beads of perspiration from her brow with the back of her hand, she said to Dooman-*ne*, 'You couldn't go this morning?'

'No, I wasn't able to.'

'What are you talking about?' asked Magdal *ne*.

'It's the fifteenth day and I couldn't go.'

'You mean the offering for old Bawoo? Does it really matter if you didn't? Gannan may be old and bent but she is still there.'

Haman *dek* asked, 'How close a relative was he?'

'Further than an eighth cousin. They say he was eighth cousin to my departed father-in-law.'

'As they say, "One kitchen sees eight cousins", it doesn't take long for kinship to expand. So, as for relatives you are the only ones?'

'There are several others but they are scattered to the north or the south and we don't know where they live.'

66

'Well, with no children . . .'.

'On the first of the month Dooman's dad could go . . . but somehow I had fixed today for this work here and then saw that it overlapped.'

'Not to worry. "One bridge might as well be a thousand miles!" When you've got your own work to do, how could you leave it to go there? Your mother-in-law is really lucky to have children like you, I can tell you that. Not all of them do what they should do.'

'We've completed a shroud for the auntie at the *champan* house as well. She was called a serf, but in fact her ladyship depended so much on those two. If only uncle hadn't died at such an awkward time – he was just unlucky . . .'.

'How could you have time for it – in the middle of all that upset?'

'That's true enough. What a night to die! I've never seen anything like it in all my life. While a creature like me, without a husband, has to exist on two bowls of gruel a day and try to bring up children, the daughter-in-law of a great family can lose her head over a servant.'

Raising the wick of the lamp, Dooman *ne*, perhaps disapproving of the way Magdal *ne* had spoken, frowned.

'These affairs – can they be controlled by human will?'

'Were things between the two of them bad from the beginning?' asked Yamu *ne*.

'They say they were never in harmony.'

'*Songnim*, you know very well – were relations bad with the other wife, the one who died?'

'The deceased lady? They were as loving as two doves. They were so young when they married – she was fourteen and he was thirteen.'

'Was she good-looking?'

'About that, well . . . there's an old saying, "A beautiful wife may be treated harshly, but never an ugly one." She was gracious, but not pretty – not compared with the present lady . . . and she'd lived twelve years without a child. If she was still alive, she'd be about my age.'

'So there must be a big gap between the master and the mother of our young Miss?

'That's right. She'd have been about twenty-three. So there's a difference of more than ten years between them.'

'Oh, She's green. Whatever they say, it's Kuchon that I'm sorry for. Wasn't he beaten to death?'

As soon as the name of Kuchon had left Yimi *ne*'s lips, Kangchong *dek*, who had been eating the noodles, said, 'What's the use of feeling sorry for someone else's man? You are too emotional, Yimi *ne* – that's your trouble. Emotional women are liable to wag their tails at men and fall into disgrace.'

'I never heard such rubbish. So, because I'm emotional I've seduced someone, is that it?'

With flushed face, she was ready to fight.

'In principle, I mean.'

'Indeed?'

'I was referring to the so-called lady of the *byoldang*, so why are you making a fuss? It's a kind of sin for any woman to be too pretty. I've never seen a pretty woman who wasn't the downfall of some man.'

It could have turned into a fight, but for the topic of Kuchon, which aroused so much interest that they all started chattering, and the tautened feeling between Yimi *ne* and Kanchong *dek* was pushed into the background. The women told different tales each according to her imagination or on the basis of gossip they had gleaned. Some said that Kuchon had been beaten to death while others said, no, he had had his nose cut off, or no, it was not his nose, but his ear, and also he had had his hair cropped. Someone else said that he had run away, taking the woman with him, as if he had been a ghost, and that it was only after he had already disappeared that the household was turned upside down.

For three generations now Dooman *ne*'s family had been delivered from the humble state of serfdom to that of tenant farmers on the land of Choi *champan*, but nevertheless between these two families the bonds of the master-servant relationship were maintained at least in spirit, so she alone discreetly kept her mouth shut lest the reputation of the master's family be disgraced, even though she had more accurate information than any of them.

'They say that Kuchon is no ordinary commoner. He was educated at some hermitage in Kuchon-dong, Mooju, that's what I heard.'

Despite the insult inflicted by Kangchong *dek*, Yimi *ne*'s interest in Kuchon did not waver. Pushing the noodle bowl that she had emptied down to the lower end of the room, Kangchong *dek* obstinately took up the argument again: 'Education! Some damn education! According to what I hear, he was living as a monastery servant. Anyway, it's "Stroking the genitals of a dead son." At this stage, what does it matter whether he had any education or not?'

The women, feeling that she was going too far, gave Yimi *ne* looks that said 'take no notice.' Yamu *ne* added, 'He was a man with a past – some people say he had been mixed up with the Dong Hak.'

The conversation now turned to his origins, the contents of the tales based on pure conjecture and floating rumours, ever broadening. Some thought him the illegitimate son of a grand family in Seoul, while others said that he had been born to a *kiseng* or a concubine who had waited on the governor of a provincial town; others would add that a man with such a distinguished appearance and well-built figure could not have come from ordinary folk. Of course, no one would praise him for what he had done, but one couldn't deny that it is possible for such things to happen. Even with good family and wealth and all that sort of thing, how could any woman, unless she had exceptional virtue, not be stirred by a man with fairy-tale looks who was ready for her sake to risk his life? At that green age, though she had been living with a so-called husband only a yard away since giving birth to a girl, she had apparently led such a life that she might have been separated from him by a wall of a thousand miles. After that, what she did was not altogether surprising. As for the master, what do you yourself think of him? Even to eyes like ours, where is there a single attraction? Like a mantis, he seems to be more clothes than a man. And look at his eyes – don't they remind you of an adder slithering through the grass? They give you the creeps. People's minds and the way

69

they see things are all the same, so you can imagine how that poppy-like young beauty must have lamented her fate.

'When a woman is due to have a baby, she becomes blind to everything, they say.'

At Yamu *ne*'s words Magdal *ne* blinked her eyes, which were rather small in proportion to the width of her face. As the chat took a turn more sympathetic towards the lady of the *byoldang*, Yimi *ne* and Kangchong *dek* joined forces to oppose it. This time, for once, forgetting their quarrels, they agreed in a merciless attitude towards their own sex. Yimi *ne* asserted that it was because the lady of the *byoldang* had wagged her tail that the blameless Kuchon had been done for, and so she was the one who deserved death, while Kangchong *dek* said that the bond of husband and wife cannot be undone even under circumstances in which the sky collapsed and the earth erupted, and so in this case the woman was a hundred times in the wrong. This was both a defence against mistrust of her husband and a threat to the pretty Yimi *ne* who floated before her, plump and smart, like a hen kept for breeding. Dooman *ne*, not wanting the gossip to go deeper, said, 'As the saying goes "You can cheat your horoscope, but not fate". It had to be regarded as a predestined bond.'

Haman *dek* folded her arms and, swallowing hard, said, 'There is this story . . .'

Whenever she started off in this way, a long tale was due to issue from her lips.

'Once upon a time, a crockery seller stayed overnight at the house of the Prime Minister. On the morrow, after the merchant had left, the Prime Minister's wife was found to be missing. She had just disappeared into nowhere. The fact was that she had run away with the vendor. The great man felt ashamed, but he was even more troubled by curiosity, to the extent of refusing either to eat or drink while he deliberated on the matter. He could not understand why his wife, the mistress of the household of a Prime Minister, with no one to envy in the whole world, should have to follow a crockery vendor. So, resigning his office, he set off on a journey, wandering all over the eight provinces in search of her, so that he could find out her reasons. One day he found himself in the depths of the mountains. The sun had set and the track had become impassable when he happened to see just ahead of him a mud hut, isolated and covered with canes of Indian millet. He stayed the night there and, when morning came, a woman brought in the breakfast table. Lo and behold, whatever was this? It was his wife! Staggered, he said, "Madam, lift up your face and look at me. Don't you know who I am?" With her face still lowered she said, "What does it matter whether I do or not? It is all predestined, so please say no more and just go back." '

'You mean he left the rascal and the wench unpunished?' interrupted Kagchong *dek*.

'Just listen. After leaving the millet-stalk hovel he shed tears at the thought of this woman whose once-soft hands were now like a rake, whose clothes merely covered her flesh, ragged as a beggar, with food so rough that even the horses at home would not have eaten it, living as a slash and burn farmer in the hills. He reflected upon the fate and bondage of this wife for whom there was no other way. On returning home he opened a book called "The Record of Former Existences", from which he gained an insight into the whole affair. According to the record the Premier had been a Buddhist monk, the crockery trader a bear, and the woman a louse . . .'.

'Good heavens!'

'One day the monk, while walking along a mountain path, had caught the louse crawling on his body. Forbidden to kill any living thing, he was in a dilemma, not knowing what to do with it. When he caught sight of a bear lying dead nearby, he left it on the bear's skin and went on his way. That's the whole story. So don't you all agree that such matters as the bond between two people, and whether you are rich or poor, are all decided by your former life?'

Bemused, the women all looked at her, their eyes seeming to betray their thoughts on 'What could I have been in my previous existence?'

As Haman *dek* wiped the perspiration from her heart-shaped face, she smiled. Dooman *ne* turned up the flickering wick of the lamp.

'Mummy!'

71

Mingling with the barking of the dog, a child's voice was heard outside.

'Is that Yimi?'

Yimi *ne* opened the door and looked out.

'Daddy's home.'

'So he's back? Let's go home then.'

With a gesture of gathering up her swollen belly she rose to her feet.

'Daddy's brought some liver.'

'Liver? Excuse me, *songnim* for leaving early.'

'Aren't you going too, Kangchong *dek*?' teased Magdal *ne* after she had gone.

'If he's home, what about it? Do you expect me to be like Yimi *ne*? I've left his supper ready, so he'll tuck into it, I suppose.'

'Look at her bad ways!' Haman *dek* clicked her tongue.

'I'm not going to pamper him like a *kiseng*. If he is home, let him be. Is it a decent thing for an ordinary housewife to dash after him as if I was possessed by a starving ghost?'

'Nonsense. It's about time you learned to control your temper,' scolded Dooman *ne*.

Kangchong *dek*'s face was now suffused with a look of peace and contentment. Like a shepherd who, having herded his flock from the freedom of the fields into the pen, feels safe and can treat himself to a drink in an inn, she now looked ready to enjoy her outing with her heart at ease. While listening to Dooman *ne* telling of the scarcity of offspring in the Choi *champan* family, they peeled raw sweet potatoes and ate them till late in the night before they returned to their own homes. When Kangchong *dek* returned Yongi was lying down with a wooden-block pillow at the back of his head, staring blankly at the ceiling.

'Aren't you asleep?'

'No.'

Sitting up embarrassed, he groped for his pipe.

'I went to Dooman *ne*'s to give her a hand as I heard they were making the shroud today.'

'Shroud?'

72

'Grave clothes ready for her mad old mother-in-law. As Dooman's dad is thrifty and diligent, they seem to do all the proper things.'

'Even if I had a mind to do all the proper things, who is there in the family that's likely to need a shroud unless it's yourself?'

He lit his pipe.

'That's right. Just waiting for the day I die. Then along will come that bitch of a woman for whom you'll make the leather shoes – isn't that so?'

'You go on diligently, too, with your weaving. Then when you die, I'll put the clothes on you and bury you properly.'

'H'm, being sarcastic are you? Because I told you that they made a shroud, do you think they did it with cloth she wove herself? I hear they went to market and bought the hemp with real money!'

Though his eyes were on her face, as he sucked his pipe Yongi seemed to be preoccupied with other thoughts.

Chapter Eight

YOON BO was snapping dried pine branches into short
pieces.
    'What do you want?'

His deep ringing voice came rolling over the low-lying thatched
roof of the house. Yongi, who had stalked in carrying a bottle of
wine, stopped and glanced round like a man inspecting the site.

'I see, you've brought some wine for my birthday.'

'Yes.'

'I was feeling peckish and about to set off to the tavern.'

Yongi smiled.

'What have you done with your *miyok* soup?'

'After touching the floor several times with my forehead, I ate
it. What else?'

Being in a good mood, even though his lips were closed, Yoon
Bo's face was all a smile, the corners of his eyes pulled downwards.
A great carpenter, he was renowned for his skill and ability not
only in the town and the area around it but in other provinces as
well. But the house where he himself lived consisted of just one
room that opened straight off the yard along with a kitchen, a mere
make-shift hut without even a garden wall. Like the saying, 'No
kitchen knives in the blacksmith's house,' or 'Dressmakers and car-
penters, cutting and chopping day and night, are never well off ',
his life was indeed one of great poverty. Without even a puppy for
family, he roamed in strange places and like a migrant bird would
come back to sit by the river and dip his fishing rod. As he himself
put it, for a man without one dependent in the whole world, what
was the use of a house? But knowing the dates of his parents'
deaths, which he could not overlook, he must have a place in which
to offer the spirits at least a bowl of water on these days, even
though it be but a hovel.

'If that is your theory, why don't you concern yourself with your own descendants?', the village elders would sometimes chide.

'Can such things be done by a man's own will?' he would return.

'You have to see the sky before you can pick a star. I've never heard of a man producing a son on his own.'

He would sometimes laugh and say, 'Well, do dead lips really eat? Once the earth is in your eye sockets that's the end of it. Where are spirits? Putting out a bowl of water for the dead is just your filial duty and a way of remembering what your parents did for you, isn't that so? My own generation is enough. Why should I want any sons to carry on this life of wind and dust?'

He gathered together the remaining pine branches and broke them up. Dumping them on the kitchen floor, he looked over at the hill beyond the river for a while and flared his nostrils, where the pock-marks were conspicuous, saying, 'It looks as if the wind's getting up but what are you just standing there for? Why don't you come in?'

Yongi, who had been standing blankly, went into the room, almost crawling. Inside it was dim, with a fetid smell. At the upper end, where downy dust had gathered, was a solidly built wooden chest on which soiled bedding lay folded. A tool bag occupied a corner at the same end.

'Damn it, the wild boar must have been down last night,' said Yoon Bo as, awkwardly, he brought in earthenware cups and a bowl of chili sauce.

'I had some sweet-potatoes buried away at the back of the house but they've been ruined.'

'It's all because you don't have a fence.'

Squatting, he put the things down on the floor. He pulled out a dried pollack that had been stored between the chest and the wall, twisted off its head and tore it into strips.

'In this village there is something to eat, so it may be worth having a fence round the house, but for the really poor, what's the use of it? It would be pathetic. And the wild animals have to eat, or how would Kang *posoo*, the hunter, keep going?'

Yongi filled a wine-cup to the brim.

'*Hyong-nim*, please take the cup.'

75

Emptying it with one gulp, Yoon Bo handed it in turn to Yongi and poured out more wine.

'You, too.'

He dipped a piece of pollack into a bowl of chilli sauce.

'It looks as if you'll have to settle here for the winter. Are you going to be all right?'

Chewing steadily, he said, 'You mean will I have enough to eat? Well, when New Year is over, I'm thinking of going somewhere far away. I'm getting restless.'

'There still seems to be lots of troubles. They say there's been another conspiracy in Seoul.'

'That's nothing.'

Yoon Bo cut him short in a voice full of reproof and impatience.

'The great empire of China has now surrendered to the Japs. That's a sign of decline, I think. They will come swarming over here like ants, and they say that at the ports their traders are already getting busy. What's the use of having a scarecrow of a king if the real power lies in the hands that hold the guns? Huh, when the Dong Hak, rising up like a swarm of bees, couldn't do anything, what can you expect from a few scoundrels whispering together?'

He spoke with scorn.

That year, so far, a couple of attempts to overthrow the government had been discovered. One, centred on Han Sunhoi, former Secretary of the Office of Defence, and Yi Keunyong, Commander of the Royal Bodyguard, had miscarried. In July another plot had been discovered and the leaders, Song Jin-yong, a former police officer, and Hong Hyon-chol, a former member of the Crown Prince's Tutorial Staff, had been executed. There had been similar events in previous years. Yongi had heard tell of them from travellers. Since the amateurish uprising of 1884, led by Kim Ok Kyun, reckless and overconfident, and Pak Yong Ho under the banner of the Enlightenment Party, and trusting in the untrustworthy Japanese, there had been, to mention but the main events: the Dong Hak rebellion and the subsequent Sino-Japanese war; the assassination of Minbi, the queen, in her palace, by Japanese intruders; the beating to death in the street of Kim Hong-Jip, premier of a pro-Japanese cabinet, and Chong Byong Ha, minister of agriculture, trade and

76

industry; and the death of Auh Yoon-Joong, the finance minister, at the hands of a wild mob. Beneath these sporadic riots lay an every-bubbling cauldron of disturbance, disquiet and confusion. A group of Confucian scholars, rising against the decree banning top-knots and the assassination of the Mother of the nation, led a volunteer army in attacks on the Japanese and on local rulers, and civil disturbances flared up whenever the seeds of fire scattered here and there caught the right wind. Nor should one underestimate the strength of the Dong Hak, whose organization, gone under-ground since the loss of innumerable leaders, including Chong Bong Joon and Kim Kae-nam, still held together in its beliefs and in resistance to oppression.

Meanwhile, now that China, the country's long-standing guard-ian, had been beaten, and retreated, the newly rising power, the so-called 'Great Empire of Japan' in whose eyes no rightful owner of Korea remained, vied with Imperial Russia to grab the tempting lump laid out on the chopping board, and other powerful nations with whetted appetites kept their eyes open, ready to snatch any opportunity. Alongside this was the continuous struggle for power among the Koreans themselves, some with the backing of foreign powers and others taking advantage of royal connections. Foreign ideas and systems, while causing political confusion through the continuous making of new laws and unmaking of them, literally 'A law in the morning, repealed in the evening', had reduced to chaos the sense of values built up through the five hundred years of the Yi dynasty. Indeed, chaos was everywhere – the higher the rank, the greater the confusion, and the nearer the centre, the more extreme. In circumstances such as these, where a host of spectres seemed to walk in broad daylight, Yoon Bo might well say that the authority of the sovereign could not be of much importance, nor the schemes of a few ambitious buffoons, simple-minded patriots or clownish characters in western suits and horsehair hats to subvert the government.

'These are only trifles. What really matters is that now the great land of China has fallen, the Japs and the Russkis are trying to bash each other's heads in, while the gentry, regarding them as enlight-

77

ened and ahead of us, cut off their topknots and madly try to appease them. What does this enlightenment really amount to?'

'. . .'

'As I see it, the so-called "enlightenment" is nothing very wonderful. In a word, you can call it a good tool for killing people. Either that or ruthlessly plundering other people's possessions. It is true. "The weak cannot beat the strong", but look at our masters carrying the marauders on their backs! I'm a simple man who doesn't know very much, but I know the old saying, "If it's not the right road, don't go down it", and it makes me wonder how it can be right for anyone to hand over to strangers the land of rivers and mountains that bore and bred him. It's true that we, the low-born, have never received much of our country's gracious favour . . . but the world is too miserable and I have no heart for work. I would be happy just to sit by the blue river, fishing all the year round, and live on carp, but it looks as though even that much is not going to be easy.'

Again they poured out more wine for each other. It was not that Yongi could not understand what Yun Bo said, but being ignorant of the world outside the village, he did not have the same degree of insight. After a few moments' silence, he opened his mouth to say,

'*Hyongnim*, it's about time you changed your mind.'

Yoon Bo cast him a quick glance as if expecting him to bring up the subject of the Dong Hak Party.

'How much longer do you think you can go on depending just on your own strength?'

'When did I ever trust in strength? If I'd just relied on that, I'd have long been dead.'

'You must somehow try to settle down.'

'I haven't the slightest intention of doing that. Say what you like, the best life of all is flying free like a bird. Don't you understand?'

His eyes flashed.

'No, I don't.'

Yongi purposely pretended not to.

'A man's life is like a dew drop on a blade of grass and it lasts at the most no more than seventy years, even though he pounds the foundations and builds a house as if he's going to live for a thousand or more. What is there to rely on? Ageing, ailing and dying come the same to the king on his throne or a man living rough like myself. I am not a man with any particular faith, but I know that happiness lies in your own mind and what I like best is to trot around freely swinging my arms.'

'You'll never settle down if you go on thoughtlessly like that.'

'That's why I don't fix myself in one place. If I had looks like yours, as smart as a soup bowl licked clean by a dog, I'd have married long since, and thanks to the wife and the kids I would have enjoyed life, and suffered too. But what woman would come and look after a chap with a face like mine? Anyway, after trying it, I like this free and easy way . . . As the saying goes, "Greed will kill a man". Look at that fellow, Yi Pangi, as thin as a dried pollack. Hasn't he driven himself crazy with work?'

'He has a big family to keep.'

'That's just what I mean. However hard he works can a peasant ever expect to leave his sons any land of their own?'

'Well, you like the carefree way of your own life while he lives for the sake of his family, enjoying the hard work. Isn't that fair?'

Yongi grinned as if it was his turn to tease.

'It's just as well they don't all want to live like I do. There'd be trouble and the seeds would dry up. Only me and King *posoo* will live like this.' He gave a carefree laugh as he mentioned the bristly-bearded hunter who followed a similar course.

'You must be very contented.'

'Yes, of course I am.'

Truly, he was a man with no worries. He was an excellent carpenter and had never once taken on a job that he did not want just for the money. When, pleased with a contract, he set off, his neighbours, though it was none of their business, would expect that surely this time he would come back with a lump sum and buy a strip of land, or have enough left to do some repairs to his house, and get some poor woman to look after him, but he always returned with his pockets empty, and from the next day would saunter out to the shore of the river with his fishing rod over his shoulder. It was a total mystery where and on what he spent the money. He drank quite a lot, but he did not seem to care about women or gambling. Sometimes he would just take off without a word to anyone, his tool bag on his shoulder, and after roaming distant villages paying for his few needs by repairing a gate or putting up a cow shed, he would come home again. Almost everyone in the village thought that he had been a member of the Dong Hak, even Lady Yoon, but this widespread belief was not quite in line with the facts. He was not a member of the party, nor had he ever been a farmer.

In the first month of 1894 the grievances of long-suffering farmers and the indignation of oppressed Dong Hak believers had exploded in a civil uprising at Goboo, under a bold and able strategist, Chon Bong-joon, the Dong Hak leader of the area. What had provoked the farmers was the heavy water tax imposed on them by Cho Byong-gap, the governor of the region, an official notorious for his greed, who, with the intention of further exploitation, had reconstructed the Mansokbo irrigation reservoir, although it had been in perfect working order, using the farmers' labour, and then not only not paying them, but adding an excessive water tax. Yoon Bo, who happened to be staying in the area when this occurred, had run to the market at dawn and with a bamboo pole on one end of which was tied a white cloth, joined the crowd of over a thousand waiting the first cock crow. This uprising in Goboo, settled for the time being by the expulsion of Cho Byong-gap, was a victory for the peasants, but was soon to be reversed. The government dispatched an inspector with a makeshift policy based on a misjudgement of the situation, which led to renewed oppression and reckless violence. When Chon Bong-joon rose again he was able to mobilize more people. Better-organized groups joined them from many other places, and some of the great Dong Hak leaders, including such giants as Kim Kae-nam, Kim Deuk-myon and Shon Hwa-jung, came forward, bringing their militia. Having secured a stronghold at Paiksan mountain in Goboo, they went a step farther than mere revenge on the greedy and erring officials by setting 'Serve the Country and Protect the People' and 'Boycott the Japanese and the Westerners' as their revolutionary aims. The initial form of a civil uprising changed into something more like open war as they went on to occupy the walled city of Chonju.

Throughout this time, while the initial uprising was becoming more warlike, Yoon Bo was always in the front rank, shouting like thunder, as with a body as solid as birch wood he flew about stimulating and cheering the others. The great carpenter who, though quite illiterate, had built houses as firm as an iron tub by guesswork and intuition, seemed in war also to have the same ability, by guesswork and intuition, to gather the volunteers, organize and manœuvre them. He appeared to be excessively radical and passionate, but in his heart he did not care for warlike people such as Kim Kae-nam, the Dong Hak leader of the Taein area, a man who had the same standing and prestige as Chon Bong-joon. Though he was a leader at the summit, and Yoon Bo but a soldier at the bottom, the latter had not approved of his acts of destruction, such as unnecessary killing or burning on their way toward their goal. Yoon Bo believed that a good seamstress can cut the pieces without chopping up the material, and an able carpenter handle the timber without hacking it to bits, and for him, this should also apply to warfare. Neither a peasant nor a Dong Hak believer himself, if he had anything in common with them it was no more than his social status. Not only did he have no immediate interest in the affair, but no ambition, and because of this it could be said that his motives were more pure. In any case, it was doubtful whether, ignorant as he was, he had ever been aware of the meaning of the revolution. It might be closer to the truth to see his action simply as an expression of valour. When the Dong Hak army handed Chonju over to the government forces, Yoon Bo, who by nature hated any kind of organized belief or instruction, calmly fell out of the ranks in the same way that on completing a house, he would gather up his tools and depart.

The Dong Hak rose again in the ninth month of the same year with the slogan 'Reject Japan: Save the Nation'. They had taken up a position with a river behind them so that retreat would be impossible, but the fight ended in a tragic and irreparable defeat, leaving the hills and fields soaked in blood. Yoon Bo had not taken part in this battle. Many Dong Hak leaders, including Chon Bong-joon, Kim Kae-nam, Son Wha-jung and others were now dead. Yoon Bo, after roaming around, chased here and hiding there, had returned to the village last spring, and it was not a bad place in which to lie low. Apart from the general rumour that he had been associated with the Dong Hak, nobody knew any details. It was also said that for some peculiar reason Lady Yoon was very sympathetic towards them. There had even been a passing rumour that she had helped them, but it probably arose from the fact that when they had been sweeping through the district, killing and injuring numberless people, destroying and setting properties on fire, and even in the pine wood by the river in the nearby town executing local land owners, petty officials, army officers and the associated gentry, no damage had been inflicted on the Choi house, and a few servants who attempted to escape had been caught and beaten. There had even been another rumour that Lady Yoon had supplied them with funds and other assistance, though it had been hushed up and soon forgotten. Even so, it was not the case that Yoon Bo was being specially favoured by her, nor had he on his side ever shown any respect towards the Choi *champan* house.

After the drink they lingered on for a while chatting and then Yongi followed him to the river bank, the carpenter carrying his fishing rod.

'Look over there,' he said, noticing it first.

'Isn't that Dr Mun from the town?'

Dori was holding the reins, keeping one eye on the river as he walked, and sitting on the donkey was the doctor, his long coat and his white beard fluttering in the river breeze.

'Does that mean the Master is ill again?' said Yongi, but Yoon Bo took no notice of what he said.

'Of course! It must be Gannan *halmum* that he is coming to see.'

'Yongi! You will never be anything but tied down to other people.'

As he spat out these words Yoon Bo looked into his face resignedly and went down the beach towards the river. Yongi, gazing in turn at his back as he trudged over the sand, pressed his lips tightly together but did not seem to be really offended.

'The mistress at the *champan* house, is she well? . . .'

Wolsun's voice came on the wind and whispered in his ear.

On reaching the gate of the house, Dr Mun got down from the

ass and went into the house while Dori, after putting the animal into the stable, called for Kilsang.

'I-sang no here' said Gad-dongi, the son of Kim *subang* as he walked up with dribbling lips.

'Where's he gone?'

'Dunno. Hee-hee-hee. . . .'

For no reason at all, he just laughed, his mouth hanging open. Four years older than Kilsang, he was now seventeen, but he was an imbecile and this had driven a nail into the steward's heart.

'Look here, boy. Take this to Bongsoon's mother, will you? Tell her it's from Wolsun in the town, understand?'

Dori handed him a small package. Samsoo glanced at them as he passed. Continually 'hee-hee-ing', Gad-dongi ran off.

Kilsang was in the junk shed, in which were piled up such objects as wine jars, straw mats, ladders, and old tools, and being in the shade all through the year, the air was dank. With his back against a big jar, he was lost in something he was making, showing a careful and delicate dexterity with his pocket knife in peeling, rubbing and smoothing his material. The objects he was handling were masks. He had not yet put the colours on them but, from the look of them, one was possibly a shaman's assistant, and the other a young gentleman scholar. The two masks, lit by the faint light inside the shed, looked uncanny, partly because they had no colour, but largely because of their exquisite outlines and features. Masks were usually made of such materials as wood, gourds, pine bark, or thick paper, but Kilsang had a different method. He made a rough shape with thinly split and smoothed bamboo sticks, over which he pasted a first layer of paper, then odd scraps of rice-paper and pieces of old wallpaper were torn into small pieces, soaked in paste, and put over the frame to give it flesh. He waited a few days for it to dry before putting on more flesh and shaping it. He was now adding the last touches with his pocket knife. While living at the monastery he had been taught to draw by the master-monk, Haegwan, whose task it was to paint holy pictures. The idea of the masks had come to him from seeing those of a troupe of players who had once stayed for a night outside the village. Kilsang had come originally from Yongok monastery in Kurae.

'Judging from his physiognomy, he doesn't seem to be the type to end up as a monk. If you would look after him it would be an act of merit.'

This is what Ugwan *sunim* had said to Lady Yoon during a visit. At the time of departure, when Kilsang stood behind her palanquin swallowing his sobs, the elderly Master, his eyes rolling like coals of fire, had thundered, 'You rascal, Kilsang! Remember the saying "Out of a ditch can come a dragon!".'

It was not a very long way from Kurae to Pyong Sa Ri. Kilsang could not think why the elderly Master had decided to send him to the Choi house. To his eyes, with no knowledge of the world outside the monastery, everything was wonderful. He wondered where the beautiful Sumjin River flowed to and he marvelled at the sight of the rafts with their crews and the boatman in a market boat sliding down the river with the current. Where would be the end of the sky? The world seemed to grow wider and wider and it made his heart flutter. It had been a few months before the arrival of Kuchon when, following the mistress's palanquin, he had entered the house where, in the court yard of the *sarang*, pink blossoms of *suksanwha* were blooming abundantly, earlier than at the monastery. He had thought that the Master's eyes were even more frightening than those of the *sunim*. Standing in the strange surroundings of a strange house he had been looking around him in bewilderment when Gannan *halmum* came up and said, 'I hear you are from the monastery?'

'Yes, ma'am.'

'Is the great Master well?'

'Yes, ma'am.'

Standing by her, the old man Bawoo, blinking, listened to his answers.

'Anyway, he is a man with a strong constitution.'

The old couple seemed to exchange a meaningful glance and said, 'Be obedient . . . If the master here scolds you, don't take it to heart . . . If you stay on here it'll be better than becoming a monk, won't it?'

Gannan *halmum* picked up the hem of her skirt and after rubbing her nose wiped her eyes. For some reason the impression of that particular scene remained vivid in his mind.

Once, after he had been there several days, a gentleman calling on the master saw him, swallowed hard and said, 'What a boy! He would make a fine *tong-in*!' He was an impressive figure of a gentleman-scholar with a broad-brimmed silk hat. Wondering what a *tong-in* was, he had remembered it and asked Gannan *halmum*.

'It's a boy who runs errands for the governor, isn't it? He must have said it because you're such a fine-looking lad.'

Another unforgettable event had been the arrival, that winter, of Kuchon, looking like a beggar. Kilsang, unable to get over the sense of being a stranger, was lonely and had felt affectionate towards him from the beginning. At sunset Kuchon would stand endlessly, staring blankly at the distant mountains and watching him, hidden, from a distance. Kilsang had felt a pain as if his own heart was being rent. One day when the master was away Kilsang, sprawled on the ground, had been drawing with charcoal. It was a picture of Avalokitesvara with a bottle in his left hand and a willow twig in his right. While adding strokes to the lower part of the figure, he idly turned his eyes and caught sight of a large straw shoe. Unthinkingly he looked upwards till he met the dark eyes of Kuchon.

'It's the Compassionate One!'

'Yeah!' He was delighted.

'Where did you learn that?'

'I used to draw every day at the monastery.'

'Monastery?'

'Yes, Yon-gok-sa, with Haegwan *sunim* . . .'

Kuchon's eyes seemed to indicate that he hoped to hear more.

'He said that someday I would become a sacred painter and he made me draw plants and flowers every day.'

'Did you learn to read and write as well?'

Kuchon's tone of voice had changed.

'Yes, sir. A little.'

Unaware, Kilsang's 'Yeah' had also changed into 'Yes, sir.'

'If you don't keep practising, you'll forget.'

'The old master used to say that too.'

Kuchon's eyes wavered.

'And he used to add that the world will change.'

An ironical light passed across Kuchon's wavering eyes. After that, whenever he had time to spare, Kuchon would beckon him, and taking him out of sight of the others, teach him in secret to read and write. Master Haegwan, being quick-tempered and changeable, had often rebuked or clouted him even when he hadn't done anything wrong, yet he was even more in awe of Kuchon who, unlike the monk, spoke little and looked austere.

He was just getting the colours ready to paint the masks when there was a call from outside. It was Guinyo, who told him that her ladyship wanted him. As he ran out, Dr Mun, having left the hall, was just stepping on to the shoe stone. Confused, he quickly bowed. As a life-long friend of the old Master at Yon'gok-sa, the doctor had often been seen there by Kilsang. At his bow, the doctor nodded back. A gaunt old man, his face wrapped in a snow-white beard, he had a calm and kindly expression. Lady Yoon, her hands joined, stood in the hall and, though her face had its usual stiff and hardened look, her manners were respectful, as though she were waiting on a father-like teacher, something never shown towards anyone else.

'See the doctor to the *sarang*.'

Like her stiff expression, her voice had no inflection. Even after he had gone out of sight she remained there with her hands still joined.

'The doctor from the town is here, Master.'

'Tell him to come in.'

It was a gloomy voice. Kilsang stepped on to the verandah and opened the door. The doctor, entering the room, said, 'How are you?'

It was only then that Choi Chisoo turned from his book. His eyes were unfriendly and with none of Lady Yoon's respectful manner. Without shifting from his seat, he said, 'Do sit down.'

They bowed formally, the one in acknowledgement of Chisoo's status, with dignified civility, the other merely with a customary expression of gratitude towards his principal physician. After the greetings, Dr Mun, pushing back the lower ends of his coat, settled down. Guinyo, a graceful figure dangling a tress of long hair loosely plaited, brought in the meal table. Kilsang thought that, unlike on previous occasions, the doctor would not have come to take the master's pulse, as he had not been ill lately. In case he might be needed for any errand, he strolled up and down outside, but his mind was away at the junk shed. The masks had only to be painted and all would be done. Filled with the desire to get them finished, he finally ran off to the shed. After holding his hands to his mouth, blowing on them and rubbing them together, he set to work to blend the colours, gently holding back the great joy of the final moment of achievement. Soon the two dead masks would come alive. He held the tip of his tongue between his lips as he moved the brush. By the time the shaman and the gentleman scholar had been completed it was late afternoon. Holding them on high he ran out into the yard.

'Kilsang!'

'Yes?'

Stopping in his tracks, he realized he was by the back door of the kitchen. Bongsoon *ne* stood facing it with folded arms.

'The doctor – he hasn't gone yet, has he?'

'No.'

'What is he doing, do you know?'

'I think he is just talking in the *sarang*.'

With her arms still folded, Bongsoon *ne* anxiously glanced round the corner into the front yard and said, 'I wish I could get him round to take Gannan *halmum*'s pulse . . . I must have a word with her ladyship . . . Kilsang!'

'Yes?'

Yoni *ne*, sitting sideways on the hob, was frying, while Yoni and Yochi *ne*, a casual helper, were trimming some ginger. As if she had a cold, Yochi's mother kept wiping her nose with the back of her hand. Having recalled Kilsang, Bongsoon *ne* could not think of what to say, so she said as if suddenly reminded. 'Where are you off to?'

'To see Bongsoon to the *byol-dang*.'

'What do you want to go there for?'

'To show her these.'

He held up the masks.

'What on earth are they?'

87

She blinked.

'Masks.'

'Let me have a look.'

Going closer to the door, he held them up.

'So they are! Where did you get them from?'

'I made them myself.'

'You?'

'Yes.'

'Hey! Come and look at this! Aren't they amazing?'

Yoni and Yochi *ne* put down their work and came over.

'Did you really make them all on your own?'

Yochi *ne* wanted to make sure.

'Yes.'

'You certainly have a rare gift. Look at it! This gentleman scholar, he's no dimwit, and almost too pretty to be a man.'

Yoni took the shaman over to show her mother. Stopping her frying, Yoni *ne* clicked her tongue and added, 'How you've brought out her pitiful look! As the saying goes, "Too much talent makes a man a beggar." Don't do such things any more, my lad.'

Bongsoon *ne*, as if her previous worry was forgotten, seemed to be deeply moved.

'Don't say such a thing. If you haven't got much luck, you must have some talent – that's only fair.'

No doubt it was an indication that the emotions of the seamstress were finer than those of the cook, and it could also be seen as defending the dexterity of her own fingers, the talent by which she earned her living.

'The young lady will be delighted. As thanks for all the care you've put into them, you shall have a prize. At the New Year Festival I'll send you to see the Five Masked Players. What do you think of that?'

'Really?'

'All of you children have had a bad time lately, so I will let Bongsoon go as well.'

'Will you really?'

'Of course. Why should I tell you a lie?'

88

Without thinking of the possible complications, she had spontaneously made him a promise.

Chapter Nine

KANGCHONG *DEK*, leaning towards the light from the door, threaded the needle, snapped the thread with her teeth and, throwing the skein into the sewing box, watched Yongi's movements with fierce eyes. Yongi, wrapping his trouser leg tightly at the ankle, turned it over the bone and bound it with a pale blue ribbon.

'Leaving the house without a scrap of fire wood . . .'.

Sewing a patch on the side of a cotton sock with coarse stitches, she rumbled on, 'Five masked players or eight of the buggers, what does it matter? Does he think I don't know what's in his mind? Truly it rots my liver. Why don't I pack in this wretched life and go to a nunnery?'

Yongi stood up and put on his outer coat. It was of cheap cotton, with uneven threads and speckled as with fly spots, but thanks to the wearer's good looks it seemed quite smart. Already wearing a headband, he took down his horse-hair hat and blew the dust off it.

'What joy do I have in the world? Do I have any pining kids to look after or a loving husband to comfort me? Do I have the pleasure of building up the home bit by bit? When I go into other people's houses it smells warm and cosy but this damn place has a chilly air like an empty cupboard. Even the fences rot and fall down, and does he ever lift a hand to them? Other people bring in firewood and stack it up to the eaves so that just to see it makes you feel warm, but in this place there isn't as much as a stick to beat a passing dog with. Is there anyone in the whole world as lazy as he is? He wouldn't even pick up his A-frame until the wood pile was all gone.'

That other people had wood piled up to the roof or that there was not a stick to hit a dog with might be an exaggeration, but it was true that Yongi had not gathered enough to see them through the winter. A sunbeam that had slipped through the gap between the sliding doors passed over a dust-covered tea bowl and stopped short of the edge of her skirt. Pushing the bowl out of the way and folding up the edges of his coat, Yongi sat down and filled his pipe.

'If I had known it was going to be like this, would I have married him? Everybody praised him, saying how good-looking, strong and good natured he was, envying me till their mouths ran dry for marrying so well. What's the use of good looks? – or strength – when his heart is somewhere else? "As long as their hearts are one, even beggars are happy." While others have one year, do I have a hundred?'

Yongi just puffed at his pipe and the smoke rose through the cobwebs between the small seed bags that hung clustered on high. It also rolled and swirled in the shaft of sunlight coming through the crack in the door, and slipped out.

'Really, whenever I see Dooman's father, day and night thinking only of his home and his children, I envy his wife and wonder how it is that she was born so lucky. If it was clothes or food that I'd wanted that much, I'd have become a thief before now.'

On the sock she was patching teardrops fell. Not bothering to wipe them away, she just sniffled through her blocked nose.

At last Yongi glanced sideways at his weeping wife. A trace of embarrassment passed over his face.

'Do you think I want to go for myself? Bongsoon *ne* asked me to take the children and I agreed, that's all.'

'Silly woman! Why did she have to pick on you?'

'. . . .'

'What can they see in that bitch? Why do the Choi household make such a fuss of her? With those dog's eyes, what do they see in her?'

At last she had openly referred to Wolsun, and there were some grounds for what she said. Many years ago Wolsun had been married to a man from another region and gone away, and then two years ago she had drifted back like a fallen leaf. Not a word had been heard of her all that time, not even whether or not she was still alive. Her shaman mother had been dead two years. In the empty house with its overgrown garden Wolsun, with a bundle under her arm, was seen weeping. In the old days, when her mother had frequented the Choi house, she used to follow, holding her skirt, and Bongsoon *ne* had loved her as if she were a younger sister. On hearing the rumour of her return, she had gone to the empty house.

'My goodness, you heartless lass, you didn't even know your mother had died. How could you go on without ever sending a word? And why are you in such a state?'

Wolsun just went on weeping. At night as well, while sleeping with Bongsoon *ne*, she kept sobbing, saying, 'I tried so hard, but . . .'.

'In the end Gannan *halmum* put in a word with Lady Yoon and obtained a small sum of money for her with which she had set up a tavern near the town, where the road forked. Kangchong *dek* was referring to this when she spoke of people making a fuss of her.

'This is nothing to do with her ladyship. It was Bongsoon's mother, for the sake of the children . . .'.

'That dull woman! To get any flavour out of her, you'd need a sack of salt. Why such a thing as a play? To make her child into a shaman, eh? The spectacle of adultery with a servant . . . is that a good example for the kids? If she must do it, why can't she take them herself instead of ordering other people about? She's nobody in herself, she just relies on the power of the Choi house . . .'.

Even though she had thrown a fit, crying and sniffling, Yongi was not one to be deterred from his trip to town, but he did not like to see a woman in tears, or nearer to the truth, he was afraid of it. However much she nagged him, he would put up with it silently and when it went too far tactfully turn it into a joke. Seeing the way he handled the situation, the villagers said it was because he was living up to his name, which meant 'forebearing'. But in reality he had never once yielded to her. Whatever the circumstances, on market day he would go to the town, call at Wolsun's wine-shop, buy and drink a cup of wine and return home. He had been doing it, without fail, for more than a year and his wife knew better than anyone how stubborn he was. What had, unlike at other times, brought her to tears in spite of knowing that she could not stop him, was the thought of the night, a night tense with the thrill of the masked players' performance, and the fear that her husband would have to stay over as he was taking the children with him. A yearning to appeal to him not to go just this once, at any cost, rose to her throat. She wholeheartedly wanted to stop him, even if it meant tearing his coat to shreds, yet she did not dare, not because she did not have the strength, nor because she cared about wifely decorum, but because she knew the steadfast obstinacy that lay at the bottom of his heart, despite his outward appearance of goodness. She was vaguely aware that it was thanks to this obstinacy that he had stayed with her all these years, upholding the bond once established between the two of them, strengthened by filial devotion to his dead mother. Despite the fact that, roughly brought up at her home town of Kanchong, she had no beauty or charm, nor much skill as a housewife, he had never once caused any scandal with another woman. A prudent intuition that such doggedness, once it had taken a different turn, would be impossible to bring back again was the only reason for her to exert the least self-control. The sun had advanced much further westward, judging from the way the sun-beam that squeezed through the door now stretched as far as her knees.

Each time her sewing hand pulled out the needle it revealed a white wart on the side of her thumb.

'Birds of a feather flock together, and loose women's children . . .'.

She was unable to complete the sentence, for Yongi's pipe struck hard on the ashtray. Startled, she cast a quick glance sideways. As he banged the pipe again, gave it a suck, and tucked it in to his waist band, his face was flushed. At that moment there came the noise of running footsteps from outside the gate. On the frozen ground they sounded clear and vibrant, as did the girl's voice that called: 'Uncle!' 'Uncle!'

This time it was the excited cry of a boy, and then a flurry of footsteps resounded inside the yard.

'So here you are!'

Yongi opened the door with a clack and looked out.

'I'm out of breath! We've been running like mad because Gad-dongi wanted to come along too.'

Bongsoon spoke in a ringing voice. Rolling her eyes, Kangchong *dek* stared at the children. Dressed in their New Year best, they sat on the low wooden verandah leaning forward and laughing as if to split their sides. Bongsoon had on a yellow silk *jogori* and a blue skirt with a purse of red cloth dangling from her waist. A silk scarf, very likely her mother's, was tied round her face, wrapping her jaws so tightly that her eyes seemed to bulge, and fastened firmly at the top of her head. Kilsang was wearing a pair of cotton pantaloons with a *jogori*, also with a cloth purse of dark green dangling on a cord with two tassels, one lime and other yellow, which made him appear even more attractive. His hair, tied up with a black ribbon of fine gauze, looked soft. Padded with fresh cotton-wool, both their *jogoris* were light and warm.

'Let's go!' cried Bongsoon, bouncing up and down.

'Right oh.'

Even as Yongi spoke Kangchong *dek* spat out, 'Someone's dying to get away.'

Yongi stooped to go through the door.

'Isn't it cold?'

'Not really,' said Kilsang.

'Well, see you then . . .'.

Yongi looked back at his wife.

'Thanks to the Governor, someone's blowing the trumpet.'

Unable to control her temper, her eyelids quivered.

'Off we go, then. It's not as cold as I thought.'

Yongi took long strides. Chased off by Kangchong *dek*'s stare the children, without a 'goodbye' followed him almost running, the bright stripes of Bongsoon's brocade shoes disappearing round the gate.

'That old passion is there. It's as simple as making a wooden scraper from a flat board. May his legs snap on the way home! Make him a cripple and he won't go out any more.'

Kangchong *dek* hurled away her sewing box.

'Uncle, we're staying the night in the town, aren't we?' asked Bongsoon.

'Yes.'

As if unable to fit in with their small steps, Yongi strode on without slowing down. The children, especially the girl, were almost running to keep up. The country road was scattered with pebbles. Hard dried cow dung rolled here and there. Kilsang looked up at the sky. It was not as blue as autumn, but clear. Being winter, it was not likely to rain.

'Uncle, we are going on the ferry, aren't we?'

Panting, Bongsoon asked again.

'Yes.'

They came face to face with Yimi *ne*, coming up the road with a bottle of wine.

'On your way to town, eh?'

'Yes.'

The front of her white cotton *jogori* with maroon trimming and ribbons was bursting open, and her black skirt was also blown out as if she was not far from giving birth, but her face looked well. Evoking a sense of tenacity like a waterside weed, she always seemed, whatever the circumstances, to overflow with health and vitality.

'We are going to see the masked players.'

Standing next to the boasting Boongsoon, as if supporting her statement, Kilsang felt proud.

'Aren't you lucky!'

Speaking superficially to the children, she turned a smiling face towards Yongi.

'It's already seven days since the New Year – who would have any wine left by this time? But he bothers me like hell, so I've been out to get him some.'

'He should've gone himself, instead of sending you.'

'What can you do? He's not like you.'

Shamelessly she sought his eyes with a smile that seemed to release sensuality and sprinkle it over his face. She was a pregnant woman rather than a mother. It was not licentiousness; it was nature.

'You look just like a bridegroom.'

'You'd better be on your way.'

He said this with anger in his voice and resumed his pace. The children began to run again. As he ran, Kilsang looked back. With the bottle resting on the ground, Yimi *ne* still stood there blankly.

'Manuring the barley, are you?'

This time Yongi spoke first and loudly. Off the road, on a path, Yongpari was walking ahead of them with manure buckets at each end of a pole across his shoulder.

'Going to town? If I'd known I'd have gone along too.'

With his long mooli-like face, Yongpari stood with the buckets suspended, white breath curling from his half open mouth.

'Is it the last day of the year? What's the rush?'

'What can a farmer do but work? A day or two off at New Year and my back aches after a couple of loads.'

'If we couldn't die before the work was all done, we'd never die. "The mouths of the living don't collect cobwebs", as they say.'

'It's easy to talk, but life is not all that simple. You'd better get going. Look – the boat's coming.'

The road to the river curved away to the left and Yongpari's field path turned off to the right. The distance between them grew. At the ferry only one man, a stranger, stood waiting – the playful young people of the village had long since left by road. As soon as the boat, coming from the direction of Hwagae, touched the white ice-covered shore and put out the boarding plank, Yongi went up it, carrying Bongsoon. Kilsang followed and so did the stranger. The boatman pushed off from the sandy bottom, backed into the middle of the river and began to scull. The passengers, silent until they were on their way, now began to talk. The sun still had some way to go, and the bamboo grove behind the high floating roof of the Choi *champan* house shone frosty in the evening light. Taking some peeled chestnuts from the bundle she had been carrying, Bongsoon crunched them in her mouth.

'Kilsang, do you want some?'

'Please.'

He took some and crunched them.

'Uncle, would you like some dried octopus?'

Yongi chewed it hard.

Shadowed by the mountains, the water was a deep green like dark jade. To the rhythm of the scull the view of the village gradually receded behind the bend of the river. By the time they reached the tavern the last rays of sun from the ridge of the western mountain shone on Yongi's back.

'My little darling has come! My goodness, your fingers are frozen stiff!'

As Wolsun grabbed hold of Bongsoon's hands, her eyes were filled with tears. Her face looked bluish, perhaps reflecting her *jogori* of pale blue silk.

'Let's go in quickly, Kilsang.'

She pushed the children from behind to urge them into the house and Yongi took off his shoes to follow.

'Why did you close the shop?'

'Because the children were coming . . .'.

Without finishing her sentence, she picked up Bongsoon and, pushing aside the quilt that had been spread at the warm end of the room, put her down there. Being made a fuss of, Bongsoon felt superior, as if she had become the young Miss Sohi. Looking over at Kilsang, who sat on his knees at the cooler end of the room, her face seemed to betray the thought that she would like to boss him as Sohi did: 'You rascal, I'll beat you! Bare your legs!'

'Children are one thing, and business is another . . .' mumbled Yongi.

'One day's earnings – what difference would it make? Kilsang, come here. It's cold down there. Tell me about her ladyship. Is she well?'

'Yes.'

'And the Miss?'

'The young Miss . . . she cries all the time.'

'Oh, does she? . . . I'll get some *dok* soup – wait a minute.'

She stood up to go.

'Don't bother. We weren't expecting anything.'

For the first time Wolsun looked at Yongi. Until then they had awkwardly avoided each other's eyes as if, with his children, he was calling on a brother's widowed wife. Wolsun went out of the room putting on an apron. As though she had had it ready, she soon brought in the steaming soup.

'I must light the lamp.'

'Let me do it.'

Yongi lit the oil lamp. The flame flickered and then brightened. From the market, where the plays were to take place, came the humming of the crowd. The children, over-excited, were hardly able to eat. Kilsang, sitting awkwardly, opened his mouth, 'The show . . . if we don't get places . . .'.

'Don't worry, love. I know some of the players and I've asked them to keep seats for you.'

As if wanting to make sure, Kilsang added, 'I hope they will be right at the front, because we are so small.'

'Of course they are at the front. Now stop worrying, and eat up.'

Bongsoon, who had been hanging on Wolsun's lips, cast an accusing glance at Kilsang.

(She's a close friend of my mum, and she knows best!)

Yongi finished the last drop of his soup before leaving the table. From the square came the sound of cymbals and drums.

'Auntie, we'd better be going now.'

This time it was Bongsoon, who had been so good, who fretted.

'There's still a long time to go. From now on they will be putting up the tents, making the fire, and things like that. Why go early and shiver?'

'You're coming too, aren't you, auntie?'

'I'll just take you along there and . . .'

'Don't you want to see it?'

'I've often seen it in the past.'

The eyes of Yongi and Wolsun met as if drawn by a magnet. Wolsun's face looked as if she was about to cry. 'Why don't you ever accuse me?' he said to himself as he dropped his eyes, thinking of how she would have gone alone to some temple on New Year's Eve to pray for the repose of her dead mother while in other homes families gathered to prepare food; how she would have wept with a piercing sorrow even more severe than the penetrating chill of the temple hall; how easily she used to become scared and tearful when she was small – she would burst into tears even if someone shouted at her, or at the tale of an old man coming round with a sack on his shoulder to steal children, and if the young master, Chisoo, told such stories, she would be even more scared and tearful. The children were fidgeting, their whole attention turned to the noise from the square.

'Well, then, let's go.'

Seeing them fret, Wolsun smiled and rose. Taking off her apron she picked up a silk scarf and tied it round her head. The children dashed out before her. The evening air was bitter and all round was dark, while a continuous stream of people were walking towards the market square.

'So you've come too, Yongi *hyongnim*?'

Someone spoke from a group of young men a little way behind. As if they had been drinking somewhere on the way, they staggered unsteadily. Stepping aside from the children and Wolsun, Yongi said, 'A drinking bout in broad daylight, eh?'

'Yes, we've had a cup. If not on a day like his, when do we have the chance to? . . . ahem!'

Giving off a rougher air than mere tipsiness, they cast coarse glances at Wolsun. After brushing past Yongi they giggled at something said between themselves and then poking each other's ribs, burst into another bout of laughter. Yongi frowned. Wolsun walked on with lowered head. Her white silk scarf fluttered a little. (These days youngsters are so shameless – perhaps it's the rotten state of the world . . .) He was gripped by unbearable sadness. It was not so much with the young people as with himself that he felt angry.

'Wolsun.'

'Yes?'

'I can see the show from anywhere, dear, so you take the children and find places for them . . .'.

Wolsun, startled by the 'dear', but understanding his embarrassment, just said, 'All right.'

He soon disappeared into the crowd and walking behind the children, she went to the changing room, made up from well-worn canvas stretched here and there between wooden poles, and looked for Mr Hwang.

'I've got a straw mat reserved for you.'

The old drummer gave her a good natured gummy smile.

'It's to sit these little darlings, eh? Whose dear daughter could this be? And whose precious son is this? What fine looking people!'

He smiled broadly at the children, showing his toothless gums. In the old days, when Wolsun's mother was still alive, they had been close friends, Mr Hwang enjoying in a small way some fame as a drummer. He had been handling the drumstick since he was ten, thoroughly mastering the technique, and the years of his prime, during which he had backed the voices of some famous singers, had been a golden age. As the saying 'Great songs need a man, a drum, and a woman' indicates, however good the singer's voice, if the drummer is poor or out of temper, the performance will be a flop. Good at accompanyng a variety of songs, as also at providing rhythm for dances, he had been extremely proud, so much so that when upset he would go beserk, ruining the songs of famous performers or throwing his drumstick into the air, and eventually he found himself on the downward slope. To soothe his ill-temper he had resorted to wine and women, and in this way speeded his own downfall. He had ended up in his old age as merely the drummer to a five-mask troupe, but time had rubbed him into a gentler character. By the flame of the wood fire that lit the changing room his wrinkled face seemed full of rippling furrows that told the sad story of a man who had lived all his days relying on one drumstick, with no house to go back to, nor children.

After gazing absently at Mr Hwang, who was all smiles for the children, Wolsun said, 'Uncle, your clothes are too thin.'

He turned his head, 'I don't feel the cold, I'm so used to it . . .'.

'Even so, at your age . . .'.

Suddenly the mild expression on his face changed.

'Wolsun!'

'. . . .?'

'How you look like your mother! Just now I was astonished, thinking it was the old Wolsun *ne* standing before me.'

As if the past thirty years which he had reckoned as dead and gone had suddenly risen up and appeared before him, he was staring at her closely.

'When I saw you in the daytime, you weren't like this . . .'

'You are funny, uncle . . . we are mother and daughter. Who else should I take after if not my mother?'

'Huh, you are quite right. How time goes by! As they say, "Young yesterday – white hair today". I wonder if Wolsun *ne* is still holding up a trident and casting out devils in the other world?'

'Don't say such an awful thing. All the contemptuous treatment she suffered in this world – is it going to be the same in the other one as well?'

Tears rose to her eyes. The old man smiled faintly as if awakened from a dream.

'That's true . . . don't feel sad about it, and, by the way, can I order a bowl of hot soup for the morning?'

'Yes, of course.'

While they were talking, the children were enchanted, exploring the changing tent. There were costumes piled up, masks, various musical instruments, and the players who chattered as they casually came in and out. The children seemed to be attracted and drawn into this marvellous land of magic. Wolsun led them to the mat on the front row that an errand boy of the troupe was keeping for them.

'Sit here quietly while I fetch the fire pot.'

She soon reappeared, bringing an earthenware pot with live coals buried under the ash.

'If you feel sleepy while you are watching, just drop off.'

She handed out snacks, pushing them into their hands, took the scarf off her own head and put it round the neck of Bongsoon who had one already, making an extra layer, and rose to go. By now the crowd packed the show ground and was making quite a din, while in the nearby gambling corner a bright bonfire flared merrily, its tongues of flame making as if to swallow up the night.

At last the music of the prelude burst out. The Divine Eastern War Lord of the Spring made his entrance in a green mask. The Divine Western War Lord of the Autumn made his entrance in a white mask. The Divine Northern War Lord of the Winter made his entrance in a black mask. The Divine Southern War Lord of the Summer made his entrance in a red mask. The Divine Central War Lord made his entrance in a yellow mask. In military coats of the same colour as their masks, their grotesque brilliance dazzled the eye. When the music changed to that of the shamanist ritual, the five divine marshals danced to the rhythm in high spirits. The musicians, some wearing blue coats and some yellow, beat, scraped or blew the short drum, long drum, fiddle, flute and fife. The five spirit

figures danced on, interchanging their positions, the dancing growing more spectacular as the music changed from *bonryongsan* to
taryong rhythm. While Kilsang watched as if dazed, Bongsoon's eyes
sparkled. The spectators were as noisy as ever. The play moved into
its second stage. The divine figures had disappeared one after the
other and in their place came another five with lepers' masks in
blue, white, red, black and yellow. They tottered about in the
dance of the disabled, showing mutilated arms, limping or hopping.
Watching these bizarre, comic and even pitiable dancing monsters
reflecting the blaze of the bonfire, the spectators laughed with
excitement, and then fell silent as they became absorbed in the
dance. It was then that Yongi slipped out of the fairground, to face
instantly a darkness that seemed to press into him, a deep blackness
from which he felt unable to plough his way out. He went into a
tavern not far from the market place. The woman, who had been
dozing off, jumped up.

'What, is it over already?'

'No, it's only in the second stage.'

She flopped down again, still dazed, slowly scratching her head.
Unable to trade during the New Year Festival, they were ready to
make a killing at the end of the play, and waited with soup boiling
vigorously in the cauldron and several jars of rice wine.

'You gave me a shock! I thought the show was over.'

'Even though it isn't, there's a customer here, so what about a
drink?'

Having sat down, he drank a bowl of *makulli* at one gulp and
without bothering to touch the food, handed it back to be filled
again, once, twice, three times, four – still he held out the bowl.

'Take it easy or you'll choke yourself. What a way to drink! You
ought to eat something with it . . .'.

The hostess, suddenly noticing his good looks, kept glancing at
him. After the fifth cup, instead of reddening, his face went white.
With deep sunk eyes, he looked frightening. After paying, he
stepped out into the bitter night wind and walked unsteadily. He
went down a road where the houses were few, with gaps between
like missing teeth – a desolate, pitiless and deserted road. He uri-

nated at the side of it. The sound of the flutes and drums came as if from a distance.

'Even if he's a leper with flesh rotting away, a gentleman is still a gentleman, eh? Even if she's the most beautiful woman in the world, a shaman is still a shaman – is that it?'

After pulling up his trousers and fastening them at the waist, still unsteady, he reached the front of Wolsun's tavern.

'Wolsun!'

It was a thunderous voice. 'Open the gate!'

He banged on it with his fists. It opened with the force of them and in the courtyard she stood transfixed.

'Drink . . .'

She was going to add, 'Haven't you had too much?' but could not bring out the words.

'Why shouldn't I? Wine and women are not for poor peasants, is that it?'

Bringing his face close, he spoke as though in a whisper, 'You are the thorn that is stuck in my throat. Why couldn't you manage better? Why did you have to come back?'

After saying this, he wept. She weakly attempted to escape, like a girl facing a father with a cane. A strange sound came through his teeth as he gritted them to choke his sobs. Dragging her by the wrist, he went into the room, threw off his hat and extinguished the lamp. Then grabbing hold of her free hand with his other one he flung himself on to the floor.

'There's never been any time or place when I wasn't thinking of you. It's all my fault. Why don't you hate me?'

Pulling her into his arms, he rubbed his face against hers. As their tears joined in one stream, their bodies became one and, floating higher and higher they performed the ritual of a tragic love that could not be undone for all eternity.

Chapter Ten

WHEN the weather was at its coldest the ice was thick along the edge of the river, but as it turned milder broken lumps floated away, shining in the sunlight. Now, even they had melted and the water, carrying foam to the edges, slapped the sandy shore. Spring frost formed on the crushed brown tips of the barley shoots and on the reddish furrows, and here and there in the bottoms of the paddies stood piles of manure or compost. From the look of the gaunt mulberry trees, bent like a dog's leg, spring seemed still far off, but in the courtyards of the *byoldang* and the *sarang* the plum trees carried buds of white blossom ready to burst out at any moment. Soon tender green leaves would appear on the big willows that stood along the river bank and on the turf that had been left black after burning.

The yard of the servants' quarters seemed quite empty, but someone was there. In front of the verandah, Gannan *halmum*, with twitching lips, took slow steps towards the well, as if practising. Indeed, she was testing her legs, humming to herself the 'Song for the Encouragement of Virtue'. The house was all quiet. Nobody came or went. After circling the well she returned to the verandah and, leaning heavily on her stick, sat on the edge. There was no sign of anyone in the direction of the *byoldang* either, for yesterday Lady Yoon had set off with Sohi for the Yon-goksa. Several servants had gone to carry the palanquin, as well as Samwol and Bongsoon *ne*, with her daughter. The rest were out in the fields. Yoni and her mother chatted with Kim *subang*'s wife at her house at the rear. Kim *subang*, while listening to Choi Chisoo giving some instructions, cast anxious glances towards Gaddongi, who, from beyond the fence, was throwing stones in the direction of the *sarang*. Guinyo, wherever she might be, had been out of sight from the morning. As if they sensed the absence of people, rats scurried about the yard and, coming close to Gannan *halmum*, stared at her as though they were curious.

'Mr Rat,' she mumbled, as if it was someone to talk to, 'even you look down on me. Because I am old and sick you think I'm as good as dead.'

Her face was all bones and skin, like the dry patch at the joint of the mulberry tree that stood alone on the bank, gaunt and bent, even in spring. Deprived of the sun, her complexion had turned the colour of withered cabbage and her mangled half-white hair, much of it already gone, not fit to be brushed up or coiled, hung loosely round her face. Though she was nearing the age of seventy, her state seemed to be due more to the effects of a merciless illness than of age. She had never had any children and Gannan *halmum* was but a nickname. In earlier days when her husband was the steward, she had been known as Kim *subang-dek*, but as she grew older and turned white, the present Kim *subang* had taken over the title and duty from old Bawoo and the old couple were known as Grandpa Bawoo and Grandma Gannan. Last year, after his death, a second one had been anticipated, but as the winter went out she unexpectedly improved, little by little.

'The seasons come round without fail, the river has thawed, and shoots appear on the trees, but is there anything as unreliable as human life? The wicked old man how could he go off and leave me, with nobody to see to things when I die? When he was alive he used to say "Old woman, I will bury you safe and sound . . ."'

Gad-dongi looked into the yard and, perhaps not seeing her, went out again pulling his trousers at the waist.

'Seventy years of human life is only a passing moment. Things of the past seem to have happened only the day before yesterday . . . When I went to the Paikryon hermitage with the young mistress it seems only a couple of days ago . . . Now she also has grown old . . .'

Face to face, she called her 'your ladyship' but to Gannan she was always 'the Young Mistress'. To her, she remained young, tender and pretty as a flower.

After sitting for some minutes she absently stood up, leaning on her stick to test her steps. After taking a few paces she would pause, and then go on. In this way she went out of the gate of the servants' quarters, and halfway down the slope, almost crawling, she let go of her cane and flopped down on to the ground.

'This is how I will go, the way a straw fire dies. Oh, my breath . . .'.

Far away in the water-parsley field village women could be seen gathering the crop. She could almost feel the chilly, water-logged mud squelching under her feet, the tender leaves softly tickling her shins. Having endured the winter the green leaves would be soft and their scent pungent. How fond her old man had been of dace soup with water-parsley! The thought of him came to her suddenly.

'Silly me, everything I see reminds me of him.'

She stood up and resumed her walk down the hill. The end of her walking-stick that groped on the ground looked hazy, but she went on, gritting her teeth. An ox-bell sounded from behind her and then she saw the beast's breath.

'Out of the way! Out of the way!'

A thunderous voice hit her on the back of the head. Confused, she flung herself on to the ground.

'I wondered who it was. Is that you granny Gannan?'

'. . .'.

'You'd do better just to stay in your room and eat what they bring you. What have you come out for?'

Chilsung spoke in a croaking voice like a stork.

'I miss people so much, that's why I've come out . . . are you on your way to plough the paddy?'

'Yes.'

Looking at the ox that stood with a plough on its back she asked, 'Is it your own?'

'If my mother had worked for the Choi house we might have had one, but no chance of that. It's Yongi's.'

'Yongi's? . . . I've just come out because I miss seeing people.'

'Are you out of danger now, then?'

'Not really – it would be better for me to pass on but . . .'.

Chilsung remembered the beating he had had from Bawoo when he was a kid for damaging the Choi melon field.

'That's right. Living too long is a kind of sin.'

He struck the ox on its flank to prompt it to move on. Its white tongue hanging out, it lowed and began to step out. Gannan *halmum* stared resentfully at his broad straight back. Though she liked to keep saying that she must 'go', his uncharitable remarks had upset her.

(When they reach that stage, they ought to be buried alive.) As if convinced that old age or sickness would never come to him, he struck the ox again on its flank, crusted with dried dung. It bellowed as if to say, 'You are not even my master, so what right do you have to bully me like this?'

The sky with clouds like clumps of cotton wool could not have been more peaceful. Everything looked peaceful – the farmers walking by the fields, the raft floating down the river with the current, and the calf that followed its mother grazing in the field beside it. The farmers, wanting nothing more, nor anything less, and nature, also wanting nothing to be added or taken away, were both at this time in harmony and at peace. Having reached the front of Dooman's house, Gannan leaned against the brushwood gate, gathering her breath. The dog ran out. Along with its bark came the sound of a handmill grinding in the yard and the smell of decaying compost from a shack near the gate. Inside the yard there was only the sound of the mill, not even any children around, and the dog, dropping his tail, retreated and perhaps because of that, no one even looked out. Like a spoilt child she had expected some one to rush out to support her but, as it turned out, she had to walk across the yard clearing her throat.

'Isn't mummy at home?'

Dooman *ne*, turning the mill by the brushwood fence that surrounded the big jars of soy sauce and bean paste, stood wide-eyed.

'Good heavens, auntie! What brings you here?'

She ran up, took the walking stick, and holding Gannan up, helped her to the verandah.

'Phew! I was longing for some company, so I came out, but I'm all out of breath and giddy . . .'.

'I've been meaning to come and see you all this time but I never managed it . . .'.

'What are you doing?'

'I've soaked a handful of rice and I'm grinding it to make some broth for mother.'

'How hard you work.'

'Good of you to say so.'

'Where's Dooman's dad?'

'He's started the spring ploughing.'

'The children?'

'Gone to gather firewood.'

'Where's young Suni?'

'She's taking her dad his lunch.'

'Just like their mum and dad, your kids are smart, too. This is a house that will prosper.'

'You should be resting in bed. How did you manage to come this far?'

'The nights are too long . . . and the days are too.'

'Still, it's great to see you getting about like this.'

'Well . . . I'll go on like this for a little while and peter out the way that a straw fire does. I've lived my time. How is my sister these days?'

'Not too bad. Mother! Mother! Aunty's here!'

Bringing her mouth close to the door, Dooman *ne* shouted loudly enough to split an eardrum. From the room came: 'Wha' ya' say? Rain come? Sha, it shoodacome.'

What she meant was 'What did you say? Rain is coming? Sure, it should.'

Not only was Dooman's grandma out of her mind with age, and deaf, but her tongue had stiffened. Supported by Dooman *ne*, Gannan *halmum* entered the room where she lay. It was dark and smelt bad. Lifting up one end of the quilt under which her mother-in-law lay, Dooman *ne* sat the visitor down.

'Auntie — I will quickly go and get the broth.'

Gannan said, 'Child, if it's for me, leave it and don't bother,' but Dooman *ne* went off in a hurry. Being a patient herself, Gannan seemed at home with the bad smell in the sickroom. The whitish eyes of Dooman's granny stared at her, though it was doubtful whether she recognized her. Gripping her fist tightly, Gannan *halmum* called loudly, 'Sister!'

'Aah.'

Dooman's granny sounded as if she was responding.

'It would have been all right for you to live longer, sister, but look at you – you can't control yourself . . .'.

Then she lowered her voice and said, 'You have such a dutiful son and daughter-in-law, but you don't realize how lucky you are – tut, tut, tut . . .'.

Not only because she had no strength left to shout but also because there was no point in it.

'Rain mus . . . las year, the vil up wat fight, pai waist brok . . .'. which meant 'Of course the rain must come . . . last year there was a fight over water with the people of the village further up and our Pangi's dad hurt his back . . .'.

'Last year, you say. Don't you realize how long ago it was, sister? It was over thirty years ago. What a good memory you have . . . it is true, sometimes you suddenly remember something in the past as if it was yesterday. Even when you lose your memory you don't forget your husband, is that it? Buddha, have mercy on us!'

In place of a sigh she recited a prayer.

'I was in such a hurry that there are lumps in it.'

Her hair covered in ash, as if she had been burning damp pine twigs, and dripping with sweat, Dooman's mother brought in a table on which were laid two bowls of sesame-seed broth and a bowl of fresh wild greens, lightly scalded and tastily dressed.

'Child, don't worry about me. With me, it is just my mouth that refuses to eat – otherwise I don't go short.'

'Even so, you can't go back without eating anything. Please have some.'

When, after much urging, Gannan *halmum* picked up the spoon, Dooman-*ne* sat her mother-in-law up with an arm round her and fed her with a spoon like a small child, blowing on each spoonful of soup to cool it. For an old woman whose mind was gone, and who merely breathed, she had a strong appetite. When she had emptied the bowl, Dooman *ne* laid her down saying, 'If she has any more, she'll have loose bowels.'

Then, noticing there was a lot left in the other bowl, she added hastily, 'What's the matter with you?'

'I've eaten a lot. At home I can't eat even this much.'

'If you eat so poorly, how are you going to keep going? I wish I could go and see you more often, but there's Samwol and Bong-soon *ne* both taking care of you, and I don't want to look as if I'm trying to interfere.'

'You needn't worry about that. With your own family to look after, you shouldn't come too often. As for Samwol and Bongsoon *ne*, they are full of your praise – they say that even if you had been my own niece you couldn't have done more.'

'Not at all.'

Smiling modestly, Dooman *ne* bent her healthy body forward and wiped the dribbling mouth of her mother-in-law. As she step-ped out of the room with the table, the dog yelped as if it was being killed.

'Look at her! Stop it! What are you beating the dog for? Crazy bitch!' screamed Dooman *ne*. After a moment of turmoil in the yard, it became quiet and she re-entered the room.

'What was it?'

'It's Dochul *ne*. She hasn't been around for some time now, and I thought she must have dropped dead somewhere . . .'.

'For a mad woman, she's on the quiet side. What made her go like that?'

'They say her sickness gets worse in the spring.'

'I've heard that too.'

'Aunt, by the way . . .'.

'What?'

'A few days ago,' Dooman-*ne* frowned, 'Kangchong-*dek* went off to her mother's . . .'.

'To her mother's? Why?'

'Because of Wolsun.'

'Wolsun? That girl? Hasn't she set up a wine shop in the town?'

'That's right. And Yi *subang* has been . . .'.

'You mean Yongi?'

'Yes.'

Gannan understood at once.

'Poor, poor lass. Thanks to her mother's generous heart, I thought she would have a happy life, but how unlucky she has been.'

In the same way that Lady Yoon was 'the Young Mistress' to her, Wolsun, nearly thirty, was still 'a lass'.

'Born to a sad fate, how can she help being unlucky?'

'You are right, dear. It was exactly because of that that in days gone by Yongi's mother prevented him from marrying her by refusing to eat or drink. So Yongi's wife went back to her parents. And then what happened?'

'She went away saying she couldn't go on living with him, but a couple bound by law – can they break up? It's just her bad temper, putting on a show of threats. The thing is that on her way back, on the brow of that hill – what's the name of it? – she saw Kuchon.'

'What did you say?!'

Gannan *halmum* was so startled that she nearly jumped from her place, her eyes, which had been dull, opening wide. 'Kangchong is the other side of Sanchong in the Haman area, isn't it?'

'That's right!'

'That's not far from Mount Chiri.'

'That's right!'

'So it seems to me that he must be hiding somewhere on the mountain.'

'What did he look like? What about the *byoldang* mistress?'

She drew close to Dooman *ne*, tightly clenching her rake-like hands.

'Probably she was ill. He was carrying her on his back, both of them looking like the beggars of all beggars.'

'Beggars of all beggars!'

'The mistress, as she was on his back, had her face hidden, though she would not have known Kangchong *dek* anyway. Apparently Kuchon saw her clearly, but with no sign of shame or attempt to avoid her, he just went past, staring straight ahead without even blinking.'

'He would have been like that . . .'

Tears came to the old lady's eyes.

'Kangchong *dek* said that as she stood there looking at his back with her on it, tears rose to her eyes.'

'The poorest of all beggars – Hwani!'

'What did you call him?'

'Nothing.'

'Hearing that story made me think of human life . . . the wife of the only son of a great family giving birth to a child and it ends up as a beggar – who could have dreamt of such a thing?'

'I'm feeling faint. I must lie down.'

'Yes, lie down.'

She went to the inner room to fetch a pillow and put it under the old woman's head.

'Beggars of all beggars!'

'Hasn't there been any word from her own home?'

'What word could there be? Of course it is possible that they have not been told by this side, but even if the news reached Seoul, a thousand miles away, they would have done nothing but count her as lost.'

'What sort of family are they?'

'Rather poor, but scholars with an excellent family tradition. Having such a strict tradition, would they even bother to find out whether she was dead or alive?'

'I heard that she was related in some way to his first wife.'

'Not quite, but the marriage was arranged through a connection of her family.'

'Why was it that both the marriages were with Seoul families?'

'It was because the grandmother came from the Cho family of Seoul. She had arranged to take the first granddaughter-in-law from her family.'

'For the sake of a descendant, doesn't the Master need to remarry quickly?'

'. . .'

'When you consider the great responsibility of carrying on the household and the ancestral rites and duties, even now it is too late.'

'Well . . . if by remarrying now he could have a son, he would have done so already, but as its a family where descendants are rare – I don't know . . . What they call "seed" often falls where it is not wanted, but . . .'.

She mumbled as if to herself.

'Mummy, I'm back – I've given dad his lunch,' called Suni. She looked more than her fourteen years as she came in with the lunch basket on her head. Noticing a strange pair of shoes under the verandah, she opened the door of the small room to look inside.

'Oh granny, is that you?'

She smiled, showing a crooked tooth. Her smooth round face was like her mother's.

'Yes, my pet.'

From her lying position Gannan looked up and smiled back at her.

'You are well enough to walk about, then?'

'I had to come because I missed you all so much.'

'Did your dad eat up all his lunch?' asked her mother.

'Yes.'

'The rice had gone cold, hadn't it?'

'He dumped it into the rice tea and ate it all.'

'Would you like to go to the kitchen, clear it up, and pound the barley again? I've kept it wet.'

'Yes, mum.'

She went there, with the basket. Dooman *ne* lifted her mother-in-law, helped her on to the chamber-pot, and then lay her down again.

'If you look closely at life, as they say, the man with a crop of ten thousand sacks has ten thousand worries, and the man with a thousand has a thousand worries . . . but what I've really come for today,' Gannan *halmum* turned over to face Dooman *ne*, 'Is to consult you about something . . .'

'Yes, what is it?' Dooman *ne*'s face became slightly tense.

'It's about your second son . . .'.

'. . .'

'If people like us, in the position of servants, talked about "adoption" it would be presumptous – my dead husband told me never to let the word out of my mouth – but, the more I think about it, the more I'm convinced there's no other way.'

'Yongman?'

He was her second son. An awkward expression rose to her face.

'No need even to call it that, nor do I wish to be taken care of

113

by him in my life time. It's only after I have gone that it would concern him.'

'. . .'

'Even though they say that if the ancestral sacrifice has to be done by the mother's side, your descendants won't prosper. If you think about it, we are all from the same Kim family, aren't we – though it's a distant relationship.'

'That's true.'

'As long as I am alive I can put out at least a bowl of water on the grave, but once my eyes have closed, where would the poor spirit get even a drink? Her Ladyship has said that she will put us in the care of the monastery, which might do if I had no relations at all, but I thought that at least I could have a word with you . . .'.

'Of course.'

Though she said this, a worried expression clouded her face.

'Even though it's a distant relationship, your father-in-law and mine were second cousins, so we are not entirely unrelated.'

'Of course you are right.'

'As I said earlier, there is no need to call him an adopted son or anything like that. It would be fine if he could just remember to put out a cup of water for us on our anniversaries.' Dooman *ne* could not readily give her consent. It was not a trivial matter, nor was it only a question of care and devotion. For a peasant one ancestral sacrifice was a frightening affair. Especially when they themselves had nothing to pass on to the second son, how could she make a promise and burden him with a life-long duty? Once you took it on, it was an iron rule to serve the deceased ancestors well, or else disasters were bound to come to the family, as often happened. Thinking about all this, she felt totally at a loss.

'I am not asking like this without giving it thought. I will speak to her ladyship about endowing you with a patch of rice paddy . . .'.

Dooman *ne*'s cheeks glowed red at once. It was more than she had ever dreamed of. 'I'll find it hard to speak to her. But if I do, she won't look down on me . . .'.

'How could you . . .'.

'Of course she won't, though it is still hard to bring it up.'

'I will have to talk it over with Dooman's dad . . .'.

'Of course you must. It's to talk to you about this that I made a desperate effort to come down today. It's a sad thing to have no children.'

'I — I do appreciate it.'

Confused and excited, Dooman *ne* did not quite know what to do. 'Now that I have said what I wanted to, I must get back, but I feel so giddy, I don't know whether I can walk.'

'I . . . I'll take you on my back.'

'Can you really?'

'Yes, of course.'

Suni was pounding barley in the mortar with a small wooden pestle. Her short skirt worn over pantaloons fluttered up and down with the movement of the pestle. Each time she lifted it in the air her heels went up too as if she was being forced up by the wooden stick. She had skinny arms.

'Granny, are you going?'

'Yes, I'm going.'

And hoisted on Dooman *ne*'s back, she went out through the brushwood gate.

'Goodbye, granny.'

'Goodbye, my dear.'

Dooman *ne* did not feel the weight of the old woman at all. A good piece of rice paddy was no trivial matter.

Chapter Eleven

'OH! Really? Oh – oh – really!'
   The teacher, Kim *hunjang* brandished his long pipe in a state of agitation. Yoon Bo, stalking down the road after attending his parents' graves, called from behind: 'What lovely weather! On such a beautiful day, what can be the matter with you, sir?'

Kim *hunjang* turned and said, 'Really, I believe the world has come to an end. It has, indeed.'

'What's new about that? Hasn't the world long since had its end announced?'

'That ruffian, Suh . . .'.

He hesitated, unable to finish the sentence, while Yoon bo smiled broadly, showing his sparse teeth.

'I get it. You saw Suh *subang* carrying his wife on his back.'

Glancing at Suh Keumdol's fence of Indian millet canes behind which flickered a cock-comb, Yoon Bo broke into a broad smile again.

'However low they may be, and though it is said that the world has become shameless to the point of ruin, human beings must never turn into beasts – of course they mustn't.'

'It is because of her stomach worms that he has to put her on his back – I think the clever worms know his back is good medicine, you see.'

'Not just a wormy stomach, but even if her bowels were cut out – ahem – ahem – one has to think about the eyes of others, the eyes of others! A man with a daughter-in-law, and supposed to be a decent farmer!

'Suh *subang* is a man with a happy nature. You would feel differently if your wife was still alive. They say that husband and wife grow fonder of each other as they grow older.'

'Rascal! How dare you suggest such a thing for a family of good birth? I'll tear out your tongue, you villain.'

His drooping eyelids bulged as they tightened into a triangle.

'Really. There doesn't seem to be anything to get so angry about . . .'. As if enjoying himself, Yoon Bo stood smiling at him. Kim *hunjang* in his turn looked sideways at Yoon Bo.

'You rascal! "When a big fish jumps the little fish jump too." How dare you mock a gentleman?'

Even so, Yoon Bo, still grinning, showed no sign of parting and was probably waiting for his anger to run its course. The village people treated Kim *hunjang* as if he were very old and worthy. This was largely due to his face, which was wrinkled like a piece of dried marrow and covered in a cob-web of lines. He looked as if he were seventy at least. From under his hat tresses of half-white hair poked out, his thin beard and eye brows were like well-beaten flax, and his voice lacked energy. Nobody, including himself, was inclined to believe that he was in fact a year or two short of fifty. It was only when they realized how straight was his back, and how he managed his farming as well as a man in his prime, that they said, 'Well, of course, he hasn't had his sixtieth birthday party,' making a guess at his age, but it did not stop them treating him as an elder.

This premature ageing was probably the result of his family misfortunes. He had buried three sons, one after another, in the hill behind the village, and then his wife, who had died of a broken heart from her losses. Now he managed to eke out a poverty-stricken life with his youngest daughter, the only survivor. But as a country gentleman from a family which, since their great-grand-father had held a minor post, had not once gained the honour of passing the public examinations, he constantly lamented, 'If I close the door of the family like this, how can I face my ancestors?'

Whatever his inner feelings, he was as mean to his only surviving daughter as if she were a dog with mange. His mind was possessed with thoughts of how to obtain an adopted son, or of to whom he could leave the care of the ancestral graves, as if the rest of his life were just for that one task. After he had given vent to his anger, it seemed to have worn itself out, as Yoon Bo had expected. He gazed at Yoon Bo's new straw shoes pressed firmly into grass wet with morning dew and then at the tool sack on his shoulder and said, 'You've got a job?'

'Yes, sir.'

'Um . . . I see.'

'Good-bye, till I come back, sir.'

'Well . . . just look over there.'

'Why? What is it?'

He looked towards where the pipe was pointing. The morning mist was slowly lifting.

'Can't you see them all at work?'

'Yes, ploughing the paddy.'

'The land is good to us.'

'. . . .?'

The teacher quoted five Chinese phrases, and went on, 'But the land is not like that, is it? It awaits as ever the will of heaven and the care of man.'

'I didn't get it, sir.'

'When hungry, flatter the one who feeds you. When full, turn and go. Gather where it's warm. And turn away from where it's cold. These are the ways of men.'

Yoon Bo stood and blinked.

'Going far?'

'Me . . . ?'

Kim *hunjang* nodded.

'I'm going to Jinjoo.'

'You'd better change your ideas. In the old days you'd have had no chance of getting away with it. It's all useless.'

He spoke with vehemence, as if, on second thoughts, he was angrier than before.

'What does it matter if it was useless, or whether I change my mind. Isn't everything ruined now?'

'I could have had you turned out of the village . . .'.

'If you'd tried, do you think I would have just gone?'

'I could have done that but – ahem, ahem – I thought well of your filial piety. That's why I let you off. The wise men of old said "Know before you act." What do you know about anything?'

'Such learned words don't mean much to me, but master . . .'.

He put his sack down on the verge, moved close, and whispered,

'Allow me to ask one question – what is your view on the "Army of Justice?" Are they as bad as the Dong Hak?'

'Ah, um, there is no comparison. How could you call them bad? – literally an army of righteous men of honour, the flower of the nation.'

'If that is so, it seems to me that the "Army of Justice" want to chase out the Japanese, and the others want to stop and punish the officers who steal and scheme to betray the country. In my view they are equally worthy, so why call the Dong Hak bad and the "Army of Justice" good?'

'You rascal! How can you say that loyalty and disloyalty are the same?'

'So, exactly the same thing when done by the people is disloyalty and when done by the gentry is loyalty? Is that it?'

At last he seemed to realize that he was being made a fool of.

'Shut up, you idiot! Be off at once!'

Dipping the soles of his straw shoes in the stream by the path, Yoon Bo craftily changed the subject.

'By the way, sir, where are you heading for through the morning dew?'

It was not the first time that the two of them had engaged in this kind of exchange. Despite their difference in status and opinions, they were in a strange way congenial and, indeed, felt mutual affection. Rebuking the other at one moment only to realize that he was being teased the next – in this way there flowed between them a subtle friendship.

'I've been to Kim *jinsa*'s in the next village. It looks pretty hopeless.'

In no time his tone had changed to that of consultation.

'I hear that chap Uksoi has run away?'

'That damned ruffian has abandoned the helpless family of his late master – really, the world has become a wilderness. If he can be caught, he ought to be put on the rack and killed – he ought to be flogged to death.'

'He's not entirely to blame. What a time he must have had before

119

he decided to go! He went without a meal as often as he had one. Besides, having to serve a pair of widows must have been stifling. It was only because of his stupidity that he stayed on so long . . .'.

For a man who had come out for a long journey, Yoon Bo was leisurely, and the teacher equally so. He had no thought for his daughter, who had had acute stomach cramp in the night and was still in bed.

'Why – do you reckon that fulfilling your human obligations is as easy as eating cake lying down? For servants there are certain duties and likewise for masters there are different duties.' At this moment Kim Pyongsan came strolling down the path, with no hat over his topknot, his hands tucked in the top of his trousers, after a night of gambling in the next village. Seeing them in his way, he snorted loudly. As Yoon Bo turned, Pyongsan walked straight between the two of them. Lifting his head, he stared straight into Kim *hunjang*'s face and then, turning his short neck, stared also into Yoon Bo's and, with another snort, continued on his way. When it was too late Kim *hunjang* gathered his phlegm and spat loudly on the roadside.

'Farewell for now then, master.'

Yoon Bo picked up his sack and walked off briskly. He heard from behind, once again, Kim *hunjang* spitting loudly. Pyongsan, walking ahead, turned and said in a coarse voice, 'Setting off to work, eh?' as if to suggest, 'It is not you that I feel bad about.'

'Whether or not you'd call it work, certainly I'm off . . .'.

His reply was in a neutral tone, neither respectful nor slighting.

'Bloody hell! I've been up all night . . .'.

'So you had a good session.'

'Hopeless!'

Yoon Bo was keen to get away but Pyongsan moved his fat body quickly so as not to fall behind.

'From the way you say it, you must have won a lot of money.'

'Won? I lost absolutely everything.'

'You didn't have anything to lose.'

'Huh, huh, huh, . . . that poor wretch, the whole capital for his trade went up in the air.'

'I see you've ruined the living of some poor tradesman. You

gentry have a whole variety of ways for robbing the lower orders, all sorts, like a pedlar's wares.'

As if pleased at being classed with the gentry, Pyongsan giggled. Yoon Bo, mumbling as if singing to himself, walked off toward the ferry without a farewell. Thrusting out his bulging paunch, Pyongsan strolled on along the road towards his home. His neck seemed to be buried deep in flesh. Like a pudding basin, his head got narrower towards the top, while below both cheeks bulged out with flabby fat. Stiff and thick, his hair in the front grew very low so that the height of his forehead was barely an inch, and across the middle of it ran a thick line.

'Oh, my stomach!' he bawled, with hollow coughs, as he entered the yard across which came the sound of weaving. Seeing their father, the two brothers ran off to the back like squirrels.

'Would you like the breakfast table brought in now?' asked his wife as she released herself from the loom in the small room and hurried out to receive him.

'Ugh! I must catch up with some sleep first.'

He went into the main room and leaving the door flung open, spread-eagled himself on the floor. And in no time he was snoring away. Once asleep in such a state of exhaustion, he would not be likely to get up before the early afternoon. Closing the door, she beckoned the children and saw to their breakfast. For herself she dumped a lump of rice in some rice-tea, and as she picked up the hoe she said, 'Father is asleep. So, when you have finished eating, take the table to the kitchen and go out and play. Do you understand?'

Twelve-year-old Gobok, thrusting out lips like his father's and looking angrily at his mother from downcast eyes, expressed his discontent, but seven-year-old Hanbok nodded in agreement.

Here and there among the paddies were set squares of rice seedlings, their tender leaves quite advanced. Most of the barley fields had been hoed so that the dark furrows looked fresh. Pyongsan had sold off their few patches of paddy for gambling capital, so all they had left was a piece of dry field where two large rocks took up much of the space. Preoccupied with earning money by weaving day and night, Haman *dek* could scarcely spare a minute to weed even that small piece, and it was overgrown. (In this state what chance does the barley have to grow?) Squatting down, she started weeding. It seemed that this year they were worse than ever. (I must hurry up and get back . . .) In a flurry, the more she hurried the less progress she seemed to make. Because of the rocks the actual land where barley grew was not very much, yet to her one length of furrow seemed an infinite distance. (I wish my eyelids would stop fluttering so much. What's the matter with me? And this ringing in my ears.) Sweat rose on her red flushed face. After she had been bending over weeding for half the day she caught sight of Suni carrying lunch things on her head for her father. She rose weakly, her face now very pale.

'Child!'

'Yes?'

'Taking lunch to your dad?'

'Yes.'

'If you have some water, could you spare me a drop?'

Suni put her container down at once and poured some water into the lid of a bowl. She took it down to the furrow where Haman *dek* was and passed it to her.

'It's like drinking the water of heaven. Phew.'

'Please wipe your face. Why don't you take it easy and have some rest?'

Instantly her eyes became hard.

'Off you go.'

'Yes.'

She gazed blankly at Suni's back as she walked along the path between the fields with the basket on her head, her pigtail dangling. To be pitied even by a little one – the child's goodness had hurt her pride. When she was back home, the sound of the snoring was as before and the yard was empty. After dropping her hoe by the jars and washing her hands, she took the cloth off her head to wipe her hands and face, and then lifted the lid of one of the jars. Her hand groped into the salt in the jar, and taking out an egg she thought to herself, 'Weren't there four? . . . it's Gobok again!' For making a silk *jogori* for a girl in the next village who was getting married she had been given some eggs which she had hidden in the salt jar. Had she managed to hatch a chicken and keep it, before it could lay, she would have had to offer it to her husband to eat. Had it been a piglet, or even a calf, it would have been the same.

'Wretch! What do you take the master of the house for? For your foot wrap, eh? – low bred, ignorant wretch!'

To avoid his kicking the table over there had to be, by whatever means, at least one tempting side-dish on it apart from *kimchi* and soya-bean soup. Fortunately he was frequently off roaming about the town, sometimes for several days, so it was for when he would be at home that the eggs had been hidden away like treasure. And now two were missing. (There is no hope for that boy. I have had to be firm with myself not to admit this, but Hanbok is my only hope.)

The spring onion soup was just boiling when the coarse voice of her husband came, 'Bring the table now!'

'Yes.'

She put beaten egg into the boiling soup and taking the bowl of rice out of a pot, she put them on the table. On receiving it, Pyongsan, as usual, commented unkindly saying this is too salty and insipid, poking the rice roughly with his spoon. But thankfully for his wife, he ate it without making further trouble, emptying the bowls of soup and rice. Though only a trifling sum, the gambling had not been bad, he had had his fill of sleep and satisfied his stomach with spring onion soup, and seemed to be in an unusually good mood. When he arrived at the tavern he called out loudly, 'Hey, Kang *posoo*! It's been a long time . . .'.

A man with bushy whiskers looked up from the cup from which he was drinking and parted his lips in a smile.

'Hah!'

Drawing close, Pyongsan inquired, 'How are things with you these days?'

'It's always the same with me. As always, too, you look very well, Kim *saengwon*.'

Pyongsan's ruddy face became even brighter. It was rare for him to be called *saengwon*, a gentlemanly title, and there was never any flattery in what the guileless hunter said.

'Not seeing you lately, I wondered if you hadn't become a squashed hat.'

'When I am tired out there's nothing I can do and the animals don't just wait for me to catch them, so I wouldn't be surprised if some day I get eaten by a tiger, never mind being a squashed hat.'

'Don't worry – you are still in your prime. Have you been to the market?'

'No.'

'What then?'

'I have some business right here.'

'What kind of business?'

'Well . . .'.

'Must be good business?'

'Can't be bad, I guess.'

With a large strong hand Kang *posoo* wiped the wine off his whiskers. Pyongsan energetically banged on the table.

'Why does no one bring any wine? I'm paying today!'

The woman ignored him.

'Look here!'

'I won't serve you!'

Her voice was shrill.

'I'm telling you to bring some wine.'

'And I'm telling you I won't.'

'Why?'

'Even a flea has shame.'

'Huh, do you think I haven't got any money? Don't worry.'

He rattled his pocket. Still looking displeased, she snubbed him with 'What bad luck', as she poured out the wine. As if used to such insults, he took it patiently, quite unlike his manners at home. He was in a very good mood. He had not forgotten the several occasions when he had lured the hunter into the gambling shop and profited greatly from his capital. Once he had obtained a bear's gall for next to nothing and had sold it for several times what he had paid. Though renowned as a demon in the hills, when he came down from them the hunter became a simpleton whom Pyongsan could handle as he liked, a solid source of nourishment. If he had been to town, it must have been to dispose of his catch. Once the money was in his pocket, where would it go? It was already as good as in his own. So it was natural for him to be gallant, offering to pay for the drinks which he demanded by beating on the table.

'So, what is this good business of yours, then?'

'A certain female . . .'.

In the middle of the sentence Kang *posoo* abruptly shut his mouth with embarrassment. Pyongsan's eyes flashed brightly.

'H'm . . . a certain female, eh?'

'No, no, I didn't mean to say that. A certain person made an urgent request . . .'.

'Was it for a bear's gall?'

He shook his head.

'Will it bring in a tidy sum?'

'You couldn't call it a tidy sum, but it was wanted regardless of price.'

'When are you leaving?'

'I will fix the deal tonight and probably go in the morning.'

'I see. Come on, drink up, man.'

'I need sleep more than wine.'

He yawned as he took the cup.

'Is it a tiger skin?'

'Do you think it was that easy?'

'What is it then?'

'Well, I'd rather . . .'. He only smiled secretively and would not easily be persuaded to tell. He smothered another yawn.

'I'm sleepy. I had a bad night.'

'Then there is no need to go on with needless drinking. Go into the back room and have a sleep,' put in the woman, as if with the intention of separating them.

'That's a good idea.'

Seeing him pass into the back room, Pyongsan furtively rose. As he was about to slip out the woman called, 'Who is going to pay?'

'That's right.'

He stepped back and counted out the money.

'What about all the credit you owe me?'

'Look woman, don't fuss like a wasp. Am I going to pass away tonight?'

'You can't be sure can you? Don't we always ask each other how we passed the night?'

Pyongsan cleared his throat loudly as he entered the village. When he reached the shade of the village tree he squatted down awkwardly and looked out over the fields. His original idea had been to have a drink and then go on to the town, but now, with Kang *posoo* on his mind, his legs were tied down. (That ruffian – after saying 'a certain female' he broke off. 'Female', 'Female' . . 'Regardless of the price?' 'Regardless of the price' . . . by any means possible I must drag him down to the town tomorrow morning . . . but how . . .?)

In the fields below men and women alike were busy. His own two sons were the only ones hanging around the threshing ground, for other children had to work when their parents were busy. Even if only a five-year-old was left behind, he would be put out on a straw mat to chase away the birds from the yard where moth-eaten millet was spread out to dry. Gobok could be seen punching his brother Hanbok for something he had done wrong, and he was crying. (Regardless of the price . . . however high or low . . .) Measuring the height of the sun, Pyongsan stood up.

'That rogue – why is he hanging about here? This is a farming field, not a gambling field.'

'His flesh looks good. Take a cut with a sharp knife and it would make a fair lump, wouldn't it?'

'Tender, too.'

'Of all meat, human flesh is the tastiest, they say.'

'That will do for a tiger-tempting tale. Stop it now and get on with your work!'

Dooman's father, Yi Pangi, told off the young ones for their nonsensical chatter. The tendency to regard Pyongsan as someone as harmful as a snake or a scorpion was more evident with the women than the men. Any woman who saw him on the road would avoid him by turning down a side path. Yongpari, working on a dike, called out loudly, 'Look! What's that over there?'

Pyongsan, passing, turned to look where he was pointing. A man on horseback, in a western suit and hat, had entered the village. Children leading oxen to graze on the roadside scattered and ran.

'I've never seen anything like it. Isn't it a Jap?' Yongpari asked Pyongsan uneasily.

All the others, farmers and their wives, stood up and gazed in fear at the distant figure as he rode past.

'He must be going to the Choi house,' mumbled Yongpari as he saw the horse going up the hill.

Pyongsan snorted and said, 'Ah, it's that fellow from the Cho family in Seoul.'

'Pardon?' said Yongpari, bursting with curiosity, but Pyongsan passed on without another word. When the sun had completely gone down and dusk was gathering he returned to the tavern.

'The soles of your feet will catch fire,' said the woman as she gave the table a wipe and put aside the dish cloth.

'Where's Kang *posoo* gone to?'

'I don't know.'

From the back room came the sound of snoring. Breaking into a smile, Pyongsan said, 'Is he your man? Why are you trying to keep him tucked away?'

'Oh, my! You ought to be struck by lightning for saying such things when my own husband is here alive and kicking.'

'Ha ha ha . . .'.

'You need a change of heart.'

'What's wrong with it?'

'If you don't, you won't die a decent death, and I shall be sorry. A clumsy, innocent man, like him – don't you feel any pity for him?'

'Why, am I going to eat him up?'

'Do you think you will get away with your sins?'

Regardless of her words, he went home assured that Kang *posoo* was there, but so preoccupied that he could not sleep, partly because he had had his fill in the daytime. He feared that the woman might scheme to separate them and send the hunter away. (Just wait until the first cock crows.) But, unexpectedly, it was Kang *posoo* who came to see him. Standing by the door, he called in a low voice.

'Can you come out for a minute?'

'Sure, sure I'll come.'

He put on his clothes hurriedly enough to get both feet into

127

one leg of his trousers and stepped down into the yard, where the moon, still hanging in the sky, cast a whitish light.

'I've come to consult you about something.'

Kang *posoo* pulled him along past the rubbish heap and under the apricot tree. From a small room where the oil lamp flickered came the sound of the loom.

'What is it?'

'Well, this is something rather unusual.'

'Oh, you make me lose patience. You couldn't sell it, is that it?'

'I sold it all right, but what I got for it was a pair of gold rings.'

'Indeed?'

From Pyongsan came the sound of swallowing hard. He was truly surprised.

'Please don't tell any one.'

'Of course not. So what are you going to do with them?'

'It's the first time I've ever seen gold rings.'

'It would be.'

'I want to sell them but I daren't.'

'Leave it to me – I'll see to it.'

'That's why I came.'

'But I have to know the inside story . . . What was it that you sold?'

'Well, it's a bit embarrassing.'

'Come on. You've been like this all day. Hasn't it simmered long enough yet?'

'It's embarrassing to talk about, but you know that thing that is said to bewitch a man, so that if a woman possesses it he can't pull himself away from her – the vixen's thing.'

'What?' After a moment of confused silence Pyongsan burst out laughing and clapping.

'So, tell me, who is this treacherous bitch who has had it from you?'

'I've promised not to tell.' He shook his head, but in the end Pyongsan succeeded in making him open his mouth. He learned that the treacherous female was the maid at the Choi *champan's* house, Guinyo.

Chapter Twelve

AS the guest from Seoul, having paid respects to Lady Yoon, followed Kilsang towards the *sarang*, the eyes of all the servants standing around, male or female, turned towards his back. It was Cho Junku, a second cousin of Choi Chisoo, who had been there six years before at about the time of Sohi's birth. He was the eldest grandson of the brother of Lady Cho, Chisoo's grandmother. As soon as he had disappeared towards the *sarang* the men and maids started whispering.

'He was here a few years ago – don't you remember?'

'That's right. Then he looked grand in his horse-hair hat and *dopo* but now he looks awful.'

'Dreadful. A crow would call him "uncle"!'

'A swallow would call him "grandad".'

Giggles all round. A gentleman of Seoul in the new style, he wore a dark western suit with hat and shoes to match. With short legs in proportion to his body and a large head, he would have looked grotesque in any case, but they seemed to think it was due to his western attire. It must have been hereditary as the late Lady Cho had also been small and short in the leg.

'I've seen Jap soldiers riding by, but the same narrow trousers didn't look so ridiculous on them.'

'That must have been a uniform, which is different.'

'Uniform or not, they are all the same narrow trousers, aren't they? To be sure, those chaps looked smart.'

'I bet it was because they had long swords and your heart shrank to the size of a pea. That's why they looked so splendid. Besides, why on earth does he tie that piece of stuff round his neck? it couldn't be a hat string.'

Water flows downstream, as they say, and from the way the servant behaved it was obvious that he was not a welcome guest to

Lady Yoon or Choi Chisoo. Entering the courtyard of the *sarang*, Junku asked Kilsang, 'Where is Kim *subang*?'

'He has gone to Gurae.'

'To Gurae?'

'Yes, sir.'

'Is he in the *sarang* then?'

'You mean the master?'

'Yes.'

'He is in the Garden House.'

Junku said scoldingly, 'Then go at once, boy, and tell him that his elder cousin from Seoul is here.'

'Yes, sir.'

As he watched Kilsang running off, Junku did not step up on to the verandah but remained standing in the shade of the plantain tree. He took off his hat and wiped his face with a handkerchief. His forehead where it had been under the shadow of his hat was startlingly white. Despite his poor figure his long eyelashes and clean-cut face had a touch of nobility.

'So, it's still an era of peace and prosperity here.'

He folded his used handkerchief neatly before putting it away in his pocket, and with his hands behind his back, looked down at the toes of his shoes. Then straightening himself, he gazed up at the sky in which a hawk circled with outstretched wings. After wheeling several times it flew away towards Dangsan, leaving the cloudless sky empty. Now only the sound of women singing in the fields could be heard, borne on the dusty wind. Flushed, Kilsang ran up.

'Sir, my master bids me escort you to the Garden House.'

Junku shrugged and went briskly through the gate. When they were there Kilsang called, 'I have brought the guest, master.'

Instead of an answer, the door opened. A scholar of about Chisoo's age, seated and stroking the sole of his socks, stared at Junku stepping up on to the shoe stand and then, with a look of embarrassment, turned his face away.

'Do come in.'

Chisoo, in a sitting position, spoke casually, as to a next door neighbour.

'You seem to have a visitor . . .'.

'Don't worry about that.'

Once in the room Junku took off his hat and, hitching his trousers at the knees, sat down. Through the open door came a breeze laden with the scent of pine woods.

'You must have had a long hard journey.'

Chisoo spoke again in an ordinary tone of voice and after pausing a moment with a meaningful glance at the scholar, he said, 'Let me introduce you. This is the person from Seoul I mentioned before.'

Then to Junku, 'This is Yi Dong-jin of Hadong.'

When the initial greetings were done and they sat back again, they felt awkward. As it was a first meeting, without Chisoo's help it was difficult for either of them to open their mouths, and as he did not speak they had to be silent. At last, he said, 'What has brought you here this time?'

'Nothing special − just for a change of air.'

'Your family are well?'

'As well as can be. Your complexion is still not good, is it?'

Chisoo tightened his thin lips. His manner was as chilly as the winter breeze on the Sumjin River, but Junku, as if accustomed to it, was calm, though he could not but be conscious of the presence of Yi Dong-jin. When sitting down Junku was slightly taller than the other two. His regular features and the polished air of a Seoulite gave him an edge over the others and, though two years older than Chisoo, he looked younger.

'So, nothing special has happened all this time?'

'There was something special.'

Suddenly Chisoo's voice became sharper.

'There was an incident in which a woman fell for a servant and ran off with him.'

He chewed the words and spat them out. Junku's eyes tightened. Though he knew about Chisoo's occasional fits of hysteria, he had not expected him to bring up his own affairs so openly.

'I've heard a bit about it . . . so it looks like an end to the line.'

It was not what he should have said, but it slipped out unawares.

'You know, don't you, that even had she stayed on, it was the end of the line anyway, as I am useless now.'

He gave a roar of laughter as though for some mysterious reason he was greatly enjoying himself. Stroking the bottom of his socks, Yi Dong-jin listened without a word.

'It's the family line that's the worry. What are you going to do about looking after the ancestral tombs and the rituals?'

'Why, haven't you heard? Followers of Western religion are already smashing up their family shrines anyway.'

'I hope you are not going to bring in your mother's family and let them dominate it all?'

Junku spoke in a joking way, but it sounded unnatural. Yi Dong-jin's eyes became a little fierce as he caught Junku's and he looked away.

'There's not a drop of Choi blood anywhere to be found, even if required for medicinal purposes, as they say. Only Cho's and Yoon's are available.'

'What nonsense you talk. What it comes to is this: you have to depend on the maternal side for the ancestral rites.'

'There's no need for you to worry. From ancient times it has always been the hens in our clan that crowed and brought in the dawn. By the way, have you seen my mother yet?'

'I've just been to pay my regards but she seemed to be angry about something . . .'.

'Angry or pleased, who can know what's in her mind?'

'It might have been my bad conscience but I couldn't help thinking that she was blaming me for what has happened to you, so I fidgeted as though I was sitting on a pincushion.'

'Well . . . if I'd done just as you told me to, and along with our powerful relatives, gone only to high-class courtesans, this wouldn't have happened, I suppose.'

He roared with laughter again. He seemed determined not to treat his elder cousin with due respect. Judging from the subject of the conversation, they were referring to some dishonourable deeds, and to pour them out in this shameless manner could only indicate that he despised his cousin.

'And my aunt will misinterpret it, thinking that it is all my fault for inviting you to Seoul and leading you astray.'

As he spoke Junku cast a glance now and again at Yi Dong-jin as if to say, 'As it's all come out, there is no call for me to be restrained.'

'Well . . . do you really think so? Or wouldn't it be rather that she was displeased to see you in the new style, with your topknot gone, and in a western suit?'

While Junku smiled wryly, Chisoo continued the attack.

'Or is it possible that she's thinking that you've come to ask another difficult favour like the last time?'

Junku's face, so far calm, fell, but only for a moment. He avoided Chisoo's eyes, which smiled with cruelty.

'I haven't come for that sort of thing this time. Even if I fell so low as to be "Out on the street, exposed to wind and dew", would I be so shameless as to ask for her help again? It's just that things are very disturbing in Seoul, so I came for a change of air.'

Dong-jin spoke for the first time, 'Have you come straight from there?'

'Yes.'

'Tell us what it is like. Buried here in the mountains, we are more or less blind men with open eyes.'

'Well, what can I say?'

'What do you want to know for? Are you intending to go and beat the drum and gather a mob yourself?' said Chisoo to Dong-jin in a voice that was too hard to be a playful rebuke.

'Huh! You just keep quiet. If I could, why not? So, tell me, how far have they gone with changing their clothes and cutting their hair?'★

'People in western suits are still very rare but short hair is more noticeable.'

'I hear that the opposition was stronger from the side of the common people.'

'That is probably true. Even the sedan bearers of the foreign

★ A Short Hair Edict was one of the sweeping reforms introduced under Japanese influence in 1894, forcing men to cut off their topknots, but it was soon abandoned because it aroused such strong opposition from the public.

missions ran away, scared of having their hair cut. Public feeling was high, especially after the assassination of the Queen.'

'Even these days, I've heard, the "Army of Justice" emerges now and, again on the outskirts of Seoul?'

Junku noticed the vein bulging on Dong-jin's large hands as they stroked the soles of his socks.

'It may be so, and not only around Seoul. They seem to raise mobs and cause disturbances all over the place. Even an issue like the Short Hair Edict can turn the whole country upside down. How pitiable and farcical it must seem to foreigners.'

Having sensed Dong-jin's feelings from the atmosphere, Junku had made the first move by ridiculing them.

'Well . . . I suppose we country scholars, being ignorant of the ways of the great world, have no right to criticize.'

'But you won't forever remain in peace out of reach of the great powers simply because you live in a remote village.'

'That's true. And you can't say it's been altogether peaceful here, either.'

'As I was riding down here, country scholars seemed to look at me as if I was some kind of animal. If we go on like this, when are we going to be enlightened?'

Having said this, he snorted as if to say, 'You two are looking at me like that, too, aren't you,' and went on, 'It is deplorable that they should be so narrow-minded. Not only are they unaware of how the world turns, but by continually opposing such trifles as shorter hair, they drive an already troubled country into even more of it. In this way, there doesn't seem to be the slightest hope of bringing about any reforms, does there?'

'That may be so, but you can't say that it's just a question of the Short Hair Edict. Whose hands are going to control our national affairs? Isn't that what we are really concerned about?'

'As they say, "It doesn't matter which road, as long as you get there." Instead of taking account of what we might gain from it, you waste time arguing about the rights and wrongs of it, while others get a thousand, ten thousand miles ahead of us. Is it the time to argue about trifles like clothes?'

At this point Chisoo rose and went out, possibly to go to the privy.

'Anyway, so-called customs are bound to follow the more advanced, so sooner or later . . .'.

Yi Dong-jin cut him short.

'Just by imitating the externals without knowing the substance one does not necessarily become civilized. It may seem rude to speak as if I was referring to you, Mr Cho, as an example, so please excuse me. Ha! ha! ha! . . .'.

Junku, trying hard not to look defeated, said 'From the beginning man has wanted to make life more convenient. I think that's how tools came about and everything developed. Isn't electric light more convenient than oil?'

'Oh, yes, draining the water out of the lily pond in the palace garden to light an electric bulb was an amazing thing. Oh yes, so-called "convenience" is an absolute necessity of human life, I do agree with you there.'

With a repressed snort, Junku said, 'We may call them "Jap pirates" or "aliens", but we should realize that they regard us as barbarians. However much the narrow-minded gentry may boast about their country as the "land of etiquette", to the eyes of foreigners all this pomp is nothing more than a bizarre spectacle in a primitive land.'

'Barbarians, eh? . . . Fundamentally, such things as courtesy and manners are not for the sake of convenience. Things like ethics and morals, too – they are as cumbersome as our attire.'

Junku made no answer to this. It seemed as though he now realized that Yi Dong-jin was formidable.

'Mr Cho, what you have said has set me thinking about many things. If one would chose rather to starve than to lose one's dignity, it is because one is a man and not an animal, but on the other hand one must not entirely lose the animal's instinct for grabbing food . . . that's the only way to stay alive. If that is so, what's wrong with changing your clothes and cutting off your hair? Wouldn't you even go as far as digging up your ancestors' graves?'

'That's right. To achieve one's aim, one needs the courage to face up to insults, and patience, too,' replied Junku.

At that moment Chisoo returned.

'So down here it is still an era of peace and prosperity, eh?'

As if to dismiss what had so far been said as merely trivial, Junku turned to Chisoo with a new theme.

'Not really.'

'Well, at least outwardly it seems so.'

'One never knows when they will all pick up their pitchforks and charge.'

'Never! After seeing tens of thousands of Dong Hak fall like autumn leaves, they wouldn't break into any rash and thoughtless action, would they, not unless Japanese power recedes?'

'Don't there have to be continuous uprisings, one after the other, so that the Japs can sweep the board once and for all? To tell the truth, they ought to bow down to the spirits of these Dong Hak with an offering of a bull's head. Who else do they have to thank for the chance to strike at China? As their interpreter, you should know.'

Noticing the expression on Dong-jin's face, Junku looked displeased.

'No need to call me an interpreter. To understand what was going on outside I read some foreign literature which, naturally, led me to become acquainted with them, that's all.'

'You don't have to feel bad about it. What's wrong with being an interpreter? It is not like the old days, is it? They say that they are the ones who sway national affairs one way or the other and if you manage well, you can gather enough silver to fill your storeroom.'

'I admit there is something in that.'

Junku looked gratified but then Chisoo, entirely out of context, snapped, 'This is a world in which a low-bred rabble in straw shoes with bamboo spears run wild like madmen.'

Yi Dong-jin was quiet, a sour smile rising to his lips, as if thinking to himself, 'There he goes again – another storm is on its way.'

'It's all wrong – from the abolition of serfdom in the year *Gabo*. They are rotten right through and they've gone crazy – like scoundrels that flatter low-class women!'

136

'What a thing to say – do you realize what kind of a world you are living in now?'

'What kind of world, indeed! Do you mean that the world itself has changed? It hasn't. It's only the guts of the gentry that have gone rotten.'

'Huh, you are looking at it only from your own point of view, and when that goes too far it becomes prejudice.'

Chisoo laughed hysterically.

'Quite right. I'm sure it's just prejudice. Nevertheless, I will not bow down to the lower orders to preserve my own property and life. You wait and see – soon these beggars are going to grab the gentry by their topknots and sit on them until they are finished.'

'In a time like this such things are only a small problem.'

Chisoo took no heed and went on, 'It is like making a hole in a cage of starving wolves instead of thinking about how to keep them in. That's the end of it – they will try to get at the very intestines of the gentry. Do you think they rebelled because they were hungry and naked? Or because they had been exploited by greedy officials? Was there ever a time when the common people were well fed or well dressed? Had the walls been high and strong, they would have accepted it as their fate even if they were so hungry that they died with the skin of their stomachs stuck to their backs. There has to be a loose corner, or a hole to crawl through before they venture out to shout and brandish their implements and when they realize that the defence is weak, only then, will they all tumble out and yell. Have you ever seen an ill-treated man that wasn't cunning?'

Chisoo's eyes seemed to pierce Junku. The abuse might have been aimed at him.

'If they were forced to crawl on their knees, they would, because even if they have to live on cow feed, they know life is precious – can you imagine them risking their one and only life to eat rice instead? Fools, do they think they are dealing with people who can be won over with sweets? The idiots, why can't they see that once they give an inch they will have to give away the lot. They are fools.'

'It's not really as simple as you make out, is it?'

Junku made a mild protest.

'For instance, take the case of the Dong Hak. You can't simply say that they rebelled for bigger bowls of rice. That was not all. There was a formidable religious strength in it, though it was a heresy, no doubt. What about the Catholics? When they are willing to sacrifice their own lives, who can defeat them? As you say, when a fellow complains about a small ration, starve him for a while and he will be glad to eat anything, but once he gets the notion of having a happy life in the next world it's a different matter altogether. Similarly, in the case of the country, when it's like a stirred up beehive something has to be done. The policies have to be flexible to get round the crisis – appeasement or restraint.'

'Whichever way you look at it, it's all the same. Earlier on, when I called them scoundrels, you said it was prejudice. Do you think I condemned them as wicked just because I want to preserve my own life and property?'

Chisoo spoke as if he was about to strike Junku.

'In that case, I would be one of them myself. Ignorant people are so crafty that they will make a move only when the price is clearly indicated, whether in this world or the next, and when it has nothing to do with their own interests they don't take part in it. In short, they have no principles. They are not people who would risk their lives for the sake of integrity or an ideal, even though they might sell themselves for their own advantage. I admit there were people such as Jun Bongjoon and Kim Kaenam among then, though they were probably no more than men of ambition. Anyway, they knew how to make use of the crowd and though they were our enemies, I admit that one of them was worth more than a hundred boastful officials in Seoul. The rotten gentry that fawn on the lower class like dogs, or the ones that bestow benevolence with the cunning of wolves, aren't they all the same brood? Those rascals would burn their robes or their family trees to save their lives if necessary, and live on even as butchers.'

'Ha ha! Leave it there. However eloquent you may grow it won't make any difference. I have no doubt that the Choi *champan* household are wolfish gentry.'

As if to come between them, Dong-jin laughed heartily. Adding,

'I must leave you now,' he stood up to go. Chisoo, who had seemed to be over-excited, made no fuss and rose to his feet also, ready to move. Turning to Junku, he said, 'We might as well go down, too.'

They came out of the Garden House together. Now, as he walked close beside Yi Dong-jin, Junku was hardly tall enough to reach to the bottom of his ears, making a poor impression. Under the chestnut tree to the left of the pavilion Dong-jin's servant waited with the tethered mule. Absorbed in the antics of the madwoman Dochul *ne*, in front of the pavilion, he now sprang up, dusting his bottom.

'I pray, I pray, I pray to thee, Guardian of the sites. On the day of my son's great home-coming, when he has been designated Governor, I shall have the great table laid out ready with rice cake . . .'.

Joining her hands, she repeatedly bowed towards the plaque over the door of the pavilion. Dong-jin passed close to her as he went to his donkey.

'See you soon.'

With a word of farewell to Junku, he mounted it. In the light of the setting sun the pitch black of his horse-hair hat and the bright folds of his white *dopo* were beautiful. The servant held the reins. As he moved down the slope the ribbons from his hat and coat fluttered in the breeze. As Chisoo and Junku were about to move away Dochul *ne*, giving off a sickly smell, hurtled towards them like a stone from a catapult, screeching, 'I pray thee, General of God's army!'

As if to embrace the whole sky, the entire earth, trees and plants, seas and rivers with her arms, she stretched them in a great circle and bowed in worship before Chisoo. Her flesh, where it showed through the tears in her clothing, was mottled with dirt. A bee circled her face, on which blood from scratches and pricks had congealed. Chisoo's face was scarlet and even his eyes seemed bloodshot.

'I pray thee, great General of God's army, bless and shine upon my son's path to office, let his name reach the royal throne so that his mother's wish, stained with her blood, may be granted!'

'Bitch! Get out of my way!'

'I pray thee, General of God's army . . .'.

Chisoo's arm seemed to strike the air and Dochul *ne* fell to the ground, only to spring to her feet again. She began to clap.

> *'Fire spreads fast!*
> *The flames flare up!*
> *The roof, the earth, the corners are falling —*
> *All people gather at Mount Paiksan in Goboo.*
> *General Nokdoo, in white robe and hat,*
> *String of one hundred and five beads in hand,*
> *Recites the prayer twenty-one times.*
> *Ah, Ah —*

She floated in a dance.

'What an extraordinary madness!'

Junku frowned.

On Chisoo's face the blush had been replaced by a chilly smile. They walked down the sloping path.

'In the first month, on the eighth day, when the dawn cock crows . . . birdie, birdie, blue birdie! Don't sit on the *nokdoo* beans . . .'.

Snatches of her chant reached them from behind, carried on the wind.

'She is certainly mad, but it doesn't seem to be any ordinary madness.'

Junku turned round.

'She belongs to the so-called Enlightenment Party.'

Lowering his eyes Chisoo smiled.

'Her brat gained some fame in the Dong Hak faction and was shot.'

'What do you mean, "Enlightenment Party"?'

'In the sense that they tried to uproot existing things they can be called "enlightened", can't they? The fact that they actually set out with the slogan "Equality for all" shows in itself that the Dong Hak were more enlightened than the "Enlightenment Party" of Seoul. Don't you see? Ironically, she cherished the dream of seeing her son made governor.'

140

After a mocking laugh, he added 'She can't be the only case of that sort, can she?'

With a bitter face, Junku looked back. Under the chestnut tree she continued to dance.

'Peasants with nothing but vegetable patches, when they got to the Paiksan mountain in Goboo, the headquarters of the Dong Hak, you can imagine how they saw in their mind's eye an alluring expanse of fertile land. Why, "equality for all" – is that anything new, and solely the idea of Choi whats-his-name, the founder of the faction? Ha, maybe the day will come when the family tree of a gentleman will be as miserable a document as that of serfdom and then there will be another uprising of "equality for all," eh?'

Village girls coming back from gathering mulberry leaves, seeing Junku, hurriedly turned into side lanes, taking him to be Japanese. Not only Junku, but Chisoo also was frightening. The former looked like a beetle and the latter was thought of in the village as a mantis.

In the *sarang*, Chisoo sat down to supper with Junku. After putting the table down, Guinyo, as she stepped backwards, cast a sidelong glance at Junku, who had been eyeing her already. At the threshold, narrowing her big dark eyes, she cast him a bold look, but it was not an amorous one. It might have been asking, 'What's your business here?' Now Chisoo was silent, as calm as the sea when the wind has died down, a completely different person from what he had been a while ago. (How am I going to put up with this man's caprices? Still there is no way but patiently to wait and see.) When he had finished eating, Junku swilled his mouth with rice tea and sat back. As she removed the table Guinyo looked at him once more, again not an amorous glance.

'What a strange young woman!' he thought to himself.

Chapter Thirteen

GANNAN *HALMUM*, in and out of bed, got through the spring without any serious trouble. By the early summer she was up and about, saying that if she kept still, she was afraid her joints would go stiff and she wouldn't be able to move. In the shade by the shed, Dori, who was fixing a new handle to a scythe, said with a teasing smile, 'Granny, when the earth was frozen solid I thought we'd be breaking some spade handles trying to dig your grave, but look at you now! Your hair is growing black again. Take it easy now, granny, and stay alive until I've got married and had my first son?'

'You rascal, that's a curse.'

Picking up scattered grains from the ground and putting them into a wooden bowl, despite herself, she broke into a broad smile, her lips showing the tremor typical of the old.

'What do you mean, curse? You mean you want to live even longer? I'm to stay unmarried till my own hairs go white, eh?'

'You're crazy.'

Bogi, straightening up after turning up the bottoms of his trousers, joined in.

'Granny, please hold on to Dori to stop him marrying and live long. I can't bear to think of him getting married and the blind fertility spirits giving him his first son.'

'You are crazy! What sin have I committed to be condemned to go on living until I can't control myself?'

Samsoo, coming round from the backyard, added as he went past, 'You are right there, granny. But please when you do go, make it spring or autumn. Summer corpses or winter corpses are equally dreadful. Frozen ground is no good and neither are bluebottles buzzing about.'

'I see. Don't worry Samsoo. When I go I'll leave a will that forbids you to have anything to do with it.'

'Oh, yes,' he said as he went out, ' please do!'

(Wicked rascal! I wiped his nose and washed his face and brought him up like my own son! As the saying goes 'The one who's been greatly favoured curses you greatly, and the one who's received less curses you less.' How true those old sayings are!)

Dori, closely examining the scythe, said, 'How did this happen? – teeth missing. I bet that rascal Kilsang's been meddling with it again.'

There were two dents in the blade.

'Granny!'

'What now?'

She turned her irritation on Bogi.

'Don't take any notice of what that rascal Dori says, but go on living until I am married and have five little sons – what about that?'

'You have the mind of a thief. You are trying to get granny to put in a word with her ladyship to have you married before me – is that it?'

'Just look at these boys, playing with me like a ball. Now stop your pranks and get on with your work. I'll be merciful to you and die soon, so leave me alone. I don't care whether you go to the girl's house and hang yourself there or take her away upside down on your back.'

'Huh, really. I think in this village the supply of girls has dried up at the source.'

Bogi hoisted his A-frame on to his back and walked out. Dori, picking up another scythe from the shed, also fixed his A-frame and went out, saying, 'You must live long. Isn't it true as they say "A dead prime minister is not as good as a live dog"?'

'How is it that nowadays youngsters don't realize how precious grain is? Aren't they afraid of Heaven, spilling it all over the place?'

Picking up the bowl, she stood up, groaning, 'Huh, my back.'

She put it down on the mortar by the shed.

'How long the nights are, and the days too! Oh dear.'

She had not been saddened too much by Samsoo's heartless words for even more she had been gratified by the roughshod affection shown by Dori and Bogi.

143

'Phew! Buddha, have mercy! May I enter Nirvana in my sleep.'

It was the season when everyone was busily on the run. Bees hatched out, silkworms, after waking from their early sleep and visibly growing, had entered into another sleep, and soon the picking of mulberry leaves would become more urgent. Cotton seed was sown and cut grass put in the paddies, while the fields of flax were knee-deep. As the sun daily grew hotter, all living things abounded and thrived. If only there was a little more rain, the greenfly on the leaves would be washed away. Until the barley harvest the women would be tied down, not only with the silk worms, but also with finishing the spring weaving. Indeed, the harvest was not far away – hadn't they already tasted the unripe grain? Starting from the sunniest spots, it would gradually ripen. Gannan *halmum* entered the yard of the *byoldang*. Lady Yoon sat on the verandah by herself but without noticing her, Gannan went to the edge of the pond.

'Without the owner, only the weeds do well.'

Mumbling to herself, she bent down to pull them out. Japonica blossom constantly opened and fell, scattering pink petals over the yard. Watching the old woman's back as she squatted down, Lady Yoon was silent. In a thin silk skirt and *jogori*, she looked emaciated and her complexion was sallow.

'The flowers blooming as splendidly as this, while they are the beggars of all beggars . . . oh, dear, oh, dear . . .'

She went on pulling out the weeds moving about slowly in her squatting position.

'You can cheat on your horoscope but not on your fate . . . Ah, ouch! A damned ant.'

She picked it off her neck where the skin was loose and puckered. Crushing it, she said, 'I'm as withered as a dried pollack and you won't get a bite out of me.'

Lady Yoon, who had been silently observing her movements, called quietly, '*Halmum!*'

As if struck by thunder, the old woman sprang up startled, straining her back.

'Ah, ouch!'

Her ladyship waited for a moment.

144

'Yes, young Mistress.'

'Are you feeling better now?'

'Thanks to your ladyship's grace – though it would be better if I just departed – I seem to be recovering little by little.'

'So you must.'

'I've lived as long as I can expect to.'

'Who can say? You might outlive me.'

'What an awful thing to say, ma'am.'

'Is there any order of young or old in death?'

The mistress seemed to open her mind a little towards the old woman. (Lady! Master Hwani and the lady of the *byoldang* are now like the beggars of all beggars . . .) Gannan swallowed the words hard. Lifting her gaze to the sky, Lady Yoon said, 'There's going to be a drought.'

'I am afraid so, ma'am. It would be a blessing to have a heavy shower for once.'

'It's up to the One Above.'

'You are right, "young Mistress", I mean your ladyship.'

'How stubborn you are to still call me that . . .'.

Despite herself, Lady Yoon laughed.

'Kim *subang* was talking to me about you.'

'Yes, ma'am?'

'After listening to him, I thought what a good idea that was of yours. It would be much better that way than putting your name on to the monastery list . . . The wife of Yi Pangi – what's she like? Is she genteel in her ways?'

'Yes, ma'am. She is diligent, tidy and clean, and a filial daughter-in-law too.'

'How many children do they have?'

'Two boys and a girl, ma'am.'

'Not many.'

'I am ashamed of myself. I have grown old without doing any-thing for you, and to depend on you in this way is sinful enough, and then on top of it . . .'.

'Don't say that. It's remiss of me not to have thought about it earlier.'

Lady Yoon slowly stood up. Her tall and well-proportioned

figure, dressed in white silk, had an air that was quite magnificent. Gannan *halmum* followed her with bent waist as far as the gate of the *byoldang* courtyard and looking towards her receding back, she swallowed hard once again (Lady! Master Hwani and the young mistress are now the beggars of all beggars!).

Going back to the spot where she had been weeding, she looked up at the sky, as her mistress had done a little while before, through the branches of the willow. (Dear husband, the mistress has granted it to us. Yes, husband, though we have no children, we won't go thirsty. We now have some land to provide for our departed souls. Yongman will lay out at least a bowl of water for us. Husband, do you hear, our own paddy for the departed . . .) She stood up with her face looking more sad than happy and then dropped down to carry on with the weeding. (I knew it would be granted. Of course her ladyship wouldn't turn down my appeal, of course not. Dear husband, I can close my eyes now and go in peace.) She could see vividly before her eyes the paddy full of water and well grown rice plants waving their dark green blades in the breeze.

'Granny!'

Samwol came into the courtyard carrying Sohi on her back. The little girl was sulky.

'Why do you have to do it yourself? You can ask Dori.'

'My child, what's the use of being idle? You must work as long as your limbs are firm.'

She smiled broadly.

'What are you so pleased about?'

'I'm pleased with the fine weather and with everything in the world, for I now understand the reason and principle of getting old.'

She made irrelevant remarks, but could not help her mouth widening into a smile while her lips trembled as often happens with old people.

'Let me down.'

Sohi fidgeted.

'Yes, Miss.' Samwol put her down. Squatting on the ground opposite the old woman, she asked half-heartedly, '*Halmum,* what are you doing?'

146

'I am weeding, Miss.'

Then to Samwol.

'Where's Bongsoon?'

'She's gone with her mother.'

'I heard that her uncle had died.'

'Yes. With the funeral and so on, it will be three or four days before they are back. So I have to wait on the young miss all that time.'

'*Halmum?*'

'Yes, Miss.'

'Why is your hair like that?'

Another half-hearted question.

'Because I am old, that's why, Miss.'

'Because you are a bent and crooked old woman, is it?'

'Yes, a bent and crooked old woman, Miss.'

'Bongsoon called you a wheezy old thing.'

Gannan *halmum* and Samwol cackled with laughter. Meanwhile, Sohi was gathering the fallen petals of japonica in her skirt. She appeared to be dispirited.

'She seems to have put it out of her mind lately.'

'Still the thought of it often comes back to her and makes her fret.'

'It's only natural, isn't it? She is at the age when a girl most needs her mother . . .'.

Then, changing the subject, she called, 'Samwol!'

'Yes?'

'I suppose the fern season is over by now?'

'Why?'

'It's just that I fancy some shoots.'

'I'm not so sure. There might still be some tender ones on Dangsan.'

'As I get better little by little, I fancy all sorts of things.'

'To save a dying man, someone went off in the middle of winter to look for bamboo shoots. I'll go and look for some.'

'Shall I go with you, walking slowly?'

'Do you think you should, Granny?'

147

'You'd reach it with your nose if you fell over, and if I don't move about my legs will go stiff . . .'.

'Let's go together then. We'll take the young Miss and go slowly, resting now and again. Let's go Miss – to the hill to pick some fern shoots. With Bongsoon's mother not here she seems so crushed . . .'

Samwol, hitching up the end of her skirt, wiped Sohi's nose and took her hand. They walked round the back yard and came out on the vegetable field by Kim *subang*'s house. Kilsang was playing foot-shuttlecock with Gad-dongi. Gad-dongi's younger sister Nami was thinning out radishes. Gannan remarked, 'That's stupid, big boys like you . . .'

Gad-dongi, dribbling, answered by rolling out his tongue and making beastly noises, 'Wha, wha, wha, au, au, au . . .'.

'You naughty boy.'

Brandishing her stick, she pretended to hit him.

Samwol asked Nami, 'How's your sister – has she plenty of milk?'

'Yes.'

They had passed the vegetable patch and were walking up the slope. Samwol said, 'Now they have their first grandchild, do you thing Kim *subang*'s wife will be a bit more dignified?'

'You can't give away your habits to a dog, can you?'

Gannan chatted as she walked up the slope between rests, leaning on her walking stick. Sohi holding Samwol's hand walked on glumly.

'How did that slovenly woman deserve to be matched to someone as genteel as Kim *subang*? If a woman makes a wrong match, it's a handicap for life, but if a man meets the wrong woman, that's paralysing, too.'

'By the way . . . gran.'

'What?'

'You know that visitor from Seoul?'

'. . .'.

'He really is funny. Guinyo was saying that after making Kilsang dust off, blow, and dry his clothes, and then dust, blow and dry the thing he wears on his head as though they were a gold crown and court dress, he had them put away as if they were ancestral tablets.'

'He must be as fussy as a woman.'

'Bongsoon's mother made him a change of clothes and he asked

148

her to make another one. He must be intending to stay a long time, mustn't he?'

The valley was covered thick with leaves. Here and there, where the sun penetrated, pale green patches wavered but the air in the wood was chilly and dank. From the streams, though invisible, covered by brambles and vines, came the babble of tumbling water. A wild pigeon, sensing their approach, rose with a flutter of wings and made Sohi jump.

'Take her on your back – there might be snakes about.'

Gannan *halmum* alerted Samwol who, handing over her basket, hoisted Sohi onto her back.

'Samwol!'

'Yes, Miss.'

'You know, a long time ago, Bongsoon picked me some wild berries.'

'It will be some time yet before they are ripe.'

'How many days?'

'Not until the barley harvest – about a month.'

'How many days is that?'

'Just over thirty.'

'Less than the age of my grandmother, isn't it?'

'Of course. About the age of your father.'

'They were so tasty.'

Tightening her arms round Samwol's neck, Sohi swallowed.

'I wouldn't say that – rather bitter, not sweet at all.'

'They are!'

'Toffee is nicer than wild berries, or honey.'

'No, no! The berries are better.'

She beat Samwol's back with her fist.

'What's nice about wild berries? They're not at all sweet.'

'They are!'

'Well, I think honey and toffee are nicer, Miss.'

'I'm telling you! Berries are nicer!' Sohi pinched Samwol's neck and grabbed hold of her hair.

'Ow!'

'Say the berries are tasty!'

'Yes, yes, Miss, the berries are tasty.'

149

'So I was right.'

Gannan *halmum* suddenly stood still. Beside a tree stump was a grey rabbit. It was engrossed in eating something, twitching its mouth, when suddenly its eyes met hers. It was so sudden that it seemed confused, unable to run away. Letting herself down quietly, Gannan laid aside her stick and held out her hands.

'Little rabbit, little rabbit, come to me!'

As she spoke it shot off and disappeared like a puff of smoke.

'Ho, ho . . . ha ha! Did you say "Little rabbit, come to me?" ha ha . . . Oh! My stomach, it hurts!'

Samwol lowered the kicking Sohi to the ground and held her stomach.

'Gran, ho! ho! Did you think that if you said, "Little rabbit, come to me", it would really come? Oh, it's so funny it kills me!'

'I was a bit confused, that's all. What's so funny about it?'

As she said this the old woman also laughed helplessly, flopped down as she was.

'Where's it gone!'

Sohi shrieked, and then, stamping her feet, screamed, 'I said where's it gone?'

'It's run away,' said Samwol, and sensing trouble, she purposely looked towards a distant hill.

'It's a long way off by now, Miss.'

'Go and get it.'

'It's run away, Miss. We can't.'

'I'm telling you to fetch it.'

'It wouldn't be caught by us.'

In the middle of the wood they were in a plight, not knowing whether to go on or turn back, when Kilsang appeared running breathlessly.

'Kilsang! They chased away the rabbit. Samwol did it, no, I mean *halmum* did it!'

Speaking in a tale-bearing tone, she burst into tears. Kilsang was at a loss, but when he heard Samwol's explanation he said, 'Never mind, Miss. Next time I'll catch one for you. I'll set a trap and catch it.'

'Listen, Miss,' coaxed Samwol, 'Kilsang will catch it for you.'

'I don't care! Fool, idiot! Wheezy old thing! Why did you chase it away?'

She ran to where Gannan sat on the ground and pummelled her shoulders.

'Oh dear, really, what can I do? It'll be the death of me that wretched rabbit!'

She gazed wide-eyed in the direction in which, like smoke, it had disappeared.

'Stop it now. If you cry, a fox will come and carry you off.'

Her crying abated, but not because she was afraid of the fox. She realized that however much she cried, Samwol or Gannan would never be able to comfort her in the way that Bongsoon *ne* could. Bongsoon *ne* smelt like her own mother, but there was no such smell around either of these two.

'I want to go home! I'll go home and tell Bongsoon *ne* about you!'

She stopped crying abruptly.

'You know she is away,' said Samwol rather teasingly, but Sohi ignored her and, taking on a false air of dignity, she said, 'I hate you, *halmum*! And you too Samwol! I don't want you to come back. Don't come back!'

'That's right, Miss. Let's just you and me go home together – how's that?'

Kilsang offered her his back, relieved that she had stopped crying.

'Kilsang, why did you come?'

'I just felt like it,' he said as he carried her down the path through the wood.

'We might as well go too.'

Gannan stood up leaning on her stick.

'Yes, let's.'

'She gets like that because she is missing her mother.'

'I know. If Bongsoon *ne* was here, she would have made a bigger fuss, crying and fainting, poor child.'

'I think Bongsoon *ne* is really good. She has a heart of gold.'

They watched Kilsang and Sohi disappear down the hill as they followed slowly, resting now and again.

Killsang said, 'Miss!'

'Um?'

'I'll catch the rabbit for you.'

'Umm.'

'Without damaging one hair, in a trap.'

'Um. What do rabbits eat?'

'Things like grass, or fruit.'

'No rice?'

'No.'

'No rice cake?'

'No.'

'Once, my mother gave the birds some rice. They'd just come down in the yard, you know.'

Kilsang closed his mouth. From the valley they had now reached the Dangsan pavilion. He said, 'Miss.'

'Um?'

'What do the clouds look like to you, up there in the sky?'

'Where?'

'Over there, where they are billowing up.'

'What about it?'

'Doesn't it look like a man on a horse?'

'I don't know.'

'It would be great, wouldn't it, to ride on a big kite and fly up to see it? To fly up and up right to the top of the sky. That would be fantastic, wouldn't it?'

'What would you want to go up there for?'

'The master monk at the temple told me that if you go on up and up, you come to Soomisan mountain. On that mountain, he told me, all the houses are built of precious metals and stones.'

'What are precious metals and stones?'

'You know, like the decorations you wear on New Year's Day, and the greenish beads on them – things like the ring her ladyship wears on her finger – that's precious metals and stones.'

'Ah, I know, I know. My mother has rings in green, yellow and white as well, and then she has hairpins and . . .'.

In the middle of the sentence she bounced as if she was on a horse and stretched out her arms 'this much, she has this much of them.'

'. . .'.

'She said she would give them all to me – things like beads, rings and hairpins, all of them – she said she would give them to me.'

Kilsang said nothing and she was disappointed. Recently, she had not made scenes demanding her mother. She seemed gradually to perceive that her mother's affair was something of a disgrace, though she had no idea of what it was all about, and that she ought never to mention her again. Only when she was overcome with a surge of longing for her, would she cry violently, seizing on some trivial matter as an excuse. There were times when she wanted someone to talk to about her mother, whoever it might be. She would try to bring it up in a round about way as she had with Kilsang just now, but there was no one who wanted to talk.

Altogether, she had matured. The sorrows of her life had endowed her with wisdom beyond that of other children.

'Kilsang.'

'Yes, Miss.'

She had called him for no apparent reason, and then pressed her cheek against his back and looked up at the clouds. From the peak of the mountain across the river they rose up and piled themselves higher and higher.

Chapter Fourteen

THE last remaining passengers on the ferry were two men, both in their thirties, on their way to Hwagae. They had come on board at the landing at Hadong in the early evening at the same time as Wolsun. They seemed to be farmers, with the comfortable look of those who owned a biggish piece of land. It was now completely dark and Wolsun, squatting on the floor of the boat, pulled her hempen outer skirt over her head to keep out the river breeze. It was a moonless night, but the light of countless stars made a faint glimmer all round. Although it was early summer, the river breeze, saturated with evening chill, sent a shiver under the skin. The sound of the oar and the waves slapping the side of the boat rang out lonely and desolate as if it were a departure for the other world. Stretched to the full by the rising tide, the surface of the river seemed to glisten on its own rather than by reflecting the starlight. The lights of the little village where they had put down passengers a short while before gradually dwindled. Only the sound of the oar and the slapping of the waves could be heard. One of the two men, who until now had sat in complete silence, seemed to have taken out a pipe and filled it with tobacco and then he lit it. Near the side of the boat a fish leapt with a splash.

'Coming to think about it . . .'.

He broke off and repeatedly sucked on his pipe. Like a live coal the tobacco glowed and dimmed, and each time his face, dark with beard, the brim of his hat blown back by the wind, showed reddish in the glow.

'Dr Mun's words turned out to be exactly right.'

As there was no reply, he went on, 'He may be stuck in a village backwater, but he is a great doctor.'

'A great doctor? What kind of a great doctor is it who can't save a dying man?' replied the other nonchalantly.

154

'Man, when even the Emperor Chinshi of China couldn't find the elixir of life, who can hope to live for ever? When I said he is a great doctor, I was thinking of how he knew beforehand that he was going to die.'

'Fortune-tellers and shamans would know that – what's so great about it?'

'But quacks are not like that, are they? After he had taken his pulse, Dr Mun said to Sangku, "I can't provide any medicine, so give the patient anything he asks for." That was all that he said.'

' . . .'

'But how could Sangku accept that? They were brothers and he must have thought, "How can a green youth die like that?" They say he stood up to the doctor saying, "How can you say that of a healthy young man?" Maybe it was just out of anger, but he gritted his teeth and said, "Just see if he dies!" He got hold of all kinds of medicines but what was the use of it when the disease was already in his bones? It was only a waste of money.'

'At this stage, what's the point of talking about the dead? I couldn't bear the sight of his widow weeping, and her big with child.'

Swallowing hard and drawing urgently on his pipe, the other said, 'That's right – a fatherless child. He's left his seed all right but it's a dreadful fate for the young widow.'

After that the two returning mourners were silent.

Another woman like Bongsoon ne, thought Wolsun as she buried her head deeper into her skirt.

'He must have been young, then?'

The old boatman who up to now had only moved the oar put in a word.

'Twenty-three, in the full bloom of youth.'

The man knocked out his pipe on the side of the boat and tucked it in into his waistband. The boatman said, 'Dr Mun – there's no doubt that he's a great doctor.'

'If only they had taken his advice, at least they would have saved their money . . .'.

The boatman went on, 'Once in my prime, I became ill and it gradually got worse until I was almost at the point of death. There

was not a well-known medicine that I hadn't tried. I even drank
water from a corpse, and what about all the exorcisms I had? All
quite useless. Whether it was my fate, I took ten doses of medicine
from Dr Mun and I was completely healed. That was it. It wasn't
expensive medicine either, and I didn't have to take it for long, just
ten doses – that's all. So what I'm saying is, above all, you must be
skilled at taking the pulse . . . no doubt he is a great doctor. That's
not all – he understands the poor, and if someone is sick he never
refuses to go, even in the middle of the night and no matter how
far. There is really no one like him. Those quacks, not worth a
dog's horn, with their fat stomachs, haggling over whether to go
or not, and trying to make a fortune out of a few doses of trash. If
Dr Mun had been like them, he'd be sitting on a pile of money as
high as a house, but he is such a good man and so wise. When he
is on the road, if he meets a child with a cold, he just takes a tablet
out of his pocket and pops it into its mouth – you will never find
another man like that.'

The man who had been smoking said, 'The trouble is that he is
too forthright. With sick people, however fatal it is, they won't
believe that they are going to die.'

Wolsun also remembered. It had happened when she was small.
Wherever it may have been, he had put into her mouth a reddish
tablet. It had been cool and refreshing. At the village landing place
she got off the ferry carrying her bundles. As he pushed the boat
off with his pole, the boatman said, 'Wolsun, watch your step. It's
dark.'

'All right, goodbye.'

The boat was gone and she stepped out of the wet sand by the
water's edge and on to dry loose sand that slipped out from under
her feet, making her ankles tired. It seemed as though the beach
stretched on for ever, and the sky as well – how could there be so
many stars? It brought thoughts of her mother offering the sacrifice
to the Dragon King here long ago. She could see the sacrificial
food set out in the flickering light of the candles. Her mother sent
up into the black sky the sacrificial paper burnt on the candle flame
and carried out the ritual with her arms moving as gracefully as

those of the Bodhisattva of Mercy. Her white skirt had fluttered in the breeze.

('How did you fare so badly and come back like this?' That is what Yongi said to me. Why do you think I did so badly and had to come back? Mother, my poor mother! 'Defy fate and make your life' you said, but my destiny was just like yours! As I told you, I have no mate, no lover, just like you, for if it wasn't you, who could your child take after? I've come back because I am dying to see him – just for once to see even the fence of his house – that's why I've come. Mum, you will call me crazy or possessed, won't you? I don't know. I was going crazy, obsessed with wanting to see him. I don't care any more.)

The water of the river glimmered indifferently, as did the stars in the sky, and only the dark mountain side calmly watched the wandering girl.

Long ago, when she was crying and refusing to be married, her mother, vigorous, witty and unemotional like a man, had beat her on the back, saying, 'You crazy thing! You possessed thing! If you want your own way, why couldn't you have been born in the right place instead of dropping on the doorstep of a shaman? You crazy thing! You possessed thing! Why do you have to drive nails into my heart like this?'

She too was crying.

'Go and live somewhere where they don't know what your mother is, and defy your fate. As they say, "Don't even look at a tree that you can't climb." What does it matter if he's old? Or if he's lame, as long as he takes care of you? And when you have children, enjoy yourself in your old age. Never think of looking for your mother. As for me, I'll go on and on – do an exorcism or two, and on and on again until I die and that will be the end of it. Won't the lady of the Choi *champan* house at least take care of me when I'm dead?'

'Why on earth should she see to your funeral?'

She had given a mysterious answer to her daughter's words: 'All that is due to a bondage from a previous life – what they call "karma".'

Strong waves from the high tide were beating on the sand.

(Mum, why does this beach go on so endlessly?)

She was wandering on the sand instead of going up the bank. She was waiting for the night to get deeper so that there would be nobody about on the road. Hugging her bundle with both arms, she rested her cheek on it.

All this time – about a month – Yongi had not once shown his face. At first she had thought he was busy with his work in the fields and then she had thought it was because Kangchong *dek*, sensing something, had stopped him. Whichever way you thought about it, he had been unkind. Especially at night, after clearing up the shop, when without changing her clothes she lay curled up like a shrimp, making a pillow with her arms, her ears straining for sounds from outside, she reproached him and could not sleep. On market day, shamelessly, she sought out people from the village to ask about him.

'Yongi? Ill? Why should he be ill? Just now, as I was coming, I saw him going out with his ox.'

(Heartless man . . . he was like that in the old days too.)

Since the night of the masked players he had been several times, fleetingly, in the middle of the night – moments painful in the meeting and more painful in the parting. On the next market day she again asked Yongpari if he was all right. 'As far as I know.' Sorry for her, he had quickly vanished from her sight. After wandering for some time on the beach she went up the embankment and on to the road to the village. From the huddled houses filtered faint gleams of light, and at some of them people were coming and going in the yard. As she came close to Yongi's gate, left open, a noise from the yard made her hide in a patch of millet that had grown waist-high. Through the leaves the yard could be seen, dimly lit. As if they had been working late and had only just cleared away the supper, a lamp hung from a pillar of the verandah and, although no one was visible, shadows flickered by the jar stand – maybe Kangchong *dek* was washing up.

(Whatever have I come here for? Am I possessed? I must be mad. There is nothing the matter with him, nothing at all . . . by stopping completely, does he mean to say 'I don't care'? Heartless man – but he was like that in the old days too.)

158

Tears surged up. The salty taste of them mixed with the smell of millet leaves grazing her nose.

'I am going to see *songnim* at Dooman's. You can go to bed first or not as you like.'

Kangchong *dek*'s voice sounded near and the next moment her smallish figure appeared at the gate. With folded arms she looked around for an instant and passed in front of the millet patch.

'That damned bitch – I'd like to crush that prattling mouth of hers,' she was muttering.

Then her figure was no longer seen through the leaves.

From the sky the stars were pouring down like a snow storm. In mid air each of them whirled on its own. But they were not really stars – they were reeling sparks that rose before her eyes, a wild dance of them that came from her beating heart and her giddiness. How much time had passed? She came out of the millet field intending to go to her old house, which stood apart from the village. As she passed the open gate, she stopped. Sitting on the verandah, lit by the lamp on the pillar, Yongi was smoking his pipe. He was looking down at the ground.

'Look.'

She was sure that it was uttered only inside her own throat but Yongi, startled, looked up. 'Who's that?'

'. . .'

'Who is it?'

'. . .'

He threw away his pipe and ran forward.

'Who? Who is it?'

Even after he had clearly seen who it was, he still asked.

'I'm going to see my house. I was just passing by . . .'.

Her voice was icy.

'House . . . to see your house?'

For a while he circled like an animal in a cage.

'Well, go and wait there then. I'll come – I'll come soon.'

'Don't.'

Turning away with her bundle, she again looked back and said, 'Don't.'

He was still turning to and fro in front of the gate. She could see nothing in front of her, not even the crowded stars in the sky, but she walked on, following the fence.

'Don't, don't, please don't. At daybreak I'm going to catch the ferry and go.'

As she shaped the words between her lips, she heard them coming back and ringing in her ears like cymbals. Having reached the lonely hut, she felt for the ring that held the door, released it, and stepped inside. A strong whiff of mould stung her nose. Rummaging in her bundle, she took out a candle and flint and lit the candle. The shadow of her head trembled on the mottled walls. Perhaps a pedlar had spent a night in the empty house, for in relation to the time it had been left, not much dust had collected on the floor. Holding up the lighted candle, she went to the altar where the spirit tablet was kept – it was just as it used to be. She blew the dust off the holder and put the candle into it. The paper flowers in porcelain jars each side of it were so bleached that the once-bright colours were not only indistinguishable but covered with whitish dust. Since the death of her mother not as much as a single spoon remained of her household goods, but as though even thieves feared the punishment of the spirits, around the altar nothing had been touched. The incense burner also was just as it had been, while at the upper end of the room was a battered chest. Naturally, any clothes inside it would have gone, but ceremonial garments might be left – an outer coat or a flower hat. She put lighted candles in the remaining holders and a smoking stick of incense into the burner. She flung open the door, and as the air rushed in the candle flames wavered, and the smoke of the incense. Taking out a dry rag which she had prepared, she went to the stream in front of the house, wetted it, and brought it back. After wiping the floor she went to the stream again, rinsed it out, and then washed her face. When she returned to the room, she took out of her bundle a white porcelain wine bottle, honey biscuits, fruit, grain and *dok* and arranged them before the spirit tablet. She poured and set out some wine, and then took the things out of the chest and put on the outer coat. She did up the belt and put on the headband, on top of which she placed the flower hat. She picked up the bells and the fan. She snapped the fan open and gave the bells a shake. As their clear sound rang out through the dark night, she felt the breath, eyes, and strong voice of Wolson *ne*, her mother.

'Mother!'

The sounds of the drum, flute and cymbals, the brilliant colours of the sacrificial food on the altar in piles a foot high, paper flowers, white, yellow, pink, and blue, the blossoms of peony and lotus . . . the eyes of her spirit-possessed mother drew close, gradually filling her whole vision. Her fast breathing could be heard. The vision of her mother shaking the bells and snapping open the fan —

> *Uhu — eheya —*
> *Here comes Birideghi, uhu —*
> *Birideghi's father,*
> *He was the warrior of the Chon-Byol Mountain,*
> *Birideghi's mother,*
> *She was Byong-un, the lady of the Keum-Tal,*
> *The Chon-Byol warrior hearing that*
> *If he married Byong-un of the Keum-Tal,*
> *He would beget nine sons —*

(Mother, you might as well let me be possessed by the spirits. Then I shall forget all my sorrows. The spirits will get hold of me, won't they? You used to say that the reason why we can have no close relationship with other people is because the spirits come between us, didn't you, mum? You used to say that, for my sake, you should disappear without trace, and that I must not become a shaman, but bear children and live a normal life. Where are they? Now I'm thirty and where are the children that I am to be happy with? Between heaven and earth, I am all alone. Let me be with the spirits. Otherwise, I shall die! Mother! Mother!)

Yongi, after seeing her off and walking up and down the yard, went up on to the verandah, picked up a wooden pillow that was left there and lay down.

(The night air is quite chilly, and how cold the floor is!) The faint light from the lamp rested on his closed eyelids. His deeply indented face with prominent nose, cheek bones and brow, looked like that of a dead man. From the shed came the sound of the ox chewing the cud. Far away, frogs croaked in the empty rice fields and from under the floor came the crying of crickets – the cry of the crickets, the cry of the crickets – it came again and again.

(The floor is cold – the floor is cold!)

He sprang up. He put on his shoes and went round the back to pick up a bundle of pine branches. He returned to the front, blew out the lamp and went out of the gate. A light showed from Dooman's. In the distance a dog was barking. When he had entered the yard of the shaman's house, he carefully shut the gate, went straight to the kitchen and touched the fireplace with his hand. It felt cold. He untied the bundle of wood, snapped them into pieces, pushed them into the fireplace and lit them. After smoking a little at first, perhaps because of a good draught, the fire went smoothly under the *ondol* floor.

'Poor thing!' He muttered as he watched the flame.

'She looks to me for support? What is there to hope for from me? What is there, hum.'

He broke more wood and pushed it in.

'Yongi, you rascal, if you pluck out one of those sparkling eyes of yours, if you do that you might marry our Wolsun . . . Don't follow her around. You've made the spirits angry and one of your eyes will fall out.'

Before him rose the face of Wolsun's mother as she sat flopped down in the yard looking at him with dreamy eyes.

'Then pull it out – I can manage with one, can't I?'

'It's all useless, quite useless.' She had stood up with a chuckle.

In no time the flames had gone, leaving only embers covered with white ash. He stood up and went round to the room. The colourful things inside could be seen through the torn paper on the door. He pulled at it. It would not open. He pulled harder. There was only a rattle from the metal ring – it was locked.

'Open the door.'

'. . . .'

'I said open the door!'

'I won't.'

'Don't be silly – open it.'

'. . . .'

'It was my fault.'

'It'll only cause a terrible row. At daybreak I'll slip away so quietly that even the mice and the birds won't know. You go home.'

'Can't you do what I say?'

'No, I can't.'

He broke a corner of the lattice, and pushing his hand through, released the ring on the door.

'Ah!'

With the flower hat on her head and wearing the ritual robe with its bell – it was in this guise she stood and glared at him. His face became all at once distorted, his temples throbbing.

'Why are you doing this?'

He snatched off her hat. The ribbon under her chin snapped.

'Why are you doing it?'

He trampled on the hat, pulled off the head band and threw it away and tore the robe in shreds. He was like an angry beast. He rushed to the place where the spirit tablet was set up.

'Don't – don't do that! You will be punished!'

She screamed, grabbing his waist.

'Why? Why couldn't we come together? It can't be that you don't know the reason?'

'I do know, I do.'

She trembled like an aspen.

'Then you know you shouldn't be doing this.'

'I know, I know.'

'I don't care if I'm blinded or struck dumb. I'll burn up the whole lot! Where are the spirits?'

He had turned white.

'Let's forget it. Let's stop. What can we do?' Lowering his voice, he suddenly snatched the trembling girl in his arms. 'Wolsun?'

'Yes.'

'Shall we run away?'

'If that's what we wanted, we'd have done it long ago. At this stage . . . if only I can see your face, that will be enough. If only you had let me see your face, I wouldn't have come here.'

After patting her on the back, he put out the candle. As if he wished her slender body to be broken and crushed so that it would finally disappear from the world, he embraced her with all his strength while she, suppressing her screams, muttered incoherently.

'Go, please go. It shouldn't be like this, I so wanted to see you. Just to see your face or even the fence . . . we mustn't do this.'

'What is there we mustn't do? There's nothing we can't do!'

He was violent. It was not an act of love, but of trampling on her and trampling on himself. Frightened by it, she struggled with all her strength to stand up but in the end she went limp like a weak animal ready to suffer pain. Ecstasy and pain, the climax was over, and darkness and silence enclosed them. Resting his head on her breast, he was still. In the dark there was no spirit tablet, no sacrificial food, no powerful chant of Wolsun's mother, nor the faces of his mother or his wife. No village, no wine shop at the fork in the road. There was only the cries of frogs along the rice fields and the sound of the cuckoo in the woods.

'Wolsun!'

'. . . .'

'Never go away.'

'. . . .'

'Why, do you want to be a shaman?'

'I couldn't.'

'That's right, don't.'

Slipping off, he put his arm under her head as a pillow and stroked her hair.

'I'm a shameless creature.'

'. . . .'

'After putting you in a wine shop . . . then, going to see you in the night I thought about my situation, kept on thinking about it. I was too ashamed – that's why I couldn't come, though I knew that you would be waiting with your eyes popping out, knew that you couldn't sleep in the night. Yongpari told me that you were asking after me. It was tearing my guts. I thought a thousand, ten thousand times of throwing up everything, giving it all up and running away somewhere where I could live just with you. But it can't be done. It wouldn't work. I can't leave these hills and rivers. Even if I go blind and my limbs are broken, I can't escape my duty as a son and my human responsibilities.'

'How the cuckoo cries!'

She spoke with her face buried in his chest. Stroking her hair again and again, he said, 'Probably there's going to be a drought.'

'On the way, on the ferry boat, the river wind was quite cold.'

'It would be at night.'

'I shouldn't have come?'

'Oh, no. I'm glad you came. I was just thinking of you. At first, I thought it was a dream. You were standing there like a ghost.'

'Early in the morning, at the first light, I will go. I can't stop to see Bongsoon *ne*. And if her ladyship hears about it, how badly she will think of me!'

'. . .'

'She will, won't she?'

'Let her. If that was all we had to worry about . . .'.

'Look, look here! You must go . . . please go.'

Suddenly she spoke sharply, but her hands were contrarily grabbing the hem of his jacket. His arms were trembling.

'Why?'

'Hurry up and go. I won't fret any more.'

Letting go of his jacket she tried to sit up.

'What are you going to do?'

'Light the lamp.'

'Don't do that. Let's stay a bit longer like this, and . . .'

In the darkness, he kept his eyes lightly closed.

'Go to sleep. When you fall asleep, I will go.' It was impossible to sleep but she pretended to, and he suppressed his breathing. It must have been long past midnight. He removed his arm from under her head and, sitting up, for a long time listened to her breathing and then slipped out. Trying to listen only to the cries of the cuckoo, she held her breath harder than ever and stared into the darkness.

Next morning, at dawn, with her bundle under her arm, she went down the road. She would walk to the next village and wait there for a ferry. The stars were as before. Countless, they twinkled. But the path was very dark and the dew-laden grass at the edge of it soaked her socks. The village was still asleep and quiet, but the cock crowed several times. At this sound, flustered, she quickened her steps. Then, just as she was going round the corner of a wall, 'Ouch!' The scream came first from whomever had bumped into her rather than from Wolsun. Although it was in the darkness of the dawn, they had collided so violently, faces almost touching, that they could recognize one another. Wolsun ran off without any greeting, and her opposite number, Yimi *ne*, also for some reason retreated in great embarrassment. She had been to the privy and then remembered a marrow that dangled temptingly from Magdal-*ne*'s wall. She had plucked it and had been on the way back, holding it under the fold of her skirt. After reaching her yard in one leap, she thought to herself, 'There is no way she can know what I have done, and she doesn't even live here, so what is there to be afraid of? Anyway, what did that woman come here for? Why should she be running away like that? It's queer? Mm, that's it. It's Yongi. So that's how it is!'

She put the marrow she had kept hidden in her skirt on the kitchen range and covered it with a basket.

'So it's Kangchong *dek* who's being deceived! Now I can see Wolsun is no ordinary bitch. With eyes like a dog's, I can't see what it is that fascinates him.'

She was so jealous that she could not bear it.

'So Yongi is now on the way down. Having a relationship with a witch — it's bound to bring bad luck. As for the bitch herself — to have crept right into the village where his wife lives with her eyes wide open — she must be ever so bold.'

From inside the room came the sound of a child crying. Softening her swollen breast with the palm of her hand, she went inside. After putting the child to suck, she said, 'Ha, so it's Kangchong *dek* who's being deceived!' Her eyes flashed.

Chapter Fifteen

IN THE evening as she tipped the corner of the matting to gather up the barley, Magdal *ne*, who had been at it all through the morning, started again, as if she still had not got over her anger.

'Whose wicked hand took away that precious marrow of mine? Did they think we hadn't eaten it because we hadn't got any teeth? I was treasuring it to make marrow mash when it was ripe. If things are going to be stolen as often as this . . . Magdal! Do you hear? What's the use of being stuck there in front of the fire? Can't you come quick and help me with this sack?'

Her daughter, who had been lighting a fire under a pot with barley in it, threw down the poker and, rising from her squatting position, came out like a child learning to walk. She must have been fourteen or fifteen but she looked almost like a dwarf.

'Mum, stop it now. Grumbling about it won't make a missing marrow come back.'

As she spoke she held open the mouth of the sack. Scooping the mound of barley into it, her mother said, 'Shut up. Do you want me to act like "a dumb man with stolen honey in his mouth" after losing something as precious as gold?'

'Even so – well, it's gone . . .'

'Come to think of it, it's all because they look down on me. They think that as I'm a widow without a man, no one will speak up for me. Damn it, what a rotten fate!'

'Is it only our things that have been stolen? It's a regular habit with that rascal.'

'Is it only once or twice?'

Just at this moment Kim Pyongsan, having left his house, was walking through the village. Seeing him, Magdal *ne* threw down her scoop on the mat and ran out of the gate.

'Whoever heard of such a thing? The village shouldn't become fouled like this. It won't do! Something must be done!'

She was screaming at the top of her voice.

'I know whose damned offspring has done it. Of course I do! Doesn't he steal eggs from the hen coop? And strip beans from the bean plot? As for the aubergines, they go as soon as they appear. And now even the marrow on the garden wall is taken away . . . If the village becomes as disreputable as this, how can anyone sleep in peace?'

Waving her arms in the air, she yelled and yelled. She was doing it, of course, for Pyongsan's benefit. The thief who had sneaked the eggs, and roasted and eaten the beans, was his elder son, Gobok. The stealing of the eggs and eating of the beans had been spotted there and then and severely dealt with but, in this case, the picking fingers had not actually been caught. Moreover, although behind his back Pyongsan was called a 'dog-leg gentleman' or a knave who lived on fees from gambling dens and was not regarded as a decent citizen, he was still a so-called gentleman, so she could not pour out her abuse to his face but had to shout it indirectly. He snorted,

'Huh, is a new governor arriving? What's all this noise about?'

In the same way that Magdal *ne* pointed at Gobok as the marrow thief, he also seemed to suspect that it was the work of his son, but, as if to say 'It's none of my business,' he looked at her squarely as she gabbled on, foaming at the mouth. Her eyes bulged. Slowly swinging the arm that held his fan, his reddish face even breaking into a smile, he went past her in an arrogant manner, with jaunty stride, at which Magdal *ne*, turning sharply, began to rave again at the back of his head.

'Whose damned offspring is it that befouls the village, and not just once or twice? When thieving becomes as common as this, how can we allow such a person to stay in the village? It's not just once, or twice – going on like this, we can't just leave it. Have you ever heard of anyone who does no work and doesn't steal? As the saying goes, "Only if the water is clear above will it be clear below." May the hands and wrists that took my marrow rot away overnight! How can they do anything else? Did we leave it there because we had no teeth ourselves? Did we plant it to stuff the guts of people like that?'

Regardless of all this, Pyongsan was already far away, his hand with the fan swinging, walking up the road with his jaunty stride. Magdal *ne*'s voice grew faint.

'Offshoot of a dirty lineage. As they say, "A needle thief becomes an ox thief," and "A tree can be judged from its seed leaf." In this way other people's children will be spoilt, too. A man of the gentry? What a fine sight! Rotten creature of a gentleman!'

As she pulled the top of her skirt right up under her arms and tied up the strings again, still mumbling, Pyongsan was walking up the rise to the Choi *champan* house.

'Hands of a rascal whose tongue should be pulled out! Bandit! A brute who would sell and eat up the whole country, and China as well.'

'What's the matter with you!' asked Yamu *ne*, on her way back from the field with a hoe.

'It's beyond words.'

'Why?'

'With nothing better to do after all his other tricks he's even taken the marrow off the garden wall, the dirty thief!'

'Who?'

'No need to say, it's plain enough. Who else but the damn son of that great gentleman of the name of Pyongsan, or Dog-san?'

'I know he is good at doing things like that, but what did he want a marrow for?'

'He was hungry, so he cooked and ate it, of course.'

'His mother being as she is, how could he take a thing like that into the house without getting a thrashing?'

'Why would he tell his mother before he ate it? Sitting at the loom, she forgets how the world goes by. How does she know whether it's porridge that's boiling outside or whether it's soup?'

'I suppose that's true . . . with such habits he is going to make her ill.'

'Only if the water is clear above, will it be clear below.'

'I've warned my boys not to be friendly with him but it really is annoying for the village to be befouled like this.'

169

'What's the use of talking? If he's like this already, I bet he'll chuck his own father out of the house by the time he's a bit bigger.'

'Though they say "People with children shouldn't call other's children adulterers or thieves" . . . it's such a pity that he has taken after his father. When you think of his mother, it would be hard to find any one like her in the whole world, she is so dignified and so correct in every way, so learned, and nimble with her fingers. As the saying goes, "If you've not been lucky with your husband, you won't be lucky with your sons either." It's true, and now she's got cause to be ill.'

'You're right there. For her sake, I've put up with a lot but we can't go on hushing it up endlessly. The elders of the village will have to get together and take some action – turn him out or something like that.'

'We can't go that far. He does it because he's still a child. If he goes on like that when he's old enough to know better, then of course we must turn him out or something . . . My goodness, I'm forgetting! I'm late for getting the meal, the sun's nearly set.'

She turned in a hurry to go. Magdal *ne* detained her.

'Listen to me.'

'What?'

'Have you heard about it?'

'You mean about Choi *champan*'s?'

'That's one thing – Kang *posoo* has gone after Kuchon, but that's old stuff. Haven't you heard about what happened at the shaman's house last night?'

'No?'

'They say Wolsun has been and gone.'

'What's wrong with that?'

'What's wrong indeed! She was seen sneaking away like an alley cat at first light.'

'Why should she do that?'

'Huh, really! Look at her, asking why! She came to see Yongi, of course, and after relieving her passion, without his wife knowing, frightened of being seen, she ran away early at dawn.'

'. . . I see. I guess Kangchong *dek* must have leapt a thousand feet in the air – ten thousand.'

'If she had, it would've made a good show, but I don't think she knows anything about it, like a deaf raven.'

'Then where did it start from? Has someone with nothing better to do been staying up all night to spy on other people's love affairs?'

'They say it was Yimi *ne* that saw her. At dawn, on her way back from the privy.'

'Even if she did, she could have kept it to herself. Why does she have to make such a noise about it? She is uncommonly wicked herself. I can't see why she's making such a fuss when it is not even her own husband. That's why she has squabbles with Kangchong *dek*.'

'How can she keep her mouth shut when her guts are itching? That's not all. They say that someone else saw a light inside the shaman's house, apparently on their way back from night fishing. Then, guess what that silly woman Yimi *ne* did? She went over to Kangchong *dek*'s and in a roundabout way she asked about it.'

'She is really is naughty.'

Though Yamu *ne* said this, she was so curious that she could not go away.

'She went there and asked if Yi *subang* had been to the town last night. With no idea of what was going on, Kangchong *dek* said brightly. "What would he go to town for now that he's made a clean break with that woman? He doesn't go there even on market days". You can understand that she spoke like this because she doesn't like Yimi *ne*. "Then, was he at home last night?" she cheekily went on. "Of course he was. When I came back late after finishing a small job at Dooman's he was fast asleep and snoring." Then she burst into anger, accusing her of prying into whether someone else's husband was in or out. So you see, during her absence, the pair of them throughly enjoyed themselves. As they say, "Not knowing what all your three neighbours know about your husband." Now it has reached the stage where the woman makes the advances. Wolsun is no ordinary wench.'

'What a fuss! How can you be so sure until you hear both sides? As for Kangchong *dek*, it's perfectly true, she's over jealous. At the age of thirty she has failed to produce a child and, wherever it comes from, they must have a son, mustn't they? Women's minds are all the same, I know, but she has no right to complain before she has produced a son to carry the sacrificial table.'

'If Kangchong *dek* hears of this, she will want to kill and eat you.'

'No use having a voice, if you don't speak up. What I'm saying is only the truth. Ugh, I'm, forgetting, I shouldn't be standing here like this. Supper won't be ready until midnight.'

This time she shook herself free of Magdal *ne*'s grip and scurried away.

'Damn her – to find the right place underneath your nose and put it in, that's all there is to a meal even in the middle of the night, so why such a rush? The way all these bitches with husbands show off! I must be the only one in the world with such a sad fate.'

While she was burbling on, Kim Pyongsan almost brushed her as he passed. As he did so, he lifted his arm and flicked open his fan, nearly poking the tip of her sunburnt and flaking nose.

'My goodness!'

He calmly walked on, fanning himself. She could not think quickly enough to hurl anything at his back, nor could she dare to abuse him directly. So once more she growled, 'My goodness!' and began to screech, bringing up again the story of the lost marrow. This time with added vigour, spitting out one after another all kinds of curses.

'Curse the rascal who has taken my marrow, may his offspring be beggars for ten-thousand generations. May his wrists shrivel with leprosy!'

The village urchins began to gather in a swarm. Men coming back from the fields, hearing her screaming, went past quietly smiling to themselves. Chilsung, who had not only enjoyed the side-dish of marrow at breakfast, but knew where it came from, took her side as he went by and said, 'Huh, what damned rascal's fingers could have done such a thing?'

'Doesn't it seem obvious to you? Who indeed, but the same one who always does these things? A scoundrel who could ravage the whole of the country and put it into his stomach, and China as well! The men of the village should get together to turn him out, or at least do something. We can't let the place be fouled like this.'

'I think we certainly ought to take some strong action sooner or later.'

Grinning, he twirled the stick of his A-frame as if to chase the kids away.

In no time dusk was falling all around and an evening mist could be seen spreading over the dark hills across the Sumjin River. From the wooden-board chimney of each house rose the smoke of supper cooking. The children dispersed. They were hungry and went home towards the smoke, each his own way.

Producer of many litters, Dooman's ancient bitch Boksil, sitting lonely outside the gate, saw Gobok's brother Hanbok running hurriedly by and barked at him.

Smothered in Magdal *ne*'s abuse, Pyongsan returned home and called loudly to ask if supper was ready. While his wife hurriedly ran into the kitchen, Gobok, furtively eyeing his father's expression, stepped backward and ran out of the house. The marrow was clearly not his doing, but because of his previous crimes he could not say a word to protest his innocence, though he had overheard what Magdal *ne* was shouting. If his father caught him, he would deny not only the marrow, but all his previous misdoings, but he was scared of the beating that would come first. After staring blankly at his retreating son, Pyongsan stepped up on to the verandah. (Hum, what's the difference between yours and mine? You should have the guts even to snatch things out of other people's hands – that's the way to survive!) Haman *dek*, knowing nothing, brought in his supper almost too politely, so that she got on his nerves. When he had eaten it, to alleviate the drowsiness induced by a full stomach, he lay on his side, resting his neck on a wooden pillow. In the next room, concerned about her husband's mood, she had left the loom and was sewing a patch on his socks while in a low voice she taught Hanbok to read. He sat with book open before him, a book worn, and faded to the colour of tobacco.

(Will this wench turn up . . . still, what else can she do?) Lying on his side breathing heavily, Pyongsan turned over, lay on his back and stared intently at the beams across the ceiling. (No one can know his fate. There's no law that says I have to go on like this till the end of my life. Have I no guts? Death to all those low-class bitches and buggers! If it was like the old days, if it was a proper world, would they dare? . . . did I want to fall into this kind of life? Fine, let's see! I can't throw away this bit of luck that has rolled my way. I'll make it a real bonanza!)

The night was dark, so dark that the stars, so brilliant the night before, were nowhere to be seen, not one, and a warm wind swept by. Perhaps the rains would begin tomorrow, for the cuckoo seemed to be pouring out its last strength. With a quick glance towards the small room from which a gleam of light leaked out, he crossed the yard and went out. As he turned the corner of the wall, the noise of weaving began, as if his wife had sensed that he was going.

'Toad-like idiot. Work and work until your bones wear out, and where does it lead but to a miserable death? Still, that's her fate.'

He was going up the back way to the pavilion, that is to say the way round the hill that avoided the Choi house. There was a rustling sound as his clothes brushed against the thick scrub. At the back of the pavilion, as if cleaving the darkness, he turned into the narrow path that led to the Fertility Shrine. (What a wonderful night! If someone was slapped on the cheek, or stabbed to death, nobody would know. Whenever it may be, his downfall must come sooner or later, and as for luck, it's so capricious that it rarely stays long in one place. Isn't it true that but for those tough womenfolk he'd have long since been ruined?)

He groped his way over the stone bridge that lay across the stream. When he reached the shrine he rested on the terrace and looked all round. Only darkness, with the sounds of the stream, and the trees and grasses shaken by the wind. (By nature, wealth is meant to come and go. When it rots in the storeroom, it naturally breeds evil. Now in the stores of that wretched house, it's been decaying for over a hundred years, and I'm going to take advantage of its evil to make a grand splash. In other words, Kim Pyongsan is not going to live for ever on the tips from gambling dens. Now then, why doesn't this wench turn up? Still, she has no choice. After so much effort, at last I've got hold of her tail. There's no way out. Fly or leap as she may, there's no way she can manage it on her own.) As his eyes got used to the dark, little by little, things became visible. The trunk of the big hardy orange in front of the

174

Shrine came dimly into view. Thinking that Guinyo might be hidden behind it, he went over and put out his hand. There was nobody, just empty space. As he sat down after returning to the terrace, there came the sound, not of rustling leaves, but of clothes brushing the bushes and feet on fallen leaves. (I knew it. You had to come.) With his buttocks pressed hard on the chill of the stone, he cocked his ear. She had pulled her outer skirt over her head so that only her eyes showed. In the darkness they seemed to give forth light. She said composedly, 'What did you call me out here for?'

'If you didn't know you wouldn't have come.'

He also spoke coolly.

'I've no idea what you are talking about. Didn't you say something or other about some rings? What do you want to say about them, then.'

'A pair of rings, not worth the blood in a bird's leg – there's no need to bring that up.'

'If there is no need to bring that up, I don't have any other business with you. I thought perhaps you were wondering about where they came from. I'll be off then.'

'If you want to, go. But you won't.'

'What do you mean?'

Her voice was shrill.

'You are only a servant, but arrogant and wicked, I know that much at least. But listen! "Above the one who leaps there is one who flies." '

'Don't make useless guesses. What is there to leap or fly about? That Kang *posoo* must have told you something, but if you are trying to make me out as a thief, it won't work. The *byoldang* mistress – it was late autumn last year when that incident happened – when she asked me to look after the young miss, she pulled a pair of rings off her finger and gave them to me.'

'I just said don't bring that up – there weren't any witnesses so who cares whether it was one way or the other?'

She was silent. In truth, they had not been given to her by the mistress. At the time of her departure, she had taken them off and

175

laid them on the top of the chest, and Guinyo had taken them secretly.

'Guinyo.'

'. . . .'

'At this stage, why don't you open up? To a house with wealth like theirs, what's a gold ring?'

'What do you mean by open up?'

She was looking for his motives. He said scoffingly, 'However well you keep a fox's thing it won't be any use, nor will it help to offer prayers at the Fertility Shrine. You won't give birth to a wooden block, let alone a son.'

'. . . .'

'I know all about it. I was curious over what you were up to. If you and I join hands, then it's just possible that your dream will come true. A dark scheme never succeeds without an accomplice. When hands and feet go in harmony, only then can you say that "It pleases your sister and her husband as well".'

'. . . .'

'I'm telling you, Choi Chisoo hasn't enough virility. Even if you had the skill to swing the sky on top of your head, there's no hope in that. You need another man, someone else. I don't mean to offer myself. Not only because I have my dignity to keep up, but because I can't be certain that I have it in me.'

Guinyo chuckled.

'Who knows whether or not he has the virility? You have to see the sky before you can pluck a star.'

'What do you mean?'

'I don't think it's that he lacks virility. By nature he doesn't care for women.'

Saying this, she let out another chuckle, as if to say that she would love to see his dumbfounded face if it had been light, but he was neither embarrassed nor surprised.

'I might have guessed. The more's the pity – the helpless way you behave.'

He stood up, and walked close to her, 'Guinyo.'

She seemed to be at a loss. Inwardly he also felt the same. They felt as though a pile of pure gold was collapsing quietly, and being

176

scattered, felt like an old man awaking from an exquisite dream and staring at the bone-like beams across the ceiling with a sense of emptiness. But it was not an absolute despair. Just stretch out your hand, it seemed, and struggle a little more, and something might be grasped. With a helpless sense that the dream might topple, they realized that because of this common psychological need, they had joined their hands more firmly than by words. The prospect that by joining hands they could work for their common interest was the only relief in that moment of helplessness. There will be a way. Only if you and I can agree . . . do you understand? Wait a little and see. Certainly there will be a way . . . "Please your sister and please her husband as well" – Do you understand? I will arrange it and, by whatever means, you just get pregnant. Once a servant girl like you sets out with a great ambition, you must see it through to the end – of course you must!'

A few days passed. It was before breakfast. Yongi, with his A-frame, set off to cut some long grass. As he walked past the road through the village, he saw in the distance something odd coming towards him. In the whitish morning mist, it turned out to be a child with a winnowing basket over his head. It looked as if the basket was walking up to him. Beside it came Dooman yawning, as if not fully awake. The child underneath the basket was Yongman, who must have wet his bed during the night, as this was the traditional punishment. 'You're going to beg for salt, Yongman?' said Yongi as he hid his amusement, while Dooman smiled in the middle of yawning. Yongman glared at him, rolling his tearful eyes. After passing him, the children went through the gate of Yamu-ne's. Soon after her voice was heard, 'Did you ever give me any salt?' and the sound of a cheek being slapped, then the sound of Yongman bursting into tears. Yongi had been smiling, but the smile disappeared from his face as he thought of his own childlessness.

In the pepper plot of Kim *jinsa*'s house, where now only two widows lived, the weeds were taller than the plants. Yongi walked slantwise up the embankment above the plot, put down his A-frame and began to cut the grass. The sap stained his fingertips. On the river, rafts of logs floated by. In the middle of cutting the grass he stopped and, sickle in hand, looked blankly at the water. (Is it market day today?) He was about to resume work when he saw in the distance two men walking side by side, coming from the hill on the back path. It was Pyongsan with Chilsung. Chilsung seemed to recognize Yongi but for some reason quickly turned his face away and went out on to the road by the embankment following his companion. It seemed a bit early to be going to the market? He wanted to ask Chilsung whether he was, but because the sight of Pyongsan was an eyesore, and the way Chilsung had turned his face away was strange, he just bent down, grabbed a handful of grass and brought his sickle to it.

Chapter Sixteen

ON welcoming Junku at the garden house, Chisoo had mentioned the affair of the lady in the *byoldang*, but since then he had never again referred to the shameful incident. With his arrogant nature, it was unlikely that he would forget it, or hush it up and bury it in the dark, but Junku could detect no sign of action from his side. It had been in the year following Junku's first visit to this place, six years before, to raise a not inconsiderable sum of money – Lady Yoon had calmly granted his request – that Choi Chisoo had turned up in Seoul, without warning, accompanied by Kim *subang*. In those days, Junku had had no understanding of Chisoo's character – his long neck and his delicate health were all that he knew of him. He had taken him for no more than a countrified young gentleman brought up by a mother widowed young, with no notion of hardship, who had done just what he pleased; someone foolish and ignorant of the world. Though it was true that he had only to hide the sharpness of his glance to look rather foolish, it had been a gross mistake on Junku's side to regard him as such. With the intention of opening up a road to success in the world with Chisoo's wealth, by duly manipulating him, Junkoo had been in too much of a hurry, with the result that he had all too easily given himself away.

'Think about it. Though lately, for three generations, your fore-bears have died young without attaining any position, the grand-father of your grandfather reached the rank of *champan*. Do you want to remain as idle as this? Unlike the old days, it is not at all difficult to get a post. Saying it is difficult, that's just the excuse of poor scholars. For some time I have been in close contact with foreign envoys so I can always pull strings. What about it?' From the start, Junku tempted him with mean and shameless words and conduct. According to his arrangements, Chisoo, with a bland smile, mixed with the sons of powerful families – in fact distant

179

cousins of theirs – and swept through the *kiseng* houses spending money like water. Even so, he did not really want any official rank – he just quietly observed the way Junku carried on. Cowardly and base, he put on vain airs with a boastful and assertive manner, at one moment gabbling away as if he was an expert on foreign things, only to reveal his hopeless ignorance the next. In this way he had finally reached a stage when, as if to say that the always smiling Chisoo smelt milky, he tucked him away in a corner, and began bargaining over his own interests. He was quite unaware of the mockery hidden away in Chisoo's eyes. One day when Junku came to his lodgings Chisoo said calmly, 'So far, thanks to you, I have been able to see all kinds of good places. Now I will show you some interesting ones.' All this time Chisoo had never once been to Junku's house, as he had declined to stay there, perhaps because of what he had been told about it by Kim *subang*, who often came up to Seoul. Junku had asked him once, but after he declined he had never repeated the invitation, so it was Junku who always came to where he was staying.

'A good idea. You must have gained some confidence by now.'

He had laughed boisterously in a way that did not suit his physique, but Chisoo said nothing. The dim alleyway into which Junku was led was a shocking place – a shabby and sordid brothel frequented by outcasts, a place in which women merely sold their bodies, with no music, dance or elegance.

'Man, what do you think you are doing?'

'Why?'

Chisoo had responded to the sharp rebuke with a smile.

'Is this a place for scholars to set foot in?'

'If you are going to discuss the affairs of the country, you have to know it from the top right down to the bottom.'

'You should discriminate. Quickly, let's get out of here.'

As if the edges of his coat might be contaminated, Junku pulled at his arm.

'If you only seek respectability, how will you gain enlightenment? Was there any respectability in the houses of the high-class *kiseng*s'?'

'No, but there was a kind of elegance, wasn't there?'

Chisoo shook his arm free and grabbed Junku's. Dragging him

into the shabby house that seemed to be tilting over, he said, 'Those
gentlemen of Seoul from whose decaying guts blood and pus ooze
out! They should be humbly thankful even for a place like this. To
their rotting nostrils the smell of the prostitutes should be sweeter
than perfume.'

At this, Junku, at last realizing Chisoo's true character, shuddered.
Momentarily he felt like pulling out his own eyes with regret for
having taken him for a widow's only son, ignorant of the world.
He now realized that all his schemes had evaporated. Junku had no
choice but to pass the night in a prostitute's room. He was not by
nature given to lechery and treated his body as if it were holy.
Because of an obsession with cleanliness, he stayed awake all through
the night in trepidation lest he touched the woman with the edge
of his garments, let alone put a hand on her. But Chisoo, it appeared,
was not like that. On the next occasion, he dragged Junku as far as
the port at Inchon and humiliated him in a low-class whorehouse
known to cater for Chinamen. His behaviour in troubling Junku
in this way was both tenacious and cruel.

Though in associating with such women he had no restraint, he
did not seem to gain any pleasure from it. His behaviour was more
like a struggle against something, violent and destructive – probably
he was filled with an abhorrence of women. It also seemed as
though his psychology was such that he needed to trample on them,
and it exploded in the form of this ugly dissipation, the tormenting
of Junku being incidental.

Chisoo had never loved the beautiful lady of the *byoldang* and he
had been a cold son to his mother. After about six months in Seoul,
his health was ruined. When he came back to the village, like a
skeleton, it had been Dr Mun who at least saved his life. He had
told Lady Yoon that there would be no offspring. Apart from her,
this was known vaguely only by Kim *subang*, the simple and faithful
servant, and Choi Chisoo himself, while Junku had guessed from
the resentful manner of Kim *subang* when he occasionally came to
Seoul.

After he had been at the Choi house for a fortnight, Junku went
to Pusan. When he came back he had had his hair cut and was
wearing a white summer hat. He stayed on another fortnight and

showed no sign of going back to Seoul. When Chisoo was not in too bad a mood Junku played Go with him or went to the archery field to shoot or cautiously talked about current affairs. Junku was not unaware that in his efforts to suit Chisoo's mood the views he expressed were not always consistent and he also knew that his comments on current affairs were no more than objects of his cousin's scorn. However, under Chisoo's pressure he felt unbearably constrained unless he gabbled away on whatever the subject might be. He had not the strength to stand up to Chisoo's silence, and was in his heart, extremely scared of him. The combination of his weakness, through revealing his own inner schemes, and Chisoo's tenacious character, overwhelmed him. So when Chisoo's forehead began to show blue veins he would escape and hurry down to the village. Once out of his cousin's sight, he became a dignified and benign nobleman from Seoul. He made great efforts to be friendly with the farmers in the village. On his way to and fro, when he happened on peasants who had come up on to the banks of the paddies to rest, he spoke first, kindly answered their questions, and did not decline even the farmer's wine when it was offered, sacrificing his obsession with cleanliness. The village people, who at first had been cautious of him with his western-style clothes – since changed to hemp as fine as the wings of dragon flies made by Bongsoon *ne* – began to feel friendly towards him for his pleasant and kindly way of speaking. When had any gentleman been so amiable to commoners? Especially as he was impressed on their minds as a personage of high rank from Seoul, and they did not want any change in the social order.

They were basically very respectful towards higher authority. They did not greatly respect Kim Pyongsan because he was from a lower rank of the gentry, but the reason they hated him and held him in contempt was that, as a gentleman, he went round with outcasts, setting up gambling dens and disgracing the dignity of the gentry. It was the same with Kim *hunjang*. Though they had close, affectionate feelings for him, they could not revere him – a man who had lost the prestige of a gentleman for, like an ordinary farmer, he did the work himself without a single servant. The reason they regarded Choi Chisoo of the *champan*'s house as something of a god was not because he was a kind landlord – it was rather his air of upper-class superiority, so arrogant and totally unapproachable. But with Junku it was quite different. Though he accepted and drank their wine, there was an air of luxury and elegance about his manners and his dress. He was so knowledgeable and told them fascinating stories of Seoul, talked about national affairs or foreign lands, and of his dealings with people of such importance that it was difficult even to imagine them – all this was enough to arouse the admiration of the peasants, and when such a man showed his magnanimity by drinking their wine, without making excuses, they could not but be moved.

'You can't even imagine this happening with the Master of the House.'

Moreover, when he supported the farmers and criticized the gentry, they would wonder, despite vague doubts, whether perhaps the more enlightened gentry were on their side.

'So, is this the way the world goes? If you are good at reading and writing, and clever, you can get a government job even if you are a commoner?'

'The riper it is, the lower the corn bows its head – that is a well known truth. He must have been brought up on good food and good clothes in a family of high rank yet, without showing the slightest sign of it, he knows how to treat children or old people. It may all seem an ordinary thing, but it is not easy to do. Do you reckon just any one can do it?'

An old peasant, moved by the way he was treated politely for his age, praised Junku, and in praising him it was natural for them to fall into finding fault with Chisoo.

'He has the family background, and the wealth. If, with all that, he still can't win office, he must be a real failure.'

'What's the use of a good family? Wealth is no use either. The person himself must be outstanding to bring honour to the family and its wealth. You can take all the things up to Seoul, pack after pack, but what's the use of them when the person is so poor? There's nothing to be done.'

'The gentleman from Seoul – he looks as though he might do

183

something great, whatever it may be – a man of that calibre. His short height is a fault but how fine he looks! He is very well built.'

Meanwhile, in the Choi household, unlike the village, Junku's position was not at all favourable. Lady Yoon and Chisoo had good reason to neglect him, and the servants also, not only because they sensed that their employers did not welcome him, but on their own account, saw him as disgreeable. Bongsoon *ne* let out a cautious complaint: 'I shouldn't say things like this and I know he's a relative, but to come without a single change of clothing – mind you he first came in that western suit, or narrow trousers, or whatever, that no one else wears – and to make such a fuss about it, even more than the master himself, changing them when they're the least bit dirty – it's not as if hemp clothes are easy to handle.'

'I know,' added Samwol. 'For some reason, I hated him from the start, even though I had nothing to do with him – his face is as smooth as a porridge bowl licked clean by a dog.'

'Stop it. You mustn't talk like that.'

'Guinyo thinks he's good-looking, with his straight forehead and white skin, but to my mind a man should have bolder features . . . why are his hands so much like a woman's? And what short legs he has!'

'That must be hereditary. The late mistress had short legs too.'

'As for our master, apart from his fearful temper, he is tall and sraight, and when he's in his *dopo* and Tong-yong hat . . . for a man, a good physique counts more than his face . . .'

'Oh, yes, as for being smart when you're dressed up . . . Whatever he puts on, he shines in it. That's true of her ladyship as well . . .'

'What on earth has he come here for that keeps him so long? I wonder what he does in Seoul.'

'Well, . . . Kim *subang* says his family situation is chaotic.'

In the servants' quarters the men also gossiped. 'I reckon he has reasons why he can't go back to Seoul. He's come here in exile.'

'That's very likely . . . like a tender pear, he seems pleasant enough . . .'.

'That's true.'

'But there's something not quite right about him . . .'.

'It's because we don't know him well enough.'

184

'However good a man is, he can't please everyone. The thing is that when he goes down to the village, children like him, grown ups like him, and he even drinks with them, and I hear that he says things such as that when we are all enlightened there will be no more "commoners" and "gentry", as though he was stroking their backs. He must be uncommonly shrewd and able.'

In the middle of all this only Samsoo rebuked them, saying 'Huh, he treats them like human beings, and it's too much for them – that's all.'

On one occasion Bogi said, quite casually, 'Is he our master? Why are we making so much of him?'

At this, Samsoo leaped in with 'Idiot! you'll never be anything but a slave!'

'What did you say?'

'Why? Don't you like to hear it? Why not? I thought you'd like it.'

Bogi was breathing heavily as Samsoo went on, 'Why is he blamed for not being bad tempered? Why is it a fault if he treats serfs and commoners like human beings, um? If it was the gentry who were blaming him, that would be a different matter, but from you, a servant like you . . .'.

Dori interceded, 'Look, what is there to fight about? Samsoo, you too, there's nothing to get heated about, so leave it alone.'

'Yes, I am getting heated. It's only when they treat you like dogs or pigs that you look up to them and timidly crawl before them. People like you who look down on him because he deals equally with everyone, high or low, are not fit to be anything but slaves all your life! A bunch of wretches that deserve to be servants for a thousand, for ten thousand years, for ten thousand generations!'

'Did you say "wretches"?'

Soodong, who was his senior by more than ten years glared at him.

'I didn't mean you, Park *subang*,' he said and abruptly departed.

Chisoo had left on the previous evening to call on Jang-am *sonseng*, who was ill. He had not come back that night, and was still not back by mid-morning. The sky lowered and it looked as though it was going to rain. Junku, sitting bored in the hall, glanced up at the ash-coloured sky that seemed about to descend on them.

He did not want to prolong his stay. During their first conversation, when Chisoo had said 'probably she thinks you are here to ask another difficult favour like the last time,' he had replied, partly because they were in the presence of Yi Dong-jin, 'I haven't come for anything like that – even if I fell as low as to be "Out on the street, exposed to wind and dew," would I be so shameless as to ask for her help again?'

But in truth he had come to escape from tormenting creditors.

(Where can I go? And in weather like this, too.)

Instead of feeling a sense of freedom in the absence of Chisoo, he was unable to bear the loneliness.

(That's it! I might as well go and visit that old fool.)

The thought of Kim *hunjang* had momentarily flashed across his mind. They had once exchanged greetings and though the teacher had shown slight disapproval of his haircut, he had expressed sufficient respect for his social status. He went down to the village and asked a passing child the way to Kim *hunjang*'s house. At the gate he loudly called to the servants, 'Come and open the gate!'

There was no sound. After clearing his throat, he again shouted, 'Open the gate! Is nobody there?'

At this the straight figure of the teacher himself appeared at the entrance and seeing Cho Junku, a blush rose on his dry-leaf-like face.

'To what do I owe this honour?'

'I was so bored, I've come along for a chat, if I may.' After a moment's confusion, the teacher said, 'This is such a squalid place, but do come in.'

Showing him into what was only in name a guest room, he was extremely embarrassed.

'Being in the state of "self and servant in one", things are not very respectable, I'm afraid.'

He was considerably moved, and at the same time ashamed. The twelve-foot-square room, used as schoolroom-cum-guest-room, with a lobby attached to it, smelt musty, but was neat and clean, and as he sat and faced his guest, his posture was straight and correct. Though he was sure he had just heard Junku say he was bored and had come for a chat, it was such an unexpected visit that his face tensed at the thought that he might have some other matter on his mind. He first offered him tobacco, though it was only a formality.

'I must not smoke.'

It was true that he did not smoke, but it was as a younger person that he politely declined. At this moment there came the sound of heavy raindrops drumming on the lids of the sauce jars. The room grew dark. Kim *hunjang* opened the door. Black clouds ran fast across the sky.

'It's welcome rain' said Junku even more modestly.

'Yes, at just the right time.'

'If only the seasons are favourable, life in a country village must be very pleasant.'

'Maybe.'

He broke off to open the back door of the room and called to his daughter inside, 'Bring in the table, will you? I think there is some plum wine left.'

'I am awfully sorry. I just came along out of boredom, but I am putting you out.'

'Don't say such things. I am most grateful to you for coming along to a shabby place like this.'

'After spending some time here, I think I can appreciate the mind of scholars who live buried in the country. The mountains and rivers are so lovely and the people so hospitable.'

'Yes, it's all right as long as you have no ambitions . . . but how can there be no regrets? We are all unworthy of our ancestors.'

'With the world in such turmoil what chance is there for true scholars to make their name?'

These words seemed to give him some comfort.

He said, 'Without talent or much learning, I never expected to attain high office, but another member of my family who was highly promising died young and never had the chance to fulfil his hopes. He passed away, leaving his household in a sorry state. Kim *jinsa* of the upper village was a second cousin of mine.'

During a brief pause, a look of pride flitted over his face.

'Distinguished in scholarship, bearing and judgement, he passed

187

the examination for government office at the age of twenty . . . he was expected to bring glory to the family, but it all came to nothing.'

Tears came to his eyes.

'If he were still alive, he would now be forty-three – he was five years younger than me – and his posthumous son whom we thought might fulfil his father's hopes went even before he was twenty. Two young widows are left – it's dreadful.'

While he talked in this way he never said a word about himself.

'Oh, really! What a very sad story!'

At that moment the wine table was brought in, and Kim *hunjang*, as if feeling that probably he had said more than he should to someone on his first visit, smiled awkwardly. He filled a cup and offered it to Junku.

'This is plum wine. I don't suppose the brew of an out-of-the way village will suit your taste.'

They chatted about this and that and as they grew slightly intoxicated, they became more open about various things. Kim *hunjang* went as far as to imply his disapproval of Junku for cutting off his topknot, while the latter, bringing out his own speciality, current affairs, began to talk less cautiously than he might have done with Chisoo, partly due to the wine and partly because from the beginning he inwardly regarded the teacher as a country bumpkin.

'At present, the state of this country is just like that of a tasty lump of meat. Whether you call it the nation or the royal court, they are fighting over it like devils, robbing and being robbed, chasing and being chased. In this situation, how easy it is for the foreigners to spread their wings. Mining concessions, rights for the construction of railways, even the felling of trees in the forests – all these things are put into the hands of foreigners, just to fill their stomachs. Who is to blame for it all, do you think? I am telling you, it's the fault of the conservative faction. The keep-to-the-old-ways party have ruined the country. Had they kept the doors open from earlier times, and had their eyes been open to learn these new advances, we should never have come to this. I have thought about it, and read some books about other countries and looked into their circumstances, and I have come to the conclusion that nothing will come from the way things are going. They should have long since built up military forces. Now, far too late, they are talking about such things as fortifications and rifles and inviting army instructors and so on. What can you expect of them?'

He paused for a moment. As if some idea had just occurred to him, a serious look came over his face and then he broke into a broad smile.

'That's it, that's right – talking of guns and foreign army-instructors and so on – isn't it a case of "sending for medicine after the patient is dead?" The country is now about to be eaten up once and for all so what is the use of getting agitated about it?'

Kim *hunjang*'s face looked blank. He felt the need to express an opinion, but he completely lacked the kind of knowledge needed to talk about national affairs. All he knew were the thoughts of a hundred years ago. On present day matters, especially things from the heart of Seoul, so convincingly conveyed by Junku, he could neither blindly accept them nor refute them.

The rain was streaming down steadily. Junkoo stared out at it. His face showed that he had now lost his earlier interest in current affairs. He seemed more concerned about the rain – if only it would stop! In a deflated tone he went on, 'Anyway, in the future, unless people go abroad and widen their knowledge or at least are alert to world affairs and fully understand what things are like in advanced countries, it will be difficult for them to conduct themselves properly. You can't just say that it's servile imitation or a sign of decadence. That is how the Japanese got in first. Look how that worthless island broke the power of China and now challenges Russia! It is all because they were quick to open their doors, promptly absorbed Western ways, and put their efforts into raising an army equipped with the latest weapons. In other words, they had foresight. Now they have proved their superiority by power. We may try to write them off as pirates and so on, but that's nothing but empty pride. Uprisings such as the "Army of Justice" are no more than the cries of bundles of straw. We must be smart too, to snap up from them what we need and make concessions in order to gain. Vain pride, what's the use of that? Just wait and see – Japan will overpower Russia. Russia is a great hulk, empty inside. Like

China, it is big and old fashioned while Japan is a newly rising nation . . .'.

While continuing to pour out words with which his tongue was familiar, his mind was on the streaks of rain. It was when phrases like 'uprisings such as the Army of Justice' and 'cries of bundles of straw,' issued from his mouth, that Kim *hunjang*, with a strangely perplexed expression, began to show definite disagreement.

At last the rain stopped. Junku stood up.

'Well, I have been talking too much.'

'I am sorry to have given you such a poor reception.'

'How can you say that? I have caused you so much inconvenience.'

Kim *hunjang* went as far as the outside of the gate to see him off.

'How can a man from a distinguished family go so far . . .' he thought, while once again exchanging farewells outside the gate and Junku mumbled to himself, 'A gun . . . a foreign army instructor . . . that's it! It's worth putting into Chisoo's head', and taking hurried steps with his short legs, he went down the village road. Even though he walked fast, the cautious Junku reached the house without a spot of mud on his white socks, though it might be said that the earth had been so dry that it had sucked up all the rain. On the stone outside the *sarang* stood Chisoo's shoes, side by side. It was most unlikely that he would have returned in the rain, so it must have been just after Junku had gone out. He stood for a moment. From the waving leaves of the plantain drops of water rolled and fell. A cool and pleasant breeze brushed his face. After taking a deep breath and calling 'So you are back,' he opened the door. Chisoo sat there with a blank expression.

'Was he seriously ill?'

'. . .'

Junku sat down in front of him.

'I was rather bored so I went to see that Kim *hunjang* or whatever his name is.'

'. . .'

'While you were away I was thinking like this . . .'.

'. . .'

'Whatever happens, it seems to me that you must take more care

190

of yourself. Medicine is all very well, but don't you think it would be better if you had some exercise? So I thought, what about hunting?'

'Hunting?'

'Yes, have you ever tried it?'

'I did, a long time ago.'

'In those days, it must have been a tiresome business. Now without bothering with beaters, there's a simple way of doing it, with a rifle.'

'A rifle?'

'I don't mean the sort of matchlock guns that trappers use. Get hold of a good rifle. The pleasure of hunting is quite extraordinary. In Seoul I have been out with foreigners. From here Mt Chiri is quite close, and that's the perfect place.'

'A good rifle, you say?'

His eyes showed his keen interest.

'It will be expensive, but with the help of foreigners, you can get hold of one.'

Chapter Seventeen

IT had been sixteen or seventeen years ago, long before the birth of her daughter, Bongsoon. It was night and snow was falling lightly. Her husband, already on the run because of his involvement in the popular uprising, was from the early days often away from home and when he finally disappeared without trace, taking another woman with him, Bongsoon *ne* had settled as seamstress at the Choi house, waiting for a man who had made no pledge to return. On that night, as Bongsoon *ne* sewed Gannan *halmum*, weaving, told her of the death of Chisoo's father who had departed this world at the age of twenty-one, in the late autumn, when they had all been busy storing chestnuts underground in the backyard.

'Even now the thought of what happened that night makes me shiver.'

Joining a broken thread, she shuddered.

'My husband was away at Curae with Soodong's father, Park *subang*, who was then responsible for the running of the household. Perhaps it was fate . . . it was unusually windy and cold. Just as in February, when the witch of the wind comes down, there was a kind of creeping cold. Perhaps it wouldn't have happened if Park *subang* had been here? From the early evening the baby, our present master that is – he'd just had his first birthday – had been so fretful that her ladyship and myself were in a sweat, taking turns to soothe him to sleep. From birth, he's never been strong, always ailing. Coming after the loss of their first son, in a family where children were rare, he was so precious that at the first sign of a temperature the whole household was disturbed. When we saw him fall asleep, after a long struggle, I went to the other room and probably slept a bit. I suddenly opened my eyes at a great noise of dogs from the direction of the bamboo grove. A wave of cold swept over my whole body. There was the baying of the dogs and then yelps of agony as if their guts were being torn out, enough noise to carry away the whole grove. They were dogs, but of no ordinary kind. They were enormous, and as strong as tigers. When those two made such a din, I knew it couldn't be any ordinary matter. I thought the mistress must be frightened – I must go across and see her at once! That's what I intended, but I couldn't move. My teeth were rattling, and I felt as if something was going to burst through the door and come for me. Desperately screwing up my courage, I just managed to get to her room where she sat sewing by the sleeping baby. I had gone in case she was frightened, but on seeing her so calm, I lost my own fear. Since then I have always regarded her as someone special. She is quite fearless and never lets any feelings of like or dislike show on her face. "What could those beastly dogs be making such a row about, ma'am?" I asked. She did not reply at once. After a while she said, as if to herself, "It sounds as if we are going to lose two good dogs!"

'They call them dogs,' I said, 'but they are so enormous, and when two of them like that make such a row it must be the mountain spirit himself who has come down.'

'To this she said, "It may be. It must be some big mountain beast. Probably our prayer lacked devotion."

'In fact, such thoughts had crossed my own mind because it was the very day on which she and her mother-in-law had returned from the temple, after prayers and offerings for the long life of the baby. Somehow I felt alarmed and had a premonition of disaster. Even so, I couldn't say anything like that, could I? So I said, 'It couldn't be that, madam. Four-footed beasts can wander anywhere, can't they?' but I was scared, as if the cries of the dogs falling on their backs as they died were tugging at the roots of my hair. I sat up all night, you see. I heard later that in the inner quarters the old lady stayed up all night offering prayers.'

'Was it really the mountain spirit coming down?' asked Bong-soon *ne*.

'Well, it wouldn't have been too bad if it had just carried off the dogs.'

'You mean someone was killed?'

Bongsoon *ne* stopped work and looked up at her.

'Not exactly that either. When the morning came, I dashed out, and what did I see? Right in front of the inner gate of the *byoldang* the two dogs lay stretched out asleep – the ones I had been sure were dead. Without thinking I shouted, "Ma'am, the dogs are lying here asleep!" and kicked them lightly. Lifting their heads they looked at me with such terrible eyes. I've never seen anything like it in the whole of my life. They were blood-red as if their eyeballs had burst, as if they had been tearing and devouring a corpse all through the night . . . Then things began to go wrong – though it was all right up to mid-day. In those days Soodong's father, Park *subang*, used to live at the back as we do now. Around midday there was some hubbub at the back of the house. Who could guess what it was? We were as ignorant as the ravens. Those stupid servants had found a dead deer in the bamboo grove. Apparently the rascals, blinded by this – and quite unaware of the pious acts, the Buddhist dedication, that had just been made – carried it into the house at the back, a deer bigger than a half-grown ox left by the dogs who had been burrowing into its guts. Park *subang* was away and his wife with the baby on her back was somewhere in the inner quarters, and they knew that the master too had been away at Jinjoo for some days. It was an unusually good opportunity as there was no one to be afraid of. In fact, the master was already back in the *sarang*, though they didn't know. Being crazy about the venison, they could not know – or was it fate that things were to go wrong? Anyway, he must have gone out to see what all the noise was about in the back quarters – he was so manly for his age. He was quite different from the present master, he had a look of magnanimity, with a fine body; he was well educated, but enjoyed hunting as well, and before he was twenty he had already resorted to a *kiseng*'s at Jinjoo, so he must have been very mature. Perhaps because of this, he was well acquainted with worldly affairs and skilful in handling servants, never scolding them but now and again making them realize their faults in a joking way. The village elders always said that, as he was not fussy, things would go well for him and that, being a great man like his great-grandfather, the *champan*, he would reach high office. The old lady also prayed day and night that she might live to see the day when her grandson entered the government and returned home in glory – only she was a little fearful about his chivalrous character. You can imagine what it was like when such a master went out to the back of the house. The damned ruffians who had been stuffing themselves with the venison, overcome, couldn't go on putting it in their mouths, could they? Then, it seems, the master smiled and asked who had caught the deer? Soidori, one of the older ones, the grandad of Samsoo, who must have been over thirty then, as he was a year or two older than my husband, Kim *subang* – probably he was less awed by the master than the rest, as he had carried him on his back when he was young – he answered, "It was done by the dogs, sir."

"Great big men like you eating something killed by animals? You are a shameless lot!"

'It made them relax. So then, they were rash. What did Soidori do but offer him a piece of the meat? When the master had been young, he used to pick chestnuts for him and things like that, so of course he did it without thinking. As for the master, what would he want it for? He ate it just so as not to embarrass Soidori.'

'My God! He should never have done such thing after making an offering to Buddha!'

'That's right. It was them, the ruffians, that deserved death, though the Buddha would have regarded them as dogs anyway – but it was careless of the master, too. Still, there was no way for the menfolk to know what the ladies had been doing, and what do men care about religion anyway? They treat monks like . . . In short the retribution fell on him. On that very night the trouble started and the whole household seethed like boiling water. Straight away he lost his speech and, beating and tearing at his stomach, he was gasping for breath – there are no words to describe it. It was unbearable to watch. In the middle of the night the doctor was brought in, not Dr Mun, but his predecessor Dr Ha, but it was no use. When she finally heard about the deer the old lady fainted. Whatever happens, you can never say that there's no Spirit in the world. Didn't I plainly see it all with my own eyes ? – certainly I did. At dawn, when I was boiling rice gruel in the kitchen . . .'

She stopped spinning and scowled, 'You can't imagine what a horrible thing I saw when I lifted the lid.'

Bongsoon *ne* swallowed hard.

'In the gruel there was a boiled centipede, and without a grain of exaggeration, it was as big as a shoe!'

'A centipede!'

'It went hazy before my eyes and cold sweat ran down my face. As part of the punishment he was not to be allowed to put anything down his throat. My heart fluttered, but what could I do? Rushing about like mad, I ground some rice, made more gruel, and took it to him, but there was no way he could swallow it. It was spooned into his mouth, but it just ran out of the corner. He carried on like this until a little after midday, and then drew his last breath. The old lady, after beating the floor in anguish, swooned, while her ladyship and the young mistress looked lifeless − it was too painful to see them in that state. Soidori, Samsoo's grandad went straight out and hanged himself, leaving Samsoo's dad behind. He had a kind heart. How could he have made such a mistake? When I think about it I feel sorry for Samsoo, so I do things like wiping his nose, and give him things to eat . . .'

'What happened to Samsoo's father then?'

'The rascal? Who knows? Wherever he'd begotten him, he brought Samsoo, almost newborn, left him in a servant's room and ran off. He was a boy of only eighteen, so either he had seduced an unmarried girl or the child's mother had died . . . as Samsoo grows older, he looks just like his father, so it must be his seed.'

Realizing she had digressed, Gannan *halmum* quickly returned to her story.

'So the two dogs were killed and since then we have never had one. From then on the old lady took to bed with a stroke and after a year she passed on . . .'

Apart from this, Gannan *halmum* had told her other stories, not in much detail but roughly, of how the Choi *champan* household had been established. Prosperity had come in the time of Choi *champan*'s mother − that is to say it was she who, as a young widow, after her husband's death, had laid the foundations for the prosperity of the present day.

'I guess that though they were a good family, they were very poor. They say the grandmother of the *champan*, wishing the household to prosper, did the "Six Sacrifices".'

'They say that can be done only by exceptional people with exceptional dedication.'

'Of course! It can't be done with just ordinary devotion. It has to be done six times a year. While you are at it, fasting of course, if you doze off just once, the whole thing comes to nothing because the divine officer on watch behind you will report it to heaven. If it was, who wouldn't do it? So, whether thanks to this or not, the house began to prosper, and the *champan*'s mother must have been a great lady too. They say she bled herself in building up the household. Leaping one generation, the *champan*'s daughter-in-law, her late ladyship who dies of a stroke, she also increased the family fortune as much as a man could have done. Then, leaping another generation, came the "young Mistress" – I mean her ladyship. Though she brought a big dowry from her own home, being sharp and clever, she has increased the property even more, without losing people's affection. So, with a gap of one generation between them, the *champan*'s grandmother, his daughter-in-law and his great-granddaughter-in-law are the three great ladies of the family, but strangely each of them became a widow at an early age with an only son. It's not that they didn't have other children, but they never seemed to prosper. But how many people are lucky enough to bring up as many as they give birth to? I can't say much about his grandfather, but the present master is the fifth generation of only sons. His grandmother used to go to the temple a lot to offer sacrifices, and built a shrine for the fertility gods, and offered devotions, but it looks as though scarcity of offspring can't be resolved by human power.'

'So that's how the master's father died. What about his grand-father, did he die early too?'

'Yes, before he was thirty . . . his wife came from a Cho family in Seoul – you knew that, didn't you? On his way back from Seoul he fell off his horse and then . . .'. Gannan seemed to be uncertain about this event and did not want to take it any further. Apart from how the master's father had died, all that Bongsoon *ne* could remember about the family was that the *champan*'s grandmother had done the Six Sacrifices, but the stories that had been handed down in the village were more detailed and gruesome. It was so long ago that they were now like legends. They were not supposed to be publicly revealed, but nevertheless they repeatedly cropped up like the seasons that visited forest, river and fields – they could be called the village history. There were many anecdotes about the *champan*'s mother, all of which revealed her extraordinary meanness. Saying that the grubs in bean paste are as good as the paste, she had sucked them before she threw them away: she had rounded up all the servants in the middle of the night and sent them to the river to cast nets and scoop up fish till daybreak to take to the market and sell; in the winter this wolf-like woman, without taking a wink of sleep herself, went round every room to check that no fire had been lit; as the servants slept curled up like shrimps in the freezing rooms, she shook them to wake them even before the dawn, and sent some of them off to the market with firewood, and others to the hills to gather it; at the time of boiling soya beans to make sauce, she gave them no rice, saying that they were eating the beans, and at the time of pickling cabbage there was no rice because they were eating cabbage, and so on. Bong-gi's grandfather, who had died a few years before, had told another story, saying that as a child he had seen it with his own eyes: 'This happened once. There was a drought that year and the monks were making an offering. Seeing the hungry look on the faces of two pedlars who had stopped to watch, one of the monks gave them some rice. The wicked old woman swooped out of nowhere and snatched the bowl. Then she emptied it, rinsed it, drank the water herself and rebuked the monk, saying, "In this dry weather, with rice as precious as grains of gold, don't you realize you can't just give it away?" His face reddening, he said, "Huh, really! If she doesn't fall into hell after this, there's no justice in the world!" '

That much was believable, but the villagers preferred more fantastic tales. A servant girl, ravenously hungry, ate a handful of rice while she was washing it. Seeing this the old lady hit her on the head with a club. Whether it was the doing of an evil spirit, the girl died instantly and her resentful ghost hung about the corners of the roof and the yards until finally it got hold of the seed of the family line, the only grandson. All of a sudden he was in the throes of death, rolling his eyes, and the whole household was turned upside down. A blind medium did the rituals, and the ghost came up – it was the servant, of course. The medium urged it, shouting loudly, to own up to what it was doing, and it confessed that it was the spirit of the one who had been hit with a club and died resentfully. So, offering a generous sacrifice to placate the grievance, he led it into the path to the Buddha, and just managed to save the seed of the family line . . .

It was said that when the old woman died she became a great snake. A servant girl went to the chest to get some rice and heard a sound coming from underneath saying, 'A little at a time, A little at a time.'

Looking down, she saw a big snake. She burst out in anger, 'When you were alive you used to chant "A little at a time, A little at a time," day and night, and now even after you are dead you are still at it!'

She poured boiling water over it. With the skin scalded off its back, the snake used to go round shedding tears and it was said that such a white snake still remained as the guardian of the site.'

It was also said that this tale had reached the ears of Choi Chisoo's great-grandmother and the woman who had divulged it was nearly beaten to death.

Of all these tales, the one most damaging to the family reputation would be this one. One year there had been a bad drought in the village, a frightening one in which fields were scorched yellow, and even the river dried up so that the fish lay dead. The government released some famine rice but there was a limit to it. The alleys were strewn with the bodies of those who had starved to death, and there were no animals to eat them. At this time the mounds of grain in the store room of the Choi household were exchanged for the land deeds of the starving farmers who, giving up a piece of paddy yielding sixty sacks for a few measures of grain, had no time to think of the sad injustice of losing the land passed down through the generations, so desperate were they to save their lives. At this time a widow with seven children, no longer able to bear seeing their life flickering out, and hoping to wet their throats with gruel, had crawled to the doorstep of the Choi house carrying a bowl and begging piteously. But there was no way in which grain, precious as golden pieces to be exchanged for the deeds of land, would be given to her, so she died cursing them. 'That's it! With nothing to eat, I lead my children to the world beyond, but I will see to it that there will be no family to enjoy the treasure piled up in this bastard's house!'

Because of legends that the lack of children in the Choi family was due to the resentful spirits of the starved widow and her children, until quite recently, it was said, virtuous scholars, when they entered the village, turned their faces towards the river to avoid the sight of the whale-like roof of the house and spat at the monument to the high-ranking member of the family. It is imposs-ible to know to what degree these stories were based on fact, but there could be no doubt that there had been some acts of wickedness behind the accumulation of such great riches.

In the hall of the *sarang*, Chisoo and Junku faced each other in a game of Go. Apart from the sound of the stones clicking on the board, the sultry afternoon was quiet. As he stood beneath the eaves in the backyard, Kilsang was lost in watching the clouds rolling across the sky. (Really, where are they all going to? Why can't you ride on them? If I could, how I would love to go and see the old *sunim* again!)

'Kilsang, you rascal,' he used to say, 'If you don't appreciate the value of even a single grain of barley, the day will come when you suffer hunger.'

He felt an unbearable yearning for Ugwan *sunim*. He had been a stern and terrifying old monk. How everybody used to tremble in front of him – Kilsang as well! – yet the first face he could remember was not his mother's but the monk's.

On the path through Kim *subang*'s vegetable plot Guinyo went by. Turning his gaze from the clouds, Kilsang stared at her back, where maroon ribbons flapped on her pigtails. From where he was playing Go Chisoo also had a flickering glimpse of her through the bamboo blinds. Her lips thin and red, she was smiling faintly with a slight twist of her mouth. Kilsang followed the outside wall of the *sarang*, writing on it with his finger and then looked up at the crimson blossoms of the pomegranate. Again his eyes were turned to the floating clouds. (Why did the old master send me here?

Didn't Haegwan *sunim* say I'd be an artist?) Ugwan had been a frightening master but out of all the novices, his eyes had most often fallen on Kilsang. He remembered that it had been a look of sadness. When he said 'You rascal!' his eyebrows would wriggle, but when he leaned on his staff and gazed at the misty clouds that hung about the waists of the mountains – how sad he'd looked!

'What rotten weather.'

Having finished the game, Chisoo gathered the Go stones and put them into the bowls.

'It's sweltering.'

Junku took out his handkerchief and wiped his forehead.

'Wouldn't you like to go up the hill?'

'The hill?'

'We might see something interesting.'

'Interesting?'

Junku's face changed colour – he was reminded of the time when he had learned his lesson about the word 'interesting'. In Seoul when he had been dragged into a prostitute's den, Chisoo had used that word. There couldn't be a whorehouse on the mountain, but one could never guess what wickedness might be in store. Yet, knowing Chisoo's stubborness, he could not decline, so he felt uneasy. Chisoo was smiling. Didn't they say that Jo-Jo (hero of a Chinese classic) had been ruined by a smile? Chisoo's smile also did not seem to be a favourable omen. When the short Junkoo and the lanky Chisoo had walked up to the pavilion, they saw Dochul *ne* crouched under a chestnut tree, searching for lice, bare to the waist and with her legs showing through her torn skirt. Junku, after smirking, turned his face away while Chisoo looked at the sight with expressionless eyes.

'Come on, man.'

Junku pulled at his elbow. When they had gone past, Chisoo said, 'I hear you've been going down to the village quite often?'

'Well . . . I get bored.'

'And drinking with the lower classes.'

'What do you mean? . . . I would have thought, in eating and drinking, high and low didn't . . .'.

'Of course not! An excellent thing to do!'

As they entered the woods, Junku again felt uneasy. He looked back the way they had come. Under the chestnut tree Dochul-*ne* looked small. As if to make his head turn back again Chisoo said, 'Branch off here and go straight on and you come to the shrine of the Fertility Spirits.'

'Fertility Spirits?'

They turned from the path that went on towards the valley. After they had gone some way, they came to a thin stream with a stone bridge that looked too grand for it. It was only when they had crossed it that Chisoo replied, 'That's right, the Fertility Spirits.'

'Does that mean a place where people go to pray for a child?'

'That's right. Didn't you see it when you were here before?'

'When did I have time? Besides, you can see them anywhere.'

'I don't think they are all that common.'

'I can't distinguish a Fertility Shrine from a Guardian Spirit Shrine anyway.'

As they followed the lonely path, Chisoo said, 'They say it was built by my great grandmother.'

'Really?'

'It didn't work though.'

'It's nothing but superstition – it was a useless thing to do.'

'Here we turn off again. This path will take us up to the back of the shrine. If you go straight to the front of it, there is a stream, bigger than the one we passed, and the Guardian Spirit Shrine. The river is an ideal place for women to bathe.'

Junku smiled faintly as he thought to himself, 'Hum, so you want to hide and watch the women bathing?'

However, when they reached the back of the shrine Chisoo, without going any further, turned and said, 'Don't make a sound.'

Almost pushing him forward, Chisoo made him stand near the back wall of the small shrine. Realizing his guess had been wrong, his face fell. He was also a little scared at being pushed by Chisoo. At a distance the roof of the Guardian Spirit Shrine, and its once brightly painted eaves, now bleached, could be seen through the bushes, and the path that led to it could also be glimpsed between the trees.

'What on earth are we doing here?'

Chisoo put his finger to his lips, his eyes full of mischief. Indeed he looked like a boy, clearly the only son of a widowed mother. The next moment his eyes seemed to have caught something. Having cleaned herself in the stream, Guinyo, holding a towel, was walking towards them. Chisoo had turned so that he stood with his back to Junku.

'Don't make a sound or it will spoil the fun,' he whispered. Some time later there came from the front of the shrine the sound of the door being opened with the rattling of the metal latch. It was followed by the crunching of feet on the ground inside and then on the wooden floor. There was a long silence and then a voice was heard: 'Three Gods of fertility and God of the trees, Spirit of the Mountain, Chonjorang God, and Eunjorang God, I, nineteen-year-old daughter of the Kim family, cherish a wish to have a seed-son. Grant me a seed-son to carry on the line of the great Choi family.'

Junku's eyes opened wide. (Seed-son of the great Choi family? Isn't that Guinyo?) He glanced sideways at Chisoo who was gloating. Her prayers of pleading continued to make themselves heard. Probably she was endlessly rubbing her palms together and bowing her head. At last the sound of prayers came to a stop and footsteps were heard receding to the outside of the shrine. A cuckoo shot out of the wood like a catapulted stone and shrieked as it flew away. Junku, amazed, mumbled to himself, 'What ambition!' Then he said to Chisoo, 'Man, you have laid hands on that bitch, haven't you?' and broke into chuckles. Chisoo joined him.

'Don't you find it interesting?'

'Ha! ha! Really! That creature's got her lungs greatly blown up with air.'

'The vision of herself with great wealth would have flickered before her eyes.'

'You are also to blame.'

Chisoo stopped laughing, his chuckle receding to a trickle, and then a vicious glint flashed in his eyes.

'Did you say that I'd laid hands on her? Why should I when it's more fun just to watch without actually touching her?'

'Really?'

Without further clarification Chisoo went on, 'It's all a matter of perseverance.'

'. . .?'

'Men can't beat women for perseverance. They are full of greed too, and even when they are not greedy . . . because of petty jealousy, a small grievance or hatred, they will often commit murder.'

'What, exactly, are you referring to?'

'The running of the Choi household, isn't that a typical example of female perseverance?'

He stopped short and said, 'Let's go down.'

Until they reached the stepping stones he kept a heavy silence, but when they had crossed the stream he turned to Junku, who was following behind, 'Would you like to go to Seoul and try?'

'What?'

'Try and get me a rifle'

'Yes, yes, of course!'

He nearly tripped over a stone as he hastily agreed.

Chapter Eighteen

ENVELOPED in the smoke from a mosquito fire, Yongi squatted in the courtyard with his pipe in his mouth. Humid air seeped through the holes of his coarse flax vest. Because of the acrid smoke in his throat he coughed as he continued to suck at his pipe. His back was stiff from weeding all day, bent over in the paddy, but his bodily pains were nothing compared to the hardship of restraining himself from running down to the fork in the road and Wolsun. He slowly rose to his feet, stared at the ground for a long time and then squatted down again. He knocked out the ash, refilled his pipe, and lit it. More than ten years ago when, as a slip of a child, she had left the village with a man from another region and Yongi, hidden behind barley sheaves, had watched her go, something hot had risen to his eyes. (Wherever you go, just be happy!) He had tried to forget her but then, after more than ten years, she had turned up again, and set up the tavern in the town so that every market day, coming and going, he briefly saw her face and took comfort in a cup of wine, but now things had changed. Since the night of the masked players, she had become his own flesh and blood. Her soft skin and the smell of her body were ever circling around him. Although, for the sake of his manly pride, he had stopped going there and restrained himself till the bones in his body almost snapped, he could not accept that she was not his woman. After her visit to the village he had been into town once, staying over night. This had caused a great row in which Kangchong *dek* had thrust herself at him screaming, 'Kill me!', but even at such a moment he could not give up the idea that she was his woman.

(Can't I put up with this yearning? We are no longer separate.)

His feelings when, hidden, he had watched her retreating figure and wished her happiness wherever she might go, or his feelings when he had glimpsed her face only on market days on his way there or back, even the heart that could never think of her without choking – all this had been mere make-believe. It was only after their physical consummation that he had begun to take in, for the first time, the meaning of such things as ingrained sorrow, the lonely pine tree on the rocky hill, the mournful cry of a solitary wild goose. He had become hard working and, whatever trouble might be caused by Kangchong *dek*, like the blinded mule that turns the millstone, he silently trod round the base of his life, consolidating his mind in the circle of love: revival, dedication and again, love. (We are no longer separate – can't I control this yearning?) He let out a deep sigh.

'Yongi!'

A voice called from outside the wall, on which gourd flowers were white, and Chilsung thrust himself into the yard. With the moonlight behind him, his top-knotted head looked big and dark.

'Let's go to Yongpari's.'

'Have they killed the dog?'

'Yes. For once, we are going to have some meat.'

Yongi knocked out his pipe and tucked it into his waist band as he stood up.

'My wife is not back yet. Your's isn't either, is she?'

Chilsung looked across towards the house.

'She'll come when she's ready . . .'.

'I bet the work is all done and they are just sitting around and chattering.'

'. . .'.

'Is she still jealous?'

'. . .'.

'Even if a man has gone a bit astray . . . she went too far.'

He seemed to be referring to what had happened a few days before, when Kangchong *dek* had dashed about with a knife crying, 'Kill me!' and Chilsung had restrained her.

'It's all because you are too soft. If I were you I'd give her a good thrashing and cure her bad habits. They say "Spare a wife from beating for three days and she'll turn into a fox".'

'She's so small, where is there a corner to beat? Anyway, if there's meat there should be some wine as well?'

'Of course, you can't eat dog without wine.'

The two of them, both strikingly tall and sturdy, walked out of the gate. The moon shone in front of them, casting two long shadows behind. As they went along the dike frogs croaked in the water-filled paddies. Meanwhile, at Dooman *ne*'s the women of the village had eaten their fill of a neatly laid-out supper – new barley, peppery soup and *kimchi* made with young raddish leaves – and swilled their mouths with hot rice tea, after which some went home, some sat on the verandah and others cooled their sweat and talked on a mat outside. During the day, under a tent pitched on the river beach, they had sweated freely in the communal task of steaming and peeling hemp and bleaching it in the water and in the evening they sweated even more in making sure they ate as much as they could of the supper to which each had contributed.

'. . . sitting up all through the night, they had finished making the official robe, but how sleepy the maid was! While pressing it, she nodded off and burnt the collar. The hour for his appearance at the court was near, and his wife felt black despair. Without thinking, she hit the girl in the face with the iron. Of course, she herself was totally confused, and it was a kind of karma from a previous incarnation. Anyway the girl died, and in her panic the wife put her underneath the floorboards in the stable . . .'

Haman *dek*'s story had entered its simmering stage while on the verandah Yamu *ne* and Magdal *ne* were disparaging Yimi *ne* in whispers.

'That woman, You wait and see, she will never be well off. She gobbles down more food than anyone else – and did you see the bowl of grain she brought this morning.'

'Bowl? – more like a saucer!'

Yamu *ne* tittered.

'I'd want nothing more in the world if only I had Yimi-*ne*'s sacrificial food! How on earth can she be so mean? Even a woman like me with no husband shares things out. As they say "Even love is give and take". If you want to receive you have to give.'

'Husband and wife are just the same. I've never known anyone who had a drink from Yimi's father. A little while ago Suh *subang* went to see him about something or other. They were just having their supper. As you know, Suh *subang*, though he always laughs good-naturedly, is particular about his manners, isn't he? He says that he saw Yimi's father take the dish of meat off the table and hide it behind him. Suh *subang* calls him a mean bastard. It's funny how they're both the same.'

As they moved out on to the mat, Haman *dek*'s story seemed to be reaching its final stage.

'. . . the visitor saw a lad and a girl with a green bundle under her arm enter the big gate. The moment they came in the girl picked up a crowbar and the man a length of straw cord. Then they tied up the son of the house, who was in the middle of a meal, and the woman brought the iron bar down on his head. All of a sudden, in the middle of eating, the son grabbed his head and rolled about on the floor, but he could not see the ghosts. The visitor briskly entered the house. On seeing him, the girl ran off. He chased her and saw her suddenly disappear under the floor. At the visitor's orders, the servants removed the floor boards, and there they saw the girl lying as if asleep, not a bit decomposed. At this stage the wife could do nothing but tell them what had happened from beginning to end. So they brought up the spirits of the maid and the boy together, joined them in marriage and, by offering a rite to pacify them, got rid of the resentful spirit.'

'So, if it hadn't been for the visitor, the son of the house would have died? It reminds me of the tales of the Choi *champan*'s family.'

'Even a ghost couldn't do it single-handed — she had to take a man with her.'

'By the way, what's happening at the Choi house? It's more than six months and we are entirely in the dark. It's not likely that such a great family will just let it go, so they must be doing something . . .'

'Oh, not that again.'

Dooman *ne* restrained Magdal *ne* as if fed up.

'It's all one's fate. I may be wrong but I think it's just as well it happened. Otherwise who knows? If one of them had died and become a love-sick spirit, there would have been real trouble,' said Yamu *ne*.

'That's true. I remember, when I was small, watching a rite of pacification on the top of the "Pining Rock",' said Yimi *ne* as she scratched her head, probably itching from sweat.

'The shaman beats the cymbals and urges the spirit to go like mad, and, if it doesn't drop off, then all together they push the person down the rock – isn't that how they do it?'

'What's the use of living like that? One might as well die. They say that if the person says, "I'm going to brush my hair," then the love-sick spirit that is stuck under her jaw drops off. When she has finished her toilet it comes back and sticks itself on again – how spooky!'

Feeling scary, as if a whip-snake might creep out from the shadow of the persimmon tree through which the moon light wavered, the women moved up and sat closer.

'I've heard that if the one who's possessed by the love-sick spirit, before she breathes her last, has a bloodstained petticoat put over her and and is sat on the privy, the spirit doesn't come back.'

'They say that a peach tree calls the spirits. A long time ago, a man called Ahn Bom-shik lived in a village . . .'

Kangchong *dek* was bringing up a tale when Yimi *ne* cut her short: 'That's just a shaman's song . . . We all know from the old days that we shouldn't plant a peach tree inside the garden wall.'

If it had ended there, all might have been well but, while shamans were the subject, someone said that there hadn't been a rite worth seeing since Wolsun's mother died.

'They are all novices. I heard that there was going to be a requiem and I went as far as Hwagae to see it. Even the so-called best in the district was no good, nothing to compare with Wolsun *ne*.'

This unwitting word from Dooman *ne* had the effect of upsetting Kangchong *dek*. At once she became abusive about Wolsun's mother.

'Those spirit-mongering bitches! That's why she died such an unnatural death – Wolsun *ne* or whatever she was called – she froze to death – isn't that right? On her way home after a drinking bout.'

'Well, really!' muttered Dooman *ne* with embarrassment.

'Kangchong *dek*.' Haman *dek* addressed her gently. 'You shouldn't be too sharp about it. Men are bound to go astray at times . . .'

'*Songnim*, you have a heart as big as sky and the sea, bless you.

209

You even give him money for drinks, and gambling too, and still uphold him as the master of the house and wait on him as if he were a god, but I can't be like that.'

She spoke roughly, but Haman *dek* went on as politely as before with a smile on her heart-shaped face that seemed to say, 'Should I look down on you? That's why I am telling you this. Compared to me you are as lucky as a golden Buddha.'

Dooman *ne*, pitying them, tried to help.

'Don't be so quarrelsome! Did Yi *subang* ever ill-treat you because of his little affair? Lately, he has been working harder in the fields than ever before what is there to make such a fuss about?'

'What else can he do but work when he hasn't a penny to his name? All he has is that great thing of his. "A numskull with a club setting off on a grand tour," as they say. How could he even think of having a concubine in a low-class family like ours?' Kangchong *dek* spoke jeeringly in vulgar language.

'Enough is enough. What will you do if, after all this trouble, one of them dies and becomes a love-sick ghost that sticks to the other. Anything is better than one of them dying.'

Following up these words from Yamu *ne*, Magdal *ne* chimed in 'You have to satisfy your desire in some way or other or you become ill.'

'Why say that? If there ever has been any desire or sorrow, it's been on my side. What kind of grievance can there be on the side of that dirty pair?'

'What a way to speak!'

Dooman *ne* again gave a hollow laugh.

'If anyone is to die, it will be me. My blood will dry up and I'll die. That's it, I'll die and become a love-sick ghost for a thousand, no, ten thousand years!'

Tears rose to her eyes.

'Look here, Kangchong *dek*, you must grow up. What can you do with a mind as narrow as the guts of a minnow? After going on like that for a while, he will come to his senses, and that will be the end of it. You are properly married through the six rites and that is the important thing – why go on about dying and living and all that? If you put your heart into your housework, there's no

210

time to brood on it. I've seen your cotton field and its a jungle. Don't we all know what Yongi is like? – he is not the sort who would ever ill-treat his wife.'

As Dooman *ne* exhorted her, Kangchong *dek* was looking for her shoes.

'I'm going.'

She was about to leave when Yimi *ne* called out, 'Kangchong *dek*, don't just struggle on your own. Don't you think you should watch out for a light in the shaman's house?'

Yamu *ne* frowned and jabbed her in the ribs, but it was too late. Kangchong *dek* had seen it all, including the poke. She turned back and came close to Yimi *ne*.

'What did you say? Please speak more clearly.'

'I'm not afraid to say it if you want me to.'

'That's right, that's what I'm asking you to do.'

'Wolsun came in the night, slept in the shaman's house and went off again, but you don't seem to know.'

Dooman *ne* clicked her tongue.

'Slept and went? Do you mean with my husband?'

'Well, you will have to go and ask her yourself about that. She should know.'

Without another word, Kangchong *dek* shot out of the brush-wood gate. She walked along the path through the paddy fields. The moon, immersed in the stream by the paddy, followed her.

(That woman has been and slept with him? That damned bitch!),

If Yongi had been in front of her, she would probably have scratched and pummelled him. Even without cause she had often felt such a mad impulse rising within her. As she entered the gate of her own house, the yard was empty and the mosquito fire had faded and gone out.

'Kill me! Kill me!'

She pulled open the door. The moonlight shone in. She looked anxiously about the room but it was empty. She ran to the privy – but no one was there.

'Look! Where are you?'

Only the sound of insects came from the corners of the yard.

'I see! You've gone there again! Let's make an end to it! You'll see one of us die!'

She ran to the shed and picked up a sickle. Its blade flashed white in the moonlight.

'Why should it be me? No, whatever I do, I won't die alone!'

Throwing it away, she hitched up her hemp skirt, fastened the string tight around her waist and dashed out as on wings. All the way to the town, a distance of seven miles following the endlessly curving river through fields and woods, the moon immersed now in the river and now in the ditch, chased her faster than before, while frogs croaked as if in pandemonium.

When she stood in front of the tavern at the fork in the road, there was not even a puppy in sight and the low-lying roof of the unlit house seemed to overwhelm her small figure. For a long time she tried to get her breath back, but her pounding heart ached as if to burst. Her dry lips were trembling violently.

'Is any one there?'

Her voice faded inside her throat.

'Look here!'

Shouting loudly, she beat on the gate.

'Uhm!'

She kept on banging.

'Why can't you open it?'

'Who is it – in the middle of the night?'

It was Wolsun's voice.

'Open up! You bitch!'

'My goodness . . .'

With this a gleam of light showed from the room.

'Who is it?'

A trembling voice was heard at the gate.

'You know who I am, don't you?'

'. . .'

'Open it at once!'

'What do you want? Can't you wait until dawn?'

'How dare you! If you don't open it, I'll smash it down. Do you think I'll just go back? Did I come here just to go back?'

There was the sound of the bar being removed. As soon as one side of the gate was open she leapt through and shouted towards the room, 'Let's die, you and me! You only die once!'

Stepping over the verandah, she noisily slid back the door.

'. . .?'

There was nobody there.

'Where's he gone?'

Wolsun, who had been standing nonplussed, said, 'Who are you looking for?'

'You sly creature! Who would I be after but my husband?'

'He hasn't been here.'

'Hasn't he?'

As she had done at home, she searched the empty room, groping over the floor, ran to the privy, and looked into the public room. Then she said, 'Didn't he really come here?'

'No.'

She flopped down. As if her heart beneath the white under-blouse was fluttering, Wolsun pressed her breast with her right hand. Lit by the lamp and the moon, her face twisted as if to burst into tears and then, becoming tense again, hardened like wood. After a while Kangchong *dek* stood up abruptly. Her hatred of Wolsun had been ignited.

'You bloody bitch!'

She ran at her and tore her vest.

'Why, what for?'

'You don't know? You bloody bitch! How dare you? – coming as far as the village and tempting him out!'

Wolsun's vest was torn and her skirt was slipping but before she had a minute to put them right Kangchong *dek* rushed at her again, grabbed her hair by the roots and twisted it.

'Let me go and we can talk.'

'I won't! I wouldn't relent even if I had your liver out and ate it. Do you think I'll go off and leave you in one piece? Let me have a good look at you – see how much smarter are you than me – to melt away men's guts!'

As Kangchong *dek* flew about, knocking Wolsun over, pummelling her and shredding her clothes, her small body looked like a jumping bean. Her hair fell loose so that each time she brought her fists down on Wolsun the cascade of her hair came down on her face. If Wolsun had stood up and fought back she would not have been assaulted to this extent, but all that she did, while trying to dodge, was to say in a tearful voice, 'Please stop. We used to . . . from a long time back . . . Oh, please stop it . . . before he met you . . .'

'You bitch! You devil! Still you won't give in! You are the sort that eats up every man that comes your way! How dare a shaman like you try to ruin somebody's home!'

Even so, Kangchong *dek* felt her spirit deflating. One-sided pummelling was pointless and she felt foolish. As the strength went out of her fists, she began to feel that something was wrong. (That man – where could he have gone to? Perhaps he's with his friends? It's pretty certain that he hasn't been here. What about when he finds out about this?) She was suddenly scared. She did not know what might come out of his stubbornness. (I must be back before dawn . . .)

'You, bitch! Still you won't give in!'

Even though she maintained her bluster, inwardly she was worried about how to bring her attack to an end.

'Please stop it.'

'You bitch! You can't say you were in the right, can you?'

'I'd meant never to go but . . . how could I say I was in the right?'

She tried to pull herself free.

'That's right.'

Kangchong *dek* let her go, and tried to put up her dishevelled hair.

'If you ever try to call my husband here, or set foot in the village, then mark my words, you won't live out your natural life.'

Uttering more threats as she smoothed her clothes, she gave a quick side glance at Wolsun, flopped on the floor weeping, and went out with hurried steps. From the gate she shouted,

'I've no time, so I'm off now, but if you don't watch out . . . !' and stepped out into the road. A little further up, the empty market place could be seen. As before, not even a dog was in sight as she flew off.

From fields where the daytime heat was lost came a chilly breeze which cooled the back of her sweat-drenched neck as she hurried along beside the tree-girded river. It cooled her sweat but not her heart. She was the one who had done the beating but she felt as if, rather than venting her anger, she was running away defeated, so much so that, had she not been in such a hurry to get home, she would have gone to the shore to throw herself down and have a good cry.

'This rotten fate! If only I had a child, my destiny wouldn't have been like this – "Elixir only in name," "A dog-apricot with a pretty colour" – what's the good of the six rites of marriage? All his heart is with that woman and only the husk is left for me. What comfort is there for me to dig the soil and weave? Oh, sad and pitiful woman – that's me – a poor wretch. Oh, hell!'

At last she burst into tears, still running. On the way there she had been too enraged to notice anything, but now she was scared. Summer nights are short. During this brief period, she had walked fourteen miles, seven each way. By the time she reached home all around her was turning to jade and she could see dew drops on the gourd flowers on the garden wall. The brushwood gate hung open just as she had left it.

'What does this mean?'

He was not there – not in the privy, nor in the room or the kitchen, nor was there any sign that he had been there while she had been away. At the thought of being cheated, her whole body trembled. But like a used-up piece of cotton wool, she could not budge – she had exhausted herself in running madly for fourteen miles and beating and shouting at Wolsun, after a day in the tent where she had worked until her hempen underclothes were soaked in sweat. She hadn't realized it until now, but her left elbow was burning, perhaps sprained while attacking Wolsun.

As the sun was about to rise, with a reddish light glowing all around, Yongi briskly walked in. Seeing her crouched on the verandah, he said, 'Why haven't you let the fowls out . . . ?'

From the coop a cockerel crowed. Her eyes were nearly popping out.

'What's the matter? Have you gone mad again?'

He was turning toward the cow-shed when she rushed at him from behind and grabbed his belt.

'Kill me, and go and live with that bitch!'

'Don't be silly – from the first moment of dawn . . .'

'He pushed her off. She gave a moan of pain and, grabbing her sprained arm with the other hand, flung herself to the ground. Again a cry of pain.

'Don't make such a fuss.'

'It's my arm . . .'

From the way she cried, he realized that it was not altogether pretence.

'What's wrong with it?'

'My arm? My arm wouldn't be enough. Break my legs as well. Then you can easily go to town and . . .'

In the middle of it, she yelled again from the pain. Yongi started to rub it.

'You give the medicine and the disease as well! Ouch! Oh!'

'What a way to start the day! Let me have a look – you must have sprained it.'

She thought if he'd just come from there, he would know about the row. But he seemed to show no sign of knowing.

'Look . . .'.

'. . .'.

He went on rubbing her arm silently. The sun was rising. Like the sun, his eyes were red and bloodshot. So were hers.

'Where were you last night? Do you want to be the death of me?'

'That's enough for now.'

He frowned as he rose.

'I'm asking you where you were!'

He turned on his way to the shed.

'At Yongpari's. Why?'

His next words came in a gentler tone.

'They killed the dog, you see. We had a round of drinks.'

'You mean the whole night passed in a round of drinks?'

'It was too hot. I went to the pavilion with Chilsung and slept there.'

She closed her mouth.

Chapter Nineteen

THE cotton plants sown between the rows of barley began to thrive after it had been cut and threshed. The sun scorched down. Under the village tree the old men sat with their pipes in their drooling mouths and talked in a drone. The children played by the river, splashing each other. Along the furrows, now plainly a cotton plantation, the women, bent over, were piling up soil round the plants as they dug out the barley roots with their short hoes. Alive, the barley had blocked out the sun and sucked the nourishment from the soil, but now that it was dead its roots would decay and fertilize the cotton.

A peasant started to sing.

> *'Cholla Province,*
> *In the Mount of Camelias,*
> *Wasp-waisted, my mother.*
> *Love for her lover is all very well*
> *But where's the love for her poor child?*
> *Leaving me, like the half-moon,*
> *She has gone after her lover and is nowhere to be found.'*

It was Dooman *ne*, and her song, clear and piercing, resounded far across the hot fields. Of all the women, she had the best voice.

'Yes, a song for the young Miss at the House to sing.'

'Love for her lover is all very well, but where's the love for her poor child? Leaving me like the half-moon, she has gone after her lover.' As the old saying goes "Tales tell lies but songs the truth." Such things must have often happened in the old days.'

As if thirsty after her song, Dooman *ne* went over to the edge of the field where a jar of water had been left, dipped a gourd shell into the tepid water to drink and said,

'Hey! all of you. What about a break?'

They put down their hoes, stood up one after another and moved up the slope to where a leaning pine tree spread its branches.

Yimi *ne*, who had been sulky all along, unwound the towel from her head to wipe her face and removed her straw shoes to shake out the soil, saying, 'Talking of things you hate, what I hate most of all is hoeing the fields in summer.'

Magdal *ne*, taking up her words, chanted as she floated in a dance, 'What's the good of hating it? If only I were a *kiseng*, I would latch on to a big landowner and build a great mansion with fancy walls and gauze windows . . .'.

The women burst into laughter, and Yamu *ne* said, 'You're crazy. With a face like a boatman from Daema Island, if you could latch on to even a smallholder, I'd light a fire on my finger and go up to heaven.'

'Shut up. It's only the summer sun that's made my face look like this. When I was young, there were plenty of young men after me.'

Again they all laughed loudly.

'Haman *dek songnim* hasn't been out today?'

It was Yamu *ne's* turn to ask Dooman *ne*.

'Don't talk about it.'

'What's the matter?'

'I hear she's in bed and can't even move.'

'She's been thrashed again? Can't that horrible hand be removed? A hand that steals, beats its wife and gambles should be chopped right off.'

Magdal *ne*, who had been so cheerful, burst out as if her forgotten anger had boiled up again.

'Be quiet. "Speak of the tiger and it appears!" There he goes — he might hear you,' said a younger woman, pulling at her sleeve.

'Hear me? Let him listen. A hand that steals must be chopped right off . . . Why? Am I saying something wrong?' She bawled loudly, but leaving out the reference to gambling and wife beating.

'Nowadays he hardly ever goes to the town — just stalks round the village.'

'From the way he stays away from the town, I bet he's done something that deserves a thrashing. As a gambler who can't go gambling, his body is itching so he beats his innocent wife.'

Everyone added something except Yimi *ne* who, with her mouth shut, stared at his back. Seeing him disappear, Dooman *ne* said with a worried look, 'Oh dear, the poor boys will be looking miserable with their mother out of action . . .'.

'As she was marrying a man above her in rank, she apparently brought some dowry land with her.'

'Do you think it's still there? – I bet it's gone long since. What's so good about the gentry – if you have to tighten your belt?'

'If you just hold up your pedigree, does rice fall into the pot?'

'Even if he sat me on a golden cushion, I wouldn't have it. There he is, sound in every limb, and all through the four seasons he hangs around with his hands in his pockets and a face as red as a lobster, while his wife doesn't know how to fill the bellies of their poor little kids. They call him a gentleman, but what's the good of that? It's only a low military rank and there was never a monument for any of them, not one minister or judge.'

'I'd rather be a widow.'

Yimi *ne*, who had been silent, opened her mouth to say, 'I don't care whether it's doing rites or eating cakes – I'm more worried about my own family.'

'Why?' asked Magdal *ne* as she twisted her neck to look at her.

'I mean Yimi's father . . .'

'What's wrong with him? He's hard working, strong and looks after his family.'

' "Trust your axe and it chops your feet", as they say.'

Yimi *ne*'s face, tanned to the colour of corn, was as pretty as ever and looked healthy. After giving birth to a son in February, she had recovered well and now her face was glowing.

'Has he got a woman somewhere?'

Magdal *ne*'s eyes sparkled.

'I wouldn't worry if he had. Why, do you think I'd be as jealous as someone we know? Every night he comes and calls from just outside the gate, 'Chilsung! Chilsung!' It drives me mad.'

'Who does?'

'Who? Him – that Pyongsan, or whatever he's called.'

'Whatever for?'

'I've no idea. That's why I'm so worried. Yimi's dad – he hasn't a penny to spare for gambling, so at first he used to get out of it by asking me to say that he wasn't in. But he has the skill – he learnt it in his wandering days. So isn't he likely to be mad about it after playing once or twice? The last few days he has come home at daybreak and stayed in bed like a corpse until the sun was high . . . really I'm worried to death.'

'Come to think of it, I saw them once – the two of them going off together.'

'Whatever happens, I won't put up with it. If he goes on like this, I'll set fire to our little thatched cottage and bring it all to an end. Look at Haman *dek songnim* – why should I be like that?'

Just at this moment, across the fields on a path through the paddies, Yongi appeared, feet bare and with his trousers rolled up, as if going to his lunch after irrigating his field. Yimi *ne* stopped speaking and brazenly stared at him.

'What's his wife doing – not even bothering to bring his lunch?' Dooman *ne* clicked her tongue.

'You'd think that after going there and beating her that much, half her anger would have gone,' said Yamu *ne*. After watching Yongi disappear, Yimi *ne* abruptly stood up, walked down to the field and picked up her hoe. The others followed. Dooman *ne*, with her fine voice, raised it in song and the others joined in as they went on until the sun was setting.

That night Yimi *ne* nagged her husband until late, saying while the others were wearing themselves out to get water into their paddies, why was he giving up? Since their marriage she had scarcely ever been the one to nag. It had been rather Chilsung, working hard himself who had driven her to it, as if he had acquired an ox. She had done so vigorously, with an equally vigorous appetite and, apart from times of confinement, had rarely been ill enough to stay in bed. Her husband was to some degree pleased that she was healthy and worked hard, but whenever he saw her stuffing rice into her mouth till her cheeks bulged he lost his temper for no apparent reason and complained that while others ate gruel, she had to have rice. But, unlike other women, she did not take it seriously. She would only cast him a sidelong glance as she pouted.

It could be said that in conjugal love they were strangers, but one in mind and body as far as material interests were concerned.

On the following day, before sunset, she was pounding barley while Chilsung made bundles of young radishes ready for market when there came the sound of Pyongsan calling from outside. Looking down at the radishes he hesitated before he went out.

'Let's go to town.'

'Now?'

'Um.'

'I've got to do the radishes to take to the market tomorrow . . .'.

'Don't talk so much and just follow me – there's a better way to live!'

This was the phrase he recited whenever he took Chilsung out. Getting ready in a great hurry, he ran out pretending not to hear his wife's grumbling.

'I feel as if I'm bewitched by a fox. As soon as you say "Let's go" my feet just go out before me.'

He spoke in a rather uneasy tone of voice.

'It's all been arranged that way.'

As they walked together, Chilsung glanced at Pyongsan's small eyes, like two slits made by the tip of a dagger. As he had said of himself in a heated argument with Bong-gi some time ago, Chilsung was not the sort of man who would put up with the loss of a penny. Anything free he would not refuse, even if it was caustic soda, but of late he had felt uneasy about Pyongsan who bought the drinks every time and gave him money to gamble with, yet never revealed his real intentions.

(Why? Am I a scarecrow? What fool would refuse things that come free? Certainly he can't ask me to spit out what I've eaten, can he? Even if he did, I haven't got a penny to my name. Was it me who asked him to buy the wine or give me gambling money?)

They walked up to the main road. It was not yet dark but the crescent moon was out. The fields were mottled in light and dark. Already from afar came the call of a fox.

'This wide expanse of fields – who do they belong to?' asked Pyongsan with a smile.

'They're all Choi *champan*'s, of course,' replied Chilsung with a similar smirk.

'Out of this, one half – will that do for you?'

'Pardon?'

'Why? Don't you want it?'

'Well, if you can have what you want if that's the case, who wouldn't?'

'H'm, a man's greed . . . there's no limit to it.'

Pyongsan laughed in his croaky voice. As Chilsung rubbed his face with the hand with a missing joint there was a sound of swallowing hard. They met the ferry on the way and got into town before it was too late. They spent the night at the gambling den, the capital coming from Pyongsan. He had a considerable sum of money from cleverly handling Kang *posoo*'s ring. By careful scheming he did not have to spend much himself, and as he was counting on the other ring, still with Guinyo, for further funds, when he was with Chilsung he could give the impression of spending freely. On this night they won a good deal – of the two, Chilsung had done better. After repaying the loan to Pyongsan, he was able to thread quite a pile of coins and tie them round his waist.

They left at dawn and slept until midday at an inn. As he awoke, stretching his arms and yawning lazily, Pyongsan said, 'We must have a drink.'

'Let's go to Wolsun's,' said Chilsung as he sprang up.

As they entered, Wolsun put out her somewhat swollen face and said, 'We're not open today.'

'Not open? When guests call, even in the middle of the night, you should set out the table – that's the proper way for a hostess. Do you hear me?'

(Even at the point of death, a gentleman is a gentleman, eh?)

Chilsung smothered his laughter.

'As I didn't intend to open, I haven't got anything ready. Please try somewhere else.'

'Haven't you got even wine?'

'There might be some left, but I'm not well . . .'.

'From the look of your face you must have made some chap sweat a lot last night, ha! ha! . . .'.

'What?'

At that moment, blue sparks leapt out of her eyes – like the phosphorescent light that one sees around a tomb on a rainy day. Her face had turned as white as paper.

'A woman who sells wine has to put up with a few words of that sort. Come on now, let's have something to drink.'

Overawed by her manner, Pyongsan coaxed her as he stepped into the public room. A smile passed over her face – a ghostly smile. Taking up her place, she put in front of him a cup brimming over with wine.

'Is this your last day of business?'

Speaking as if to scold her, Chilsung gave her a wink as if to say, 'Don't take any notice.'

Each had four cups or more. Every time the cups were put out they overflowed and spilt on the table.

'Do you really mean not to let us have a side dish?'

Pyongsan raised his chin and glared at her. As he did so, flesh stood out on his neck, bulging like a tumour and looking reddish. Spitting blue sparks, Wolsun's eyes glared back at him.

'Really, look at her! Does she think we are here for free wine? Why does this thing treat us so haughtily?'

He brandished his fist in front of her eyes as if he was about to hit her.

'Yes, it's free – free wine to chase away wandering ghosts.'

'How dare you, you bitch, eh? We come to buy drinks from an unlucky witch like you and get this cheek . . .'.

'From the beginning you were in the wrong place, sir. You should be in a Tea House in Seoul.'

'What insolence!'

He stretched his arm across the table to grab her blouse.

'Please leave her alone. It's probably because she's not well.'

After calming Pyongsan, Chilsung went on, 'Wolsun, you shouldn't speak like that without thinking. It doesn't matter with people like me, but you can't speak like that to the master of a Military Officer's house, you see.'

The last words had a tone of gentle mockery. Unlike Kang *posoo* who, on hearing that Pyongsan was of the gentry, blindly addressed him as *sengwon*, it seemed that Chilsung, living in the same village and knowing him well, could refer to him as the Master of a Military Officer's house only with irony.

'A shaman summons the spirits of grandma and grandpa at the butcher's in just the same way as at a cabinet minister's.'

'Shut up now. It was just my quick temper, ha ha . . .'.

Much pleased to be called 'The Master of a Military Officer's House', he laughed, showing his crooked teeth and looking as gallant as the war lord of a Chinese legend.

'Come on, pour some more wine.'

He pulled her by the arm, but shaking off his hand she stood up, crossed the hall and snatched open the door of her room. Inside it a large bundle could be glimpsed. Then she slammed the door.

'She's never been like that before.'

Chilsung shook his head. To save his face, Pyongsan put on vain dignity and said, 'H'm, charming. Being like that she's even more attractive. If I had known, I'd have come last night and patted her bottom, ha ha ha . . .'.

'You should be stabbed to death! May you turn into a wandering ghost and never be born again!'

Curses came through the door like the sound of a howling animal. Chilsung felt a chill down his spine, and Pyongsan's face changed colour. Wolsun's voice was as eerie as an incantation.

'Let's get out of here. Come on!'

Chilsung hurriedly stood up, taking Pyongsan by the arm. Even though they were sober, they went out together pretending to be completely intoxicated and leaving not a penny on the table. Both of them were well aware of what they were doing. They carried on like this, pretending not to take any notice of each other, until they were well beyond the forked road, swaggering this way and that in a shameful imitation of drunkenness. Once out of the town, in no time they had let go of each other and walked along normally, and the miserly Chilsung even remembered to dip his straw shoes in the stream of water to save them from wear. Strong, and familiar with the road, they managed to reach the entrance of the village before sunset. Pyongsan stopped in front of another tavern.

'Do you want more to drink?'

Shaking his head, Pyongsan moved in the direction of the woods opposite the shop.

'What are you going to do . . .?' asked Chilsung as he followed.

'It's cool here. Let's talk while the sweat dries.'

Pyongsan sat with his legs dangling on a rock that lay by a pine tree. Chilsung gawkily stood in front of him. Between the trees the tavern could be seen, and the road.

'Really, this is the coolest place of all.'

Without saying anything, Chilsung felt the bundle of money as he took out his pipe, only to put it back again.

'What hot weather. They must be working in the fields, all of them, like a swarm of ants.'

Again it was Pyongsan who spoke.

'I suppose so. I should be hoeing too. My wife was having a fit . . .'

Sensing that there was something to be talked over, Chilsung brought in his wife as an excuse for slipping out of it if the proposal did not suit him.

'Do you want to do nothing but dig the soil for the rest of your life?'

'What else can I do? What can a peasant do but dig the soil?'

'Cowardly nonsense.'

'Even if I wasn't a coward, there's no other way. For a peasant, you either dig the earth or become a pedlar – what else is there?'

Chilsung, while showing his firmness, cast a quick glance at Pyongsan as if tugging at a fishing line. After a few blank moments he mumbled in a low voice, 'If you have great courage . . . and if you are lucky . . . I don't mean by this that you should sell your little cottage and put it into gambling . . .'

'Tell me what you do mean.'

Mentally Chilsung pulled harder at the line.

'It has been planned long since. If all goes well, you and I – more so for you than me – will see a complete change in our fortunes. It's true that good luck doesn't come so easily.'

' . . .'

'Nor is it likely to be gained in a day or two – indeed it may take much longer than it looks. But go on digging the soil for ten

225

years and you've still got no more than rags on your back. From that point of view, you can't call it a long time . . .'.

'Please, tell me what you are talking about.'

'Gradually, gradually . . . no need to rush. By the way, you've got three children − all of them boys, is that right?'

'No. A girl and two boys.'

'When I picked you out in my mind it was because you are good at fathering sons . . . but you have a daughter as well, eh? . . . As you've seen the wider world, you will be able to understand.'

'I haven't the slightest idea of what you are talking about.'

Even so, in his mind something vague was rising to the surface.

'Though I am a so-called gentleman, I have long since parted with books . . . so this is a story I've picked up with my ears.'

He momentarily looked pensive.

'The Emperor Chinshi of China was, they say, not the real son of the king, but of a merchant.'

'You mean the emperor who sent people to the West in search of the elixir of life?'

Chilsung tried to show a little of his knowledge, which was ignored.

'This merchant, the father of Chinshi, must have been a man of cunning and some guts, as well as foresight. While the prince was in exile as a hostage he befriended him and, while secretly helping him, offered him his favourite concubine, who was already pregnant with his own child.'

'So?'

'The prince, having returned to his own country after much scheming, became king, and as he believed that the child born to the merchant's woman was his own, naturally it became the prince, and eventually emperor − that's the story.'

'In short, it is a story of cheating the seed − that's what you mean?'

'That's right.'

'What about the real father, the merchant − did he have a good life?'

Chilsung's eyes sparkled, and as his lips moved his upper one seemed to deepen.

'Not only that – he got to be what nowadays they'd call the "Prime Minister".'

'I see.'

Chilsung felt that what had been vague was now becoming more definite but, whatever he intended, Pyongsan's face betrayed nothing. Whatever he was up to, he seemed to be beating about the bush.

'Let's move on.'

Chilsung followed him with a disappointed look, but submissively. They passed the tavern and the pine wood too came to an end.

'What wide open fields! The backs of those people hoeing must be burning. A squall of cool rain would be a mercy for them. All their lives they will wear worn-out vests, tread the early morning dew, their hunger relieved with a bowl of barley gruel, and only when the sun's completely gone will they stretch their legs in mud huts like stables. How is it different from the life of oxen or pigs? To put even a salted fish on the sacrificial table you have to weave straw shoes all through the night, and for children's weddings or family funerals you have to get into debt – you weave till your nails wear out with not a day off to straighten your back. As the saying goes, "Even in a field of dog shit, choose the right place." What's the use of a poor gentleman's pedigree? Can you boil it and eat it? Seeds must be dropped on fertile land, on a cushion of money . . .'.

'Of course. You are absolutely right, sir.'

Chilsung religiously agreed. To him, suddenly Kim Pyongsan's back looked like that of someone great. In a man he had regarded with contempt, there might be hidden unusual qualities and the strength to carry out some extraordinary task – these thoughts made him restless with excitement.

'Chilsung.'

'Yes, sir.'

'You got married late, didn't you? Is your production on the frequent side, would you say?'

'That's right. On the frequent side. Because, though I've had my topknot for some time, I've only been formally married for a bit over six years.'

'Is that so? Is your health good?'

'Never a day of illness through all the twelve months of the year.'

Soon they were coming up to the village. They saw from a distance Dooman's father, Yi Pangi, coming along the embankment towards them, driving his ox. He had been watering the paddies and on his way back, noticing the ox left there by his children, was bringing it home.

'Yi Pangi!' called Pyongsan, resuming his usual air. But whether he heard or not, Pangi only struck the ox with his whip.

'Hey, Yi Pangi! Have you married off your ears?'

He slowly turned his face but did not stop. Ears, eyes, mouth, and nose, his features were all smallish. He looked like a man of meticulous temperament.

'My wife – have you seen anything of her?'

For no apparent reason Pyongsan kept up a jaunty smile.

'You'd better keep your mouth shut or the wind will get into your lungs,' spat Yi Pangi.

Though they were of the same age and known to have been childhood playmates, Dooman's father regarded Pyongsan as less than the droppings of the next door dog. But for some reason, Pyongsan, instead of getting angry, just laughed.

'Huh, do you hear that low-bred man talking to a gentleman about the wind in his lungs?'

'You'd make a cow laugh! Gentleman, indeed! Do you call a fellow who beats his wife and takes tips at gambling dens a gentleman? Ugh! I'd hate to be that kind of gentleman. I'd rather be a butcher.'

Dooman's father, after spitting, again struck the ox on its flank. The sound of the ox-bell came with the smell of grass at sun-down.

'Huh, damn you . . . am I the enemy who dug your ancestor's graves? You whine every time you see me, trying to make trouble – I must see to it that your hide is hardened.'

Dooman's father, ignoring this, walked on and then turned round and said, 'Chilsung, you'd better watch out. Follow that gentleman and you'll end up ruining your whole family. As the saying goes, "Cunning mice, blind at night." Well, I must admit you make a good pair.'

Then he was gone.

Chapter Twenty

CHO Junku, having received a considerable sum of money, enough not only for rifles but also to relieve his family difficulties, left the boredom of the village on a mule, his face all smiles. After he had gone, Chisoo, attended by Kilsang, was confined to his study for several days, amid the smell of dust and decaying paper, sorting out his books. He failed to find anything on guns, but had come across one or two on gun powder and now seemed to be reading them. Lady Yoon, saying she was indisposed, did not leave her room. Guinyo, as if wanting to find out what was behind Junku's departure and Chisoo's retreat to his study, pricked up her ears like an alley cat with its claws drawn in and circled the house.

Now, Yi Dong-jin from the town was in the *sarang*. He looked low-spirited. Chisoo appeared cool, as if indifferent to his depression.

'The modern gentleman of Seoul – has he left?'

'Yes, but he'll be back.'

'Whatever for?'

'He's going to get me a rifle.'

'A rifle? What will you do with that?'

'I'm going to be a hunter.'

Yi Dong-jin looked at him fixedly and smacked his lips.

'Whatever it is, you always have the wrong ideas,' he said, but in a tone that suggested that he was not expecting it to have much effect.

'If I had the right ideas, do you think the world would change?'

'Your thoughts are confined within these walls – you never think about anything beyond them.'

'It is possible that a boundless world exists within these walls and nothing at all outside them.'

'Come on, you are trying to be perverse again.'

'Even if, by just plucking out one of my own hairs, I could benefit the whole world, I still wouldn't do it.'

'Damn that rascal!'

Chisoo smiled softly. He had quoted Yangtse, the ancient Chinese philosopher who had advocated egoism and hedonism, and Dongjin was cursing him.

The whole household was quiet. Bongsoon *ne* and Samwol had gone to bathe in the Dangsan stream. The servants were out in the fields and the casual kitchen workers had taken them their lunch. Only Yoni *ne* was in the kitchen, stirring pine-nut porridge with a wooden spoon.

'What I hate most is hoeing the fluffy millet. All the time I'm scraping a patch of that tasteless stuff I'm boiling with indignation.'

In the vegetable patch by the sloping path, thinning out radishes, Kim *subang*'s wife was talking to Gannan *halmum* who sat on the edge like a tumbling doll. Yoni and Nami were chattering as they picked aubergines and cucumbers to make side dishes for supper. Gannan *halmum* said, 'Still, for poor people fluffy millet is a great help. If a guest turns up, you just add some water and you get an extra bowl of cooked grain – so they say. Poor farmers, how on earth can they afford to eat proper millet?'

'I'd rather have ragged clothes – I just can't eat coarse food.'

'What about after a bad harvest? Whether it's bitter or sweet . . . you'd try human flesh.'

'What have we got to do with a bad harvest? Even if ten thousand others starved to death, we wouldn't would we?'

'That's senseless talk. Seeing others dropping dead with hunger, how could you put food in your own mouth?'

'If hard years come, our master's land will grow bigger, so why should you worry?'

'You'll be struck by lightning. Your tongue's like an axe. You'll come to a bad end with that tongue of yours.'

'I've seen people come to a bad end even without a sharp tongue. Go and look at Kim *jinsa*'s pepper field.'

'. . .?'

'Even when their servant runs away do they say anything? The widowed mother-in-law sits in the upper room and the widowed

230

daughter-in-law in another, and will they speak even if cymbals clang in the yard, or their stomachs are stuck to their back from hunger? The grass in their pepper field is long enough to graze cows – they might as well give it to someone else – I would, if I were them. They're not little chickens in a cage and Kim *hunjang* seems to have all the burdens. Only yesterday I saw him trying to plough their paddy when he can't even manage his own . . .'

In the middle of speaking, she used an earth-stained hand to hitch up her hemp garment and scratch her dried snakeskin-like thigh. In the courtyard of the *byoldang*, where the afternoon stretched out langorously, two little heads, each with a ribbon dangling, could be seen, two pairs of dainty shoulders, and two little shadows poking out from the shadow of a tree – the children sat quiet by the lily pond and on their prettily dressed shoulders the shadows of the willow hung like lace. A green frog the size of a date sat composedly on a lily leaf, looking up at the sky. Where the surface was not covered by the leaves a 'salt-man'(water stalker) circled and tiny yellow flowers waved.

'Bongsoon!'

'Yes, Miss.'

'Why do they call it a "salt-man"?'

Sohi asked as she pointed.

'I don't know, Miss.'

'Why don't you? Tell me.'

'I really don't know.'

'Why don't you? I do.' She suddenly stood up. Soil was stuck to the tips of her brocaded shoes. Bongsoon wiped it off with her palm.

'I know all about it. Kuchon, that rascal of a monk! He's a salt-man!'

'Pardon, Miss?'

Bongsoon looked up at her blankly.

'Once upon a time, a salt-man ran away, taking a pretty lady with him. That's what Gaddongi's mother told me.'

'The salt-man . . . but I know Kuchon is not a salt-man . . .'

Bongsoon, still squatting, waddled round behind the willow tree. Sohi, gasping with pent up anger and frustration, repeatedly kicked

231

the earth with the shoes from which Bongsoon had just cleaned the soil. Pebbles rolled and splashed one after the other into the pond. The frog on the leaf disappeared and the 'salt-man' stopped and froze.

'Miss! Young Miss!'

Suddenly Bongsoon called loudly. 'Come and look at this!'

'. . .'

'Here, I mean! Ants have got a big bee . . .'.

'. . . .'

'Little ants are trying to kill a big bee.'

'Where! Let me see.'

Her eyes sparkling, Sohi ran over.

'Look at these tiny things!' The bee was alive. Perhaps its wings were damaged. It could not fly. It had been about to crawl away when several ants had attacked it, one on its tail, one on its back, and one hanging on to a leg. The bee rolled over, knocking off the ants. After frantically running about they mercilessly assaulted it again – they were cruel and horrible demons. Their heads touching, the children were motionless, absorbed in watching the fierce battle.

'Miss!'

'. . . .'

'Those devils of ants – let's kill them.'

'No, don't.'

As if they had received a signal for help, more ants came running. The bee, that had been able to crawl, could now only turn.

'Miss!'

'. . . .'

'Those ants – they are devils! Let's kill them.'

'No.'

'Poor thing!'

Bongsoon put her hand out to the turning bee but Sohi pushed her away. Falling back, she said, 'Don't you feel sorry for it?'

'I want to see who wins.'

'Bongsoon, what are you up to?'

Kilsang's face appeared. 'What's this?'

'Ants – ants are going to eat up this bee – it's not even dead . . .'

232

Kilsang's hand, in no time, snatched up the bee, scattering the ants.

'What are you doing!'

Sohi screamed. Nevertheless he carefully took the exhausted and broken-winged bee to a myrtle flower and put it among the pink petals.

'Suck the honey and get better.'

Stamping her feet, Sohi cried. Kilsang looked at her with cold eyes as she screamed, 'Rascal! Monk! Salt-man! Liar! Idiot who can't even catch a rabbit!'

'Kilsang!'

Someone called him from the other side of the wall.

'The master wants you.'

Bongsoon *ne* and Samwol were back from bathing complete with their hair washed and neatly brushed. With Sohi crying behind him, and Bongsoon *ne* comforting her, Kilsang ran towards the *sarang*. Yi Dong-jin must have gone, as he was not to be seen. Chisoo, standing by the edge of the verandah said, 'Go and fetch Kim *subang*.'

'Yes, sir.' Kim *subang*, who had been eating a late lunch, came out wiping his mouth.

'Did you call me, sir?'

'Yes.'

'. . .'

'They say there is a hunter called Kang?'

'Yes, sir.'

'I've heard that he is very able.'

'That's true, sir. They say that in the hills he's a genius but down in the village, an idiot.'

Chisoo smiled faintly at this description.

'Can you find out where he is?'

Confused for a moment, Kim *subang*'s face changed colour. 'It's just that – he rarely comes down to the village . . .'.

Noting his face, Chisoo said, 'So you don't know – is that it?'

'Not exactly that, either, sir, but Mr Kim of the Military Line . . .'.

'You mean Kim Pyongsan?'

'Yes, he might know where he is.'

233

'I see . . . go and tell this chap Kim Pyongsan that I want to see him.'

'You mean personally, sir?'

'Yes.'

Kim *subang* stood awkwardly.

'What's the matter?'

'Oh, nothing, sir.'

He went out hurriedly.

(Why does he want Kang *posoo*?)

Not knowing that Cho Junku had gone to Seoul to buy a rifle, he felt uneasy about the rumour that Kuchon was in Chiri mountain.

(It couldn't be . . . that is one thing, but how is he going to get on with that rogue? Thinking 'I'm also a gentleman', he won't be humble, and the master will treat him roughly like a servant, and it may turn out nasty.)

He went down to Pyongsan's house but found it empty. (If he's not in I must see his wife and find out where he's gone to.) There was no sign of anyone coming, nor even a chicken around looking for food. He could not just wait endlessly in an empty house, so he walked out.

Sitting by the stream washing clothes was Haman *dek*, whom he had not noticed as he went in.

'Excuse me, M'am.'

Her washing movement stopped but she did not turn her head.

'I am the father of Gad-dongi from the *champan*'s house . . .'

'Go on.'

As if she had suddenly decided to keep a social distance, she continued not to look at him.

'My master wants to see the Mas . . .'

Then, deftly missing out the next words, he said '. . . Wants to see him.'

For the first time she turned round. Beads of sweat glistened on her narrow brow. She frowned, her face blotched with black bruises.

(You rascal, you can't bring yourself to call him 'the Master of the Military House of Kim', can you?)

234

But instead of her thoughts: she said, 'You might as well go and look for him in the tavern.'

Then she resumed her work, dumping her washing into the water with a splash.

(Huh, what awful things he has done to her!)

Scowling as if he had something bitter in his mouth, he set off for the tavern in search of him. He hated facing him, especially now after seeing her bruised face. Long ago — already thirty years had passed — soldiers had rushed into the house, and this incident had left the faint-hearted Kim *subang* with palpitations. Among them he seemed to recollect a face that resembled that of Pyongsan. Every time he saw him, he felt his heart trouble start again. It took him some time to regain his composure, saying to himself, 'Don't be silly, times have changed.'

It was also because Pyongsan, knowing his fear, often teased him, calling him names such as 'The Heavenly Lord's man', a common term for Catholics.

When he reached the tavern he could hear Pyongsan's croaking voice from outside. Leaning forward, he peeped in. He saw his back as he gabbled away, shaking his short thick neck. He was in the company of a man with a raffish air, who was not known in the village. This man kept swallowing wine and steadily chewing with a congenial manner.

'Excuse me.'

Pyongsan looked round.

'Can I . . .'

'. . . .?'

'Can I have a word with you?'

'Come inside, then.'

'I'd rather stay here just for a minute.'

'You want me to come outside?'

'Well . . .'.

'You ruffian! Did you break your legs last night?'

Kim *subang*'s face turned white. He gingerly walked in.

'As I don't drink, I don't usually get close to wine jars . . .'

He forced a smile on to his pale face.

'Yes, I remember now . . .' Pyongsan gave a loud laugh.

'You are going to split our ear drums. As the saying goes "A day old pup, not afraid of anything" . . .'

Pretending not to hear the hostess' sarcasm, he went on,

'That's it. I forgot that you are a "The Heavenly Lord's man". Of course you mustn't go near a wine jar.'

'Don't say such things – they can cause great trouble', blurted Kim *subang*, as if about to cry. His tightened fists were trembling. Plainly he was suffering some kind of hallucination.

(The days of Catholic persecution are over. They say that now in Seoul they are building a big catholic house on Chonghyon Hill. So times really have changed.)

Only after mumbling these words to himself was his mind at rest. Originally he had been a servant, not of the Choi house, but of the Yoon family, the paternal home of the mistress. When he was seventeen there had been a great persecution of Catholics in which the whole household had been destroyed within a year. Lady Yoon's father, who had been lying ill, was the only one miraculously to survive the massacre. Born faint-hearted yet passionately loyal, the simple-minded Pansool (Kim *subang*'s first name) had carried his old master on his back to the Choi *champan* house. He was not a Catholic himself but he could not forget the tragic scene. It still made him shudder when he thought of it, and for the past thirty years he had been tormented by an uneasy sense that such a disaster might come again.

'It doesn't matter to me whether you are of the 'Heavenly Lord's faction' or the Dong Hak faction,' said Pyongsan.

'. . . .'

'A dwarf or a giant, I don't care. So what have you come for?'

'My master . . .'

'That Choi fellow?'

Raising his voice, he cast a glance at his dissolute companion as if to say, 'See, I can even be disrespectful to a great landlord, Choi *champan*'s offspring!'

'My master wants to see you . . .'.

'Me?'

His eyes were alert.

'Why?'

236

'I don't know.'

'I have to know what it's about first, don't I? Did I have a bad dream or something last night?'

Despite his haughty air, his eyes grew serious. Kim *subang*, fearful lest his master's orders be disobeyed, tried not to offend him.

'He . . . he has some kind of request to make – I think.'

'Something to request of me? . . . unless he's going to ask me to teach him how to gamble, what could he want of me?'

Kim *subang* flushed.

'H'm, your guts must be swelling up, eh?'

The hostess's sarcastic treatment of Pyongsan encouraged Kim *subang* to burst into anger: ' "The strong and the weak are not the same," as they say. Do you think he keeps servants as fierce as tigers just for ornaments?'

Then he gladly spat out the words he had not been able to say before. 'Is the Master dogshit or cowshit? Why do you use his name so carelessly?'

Kim *subang*'s strong words were effective, but to keep up appearances before his companion, Pyongsan said as he stood up, 'Names are for calling and if he's the Master, he's your Master, not mine. Still I suppose I'd better go – I can't ask him to come to my house and make his request because I haven't got a *sarang*.'

He came out at once, rather nimbly for his heavy build. 'Kim *subang*.'

His voice was now soft, while the steward replied roughly.

'What?'

The more he thought about it the more angry he felt.

'What do you think he wants me for?'

'You'll find out for yourself soon enough.'

'He's only a distant acquaintance of mine, so what could it be?'

'Why, are you afraid he might hang you up on a tree and thrash you?'

'What a thing to say!'

'You'd better behave yourself – you know what he's like. Unless you want to be turned out of the village.'

'Who can do that?'

'He can, can't he?'

237

Indirectly applying pressure, Kim *subang* had given him a hint to be submissive in front of Chisoo. In the village they met Chilsung, carrying some tools. He looked at them in turn and questioned Pyongsan with his eyes, but he smiled as if to say there was nothing to worry about. Chilsung looked back a long time after they had passed.

Entering the courtyard of the *sarang* Kim *subang* called out, 'Master!'

'Ehm?'

Pushing aside the bamboo curtain, Chisoo looked out and saw Pyongsan, who was standing awkwardly behind the steward, his expression subdued. He stood there trying to work out whether he should go in with dignity as a gentleman, even though undistinguished, or be submissive from the beginning, acknowledging his low status, not much above that of a commoner. Stepping out on to the verandah, Chisoo went and sat down on a flower-patterned rush mat that had been put down.

'Please come up'

Unexpectedly, his tone was respectful.

'Thank you, sir.'

He instinctively bowed from the waist and cautiously stepped up on to the verandah.

'Are you well, sir?'

Unwittingly, he was being submissive.

'What can I do for you?'

'Kim *subang*, you may go,' said Chisoo to the hovering steward.

'Yes, sir.'

Looking back once more uneasily, he retreated.

'Do you know Kang *posoo*?'

'Sir?'

His face changed. The thought of how he had sold a ring for him flashed across his mind, and then he remembered how he had threatened Guinyo and made her his accomplice.

'You mean . . .'.

'I mean the man known as "a genius in the hills, and an idiot in the village." '

'Well, I know him, but what about him?'

238

'Do you know where he is now?'

Pyongsan said more calmly, 'He must be somewhere in the hills, but why do you suddenly wish to see him, may I ask?'

'I know he's in the hills.'

'So, sir?'

'If I sent someone, would they be able to find him?'

'Maybe . . . there's no reason why they shouldn't.'

'. . .'

'He has no fixed abode, but if I went with them . . .'

Pyongsan, trying to probe Chisoo's mind, watched his eyes.

'Will you try?'

'It shouldn't be too difficult. The places he goes to are obvious enough. We can try the wood carvers' huts and fire-field farmers' dugouts one by one – then we'll know his whereabouts. I found him once before in that way.'

'You see, I want to try hunting.'

'Hunting!'

Pyongsan raised his voice not so much from surprise as relief, but Chisoo, after looking at him with suspicion, turned away his eyes as if displeased.

'Yes, hunting.'

'. . .'

'I thought of having him as my teacher.'

It was said in a mocking tone, but Pyongsan was not put out by it.

'Certainly, sir. If it comes to hunting, that fellow Kang *posoo* really is the man. He's been through it all. Yes, some hunter! There's not a square foot of the hills that his feet haven't trodden.'

Pyongsan kept breaking into smiles, showing his crooked teeth. It seemed that things were unexpectedly turning in his favour.

'While I am on the subject, I can assure you no animal ever escapes his aim, once he has his eye on it. He's mad about hunting. He has no wife, no home, no children. All alone in the world, with nothing but his gun on his shoulder, he sleeps where his feet stop, eats what comes, and hasn't a worry in the world. You'd never find anyone as carefree as he is.'

'He must feel free!'

'Certainly he does. It's not that he's never set himself up with a woman, but he is so mad about hunting they won't put up with it. You know how basically women are like cats. If you don't keep stroking them, they'll run away.'

Gesticulating with hands and body, Pyongsan prattled on without a moment's pause, partly because he was coarse by nature and he was now relaxed, but he also felt an increasing upsurge of anger. Choi Chisoo's birth, his wealth, his knowledge, and his arrogance – all these became a great lump and squashed beneath it, he felt he was becoming smaller and smaller. It saddened him and made him restless.

'When will you set off?'

Pyongsan closed his babbling mouth. Unconsciously he smiled as if to apologise for his stupid prattling.

'If – if you want me to, I could even start tomorrow.'

'Would you like someone to go with you?'

'That would be even better.'

'Then go and get ready for the journey.'

He retreated from the house. He gathered up phlegm and noisily spat it out. (Me? uhm . . .) A toad waddled away near his feet. (Me? uhm . . .) If the waitress at the tavern insulted him, he just smiled. Beaten up by a gang of gamblers, after a fit of screaming, it ended there. Whenever he felt contemptuous eyes aimed at him in the village, he just snorted and that was that. But now coming out of the Choi *champan*'s house his eyes were filled with tears of sorrow.

'Bloody hell!'

He kicked the toad that was sluggishly crawling by. It fell some distance away, showing its yellowish tummy, but it soon turned over and carried on.

Guinyo was standing against the wall in a spot of shade made by the branch of a pomegranate that hung over the wall of the court-yard of the *sarang*. She closely watched his movements.

'I say!'

He raised an angry face.

'What did you come here for?' she asked as she came closely along the wall. Her large dark eyes were scrutinizing his expression with moronic intensity.

'Don't be cheeky.'

'You're speaking too loudly.'

'As loud as thunder!'

'What's the matter? As they say "Thrashed by the court, he goes home to beat his wife." '

'What?'

A wicked smile rose to his face. Lowering his voice he said, 'Chisoo wants me to go and fetch Kang *posoo*.'

'Kang *posoo*?'

Her face hardened. Pyongsan's voice was even lower.

'Don't worry, Guinyo. You are not nervous, are you? Chisoo's wife is as good as dead.'

'. . . .'

'The dead don't talk. Are you afraid the story of the rings might come out?'

'Don't talk rubbish. How many times do I have to tell you? She gave them to me.'

'Then you are worried about the fox's thing?'

She glared at him with flashing eyes.

'Ah, there's no need to be upset. As you say, that's all nonsense. I was just a bit over-excited.'

'So why does he want Kang *posoo*?'

'He wants to go hunting, though it's not clear to me whether he means animals or people.'

'Pardon?'

'He wants to have Kang *posoo* as his teacher.'

Pyongsan chuckled.

'But . . .'.

'You are worried about him is that it?'

'Who knows? He might spill it out the way a dog does with sand.'

'You'd better not concern yourself with that. It's my business as much as yours. I'll see to it that his gob is sealed as tight as a vinegar bottle.'

'If he means to go hunting . . .'.

Guinyo was thoughtful for a moment.

'It will be good fun. I think this might be a good omen.'

And as if to strengthen his determination his face became grave.

241

Chapter Twenty-One

KILSANG was running across the inner courtyard carrying a water jar when someone called to him from behind.
'Yes?'

He quickly put it down and looked round. Lady Yoon was sitting on the verandah.

'Yes, ma'am?' he repeated.

'Come here.' Though he lived in the same house, he hardly ever saw her, nor had he any occasion to address her directly. Awed, he went and stood in front of her.

'What are you carrying that for?'

'Just to sprinkle water on the *byoldang* courtyard, ma'am.'

Hands joined, he lowered his head. The ribbons on his jacket had grown short. As if that was not enough, it was shortened even more by a knot to hold a coin. It had been given to him by a guest but he felt ashamed to have it in his ribbon and feared that he might be scolded for it.

'Are you still learning to read and write?'

'Yes, ma'am.'

Startled, he looked up.

'The old master at the monastery – he was telling me that he gave you some words of advice.'

Her voice was gentle.

'Yes, ma'am.'

As he lowered his head again a red streak spread over his cheeks. Somewhere nearby the old master's voice rang out. (Do not attempt to sleep as much as others do, but read again what you've read, write again what you've written and gradually you will begin to understand the principles.) But since Kuchon had gone, he had completely forgotten about reading and writing.

'I will tell Kim *subang*. All you will have to do is to run errands at the *sarang*.'

She was silent but did not tell him to go. After a while she said, 'Let me see your face.'

He raised it. There was a tremor round his mouth. His huge eyes were brimming with tears. She closely examined his face as if she had never seen him before.

'The old master is right. You must not become a blind man with open eyes. You may go now.'

'Yes, ma'am.'

As he stiffly walked away his vision went black with excitement and tension and the feeling that her ladyship's eyes were fixed on the back of his head made him choke. With difficulty he picked up the jar and, when he was round the corner and knew that he was out of her sight, he began to run. Reaching the well without a pause, he let out his bursting breath in one go and looked up at the sky. It was blue without a spot of cloud. Dropping his eyes, he looked into the well. In the blue sky floated a face. He tossed in the bucket. The face was smashed into pieces and the sky also crumpled.

By the shed, leaning back against an A-frame, Samsoo was having a nap. The idiot boy, Gad-dongi, was stealthily crawling up to him. That Lady Yoon had called him and spoken to him personally was, for Kilsang, an event as gratifying and honourable as passing the state examinations. That was not all. That the old master still had not forgotten him and had asked her to take care of him – for the lonely Kilsang it was a measureless favour and grace.

Aiming at Samsoo's nostrils with a straw, Gad-dongi laughed to himself, drooling. His laughter seemed to make the aiming harder.

(You must not become a blind man with open eyes.)

He thought of Lady Yoon, her face and hands speckled with those dark spots that are called 'flowers of the other world' and her piercing eyes.

(I will, ma'am. I will diligently learn to read and write.)

Samsoo turned in his sleep smacking his lips. Kilsang filled the jar and ran to the *byoldang* yard. He heard sneezing followed by Samsoo shouting and then Gad-dongi crying as if he had been clouted. Under the shade of a tree Boongsoon *ne* sat on a wooden bench feeding Sohi with melon, removing the pips as she did so.

With her hair tied up to keep her cool, she was being fed in spoonfuls like a baby bird. As she ate, she kept scratching the reddish sweat spots on her forehead.

'You'll make them sore, Miss. Don't scratch them,' said Bongsoon *ne* with a frown.

People usually talk of losing weight in the summer but Bongsoon *ne*, partly because she worked in the shade, tended to put it on. Kim *subang*'s wife envied her and would say, 'Flesh as white as the inside of a gourd — "A nice plump widow" as they say, but really it is a wonder the way you put on weight in the hottest weather.'

'That will be enough for now. We don't want to upset your tummy, do we?'

Bongsoon *ne* put aside the bowl with the spoon in it, picked up a fan and, pulling out the rear edge of her jacket, sent some cool air up her sweat soaked back.

'What weather.'

After fanning herself for a while, she turned the breeze towards Sohi, watching Kilsang who was splashing water on the yard where the sun sizzled.

'Kilsang!'

'Yes.'

As he spoke, he came running towards her with the bowl in his hand.

'Look at him — as if he was going to put out a fire. Why are you in such a flutter?'

'Pardon?'

He was smiling happily.

'Why are you so happy?'

He kept on smiling.

'I called you to ask you to do something for me, but I can't think what it was now — what was it? — Oh, that's right. Go down to the village, to Yi *subang*'s.'

'Certainly. You mean Uncle Yongi?'

'M'm. Go and ask him if he can spare a minute to come and see me.'

'Yes. I'll be straight back.'

'By the way, Kilsang.'

'Yes?'

He turned.

'When is the next market day?'

'The day after tomorrow.'

'The day after tomorrow?

That's right. Let me see you go now.'

'Sure.'

When he reached the servants' quarters he heard Gad-dongi's odd sound mixed with sobs. With one hand holding up his trousers where the ribbon had come undone, he was chasing Samsoo, raising his other hand to hit him.

'Why did you start him off, only to be in trouble yourself?'

Yoni, watching as she held an empty basket, rebuked Samsoo. Samsoo pushing Gad-dongi aside, shouted, 'Me start him off? The little bastard put it up my nose . . . !'

'It serves you right for having a nap while others were working.'

'What did you say, you damned bitch?' said Samsoo as he tried to push off Gad-dongi.

'How dare you? Do you want to have a few bones cracked?'

'Why did you hit me?'

Gad-dongi clung to him doggedly. When Kilsang reached the bottom of the hill Bongsoon shot out from nowhere like a little windmill.

'Where are you going?'

'To Uncle Yongi's.'

'What for?'

'Your Mum sent me.'

'I'll go with you.'

She walked with him. Her hair also was tied up for coolness. Below her short skirt her calves were spindly like those of a stork. Whether it was a growing spell or because of the hot weather, she looked a bit thin, like a moulting chicken. They pattered down the path to the village. A cow grazing under a tree swung its tail to chase flies from its flanks and, seeing them, let out a long 'moo'. The sky was azure, from the line of hills on the other side of the river up to the brow of Dangsan. As if following a kite that had broken its string and was floating away, Kilsang, without thought for where he trod, walked on with his face turned upwards.

'Kilsang.'

'Um?'

'They say Guinyo is betwitched.'

'What?'

'They say Kuchon, too, used to go to the hills as soon as it was dark.'

'. . .'

'That was because he was bewitched as well. This time, I hear, it's Guinyo who keeps going there.'

'She goes to bathe, she told me.'

'Every day?'

'Because it's so hot.'

'No, it's because she's bewitched, that's why. Don't you see Dochul *ne* going there over and over again? They say it's because the spirits call her.'

'Who told you that?'

'Kim *subang*'s wife.'

'She's crazy.'

'When the children reached Yongi's, Kangchong *dek* was sweating away at pounding barley.

'What have you come for?'

Resting the pestle against the mortar and gathering the barley into the middle with a wooden spoon, she gave them a nasty look.

'Is uncle in?' asked Kilsang.

'He's gone to the paddy. What do you want him for?'

She exploded in anger. Kilsang flinched.

'If he has a minute to spare, could he come up to the house?'

'Who says so?'

'My mummy,' said Bongsoon, helping him out.

'What for? – to give him a prize? To praise him for becoming the sleeping-mate of that bitch?'

She never bothered to keep up the dignity of an adult.

(On the night of the play these brats came and took him off to the town, they did!)

They were an eyesore.

246

' "Birds of a feather flock together." What does she want to whisper into his ears? Is he the village layabout?'

As she lifted the pestle to resume pounding, Yongi came in for his lunch.

'What are you doing here?'

The children let out a deep breath.

'What's the matter?'

'When you have a minute to spare, can you come up to the house?'

'Who says so?'

'Bongsoon's mum.'

'I wonder why?'

Without showing the slightest sign of getting a meal ready Kangchong *dek* fiercely pounded the barley. Fortunately it was dampened or it would have been completely crushed.

'I'll come after lunch.'

Yongi sank down on a straw mat spread on the ground. A little later he went along there to see what she wanted.

'Are you going to the town on market day?'

'I haven't any particular reason to go, but . . .'

His face was gloomy.

'If you were, I have something for Wolsun.'

'What is it?'

'I've got two summer jackets ready for her. I'd be glad it you could take them . . .'

'I'll go.'

The next day he sat endlessly smoking on the bank of the paddy he had been watering. A stork stood blankly at the side of it. Whether it was dozing or meditating, it did not move. It looked as lonely as in a picture.

(It's market day tomorrow – if I go, will she avoid me again?)

Not knowing the havoc that his wife had caused, he had turned up there on the following market day to find it closed and padlocked. Worried, he had waited for her till the evening but she had not come. The next day, setting off from the village in the early evening, he had arrived after dark but, in bed, she had turned him away saying she was not well. She did not seem to want him. Not being brazen enough to question her reasons for avoiding him, he had just gone home uneasy and anxious. On his way back the night road seemed long and, as he entered the house, his despair had been so great that all its pillars seemed to be shaking. Since then, and especially over the past few days, there came more frequently from Kangchong *dek*'s lips the words, 'It's driving me mad! I'll end up by going away.'

Sometimes she also abused him, saying 'If you were dead and gone, I could live better as a widow.'

Once, he had spoken to her, even if disagreeably, and sometimes, after looking at her with pitying eyes, had comforted her, but these days he just worked on in the yard or in the fields without a word and, as for sleep, once he lay down, whether in the village pavilion or a corner of the house, that was that. Because of what she had done she knew the cause of his depression and, knowing it, was the more angry.

(It's market day tomorrow, but she might shut the shop again to avoid seeing me . . . Perhaps it would be better if I went today.)

The summer blouses from Bongsoon's mother made a good excuse for calling.

(Why should she shun me? What happened to her? Has she had enough of me? Thinking I am useless, has she given me up? Has she found another man?)

Knowing her single-minded nature, such things were impossible, inconceivable, and he would never believe them, yet he could not shake off these painful imaginings. There was hardly a woman who did not know that Kangchong *dek* had gone to the town and beaten up Wolsun, but most of the men were ignorant of it, partly because poor farmers could not be interested in other people's wives, and partly a curious trait common to all females – even those with husbands so ugly that a blind bird would not have gone to them – that they liked to tell their husbands tales of women who had gone astray but stories of erring husbands they kept to themselves. Dooman *ne*, disapproving of what Kangchong *dek* had done, once mentioned it to her husband but, not liking to interfere in other people's business, he had given Yongi no hint. Yongi came home, washed and changed, and got ready to go to town. His wife had gone out leaving the house untidy. He took a dented sickle, an axe with a blunt edge and a hoe and set off.

'Didn't I hear that tomorrow is market day?' asked Bongsoon *ne*, who was sewing when he came in.

'My tools are in a poor way, so I thought, on my way to the smithy . . .'.

He looked the other way as he spoke. Bongsoon *ne* took a bundle out of a chest and handed it over, saying 'Tell her to call in sometime, to have some sweet melons, and water melons too. And it's the peak time now for bathing in the cool water. I know she must be busy, but how is it that she never shows up, not even a shadow?'

'Probably she is afraid of causing you trouble.'

'What trouble? Food? How much can she eat? A bed – she can just sleep in my room, and her ladyship occasionally asks after her, perhaps when she thinks of her dead mother.'

Coming out of the Choi house, he carried straight on, and as he caught the ferry half way he arrived in the town earlier than he had expected. As he stepped off the boat, his mind was disturbed for no apparent reason. He had the feeling that something had happened.

(I might see something awful.) The picture of Wolsun with another man floated before his eyes.

(Never – it is not possible. I know her through and through. Mountain and rivers may change but not her.)

A long cherished thought welled up – to run off somewhere with her.

(Kuchon went off taking even the wife of his Master. My wife will get on all right without me, won't she?)

But there was something that stuck in his throat like a fish bone.

(You must never ill treat your lawfully married wife. How a woman fares depends on her man. Lead her, teaching her what she does not know.)

This was what his mother had said to him when, after his marriage, he was fretful and unable to love Kangchong *dek*. Even as she breathed her last, she had told him not to ill treat the wife whose duty it would be to carry the sacrificial table for his parents.

(If I go, who will observe the anniversaries of their deaths?)

249

Tears rose in his eyes. The smithy was in a quiet spot by the road side, just short of the tavern. As it was not market day it was not busy. Ok *subang*, the owner, greeted him, 'It's a long time since I saw you.'

'Keeping busy?'

'Not really.'

'Would you like to have a look at my tools?'

'Of course . . . what's it like this year?'

'What do you mean?'

'The crops.'

'I won't know until I get into the paddy with the sickle in my hand, will I?'

'That's true. How can you guess how much God will give?'

Puffing pipe smoke through his sparse beard, he glanced up at the dusty scene outside.

'I've got a call to make. Can you do them while I'm gone?'

Carrying the bundle, he went to Wolsun's. As on the last market day, there was a padlock on the gate.

(A wasted journey again – where can she have gone?)

He shook the gates wildly. With only a padlock they should not be so firm. Stooping, he looked closely and saw they were nailed up. Alarmed, he called.

'Wolsun!'

There could be no answer.

'Wolsun!'

He shouted loudly, but as it was not market day, there was hardly anyone in sight in the quiet street. He felt that she must be waiting in one of the side alleys and, if he searched, he would find her. He began to wander through the town and lost count of how many times he had been round. He had walked the same paths and stood in front of the oil-seller's shop many times over. Then he ran back to her house like a madman.

'Wolsun!'

After shaking the nailed-up gates, he turned his blurred eyes towards the street. 'Where could she have gone? To the temple? Not only padlocked, but nailed . . .'

An old woman hawker came along, carrying her goods in a

hamper on her head, a familiar face from market days. At other times she went from house to house.

'Granny!'

'What, dear?'

'Do you know the hostess here, the one called Wolsun?'

'I know her by sight.'

'Then, do you know where she's gone? Have you heard anything?'

'Yes, there was something. Did I hear she went off with a ginseng trader from Kangwon-do?'

'What?'

'I think they said she'd caught the eye of a ginseng trader from Kangwon-do and gone off with him.'

'With a Kangwon-do ginseng man? No, it can't be!'

'I don't even know who he is, but that's what they say.'

The old woman closely watched his face as it turned as white as paper.

'Could it be true?'

'True or not, that's what they all say. Why? Did you lend her some money or something?'

Familiar with the ways of the world, the old woman's watery eyes seemed to say, 'You gutless fellow – what's the use of thinking about a girl who's gone off with another man?'

'Money? No, nothing like that.'

He tried to force a smile but it only distorted his face. The old woman put down her hamper, sat down in front of the tavern and took out a pipe.

'If you've got any tobacco, give me a fill.'

As he tipped his pouch into her palm, his hand trembled. Spitting on the tobacco to dampen it, she said, 'So the girl has thrown you over?'

'No, not that either.'

As he said it his eyes became tearful.

'I know it all. When a big strong fellow like you has tears in his eyes – you can't deny it.'

Like a crow pecking at a corpse, she pecked at his sorrow and laughed.

251

'Love – it's an awful thing.'

Lighting her pipe, she sucked hard. In her shrunken gums there must have been some teeth left. With the sound of them clicking against her pipe, she said, 'It's best to forget about it, and you're bound to as time passes. Life goes on, one way or another, until all that's left in front of you is the graveyard – it's only for a short time when you are young that these things seem to be a matter of life and death. In my youth, I floated about like a cloud in places of entertainment, getting the price for my looks but, thanks to a wretched love affair, I fell to this. You can't tie your heart down with a string, can you? So forgetting is the cure, and once you get old it's all nothing. If you don't want to be hard up in your old age, it's money you need, not a woman or a man. As the old saying goes, "Walk with your son in front of you and you're hungry, but walk with a silver coin tied to your belt and you aren't." With money you can appease even angry spirits or the souls of your ancestors.'

Yongi, who had stood looking at her vacantly while she mumbled on with tears trickling from her eyes, said, 'It's not like that,' and quickly walked away. As he went, his trembling legs seemed about to fold up and give way.

(Wicked woman! Heartless girl . . .)

He just managed to reach the smithy.

'Are they ready?'

Ok *subang*, who had been hammering a piece of metal, put it on to the fire and said, 'It needs beating once more.'

While waiting for it to redden the smith thumped his own back. Drops of sweat fell from the face of the youngster who was working the bellows.

'It's impossible – hugging the fire all the time in the height of summer . . .'

Stopping short, Ok *subang* asked, 'Why is your face like that?'

'Like what?'

'Like a man with stomach cramp – it's as white as paper. Are you in pain? Have you been robbed? You weren't like that earlier on, were you?'

'Yes, I've been robbed.'

252

Looking out on to the road, he said whatever came to him. The old woman with her hamper on her head could be seen walking towards a village at the foot of the hill. With the dry weather, white dust was rising.

'How much have you lost?'

'A thousand.'

'You're crazy . . .'

'In value, it would be ten thousand, a hundred thousand . . .'

In the middle of this his voice faded. Whatever the smith might be saying, in Yongi's ears there was only the sound of the wind. It was not really windy, but all that he was hearing was the sound of it. As he picked up the finished tools tied with string and came out of the forge, he walked back into the quiet market square and went into a tavern. Two rough-looking men sat sprawled. Like a man dying of thirst, he drank the cup of wine that the hostess offered at one gulp and asked for another. He heard her talking with one of the men.

'He's not much of a character, but he's all right.'

'I hear he's a ginseng trader?'

'That's what they say. If he's the one who comes every year, I must know him. Apparently he's elderly, so I don't know how they'll get on. The girl never was very sociable, or very glamorous. Anyway, she's gone and I won't lose by it, but I feel somehow glad and sorry at the same time.'

'Huh, really. I had my eye on her, but "Above the one that leaps is one that flies." '

The man looked up at her from his reclining position and laughed.

'Don't you want to sell anything?'

Yongi struck the table. He gulped down a second cup, threw down a coin and went out. As he entered the village he met Dori. Thrusting the bundle foward, he said, 'Please take this to Bongsoon's mother and tell her that I couldn't deliver it.'

'What is it?'

'She'll know. Just tell her the place was locked up and there was nobody there.'

He turned towards his house. Once there, he threw the tools in

253

the shed and went into the room. Kangchong *dek*'s piercing voice rang out but he just hung his clothes on the wall and collapsed into bed.

Chapter Twenty-Two

AS Dr Mun came up to the broad shade of the hardy orange tree the river breeze on this higher ground was more refreshing. He dismounted lightly, not like an old man. Though he had set off at dawn, seven miles in the height of summer had dampened the back of his hemp coat. While the donkey was being tethered, Kim *subang* came out and bent at the waist to greet him.

'Isn't it hot?'

'Yes, indeed.'

As he entered the inner quarters, Lady Yoon, sitting in the large hall, rose to her feet. Probably because of her yellowish clothes, her face looked sallow and a little swollen. She invited him in. After he had left them, Kim *subang* turned the doctor's shoes round so that they faced the front, joined his hands to announce his retreat and left.

'How are you these days? My respectful greetings.'

After the salutation, he examined her face with thoughtful eyes.

'You've had a hard time coming to see me on such a hot day.'

It was cool in the hall and at the rear the back garden could be seen through the open door. As if it were exempted from the drought, there came from the trees a breeze laden with refreshing scent and moisture. He opened a heavy, bamboo-ribbed fan and slowly fanned himself. There was a long silence. At last, folding the fan, he said, 'You don't look very well.'

'It must be the weather, I suppose.'

'You must try and keep calm.'

'. . .'

'So, why did you send for me?'

'Well,' and after a short pause, she added, 'Are you intending to set off for Yon-gok monastery today?'

'If there is nothing to keep me here, I will go at once.'

'I sent for you because I feel so oppressed . . .'

255

'If you look at it that way, there's no end to it. All the suffering of the past is like a dream, and so will the suffering of the present be, when it's over. You must endure it.'

'You have always told me that, doctor.'

'And won't I say it yet again tomorrow?'

She lifted her eyes and gave him a sharp look, eyes that had been respectful but were now full of hostility, giving out a bluish light as if aimed at an enemy. There followed a silent exchange of thoughts.

(I have already been offered as a sacrifice to the Buddha – how can this life go on so long? Are you going to say that I still have more to expiate?)

(Lady, your suffering is the suffering of all human beings. Do you think it is yours alone?)

Dr Mun calmly took in her hostile glance.

(Between you, you have hung my life high on a tree beyond my reach. And then you all think that there is no other way out of it but to pay for my sin. I still have to punish myself, is that what you are saying?)

(Lady, what is the name of your sin? It is a sin because you think it is, can't you see that? But let it be. The point is that you can't die when you wish to – that is what it means to be human. Even if life is more painful than death itself, you have to go on living. One thing I have learned through seventy years of life as a doctor is that human life is a precious thing – not only one's own but others' as well. As for sin, everyone is a sinner, and if it has to be paid for, one has to pay. If a man dies when he should live, that is a dog's death; if he who should die lives on, it is only as an animal, not a human being.)

(That's right. I deserve death and carry on like this, so I am an animal.)

(The poor animal has nothing to pay. You have no sin. The past is an illusion. Endure, you must endure the present.)

(I am a sinner in mind. I have a wicked mind. I deserve even greater punishment than what I suffer in this life. I deserve death, I deserve to fall into hell and be hung upside down.)

Turning his gaze to the back yard, Dr Munn asked, 'The one in the *sarang*, is he all right?'

'Yes.'

All expression had gone from her face and she went on in a level tone.

'He says he is going hunting.'

'Hunting?'

Dr Mun turned his face back.

'Yes, he has even sent someone to Seoul to find a rifle.'

Cicadas could be heard. They cried as if to tear the summer day into shreds.

'That's a ridiculous idea.'

'. . . .'

'With his weak constitution, wouldn't it be as bad as taking poison?'

Samwol brought in bowls of fruit salad and the conversation stopped. Sensing the tense atmosphere, she was embarrassed, and after putting down the bowls she hastily retreated. Lady Yoon mumbled, 'Obstinacy . . .'.

'Obstinacy or no obstinacy, whose idea was it?'

'The man from Seoul, that second cousin of his, must have recommended it.'

'That unwelcome guest has started off more trouble, has he?'

'He's not the sort of man to be influenced by others. I suspect there must be some other reason.'

Her face turned white and began to twitch.

'I am sure he intends to search him out.'

Her voice was low. Dr Mun's face also changed colour. There lasted between them a long and heavy, a measureless silence.

'How could he? As basically a man of discernment, he must know it is not a time to pursue private affairs.'

His voice was low, and it sounded weak.

'If he'd been thinking like that, would he have let a year go by? He wouldn't suddenly do such a thing now. Jamg-am *sonseng* would not allow him to.'

Despite his repeated negations, Dr Mun's face showed anxiety.

'I am nine-tenths convinced of that, too. But he seems to be bringing in a hunter called Kang who is well acquainted with the hills. He is that kind of person – from childhood he has always

257

been unpredictable. Besides, he has a nature that never forgets an insult, however trifling.'

No one could have imagined Lady Yoon's face so agitated: it was truly pitiful.

'It's useless to lament the past – but when Kuchon came to the doorstep of this house, you made a mistake, ma'am.'

'He came to lash me, and I thought that I shouldn't avoid it. I had made up my mind to face up to anything that might come.'

'That child has no reason to lash you.'

'. . . .'

'A monk without a tonsure, a warrior without armour . . . an idiot.'

He remembered Ugwan's lament.

' "A monk without a tonsure, a warrior without armour" . . . what exactly does it mean?'

After thinking a moment, he said, 'Anyway, I am on my way to Yon-goksa. I will see Ugwan and talk about Hwani's circumstances. Please don't worry too much.'

She had managed to hold back her tears to the last moment. As he rose to go the doctor mumbled as if to himself, 'His father, Haewol, has been executed.'

She betrayed no feelings: in no time at all her face had regained its usual stiff expression.

After calling at the *sarang* and exchanging brief greetings with Chisoo, he was about to step out of the gate. Outside, Dori had put the saddle on the ass and waited for him to appear when there came an urgent call,

'Sir – Excuse me, sir!'

'Oh, it's you *halmum*. Are you better these days?'

Without answering this question, she said, 'I have something to tell you.'

Both Gannan *halmum* and Dr Mun looked about them. Kim *subang* had already gone out of the gate to see him off from there and there was no one in the courtyard by the middle gate. Lowering her voice, she said, 'Sir, it's about Master Hwani.'

'Tell me.'

'Somebody has seen him carrying the *byoldang* lady on his back.'

258

'Where was it?'

'She did not know the name of the place, but it was on her way back from Kangchong in the Haman area.'

'When was that?'

'Last spring. I could not tell her ladyship. When I heard it my heart was breaking – she said they were like the beggars of all beggars.'

'I see.'

Dr Mun slowly went out of the gate, mounted the mule and departed amidst Kim *subang*'s farewells. As he jolted away on the donkey under the scorching sun he repeated the words he had said to himself earlier on about Gannan – 'She lives long!'

Dori walked with the reins, his eyes on the river to watch out for an empty ferry going upstream.

'The suffering of the past is like a dream, so will the suffering of the present be when it's over. You must endure.'

These were the words he had spoken to Lady Yoon. If he could call the seventy years of his past life a dream, it had been indeed a long dream. Through those seventy years, fifty as a medical man, he had witnessed numberless deaths of all kinds. Apart from those who had died because the medicine was ineffective, or of old age, and those who fell in epidemics, he had seen people who had died in years of famine, in popular uprisings, and violent deaths during the turmoil of the Dong Hak rebellion and the martyrdom of the Catholics.

His connection with the Choi *champan*'s house, strictly speaking, with Lady Yoon, had begun with a death that he had watched over. In January 1866, in the third year of King Kojong's reign, out of the blue, a fierce whirlwind had sprung up, in which nine French Catholic priests and several Korean believers were executed. This gale grew and swept the whole country. The persecution of Catholics carried out in local towns at the instigation of the Regent's mother was a large-scale blood-letting, cruel and ruthless, in which the number of the dead was guessed at between eight and twenty thousand. In retaliation a fleet of seven French warships had attacked Kangwha Island, but the landing force was chased away by an army of Korean hunters. This incident, called the 'Byong-In-Yang-Yo,

(Disturbance by Westerners in the year Byong-In) had inflamed the public with anti-Western feeling, spurring on the process of uprooting the Catholics. Bloodshed always tends to turn the public into a blind mob, while private vengeance and plunder are crimes common in carrying out orders from above. It had been no exception in this case – numberless innocent people had lost their lives. In the following year Lady Yoon's paternal home in Namwon had been destroyed, a tragedy in which the whole family had been massacred, except for her father, Yoon Ik-ro. The only survivor, he had been brought to his daughter's married home in the middle of the night, carried on the back of his simple and honest servant Pansul (now Kim *subang*). The old man, near to death, had refused to the last to betray his belief and, blaming Pansul for carrying him away, had almost starved himself, until he had breathed his last under the eyes of his widowed daughter and Dr Mun.

He was awakened from his reverie by Dori. 'Sir Our mistress – is she seriously ill?'

'You're anxious?'

'Yes, very much, sir. I hope she will live long – she is the mainstay of the house.'

'Don't worry yourself.'

'The colour of her face is truly . . .'.

'It's because she has more worries than any of you.'

'I know. This year she seems suddenly to have got older . . . that damned man has done real damage by going off like that.'

'. . .'.

'His sin deserves death. Every time I see the young miss . . .'.

The doctor did not say anything, so Dori also shut his mouth. To this day the doctor could not forget the dagger-like eyes of the woman of over twenty years ago. Her eyes were truly like knives with which she could extinguish her own life or others. In a room where the dusk was gathering, she had been lying with her eyes closed, as if dead. Not even a strand of hair stirred. A mosquito had buzzed past his ear. (The pulse of a pregnant woman!) Her mother-in-law had anxiously observed the doctor, who had betrayed his feeling of shock. He once again heard the buzzing behind his ear. She told a servant girl, 'Light the lamp.'

She lay still as before. The light flickered across the room and the mother's shadow flickered with it.

'She seems to have been affected by the heat. Besides, her nerves are very weak. A quiet place . . . I would recommend her to go somewhere quiet to rest.'

At that moment, the woman opened her eyes wide. Dagger eyes were directed at his forehead. He tried to face them out with his own. But hers became sharper, piercing him.

(Why are you telling a lie?)

Her mother-in-law, who seemed to be shocked by the words 'nerves are very weak,' was in a flutter.

'Since she came back from the hundred days' prayer . . .'.

It seemed that, naturally, she was recalling her son who had died after eating venison, following her prayers at the monastery, and wondering whether unawares they had again done something remiss after the prayers. But above all she was frightened by the strange look on the doctor's face. As he had stepped down into the courtyard of the *byoldang*, the then steward's wife (Gannan *halmum*) had stood back with an awkward air as she looked at him with scared eyes. Lady Cho, the mother-in-law, walked in front of him with precise steps and, when he was about to go through the *byoldang* gate, Gannan *halmum* had come close and then started and stepped back again. Sensing this, he had turned round and seen her imploring eyes piercing him.

'What is it?' he had asked with his eyes. The next moment, tears were falling from hers.

'Please save her. Please save my mistress.'

He had briefly dropped his eyes and turned away without reply. It had been too late for him to go back to the town, so he had stayed in the *sarang*. He could in no way fall asleep. (What a strange affair!) From the room across the hall had come the sound of the twelve-year-old master, Chisoo, reading aloud till late. (How can it be possible?) He turned over but still could not sleep. Instead the woman's eyes with daggers in them floated before his eyes.

(Don't I know her character – as straight as bamboo!)

A mosquito buzzed. The terrible tension, earlier, in the *byoldang* came to him. Meanwhile, the sound of reading had ceased. A silence as if the whole world had disappeared, except for the call of a nightingale from afar.

(And the steward's wife . . . with tears in her eyes. What was she weeping for?)

However hard he tried, he could not solve the enigma. He had been at a loss to know how to deal with what lay ahead.

'Sir, sir.'

The subdued voice of a man. The doctor had sprung up.

'Who is it?'

'It's only me, sir. Bawoo.'

Drawing back the curtain he had looked out to see the steward with his head lowered.

'What's the matter at this time of the night?'

'There is something that I ought to tell you.'

'Come in.'

'No, no. I'm all right here.'

'Come in. There are too many mosquitoes about.'

'If I can be so bold . . .'.

'Come on, man. You just said you had something to tell me, didn't you?'

He came in almost crawling. Purposely Dr Mun did not light the lamp. His head hung low, he did not speak, nor did the doctor urge him. When he opened his mouth after a long while, it was with a trembling voice, 'Please save our mistress.'

'. . .'.

'If anything happens to her, this house will be ruined.'

'I realize that, too.'

'Who else is there? Her ladyship is advanced in age, and the master still so young.'

'I know.'

'She is not to blame. We know what she is like. She was going to hang herself in the mountain at the time.'

'. . .'.

'My wife and myself, we had to watch her day and night. How on earth could it be so unfair?'

He had wept unconstrainedly. Usually a poor speaker, and a man

262

of few words, he went on after his tears, 'I would give my own life if it could save hers – my life is worth nothing.'

'Tell me what happened.'

'I daren't tell you that myself, how could I?'

'. . .'.

'Chonum monastery, Ugwan *sunim* . . .'.

'What?'

Dr Mun's eyes flashed.

'What did he do?'

'No, not him. Go to him and you will find out what I daren't tell you. He knows about it. He should be told of the present situation . . . and I hear that you are a close friend of his.'

The next day he had gone to the Chonum-sa, where the abbot Ugwan then was. What he had learned there had been a shocking story. The man who had raped Lady Yoon, there for a 'Hundred Days' Prayers', was none other than Kim Gaejoo, 'Hae-wol' by pen-name, the brother of Ugwan. From a middle-class family, Gaejoo had been an ambitious youth whom Dr Mun had loved dearly, so the shock was unbearable. Apparently, he had happened to be at his brother's for a rest at the same time as Lady Yoon.

'He deserves death! I had no idea he was as rotten as that.'

Ugwan had sat with his eyes closed.

'Where is he now? Tell me where that rascal is!'

'Do you think he'd stay on here after committing a sin?' Ugwan had spoken calmly.

Already the donkey was passing the square at Hwagae. As it was not market day, it was quiet. The roadside taverns too were all empty.

'Sir!'

'What is it?'

'This beast – I think I ought give it some water.'

'Of course. Do.'

He dismounted in front of a tavern. He was thirsty himself, so he asked them for a bowl of water. Dori, having tied the donkey under a tree, was giving it a drink. Inside the shop were two youngish men with a scholarly air, probably having lunch. Not being a drinker, the doctor sat on the wooden bench outside and

263

spread his bamboo-ribbed fan. The sound of low voices flowed out from inside.

'There's no other way. I am sick of living like this. I must bid farewell to the ancestors' shrine, pack up and get out of this place. Go to the land of the Japs and, whether by begging from house to house or in the street . . . What hope is there? Talking of ruin, how could a country be more thoroughly ruined?'

'Everyone running about just to save his own life, and to die for a just cause is regarded as nothing more than a drop of blood in a bird's leg – the world has come to this! When I think about it, I feel like going to Kwangwha-mun Square to cut open my stomach, pull out my guts and die, but . . .'.

'It's too late now.'

'That's right, it's too late – like an octopus with its tentacles all cut off. When I was leaving Seoul this time, I heard that ruffian Ahn Kyong Soo has run off to Japan.'

'Why?'

'He was found plotting to remove the king or something like that.'

'Coward!'

'A spy of the Japs! That villain, one year he helped their soldiers to climb over the walls of the palace and, thanks to that, he was given a post, so now he has nowhere else to go, has he?'

'Then, the next year, the year of the queen's assassination, he tried to stop the Japanese mob climbing over the palace wall.'

'That's why, even with the title of Minister of the Army, he had to run away – well, I suppose, he's not the only one of that sort, is he, who'd "run with the fox and hunt with the hounds?" In the name of putting the country right, the bastards of the Enlighten-ment drew the Japs into the palace, on the slightest pretext, as if it were their own *sarang*, and the best they could do was to be their cat's-paws – what else have they done? Reform, eh? Huh, huh, huh . . . If the Keep-the-Old-Ways Party are plump pigs who have sucked up the fat and blood, the Enlightenment Party are the running dogs of the Japs, aren't they? Huh, huh, huh. . . .'

'Ha, ha, ha . . .'

The two young scholars gave a hollow laugh.

(To think that I am seventy years old.) Dr Mun closed his fan and rose from the bench.

Chapter Twenty-Three

SETTING off on a donkey held by Samsoo who, though a servant, had the neat look and the dignified air of one who belonged to a great family, Pyongsan had no reason whatsoever to feel disagreeable. He had plenty of money for the journey. Because of the drought the wind carried sandy dust, but it was a clear day without a cloud in the sky. The jingling of the horse-bell echoed over the fields. Ruffled by the wind, the river glimmered with ripples.

The moment he was out of the gate, he threw away the thought that he was on an errand for Choi Chisoo and, as if an elegant sightseer on a tour of the provinces, he stretched out his thick neck and held up his chin, displaying the fine air of a gentleman as though he had regained his lost dignity.

(Once I read some of the classics, but how futile learning is! Twenty years since I opened a book – alas, I am as good as blind.) He was despised as 'a dog-legged gentleman', with no chance at all of entering the state examinations, but riding a donkey and leading a servant seemed to make him realize that study was one of the essentials of such rank. He had never regretted his ignorance, nor thought highly of Kim *hunjang* with his reputation for learning.

(Does she think she's a lady of an illustrious family? Cheeky woman. Learning? What bloody learning! – like an egg to a dog's foot. Forget where you belong and you don't live a full life.) It was not because he was jealous of her that he would curse his wife as she taught their sons to read and to write. It was presumptuous of her, as a woman from the middle class. He had a firm sense of the distinction between middle class and gentry and a tenacious belief in his superiority over his wife. It probably explained his strong sense of inferiority in regard to Choi Chisoo. At any rate, he was in a very good mood and because of that he remembered his childhood when swaying from the waist he had recited before the teacher, and felt sorry that he had stopped reading the classics.

The journey was a slow affair. Whenever they passed a village tavern he would tell Samsoo to stop. Admittedly the hot weather must have been a hardship for anyone so fat, but the inability to pass a wine shop without calling in seemed to be becoming a habit. Whenever they entered, he was received politely, as a gentleman, and not as a gambler. Though his face was an odd shape, his complexion was good, and somewhere in his body, which had never laboured, a touch of aristocracy remained, while his husky voice greatly reduced the repulsive impression given by his gross form. Apart from his own presence, no doubt Samsoo's dignified manner as the well-trained servant of a great family earned him more respect. This was an area where, when the Dong Hak rebellion had swept by, it was said that the severed heads of the gentry had dropped like leaves in an autumn wind, yet among the people an almost instinctive fear of them still remained. After he had left, they might gossip about his odd shaped face, and so on, but in his presence the serving girls treated him kindly while the customers, glancing at each other, offered him their seats.

As he shook the soil off his socks by the roadside, Samsoo would now and again look up at him scornfully. (H'm, 'Thanks to the Governor, he can show off!' as they say. He's having a good time.)

When it was near sunset Pyongsan ordered him to go in the direction of Gurae.

'Pardon?'

'I said, let's go to Gurae.'

'You mean go there instead of to the hills?'

'I might be able to get some information – that's why. I might even find him there in the market tomorrow. Anyway, we'll go there first and decide.'

There was an uncertain look on his face, but Samsoo did as he was told. As soon as they arrived, Pyongsan settled into an inn by the market. It bustled with traders from all over the place gathered for the market on the morrow. The hostess had a large purse dangling from her shapeless waist. After they had handed over the donkey and entered a room just large enough to stretch their legs,

Pyongsan leaned back against the wall and wiped the sweat from his brow.

'Open the window.'

Samsoo angrily pushed open the window on the mottled back-wall.

'Samsoo!'

'What is it now?'

'You are too simple-minded. We haven't got any fixed date. It's a good excuse, isn't it? We take it easy and have a good time and then go back. What's wrong with that?'

'. . .'

'It's for the sake of an old friendship that I'm treating you like this.'

'What friendship?'

'With your father, I mean.'

Samsoo's face changed colour.

'I knew him well, though he was four or five years older than me . . . There's no reason for you to wear yourself out working for the Choi house. I'm not trying to tell you what to do. It's just that your grandfather, though his loyalty was matchless, in the end he hanged himself, and your father – he lived in sorrow.'

Not a word came from Samsoo. These were things he already knew.

Outside it was noisy. Someone was bawling, 'How can such a thing be possible between host and guest?' while the pattering feet of the servants could be heard as they carried meal tables in and out. Pyongsan took off his hat, headband and coat and, as he hung them on the wall, he smiled as if excited by the noise outside.

'We'll enjoy ourselves here tonight, and go on in a leisurely way tomorrow – then all will be well. Even your boss couldn't expect us to bring Kang *posoo* back at once, a man who scuttles about like a mountain crab.'

Samsoo was still silent but on his face the look of scorn for Pyongsan had lessened. Having declined supper, Pyongsan sat out in the hall drinking with the look of a man with no worries. Going about as a gentleman was all very well, but he couldn't do without the fun of cards. In a gambling den, there was no distinction between commoners and gentlemen; indeed, the clothes and style of the gentry were, if any thing a hindrance.

Lifting his cup of wine and recovering from his fatigue, he was now waiting for the time when the game would begin. In a corner some traders and a farmer with the look of a landowner were engaged in an argument. At first sight it looked as if the traders from Cholla Province and Kyongsang Province were quarrelling over some account, but it was not that – the argument was about the rights and wrongs of the now-deceased Prince Regent and Queen Min.

'Huh, really. Just think about it. Certainly she was a woman – she wore a skirt all right, but no ordinary woman. It's true – if it was an ordinary family, it was her father-in-law, but it was no ordinary family matter, was it, eh? It was a national affair. Then this crazy old man – he leads the Japs into killing the mother of the country. Is that right? Just think about it. It shows what a clever woman she was for the Japs to want to kill her, how brave she'd been when everyone else was feeble and crawling before them. However much power is a good thing, how could he go to the palace riding on the backs of those Japanese dogs? Whatever may have passed between the two of them, even in an ordinary family you can't give away your daughter-in-law. How could he hand her over to the bloody Japs in that way? Even if you had ten mouths, you wouldn't have one word to say. How could you, even if it's only for the sake of the country's dignity.'

The speaker rolled his big eyes.

'H'm, who was it, then, that handed her father-in-law over to the Chinese bastards?' retorted a Kyongsang Province man.

'True, but that's different. As for China, they have been from ancient times our Big House, haven't they? – not to be compared with those dirty dogs, the Japs. The old man went to China and had a good time and came back safely, didn't he, eh? In the old days the Japs had to bend the knee before us. Then they took what we wear for mourning and made their ordinary clothes out of it – what ignorant people to copy mourning dress of all things! Our Great Monk Sa-myong, a long time ago, beat them with a magic trick. He could have dried up the seeds of the whole lot of them.

These dog-like barbarians, wearing clogs and naked except for a loin cloth – even if the Queen committed a hundred sins, how could he do such a thing? How could he let them trample their clogs over the palace where the king, his own son, was living, and join the plot to kill his daughter-in-law? It was the same thing as selling the country to the Japs – of course it was.'

'However much you get in a sweat calling them dogs, it's no help. "The strong and the weak are not equals," as they say. The Japs have beaten China . . . so! You can't depend on China any more . . . it's like an old barn. From ancient times it's the rule that "When the hen crows the house falls", and when a woman's voice is heard outside its walls, there's no more hope for that family!'

'You're hopeless! Are you trying to say that it's the queen who's ruined the country? That's not even partly true. Who was it that gathered all the people to build a great palace, and raked in taxes until they were bleeding, regardless of whether they starved or froze? Was it a monk from Chiri mountain? Or just when the country needed them, left the soldiers to starve?'

'Huh, I don't see how you can say that. Who was it that, while her soldiers were starving, was floating basin after basin of white rice off on the water, until eventually they threw her out? Day and night, in the name of religious devotion, she called in shamans and did such wicked things – no wonder the country was ruined.'

Pyongsan, who had been quietly listening to them as he drank, joined in: 'Listen to me all of you. Whether you turn it this way or that, it's all out of the same box, so why make such a noise about it? When even scholars who have never known how to do anything but hold a pen rise up from every corner to avenge the Mother of the Nation, how can you talk such rubbish? If you've got nothing better to do, just lie down quietly and count the beams across the ceiling. Why do you get so excited? "Stroking the genitals of a dead son" as they say. What's the point of arguing the rights and wrongs of people who are already decaying under the earth? Though it's true that the day does go on too long, it stretched out like a stick of toffee . . .'

'But, sir . . .'.

270

One of the Cholla-do traders twitched his mouth as if he would speak.

'None of you has anything to get angry about or to worry about. As the saying goes, "Better a live dog than a dead prime minister." What does it matter to you whether it was the Mother of the Nation or the Prince Regent? Leave it to them whether they pound the rice or simmer the porridge – there's no need for you to worry yourselves with the country's affairs. Even people like cabinet ministers or judges take one side today and another tomorrow – it's that kind of world. Are you all dependent on pensions from the government? Why do you have to worry, if they don't?'

'That may be so, sir. But how can we help worrying – aren't we people who live by tilling the king's land?'

'The king's land? The land was given to us by Heaven, and the strong ones are the ones who own it.'

'In our village, Guksae is a giant, strong enough to pick up a sack of rice with one hand, but he is a servant without an acre of land.'

'Man, do you think strength is only physical? The man with cunning is the real strong one. Hwangwoo, the world's strongest general, failed to gain the world, but the trickster Jo-Jo got it.'

'But, sir, even if we are as nimble as Jang-Bi, as cunning as Jo-Jo, or as strong as Hangwoo, the king's land is still the king's land, that's what I mean.'

'What a stupid man! Did I tell you to do anything? All I said was to carry on digging and eating as usual. Whichever side you are on, whether the queen's or the Prince Regent's, China's or Japan's, it won't win you one extra bowl of rice – that's what I mean.'

'But, sir, how can you imagine a people without a country, or children without ancestors? You can't have a tree without a root. We people live in village corners digging the ground so we don't know whether the world is turning round in the right way or the wrong, but we hear a rumour that the Japs are going to swallow up our country – that's what worries us. That's why these stories of the prince and the queen crop up. It's also for this reason, isn't it, that the scholars are raising "Armies of Justice" all over the place?"

The farmer who spoke looked Pyongsan up and down with eyes that said, 'He doesn't look like a commoner, yet he is not even up to the likes of us poor worthless people – what a gentleman!'

Pyongsan snorted.

'Scholars who don't know how to use anything but brushes, with bones like bird's legs – what can they do? Whatever kind of world it becomes, it will be the same – the tummies of the stupid will rumble while those of the cunning ones' burst. It all depends on your own ability. Frothing at the mouth in a tavern won't change the world.'

'That's enough. It's the king's job to look after the country – there's no need for you to quarrel.'

Waving her hands, the hostess tried to quieten them.

Late in the night, Pyongsan stealthily slipped out. Chilsung had been a different matter, but he was perhaps reluctant to drag the young Samsoo to a gambling place, so he went by himself.

'Wherever he goes, he can't give up his habits, I suppose.'

In the dim lamplight, Samsoo lit his pipe.

'It makes me sick. If the master finds out he'll have a fit.'

But he had no intention of reporting it.

'It shows he has some decency. Shouldn't he at least get the credit for pushing the bloody bundle of his own child on to the doorstep to make up for what he owes.' Samsoo remembered how, when he was a child, the grown-ups used to speak sarcastically about his run-away father. As the price of the sins of his grandfather and his father, he had grown up worse off than a puppy. Whenever he thought about it he felt rage flaring up against the father who had run away and left him. Pyongsan had brought up this parent of his. There was indeed no reason for him to be grateful or pleased about that but, for some mysterious reason that he could not understand himself, he was inclined to side with Pyongsan a little, and to overlook his faults. He did not know whether it was because he felt sorry for himself sitting alone under a dim lamp in a strange inn, or because he felt resentful toward the Choi *champan* house for this sad fate.

They stayed in the Gurae tavern for two nights. On the one hand, Samsoo was worried and angry about stopping, not only for one night, but for two, while, on the other, he was tasting the pleasures of freedom. He was still a servant but, as Pyongsan was not his master, he did not have to be so attentive, while their difference of status meant that he did not have to compete with him. Besides, it was quite pleasant to look down on him when, involved in gambling, he became contemptible.

Samsoo had drinks bought for him. He could have a nap as often as he liked, and with the few pence given to him as pocket money he enjoyed roaming the market. That was not all. On their way back, Pyongsan said he would buy him a woman.

After staying two nights, they left the tavern early. They passed the market place and went on to the path through the fields. After leading the mule by the reins for some time, Samsoo took a quick backward glance.

'What are you laughing at?'

Sitting on the mule, Pyongsan was smiling happily to himself.

'Well, it's nice, isn't it? Not too hot, as it's early. The breeze is nice, too,' he said evasively.

'Will we be able to find him today?'

'Look, man, do you think he is waiting for us with a feast?'

'The master has a frightful temper you know.'

'Whether we crawl or run, if we finally get there, that's all that matters, isn't it?'

'What will we do if he is angry?'

'Who with?'

'. . .'

'Do you think my body is tied to him? How can he be angry with me?'

'Perhaps you're right.'

'Don't be too frightened. The full moon must wane. Even in the palace at Seoul, fists are close at hand and the law far way. In a situation like this, what's so great about a local landlord? At the time when the Dong Hak riot was at its height, there were certain gentry who were scared, and had secret dealings with them and helped them, and I know who they are.'

273

He seemed to be referring to the rumour that the Choi family had been associated with the Dong Hak, but, as he had no definite proof, he did not go so far as to mention a name. He suddenly gave a roar of laughter. Samsoo looked back at him again.

'I'm thinking about a cat.'

'. . .'

'A rascal of a cat. To a mouse, a cat is the king of Hell, isn't it?' After this commonplace observation, he chuckled loudly.

'In the town there was an old couple I knew. They kept a cat as if it had been their own child. At the new year festival this thoughtless pair fed it with a sticky rice cake which must have made it sick. It seemed to be in the throes of death. At this moment, a mouse came running out. Fearless, it ran round and round the cat – it was really a funny sight – and the old woman was trying to chase it away brandishing a stick and saying, "You vile creature – how dare you go on like this while he's still alive!" Wasn't it natural? How could he help being in high spirits when his enemy was sinking?'

Samsoo gave a slight chuckle too.

'Is it only animals that are like that? Its even more so with people. The power of the gentry is now just like that of the cat. There's no reason for the mice to live in fear of them.'

'The master from Seoul said something like that. When we are all enlightened, the difference between masters and serfs will disappear and, if he's lucky, even a commoner will hold high office.'

'As to how the world goes – he must know even better than your master, as he's had a wider view of it.'

'What I don't understand . . .'

'. . .'

'What I don't understand is this – he is different from us, so why should he be on our side?'

He asked with an air of stupidity.

'Ah, that? There's a reason.'

'What is it?'

'Ha! ha! ha! It's this. That man from Seoul, he has to come and beg from the Choi house, but, in my case, I can just borrow their donkeys and servants.'

Pyongsan laughed and so did Samsoo after him.

274

'By the way, what's your wish when the world changes?'

'As for me . . . well, what can I do? – "a blind man with open eyes".'

'So, you intend to be a servant all your life, is that it?'

'I'll have to see when the time comes. If I could, I'd like to be a policeman.'

'U'm, that's a good idea.'

As it was when they had left the village two days before, their progress was leisurely. Fat and flabby, Pyongsan could not stand the hot weather. They progressed by what he called 'stop and go,' so that both the mule and Samsoo had an easy time.

As soon as they reached the hills they left the donkey at a farm house and, when they had eaten lunch, set off on foot. Samsoo went in front with a sack containing a few necessities slung over his shoulder. He said, 'There's range after range of hills. I haven't the slightest idea which way to go.'

'You've never been here before?'

'No.'

'In the middle of hills, it is hopeless if you are here for the first time, but I know my way about a bit. They talk about "Looking for Mr Kim in Seoul," but in Chiri Mountain everyone knows Kang *posoo*. There are fire-field farmers all around, so you don't have to worry.'

'We'll have to sleep in the hills tonight, won't we?'

'Not just tonight. If we are unlucky, we may have to stay several nights. He's not just waiting for us on the road side, is he? The only trouble is if the weather turns nasty.'

Deep in the hills, covered with thick woods that blotted out the sky, all kinds of birds could be heard. Where a faint light just penetrated the darkness stood a poison ivy as if ablaze. As the sun was near to setting, they came to the hut of a fire-field farmer. A woman with a cloth round her head was shelling beans, sitting alone.

'Excuse me. Can I ask you something?' said Samsoo.

'Yes, what is it?'

She lifted her face. She was young.

'Do you know Kang *posoo*?'

275

'Yes, I do.'

'Where is he now?'

'About a fortnight ago, he said he was on his way to Gurae. He stayed here one night.'

'So you don't know just where he is now – is that it?'

Pyongsan put in a word.

'By now . . . it's hard to say, but he could be near Daesung or Seisok . . . Go to Seisok and ask at Chunmae's house – she will know better.'

'You mean the woman with a blue face?'

'Yes, but you can't go now – it's very rough.'

'No, that would be impossible. We'll stay here tonight if you can give us some supper?'

'Of course.'

Perhaps because they were looking for Kang *posoo*, the woman agreed without any sign of suspicion. After changing their damp clothes for dry ones, they ate a supper of potatoes mixed with millet. Soon after dark, her husband seemed to have returned but they had quickly dropped off to sleep.

In the middle of the night Samsoo woke up and went outside to relieve himself. The cries of wild animals could be heard. When he had finished in the privy, roughly fenced with millet canes, he looked up at the infinitely lonely sky as he pulled up the top of his trousers. The waning moon hung idly. The shadow of the trees trembled. The sound of Pyongsan snoring could be heard. The face of the woman that he had seen in the evening floated before his eyes. Apart from her youth, there was nothing remarkable about it, but it made his heart beat faster. It was not that he knew nothing of women, and indeed there were several female servants of marriageable age at home. But between that place with all its strict rules and this place the feeling was quite different. The desolation of the mountains in the deep of the night, the cries of the animals, as if calling their mates, and his own breathing roused in him a burning desire. He furtively crawled up to the front of the room with a millet-cane door and put his eyes close to it. At first, he could not see anything inside, but when his eyes became used to the darkness, shapes appeared. He could make out the untidy form of a man and a woman asleep in each other's arms. His eyes flashed. His body was hot as if singed by fire. He felt an impulse to seize her by her hair and drag her out, a desire to kill her. He panted and his whole body trembled.

(Hell! Even a fire-field farmer has a woman!)

His anger and resentment surged up so that if anyone had appeared before his eyes, he would have brought an axe down on them. Scarcely able to shake off a frightful power like that of a water demon trying to drag him below the surface, he went back to his room soaked in sweat and lay down with a wooden pillow under his neck. There was no way he could sleep. The sight of a man and a woman lying in each other's arms appeared before him, as if by magic, to torment him. Pyongsan slept like a man without a worry in the world, snoring and blowing his lips like a pair of bellows.

(Damn the whole world! Let it all collapse! When it comes to death, there's no difference between high and low.).

Setting off before sunrise, they had gone a fair way before it came up. The Eastern peaks were coloured with a deep pink. Rays of light shone through gaps in the sea of clouds. The sun, like a ball of fire, bounded into the sky. This spectacular and beautiful sunrise made Pyongsan look back again and again but Samsoo, with his eyes red as if filled with blood, walked on ahead like a madman. They waded through groves of bamboo and forced their way through thickets. In no time their new clothes were wet. They were chilly one moment and sweating the next, as the woods themselves continuously exuded dampness and cold. The leaves under their feet that had piled and decayed for hundreds of years and the thick moss that clung to the rocks gave out dampness and cold. Wild vines swirled like snakes round the scrub, and the morning song of invisible birds was free and rich, full of the joy of life. Along the rocky cliff a herd of mountain goats went by and they stopped to watch them before walking on. Both were silent.

'Anger the mountain spirits and you will meet disasters. The mountain is no ordinary place – you must always remember that it is sacred ground.'

Recalling what Kang *posoo* once told him, Pyongsan walked with

277

a serious mind, while Samsoo, trying to lash the upsurging passion in his body, walked on blindly. At last they met someone, an old charcoal burner.

'Old man!' called Pyongsan.

'What do you want?'

His eyes flashed. His hair was half white and his body big and strong.

'Do you know Kang *posoo*?'

'Go on further. You will see a house – you can ask there.'

'So he must be at Chunmae's.'

They walked on.

'For an old charcoal burner . . .'. Samsoo mumbled.

Pyongsan replied, 'There are all kinds of people in these hills.'

'All kinds?'

'All kinds of criminals – people who can't live in broad daylight on the plains.'

'I've heard that Kuchon is here also.'

Pyongsan smiled and said, 'The old man we just saw – he looks as though he could have been someone important in the old days.'

'Yes, I thought so too.'

'Plenty of Dong Hak and Catholics are likely to be here, and the descendants of traitors as well. This is the place where all sorts of people who dislike others, or are scared of them, hide away.'

Long past midday they arrived at the hut of the woman called Chunmae who had once before been down to look for Kang *posoo*. She had belonged to a troupe of players when she was young.

'I've seen you before.'

She lifted a face that was bluish from lead poisoning.

'We are looking for Kang *posoo*.'

'He may be here today.'

'You mean he's not here now?'

'He went to Gurae market the day before yesterday, so he'll probably be back today, if he's not stuck in a gambling den.'

'Gurae market? We didn't see him there . . .'

'I'm sure he'll come.'

He came on the evening of the next day.

'Oh, so you've been with the girls again while you had some money!'

She had her own husband, but she was still jealous.

'Why, am I your old man?'

He grumbled as he dumped his sack.

'You have visitors.'

'What visitors? Don't be silly.'

'Why should I talk nonsense?'

'It sounds like real nonsense. Have I any parents or children who would come to look for me?'

At that moment Pyongsan appeared from behind the hut with a big smile.

'Why, it's Kim *sengwon*!'

His eyes grew wide.

'What have you come for?'

'At the request of Master Choi.'

'What?'

His face changed colour.

'The master of the house wants to see you urgently – that's why.'

Pyongsan feigned the expressionless look of an officer who has come to arrest a criminal.

'Me? Why me? What have I done?'

'You'll know when you get there.'

Then he looked round. Samsoo, tired of waiting in the hut, had gone down to the stream.

'What has it got to do with me? I won't go. If it's about the gold ring, you could . . .'.

Pyongsan stepped closer to him.

'You idiot! You are going to scratch it and make a sore. I see that even though you wrestle with tigers, your guts are as small as a pea.'

He roared with laughter. Kang *posoo* laughed too, opening a mouth buried in whiskers. But, as if still uneasy, he said, 'What does he want to see me for, then?'

'So that you can teach him how to hunt.'

'What?'

'It's a bit of luck.'

'Don't beat about the bush – say what you mean.'

'The fact is the master seems to want to have a go at hunting.'

'In that case, as he's doing it for sport, he can use beaters. What is the use of a man like me who works by himself?'

'It seems that, as you say, he wants to do it alone, too. With a rifle, he says, and it seems that he has already sent someone to Seoul to get him one.'

'A rifle!'

'Um.'

'Ah, a rifle.'

At the word he pricked up his ears.

'I've heard about them – the Japs have them, and the Westerners . . .'

Pyongsan cut him short.

'That's it. So he is going to get one and try his hand at hunting. He's got the idea of asking you down to the village to teach him how to hunt or, rather, how to handle the gun and then, when he goes out, he'll take you as his guide. It means you don't have to go on living a hard life on your own – it gives you the chance to get hold of some money and find a wife.'

'Please don't talk such nonsense.'

'Why?'

'I don't want to.'

'Don't want to?'

'I am Kang the hunter, not a servant of the Choi house.'

At this quite unexpected response, Pyongsan was confounded.

'Come on, man. Do you think he means to make use of you without paying for it?'

'Pay or no pay, I don't want to be tied down.'

'It's not being tied down. You don't seem to understand what I'm saying. This man is now full of enthusiasm and he will reward you generously.'

'Whether it's reward or money, I hate to be tied down.'

'It's not a matter of being tied down all your life – just for a month or so. Even then, it's not really being tied down. Just show him your skill and give him some instruction, that's all that's required.'

'Gold or treasure, whatever he offers me, I don't like it. I'll live as I please.'

'What a stuffy and stupid fellow!'

Despite a whole night of argument, he would not relent. Pyongsan was angry and while Samsoo was out at the privy, he even tried to threaten him by bringing up Guinyo's ring. But the hunter could not be moved, and it may be that because of that he was even more reluctant to go.

'If there was anything wrong, it was the girl that did it – what have I done? I gave her something, and was paid for it – that's all.'

Chapter Twenty-Four

SHE didn't seem to have brushed her hair after getting up. With dishevelled head and hemp skirt curled up at the edge, looking untidy, Kangchong *dek* came through Dooman *ne*'s brushwood gate.

'Is Dooman's dad there?'

They were eating breakfast on the verandah.

'What a fine way to eat! Haven't you got a chin? Why do you spill it like that?'

Dooman *ne*, rebuking one of the children, said 'Come in. What's happened so early?'

'Is it breakfast time already?'

'We thought we'd get it over while it's still cool. If breakfast is late, a whole day's work gets messed up.'

The dog, Boksil, his mouth stuck in his bowl eating burned rice, barked and put his nose back into it. The courtyard had been swept clean and from the stable came the sound of the ox chewing the cud. Dooman's father, eating at a separate table, belatedly asked, 'What's the matter?'

'I wondered if you were going to the market today?'

'Yes, I must. Have you had some breakfast?'

'Breakfast or no breakfast, I have more troubles in one day than some people do in a hundred years.'

Dooman *ne* said, 'Have you had another row?' and called her daughter, 'Suni!'

'Yes, mum.'

'Fetch a spoon from the kitchen.'

She put down her spoon and ran to the kitchen.

'No, no, I haven't got time.'

Kangchong *dek* waved her hand.

'Come on. Have a spoonful with us. The rice is nicely done and quite edible.'

'I've no heart for it – and whether he's going to eat it or not, I must go back and cook something.'

Suni brought the spoon and said, 'Auntie, do have some.'

'I have to go back and do our own.'

Without pressing her further Dooman *ne* asked, 'What did you want from the market?'

'Some medicine.'

'Who for?'

'My husband, or whatever he is – he's been in bed for a few days now and it worries me to death.'

'. . .'

'If only he'd tell me what it was, I'd feel better, but he shuts his mouth tight and wont have anything to eat or drink . . . whether or not he does it to kill me, it eats me up and I just can't go on like this.'

'He's a healthy man. What could be wrong with him?' said Dooman's father. 'He's never had a day in bed in his life but now, in the fields or in the yard, it's all in a mess. I have to run here and there. I'm in a world all by myself.'

'Could it be malaria?'

Dooman *ne* cut short her raving.

'It's not that. If only he would tell me where the pain is, or even take some gruel, I'd feel better . . . I can't think of anything so I want to try medicine. I'm sorry to bother you, but if you could get some on your way to the market. Please explain it to the doctor . . .'.

'I don't mind, but really he ought to go himself so that they can check his pulse and fix the medicine to suit it.'

'I know. I am tired of asking him to go and get his pulse taken but he takes no notice. To begin with, he wouldn't even speak to me. I am worn out and my guts are rotting. Whether he's sick because he can't see the woman he wants to see, or because he hates me . . . whether you have enough or not, a family should live in peace . . . all through the year there isn't one happy day – what's the use of living like this?'

The couple were silent.

'I am trying to weed the fields, cut the hay, and run the house

283

all on my own. My inside boils and bubbles and I can't really get on with it.'

Still they were silent, until Dooman *ne*, changing the subject, said again, 'Anyway, have some breakfast.'

'No thanks.'

Pushing back the table and swilling his mouth with rice tea, Dooman's dad frowned as he glanced at her untidy appearance.

'Yongman, eat this!'

He handed over his bowl, with a few grains of rice showing among the mixture, to his youngest son and stood up. Kangchong *dek*, having ceased to rave, took some coins from a string, 'Well, I'm sorry to be such a nuisance, but please get the medicine.'

Back at home, she banged the crockery as she put some grain in a pot, and lit the fire.

'Even when he is well, the sight of him makes me mad with anger. There's so much to do and he's lying stuck in a corner like a piece of wood. Who's going to do the work? What pleasure will I get from weeding the paddies and the fields and weaving? There must be some joy in life to make work worthwhile. Have I got a brat to crawl into my arms or anyone who would feel sorry for me? And him thinking of that bitch day and night until it makes him ill.'

Poking the fire, she mumbled on, 'You're ill because you can't see her? Pray for me to die. Go on . . . Then you two will be happy together, won't you?'

The rice was boiling over and so was her mind. She had been restraining her temper out of consideration for Yongi as he lay ill, but the intuition that it was not seeing Wolsun that had made him sick brought on a rage that turned everything black before her eyes.

'Hell! Look at me! I forgot to put the soup bowl on top of the rice pot.' She ran, in haste, with an earthenware bowl to where the jars were. She was about to lift the lid of one of them when she saw him sitting on the verandah.

'Hey, you,' she said. 'Are you feeling better?'

Lifeless eyes stared at her blankly.

'You're well enough to get up and come out?'

' . . .'

284

'What about a bit of gruel?'

'. . .'

'Someone is talking to you – how can you be so stubborn and heartless?'

'. . .'

'I went to Dooman's father and gave him money to get some medicine. He was saying you should go yourself and get your pulse taken. Now stop worrying me so much and say something!'

'As if it could be cured by medicine . . .'

It was the first response.

'Then what will cure it?'

'. . .'

'Will it get better if we call a shaman?'

'. . .'

'Would an offering at the temple cure it?'

'. . .'

'Go to the pining rock and exorcise the love-sick spirit – will that do it?'

He stayed silent.

'So you're sick because you can't see the bitch you want to see – is that it? Fetch her from the town, and that will cure it?'

'Shut up!'

'. . .'

'If you go on any more I'll pull out the roof-posts!'

It was like the raging of a wild animal. Blood rushed to his white face and thick veins stood out on his forehead.

'Mention that bitch and your mouth comes unstuck. There's no need to bring her here. Go, on, Just go! Go and never come back! That'll save me from becoming a widow. I won't stop you.'

She didn't care if the rice in the kitchen turned to charcoal. She still held the bowl in her hand as she screamed at him.

'Say another word about that woman and I'll burn the house down.'

She dropped the bowl on to the lid of the jar and ran up to him waving her arms.

'What did you say? Why shouldn't I talk about her? Because she's the daughter of the highest spirit or the king's daughter? As dirty

285

as the filth in a sewer! As dirty as a bluebottle that will settle on anything! She's possessed by all sorts of spirits and gobbles up the liver of any man she meets like a vixen with nine tails! Why should I be scared to talk about that bitch? Burn the house down. I don't want to live any more either, so burn it down once and for all . . . !'

Foaming at the mouth, she looked as if she was going to run at her sick husband and tear him to pieces. Yongi ground his teeth. Greasy sweat appeared on his forehead. She could not quite go on to the verandah, so she flung herself to the ground and stretching out her legs burst into tears.

'Bloody hell! Bloody hell! What a life!'

His face went from red to purple and, as he trembled violently, his eyes glared savagely.

'I should have killed her, and myself too, there and then. I can't bear it. Why did I go that far in the middle of the night – fifteen miles there and back? Was it to see the face of that woman? How I regret it – regret that I didn't kill her there and then!'

Kangchong *dek* pounded her breast.

'I trusted the words on her lips and I've been cheated! I should have torn her into shreds but, gutless woman that I am, I walked there and back fifteen miles just for nothing. How dreadful! I could at least have broken her leg!'

Yongi stood up, 'You mean you . . .'.

'Oh! hateful and horrible!'

'. . . you mean you've been there?'

'Yes, of course! Why? Is it somewhere I'm not supposed to go? I got hold of her hair, the bitch, and I beat her like a dog in midsummer! You're sorry for her! Your heart melts! Lucky bitch to be felt for and pitied!'

Yongi's face turned as white as paper. He stepped off the verandah and strode up to her. Her ranting had ceased. He grabbed her by the hair.

'Help!'

Twisting it, he dragged her along as far as the front of the shed and kicked her.

'You're killing me!'

'Monstrous bitch!' he spat out.

He pulled on his shoes and rushed out through the gate. Sunlight sparkled in the air like drops of water. As the road to the town came into sight, there were occasional people going to market. With their oxen left on the river bank, the herd boys were splashing in the water, enjoying the summer.

(So that's it! That's what it was!)

He staggered along. Yimi *ne*, a water jar on her head, looked pleased to see him.

'I heard you were ill, and, really, your face looks terrible.'

Perhaps because she had been sweating a lot in the heat, her face looked milky and smooth as though it had been washed. As if he did not see her, or even hear her voice, he bumped into her as they passed.

'Oh, my!'

Momentarily losing her balance, she quickly righted herself, bringing her hands to the ears of the jar, but some water spilt on her clothes and dripped down her face.

'Damn! Does he think I'm a ghost or something?' she grumbled angrily but, without looking back, he was already past and gone.

'He's become really queer. He certainly does need the love-sick spirit casting out. I can understand why Kangchong *dek* goes into fits of madness.'

Yimi *ne* felt put out. She had always been sorry for herself as a married woman who fancied someone else's husband, but she had been confident and rejoiced over her superiority to Kangchong *dek*, and now Wolsun had taken this away from her.

'Huh! There's not a single spot in that bitch that's worth looking at. It beats me what makes him go mad about her. He must be blinkered.'

Going wherever his feet carried him, Yongi climbed Dangsan, where the sound of Dochul *ne* babbling in front of the pavilion came to his ears, and he went deeper into the woods. He passed the turning to the shrine of the fertility spirits and went up into the valley. Cutting across the sounds of the water and the other birds, now chattering, now whispering, came the intermittent call of a cuckoo. Through the tattered gaps in the leaves the sky was blue.

In a cool, deep place in the valley, he lay down on a level spot beneath a rock. The musty smell of decayed leaves assailed his nose.

(Why am I so weak? It feels like death.)

It seemed as thought his body was sinking into the earth. Darkness came down as if to enfold him. In the midst of it was a beam of faint light, very pale, a bluish streak of sorrow and resentment, rather than a light of hope.

(Poor thing!)

She had had to turn her back on the village for the second time. Whether it had been with a ginseng trader from Kangwon-Do or a wealthy old man was no longer worth thinking about.

(Where?)

In the illusion of being sucked into the earth, he waved his arms. Wolsun seemed to be standing near him, smiling.

(If only I knew where, I'd go after her — a thousand miles or more.)

Her tender arms were round his body. Her smell as well. Fierce desire woke his exhausted body like sparks of fire. Was it intercourse with a phantom or with the dead? His body shook fiercely. He tried to hold the thread of his rapidly dimming consciousness.

(I'm going to die. Stupid woman, wherever she goes, how can she forget me? Ah, ah.)

'Yongi, I'd rather die than become a shaman. Even if you marry someone else, I won't do it.'

The little girl had smiled shyly, or rather, as if exhausted. Unlike her mother who, in the right mood could stretch her throat and be carried away in an incantation, or oppose any ill treatment boldly, like a man, Wolsun had no power with words. So when someone like her spoke in this way it meant she had done her utmost to express herself. But as he had leaned against the rear wall of the fertility shrine, Yongi had said not a word in reply.

'I am going to be married. The bridegroom is a pedlar they say. Twenty years older than me and a cripple.'

Leaning against the bales of straw stacked against the water mill, she spoke of it as if she was talking about someone else.

'What does it matter where I go? I don't care, though Mummy is sad.'

Telling it as if it was someone else's story, tears fell from her eyes.

'Mum says that rather than go with a young man and be treated badly as a shaman's daughter, it's better to go with an elderly cripple who won't desert me . . . what does it matter where I go? I don't care.'

Perhaps if she had said, 'He's handsome, rich and going to make me happy,' Yongi might have said, 'Let's run away.' Probably, in the end, he wouldn't have been able to abandon his widowed mother, but at that moment he might have said it. This time he had no idea what kind of a man the Kangwon-do ginseng trader might be. He could be old and pockmarked, or one-eyed, or have a limp.

'What does it matter where I go? I don't care.'

Words he had heard more than ten years ago rang in his ears. If she could not live with him, she didn't care whether it was a one-eyed man or a cripple. Whoever it was, it would be the life of a rootless wanderer.

Long after midday, he just managed to come from the valley. A little way past the turning to the fertility shrine, he fell exhausted under a birch tree. A swarm of mountain ants crawled over him, but, with no strength to shake them off, he managed to raise himself and sit propped against the trunk.

'Bongsoon *ne!*'

From the wood came the clear ringing voice of a child.

'Look at those berries over there! Go and get me some.'

'Yes, I'll get some for you, Miss. But you must keep still. It's very slippery because of the moss. If you fall over, it will be terrible. Bongsoon, stay there and hold her hand.'

It was Bongsoon *ne.* He recognized her voice but could not stand up.

'I must go back, I must go back. I mustn't hang about here like this.' While he urged himself, he saw the sky broken up by the leaves and now, unlike earlier on, it looked milky white. The trees and the rocks that surrounded him seemed distant one moment and close the next. The sounds of the stream, the birds and the cicadas rang in his ears one moment and at the next seemed far away.

'Isn't it Yi *subang?*'

Bongsoon *ne*, following the children after giving them a wash in the stream, was surprised to see him propped against a tree.

'Yes.'

'What are you doing here?'

'I've been ill . . . I came out for a change of air, but I felt giddy – so here I am.'

'Yes, your face looks awful! What's wrong?'

'. . .'

'Have you seen Dr Mun?'

'It'll gradually get better on its own.'

'. . .'

'By the way, Dori brought those blouses back the other day. He said Wolsun wasn't there.'

'No.'

Sohi was greedily eating blackberries from a leaf. So was Bongsoon, pricking up her ears at the words that passed between Yongi and her mother.

'Where did she go?'

'. . .'

'She doesn't have anywhere to go, so where could it be?'

'She's gone for good.'

'For good?'

'Without a trace.'

Bongsoon *ne*'s eyes opened wide.

'She's boarded up the shop . . .'. Yongi's voice cracked. Bongsoon *ne* said no more. She realized why he had come to the woods alone and why he was sick. She knew about their past and she now thought that Wolsun was the one to blame.

'You mean she's just gone off without a word?'

'. . .'

'For the sake of her dead mother, her ladyship set her up in a wine shop and then off she goes without a word of farewell to anyone!'

'If she'd been in the state to say proper goodbyes she wouldn't have gone.'

'What state?'

'. . .'

'Where is she supposed to have gone?'

'They say she went with a ginseng trader from Kangwon-do, but how can you know for sure?'

'She is not that sort of woman.'

'It's all my fault.' His eyes were filled with tears.

'Mummy, who are you talking about?' asked Bongsoon. 'Has auntie Wolsun gone off somewhere?'

'No, it's nothing.' After hushing it up like this, she mumbled, 'How could she be so unlucky! If only she had been born in the right place, she could have had a good life . . . with no one to depend on, how bad she must have felt to go off like this without a word . . . She means well and she isn't greedy. Even so, Yongi, you can't just stay here like this, can you?'

'I'll try to get up and go . . . but my feet just won't move.'

'In this life things never go as you want them to . . . But she's gone, and that's that . . . you shouldn't let it get you down like this, Yi *subang* . . . you're not fated to be together, that's all it is, so what can you do?'

' . . . '.

'You really can't walk? I'll go down and send someone up.'

She went down the road with the children. Some time later, Dori, whom she had sent, found him lying unconscious under the tree.

'Yi *subang!* Yi *subang!*' Frightened, he rushed up and shook him wildly.

'Don't – don't shake me so much. I'm a bit weak, that's all.'

As he partly opened his eyes, his lips were white.

'Gosh, you gave me a fright – anyway, what did you come here for?'

Dori pulled him by the arms.

'Come on, get on my back.'

Pulling Yongi's arms over his shoulders, he stood up with a grunt. Yongi's body was long and slender while Dori was short and stout. On Dori's back, his legs almost touched the ground, but Dori was strong and made his way down the hill without faltering.

'In this hot weather, even if you're well, you feel tired – why did a sick man like you even try to come up here?'

' . . . '.

'We must call the doctor – you can't go on like this you know.'

'Don't worry.'

'That's not right – if you're sick . . .'.

'There's nothing wrong with my insides. If I can eat, I'll be all right,' mumbled Yongi, with his eyes shut. When they were near his house, he said, 'What am I coming back here for? In the whole world, is this the only place for me?'

'Pardon? What did you say?'

Yongi smiled faintly as he said playfully,

'Goes out after beating his wife and has to be carried home again – what a sight!'

'So, you had a quarrel.'

'Yongpari, on his way back from the fields, saw him being carried on Dori's back and came running up.

'Yongi! What's the matter?'

'He's fainted on the hill.'

'Fainted?'

Yongpari went with them through the gate. Kangchong *dek* lay in the room with the door flung open. The empty bowl was still on the top of the sauce jar.

'Missus!' shouted Yongpari. She rested her arm on her forehead, pretending not to hear.

'Missus! Get up. Look what's happened to him!'

'I don't want to hear a thing about him.'

Pretending to turn over, she cast a quick glance outside and, seeing him being carried in, she was confounded but only turned her back again.

'Missus!'

Yongpari's face was flushed. Dori lowered him on to the verandah and wiped the sweat from his forehead with the back of his hand.

'Look – don't go too far! How can you behave like this? – to the head of the family!'

While Yongpari, bursting with anger, waved his arms at her, Dori said, 'I'm telling you, he fainted up there on the mountain. Get the bedding out quickly and let him lie down.'

As if grudgingly, she sat up and gathered her hair.

'Huh! You should have taken him to that bitch in the town.'

Chapter Twenty-Five

THE fields grew a deeper green day by day from rain that came only in dribs and drabs, enough to relieve thirst, but far from sufficient. The farmers were anxious knowing that, if only they could get past this critical time, it should at least be an average harvest. The mood of the village reflected that of the heavens – whether it was generous or mean always depended on the weather. There was still enough water left to keep the bottom of the paddies soggy, but visiting hawkers and pedlars found it hard to barter their goods for grain and had to read people's faces before asking for something to eat. In homes that were short, women and children went over the fields gathering leaves of pigweed, already too tough, and made meals of wild greens mixed with grain, or a gruel of dried radish leaves. Some dug arrowroot to pound and store. Dooman's father, Yi Pangi, rebuked Bong-gi when he ran out to take back some seaweed that had been traded for grain with a pedlar.

'Don't be so silly. The luck that's on its way in will go out again.'

'Shut up. Are you going to feed me if there's a famine?'

'You shouldn't have taken it in the first place, then.'

'Was it me? That stupid woman, without even looking up at the sky, just scoops out grain – it makes you sick!'

With the bundle in his hand, Bong-gi shouted after the pedlar as, panting, he ran towards the embankment.

'The idiot – I bet he took a piece out first. Foaming at the mouth and asking for his grain back – it'll give the trader a turn,' Yi Pangi mumbled to himself as he poured water into his paddy.

Below the hill, at a swamp, young men in pairs were taking muddy water from the bottom and feeding it into the channel that ran along the paddies. Trampling the squelching mud, with the legs of their damp flax trousers rolled above the knees, they laboured with wooden buckets. The muscles bulged on legs as firm as birch trees and burnt to the colour of copper. They were bursting with energy like the burning summer sun and flourished like the thick weeds that had sprung up after a landslide the year before. Unlike the older men, who whined of a coming famine, they had no worries. As they threw their energy into the work, they also poured it out in words, gossiping and laughing about things that would have given Kim *hunjang* a fit if he had heard them. As happy as bees or butterflies trampling pollen and sucking honey, they chattered and giggled; that so and so at someone's house had a big bum and tits about to burst, so tempting to touch; that so and so, and someone else had been seen by moonlight crawling out of the millet; that such and such a widow had lifted her skirt for a measure of barley; or that every night from Wolsun's empty house came the sound of a man and woman laughing, and so on. Thick-lipped Buddol changed the subject.

'Have you heard how on the last market day that rascal Bawoo was completely stripped?'

'How was that?'

'Gambling.'

'What?'

'If it had been a pickpocket, he could at least have gone to the court, but where can you complain?'

'I see. That's why his father was after him with a stick, as if he was a mad dog. I wondered if he'd got a trader's daughter into trouble or something.'

'His father's as much to blame. He knows what his son is like, so why did he send him to sell the pig?'

'I think it was to buy things for the sacrifice, so he would have trusted him – it wasn't money to be used for ordinary things.'

'I don't think it was that. When his father had a fall on the hill some time ago, he hurt his back – that's probably why he had to send Bawoo.'

'Come to that, what do the young care about ancestors.'

'Come off it, are you so old then?'

'No, I'm including myself. On the day of sacrifice, we think about having a good feed of meat soup and white rice. We don't think about our late grandpa or grandma, do we? What did we ever get from them, to offer them a good meal? It's for people who can eat white rice all the year round, with meat as well, to wash themselves and, with pure minds, read the prayers and bow their foreheads to the floor until they are worn out. As for us, we've never inherited as much as a pebbly patch on the edge of a cliff.'

'Even so, "You must serve your ancestors well if you want to be blessed". Don't you remember what Kim *hunjang* taught us?'

'Huh, how can they give us any blessings? In the other world, too, servants will go on serving and the poor will dig poor soil to eat barley gruel. Their eyes will be on how to make ends meet for themselves – no time to think about their descendants. Even with the spirits, you need bribes – that's why ours have no effect compared with those of the gentry.'

'Chatter away like this and you'll end up by having to call in the shaman to appease them.'

'Never. What have I got to give them but barley gruel? If the spirits want their fill, they'd better go and fasten themselves to the house of Choi.'

'It gets worse! Trying to get rid of the ancestral spirits, you'll end up being turned out yourself without even barley gruel.'

'By the way – that gentleman from Seoul – I just saw him coming back again on a horse in some kind of funny clothes, like a policeman or a soldier – though he didn't have a sword.'

'Don't be stupid. How could a man of his rank be a policeman or a soldier?'

'Maybe, but there must be higher ranks in the police or the army, mustn't there?'

'Samsoo says that in a little while anyone will be able to be a policeman. If a servant can be a policeman, how could a great gentleman like him just be at the head of them?'

'Is that so? I don't know anything about it. It was just because of his clothes.'

A woman called loudly from under the village tree that lunch had arrived.

'I thought my tummy was getting sour . . .'

They stopped and washed their faces and hands in the stream by the paddies and then went in a crowd to the shade of the tree where lunch awaited them.

The woman had gone and even the girl who came later, after putting down the water container, walked off along the embankment. As she went, she stretched out her arms as if trying to catch a dragonfly in front of her eyes. It slid away and circled her plait.

'We might as well eat. My throat is so dry. I'm dying for a nice cup of *makkoli*.'

'They're all moaning about how it will be a bad harvest. Where would we get rice for wine?'

They sat round the food in a circle. Belatedly noticing Yongi, Buddol asked wonderingly, 'Why, it's Yongi *hyongnim*. What are you doing here?'

Yongi, who had been staring across the fields, turned round.

'I heard you were ill. Are you better now?'

He smiled. Out of the sun for a long time, his face was pale.

Picking off an ant that had crawled up his rice bowl, Dalsoo asked, 'I heard you were very ill, but how are you now?'

Yongi still only smiled.

'Was it malaria?'

'Probably I was just tired,' he answered tersely.

'If you haven't eaten yet, have some with us . . .'.

He shook his head. Turning his back, he stared blankly across the fields as before. As if his soul had left him, and he was alone with no one around him, he just sat and stared. The young people did not bother him any more and they were silent even among themselves as they tucked into the rice. After a long time he got up, and without a word walked off along the embankment where the girl had gone before.

Dalsoo turned and asked, 'Why is he like that?'

'Like a man who's lost his soul,' said Tajul.

Ugly, with lumps all over his face, his mouth was crammed with rice which made it look even lumpier.

'Not without reason,' said Buddol.

'What do you mean?'

'Don't you know?'

'Of course I don't, or why would I ask?'

'His woman has run away.'

'His woman? Why, I saw Kangchong *dek* this morning – coming back from the well with a water jar.'

'Blockhead!'

'All right, out with it, then.'

'Don't you remember when we went to the masked players? You saw it all.'

'Come on . . .'.

'Didn't you see him with the shaman's daughter, Wolsun?'

'That's right, you said something then, didn't you?'

Dalsoo remembered it before the others.

'I'd had a drop to drink, so I might have said something out of jealousy.'

'You rascal jealous over that old woman? Anyway, so Wolsun, his dear love, has packed up and gone?'

'That's right. I've heard about it at the market as well. A man with money has taken her off as his concubine or something. Some say that her old husband came and took her away – you can't tell which is the right story. Anyway, on my way back I noticed the shop was closed . . .'.

'So now he's sick!'

'He's touched a shaman's daughter, so he's probably had his soul snatched.'

'I mean . . . I mean . . .'. spilling rice, the ugly Tajul, said quickly, 'What I mean is, however good you are, or good looking, it's no use. Without money a man's a scarecrow. You've only got to have money, even if you're a cripple, and you can do what you like with a woman.'

'Hum, so you think it's because you haven't got any money that you have no luck with girls, not because you look like a leper?'

'In a way . . .'.

'Well, in the case of the young mistress at the Choi house, it doesn't seem to be so.'

Tajul, getting angry for no apparent reason, jabbed the rice with his spoon and said, 'Don't talk rubbish! I've never seen a woman that doesn't want money. Lift their skirts for a bowl of barley – that's what women are like.'

Yongi was stalking up towards the Choi house. He passed under the shade of the hardy orange tree and round to the backyard of the servants' quarters. It was empty. After a while Samsoo appeared, carrying fodder to the stable.

'Is Dori working outside?'

'I think he's at the back of the *sarang*.'

Samsoo didn't sound particularly friendly. Yongi sat on the edge of the narrow verandah. It's such a long time since I was here, he thought. Nothing had changed. He reflected on his childhood, most of which had been spent in this yard, always being thrashed by Chisoo.

'Mummy, I am stronger than him, so why should it always be me that's beaten?'

His mother had stared at him for a while.

'You are the stronger, so there's nothing to be sad about.'

'I'll hit him back.'

'The young master is weak, so you must put up with it. The same way that the big brother must be tolerant of the younger one. Because you are stronger than him . . .'.

'You want me to be beaten day and night because I have more strength?'

'When you meet someone stronger than you are – then you can hit him.'

'If he's stronger, will he let someone like me beat him?'

'If he's good, he will . . .'.

'What about if he's not – then I'll be beaten again.'

'It's better to be a good man rather than a bad one.'

'But – but . . . even then . . .'.

'. . .'.

'So if I'm strong, I'm beaten, and if I'm weak too. It's nothing but being beaten.'

As if lost for words, she had said nothing. Then, after a long time, she had raised her eyes to the distant hills and said, 'As a servant, how can you hit a gentleman?'

Hearing this, he had wept.

Because of the stone walls round the house and the tiers of tiled roofs, as he looked up from the verandah of the servants' quarters the sky was narrow. Clouds hung motionless, like ragged cotton wool.

'What are you sitting there for like a lost soul? Do you want to speak to Dori?' asked Samsoo. 'I'll go and fetch him if you like.

'There's no need to do that. Did you say he was in the *sarang*?'

'Yes.'

'What's he doing?'

'He'll be pulling up weeds.'

'What about Kilsang?'

'He's gone to town to fetch something from the doctor's.'

'Why, who's ill?'

'Gannan *halmum* was vomiting last night, so he's gone for some medicine. She seemed to be eating rather greedily.'

Yongi stood up. Afraid of meeting Lady Yoon, he went along the side of the shed. He crossed the backyard and walked along by the walls of the *byoldang*. He stopped in front of the open gates. When the mistress had been there he used to go past hurriedly.

Sohi lay asleep on a wooden bed looking like a picture. Bongsoon slept with her, lying on her side with her face turned away. Sohi lay flat on her back, only her head slightly tilted towards him. As with the saying, 'Who should a mother's child resemble if not her mother?', in her face he felt that he was seeing the beautiful face of the lady of the *byoldang*. Through the face of a woman he had seen from a distance only once or twice, returning through that of Sohi, Yongi, now more than thirty, was drawn back to childhood memories like sunset colours reflected from far down the river.

He had had a sister called Suboni. Three years older than himself, in the summer of her eleventh year, she had died of smallpox. She had been a pretty little girl. It had been a night of pouring rain. Since the beginning of the rainy season, the villagers had been out every day mending the dikes or reinforcing them, but they could not sleep. At his house, too, his father and mother had been sitting on the verandah watching the rain. Yongi, now convalescent after smallpox, had woken up, and, holding tight to the hem of his mother's skirt, he also stared at the thick streaks of rain coming down like arrows. The lamp, hung below the shelf, shed a milky glow on them. Then, suddenly the door flew open, and Suboni ran out crying wildly.

'You made rice cakes for Yongi, and herbs and rice with beans, and thousands of other things, and you give me nothing – why? why?'

She clawed at her face, ugly with blisters.

'My darling!'

His mother, startled, sprang up. His sister had caught the smallpox from him but, as her spots were not troublesome, her parents had not worried so much, and also, because of the compulsory work on the dikes, they had been less attentive. At the same time, they had omitted offering prayers to the spirits with food, not because she was a girl, but because it came just after Yongi had got better.

'You made rice cakes and herbs for Yongi. You gave him thousands of things.'

'Oh, dear, we're in trouble! You mustn't come out in the cold. Darling, let's go in.'

Her mother tried to carry her inside but she kicked and screamed and tore at her face.

'What shall we do? A girl – she's going to ruin her face.'

Her father, who had been silent, quickly washed his face, put on gown and hat, and fell on his knees in front of the screaming girl.

'Distinguished guests (smallpox spirits), as humans, we have wronged you through our stupidity. Let your anger cease and have mercy on us just this once. When the dawn comes we will set up a great steamer and make *dok* and cook rice and treat you well as guests. When you go back, we will call the groom and wrap up travelling money . . . what do we humans know? Whatever you do, dear guests, bless the eleven-year-old daughter of the Yi family, as you do the sun and the moon, and set her right . . .'.

He pressed his forehead on the ground as he prayed. But she died at sundown the following day. After the small coffin had been carried out, wrapped in a straw mat, Yongi saw Chisoo weeping by the fence. At that time Chisoo was ten. After this Yongi decided that, as his mother had taught him, even if he was beaten by Chisoo, he would not hate him. But Chisoo did not hit him any more –

instead he began to hate Wolsun, teasing her and calling her ugly and a cry-baby.

Dori, bent over by the stone wall of the *sarang*, was pulling out weeds.

'Better now?'

'I can just about walk.'

'You look pale.'

'That's because I've been out of the sun.'

'Why did you come?'

'I want to buy you a drink. I caused you a lot of trouble, didn't I?'

'Don't worry about that. How can I go off drinking in the middle of the day?'

He cast a quick glance towards the verandah. Because of the angle they could not see who was sitting there, but they could hear them talking.

'The idiots! They wandered round for ten days and came back with nothing.'

'They couldn't find him? That's quite possible if he doesn't have any fixed abode.'

'It's not that they didn't see him – they did. So they should have brought him back, shouldn't they, even if they had to put a ring through his nose?'

'That's easy to say. But how on earth do you pull a man along by the nose?'

It was Chisoo and Junku talking. Dori broke into a smile.

'You know what happened?'

Lowering his voice, he said. 'You know how Kim Pyongsan went to Chiri Mountain to look for Kang *posoo*, and Samsoo went with him?'

'. . . .'

'Keep it to yourself, but they say that that lad Samsoo had a real good time. He's come back looking as smart as if he'd just had a bath. Obviously Kim Pyongsan, the gambler, did it to keep his mouth shut. It's true, they did meet the hunter, but for ten days they just went round enjoying themselves, and do you know what they did?' His eyes were full of envy. He stood up and put his mouth to Yongi's ear.

'That gambler, Pyongsan, bought him a girl – yes, a girl. Don't say a word to any one.'

Embarrassed, Yongi blinked while Dori innocently gloated.

'That's not all. They gambled as well. He's going to end up by ruining himself. Not exactly a good example. That Kim Pyongsan or whatever his name is, he wouldn't find it hard to ruin someone's life, would he?'

'Is any one there?'

'Yes, sir!'

Dori, flustered, went running. Chisoo stood on the edge of the verandah.

'Bring me a drink of water.'

'Yes, sir.'

Yongi who had been standing vacantly, walked towards him.

'Greetings, master.'

He bowed from the waist.

'H'm, are you well?' said Chisoo in a friendly tone.

'Yes, thank you, sir.'

'You look pale – have you been ill?'

'Just tired, sir.'

'Really?'

'It's a long time since I saw you, sir.'

Chisoo looked at him quietly. Strangely, a warm light seemed to come from his sharp eyes.

'Well, I'd better be going, sir.'

Again he bowed from the waist.

'Who was that?' asked Junku after he had gone.

'A peasant . . . from the village.'

'For a peasant he's quite good looking.'

'We grew up together.'

'. . .?'

'His mother used to come in as one of the casual workers, but it looks as though his ancestors were of better class.'

Saying this, he broke into a smile as if mocking Junku and went on, 'That chap, Yongi, understands human dignity. If he had learned to read and write he would have been a poet, and if he rode a horse, with a spear in his hand, he'd stand in the front rank.

Whenever he tends his parents' graves, he is soaked in tears up to the ends of his hair, and he regards women as jewels – that's it – he is an example of the honourable peasants of this country!'

At the end of his words, Chisoo chuckled. There was nothing funny about what he had said but, Junku, following him, began to laugh as well until he realized that he was being mocked. The laughter on his face was gradually replaced by a dubious frown.

Why does this man always make a fool of me? he thought.

He changed the subject.

'About this fellow Kang *posoo* – do you mean you must have him here?'

'By all means.'

'How long is it since they came back?'

'Just over a fortnight.'

'So you don't know where he is now?'

'We can find out easily enough.'

'There is one sure way to bring him down.'

'. . .'

'From what I hear, he's obviously not a man who can be bought with money.'

'That rascal Pyongsan is pretty cunning. It looks as if I'll have to go myself.'

'What if he won't come even for you?'

Chisoo said without blinking, 'I'll kill him.'

'Ha! ha! What nonsense! Let me go. One rifle will be enough – if he's been crazy about hunting all his life.'

'. . .'

'Take the rifle and just let him have one look at it. He'll be like a bit of iron caught by a magnet.'

'. . .'

'For a hunter his gun is his life. No doubt he's going round with some kind of worn out old matchlock over his shoulder. When he sees a new style rifle, he will go crazy.'

'You mean give it to him?'

'No need to go as far as that. I've got an idea – I brought two so that's just right, isn't it? I was going to enjoy hunting with you, but that doesn't matter.'

Yongi walked unsteadily down the slope. Yongpari was resting on the bank with a pipe.

'Better now?'

Yongi went up to him, 'We need rain.'

He looked up at the sky.

'Yongi!'

'. . .'.

'My wife went to Jinjoo and back a few days ago . . .'.

'. . . .'

'She met Yoon Bo.'

'Yoon Bo?'

'H'm. And he said he'd seen Wolsun.'

Yongi's face convulsed.

'She was going somewhere with an old man and another woman. When he asked her where she was going, she kept on crying and just said it was far away, and wouldn't tell him where it was.'

Out of the corners of his eyes Yongpari examined Yongi's expression.

'It's not your destiny. You've got to pull yourself together, or what will happen? She said she was going a long way away so she's not likely to come back. She hasn't any children to tie her down, so she won't be too badly off on her own, will she?'

Yongi just went on looking towards the far-away fields. The young people were still pouring water into the channel, chattering as before. By the river, standing beside a calf, Suh *subang*, with his grandson on his back, was talking to Kim *hunjang*.

Chapter Twenty-Six

POSTS such as local magistrate were not worth mentioning. Six generations back an ancestor had been a Third Minister. Now empty-handed – the family had been ruined in his father's time – and an unworthy descendant, unable to enjoy the prestige of office, Cho Junku could bring no honour to the family name by referring to his middle-class job as an interpreter. Even so, he probably felt no shame, for times had changed and it was said to be a position which, handled well, could put you in touch with the strings of power and seat you on a cushion of money. Riding the winds of enlightenment, he intended to find himself a good place. In the garden house on the day of his arrival in the late spring of the previous year, when Chisoo had teased him saying, 'As their interpreter, you should know that,' he had been rather put out and said, 'No need to call me an "interpreter." To understand what was going on outside, I read some foreign literature, which, naturally, led me to become acquainted with them, that's all.'

When Chisoo had replied, 'You don't have to feel bad about it. What's wrong with being an interpreter? It is not like the old days, is it? They say that they are the ones who sway national affairs one way or the other, and if you manage well you can gather in enough silver to fill your store-room,' he had seemed to be implicitly in agreement: 'I admit there is something in that.' Now, however, he had been insulted over the title of interpreter by Kim *hunjang*, who until this point had never failed to respect him for his family connection. Bored after returning from Seoul with the guns, Junku had gone to see him. After displaying his knowledge of rifles and hunting, he had naturally gone on to talk, with some exaggeration, about his work as an interpreter and his close connections with foreign envoys. It was here that Kim *hunjang*'s attitude began to change. Until then he had been careful in his manners and had held back his own opinions, but now, treating Junku as if he were a child, he even went as far as to lecture him on human obligations and how a gentleman should behave. As he argued fervently, swaying his top-knotted grey head, Junku asked sarcastically, 'Do you think the "honourable poverty" of gentlemen feeding on vegetables and water can stand up to warships and artillery?'

'So you are saying that those who have cut off their hair and throw away their robes and even pulled out their guts – that they are now stopping the warships and the artillery? Well, Mr Cho, as you seem to be the mouthpiece of the Koreans, and the Japanese as well, you must be familiar enough with the situation.'

'Huh, mouthpiece, indeed! That's a very unpleasant way to put it.'

'People old and young, who are after power and wealth, like a swarm of flies after honey, touch the ground before foreign dogs with foreheads that used to bow only before the king or the tombs of their ancestors. How can a nation that has lost its honour keep its land? The country has been brought to ruin without needing any guns or warships.'

'In a land known as "the country of courtesy", is there anything wrong in treating foreign envoys with politeness?'

But Kim *hunjang*, seeming not to hear, was to have his say: 'Some enlightened gentlemen got hold of a few odd Japanese guns and swords and trampled over the royal palace to hold the king to ransom. When this treacherous plot failed, they ran off to that island country. Now I hear they've been behaving childishly over there, complaining that they are not well treated. Huh, really – for their own safety, they run off to another country and even there they make a fuss. Are you trying to tell me that the men who plotted such treachery are going to put the country right and deliver the people from exploitation? This damned enlightenment is like a nicely coloured dog-apricot. How can men who trust only in guns care for the will of Heaven? Even though the Dong Hak were a rabble of fools – yes, they were a rabble – they did uphold the mottoes of "Out with Japan – Out with the West", and, regardless of the consequences, they went right through to the end. Doesn't it seem that after all it is the lower orders who have kept the nation's honour?'

'You may live in the backwoods but you'd shame the intelligentsia in Seoul, from the way you know the detailed movements of the exiles in Japan.'

'Why not? Do you think I'm deaf and dumb just because I live in the backwoods?'

'Of course not. However, it's a case of knowing one thing, but not the other ten. Don't you see that it was the Dong Hak movement itself that was responsible for bringing in the Japanese army? "If you win, you are a loyal subject, and if you loose, you are a traitor." Whatever you do, the final result is all that matters. Don't you agree?'

As he said this, Junku was reminded of Chisoo's words that the Japanese ought to offer a cow's head to the spirits of the Dong Hak rebels and bow in thanks. Once again, Kim *hunjang*, without reply, went on with his scathing remarks about the role of an interpreter, his face full of hatred: 'Even a eunuch with a life more shameful than death, or a shaman with her lowliness branded on her, if they had to speak for their country, forgetting their social status, they would command the hearer's heart with their eyes alone. But to those who are crazy for power and wealth, you, "Mr Interpreter," mouthpiece of the Japanese, who brandish guns and swords and roar as if they would eat up the whole country, you must be a precious person, even more precious than an ancestral tablet. What a matchless honour it must be for you, and indeed for all your illustrious ancestors under the ground, who no doubt are bouncing up and down with happiness'. He went on like this pouring out insults in a way that was quite uncharacteristic, and to Junku unbearable.

'Sir!' he called with anger in his eyes.

'What is it?'

"In the court, higher rank: in the country greater age". Making allowance for your seniority I have put up with all this, but don't you think the joke has gone too far?'

His protest was not made at all crudely. Kim *hunjang*, who, in his excitement, had run on blindly, seemed to realize that he had overdone it. He lowered his voice and said, 'Please don't take it as personal. I was only talking about the deplorable way that things have gone.'

307

'In that case, I will accept it. But as they say, "To sprinkle ashes on the food that you can't eat," in the way that the common people do, that wouldn't . . .'.

In the end Junku had quite easily repelled him. There was a great difference in their social status and, as the old man was neither as well-informed nor as clever as the polished gentleman from the capital, he could not but be silenced.

However one looked at it, one could not deny the rising value of interpreters in a period when the brave advance of the civilized countries, sharing the pioneer spirit of hunters of men who had staked out their claims in ownerless lands, having landed in Korea, had their dreams of conquest encouraged by every aspect of a people who in an atmosphere of political degeneration swaggered about with horse-hair hats and long-stemmed pipes. In the first place, as the mouthpiece of the invaders in their initial task of acquiring profitable concessions, he was someone worth bribing. He was useful also as a kind of middleman for those who saw carrying foreign powers on their backs as a safe way to make puppets of the all-but extinguished royalty and so attain to power – though it cannot be said that all interpreters were as corrupt as this. However, despite such opportunities, Cho Junku was as penniless as ever and in the state of having to wait on the favour of Choi Chisoo, prattling in his leisurely fashion in his village retreat, or of Lady Yoon. Putting aside the question of how much ability he had in Japanese, or in what way he had taken in the idea of 'Enlightenment', in fact, his position was a vague one in which, as he had said himself, he could hardly be called an 'interpreter.' Apart from any question of his own political ability, the area in which he could exercise his influence was quite insignificant. He would have needed strong ropes to clutch in order to climb up and move in one direction or the other, or to set up schemes, but the only people he had been able to follow around jabbering a little Japanese had been those with nameless jobs in the consulate, or a crowd of others of similarly indeterminate position. Apart from making a few Japanese acquaintances, he had gained nothing. Even so, this meagre personal experience had served him well in obtaining the rifles for Chisoo. Among those he had met was a hunting enthusiast called

Minobe. He regularly jeered at the Koreans' love for their long-stemmed pipes, while the chamber pots they kept in their rooms caused him to spit and call them barbarians. He was a man who was content only if, whenever he saw some custom that inevitably differed from that of his own country, he could pull it to pieces. He was a chauvinist with a firm belief in the superiority of the so-called 'Great Empire of Japan'. There was one exception to this, and only one – he was prepared to praise Korea as having some of the world's best hunting grounds.

It was doubtful whether he had personally investigated all the world's hunting grounds but he seemed to have diligently studied books, and in view of the legendary accounts of a tiger killed by the Japanese General Kato at the time of the sixteenth-century invasion in a peninsula not likely to have much in the way of wild animals, it was not unreasonable for him to praise the country's hunting grounds. Anyway, thanks to several occasions when he had accompanied Minobe as interpreter on hunting expeditions, he was able to obtain two Japanese rifles, converted for hunting, and it was these guns that eventually tempted Kang *posoo* down from the mountains.

In the yard of a mountain shack where white hare-bells were in bloom, the evening mist was rolling in. Kang *posoo* was stroking the rifle brought by Junku. He had already explored its capacities and tested it many times, but he was still far from ready to hand it back.

'With a lot of money, is it possible to get one like this?' he asked as he wetted lips hidden in his beard.

'Do you mean you've got that much money?'

'Oh, no. How could I?'

He smiled ruefully, and then sadly mumbled, 'A homeless wanderer – how could I have money? If I earn a lot, I eat a lot, or if little, I eat less . . .'

Pyongsan, who had been just looking on with his hands behind his back, put in, 'When he earns a lot, he'll be chasing women.'

Choonmae poked out her bluish lead-poisoned face and added, 'That's right, sir. When he's eaten, a man should think about what to eat the next day. If he wastes all his earnings on gambling and women, he won't die a decent death, will he?'

'If only I had a gun like this to hunt with, I'd want nothing more of life . . . as the old saying goes, "When a great general is born, a great horse is born too." For a hunter, a gun is his life . . .'

He mumbled on to himself.

Whatever Pyongsan or Choonmae might be saying, their words did not seem to reach his ears.

'It is not the sort of thing you can obtain just with money,' said Junku, as if to nail him down.

'A precious thing like this brought on a ship from a far country – do you think anyone can get one just for money?'

'You mean only gentlemen can have them?'

'Gentlemen?'

Junku smiled at him contemptuously as, crestfallen, he looked in turn at Pyongsan, Choonmae and again at Junku.

'I got hold of it through my special friendship with some Japanese. In times like this, you certainly can't get one just by being a gentleman.'

'That's true. At a time like this when we are raising an "Army of Justice" and killing Japanese soldiers they won't easily hand over things like guns, will they?' said Pyongsan flatteringly.

After a night on the mountain, Kang *posoo*, lured by the rifle, followed the party down. When they reached the Choi Champan house, Chisoo, who had been expected to be anxiously waiting for them, was surprisingly cool – not cold, perhaps, but not particularly pleased. His expression, as he looked down at the hunter with narrowed eyes, was dark and complex.

'H'm, so once in the mountains, you are a genius? . . . ha! ha! ha!..'.

He spat out the words and then for no apparent reason burst into laughter.

'Kim *subang*!'

The steward came running.

Chisoo indicated the hunter with his chin and abruptly walked off towards the garden house without a word to Junku or Pyongsan after their hard journey. Allocated to a six-foot square room in the servants' quarters, the hunter was a pitiable sight, like a caged animal. Accustomed to hearing the sounds of the wind and the cries of beasts as he lay in a charcoal burner's hovel or a fire-field farmer's hut, or often in a cave vacated by a wild animal, and to drink blood from the slit neck of a wild boar or a deer, he had roamed as freely as if he himself had been one of the beasts. After such a carefree life, to be confined within a maze of lofty walls, and see each sunset and dawn come round to the accompaniment of such tiresome customs was hard to bear. Like an animal hood-winked by a lump of meat and caught in a trap, lured by the modern rifle and shut up in the servants' quarters, he hated the comforts and the food, and thought only of the hills. If he wanted to run away, there was nothing to stop him, but he could not shake off the fascination of the rifle. All he had done since arriving had been to go up the hill behind the village with Chisoo and Junku to practise shooting – or, to be more accurate, to watch Chisoo practise, as he was by now quite well accustomed to handling the gun. Compared with Junku, who had picked up a few tips in accompanying Minobe on the trail, Chisoo, perhaps because he had mastered archery as a young man in his twenties, was quick in learning both to handle the weapon and to shoot straight. He seemed to be concentrating and did not say a word to either of the others unless it was necessary.

In a room where the light had gone out – it must have been deep into the night – the hunter, after rising, squatted for a long time on the floor. He had intended to go to the privy but felt reluctant.

(I should have stayed the night at the tavern. Damn it, I'm choking – I can't go on like this.)

The vast house seemed eerie and utterly desolate as if even the mice were dead. Even in the day time he was scared to move about the place with its multiple rings of walls, each with several gates. He was never sure of where he was or where he must not go. Once he had inadvertently walked into the inner courtyard.

'Who is it?'

He had been frightened by the eyes of a middle-aged woman calmly staring at him from the hall.

'Out of there at once!'

311

Kim *subang* had run up and pulled at his sleeve and so he had come out in confusion.

I've heard about 'twelve gates', but really there are too many here, and too many forbidden places too. There isn't room to turn round. Food and something to wear is all you need. I wouldn't be a gentleman even if they asked me. I can't stand it, it's like being in a suit of armour, he thought.

He struggled to his feet, opened the door and went out. He sought his big straw shoes on the stone and stepped down into the yard. The tiles on the tops of walls stood out darker than the darkness, while the stones of the wall showed up whitish. The very faintest glow hung around the yard of the servants' quarters. He was about to turn the corner towards the privy when something fluttered before his eyes.

'M'm'. His hair stood on end and then he saw two eyes flash.

'Oh! Is it Guinyo?'

Before he had finished speaking the woman had disappeared round the corner. He guessed that she too had been to the toilet, but it was bad of her, he thought. Among the strange faces all around, hers was the only one he knew, yet, whenever they met, she entirely ignored him, an attitude that seemed very mean.

The next day, when he came back from the hills, he washed his face by the well to cool himself. After that he intended to run off to the tavern.

'Kang *posoo*!'

'What?'

He raised his dripping face. Guinyo stood there with smiling eyes. He was pleased to be spoken to but answered with sarcasm, 'Huh, you might as well have been a thousand miles away. Why this change?'

'There are too many eyes around, that's why . . .'.

'. . .?'

'How slow you are!'

'Why, do you think I would tell tales? I drink to be sure, but I'm not one for empty talk.'

Guinyo pouted, 'Yes, that's true enough.'

'Why?'

312

'What you said wasn't empty, was that what you meant?'

'What?'

'What you told Pyongsan or whatever his name is – that was true enough, wasn't it?'

'That? Well that was different. I just didn't know what to do with it – that's why . . .'.

'Talk of the past and a tiger will carry you off. You'd better be careful in future.'

'Of course I will.'

'That's that. But you must be lonely all by yourself in a strange house.'

Again she smiled with her eyes, a smile that made his heart miss a beat.

'Beside, the master's temper . . . but what's the use of talking about it? Just try to be patient while you are here.'

Kang *posoo* stared blankly as she disappeared with a wave of her skirt.

'Oh dear!'

He rubbed his still-wet face with his rake-like hands.

'Oh dear!'

After that, on the nights when he slept there instead of at the tavern she would often smuggle food or wine into his room. (She shouldn't. There'll be trouble when it's found out.) At first, he had felt as if they were guilty. But gradually a strange change occurred in his mind. Often his heart would miss a beat as it had when he had noticed her smiling eyes, and then, for no reason, he became restless or felt so happy that he smiled to himself. (It's madness, madness. Because I've been shut up in a house for so long, I've gone mad.) He stayed in more often. For a bushy-whiskered woodsman of nearly forty, the sickness was coming rather late. He had thought that he was not fated for love. When he had the luck to catch a large animal that brought in a lot of money, he gambled and occasionally paid for a woman, but only because he wanted her body – he had never felt affection. He had even tried living with a woman a couple of times but as when he had bought them with money, he had not felt love. After wandering in the hills for months on the trail, he would turn up again like a regular customer

313

at a tavern, only to find that the woman had disappeared. One of them had gone off with a younger man and the other, perhaps unable to believe in the future, had sold off the household goods and disappeared without trace.

'Damn it! She's gone off again.'

He would be wildly drinking in anger at a tavern and someone would say, 'How did you come to lose your woman again?'

'It's just my fate.'

'It's because you can't do it properly – isn't it?'

'Just ask your wife!'

'You rascal!'

'Better than you, I reckon.'

'H'm, you talk big, but who can tell?'

As he babbled on he would soon be drunk and entirely forget the woman who had run away.

'The way I am – how can I keep a woman? What I hate most of all is to be tied down. Come to think of it, she was quite right – she did well. It didn't suit me, and she's got to think about her own future.'

'H'm, that's true. A big bear – you don't look as if you know much, but I see you can talk well.'

'As a principle, I mean.'

'You're right. A man who can't live a normal home life doesn't need a woman to decorate it. And, if you die, the animals will see to your corpse.'

'That's right. A man with a gun over his shoulder – where else should he die but in the hills?'

He used to laugh about it like this. That such a man had fallen in love with Guinyo, who, even though she was a servant, could not be compared to the tavern wenches or women in the hills and was young enough to be his daughter, if it came out, would make him the object of endless ridicule. But, thick-headed as he was, he never gave a thought to such matters. (Probably it's because she has got that fox's thing that I am in such a muddle?) He had been lying with his head on a wooden pillow until suddenly he sprang up, mumbling to himself. (That girl. She hasn't got a husband yet. Whatever did she want it for? Who on earth has she got in mind?

314

Who and where from? Wait a minute – the chap with wild eyes who came with that gentleman, Pyongsan? Or that fellow who looks like a chestnut burr, Dori?) If it was a day of persistent rain, his dreams knew no limits and his blood alternately froze and thawed. He would run madly to the tavern. It was no longer the gun that bound him, but Guinyo.

'Guinyo!'

'What?'

She looked at him out of the corners of her eyes. By the well there was no one about. Her wrists and the back of her neck looked plump and firm and she gave out a refreshing fragrance. He swallowed hard.

'You know, that thing.'

'What thing? – what do you mean?'

Her eyes became sharp.

'The one I got for you.'

'. . .'.

'Who was it for – who did you have in mind?'

His face rapidly changed colour.

'What do you want to know for?'

As she said this she wrinkled her nose. It was like the face of an angry cat.

'If I want to, I can get some money together. You only have to have the mind for it . . .'.

Glancing at her angry cat face, he spoke in a squeaky voice. Whatever she might be thinking, she looked him up and down: with his strong frame, well-developed muscles like steel, and a face buried in beard, he was not a bad looking man. With a slight smile, she turned away. Meanwhile she continued to supply him secretly with food.

'Man, why do you look so queer?' asked Pyongsan at the tavern in the evening.

'A lifetime's pretty short, isn't it?' was his irrelevant answer.

'I don't know what you're thinking, but you look like a man who's lost his soul.'

'A lifetime goes in the blink of an eye, don't you think so?'

He pressed his point.

315

'Huh, you have changed. "Fish for the water and beasts for the hills." If you really can't stand it, go back to the hills. You are not tied down, are you?'

'Oh, no, I am used to it now. I don't miss the hills all that much.'

He was flustered as if someone had grabbed him by the neck and ordered him to go. It gave Pyongsan a queer feeling, but he had no way of knowing that it was all because of Guinyo.

'Once a long time ago . . .'.

Kang *posoo*'s eyes shone with a mixture of joy and sadness. 'I don't know why, but I often think of it nowadays. I shot an elk — it was a female — and a really strange thing happened. The next day I happened to pass the spot where I'd shot it. There, where its blood had been spilt, a male was lying, dead. There was no shot wound or anything wrong . . . really it must all be due to Yin and Yang, the male and female principles, mustn't it?'

Pyongsan just stared at him open-mouthed.

Chapter Twenty-Seven

SINCE his mission to bring in Kang *posoo*, Kim Pyongsan had frequented the Choi house and, in doing so, he gave an exaggerated impression of being favoured by Chisoo, though in fact no one believed him. In truth, it was only thanks to Junku that he had entrance to the *sarang*. In terms of human quality, Junku was less worth than Chisoo, but he affected, as a great man, to patronize Pyongsan, generously overlooking his faults and befriending him. It was most unlikely that a man of the world like Pyongsan did not realize this, but he took the pretence a step further by showing gratitude, humbling himself and fawning. The hunter, desperately lonely since he came down from the hills, also clung to Pyongsan whenever he could, which gave him a good excuse to hang around the Choi house. The only one who was pleased with all this was Haman *dek*. She was also the only one to be taken in by his bragging. Though he was a husband who, while he frequented the tavern as if it was his elder brother's house, never gave her a penny, she was grateful to him for going about with a gentleman from Seoul, and worked even harder, weaving, toiling in the fields and sewing for wages, while she also took care to supply him with clothes that had no odour of sweat and spotless socks. (Being of a good family, naturally he can't go into trade or work on a farm, and it isn't easy to get a post in this troubled time. Though they do say that these days even high offices can be bought if you have the money.) These were not vain words invented to comfort her own weary heart. She really tried to follow the example of the wise women she read about in stories and took pride in disciplining herself in the female virtues, believing that when the world was unsettled even an intelligent man could not help falling into bad ways, such as her husband had. (Without a cloud, how can the Dragon go up to heaven? Of course, he is full of grievances – how can he help it? Because he is always full of sorrow, he drinks and goes wrong. They say that even a prince, if he falls into the wrong world, becomes a woodcutter.)

While she was putting a patch on a sock, rubbing her dimming eyes under the lamp, Pyongsan, who had been lying down in the main room sat up, stretched himself to the full and scratched his chest.

'I might as well go out, I suppose?'

He went out. The early evening was already past. He walked along the dike and turned towards the water mill.

'What's he up to . . . ?' wondered Junku.

He saw Pyongsan on the way back after a long chat with Kim *hunjang* who, for better or worse, was always ready to talk. He had gone there to seek refuge from Chisoo, who soon after supper had scared him as he turned away his eyes, with trembling lips and face turning pale.

'What is he going to the mill for?'

Pausing, he tried to detect what was going on there. All was quiet in the direction of the village. The threshing floor by the mill was empty.

'That's strange. I might as well wait and see. He's bound to come out again.'

He flung himself down on the grass verge. The worst of the summer heat was now over and the evening chill crept under his clothes, making him shiver.

'Ah, I see, the girl is coming.'

He stood up, and as soon as she disappeared into the mill, he stealthily walked towards it with a smile on his face.

The next day the weather was bright. The air had become more translucent. There were no longer any children to be seen splashing about on the edge of the river.

'Hanjo – are the fish biting?' called Pyongsan in his husky voice, looking down from the dike above.

'Damn! It's gone off with the bait again!' said Hanjo, holding the rod.

He quickly glanced upwards as he drew in the line to replace it. He was younger than Chilsung's generation. He grumbled, 'Luck's been rotten from early in the morning. Even the fish must be enlightened nowadays – they're too clever – they just grab the bait and run off.'

'When Yoon Bo comes, you'll be ashamed of yourself.'

'Yoon Bo? Well, when he returns, I'll pack up. He's the elder, and you can't have two fishermen in one village.'

Pyongsan squatted on the bank. Tapping the tip of his nose, he said, 'Why do you low-class people want to bother with such things as seniority?'

'Please don't talk like that. I have never once seen Yoon Bo miss making the offering to the spirits of his ancestors.'

It was an answer that implied 'Fancy – a man like you, who goes to a gambling den even on the anniversary of his parents' death, looking down on the lower classes!'

He pushed aside the basket and cast the line.

'Yoon Bo has no one dependent on him, so it doesn't matter, but you are not like that, are you? If you spend the day like this, who does the farming?'

'Are you asking me?'

'Do you think I'm asking the river breeze?'

'Ha! ha! I suppose at the Mulberry House the servants do the farming.'

This was a sarcastic reference to the shabby mulberry tree that stood in front of his house. Pyongsan laughed.

'Well, digging or fishing, it's all work. The lower classes can't live without working.'

'Of course, that's right, sir. My wife does the farming and I do the fishing. That way, we'll manage, won't we?'

'It's like the blood in a bird's leg.' ' "Collect enough dust and you've got a mountain," as they say. The thing is that this wife of mine, whenever she's got a kid inside her, or pushes one out, she always has a craving for meat, so what else can I do? I have to work hard to catch the fish and feed her up so that her thighs grow plump again and at least she can give me a bowl of porridge.'

'You young rascal, you're not afraid to say anything, are you?'

'Well, it's because I'm one of the lower orders who wasn't brought up properly.'

He pulled out a carp. It leapt about, its scales flashing white. He took the hook out of its mouth, threw it into the basket and replaced the bait.

'It doesn't really matter about us but I do feel sorry for the lady in your house.'

'. . .'.

'You could give her a little money, even if it was only your winnings . . . if the times were better she wouldn't be weaving or digging the fields.'

'Give her the winnings? That would make a cow laugh. If I did that, I bet she wouldn't last out her time.'

Even so, as if embarrassed, he gazed up at the clouds. They too were as clear and sharp as the sky. The milky blur, like a fine spray of water, was gone, perhaps a sign of summer going and autumn coming in.

'If the husband is a gentleman, the wife should be a lady, shouldn't she? She should ride on a palanquin and have a maid to wait on her . . .'.

His tone was still ironic, but clearly he was genuinely sympathetic towards Haman *dek*.

'If I could have afforded a palanquin and a maid . . .'.

He looked as if to add, 'why should I have married into a middle-class family?' But he could not complete it. Rather dejected, he again tapped the tip of his nose with his thumb and snorted. Hanjo, grinning, looked him up and down as he gazed at the clouds and then, turning his eyes towards the dike, he said, 'Here comes Sir Mullet.'

'Sir Mullet?' Pyongsan's eyes followed his to where Cho Junku could be seen strolling towards them.

'Why Mullet?'

'Well, if there's a gentleman as measly as a dace, there must be one a bit bigger, the size of a mullet.'

Pyongsan, helpless, just laughed.

'I see you take after a certain person in eloquence as well as fishing.'

'Who? Yoon Bo? Everything about him is worth copying except, of course, the pock-marks. Even Kim *hunjang* is no match for him.'

'I wonder if he's looking for me?' said Pyongsan.

Hanjo turned his head to fix his gaze on the end of his rod. Hearing no movement yet behind him, he went on.

'If a gentleman like him was governor, they'd erect a monument in honour of his virtue. In the story of Choon-Hyang, the magistrate of Namwon, Byon Hakdo, sitting in state, made it his duty to flog the bottom of the chaste Choon-Hyang, but this gentleman, morning and evening, roams the village – and he's not a dog in a house of mourning on a rainy day either – checking every detail of how the farming is going, and asking every one "Have you had enough to eat?" or "Are you well?" Really, it's a great pity he's not the governor, or at least the master of the Choi house.'

His words were barbed, and Pyongsan also seemed greatly to appreciate them. Junku was coming nearer.

'I'd better try somewhere else. When they meet this enlightened gentleman, the fish will become even smarter and just snatch the bait . . . It's already past midday and I've only caught one . . .'.

He stood up, drawing in his rod.

'Goodbye.'

He gave Pyongsan a perfunctory bow and pretended not to see Junku who, with a sour expression, tried hard not to notice his departure.

'Didn't you go to Dangsan today?' asked Pyongsan in greeting.

Pyongsan was not exactly tall but, perhaps because of Junku's very short legs, he looked quite tall and handsome despite his fatness and his boar-like face.

'No, I didn't, as it doesn't interest me very much.'

As he spoke he stared contemptuously at the receding back of Hanjo with his rod over his shoulder. Beyond the dazzling white sand the dark green water seemed motionless. The fields smelt fresh and a hastily set up scarecrow leaned back and glared up at the sky. If he had committed some crime, it might be understandable but to see someone avoiding him as if he were dirt – what could be more insulting? Besides, it was not even an equal but a man of low class who had thrown him this open insult. Even though he was in the unfortunate state of being no more than a hanger-on at the Choi house, it must have been hard to bear. Furthermore, hadn't he been showing kindness towards all the villagers? Eventually, as

321

his anger was too great to let him ignore it, he had to ask, 'That chap just going off – he seems to do nothing but hang around day and night with a fishing rod. Does he earn his living that way?'

'He does it in his spare time. He is a peasant, a bit cheeky . . .'

Their eyes clashed. Junku blinked.

'There's another one who is crazy about fishing. A well-known handyman. He's away from the village now, working somewhere. Like Kang *posoo*, an old batchelor, pock-marked and ugly.'

'I see.'

'He's a bit cheeky . . . maybe he hates the gentry.'

'Is he a member of the Dong Hak?'

'He could be, but I don't think so.'

'He just sees things from the wrong angle, is that it?'

'Maybe . . . He wouldn't be the only one to do that, would he?'

He said this as if to imply, 'You show off your knowledge with arrogance but aren't you also one of those who sees things from the wrong angle?'

Inwardly he was delighted with the way Hanjo had upset Junku. (Insect-like beggars! If you look at the world cock-eyed, what can you do? You're all fated to wither away after floundering in the muck.) Junku regained his composure. But the hatred of Hanjo at this moment would later result in a cruel revenge which even he himself could not have anticipated.

'Autumn doesn't seem far off. The trees and grass look dry.'

He spoke as if nothing was amiss.

'Well, it's already early autumn.'

'In a village the harvest season is very much looked forward to, so the autumn feeling seems stronger.'

'That's right. They say that in Seoul there are women and children who think that rice grows on trees. How could they feel the autumn in the way farmers do?'

'Do you have a large family?'

He was asking again a question that he had certainly asked before on their way through the hills in search of Kang *posoo*.

'A wife and two sons.'

'That's simple. I envy you having two boys.'

'What about yourself?'

'One son, but he's no good.'

'So, another family where children are scarce. Still, you have a son . . . that's something.'

Junku chuckled.

'If I didn't, I might well meet with a disaster.'

'Disaster?'

Startled, Pyongsan raised his voice unawares.

'I was only joking. How could it be possible?'

He stopped short and turned his eyes towards the river. He seemed to be avoiding Pyongsan's face which had altered colour. Junku changed the subject. 'Look at that ferry – it's overloaded.'

'It's market day tomorrow.'

Pyongsan's husky voice was low.

(Is he hinting that he knows something?)

'So it's tomorrow?'

'Yes.'

'Do they sell more or buy more?'

'It depends on the season. In autumn, there's more to sell, naturally, as it's a farming community.'

Pyongsan pretended to be calm, but his eyes were so unsteady he could not focus them.

'This is something that happened somewhere a long time ago . . .'.

Junku again changed the subject, his eyes following the boat.

'. . .'.

'Such things can easily happen, only they are hushed up, buried and never come out.'

'. . .'.

'We think of not having a son as the greatest sin, but I gather it is not like that in other lands . . .'.

'. . .'.

'Because of that obstinate idea, I think, tragedies more terrible than the dying out of a line have happened . . .'.

Pyongsan's face completely changed colour. Junku, his eyes fixed on the receding ferry, continued, 'It's a story about an only son who had grown old without having a son himself. Naturally, his

323

parents persuaded him to take a concubine, but what was the use of that when he had no seed in himself?'

'You mean he himself didn't know?'

Pyongsan tried hard to keep in tune with the tale.

'Of course he did. But he had manly pride, so he took one, and she must have been crafty and wicked.'

'That's often the case.'

'She was covetous of the inheritance and, unlike the first wife, she knew, from her experience with another man, that there would be no child.'

'I see.'

'Eventually, she got herself pregnant by someone else and murdered her husband.'

'My goodness!'

'It could be quite a common story.'

'Maybe. Are you saying that she escaped without any divine retribution?'

'Dead men don't talk. These crimes all come from the excessive worship of ancestors. The custom of thinking that it's a great sin to be childless and that the spirits of the dead play a bigger part than the living must be got rid of. If you look at the slaughter of those who followed Catholic teaching, it was all because they had done away with their ancestral shrines. With the whole country possessed by such bigotry, what else can you expect?'

Junku went on at length about current affairs and the state of the country in the way that he always enjoyed, but it seemed half-hearted. Pyongsan watched his lips with tense eyes. Outwardly he appeared to be listening attentively to the other's words, but, nerves on edge, he was probing his mind with outstretched tentacles. (Is he talking like this because he's smelt something? Or is it just coincidence? If he detected something, is he encouraging me? No, it couldn't be that. How could he know what's in someone else's mind? It hasn't even happened yet. So he is telling me that finally she got herself pregnant by another man and murdered her husband, and that dead men don't talk!)

'The people ought to open their eyes – the poor people. The shamans still play a big role, and the government argues the pros and cons of ancestral rites, which are nothing more than a private matter.'

His words were going in one of Pyongsan's ear and out of the other. How long had they been talking?

'Wouldn't you like to go to Dangsan?'

For the first time Junku looked Pyongsan in the face. Their eyes briefly met and dropped.

'Shall we?'

They slowly turned and walked off. It was a few days after this that Junku hurriedly left for Seoul.

Chapter Twenty-Eight

ALTERNATELY pushing out and drawing in his lips, Chilsong was binding up the basket he used for carrying manure. His stumpy finger with the joint missing played an obscene game of hide-and-seek. Crawling over the verandah, a child cried with hunger. Yimi *ne* pounding barley, reluctantly put down the pestle and gathered in the grain as she said, 'That little wretch, he can't be hungry, but look at him having a fit!'

She went to the verandah and, sitting on the edge, undid her dress. Still whimpering, the child climbed on to her lap and fastened itself on to her nipple.

'So much work, and eaten up by the kids . . . really I can't stand it.'

Chilsung said bluntly, 'No one told you to push out so many.'

'Did I make them by myself?'

The child sucked greedily, choking as it panted.

'You know that paddy of Dooman's down there', she said.

Chilsung pretended not to hear.

'It's grown beautifully. The heads are so full that when they ripen they'll break the stems.'

'Just plant the seedlings and go and lie on Dangsan and it looks after itself until the harvest – it's that kind of field, anyway.'

'That's what I mean. The floodgates of luck have opened on them.'

'. . .'

'A pumpkin rolled in there by itself. If only we had a relative like Gannan *halmum* . . . when will we ever have a bit of land of our own?'

'You never know what fate will bring.'

'Unless the world has a new beginning, what hope is there of getting away from this life of struggle?'

'No one knows their fate. Of course they don't. If the wind

blows right, my life could change and I might have two or three concubines – you never know.'

As he cut off the cord with a sickle, he smiled to himself.

'You can have ten and you won't hear a word from me. If only we could have a better life. It's like expecting blossom from a dead tree.'

'Just stroke your ear lobes and wait and see.'

'By the way, I hear that these days Gannan *halmum* is near to death. Domman *ne* has been running about like mad – she has every reason to – she'd even pull out her own hair to make her some shoes.'

'If you're old, you've got to die. Why waste a mouthful of rice on them?'

'They say it'll be a funeral soon. If she had died last winter, Dooman's family would never have had that paddy . . . the silly old crone must have got better bit by bit just to help them. And anyway, Dooman's father works so hard they've got grain put away.'

She was unbearably jealous.

'Oh, ouch!'

She slapped the baby's cheek. Nodding off, it must have bitten her nipple rather than let go. She swore and pushed the crying child away.

'Children or whatever, you're all a nuisance. I don't care whether you cry or not, if your belly's full, lie down and sleep! If you're hanging on my tits all the time, who's going to do the work? Monks from Chiri Mountain?'

Woken up, the baby cried and clung to her even harder.

'These things are a curse – nothing but trouble.'

As she shook free of the child and stepped down into the yard, she called to her daughter Yimi who was playing just outside the gate.

'Silly girl, go and look after the baby. You eat up the food and what do you do for it? You are all my curse!'

'Did anyone tell you to produce this troublesome lot, one after the other?'

'Did I do it by myself?'

With the manure basket on his A-frame Chilsung slung it on to

327

his back and walked out of the gate. His wife gathered barley into a large jar and was about to follow with it on her head. On the way she picked up a gourd bowl from the jar-stand.

'Listen, girl, just you go out to play instead of minding the baby and you'll see!' While she was rinsing the barley by the well, Dooman *ne* came up with a water jar.

'What's happened to Suni, that you have to fetch water?'

'Must be worms. She says she's got tummy ache . . . woman, why you are wasting that good barley chaff?'

'We haven't got any pigs. Besides, I got the bran out after the first threshing.'

'Still, it's a pity to waste it.'

Dooman *ne* had a pig.

Ignoring Yimi *ne*'s sulkiness, she drew water. '*Songnim!*'

Throwing away the barley water, Yimi *ne* went on, 'Kangchong *dek*, I don't know what's the matter with that woman.'

Pouring some fresher water into Yimi *ne*'s barley jar, Dooman *ne* said, 'Have you quarrelled again?'

'Every single word I say, she twists it. As they say "Lightning doesn't strike every time it thunders." I can't quarrel with her every time. It would be the death of me. Ever since her husband went astray, that woman . . .'.

'I don't want to hear any more about it.'

'Wolsun – or whatever she's called – now she's dropped out, that should be the end of it. Why should she pick on me? It's because I have no luck with people that all this trouble comes on me.'

'It's just that she's like that. If you're sensible, you'll just put up with it.'

'Even so, there has to be a limit.'

'It shouldn't be like that between neighbours. Even if it's hard to bear, try and put up with it.'

Straightening her well-fed body, Dooman *ne* clumsily lifted the water jar on to her head.

'All is well with you, *songnim*, so you are putting on weight.'

'I know, isn't it awful? I'm getting like this and my husband keeps getting thinner.'

'Really, you're so fortunate.'

'To make ends meet, I'm on the run day and night, I must be off now.'

'Bye.'

No sooner had she receded, striding off with the jar on her head, than Haman *dek* and Magdal *ne* appeared one after the other. Unlike her usual self, Magdal *ne*, twitching her thick-set lips, was wordless, and Yimi *ne*, too gave her only a quick glance. Haman *dek* also was drawing water silently. After a while, Magdal *ne*, as if she had at last made up her mind, called, '*Songnim*!' and went on, 'I never meant to say this, but there has to be a limit to what you can put up with, isn't there?'

'. . .'.

'Also, I'll feel better if I tell you for once . . .'.

Having finished drawing the water, Haman *dek* was about to put the jar on her head. 'Whatever it is, go on.'

'Not just once or twice, but constantly he is trying to ruin me. Do you think it doesn't matter if a widow, with no man, is left to die like this?'

'What a queer thing to say! Who said you ought to be left to die?'

Haman *dek*'s dried and shrunken cheeks had turned red. Apart from her sharp nerves, her face often flushed for no apparent reason.

'Being looked down on because there's no man behind me makes it worse. Why does it always have to happen to me and not to others?'

'Really, how can I know before you've told me?'

'It's not the first time, and last night again, he took all the beans and ruined the crop.'

At this Haman *dek*'s face turned pale.

'As they say, "Controlling one's child is beyond human power," but I can't go on pretending to be dumb, can I? Please speak to him, *songnim*. Until now, to save your face, I have put up with as much as I can.'

'I understand.'

Haman *dek* left them with her jar. As soon as she had gone, Magdal *ne*, turning to Yimi *ne*, waved her hands and feet and cursed

329

and abused Pyongsan and his son, and even beat her breast. Yimi *ne* smiled faintly.

'That will do . . . I've got mountains of work to be done . . .' she said as she slipped away like a mudfish, with the bowl of barley on her head. Magdal *ne* noisily blew her nose.

'Huh! Just because it's not her business . . . whether I swallow him down or chew him up, because I can't let out this anger, I'm going mad.'

When she reached home, Haman *dek*, after searching the house, went to the threshing ground where she found her son.

'What's the matter?' asked Gobok, who had been following his mother unsuspectingly, as he noticed her face.

'I've got a job for you – let's go home first.'

'What job?'

'You talk too much. Just be quiet and follow me.'

At the house she pushed him into the small room and locked it from the outside.

'Mother!'

Inside the room, he stamped his feet. From a bundle of firewood she picked up four or five sturdy sticks and went into the room and locked it from the inside.

'You scamp! You know what you've done!'

'Mother! I haven't done anything!'

His knees knocked together as he trembled.

'You must be punished. If that doesn't cure you, you and I will die together. Come on, pull up your trousers and bare your calves!'

'Mother! What have I done?'

'Rascal! Do as I say and bare your legs!'

'I want to know what I am being beaten for.'

He was as pale as death.

'Are you going to say you didn't go to Magdal *ne*'s bean plot?'

'What? I never. I didn't do it.'

The stick flew. It struck the lower half of his body.

'Ouch!'

She beat him indiscriminately, as if she was mad, on the lower part of his body and his shoulders, with tears streaming down her cheeks. He flew about the room screaming. From outside, Pyong-san's voice thundered, 'Open the door!'

'Father! Father! Save me! Help!'

She thrashed him even more severely. With a snapping sound the door fell open. Treading on the fallen door, Gobok flew into the yard like a leaping tiger. There he ran round and round until he fell on the ground foaming at the mouth in convulsions. Haman *dek* stood blankly with the broken stick in her hand.

'What is it?' Pyongsan shouted loudly.

'You damned woman!'

Rushing into the kitchen, he fetched a gourd of water and splashed it over the unconscious boy.

'I didn't, I didn't go into Magdal *ne's* plot . . . I didn't do it,' he said through trembling lips.

'What is it?'

'Father, the beans, the beans . . . I didn't . . .'.

Swiftly turning on Haman *dek*, he said, 'Woman, tell me all about it from the start!'

'. . .'

'Why are you thrashing your child like a dog?'

'I know his wickedness.'

'What? I said tell me from the beginning.'

Without once moving her sunken eyes she told him briefly what had happened at the well. Tears streamed from her motionless eyes.

'I see.'

His face changed colour and he turned to go.

'Where are you going?'

Without answering, he slowly walked away.

(She ought to have her head chopped off!)

He clearly distinguished between an indirect accusation and a direct one. When it had been in the form of 'Who has done it?' he did not worry however gross the insults might be, but when it was 'You are the thief,' he could not ignore it. (The bitch ought to be drawn and quartered.) Because the insult had come through his son and his wife – whether or not beans had been stolen was not the point – his sense of dignity increased his arrogance. Whatever his son might have done, if she had brought it up openly, her bad manners must be corrected. There could never be any question of setting up a dispute between a gentleman and a commoner. There could only be punishment. He walked straight into her yard. As if worried that in a house without a man her chickens might be stolen, Magdal *ne* was attending to the hen-house.

'What's the matter? she said in an uneasy tone and repeatedly asked, 'Why do you come to a house where there's no man?'

'You bitch!'

'Pardon?'

'I'll tear your mouth out.'

'What? Tear my mouth out? What do you mean?'

She was frightened and subdued.

'Don't pretend you don't know!'

He walked up to her purposefully and hit her on her scabby cheek with his fist.

'Ouch! He's hitting me!'

The dwarf-like Magdal ran out of the kitchen: 'Mother!'

Again his fist struck her on the nose. Blood gushed out.

'Help! My mother is dying!'

'How dare you – you bitch? You ought to be put on the rack.'

Holding her nose, she tried to run away.

'Help! Everyone! My mother's being killed!'

Pyongsan kicked her as she ran. She fell to the ground, blood pouring from her nose. The village people crowded round. Pyongsan wiped the blood from his fist on a pile of barley straw and left with a final threat, 'Bitch! Let your tongue loose once more and it's the last time you'll come out of that gate.'

Those who had gathered round turned away from him as if to avoid a mad dog. Yamu *ne* lifted her up and, splashing her face with water brought by Magdal, wiped away the blood stains.

'How ever much the people rebel, the violence of the gentry goes on just the same,' sighed Yongpari.

'The dog-meat butcher! Gentleman! What kind of a gentleman does he think he is?' Handori spat violently.

'Beating his own wife's not enough for him – is that why he beats other people's?'

Yam *ne*, mopping up the blood, clucked with her tongue. Magdal went on crying.

'Are the lower classes nameless and the laws only for the gentry? However humble she may be, can a man attack someone else's wife?' mumbled Yamu *ne*.

'To be honest, the world's got to be shaken up . . .'.

'One more uprising to scare them stiff . . .'.

'Between ourselves, the Dong Hak revolt was something – even though they lost, the gentry were subdued and the officials were quiet, and for a time we could breathe freely . . .'

'That bastard who disgraces the village – we must throw him out straight away – we can't leave it.'

'That's right!' Magdal *ne*, who had been lying down as if she was dead, suddenly sprang up. In fact, apart from her bleeding nose, she was not badly hurt.

'The meat on the chopping board is not frightened of the knife! I'll see who dies first! I'll see to it with my life!'

She jumped up and down raving like a shaman. The wives who had arrived late whispered together in wifely fashion.

'Bloodshed everywhere and where's the law?'

'The fist's near but the law's far.'

As Magdal *ne*'s mood grew more inflated the atmosphere of excitement among the men began to go down. Finally, as she brandished her fists and rolled her eyes, they even began to laugh at her. Sensing that sympathy was growing weaker, she began to wail, 'Alas! My fate! My luck! Being alone is bad enough but what's the use of living on like this! Depised like this, how can I go on?'

After this incident there was some disquiet in the village, but soon enough, like a river after the wind has dropped, on the surface at least, it became calm again, maybe because Pyongsan did not show his face there, his wife and children stayed inside, and everyone grew tired of Magdal *ne*'s song and dance.

Squatting on the kitchen floor, Kangchon *dek* was crushing garlic. (Yesterday, on the path, that bitch smiled at my husband with her eyes again. I saw it – I saw it clearly. She's got her own husband – how dare she wag her tail at someone else's? She deserves to be killed. I've long since noticed she has the air of a loose woman.)

In her excitement she brought the knife down hard enough to spoil the surface of the choppping board.

It was understandable. When she realized that Wolsun had gone, she had thought that, with her out of the way, her husband's heart would turn back but, in fact, it had gone a thousand miles further away. He did all that was expected of him. He worked in the field, did odd jobs round the house and fed the ox. He worked slowly, but he was not idle as he had been in the past.

'I knew it was coming. Would a woman who goes around drinking places stick to one man? Huh! What's he got to offer her? Money? Luxury? A man with a wife he married with all the proper ceremonies can't expect to have a woman like that. A bitch who has one man yesterday and another today, sucking their blood – of course she wouldn't stay with him. I really feel as happy as if all sorts of evil spirits had let go and left me.'

Yongi did his work without speaking a word, buried in a cold and unapproachable silence, except for when he gazed towards the river and his face became forlorn.

'It's about time you came to your senses. Being scalded once is enough and you'd better watch out that it doesn't happen again. They say, "You may catch the breeze that's to come but never the one that's gone." Just the two of us, how much do we need to eat or spend? I may have been too hard on you, but I did it with good intentions.'

She would speak pleadingly, but he continued to keep that unapproachable distance. At first, thinking that it was manly pride, she had been at ease, though a little resentful. But she gradually grew more worried. He became cooler day by day and never came near her. In bed, if she touched him, he would turn over and when, after angry mutterings, she poured out abuse, he would go in to the unused and dilapidated spare room. Eventually he cleared it up and moved in there. One day she pushed in and hurled herself at him, pouring out curses too offensive for anyone to utter, but her small body was picked up by his long arm and thrown out on to the verandah, after which he locked the door from inside and, though she lay there crying loudly with her legs stretched out, he did not heed it with as much as a cough. The next day the villagers

334

found out what had happened and teased them, saying that the midnight wailing had made them think someone had died. To this, also, Yongi made no response. Of his own accord he became a recluse and rarely met his friends.

When she had finished making *kimchi* and had packed it into a jar, she plunged her hands into a bucket of water, dried them on her skirt and, as if she had remembered something urgent, ran to Dooman *ne's* house. Boksil barked as he rushed out of the gate at her.

'Stupid thing! Why bark everytime you see me?'

Having vented her anger on the dog, she called, '*Songnim!*'

'Come in.'

'What are you doing?'

'I was thinking of grinding some malt.'

'Why, is there a sacrifice coming?'

'What sacrifice? No, for my aunt.'

'I hear she's in a bad way.'

'Yes, so I'm trying to make a sweet drink for her,' said Dooman *ne*, as she picked bits of straw out of the grain bowl.

'You try hard to be a dutiful niece, don't you?'

'We don't do much for her really. With no children of her own, she is the sorry one.'

She walked up to the grinding stones and removed the top one. Kangchong *dek* blurted out, 'They say its a good life without children.'

Dooman *ne*, as if thinking, 'Oh dear! I've slipped up again!' smiled awkwardly and gave her a quick glance.

'That's true. Children are a worry.'

Thus appeasing her, she brushed off the buckwheat powder left round the axle.

'I'm so upset . . . *songnim*.'

'Why?'

'Yimi *ne* – I'm sure she has the ways of a loose woman.'

'What a thing to say?'

'I'm saying it because she wags her tail at other people's husbands, though she has one of her own. That bitch – from the way she behaves, I bet there was something wrong with her from when she was a girl. Just think about it. Why should a good-looking woman like her marry an old man like Chilsung, and maimed, with a finger missing?'

'Kangchong *dek*, how can you say such awful things?'

'Because I have my suspicions . . .'.

In the middle of sweeping the grinding stone, Dooman *ne* assumed a serious look.

'You're going to be in trouble. If you go on talking so thoughtlessly, you'll be made to eat your own vomit.'

'Whether I'll be made to eat my own vomit or her crotch will be split, we'll have to wait and see. There's wickedness in that bitch's smiling eyes.'

Her dark complexioned face was puckered and her small eyes glowed beneath the thin eyelids. She knew there was nothing between Yimi *ne* and Yongi but, as if his indifference to her was Yimi *ne*'s fault, she seemed unable to deal with her own hatred.

'Well, my dear, it's wrong to say such things. It is only natural for neighbours to smile at each other – is she a lady living behind nine-fold walls and keeping distant from men? What's wrong with smiling at a neighbour she sees every day? – they are not sworn enemies. Being jealous counts as one of "The seven evils for which a husband can denounce his wife". If you go on fussing about such trifles, people will only laugh at you, not at her. Never speak like that to anyone. "The more you sift it, the finer the flour, but the more you talk, the rougher the words".'

Dooman *ne* put the upper stone on the axle and, throwing in a handful of grain, took hold of the handle. With a look of unhappiness she began to turn it. It was just as well she kept her mouth shut, for if she had spread it round the village in the style of Magdal *ne*, the two women would soon have been at each other's throats.

Chapter Twenty-Nine

'THE master is here, ma'am,' called Samwol from outside.

Lady Yoon, turning back the summer quilt, sat up. The dark green of the quilt matched with her sickly face to produce an air of sadness and decline. Choi Chisoo knelt before her with knees touching.

'Are you very ill?'

Hiding his expression, he dropped his eyes to the floor.

'I think I am just over-tired,' she replied, as she averted her eyes to the bureau.

'Shouldn't I send for the doctor?'

'There is no need for that.'

'Still . . .'.

Slowly lifting his eyes, he looked at his mother. Sensing his gaze, she met it. There were innumerable dark spots on her face and, perhaps because of a sleepless night, bluish rings round her eyes like the haloes of the moon. It was a pitiful sight.

(How old she is!)

Narrow eyes, in which the pupils sparkled as brightly as ever; will and strength still inextinguishable; hair and dress as always, neat and correct even though she was just out of bed: he had never once seen her in disarray.

(Same as ever! Always that appearance, and those eyes! Like metal refined a thousand times in the forge!)

Chisoo felt his mind was cooling. The hot flow that had surged up as he noticed how old his mother looked now seemed rapidly to recede. They were both well-forged pieces of metal, and it was that moment on a battleground when two swords cross. Both vied with all their strength, a breathless silence and tension tightly packing the space between them. He could sense on his skin and in his heart that his mother's resistance was thinner than before, yet sharper.

'Do you still go shooting on Dangsan these days?'

'Yes, mother.'

'Aren't you overdoing it?'

'Certainly not. On the contrary, it seems to do me good.'

'. . .'

She looked away from him. His eyes narrowed as if the sun was bright on them.

'While I am with you, mother, there is something I have to say.'

'. . .'

'I can't go on alone much longer. Not only because of what others think, but also because Sohi must have a mother.'

Her eyes, withdrawn, now fastened on him. Having said this, he could not understand why the issue of remarriage, which he had never even thought about before, should have slipped out of his mouth.

'If that's how you feel, we must look for a suitable person.'

(Why don't you object, mother?)

'It's true. Sohi does need a mother.'

(Does she really? It will only be giving her unnecessary trouble. All she needs is a future husband, some gentle person who will spend his time in reading.)

Since his return from Seoul with an infection his habit of seeing his mother every morning and evening had been dropped. It had been a natural avoidance that had lessened their mutual burden. He still had no clear idea of how much land he owned or what was the annual yield. Not wanting to be tied down, he had consciously tried to be indifferent to such things and it might be said that, to that extent, her yoke had been heavier, which was perhaps what she desired – the heavier the yoke, the more welcome as a means of adding to her painful penance.

The shaman Wolsun *ne*, brandishing a dagger, had danced like one possessed. Her flower-decked hat and ritual garments fluttered. The cymbals and drums were wild. Sweat streamed from her face. It had been going on for several days and nights. Suddenly she had thrown away the dagger, run to Chisoo's grandmother and fallen to her knees.

'Madam!'

338

His grandmother had been startled. Blinking, she had looked down at her.

'The young mistress must go to the monastery. My spiritual strength is not enough, and the evil spirits refuse to leave her.'

'To the monastery?'

'Yes, ma'am. She must flee there and stay until the year is out. Without leaving a trace, she must go there until the end of the year.'

As she bowed low, huge drops of sweat continued to fall on to the mat. The servant Bawoo stood by white-faced, while his wife dabbed her eyes with the end of her jacket ribbon.

'In that case, we must send her.'

His grandmother, blinking, had looked at the tearful Gannan and then at Chisoo. His mother had been taken away in a palanquin. The next day except for Bawoo and Gannan who had stayed with her, the servants who had gone with them returned. How humid and long had been that summer without his mother! His grand-mother had tried hard to comfort him when he missed her but he had never been very fond of her. At night he had slipped out of the house to go to the river and catch glow-worms, while in the daytime he went up Dangsan and wept as he blew on grass blades. He had felt as if his mother would never return. At other times he took a horsewhip from the stable and showed his bad temper by slashing the backs of the servants at work, and he bothered the maids to death. After the death of Subuni, Yongi's sister, he had taken a dislike to Wolsun, for no apparent reason, and this became worse until he pulled her hair and kicked her. Once Wolsun's mother had come upon him behaving like this.

'Master, I have done wrong. Young master, forgive me.'

For some reason she had followed him, begging him to forgive her, not only once or twice, but again and again. It was because she kept on begging that an idea had come to him: 'It was your doing, wasn't it – to send my mother to the temple?'

'Yes, yes. I am to blame. Please forgive me. I have lied to the spirits, so I should be punished.'

The next year, when the flower-wind of the second month was blowing, his mother came back in the palanquin. He had run out madly as far as the entrance to the village and followed her from behind.

'Mother!'

He felt a great urgency in his heart and had called out as he followed the palanquin, but no answer came from inside. When at last it was put down and she stepped out, he could not forget to this day, how, at that moment, she had been like a figure carved out of lead. Not only her appearance but, as soon as she saw him, she stepped back a pace and stared as if looking for somewhere to hide.

'Mother!'

As he called her, her eyes became wild as though they were sending forth sparks. How could his mother be like this? All was black before his eyes – the mother who had been away for so long, whom he had missed even in his dreams, whom he had expected to stroke him with a gentle hand on his shoulder and say, 'How have you been all this time?'

After greeting his grandmother, she had retired into the *byoldang*, and the doors remained tightly closed until the sun had set. From that time there began to flow an invisible river that separated mother and son. It had been rejection without any explanation. He could not understand how the mother who had been so loving and kind had become more distant than a stranger.

He had passed a dark and lonely boyhood. Of delicate health, with a hysterical temperament from the beginning, he had become cruel and grew into a domineering and arrogant young man. In the eleventh month of the year of his mother's return from the monastery, then thirteen, he had entered into a formal marriage. The few years that followed had seen a respite in his health. It had been much later that he had attempted to solve the enigma of his mother by picking three separate incidents from his innumerable memories and piecing them together. The first was what had happened on the night when Dr Mun came to see her in her sickness, before her retreat to the monastery. It was a conversation between Bawoo and the doctor. After reading, he had put out the lamp and got into bed but he had been unable to sleep. It had remained faintly in his mind until one day it clicked and became clear. The second was Wolsun *ne*'s words and manner: 'Yes, yes, I am to blame. Please forgive me! I have lied to the spirits, so I should be punished.'

The third was his mother's appearance, like a figure carved out of lead, and her wild eyes – this was the sharpest impression of all. Around these three memories there revolved always several faces: Dr Mun, the monk Ugwan, Bawoo and his wife, and Wolsun *ne*. He had often felt an impulse to ask Bawoo or his wife or Wolsun *ne* about the mystery, while, as for Dr Mun or Ugwan, he could not think of them without hatred, though he did not know why.

He had met Ugwan once when he was perhaps twenty-two or so. The elderly monk's big, energetic figure with glowing eyes had roused in him an unbearable disgust. He had inwardly cursed him, 'Greedy old monk, whatever he feeds on, he's more like a lump of passion than a man who's supposed to have overcome the hundred and eight temptations of the world.'

The conversation, which had stopped at the point where Lady Yoon had said, 'If that's how you feel, we must look for a suitable person,' was resumed as she asked him whether Jang-am *sonseng* was now a little better.

'He seems to be in a bad way,' he answered in a cool tone.

The curious hostility between his teacher and his mother – in fact they had hardly met and there was no obvious reason for it – might be something like the hostility between her and himself. On the other hand it could be that because he knew how Dr Mun, whom his mother highly respected, and the doctor's close friend Ugwan saw and thought of Jang-am that he felt like this.

'A man with aristocratic corruption in his bones. However much learning he may have, what is the use of it? Can a man who sees people as animals set a good example in word or deed? The learned man must not only seek his own path but guide the people ino right ways – sitting all alone on the lofty seat, who can he accuse?'

Once, when Chisoo and Yi Dong-jin had been sitting with him, the doctor had bitterly criticized Jang-am, but Chisoo had contemptuously made no response. From his early days he had been his pupil and had been greatly influenced by him and, to the extent that his life had been dark through his boyhood and youth, Jang-am's views had made a powerful impact. He was a scholar who, after taking a state examination only once in his youth, had spent his life as a village recluse buried among his books, a man who was thorough in his opposition to the present power structures but did not approve of popular uprisings such as that of the Dong Hak – in fact he hated them. He regarded the people as a foolish crowd and, if ill-educated men of power were overfed pigs, the ignorant public were hungry wolves. For exploiters of shameless greed, who, brandishing their power, attempt to enliven a boring life, the foolish mob is a good tool. On the other hand, if this crowd should awake, at the very moment of awakening it will become a source of destruction. At some stage this reversal of power might be called revolution, but there would be no change in its essence, merely a turn of the vicious circle – these were his views: Give them knives, and the mob will turn into butchers- just as a beast spreading its claws reveals its true nature.

The so-called 'sense of mission', too, is no more than a cloak for knowledgeable rascals. Pull it away and look inside – they are no better than others. Human dignity is not to be found in action, but in passive compliance with principle.

It is true that study is the search for truth, but truth is not in itself necessarily useful or beneficial.

When a scholar starts with the idea that knowledge is something beneficial, he is no more than an artisan – it is not something to be put in a frame made according to set rules. Truth is not for everyone. While it's being passed from hand to hand it degenerates, dies and decays, leaving a dry husk of which some quite irrelevant imitation emerges in the end and rules the public mind. Any scholar who collaborates in such fakes is no scholar, but an accomplice of the blind mob and the politicians.

He could be called a world-weary pessimist, a man who rejected present reality for a perverse belief in pure scholarship, while his view that human nature was basically evil seemed to lead him to be contemptuous, narrow-minded, arrogant and cynical and gave him a bias towards an extreme egoism. These were the qualities that had outraged Dr Mun, who felt an affection for ordinary people and was trusted by them, though one cannot deny that his feelings were also inflamed by a sense of social inferiority.

342

'Have you been to see him lately?' asked Lady Yoon once more.

'No, I haven't been able to.'

'You should have, really, shouldn't you?'

'I will before I go off to the hills.'

'To the hills?'

'Yes.'

Their eyes clashed. After flashing fire, they cooled and hardened and then silence ensued as at the moment when steel meets steel, indeed when sword blades cross, with the pouring of cold sweat. Around Lady Yoon's eyes hung bluish rings like haloes of the moon; under the thin lids, her dark eyes did not flicker: nor did his below his raised eyelashes.

(Speak, mother. Tell me your secret.)

(Evil one! Do you really want to see me thrown into a living hell?)

'Do you really have to go?'

'Yes.'

A chilly smile rose to his lips.

'To kill is a sin.'

She closed her eyes.

'But I think it will be good training for me . . .'.

At this moment Kim *subang* called from outside, 'Madame!'

'What is it?'

'A messenger from the monastery.'

'What does he want?'

'He says he's brought a letter for you.'

'I see.'

Her tone was curt.

'What shall I do?'

'Let him go and rest in the servants' quarters and give me the letter.'

'Yes, ma'am.'

A little later Samwol came in with the sealed letter.

'Leave it there.'

She indicated the bureau with her eyes.

'I will leave you now.'

Chisoo went out and Lady Yoon went back to bed. She closed

343

her eyes and lay quietly for a long time, almost as if she had ceased to breathe. When she opened them, she sat up and unsealed the letter. It was from Ugwan and concerned Hwani. It said that certainly he was not anywhere near, that he seemed to have gone to another province, so there was no need for her to worry for the moment, and that, as the search was going on, Ugwan was sure that he would soon be found, and a safe refuge had been arranged. As soon as he was discovered she would be informed. She burnt the letter and then called Kim *subang* to tell him that he could let the messenger go back.

Ugwan's letter gave her little comfort. That Hwani was being sought was vague, and that he seemed to have gone to another province was no more than a guess. Even if he had moved to another area, if it was on a track from Yon-goksa, Chisoo, soon to leave for the hills, would be able to pick it up. Once he had set his mind on finding Hwani, the meticulous Chisoo would make a foolproof plan. Lady Yoon realized the mistake she had made on that particular day in the late autumn of the previous year when Chisoo had gone to visit Jamg-am on his sickbed. It was true she had had to act in a great hurry to take advantage of his absence but she had failed to provide the erring couple with a hiding place. Was it because she had been unable to or merely unwilling? Chisoo and Hwani were both her sons. Born to their respective sad fates, both were, for her, instruments of fierce torture, unseverable ties of blood and flesh, loved with a love that pierced her heart. For the past ten or twenty years she had been like the balance weight of scales that must not tilt to either side as her sons stood distant at their opposite ends. That she could not be close to Chisoo was partly from a sense of guilt and also because of the pity she felt for her other son whom she had had to abandon without once holding to her breast. Equally, was it not because of her obligation to, and love for, Chisoo that she could not properly provide for Hwani? In short, during the past ten or twenty years she had lived as a weight on the scales, unable to lean to one side or the other, which explains why, though she had helped Hwani to escape in Chisoo's absence, she could not provide him with a place to hide. As she thought of

344

the long years she had endured, unable to stretch out her motherly arms to help, she wondered how much longer it must go on.

When the Dong Hak rebellion seemed to cover the earth and sky – was it five years ago? – the Choi house had also been invaded by a great mob of them. Prepared for the massacre of the whole family, she had sat in her room and waited for whatever was to come. However, although they swarmed in the servants' quarters, they kept clear of the *byoldang*, the inner quarters and the *sarang*. It made her even more restless than when she had been actually expecting them. Deep into the night she could not get into bed but sat with the lamp lit. It was after midnight. A sound of approaching footsteps, and then of someone stepping on to the verandah. She slid her dagger under her knees. The door opened.

'Please, don't be frightened. I haven't come to harm you.'

The man who stepped into the room was an impressive figure of about forty. She did not raise her eyes.

'Lady!'

'. . . .'

'Look at me just once . . .'.

'. . . .'

'I am Kim Gae-joo.'

Even in the lamp light, her change of colour was noticeable.

'Please forgive me. I'm grateful that you are alive.'

Her eyes turned to him. He gave her a boyish smile. His great figure seemed to tremble gently, even delicately.

'Your son, Hwani, has grown into a fine young man.'

He paused.

'I wanted to tell you that myself – that's why I came like this.'

'. . . .'

'I know this is impolite. I've always been like that. I'll leave in the morning and take this mob away.'

As if to mark the end, fire sparked from his eyes. The lamp shone from one side so that one half of his face was in the light and the other shaded, giving him a mysterious appearance, as if half animal and half spirit. One eye glowed while the other seemed cold.

345

'You haven't a word for me! So, paying my respects to that arrogant aristocratic blood, I bid my farewell, my lady.'

With a smile of self-mockery, very different from a moment before, he bowed out.

At dawn the Dong Hak mob that had occupied the servants' quarters receded like an ebbing tide. Once out of it, they were not as quiet as they had been during their stay. On the contrary, they were fiercely destructive. Sweeping down towards the town, they had attacked the government offices and murdered the officers, high or low, landlords, and local gentry who supported the public officers, and plundered weapons and so forth – a great many people were killed or injured. It was said that the white sand in the pine wood by the River Sumjin had been dyed red with blood. Because of what had happened, there had been a rumour that the Choi house had secretly collaborated with them, given them funds, and so on, but it had never been more than rumour.

While retreating from the house, Kim Gae-joo had probably told Hwani, who had followed him into battle, the truth about his mother. In September of that year the northern and southern groups of the Dong Hak had joined into one great force and risen again with the cry of 'Down with Japan and Save the Nation', but in December, after successive defeats, they finally collapsed, so bringing down the curtain on the tragedy of the so-called Dong Hak Revolt of the year of Gabo, a peasants' war that at the same time had been a national war. Hwani, as a survivor of this struggle, after wandering to escape pursuit, had gone, not to the monk Ugwan, his father's brother, but to stand before the gates of the Choi house. When Lady Yoon heard from the doctor that Kim Gae-joo had been executed in the prison at Jonjoo and his head put on display, tears streaked the face of this woman of iron.

'Ma'am!'

Samwol's voice struck her ears.

'What is it?'

'Oh! Madame! Oh! . . .'.

'Don't be silly. Come out with it!'

'Gannan *halmum* . . .'.

'She's dead?'

'Yes, Ma'am.'
Her voice broke into tears.
'Gannan *halmum* . . .'.
'She's dead?'
'Yes, Ma'am.'

.

Chapter Thirty

IN the west the sun was about a hand's span above the horizon. As if in preparation for the darkness, the woods divided into patches of light and shade and the green fields seemed to hurry restlessly before a faint breeze. Hanjo, after gathering up his fishing tackle, was on his way home and Suh *subang*'s daughter-in-law, just off the ferry, came over the dike with a bundle on her head. Her pale blue skirt and the maroon ribbon on her jacket flapped in the breeze. It was a long way from her maternal home so perhaps she had changed her socks in the boat, as they looked white and clean in her hemp-cord sandals.

'You've been to your mother's, then?' asked Yamu *ne*, who had been walking quickly down the village road.

'Yes.'

'Anyway, your father-in-law's waiting for you with his eyes nearly popping out.'

'Yes, because mother has to do the meals.'

'Don't I know! It's not because he wants to see you, but because he can't bear to see his wife working. At their age they're a dogged pair of love-birds. By the way, someone's died.'

'Died?'

'Gannan *halmum* at the *champan* house.'

'Really?'

'She was old enough. For once we'll hear your father-in-law's mourning songs.'

Kilsang came running along the path, his pigtail bobbing. Pyongsan's son, Gobok, organizing an urchins' wrestling match on the threshing ground, squealed like a pig when its throat is cut, 'Hey, you! Kilsang!'

Wiping away his tears with his fist, Kilsang kept on running.

'Kilsang – bastard!'

He was just going to run across the yard but Gobok grabbed his jacket from behind.

'Were you hit by a stray bullet? Are your earholes blocked?'

He shook off Gobok's hand.

'Someone's died . . .' '

'Who? Your daughter?'

' . . .'

'It must be Bongsoon, then.'

He laughed, showing a crooked tooth like his father's. Breathing hard, his shoulders heaving, Kilsang was about to continue running but this time he was blocked from the front. Following suit, the small boys lined up in front of him.

'Hi! Hi! Hi! You mean Bongsoon's died, don't you?'

He tried to push them aside.

'I'm in a hurry . . .'.

Gobok came close.

'Are you going to hit me? Bastard monk! I know all about it. You're doing this and that with her, aren't you? Let me see how big your thing is.'

The boys laughed. Kilsang blushed like a radish. Ruthlessly pushing Gobok away, he ran through the urchins.

> 'Holy monk! Holy monk! Where are you off to?
> With your peaked hat and knapsack,
> Over the hill, to a girl's house.
> To beg for alms, and beat the gong?
> Not for alms, not for alms,
> But to grab her hand and kiss her.'

The children, like weeds thriving in dry land, coarsely squealed and clapped as they ran behind the retreating Kilsang. The mountains and woods, the river and the fields, everything visible was raw nature, flourishing through constant reproduction, so it seemed that the children running free as they grew, had their eyes opened early to sex.

'Damn kids! Haven't you got homes, that you have to go mad here?'

349

Dooman's father, on his way with his ox, waved his whip and chased them off. Yongman, who had been sitting apart from the others, playing a game with Gobok's younger brother, Hanbok, stood up and dusted off his hands.

'Daddy!'

'Silly boy! What are you doing here – picking up bad habits? Go home at once!'

Hanbok, glancing towards his brother, shuffled behind Yongman. 'I wasn't doing it . . .'.

'Dad! Kilsang said someone has died, and he was running like mad.'

'What? Someone died? Come on, lad. Quickly!'

Guessing that it was Gannan *halmum*, he hurried home, urging Yongman, who was a kind of adopted son and chief mourner for Gannan. The cow-bell clanked faster as well. The rice plants just beginning to show their heads in the paddy were riding on the breeze in waves of dark and pale green, nodding towards the west. As they went through the scrub, it seemed to have grown even cooler. By the well, where the soil was damp, a hen had pulled out a worm and ran about to escape from a cockerel. Crouching by the stream, with her baby on her back, Yimi *ne* was doing the washing. The baby cried each time she started to beat the laundry with her stick.

'What kind of woman would disappear leaving her washing like that?'

A bowl filled with a laundry stick, socks and rags had lain there when she first came and now, as she was rinsing her washing, the owner still hadn't come back.

'I don't know whether she's married or not, but I bet she's having an affair – even though it's not spring.'

Just then Kangchong *dek* came down to the stream with a basket of newly picked beans. With a snort, she pulled the bowl towards her and put a piece of rag on the laundry stone.

'I wondered whose it was.'

Kangchong *dek* ignored her.

'I hear that Gannan *halmum*'s died.'

'Even the strongest can do nothing when they're old. There's no

350

remedy for death.' Kangchong *dek* spat out the words as she struck hard with the laundry stick.

'Dooman *ne* was hoping so much she'd at least live on till the harvest . . . Kilsang has just gone past to tell her.'

(Bloody woman! As if I would talk with her. Cheeky and with a thick hide.)

Kanchong *dek* kneaded dirty water out of her washing. As she packed rinsed clothes into her basket, Yimi *ne* said, 'Dooman *ne*'s having a flood of luck.'

'. . .'

'Two acres of paddy – that's not chicken feed, is it?'

'. . .'

'People like us run like mad all our life and get nowhere. Farming someone else's land, you're like a bird on the grass and you can never relax.'

'That's true.'

Relenting a little, Kangchong *dek* agreed.

'The more you think about it, the more unfair it seems. Even for being a servant for long enough someone gets a piece of land . . .'.

'It was the horse that ran, but the rider who got the prize.'

'Without lifting a finger – two acres of paddy – really!'

'Come to that, it's the best land, too.'

They looked equally put out, as if they had been deprived of their own share. Only once before had these two women been in harmony and that had been when they had both disparaged the *byoldang* mistress and now they were once again in a state of agreement. As she finished her laundry, Yimi *ne* brought her baby round to the front and suckled it. Her breasts, till then hidden under the clothes, were temptingly swollen and the flesh as white as the inside of a gourd.

'Lucky families do well all round and unlucky ones get worse and worse – and aren't the taxes terrible?'

'They say, "If you are unlucky, you break your nose even when you fall backwards".'

'It's a death, but nevertheless, for Dooman *ne*, it must be a happy event.'

Entirely in agreement with her, Kangchong *dek* said scornfully,

'When my mother-in-law was alive, she wasn't exactly a stranger to that house. She was always being asked to go and do this and that, wet or dry. My husband, too – he grew up with the master as his playmate, didn't he? There's not so much as a cup of cold water from them now – though it's true that neither he nor his mother were the kind to flatter people. I think you have to say nice things to receive grace from others rather than what you really feel.'

'You're right. You have to be friendly and shrewd. How awful Dooman *ne* used to be, saying "Auntie, Auntie" and pretending she was ready to pull out her guts for her. Outwardly she looks fair minded and kind hearted but inwardly she's completely different from us. She's pretty clever at making sure she gets something out of it.'

'Yes – come to think of it, *songnim* must have been calculating, the way she fussed about calling "Auntie, Auntie . . ." '

Yimi *ne* had boldly referred to her as Dooman *ne*, but Kangchong *dek*, even though out of earshot, was careful to refer to her respectfully as *songnim*.

'They say they are not even third cousins.'

'A third cousin is nobody, really . . .'.

'Even without that paddy, when others had to eat gruel they could eat grain and have some left, and when you enter her house it always feels nice and cosy.'

Without noticing that it was getting late, they lingered on.

'Bother, I'd better go and have done with supper or whatever.'

Yimi *ne* pushed her baby round on to her back and put the basket on her head. Kangchong *dek* also stood up, carrying her washing with the basket of beans on top. They walked side by side. Yimi *ne* grumbled again, 'Dooman's father dug up that stony ground by the rock in the mustard patch and this year he got three sacks of potatoes.'

'Yes, he's a man who thinks of nothing else but his work and his family.'

'Dooman *ne* too, she looks very virtuous, but she knows what's good for her, doesn't she? When we share work, it's always her house that has the most to be done. The fact is that she's smart and feeds us all well so nobody looks displeased, but isn't she giving a penny and taking a pound? She's very clever at getting something for nothing. I bet she's saved up quite a bit of money.'

'Last year she did the shroud for her mother-in-law, and got all Suni's trousseau nicely made up – you can't do things like that without savings, can you?'

'If you think about it, we are just fools – we only look clever. People who build up their living are rather different. She never looks sulky or gossips about others – "You can never spit at a smiling face," as they say.'

'I could never be like that. I wouldn't pretend even for ten thousand pieces of gold. Perhaps it's my fate to be poor.'

'Work till your bones creak and only more kids come along – when are we going to be any better off?'

'Still, you're better off than we are, Yimi *ne*. Your husband works hard. As they say, "Lifting a piece of wet paper is easier with two pairs of hands." '

'Still you've a smaller family – when you're short, one mouth less makes all the difference.'

'That's true. In our prime we ought to be able to feed two of us even if we packed up farming and went off somewhere else. My husband seems to be getting some sense now and thinking more about his wife.'

Re-awakening the caution that had been allowed to shut one eye, she drove a nail into Yimi *ne*.

Yimi *ne* raised her eye brows.

'Has Wolsun given him up for ever then?'

She was scratching Kangchong *dek*'s sores, for the jealousy she had once felt for Wolsun was now turned on her.

'That bitch – if she doesn't, what else can she do? It's not really that she gave him up – he threw her off,' bragged Kangchong *dek* with quickened breath.

'As easy as that? – it was not just a love of a day or two.'

She did not say this for the sake of Wolsun, of course. Ignoring it, Kangchong *dek* went on, 'They say that no man can resist it when a woman wags her tail. It's only natural for a man to go with a tavern wench for once. With his own wife alive and kicking, it can't last long. Will a man refuse a woman, even if there are ten of

353

them? In the end, they are the ones that weep and have their lives ruined. The man gets away with it.'

This time it was not so much a nail that she was driving into Yimi *ne* as a stake. She gave her a sideways glance. Yimi *ne* twitched her lips.

Kangchong *dek* went on, 'It's quite true – my husband is very kind hearted. In more than ten years of married life I've never once been slapped on the cheek or rudely spoken to – he really is a gentleman. There aren't many men who care for their wives like he does. When I've worked hard he rubs my back, and my arms and legs – he is full of little kindnesses. A man is a man, I see that now. As if we had never had any quarrel or squabble – partly because he admits his sins – he's kinder to me than ever before, crawling on all fours. "Did you really believe that I could ever fall for another woman while you were here? Maybe I went astray once or twice, without wasting any money, but don't be like this – come on, let's have a real good life from now on." That's how he goes on.'

As she poured out these naked lies, her eyes glowed.

(You bitch! How dare you wag your tail when this is how it is with me!).

Yimi *ne* knew it was all bluff, but she couldn't let it rest.

'That isn't quite what I've heard.'

'What isn't?' Kangchong *dek* shouted as if ready to attack her.

'They say he's made himself ill thinking about the departed Wolsun.'

'As they say, "A pear fell just when the crow flew past." He was ill before that woman left, so who is saying that? What have you heard?'

'It's not so much what I've heard as a story that's all over the village.'

'What story?'

She looked as if she was raising her fists ready for a fight.

'You call her a tavern wench but she wasn't really, was she? They say that they'd been in love since they were children together. So they're not likely to forget it that easily.'

'Who are the fools that gabble like that? If they have nothing better to do after stuffing their bellies, they might count the grains. It must be someone who got a free cup of sour wine from her, or some slut whose mouth waters at the sight of my husband, full of jealousy. If they go on clicking their jaws like that, I'll crush them!'

She jumped up and down, as if boiling over, and Yimi *ne* giggled. 'If your mind's at rest, you don't care what other people say. But that's nothing, there's even stranger stories.'

'Such as? Let's hear it.'

'Every night you want it,' she giggled.

'You strip off and cling to him but he doesn't take any notice of you – that's what they say.'

'How dare you? Who are the wretches who say such things? I'll stuff dung in their mouths!'

She jumped vigorously up and down but it was not a baseless story. Perhaps because of shame, she did not try to detain Yimi *ne*, who, saying she was late for supper, ran off as if to escape. When they got home, Yimi *ne* was slapped on the cheek by Chilsung for being late with supper while Kangchong *dek* threw away the laundry and the beans and, going up on to the verandah, stretched out her legs and burst into tears.

It was a fine day for Gannan *halmum*'s funeral. As he was only young, Yongman wore a *dopo* with belt instead of proper mourning clothes and led the procession, followed by his father and Dooman, the men servants of the Choi *champan* house with hempen hoods, and Dooman *ne* and the maids in hemp skirts and with black ribbons in their hair. It was much more elaborate than the funeral of old Bawoo. Food was plentiful and everyone in the village had their fill. Though the bier was borrowed from the village, there were several banners with funeral odes flapping in the freeze. As the funeral of a childless servant, it could not be called sumptuous but, as that of someone whom Lady Yoon had treated with explicit favour, it was quite grand. She had lived a full life and her death had not been unexpected, so no one wept passionately, but the songs of Suh *subang*, as he stood on the bier carried by twelve bearers, as always, made the women cry. They did so for their own sorrows, for the general sorrows of human life, and at the heart-

355

rending undulation of tune and words as they flew on the wind and were scattered.

> *Alack! Alas!*
> *To the land of the southern sky, alas!*
> *Flags, banners and mourners,*
> *How sad the sound of bells.*
> *To the far far land of the dead*
> *I go, and when will I come back?*

When they came to the stream they halted. The pallbearers marked time, saying their legs ached so much they could go no further and the spirit of the dead wanted money to cross the river. Dooman's mother and father and Bongsoon *ne* put coins on the frame of the bier.

> *Alack, Alas!*
> *To the land of the southern sky, alas!*
> *Now I go on this road*
> *And when will I come again?*
> *The road is curved like a bow,*
> *And like an arrow, I go.*

As they crossed the river and turned a corner, the village disappeared from view. Passers-by stood to look at the bier, and from rafts on the river the loggers watched. They were going over the brow of the hill.

'What is she following us for?' said Kim *subang*'s wife as she looked back and clicked her tongue. With her drawers down to her ankles and a straw cord round her waist, Dochul *ne* ambled along behind them.

'Leave her alone. She's hoping for something to eat.'

Nami spoke in whisper as if to check her mother's loud voice.

'Mad creature – we want it all to be tidy, don't we?'

'Leave her alone.'

356

Entering the valley of tombs,
The turf will be my cover,
Flies will be my company.
Thin rain, heavy rain,
The rain will come in its seasons,
But who will come to seek me?
Oh, alack, alas.

The banners flapped in the breeze. Over the brow, as the bier tilted downwards, crows led the way, screeching. The gravediggers, who had gone before, had the hole dug and awaited them.

After the burial food and drinks were given out.

'Oh dear, I'm aching all over – I didn't have a wink of sleep last night,' moaned Mrs Kim as she bit into a marrow fritter.

'Not a wink? You were snoring away all night,' countered Yoni.

'Cheeky girl, when did I ever snore? Listen to her!'

'Why, will a cotton gin make a noise if it's empty?' said Yoni's mother.

'You're mad.'

Samwol's eyes were swollen from crying. Gad-dongi, his mouth dribbling, chased a squirrel, throwing stones as he ran.

'That bitch has a belly like a cow. She's already finished off a great basin of rice.'

Dochul *ne* was now sucking her finger.

'Then she starves and goes without food for days.'

Dooman *ne* defended her against Mrs Kim.

'They say a strong man eats ten days' worth at one go and then sleeps for ten days, but the way she goes, her tummy will burst.'

'She's not normal, so her stomach wouldn't be normal either, would it?'

The crows that had set up camp on the branches of the pine trees screeched as if urging them to hurry up and go. After scattering the remainder of the food they walked downhill exhausted. In the middle of the eastern slope darkness came even before sunset.

'Really, her ladyship has been so generous – Gannan has died in style.'

'Better than us.'

'And the Yi's are getting two acres of paddy.'

'Don't talk like that. Does it belong to us? It's to provide sacrifices for the dead.'

Dooman's father frowned, realizing how much gossip there was about it.

'Whether the money's in your pocket or your purse, it's all the same, isn't it? Anyway, it's a lucky strike,' said Bong-gi teasingly as he carried down the empy bier. Suh *subang* looked tired out, as was natural for his age, and went down almost leaning on Yongi rather than singing to cheer them up. Even so, he had not forgotten some cake for his wife, which he carried wrapped in a handkerchief. By the time they reached the entrance to the village something extraordinary was happening back at the lonely mound of yellow earth:

'Shoo! Naughty crows! Off with you, crows!'

Dochul *ne* ran to and fro with her arms spread like a bat. She was trying to chase away the birds that had flown down to eat the food scattered here and there. They flew up only to come down again and gobble up the crumbs of rice and meat. Tirelessly she chased them away as she eagerly grabbed the remaining scraps and ate them. The angry birds came at her in a flock. They pecked at her head and face. Even then, as if unaware of the pain, she repeated her chant as she ran round the lonely grave mound in a winged dance.

'Shoo! Naughty crows! Off with you, crows!'

The sun went down and the crows left, with not a single grain of rice to be seen.

Dochul *ne* fell asleep beside the tomb.

Chapter Thirty-One

THE plight of the pedlar, who is said to be equally worried, whether he has goods to sell, or has none, was nothing compared with this, nor could it be compared to the mind of a gambler making his last throw. Pyongsan could not make the final decision as to whether or not to go over the log laid across the abyss. It might be a rotten log that would snap half way across. His foot might slip on the green moss that had absorbed the moisture of the gorge for a hundred years. Nor was there any guarantee that between the bottomless pit and the infinite sky he might not lose consciousness and step into space. If that happened, – it would be the end of everything. He would be on the way to Hades, leaving no trace. He did not believe in the other world, nor that it would be a favourable place for him if it did exist, and he did not have the slightest desire to set off for it before anyone else. To put out his foot or to draw it back – it was indeed a difficult decision.

On the other side the land was good. Fat cattle abounded; ripe grain as countless as the grains of sand on the shore of the Sumjin River; loads of rich cloth that would break the backs of the asses that carried them – a bright rainbow beckoned him from the other side, showing him dreams that made his heart beat faster. Everything was there, piled up and flowing over. Across the awning of the tavern in the market passed the shadow of a flying bird. Squatting in front of it, Pyongsan slapped the back of his neck where a mosquito sucked his blood.

'Damn thing – even in the middle of the day!'

The surplus flesh on his face and neck wobbled. The market was filled with the tumult of traders. The sound receded as the bright rainbow once again spread itself. Grain gathers like drifts of snow, countless servants bow before him, while tenants and peasants do not dare to raise their eyes.

All through the seasons, there's music, wine, girls, delicacies from mountain and sea, soft couches and treasures of silver and gold. He would build a memorial pavilion to his ancestors and couldn't he even take up some high office? It wouldn't be difficult with only half, nay, one tenth of the Choi property. The bright rainbow, the golden dream on which he lay and fell asleep every night – Pyongsan could never give up that dream.

Guinyo had sat stooped on the rock, leaning forward as if to avoid the breath of Pyongsan, who had sat beside her. He had glanced up at the sky. The stars sparkled brightly.

(They say everybody has his own star.)

Wanting his to be big and brilliant, he searched for the largest.

(That one would be the king of the stars. I can't expect that to be mine.)

From Guinyo's body came a feminine smell quite different from that of his wife, the tavern girls or the prostitutes. Stealthily he had put his arm round her waist. She kept still, without showing any sign of rejection. Her flesh was firm and, for a girl, her waist thick. It was strange. His hand was touching solid flesh but he was not at all moved. Without realizing it, his arm slackened. She turned one shoulder.

'There's something I want to ask you.'

'. . .'

'Is Choi Chisoo still ignoring you?'

She was silent, as if to suggest that it was pointless to ask something he obviously knew.

'To capture his heart at any cost – that's not what you really want, is it?'

'You know that, so why ask?'

Her words came out sharply.

'I hate him!'

'So it's only his wealth . . .'

'He's like a snake charged with poison – the very sight of him gives me the creeps.'

Even so, it sounded more like the resentment of one rejected.

'So, it's only his wealth . . .' repeated Pyongsan.

'Why do you keep saying that?'

360

'I need to know.'

'That is not all . . .'.

'. . .'.

'I'm only a lowly servant.'

'Your position will improve – of course it will.'

'That's not all. Look, Master.'

After suddenly calling him this in a teasing tone she sniggered.

'Do you think that from ancient times they were great aristocrats and my blood is just that of a servant?'

'. . .'.

'They say our ancestors weren't servants. They weren't the children of concubines either. Even a prime minister, if he's dismissed as a traitor, can have his family slaughtered over night. If any one survived such a disaster, he could become anything, even a butcher, couldn't he?'

Her tone had become arrogant.

'So what I want is . . .'.

'. . .'.

'Yes, what I want is to make servants out of all those who have treated me as a servant. But I suppose that's asking too much.'

Pyongsan felt as if he was being grabbed by the scruff of the neck. He had thought that he was the hunter and she the falcon, but it was not so – he realized that he was the performing bear and she held the ropes. In the way that, when drunk, your legs move independently of yourself, he had, without realizing it, revealed his schemes and asked her consent. Her white teeth had gleamed in the darkness.

'If you don't do it that way, nothing will come of it – don't you see? Before the earth covers his eyes there's no chance of one inch of land . . . only the girl must survive, do you understand?'

She had whispered this, but to him it sounded like thunder over his head, her hot breath had been like sand scorched by the sun, and he had the feeling that he was sinking in quicksands.

'Why of all places do you have to sit just where people are going in and out?'

The irritable voice of the hostess caught the back of his head.

'Oh dear!'

361

Moving to one side, Pyongsan scratched his neck where the mosquito had bitten him. His clothes were limp and covered with dirty marks. It was several days since he had left the village after attacking Magdal *ne*. There was no trace of his usual swaggering style for, after several days of sleeping on the floor of communal rooms in taverns, passing the time with a few cups of wine bought with commission from the gambling den, his appearance was bound to be disreputable.

As he sat hunched, looking out on the market, a ceaseless flow of people grazed his side as they went in and out of the tavern. Rather than a place for buying and selling, the market seemed to be nothing but noise. The beggar troupes that turned up every market day made a din as they went through their antics. Starting with the chant of 'The beggars who came last year . . .' they shook and twisted their hair, their toes and fingers and even their running nostrils, their eyes gently closing and then opening wide like a burning glass and staring into space as they danced madly in their ragged clothes.

'Hey, auntie, won't you do your good deed for the day? "A pagoda built with good works won't fall." Build up your merit and you're safe from hell. For daily sins, calling on Buddha is not enough. You need good deeds as well.'

They drummed their begging bowls.

'Useless devils! Don't worry about other people's souls. Pile up some good deeds and go to paradise yourselves!' shouted the mistress of the tavern. 'Really – you can't take even a widow for nothing. Do you expect to hear our songs for nothing? We've spent plenty of time learning them.'

'Damned creatures! Do you think I run the shop just to stuff your bellies? You come round every market day and what do you say? – "The beggars who came last year . . ." – last year, indeed!'

'Well, even a snake has to eat all through the summer so as to sleep in the winter. How can anyone survive on one meal a year? In a world where you can call black "white", what does it matter if you count one month as a year, or even ten days? That's not a sin, is it? Calling a year twelve months is a man-made thing and so are the songs – no one can live without a bit of exaggeration.

Whatever you say, no one in the world is more virtuous than a beggar – he possesses nothing but his bowl, and what more does he want but a couple of meals? No house, no temple, the grass is his bed and where he stands is his house – isn't he free of greed? How can anyone be wealthy without being a thief? Isn't that so, auntie?'

These vagrants who had seen all the ins and outs of the world were always eloquent, humorous, wily and tough, and arguing with them was only a waste of time. Eventually, the shopkeeper was bound to bring out some food and wine. Market days were, it seemed, a time when even the beggars and the maimed could be active and excited. On a straw mat by a busy corner a blind man, facing places he could not see, loudly invited 'Good deeds.' A cripple crawled all over the place, his forehead touching the ground countless times as he begged.

Pyongsan saw Dooman's father, Yi Pangi, passing the tavern and Yongpari, Handori, and Suh *subang*, too, with his sack slung over his shoulder. They all feigned not to see him, so he also pretended not to see them, keeping his crooked tooth tucked inside his lip. Staying close to the rice steamer, as if stuck there, Bong-gi took big bites from a steaming piece of rice cake, creasing his forehead into three lines as he examined the passers-by. When eating, as if for him all the joy of life lay there, he looked very happy.

It was some time since Pyongsan had heard Cho Junku's story on the river bank. This man who told of strange events had left for Seoul and was no longer about.

(They say the family are delicate, but he's younger than I am, and who knows how long he may live? The men of the Choi house don't live long? H'm, what kind of idiot would believe that and just wait? To have to depend on a few sacks of rice that Guinyo can put out through the back door, or trinkets pulled off her finger – it's shameful. Does a big man scheme for such trifles? Shame on you. Waiting on a servant? It's disgraceful. Might as well stick my tongue in the sand and choke. That is bad enough, but how much longer am I just going to wait helplessly like this? He'll never lay a hand on her, will he? Then eventually he'll marry again – and that'll be the end of it, to be sure. Like the dog that was chasing the hen staring up at the roof, the chance will be gone for ever.)

It was not that the idea had not occurred to him before he heard it from Junku, but hearing it spoken made him uneasy.

(Had he said it just by chance, or with some implication?)

Anyway, that such a thing had happened meant that it was possible – in fact it could be said that it helped him to consolidate a plan. Yet the more firmly you believed it to be inevitable, the more you tended to put it off – this was the mental attitude he could not overcome. The way Junku had spoken and acted had been a kind of revelation, yet it also contained the shadow of possible detection. Pyongsan could not shake off the fear that Junku might have caught a whiff of his inner secret so that, when the scheme was accomplished, he could come back at him. It was to overcome his reluctance that he had seen Guinyo and disclosed his plans.

'Only the girl must survive, do you understand? We've got to work together.'

He recalled her whispering voice. He felt a shuddering sensation as if his skin was being grazed. The sweat exuding on his back was not due to compunction, nor because he was scared of murder. He had worked it out all by himself before he heard Junku's tale but, nevertheless, the illusion that he was trapped in a bog that had nothing to do with his own scheming, and the thought that he would never be able to get out of it, pressed on him like a nightmare. Cho Junku, the secret in his hand, seemed to be saying – 'You have taken the first step, so you might as well carry on,' and Guinyo, 'I have been waiting only for you to speak first. Now you can't take it back, can you?' He could hear her cackling laugh while her large black eyes, umoved and not matching the laughter, stared at him. It was an abyss, a thousand feet deep. The log across it was fate. The deeper the unease, the suspicion, and the fear, amidst the nightmarish feeling of being chased, the more tempting was the shore beyond that bridge, shining as brightly as ever, a brilliant world of gold. To cross the bridge – or not?

He saw on the awning of the tavern the shadows of birds passing over. The bright weather suddenly crumpled and a grey current crept up from the riverside. It did not seem to be windy but the leaves shook and the birds fled east towards the woods. The noise of the market seemed to slump, only to start up again. The dye seller with a bamboo hat and a short pipe, who had been squatting uncertainly watching the sky where dark clouds gathered from afar, quickly picked up the limp, rag-like bags of dye and hurried about, still with a pipe in his mouth but it no longer produced smoke when he sucked. The old hawker who had been shouting 'I'm going to Seoul to look for my son. A lucky chance for someone to buy the lot! Last offer! Last offer!' also began hurriedly to pack.

Drapery, dried fish, herbal medicine, stationery . . . all the stalls closed down. The rice cake seller pushed her steamer closer to the eaves of the house and Bong-gi slowly stood up, wiping his mouth. A heavy shower poured down. The traders scurried in all directions like spiders. Pyongsan sprang up also but, like a man still not fully awake, instead of hurrying inside the tavern he stood closer to the wall under the eaves.

'Ha! It's certainly coming down!' he said, as if hoping someone would respond. But no one took any notice. People continuously ran in under the eaves while those with deep enough pockets went into the tavern.

'Goodness!'

Yongpari ran in under the eaves with a net bag. When his eyes met Pyongsan's he avoided them as if he was the one at fault. He turned his face away until his neck hurt but the back of it was turning red, as if belatedly his anger was rising. The sight of Magdal *ne* with blood running from her nose had come before his eyes, and to see Pyongsan, who had wiped his blood-stained hand on a sheaf of straw and walked off with a final threat, standing there in perfect health, unpunished by heaven, seemed to anger him.

'The weather's going mad in its old age – how can you have a rain storm this late in the season?' grumbled Handori as he joined them.

Rain dripped from his hatless topknot.

'It's certainly coming down!' said Pyongsan with a glance at Handori, who had already seen him but did not acknowledge it.

He spat.

'It's completely useless rain.'

365

'It's only a passing shower.'

The others chatted among themselves, including Yongpari. Put out, Pyongsan thrust out his lips and stared at the downfall. Over the suddenly scattered market the sky became agitated now, twirling in dragon shapes, and blue began to show through the tattered clouds. In place of the dark clouds, sunlight hurried from the direction of the river, shining through the rain drops. It cleared up completely. The market was in business again. The traders babbled, pigs brought to sell grunted, and a cockerel that had squeezed out of its coop ran off with raised comb.

At last it was time to close. It was about then that Pyongsan met Kang *posoo*.

'You look terrible,' said the hunter.

'It's because I've been away from home for a long time. I was thinking of slipping back today. But what's the matter with you? Your eyes are hollow and your eyeballs look white.'

'It's nothing . . .'.

He rubbed his face with his big rake-like hands.

'It's because you miss the hills?'

'M'm . . . it's not that.'

'You're being bothered too much by Choi Chisoo?'

'Oh, no.'

'What is it then?'

'Well, life is just . . .'.

He looked toward the far hills.

'Let's have a drink.'

'No, I must go. The sun's nearly set.'

'Let it set – you can go back by moonlight, can't you?'

'It won't do. I came out because I was so fed up, but it's no better here. I must go back.'

'Look man, have you got a honey pot hidden in the corner of your room?'

He flinched and glanced at Pyongsan.

'Goodbye – I must go. You can come later.'

'Let's go together. I was going anyway. By the way, Kang *posoo*!'

He stopped and looked back.

'Wait a bit and there'll be a ferry.'

'No thanks. I'll walk.'

'Really!'

There was nothing for Pyongsan to do but follow his brisk steps.

'How are things in the village?'

'What do I know about the village?'

Tinged by the red light of the setting sun, the two men walked silently as if bound for another world. The river beach also glowed red. The tall willows and the water of the river were rippling in the rosy light.

'When is he going to set off for the hills? Have you heard?'

'What did you say?'

'I mean Choi Chisoo. When is he going to the hills?'

'Before the harvest festival, I think.'

'Really? . . . the gentleman from Seoul – did he practise a lot too?'

'Not really . . . he didn't seem to be very interested.'

'He'll come back again?'

'I don't know. Samsoo said . . .' Immersed in his own thoughts, he trailed off.

'What did he say?'

Questioned again, he said, 'Pardon?'

'Really! What did Samsoo say?'

'Oh, I think he said he won't be able to come back. He's going to Japan or China with some mission or other . . . I don't know – I didn't pay much attention.'

'Is that so . . .?'

Pyongsan suddenly broke into a hollow laugh.

'. . .?'

'Kang *posoo*, I know you're dying to be married, aren't you?'

'Married? Well . . .' He spoke casually, but he was embarrassed.

'Ha! Ha! Get married then – what's stopping you?'

'It'll be easy – is that what you mean?'

'Exactly.'

'Well, to be frank, she's as lonely as I am. Though I'm old . . . I still have plenty of strength. I'll grind my bones and work hard. If only she becomes my woman, I won't let her suffer . . .'.

'No, no, of course not.'

'While I was hunting I never thought about it – never once . . .
but a man's life is pretty short . . .'

He looked up at the sky.

'It's because you've come to live amongst others, that's why,' said
Pyongsan half-heartedly as he concentrated his gaze on one spot.

'Yes, that's it. When I see the supper-time smoke rising in the
village, I feel a lump in my heart and I think I ought to live as
other people do.'

'There's nothing to worry about. It's all up to you. Why don't
you set up a home right now?'

'Right now?'

'Yes – with a widow or a deserted wife.'

'What?'

'You mean – an old man like you wants an unmarried girl?'

Kang *posoo* was crest fallen,

'A man . . . still forty – just forty . . . there's no reason why not.'

'It beats me . . . ha! ha! ha! . . . true, there's no reason at all. Look
somewhere under a bridge, find a beggar girl and put her hair
up . . . that'd be simple enough . . . ha! ha! ha!'

'Don't be insulting!'

'Ha! ha! ha!..!'

'Don't look down on me like that! If I have a mind to I can get
hold of money! I'm not a serf tied down to some one's house nor
a miserable peasant with his eyes fixed on the sky and eating gruel!
In this world, even the children know the name of Kang *posoo*. I
am the famous hunter! When I catch a tiger, do you know how
much its skin is worth? Or a bear, how much I can get for its
bladder? I'm something different from serfs or peasants! A man of
forty – in the prime of life, the prime, do you hear!'

As if persuading a marriage broker, he clenched his fists and
pleaded loudly.

'For a man, it's an upright heart that counts! The heart of this
man, Kang *posoo*, is like a white gemstone!'

As he struck his chest his eyes turned red, with tears or in anger.

'Yes, yes, of course! Pick a flower-like virgin! I'll visit you as a
guest of honour . . . what does it matter if you're fifty or even sixty?
For a man, age doesn't count.'

Pyongsan chuckled as he replied. After talking loudly, the hunter went limp again. He walked in silence. Not even realizing all round was dark, he walked on. Pyongsan was making up his mind to put Chilsung out in front of him.

(In a battle it is better to be with a shield than without.)

When they reached the village it was quite late and they parted at the fork of the road without even bothering to stop at the tavern for a drink.

Chapter Thirty-Two

IT was a pepper plot of poor soil, mostly pebbles, in which even the weeds were yellowish, and seemed not only never to have been hoed, but never fertilized either. Unlike good soil, it quickly dried out and looked as if, once set light to, it would burn up in a flash. In this wilderness hung a few thin peppers. You could catch glimpses of them, ripe and red among the tangle of weeds.

Two women, one looking barely sixteen and the other in her mid-thirties, were picking them, their heads wrapped in towels as if to avoid the eyes of others. They were the young widows of Kim *jinsa*'s family, mother and daughter-in-law. Their fingers were clumsy at picking and their faces under the towels were pale. Pyongsan, walking by on the road above, stopped as he saw them and said, 'The living have to eat, to be sure,' and walked on. It was not said with sarcasm, or with sympathy. The two women shrank as if wishing to hide even further.

From an adjacent bean plot below the hill came the cry of a pheasant. The mother wiped her eyes with the end of her jacket ribbon as if to remove a speck. She had come to the plot with her child-like daughter-in-law, widow of her son who had died of a fever the previous year. All her life she had taken for granted the poverty of a scholar's house, and its strict manners had become a part of her nature, so that to be addressed by a man who was not a member of her family could not seem anything but absolute disgrace. The right thing would have been for him to pass by as if he had not seen them. It may be that Pyongsan, on his side, had meant, 'You are out of time. It's the world's fault if the matron and the young mistress of a noble family can't get by without having to touch the soil.'

It could be that, though he took his wife's toil for granted, he felt sorry for these two working in the field. For her, it was not only the sorrow of being insulted, but even more a feeling of shame.

She interpreted his passing remark as sarcasm. She had not killed herself after the death of her husband, under the excuse of looking after his heir. Now the son who provided her reason for not dying was himself dead, and she felt that Pyongsan was mocking her for coming out to work in order to prolong an unfortunate existence that could have no further justification. 'The living have to eat, to be sure.' could also be interpreted that way, depending on how you took it.

'Dear, let's go. We will pick some more tomorrow.'

Innocently the daughter followed her home. Though nothing to compare to the Choi house, it was tiled and properly laid out, but now dilapidated, and part of the wall by the main gate through which the two women entered had collapsed.

'I wonder why they are all so short lived?' Pyongsan mumbled to himself as he walked along the stream by the paddies on which mosquito larvae played. If his own first son had survived, he might have had a daughter-in-law by now. In a farming community many children were born and many were lost just as a thin pine tree growing in a crevice between rocks would have more cones than usual, and if, out of all these children, one or two survived to carry on the family line, they thought themselves lucky. When they died of smallpox, measles, or fever and were rolled in straw mats to be carried off to a hillside grave, they had to be forgotten, as indeed they were. When he reached Chilsung's brushwood gate, he stopped. He mumbled again, 'Why are they all so short-lived?'

As he dreamily looked over the wall at the humps of the thatched roof on which pale green gourds lay heavily he was reminded of the story of 'Hungboo and Nolboo.'*

'Once upon a time, Hungboo and Nolboo . . .'.

He mumbled to himself and, looking down, saw that his shoe had a split through which his sock poked out. He called loudly, 'Damn it! Chilsung!' and unlike other times, walked briskly into the yard.

---

* A folk tale of two brothers in which the good and kind Hungboo is rewarded with riches out of gourds, while for the wicked one they produce only refuse, snakes and toads.

'Yes!'

Chilsung, squatting in front of the shed mending his tools, jumped up. He seemed to be surprised at the difference from Pyongsan's usual furtive way of calling him.

'Busy?'

'Not exactly, but . . .'.

He gave Pyongsan a quick glance. His dark, sun-tanned face was shining.

'So?'

Pyongsan turned his gaze as if to examine the house.

'My wife has a cold, so she's stuck in the room lying down.'

In case he should breathe a careless word, Chilsung quickly gave him this warning.

'H'm, worse than a dog, eh? They say even dogs don't catch cold in the summer, though I suppose the summer is nearly over.'

His thumb flicked the tip of his nose.

'That's right. There's a mountain of things to be done and her in bed in broad daylight. She's not even a thing of beauty like a poppy flower . . .'.

'What's it like this year – the harvest?'

'About usual, I suppose.'

He spoke uncertainly.

'I wanted to borrow a sack of grain.'

'Pardon?'

A look of alarm rose to his face at once.

'Considering the close relationship between you and me it shouldn't be too difficult, should it?'

'Well, that is to say – well, the grain . . . it's still lying in the field.'

As he mumbled these words in confusion, Pyongsan winked at him and nodded towards the room.

'. . .?'

'Don't I know the grain is still in the fields?'

He smiled blandly.

(You bastard! Ungrateful bastard – why couldn't you have let me have a bit of grain if I really had needed it? Not only for the sake of the capital I have put in for you, but also for the sake of the plot in which we are committed together, you can't spare me a sack of grain? 'My tongue is short, but it spits a long way.' I wouldn't really come to you to borrow grain, would I?)

His bland smile turned into a big sneering grin. After momentary confusion, Chilsung fell limp.

'As for the grain . . . we never have enough for ourselves, but if you're really in need . . .'

Pyongsan stepped up close to him and whispered.

'Come to the tavern later on.'

Shamed-faced, Chilsung was unable to speak but broke into a smile.

'If it's difficult, don't bother. I knew it would be like this, what a kind world it is!'

He spat loudly and then cleared his throat and walked out. As soon as he was gone Yimi *ne* opened the door and peered out.

'What did he come for?'

'How do I know why he came?'

He picked up and put down the tools as if he was restless.

'Do you think I didn't hear?'

'Hear what?'

'H'm, I see it now – he's completely ruined. So he has to come to my poor house to borrow grain!'

'If we didn't give him any – that's it.'

'What did I say? Didn't I tell you not to go around with him? Does he ever notice that his own family are starving? – a good for nothing gentleman. It's obvious that he's run out of gambling money. We don't look like having any, so it will have to be grain. Does he expect us to dig up soil and eat it?'

She wiped her running nose.

'I agree with you, he's a bit mad. I don't know whether he meant rice or barley, but a sack is no trifle.'

'Knowing that, why do you still keep going out with him?'

He did not reply to this. Instead he said, 'He has no idea of how the world works. Who would lend grain to people who can't pay it back? Are we supposed to just sit here with an empty pot?'

He tried to settle his uneasiness with these mindless words.

'I can't believe it — and if so, why did you say such things to him, why did you say "If you are really in need . . ." and so on?'

'I've eaten a lot of things at his expense. Words don't cost you anything. It's only the grain we have to guard.'

'Don't talk like that. Why can't you just tell him straight? Are you going to give him ten times what you had from him?'

'What are you making all this fuss for, you stupid bitch? I keep on letting you off, so your liver gets big — if you are strong enough for nagging why don't you come out and do some work instead of just working your jaws. It drives me mad. Anyway, I don't care!'

He threw down the tools he had been working on and went out of the gate. With her face flushed with fever and her nose running, Yimi *ne* lay down again.

(With mountains of work to do, I shouldn't be lying here like this. Damn it, but I can't pull myself together. If he would only get me a dose of medicine, I might be able to get up. Has he ever once told me to stay in bed and rest, or show any concern however ill I was? Just a bully — I haven't the slightest affection for him either . . . How sad and bitter I am.)

The baby that had had its fill as its mother had been lying down all day lay tumbled aside, asleep.

(It's my sad fate that I never met the right man . . . if only I'd been a virgin, I wouldn't have been married to a man like that, would I? If only that scandal hadn't gone round the village . . . I can't even go back home by daylight . . . Whether I live or die, I'm buried under loads of work with not a thing to cheer me up and my youth is fading away.)

As she lay lamenting, her daughter Yimi shouted, 'Mum! She's brought some *duk*! From Yongman's house!'

'Did you say *duk*?'

Pulling up the top of her skirt, she came out on to the verandah. 'Mummy, *duk! duk!*'

The three-year-old boy came too, hanging on to his sister's skirt and almost falling over. Suni put the bowl down on the verandah and smiled happily.

'What's it for?'

'We made it for granny's birthday.'

'We never send you anything . . . Oh! my head!'

Yimi *ne* took a bamboo basket from the shelf.

'Aren't you well?'

'Must be a cold. I took no notice of it but now I can hardly move.'

She transferred the cake to her basket and put it away on the shelf. Her little boy, who had been sitting by the edge of the verandah gathering up the crumbs, began to whimper, and Yimi also with her finger in her mouth looked up appealingly and said, 'Mummy.'

'Where's your father gone?'

'I don't know . . . I saw him go out.'

'Let's wait until he comes back.'

The boy's eyes were fixed on the basket and he whimpered again.

'Your mother's been busy, then. Oh, my head! It's splitting. Thank her for me, won't you?'

Putting the bowl on her head, Suni said, 'It's all right. I hope you're soon better.'

With few words, but very politely she took her leave and went out of the gate. Her waist was slender in her starched black cotton skirt.

At sunset Chilsung returned with a slightly intoxicated face.

'Where have you been all this time?'

Her eyes narrowed.

'Why do you want to know, all of a sudden? It's the ruin of a family when the women have too much to say.'

In spite of his words, he did not seem to be in a bad mood, but rather as if he wanted to please her.

'Oh, my head! It's splitting. The devil's got me – what else could it be? Come and eat your supper, anyway. I've just managed to crawl about and get it ready.'

Picking up the end of her skirt, she blew her nose. Chilsung was washing.

'What are you washing your face for at this time of night?'

'Because I've been sweating.'

When he had finished he took the towel from his head and dried himself thoroughly.

'Mummy, cake please!' said Yimi, as her mother brought in the meal table, indicating it with her chin.

'It's when a woman washes at night that you have to watch out,' he muttered.

It could well be in self-defence, but his wife probed his expression. She knew that Kangchong *dek* went round spreading nonsensical words about her and she wondered if he had heard something.

(What evidence is there? It might be better if there was some.)

'Mummy, the cake!' said Yimi again.

'They keep saying "cake" – what cake?'

'Dooman *ne* sent some round as it was their granny's birthday.'

'How generous. Are they going to eat it all in one day and die the next? The grain's still in the paddy – how can they make rice cake?'

'They are just showing off. Now they have got their own land, what's a bit of rice cake?'

'Well, I'm not one to refuse a gift.'

As she put the table before him, she said, 'Do you want to eat the cake first?'

'We have rice day and night, so we might as well have the cake first.'

The children were fidgeting, their bottoms moving up and down. She said, 'The kids have been going mad about it.'

He did not say, 'Why didn't you give them some before I came?' He ate it without a word in piggish style. The children choked from eating too fast and gasped for breath, tears rising to their eyes, but they did not stop. Yimi *ne* also, wiping her nose, diligently chewed and swallowed. Dooman *ne* had sent enough for the four of them but, like field mice in a famine or a family of hungry wolves, they competed to stuff as much of it into their mouths as they could.

'I see – you've been moaning that you're dying, but you can eat pretty well! You must have a sack in your stomach.'

He glared at her.

'When I am ill, do you ever get me any medicine? What'll I do if I don't eat?'

376

'Then don't say you're ill. Eating like a pig . . .'

'It's not as if I was dying . . . my stomach's all right. Why should I starve?'

She glared at him.

'I've no money for medicine.'

'You'll need it for my funeral.'

For a while there was silence except for the sound of the four of them eating.

'If you had some cake, you needn't have cooked the supper as well. Your liver is getting big and the house will be ruined.'

He glared at her again.

'Cake is one thing, supper is another.'

'How dare you contradict everything I say? I'll shut your mouth for you.'

'If your supper hadn't been ready, you'd have blown up about me lying in bed and starving you.'

'If you're wasteful like this, we'll be ruined. Other men's wives look up to their husbands as the greatest thing under heaven, but how much do you think about your husband? If you have some special food, you could put it by in a jar and give out some more tomorrow, instead of stuffing your guts just because it's tasty and trying to finish it all at once.'

'Oh, don't be so mean. Never mind! I won't eat it.'

After making a senseless row, Chilsung followed the cake with a whole bowl of rice.

'Ah, I'm full. What about some tea?'

He sat back and stroked his stomach. She took out the table, put a bowl of rice tea in front of him and, saying she felt chilly, lay down again under the quilt.

(Bloody woman, eats like a devil and pretends to be ill. If you're not out of bed in the morning, I'll dig the floor out from under you.)

He lit his pipe, and then the lamp, gave the children, breathing heavily after eating too much, a hostile glance and was sunk in thought.

(That gentleman – he could have called me out in the usual way, so why did he ask me to lend him some grain? Was he testing me?

377

He pretended he'd done it to deceive her – but really there was no need for that . . .)

It grew darker on all sides until it was comletely black. Attracted by the light that shone through the paper of the door, moths were throwing themselves at it. Meanwhile, the children had fallen asleep and now and again came the sound of his wife's snores.

(If Guinyo gives birth to a girl, it will all come to nothing, won't it? When I mentioned that, he didn't say a word. I'm dying to know what's going on in his mind. As we're together in this, it'd be nice if he'd be frank with me. H'm, he doesn't realize how cunning I am. When it's all achieved, it's the man who provided the seed who's the most important. Of course it is! You can't cheat on the seed.)

Staring at the flame of the lamp, he beamed to himself. His sunburnt face shone as if it was oiled. The clear call of a nightingale came clearly from the woods. It must be getting late.

'I'm thirty.'

He opened the door and stepped out. The heat of the day had cooled and he felt the chilly night air on his chest. From the jar in the kitchen he filled a bowl of cold water and gulped it down. He pretended to be strolling in the yard until he was sure no one was moving in the room, and then slipped out of the gate. He went past his own fence and Kim *jinsa*'s pepper plot and when he had turned towards the foot of the hill away from the Choi house, his steps quickened. He walked up Dangsan from behind and took the downward path until he reached the stone bridge that led to the shrine, and here Pyongsan was squatting. Without a word, he waved him on towards it. Pyongsan watched the sturdy back of the stallion-like Chilsung. Listening to the cries of cuckoo and night-ingale and soaking up the dew, he was to be sentry for the love affair, or rather business affair, between Chilsung and Guinyo. When Chilsung reached the front of the shrine she was already waiting. Veiled in darkness, they stared at one another without words. She spoke first, asking him whether he had seen Pyongsan on the way. He told her that he had.

'You must promise.'

'What?'

'Not even the mice or the birds are to know.'

'Of course. Otherwise, why would I have come?'

'That's all right then.'

'You're the one who's got to be careful. Women have loose tongues.'

'Huh – this is more my business than yours.'

'Someone might come. Let's go in quickly,' he urged.

'Youngsters still soft on the tops of their heads bring up ugly girls . . .'.

'That's why that gentleman's keeping watch,' she said contemptuously.

(Look at her! Full of herself. Does she think I fancy her?)

She led the way into the shrine, where she struck a flint and lit a candle she had brought with her. Chilsung was aghast.

'L – light!'

He raised his hand as if to put it out but she blocked his way without speaking. She stood the candle before the statue of Maitreya that was enshrined there. Her hair was wet. She had bathed in the stream. Without uttering the words aloud as usual, she mumbled prayers inside her mouth, making innumerable bows. Stuck fast in one corner, Chilsung did not dare to look up at the Buddha and his eyes were wide with fear. They reflected the flickering flame. Sakyamuni had said that three thousand years after him the Maitreya would come to rule the world. Those who feared having no offspring trusted this future one as an all wise and omnipotent Buddha, especially powerful as a fertility god. That was why the figure in the shrine was the boy Maitreya.

Although Chilsung was not religious, he was scared of the Buddha. Guinyo's profile as she stood in the candlelight bowing countless times was both sad and beautiful. Her face was frightening. He felt the energy go out of his body and wanted to run up and knock the candle over. But he could not stir.

At last, she raised her soft hand to extinguish the flame, like a petal on the wind. A long deep sigh escaped through his mouth. He moved round her like a wrestler entering the ring. As for Guinyo, it had certainly not been to offer her pure virginity to a man that she had made the ritual washing. It had been to offer fervent prayers to the Maitreya in the shrine. To this woman fornication was no crime. Deceit was no crime. For her, even murder was no crime. All that mattered was to plead her one great desire. For her, the god was neither good nor evil. The only important thing was whether or not it had the power to make her wish come true.

Chilsung, who had been circling her like a wrestler, quickly undid his belt and thrust himself upon her. With no resistance, as if it was a continuation of her countless bows, she received him. She took the pain of the first experience as though it was a continuation of the sharp shock and shudder of pouring the water of the stream over herself. As if his groaning and weight were part of a distant dream, she conjured the image of the Maitreya before her eyes and continued to mumble her prayers. Only when the man slid away from her did his male odour catch her nose. It was sickening. She realized also that her body was drenched with his sweat. Hurriedly putting on his clothes, Chilsung wondered why it had been so difficult.

Chapter Thirty-Three

'HELLO, where have you been?' Kim *hunjang* who had been squatting by the side of the road gazing at the ripening grain, took his long pipe from his mouth as he stood up to speak.

'Yes, well . . .'

Dr Mun rather awkwardly left his sentence unfinished as he looked back in the direction of Hwagae whence he had come and ordered his mule to stop. He dismounted and told the servant to go on and wait at the Choi house. As he turned to survey the fields, his eyes were half closed, perhaps because of the sun. Between his white beard and the dark rim of his hat passed blue sky and clouds.

'It looks like a fair harvest.'

'Yes, one way or another, up to average.'

As he replied, Kim *hunjang* looked happy, as when rain comes in the midst of drought.

'I hear you are farming Kim *jinsa*'s land as well – you must be busy.'

'Not really. The young people lend a hand. You couldn't say I am doing it all on my own.'

'Even so, it's very good of you.'

'For me, it's just family business. It's the young people who deserve the praise.'

Dr Mun gave a quick glance at his somewhat irritated face, but it softened at once, and he said, 'Would you like to have a short rest before you go on?'

'Yes, that's a good idea.'

They walked side by side, gazing at the fields.

There was a difference of twenty years or more between them but they looked about the same age. Kim *hunjang* wore a short jacket so that only the inner-cap on his half-white hair and the long pipe in his hand indicated his rank – otherwise his appearance was no different from that of the peasants, worn down by work and dried up with age, that one can meet in any village. Dr Mun, on the other hand, had grown old neatly, looking as graceful as a heron and still energetic. He carried himself far better, looking every inch the gentleman-scholar, straight as bamboo. Kim *hunjang*, though he took breeding more seriously than life itself and was like steel in making no concessions on social status, had always regarded the doctor with great respect, so he was not at all put out that the middle-class doctor looked like a high-ranking scholar while he himself, a genuine gentleman, looked like an old peasant. Sitting in the teacher's study, facing each other across the table brought in by his daughter, they passed the wine to one another.

Not a drinker by nature, the doctor seemed to have blurred vision after the first cup. He chewed a piece of bitter black mustard leaf pickled only with salt and smacked his lips.

'What's going on in the world?'

The teacher, starved of comments on current affairs since Junku's departure, quickly opened the discussion. The doctor, who moved in wider circles, often told him of events in the capital.

'Very much as usual, I think,' he said absently.

His face was more sombre than usual and one could sense that his nerves were on edge, as they might be after attending a patient near to death.

'Huh – um.'

The visitor was still silent.

'It's like leprosy setting in . . . leprosy,' sighed Kim *hunjang*, and he went on, 'After the plot of Kim Hung-ryuk, Russian influence seemed to recede a little, but I hear the Japs are now raising their heads again. They say that in Pusan you hear nothing but the clatter of their clogs, and didn't that chap who's supposed to be their prime minister even have the cheek to make an appearance in Seoul?'

'. . . .'

'They ought to have their heads cut off!'

'That absurd affair surrounding Kim Hung-ryuk who is only an interpreter . . .'.

'. . . .'

With a quick glance at the teacher's face, twisted with confusion, the doctor went on, 'With the present government, things like that happen every day. Russia isn't so easy to get rid of either. It's not only Japan, is it? How do you chase away flies that have smelt food? The government is selling off all sorts of concessions cheaply – everything's for sale, you might say.'

'Yes, but Japan is not like other countries. They are the enemy, aren't they? Aren't we leaving the door wide open for our sworn enemy? We mustn't do that, we just mustn't let it happen.'

He shuddered. Every time Japan cropped up his body trembled with the strength of his emotion.

'It's all the same.'

'It's not. Of course it's not! How many years is it since the queen was murdered at their hands? Besides, isn't our "Army of Justice" spilling blood in every nook and cranny of the country?'

'What's the use of a blind man blaming the ditch? It's easy for a petty thief to grow into a bandit – once you give a free rein to greed, what is there you wouldn't do?'

'Oh, sir, you are awful, you speak as if you're quite indifferent.'

'. . .'

'A thief is a thief and a bandit is a bandit. Who is responsible? – that's what matters. However small the country, it's sovereignty still clearly exists. Are the guts of all those gentlemen in high office in Seoul rotting away? Let alone fighting against the enemy, the eternal enemy who killed the mother of our country, let alone backing the Army of Justice, they are joining the enemy in aiming their guns at them. How can anything be more outrageous than that?'

As if the doctor in front of him was a member of the government he lashed out and gnashed his teeth.

'That's why I said there's no point in a blind man blaming the ditch. An octopus . . .'.

'. . .?'

'If an octopus eats its own tentacles one after another until only its head is left, however much black ink it squirts out, it can't save itself. We can't do anything with your head alone. You have to be able to move about . . .'.

'Are you suggesting that the sovereign is to blame?'

'He's not entirely blameless, I should say. But I am referring more to the smart ones – the learned people.'

By the 'learned people' he meant the Confucian scholars.

'Then you are implying, sir, that the enlightenment movement is right, are you?'

'I can't say that it's altogether wrong. It depends how you use it, in the way tools can be used to kill a man or can become his hands and feet. Likewise medicine, according to the prescription, can be good or it can be poison. Traditional wisdom, just as much as radical ideas, can cause disease if it's wrongly used, and hardens the arteries of a nation until it's sick.'

'That's not so. Arsenic is by its nature harmful, while things like wild ginseng or deer's antlers are good.'

'Everyone knows that! That's why there are doctors for the sick and statesman for the nation, I suppose.'

'Whatever you say, it is the enlightenment party that has ruined the country. It started when they got hold of Japanese guns and swords, overran the palace and held the sovereign to ransom.'

'A name doesn't mean much – you can put it on your nose and call it a nose-ring or put it on your ear and call it an earring. They were all deeds done by young men still smelling of milk, eager to get power – you can hardly call it enlightenment. To begin with, it is wrong to confuse enlightenment with Western ways, or Japanese. Enlightenment is equated with artillery or warships – that's why it's hated and feared. Though it's true that the Dong Hak army was blown to pieces by their cursed guns.'

The doctor stroked his ears.

'In a way, we ought to give credit to the Dong Hak who challenged the Japanese, but . . .'

Kim *hunjang*'s voice weakened as he became conscious of his status as a gentleman, while a strange smile rose to the doctor's face. The teacher went on, 'It was an uprising by an ignorant mob through which a foreign army came in and China was beaten by Japan, consequently causing the decline of our country . . . they can't escape the blame for that.'

'That's what all the learned people say. Like an octopus that's eaten up all its tentacles. They say that the foreign army came to protect the royal palace – presumably from its own people.'

Kim *hunjang*'s eyes flashed with enmity.

'Those are your own private feelings, sir. Are you trying to say that the government should have been off-hand about the Dong Hak, who were attempting to overthrow the throne?'

'What's the use of talking about the past? I am only a medical man, not fit to participate in running the country, and as a mere bystander, I have no right to criticize even those renowned scholars that kick about heroically underneath the bed cover . . . by the way, did you hear about Haewol's (Kim Gae-joo) execution?'

'Yes, I did.'

'The Dong Hak were the last strength of this nation.'

'An ignorant mob you mean.'

'The learned people – why didn't they recognize their strength and make use of it?'

'It was just murder and plunder, apart from the one praiseworthy idea of challenging the Japanese . . .'.

Dr Mun chuckled at this.

'Hearts that care about the country are all the same. Yours or mine . . . though everywhere opinions differ.'

Kim *hunjang* was not one to yield an argument but he had a particular respect for the doctor so, perhaps deciding to bring it to an end, he gave a broad smile. 'By the way, I've heard that Jang-am *sonseng* is seriously ill. Do you have any clear idea of what is wrong with him?'

'Yes, old age you know . . . there seems little hope.'

'What is he suffering from?'

'Well, what's the good of knowing its name?'

'He is so uncompromising.'

'It seems to me that it's that uncompromising nature of his that keeps him going. Really, he is a man of great learning. To think that such distinguished scholarship is wasting away . . .'

He spoke with regret. As he said goodbye and was about to leave Kim *hunjang* told him that recently, for some reason, he had felt short of breath.

'Don't worry. It couldn't be anything serious. You might as well

385

have some medicine to loosen your chest . . . If you know of anybody going to the town . . . I will send you some through them.'

The doctor slowly strode away as if reluctant to go. As he was passing Yongi's gate he stopped and asked, 'So, you're putting up a fence?'

Yongi, weaving a brushwood fence, looked round, 'How are you, sir.'

He stopped work and bowed.

'What's happened to the old earthen one?'

'I pulled it down.'

'You could have just put a new top on it – that would have been better, wouldn't it?'

'I have nothing much to do, so I might as well . . .'

'Nothing much to do – a farmer with nothing to do?'

Yongi wiped away the sweat with the back of his hand.

'You don't look too well to me . . .'.

'I am all right, sir. I don't have any pain or anything . . .'.

'Really?'

After the doctor had gone, he stood blankly for a time and then flung himself down. He took the pipe from his waistband, filled, lit and drew on it, and stared into the smoke with vacant eyes. Perhaps it was not the smoke that he was watching. His face was bony and burnt black. He had told the doctor that he was making the fence because he had nothing much to do, the truth being that he had recently become crazy for things to do. Anything he could lay his hands on he devoted himself to, forgetting to sleep or eat, as if he could see nothing else before him. Since he had pulled down the earthen wall and started to make a brushwood fence, he had worked late into the night taking advantage of the whitish glow. In the village they gossiped about him, saying he was a changed man, or possessed, or that his mind was settled and he was working till he bled for his home, and so on, but it was not because his mind was settled, but because of a desperate struggle to escape the torture of time.

Kangchong *dek*, when she was out, bragged till her mouth was dry about her husband and how thoroughly he looked after the running of the household and how he did all the work, inside or outside, for his wife, but it was all a vain show, another kind of abnormality.

'H'm, once he was mad for a woman and made me weep, but now he's mad for work! The woman craze was nothing to this! This is worse than having ten concubines! It's worse!'

At the first stage, they quarrelled every night, and the next, every other day, and then every third day until Kangchong *dek*, exhausted in one way or the other, managed to go ten days without a row, then twenty, by which time she had become a woman with nothing to do. She had a nap or she went out and, while she was out, she either breathlessly gabbled or, with her hands on her hips, laughed till she cried, as if possessed in the same way that Yongi was with work. Naturally there were frequent quarrels – following a big row with Yimi *ne*, she had been involved in another commotion only the day before yesterday, caused by her suggestion that Magdal *ne* and Samsoo, servant at the Choi house, were carrying on. The menfolk of the village, witnessing a scene in which evil words and obscenities were bandied about, had been amused at first but gradually came to frown and click their tongues. Eventually they went as far as saying that the village was becoming too quarrelsome and something ought to be done.

'Really, they are too bad. Poor Yongi, how unlucky he is with women!'

'He's too good to her. He ought to just break her legs and shut her up in a corner of the house.'

When the row was over, she had felt a bit ashamed of herself and she had taken to bed, with her head in her hands, and had not come out again since.

Yongi knocked out his pipe, put it in his waist band and stood up. He looked up at the sky as if to measure the height of the sun and then went to bring in the ox he had left tethered in the field. He passed the *jinsa*'s pepper plot and, as he approached the grass on the side of the hill, the ox recognized its master and lowed. Yongpari, who had been smoking, with his A-frame propped beside him, looked up and asked, 'Coming for the cow?'

'Um.'

'I saw you putting up a fence.'

'Um.'

'Sit down a minute. Would you like some tobacco?'

He shook his head. As he was about to lead the ox away, Yongpari said, 'As busy as that?'

'Not particularly busy, only . . .'.

'Have you got to go and cook the supper and offer it to your wife?'

He smiled teasingly. Yongi smacked his lips but he did not leave and just stared towards the dike, where tall willows stood starkly.

'Yongi!'

'. . .'

'Really, you can't go on like this.'

'. . .'

'I know what it's like because I'm the head of a family myself. You really can't go on like this.'

'What should I do then?'

'Just sit down a minute.'

He sat awkwardly on the grass.

'In this world, things just don't turn out as you want.'

'. . .'.

'We poor farmers – how can we ever hope to be better off? If there's no trouble in the family and we're not hungry – that's it, isn't it? When I see how your wife behaves, to put it bluntly, if I were your own brother, I'd say turn her out and send her back home. But, when you think about it again, how can you divide yourself from someone your parents have chosen for you to live with? That's why I'm saying this – though no one can change the nature they are born with, things largely depend on the man. Do you see what I mean?'

'If she was born one way, I was born another . . . it doesn't mean I'm thinking of separating, but I just can't help it . . .'.

He wiped his brow with the back of his hand.

'Why are you sweating like that?'

'I don't know. Cold sweat keeps coming.'

'It's because you're weak – that's why.'

'. . .'

'Anyway . . . maybe I shouldn't talk about other people's married

388

life, but queer stories are going round the village. At first they will only spit on her, but an insult to the woman you're living with is an insult to you, and though she behaves badly, in a way, I can't help feeling sorry for her.'

'. . .'.

'Do you think other people live together just because they're well suited? Even if they're like enemies, they've got the children and . . .'.

'I don't think of her as an enemy either.'

'Then why do you have to have separate rooms?'

'I know, I'm sorry for her.'

'Don't do it then – how can you when you're living under the same roof? The past is past, but when I see her being made a laughing-stock, though she may be hateful, you are hateful too.'

Yongi burst into anger.

'Do you think I don't know?'

'I feel so sorry, that's all.'

'. . .'.

'It's a sad sight for others as well.'

'Don't say any more. It's all the same thing.'

'You – really – how can you be so hard and cruel?'

'It's not that I'm hard and cruel. But since I've been ill . . . I just can't . . .'

His ear lobes reddened. Again he wiped his brow with the back of his hand.

'That can't be so. It's just because you have no feelings for her.'

Yongpari stood up, putting his A-frame of grass over his shoulder.

'Aren't you going?'

'You go first.'

Yongi lay sprawled as before, vacantly staring at the tall willows. Yongpari, passing in front of him with his loaded A-frame, saw, out of the corner of his eye, his vacant expression and shouted angrily, 'Damned idiot! Wait for her till your eyes fall out! A woman who's gone will never come back!'

Forgetting the ox, Yongi lay on the grass and stared at the floating clouds for a long time until he was sucked into a painful sleep.

He stood in front of the oil store. A boy, but with a grown-up's topknot, a boy-man, came bouncing up. In front of the shop he called loudly 'Auntie! Auntie!' and again, 'Auntie! Auntie!'

Looking closely, he realized it was Kilsang.

'What is it?'

A woman came out wiping her hands on her apron, the mistress of the shop.

'Some oil please.'

'What kind?'

'Camellia.'

'Camellia?'

'Yeah.'

'Don't you mean perilla?'

'No, I mean camellia. Tee-hee-hee . . . it's for my new bride's hair.'

The woman cackled with laughter.

'Who's your bride, then?'

'It's Bongsoon, Bongsoon, tee-hee-hee . . .'.

'My name's Wolsun, you see.'

Yongi who had been watching it all, shouted, 'You're crazy, why do you say you are Wolsun!'

'It's you, darling!'

She lifted her face and it was Wolsun. He felt as if his heart would stop. His chest was so tight he wanted to tear it open.

'Heartless woman! How dare you call me "darling!" Go after another man and call me "darling!" The worst woman in the world! Be off with you! Out of my sight! Be gone, do you hear!'

He screamed wildly until his throat felt as though it would burst. Unable to take a step nearer to her, he could only shout. His heart was choking, aching and overcome with pity, but all that came out of his mouth was abuse.

'I went after some other man? Who told you that? Who? One failure was enough to bruise my heart – would I go after another man?'

'Shut up! If you were coming back, why did you go? Why did you go? Why?'

He was about to dash to her when from nowhere an ox stood in front of him, blocking his way and shaking its horns.

390

'Wolsun! Wolsun!'

At the sound of an ox lowing he opened his eyes. All around was darkness while beside him his ox was calling.

'My ancestor is blocking the way, I see.'

He plucked a handful of grass and held it out to the ox. It did not take it but shook its thick neck. The cow bell sounded loudly.

'My ancestors are stopping me!'

He had heard his mother say that, in dreams, an ox represents an ancestor. Leading the ox, he returned home. Kangchong *dek* put her face out of the kitchen. She seemed to have got up and made the supper while he was out. When he came round after putting the ox in the shed, she said, 'You'd better change your clothes. They are going to turn me out of the village, so you'd better go and take part in the plan. I'm the worst woman in the whole world and you'll be given a prize. Huh! What do I care? I have seen all that there is to see – one apron string will be enough.'

This was meant as a threat to hang herself. It seemed that, having taken Yimi *ne*'s exaggerated account literally, she thought that she was really going to be turned out of the village. She looked dejected.

Chapter Thirty-Four

KANG *posoo* wanted to have another glimpse of Guinyo before he left. He looked here and there all over the house till he saw the back of Chisoo, who had stepped out of the inner gate after bidding farewell to Lady Yoon. His face sagging with disappointment, there was nothing to do but follow him. Before the gate, the servants waited in close array to see their master off.

Chisoo mounted the donkey without giving them a glance while Soodong, who held the reins, his small lips buried in a scant beard and tightly closed, gave them a quick look. Samsoo had a strange smile. Bogi cast him a sidelong glance. The pack mule, perhaps alarmed by the whiskery Kang *posoo*, snorted as he grabbed the reins.

'Master, we wish you a safe journey.'

Each one gave his farewell, but Chisoo, in the saddle, only stared at the river. It was an unexpectedly simple departure. They had thought that at least three or four servants would go, and possibly Kim Pyongsan as well, but only Soodong, not very strong, had been taken, along with the hunter. In a huddle the servants vacantly watched the two mules go down the hill. They went slowly along the road well beaten by the feet of mules and men, with the river on one side. Kang *posoo* looked back yearningly several times but when the roofs of the house were out of sight he lowered his eyes. His head kept dropping until his gaze was on his toes.

(It's not as if I was never coming back.)

The mule, glancing sideways as if it would never trust him, snorted again. On the donkey's back, seen from behind, Chisoo looked like a piece of luggage.

(The whole world seems empty; my heart is empty and I'm lost. I don't care about guns – or money . . .)

Their straw shoes were getting wet from the dew left on the

grass at the edges of the road. The weather was probably going to be capricious. Scattered clouds moved fast but the cold blue sky was high and clear. The fields swayed in the wind and through them a herd boy drove a cow, its calf skipping behind. They had gone about two miles and no one had uttered a word. At the front of the party Soodong's face now and again showed signs of tension, followed by deep thought.

(Who can know what's in the master's mind? However, this time there will be some definite result, for he's a terrible man.)

He could not keep out of his head the rumour that Kuchon was on Chiri Mountain. He wished he could clearly erase the image of him from his mind but what he had seen on that dreadful night when he and the *byoldang* mistress had been locked up in the store room came vividly before his eyes, especially the face of Kuchon who, as if already prepared for the worst, had been calm, not resisting, yet unyielding. Soodong had been the first one to become aware of their sinful love. He was also the one who, on that morning after finding the storeroom door flung open and the two of them gone, had been inwardly pleased and had hoped that they would escape somewhere out of reach. On returning from his visit to the ailing Jang-am *sonseng* in Hwasim-li, Chisoo must surely have been told about it by Lady Yoon but, as he came out of her room, he had even been smiling gently. He had shouted in the courtyard of the *sarang*, 'You rascal, Kilsang! Why haven't you swept up the leaves?'

and then, as usual, gone briskly into his room. The next day, and the next, the servants could see no change in his manner.

Occasionally word would go round that he had sent a party to search for Kuchon, and tension would rise, but already they had begun not to take him seriously over this. They said that the two of them had never been a loving couple anyway, and so came to regard the matter as closed.

(No, no, it can't be. Not with his temperament. I know him too well.)

From the time of the shooting practice Soodong had known that these worries would not end there, and now a small expedition was heading towards the hills. If it had been just a hunting party, Chisoo would not have taken so few. Soodong had a kind of foreboding that Kuchon's fate had already been decided.

(Poor idiot, didn't he realize that it must end like this? After breaking the moral law, how can he expect to live? No ordinary woman, either. The wife of a master as high as heaven – how could it happen unless the world had turned upside down? He was crazy, the damned idiot. And now, what's to be done?)

They stopped in front of a tavern for a short rest. As Chisoo dismounted, Soodong quickly glanced at his face. His lips, always tightly closed, hung slightly open. For Soodong, who had been thinking of his sharp expression as he led the mule, it was unexpected. While watering the beasts, he again looked in Chisoo's direction. He was staring vacantly at the river. He looked entirely devoid of any thought, almost like an idiot. Kang *posoo*, squatting in front of the shop, frowned as he looked up at the sky.

'We stay at Yon-goksa tonight, you understand?' said Chisoo, his eyes still on the river.

'Yes, sir.'

It was a repetition of what he had told Soodong before they set off. Kang *posoo*, after staring at the sky, rose to his feet and humbly approached Chisoo from behind.

'Please, master!'

Chisoo turned slowly to face him.

'Master!'

'. . . .'

'Um . . .'.

'. . . .'

'Well, it's all right . . . it doesn't matter . . .'.

'. . . .'

'I . . . I'll tell you some other time.'

As he spoke, his face reddened like a radish and the next moment went white. From beginning to end Chisoo had merely stared in silence.

When they set off again, they left the Sumjin River and entered a narrow path through the hills, reaching the monastery before sunset. As they halted, the desolate chilliness of the mountain air seeped through their clothes. Late sunlight shone delicately through

394

the age-old pines, firs and birches. After leaving the donkeys at an ordinary house below the temple, Chisoo, accompanied by Soodong and the hunter, walked up the road and entered the gate. The monastery must have been a large community but, inside the gate, it was quietness itself and the steadily fading light now turned into an enveloping mist of purple. A monk in pitch black robes came forward, swinging his arms, the ends of his long sleeves flapping.

'Sir!'

Soodong ran in front of him and bowed from the waist. The young monk quickly returned the greeting with joined palms and said, 'What can I do for you? Has your mistress come?'

'No, sir. The master himself, passing by on his way . . .'.

'Is that so?'

Flustered, he joined palms in greeting to Chisoo and examined him with scared eyes: 'I . . . I will report to the Master.'

He turned with a flutter of his robes and walked back at greater speed than he had come down. The back of his shaven head looked lumpy, as if it had been furrowed. Blinking his big eyes, Kang *posoo* stood still and stared at the monk's back. Below the slope, where a mountain stream flowed, two novices of about seven or eight looked up at the visitors, lifting their delicate faces. When their eyes met those of Kang *posoo*, bushy-whiskered like a brigand, they moved their necks like tortoises.

'Those children – are they orphans?'

It was not certain whether Chisoo was asking Soodong or the hunter.

'Some of them may be orphans but some were probably offered by their parents,' said Soodong.

'They're good looking children.'

'Yes, sir. Kilsang is good looking too, isn't he?'

Chisoo smiled a dangerous smile. Soodong hurriedly lowered his eyes.

'Good looking, eh?'

Then he broke into a chuckle. Not knowing what to do, Soodong clasped his hands. When he stopped laughing a dark red colour remained around his eyebrows. His face, which had looked vague and idiotic on the way now gleamed with malice.

'Good looking, indeed! Such bastards should never have been born in the first place.'

The monk Haegwan came running up to them. His protruding cheekbones were red from the effort.

'The abbot tells me to escort you at once, sir.'

Haegwan led the way, passing the side of the Great Hall, through the wood and in the direction of the hermitage. In front of it, a massive elderly monk of six feet stood looking towards them. As Chisoo approached him, Ugwan's eyes flashed.

'What brings you here?'

Chisoo bowed lightly and said, 'I was passing. It was getting late, so I came to seek a night's lodging.'

'You must be tired after such a long journey.'

Ugwan invited him into the hermitage. Soodong, dismissed by Chisoo, followed Haegwan down the path through the woods.

'It is a long time since I last saw you. Are you well, Master?'

Sitting opposite, Chisoo offered his greetings first.

'Yes, I must be ageing the wrong way round. My body gets younger and my mind is preoccupied with worldly cares, so how can I hope for paradise?'

He laughed heartily.

'And how is your household?'

'All is well.'

'And your mother, too?'

'Yes.'

'When I saw her last spring, she looked pale – is she better these days?'

This time Chisoo's eyes flashed. It was more than ten years since, returning alone after a trip to Chonju with Jang-am, he had called in at Chunun-sa and met Ugwan, who had then been there. As a young Confucian scholar, he had despised Buddhism as something not far removed from the world of witches and shamans, a religion of deceit and delusion, so that he had treated Ugwan with polite contempt. He had been upset by Ugwan's rudeness in receiving him in his shirt sleeves, but a youthful arrogance – the effect of only superficially taking in the influence of his teacher Jang-am — had also been to blame. The truth was that the degradation of Buddhism through its suppression by the Yi Dynasty meant that it had managed to survive only through the faith of women and children and the lower classes and, inevitably, the status of its priests, who had been the high-ranking intellectuals of the past, had fallen, their degradation and misdeeds losing them prestige even among the poor, so that from a realistic point of view it was not unreasonable for the anti-Buddhist Confucian scholars to hold them in contempt. However, Ugwan had not seemed to take any offence over his attitude.

'If the drought goes on like this, grain will be scarce this year. Begging won't be easy for monks, will it?'

Ugwan only smiled.

Chisoo was disappointed at such a poor response. He had meant to kill his boredom in the quiet mountain retreat with some verbal wrestling and he felt awkward and embarrassed. Naturally, he did not treat Ugwan's words as those of a simple monk. His overwhelming six-foot bulk and his glowing eyes were extraordinary.

(He's like a wolf. What does he feed on to make him like that? Far from denying the hundred and eight human lusts and passions, he seems to be one great lump of them.)

As he stared at him, inwardly cursing him, Chisoo thought that over the ten years there had not been the slightest change in him. He had not aged, his big eyes, under long black eyebrows, brimmed with vigour and his strong straight bones gave him the air of a general who had survived a hundred battles.

'Where are you bound for?' asked the monk without taking his eyes off him.

'I have no fixed destination. I have come out to do some hunting and at the same time to search for someone. To begin with, I intend to look in the direction of Mount Chiri.'

Ugwan's eyelashes stirred faintly on his closed eyes.

'To violate one of the five commandments?'

'What are Buddhist commandments to a Confucian?'

'Don't be too upset at words from an old man who lives under the roof of a monastery.'

'There is nothing to be upset about. By the way, if I do violate one of the five rules and earn retribution in hell, what will you do for me, Master?'

Chisoo smiled broadly.

'Who knows? I may be accompanying you.'

'You don't mean to say seventy years of wearing a habit are of no avail?'

Ugwan nodded.

'But I don't believe that there is no mercy or pardon in the rules of hell. To my mind, Buddha's rules are more generous than those of men.'

Chisoo chuckled and said, 'In that case, for the sake of sinners, it would be a good thing to do away with hell altogether.'

'I agree with you.'

Ugwan chuckled too.

After he had settled into a clean room and had supper, Chisoo strolled in the courtyard for a long time and then went back to Ugwan's hermitage.

'I was bored, so I have come back.'

Ugwan, sitting composedly in the lamplight, turned. It was not the appearance of the man who had laughed heartily earlier on. Under the reddish light his face was heavy and dark, as if carved in bronze. Chisoo, like a man with no nerves, sat opposite his hardened face.

'Are you there, Myonshim?' Ugwan shouted loudly.

'Yes, master.'

'Bring some boiling water.'

'Yes.'

As the sound of the novice's steps receded, Ugwan put several pinches of tea in an earthen teapot, put the lid on again and got out the cups. After that, everything inside the room seemed to sink into a heavy silence as if the quiet of the mountains had surged into it in masses. Neither of them attempted to speak. Only the flame of the lamp flickered. The silence continued until the footsteps of the novice were heard again. Ugwan put into the pot the boiling water Myongshim had brought and, when the tea was brewed, poured it out. Still without words, they held the cups as the scent rose, and sat as if attentive to the sounds of the night.

'Tell me – where do you get your novices from?'

It was an unexpected question.

Ugwan took a sip of tea and said, 'The good Buddha sends them.'

'Whose children are they? Kilsang – the one you sent us – whose son was he?'

'They're the children of Nature.'

'Do you think anyone can betray his blood ties?'

Ugwan did not answer. As if not to miss the movement of even a hair, Chisoo kept his eyes glued on him.

'Probably not.'

The answer came after a long pause. Chisoo smiled thoughtfully.

'I knew you would say that.'

'Well then, are you saying that you can?'

'Yes, precisely. With those who have defiled it . . .'.

'How petty,' sighed Ugwan in a low voice, but Chisoo cried joyfully, 'Sir!'

'Yes, go on.'

'How much rice land does the monastery have ?'

'I'm not quite sure.'

'I want to make an offering of a hundred sacks or so.'

'. . .'.

'For a certain man who is to die an unnatural death. Not only because of your duty as a priest to put a wandering soul on the way to heaven, but also your heart which could not betray your own blood, I think there is no one better than yourself, Master, to guide the unhappy spirit of that man.'

'No, thank you. I cannot think of anyone about to die an unnatural death who would depend on me for prayers.' His tone was strong and decisive.

'Not in my lifetime,' he added resolutely.

'I see.'

Chisoo stood up to leave. He went down the wooded hill in the darkness as if he was dancing. It was truly the appearance of a madman. In the morning, when Soodong went in to call him, he was not in his room.

'Is he up already?'

He searched the grounds but he was nowhere to be seen.

'Where can he be?'

Feeling uneasy, he went out of the gate but searched in vain.

'What's happened?'

He came back in and ran to the room, hoping he would have returned, but there were no shoes there, and no answer to his call. He opened the door and saw the room was untouched. There was no trace of his having slept there. His face turned white. Panting, he went once again round the monastery grounds, searched the vicinity of the hermitage, and then ran out of the temple gate.

'Oh!'

He stopped as he saw Chisoo walking up towards him with his head bowed.

'Master!'

'. . .'

'Where have you been? . . . I – I've been looking for you every-where!' he called joyfully.

Chisoo lifted his face. His eyes were bloodshot and his clothes were soaked in the night dew.

'Oh, Master!'

As he called, he stepped backwards. Momentarily he had flinched at the thought that Chisoo might be deranged.

'I am going to get some sleep, so stay away until I call you.'

His voice was gentle.

'Oh, so you are not going to leave today, sir?'

'There's no hurry.'

After breakfast, Soodong, who had been staring blankly at Kang *posoo*, said, 'Kang *posoo*, please say something.'

'Aren't we going today?'

That was all he had to say.

'I don't know yet about that . . . but I'm bored stiff – it's like being a dumb man with stolen honey in his mouth . . . I can't bear it.'

'So I'm not the only one – you're the same?'

400

'I'd rather there was thunder and lightning or something. I've never been so lost in all my life.'

Soodong was very restless. By custom a man of few words, he was worried now because he sensed that something bad was about to happen. Kuchon and Chisoo, his master, kept coming before his eyes tangled into one frightening vision. Chisoo's face as he had seen it outside the gate was like a riddle, yet on the other hand it seemed something quite natural.

'Women are the cause of all the trouble in the world.'

'What?'

At the hunter's query Soodong was embarrassed by what had escaped his lips. Kang *posoo* said, 'Sure, they are. They are wicked creatures.'

'. . .'

'It's girls that can melt a man's guts . . . it can be a matter of life or death.'

Soodong stared at him, his thin eyes widening, 'You seem to know a lot for a man with a gun who spends his time hunting!'

'Even a chap who lives by hunting can know the principle of Yin and Yang.'

'Anyway, it's nothing to do with you.'

'. . .?'

'It's not for you to talk so freely about other people's business.'

'What do you mean, other people's?'

In Kang *posoo*'s confused mind clouds of doubt rose in great clusters.

(Why is this chap being so arrogant? Ever since yesterday he's been sulky without saying a word. Perhaps he's also in love with Guinyo?)

Chapter Thirty-Five

CHISOO had been expected to leave the next day, but he stayed on at the monastery for three more nights. During these three days, Ugwan in the isolated hermitage and Chisoo in his room near the Seven Star Chapel hardly came out or met again. Sitting alone, Ugwan sipped the tea brought in by the novice, Myongshim, briefly listened for steps outside and closed his eyes. Even though he shut them, from all directions Chisoo's face flickered before him. This face, smiling with slitted eyes, hundreds and thousands of such faces filled the room and moved like monsters before him. It was like looking into purgatory. He opened his eyes. The brightness of the latticed paper door dazzled him — it was a sign of autumn. It came to the mountain monastery one step ahead of the village, beginning with the petals of the bell flowers. Through the thin-paper door he was aware of the world outside — the sky, the woods, the monastery buildings, the rocks and the paths among the woods all at once holding their breath, each standing in its place, transfixed, without a quiver, all things rigidly keeping their distance, as if held by a lever — a solemn space which would not allow the two of them to come nearer, not one inch — that was how he thought of the distance between himself and Chisoo. The sound of the wind that shook the wood as it passed, of the mountain stream trickling between the stones, the chanting of scriptures that seemed to carry and spread the calm, and the sound of the monk's steps and movements, even these seemed to Ugwan to be a part of the fog-like curtain that shut him off from Chisoo. It was a fierce confrontation between the measureless power of inner, centripetal forces and outer, centrifugal ones.

He sighed and closed his eyes again. He felt an endless temptation to open his heart to Chisoo and tell him the truth: 'I know it is natural for retribution to follow according to the law of cause and effect. However, as retribution for one evil act leads to another, it

402

becomes an endless cycle. Didn't the disciple Mokyon beg Buddha to tell him what to do to save his mother from being punished in Hell? In your case, it is a good woman, who came to the temple to pray for the repose of her dead husband and for blessing on her son and through an unforeseen disaster was made pregnant with the seed of sin. Can it be said that she is sinful? Who has the right to punish her? When you think about all the pain she has suffered by labelling herself a sinner, how can you subject her to the tragedy of bloodshed between her children?'

It was hard for him to suppress his impulse to talk in this way to Chisoo, sitting close to him, knees touching. He was well aware that he felt like this because of love for his nephew, Hwani, which he could not sever however hard he might try, and also aware that there was no chance of changing Chisoo's mind. Besides, it was risky and dangerous, for though Chisoo had said something about betraying blood ties with those who had defiled them, one could not conclude from this that he knew all about it. It was a secret which even if everyone else knew, he must not, a secret that had to be kept. The witnesses, Bawoo and Gannan *halmum*, and Wolsun's mother, were all under the ground and the sower of the seed, Kim Gae-joo, was also no longer of this world. This man, on the one hand like storm and fire and on the other cold and merciless like an incarnation of ambition, who had led the Dong Hak mob against the aristocrats without the slightest mercy, like a pack of blood-thirsty wolves – he was dead and rotting beneath the earth. His brother's son, Hwani, Mun, and himself – only the three of them held the secret – along with Lady Yoon herself. He was inclined to believe that it could not have been revealed.

(Stupid idiot!)

Before his eyes, the images of his younger brother, Gae-joo, and his nephew Hwani, intermingling, rose and disappeared – Hwani, who was now a fine young man, and those eyes of Gae-joo, full of distinction and wisdom. Gae-joo, after the affair, had said to his furious brother, 'Why is it a sin to love a woman whose husband is dead? Heaven gave us the body and who are we to defy it?' He had smiled weakly but as he left the monastery he had shed a few tears of grief.

403

(A father-and-son relationship – does that carry through three incarnations?)

He reflected on past occasions that had been unbearable even for himself wearing a monk's habit: a fair way out of Hwagae market was a roadside tavern where passers-by stopped to wet their throats. As it was not market day, there were not many people about. The young waitress, sitting on a wooden bench outside the shop, fanning herself, said, 'It's so hot – why don't you have a rest?'

He had often seen her as he passed by. He said 'Thank you,' but he blushed and, not daring to sit down on the bench, stood awkwardly. As she got up, she said, 'Look how you are sweating. Your robe's soaking.'

Her gentle eyes smiled. From her body came a scent like that of grass after a passing shower. He walked away as if in flight but at the temple that night he could not sleep until dawn. The hot and searing agonies like burns felt in his days as a novice had never been easy to overcome even in later years. More than once or twice at the lectern, expounding the scriptures, the white back of the neck of a woman, her hair twined with a maroon ribbon and fastened with a jade pin, had made him giddy. Truly, to be freed from lust had been hard. He reflected on the several occasions when he had broken the commandments. Had it been illusion or dream? Certainly it had been an empty phantom – of no more significance than a mayfly or the blooming of a wayside flower. Now he was old and, though with his great bulk he was said to look as if he was bursting with vigour, he felt, in body and mind no more than a withered tree. Even when he reflected on the past, he no more felt the pain of remorse tearing at his heart, nor did he yearn for days that had gone like flowing water. That was not to say, however, that he had attained the state of nirvana. The thought of Hwani, carrying his brother's wife on his back, wandering at this very moment with nowhere to settle, and of Gae-joo, condemned as a great traitor, whose head had fallen and rolled on the execution-ground. Ugwan was grieving for that father and son, their suffering through not knowing the right way, the root of all sin. A Buddhist should discipline himself in preparation for the future, but Ugwan was wasting away with sorrow over the human relationships of previous lives and the present. He had lived all his life close to the words of Buddha but he was saddened by human voices. Meanwhile, in the same way as with Ugwan, Chisoo's battle between the impulse to break out and the rationality that held it back raged on. Under its urge, it seemed as if Ugwan was waiting for him but a yard away, while when he was ruled by reason, the vision of monk became remote, as if he sat on a mountain peak with its lower slopes hidden in mist. The peak, when it was cut off by the cloud, did not seem to be of the earth but a far, far distant thing of the air. Just as Ugwan knew that, even if he opened his heart to Chisoo and begged for a man's life, it would not be accepted, so also Chisoo knew that no answer would come from Ugwan, even if he ran to the hermitage and urged him with threats to confide in him. He was also well aware of how pointless it was to judge his mother and he knew that if, one day, the secret was actually spoken into his ears, he wouldn't know what action to take or how to collect his thoughts. It would be a total confusion, an act that would squeeze his own throat.

(What stupidity. What does it matter whether he was the seed of sin? It's quite enough that he's the adulterer who's taken my wife. What do I want to know about the blood tie for? Ties of blood – ties of blood? Ties of blood, you say? Whose blood?)

Lying in the monastery room in a stupor, he moaned and then mumbled to himself (Leave it alone. Keep it under cover, that's right . . . mm..mm? That's right, you must leave it alone. Leave what? What is there to uncover? I know nothing about it. Let's see, what do I know?).

There was one fact – it had been entirely guesswork but for him it had solidified itself into a hard fact. He had never been able to obtain from anyone any clear confirmation of his guess but for him it had become solid fact. He even forgot quite often that it was only supposition. More vividly than the mirage seen by a thirsty traveller in the desert, the pattern created by his supposition was absolutely clear to him. He was not a dreamer. Even less did he indulge in fantasies. He had followed the narrowest possible path in the way of deduction and his memory of the incidents on which it was based was so vivid it could only be described as fateful.

Wolsun's mother, dancing frenziedly with a knife in her hand and sweat dripping from her face, threw away the knife, ran to his grandmother and dropped on her knees.

'Madame . . . the young mistress must go to to the monastery. I am powerless and the evil spirits are not going to leave her.'

'To the monastery?' muttered his grandmother.

'Yes, Ma'am. She must flee there and stay until the year is out. Without leaving a trace, she must go there till the end of the year . . .'.

As she bowed, great drops of sweat fell from her forehead. The servant Bawoo's face was white while his wife kept dabbing her eyes.

'Damned girl! I'll kill you'

When he kicked her and pulled her hair, Wolsun cried. She could not make much noise, but she cried. Her mother, Wolsun *ne*, left her to cry and ran after him, pleading.

'It was you who sent my mother away to the temple, wasn't it?'

'Yes, yes. I have sinned. Forgive me. Please forgive me, young Master. I lied to the spirits so I should be punished.'

Ah, that's right – even before the day she became ill and took to bed and the doctor was called, his mother had been strange. When she came back after the hundred-days' prayer at the temple, why had she avoided him and tried not to see him? In bed, after reading and then putting out the lamp, he could hear Bawoo and the doctor talking in whispers, but why was Bawoo crying? The leaden look of his mother when she returned on a palanquin, her wild eyes and strange face as she looked up at the sky, and the way she moved as if she was about to burst into tears – all these things he had observed while hidden, pressing himself close to the wall.

The memories of this time were mysterious like sorcery and therefore strong in colour. Insistently he tried to fit them together in a patchwork, but they would not produce any shape. The more he concentrated on the enigma, the less likely it was to be solved. It had looked as though it would remain an insoluble riddle, its form hidden in the depths of some bottomless abyss until the time of the Dong Hak rebellion, five years ago. The angry rebels had stormed into the village and camped in the servants' quarters. It had been a tense day, no one knowing what would happen next, and reeking with the smell of blood. As the only man of the family and master of the household, Chisoo waited in the *sarang*, glaring venomously, prepared for negotiation or, if not, murder and plunder. Time passed but no approach came from the other side. It was more like an atmosphere of caution. During the night, even though he knew it was foolish, he stepped down into the courtyard. Kim *subang*, timid but loyal, stood guard against the wall of the *byoldang* and Chisoo also turned all his attention to the inner quarters. The night grew deeper and it looked as though all were asleep, but he could hear a faint sound of movement from the direction of the inner court. At first he thought it must be a maid attending his mother, but he became suspicious, so, treading silently, he went through the gate from the *sarang*. A light could be seen in Lady Yoon's room. A man's voice could be heard. Momentarily he felt as if his heart had stopped.

(Disgraceful!)

He was about to run on to the verandah but restrained himself.

(Wait a moment!)

There was no sound from his mother. Soon the door was opened and a man stepped out with the light from the room on his back. Coming out of it, he probably would not see Chisoo standing close to a pillar under the eaves. With straight figure and confident stride, he went out of the gate. He knew instinctively that it was the leader of the Dong Hak troop in the servants' quarters. Even at this moment no question of his mother's chastity occurred to him. Her age, nearing fifty, put it beyond imagination. Only the fact that a man of low class – he abhorred and despised the Dong Hak as a crowd of outcasts – had dared to enter her room enraged him. Then, when he had disappeared through the inner gate, sensing that it was the leader, he thought that some kind of agreement had been reached with his mother. Her room looked as if it was empty and immersed in a mysterious silence. As the flame flickered, light and shade danced on the paper door. Not only the inner room, but the whole household was now quiet. Even the mob in the servants' quarters, expected to be on the rampage, perhaps because they were worn out after a long march, gave not so much as a cough.

In the moonless sky, the stars blinked dimly. The village, where the Dong Hak must also have spread, was quiet too. Only the occasional barking of a dog shook the night air menacingly. To the insoluble riddles of his memories the incident of this night had added another and he could not think of it without a dull, disturbing pain. Some time after this came a sultry day, probably in July, while the probabilities of the matter still lay hidden in the bottomless abyss. No breath of breeze came from the river, and even though all the doors of the garden house, supposed to be cool, were open, sweat dripped from his brow. At this moment Yi Dong-jin came walking up the stone steps which were entwined with red flowers. Without servant or mule, he had come on the ferry. Chisoo had heard that an uncle and a second cousin of his had been attacked during the uprising, so he had received him gravely. He looked shabby but not dispirited.

'You must have had a hard time.'

'Well . . .'

With a bitter laugh he raised and opened his fan.

'You can smile then . . .'.

'It served them right,' he spat out.

'What did you say?'

'I said it served them right.'

'You mean it was a good thing?'

'I wouldn't say a good thing exactly, but it's "cause and effect," isn't it?'

'Huh, I see, you are one of the Dong Hak.'

'Don't be silly, but I am ashamed.'

'. . .'.

'The Dong Hak acted stupidly enough, but the disgraceful way the gentry behaved as they were dragged off – if they'd known how to behave, I suppose, they wouldn't have become corrupt in the first place, would they? They disgraced their robes.'

'. . .'

'The barbarous Dong Hak weren't as hateful as the gentry who died shamefully. Maybe there were a few who had some guts. Chong Chambong, father and son, for instance . . .'.

'. . .'.

408

'The disaster fell on them also and, in the pine wood, Chong Chambong said, 'In death too, the order of old and young should be kept, so cut off the father's head first,' and he quietly stretched out his neck. I am ashamed to tell you . . . but some of my own relations are said to have rubbed their hands together like flies – really.'

'What about yourself then? You are blameless before heaven, so your whole body has been spared?' said Chisoo sarcastically.

'I can't be sure. If I'd been there I might have failed.'

' "The sins of the fathers" as they say . . .'.

The suggestion that they might have favoured the Dong Hak had not been to Chisoo's taste.

'It can't be helped. If it comes, you have to face it. But I wouldn't like to die a shameful death.'

'You can't guarantee that either.'

' "The sins of the fathers" seems more appropriate to your case than mine, as this place seems to be the only one to be left quite undisturbed. Is it all thanks to your mother's piety?'

Chisoo frowned with displeasure and Yi Dong-jin uncharacter-istically gave a nervous laugh.

'Come to think of it, that is quite likely. Do you know who Kim Gae-joo is?'

Chisoo's eyes sharpened.

'He is the younger brother of Ugwan, the monk at Yonggok-sa.'

'What!'

'As Dr Mun is known as a close associate of his, the officials are looking for a chance to arrest him too, but the old chap is faultless. Didn't you know who he was?'

'Never.'

'So it looks as though you were spared through the influence of Ugwan and the doctor. He behaved very savagely in the town.'

Chisoo's expression was completely changed.

'Apparently he was intelligent and good looking and rumour says that he's followed by a son whose looks are as fine as jade. Nobody knows who the mother was and his father has brought him up on his own.'

He had spoken casually but these words had sounded in Chisoo's ears like the faint buzz of a mosquito one moment and thunder the next. At that moment he had not understood the cause of the disturbance. It was after this that he had gone up to Seoul to indulge in a life of dissipation.

It had been outside the wall, on a day in June when the jacaranda was in full bloom, yellowish yet with a tinge of pink. After the rain the stone wall was green with moss, against which the blossom made a tangle. It was here that Chisoo, on his way down from the garden house, saw Kuchon standing lost in thought. Even as Chisoo came near, as if unaware of his approach, he remained standing by the blossom. Only when he was very close did he turn his eyes slowly to Chisoo. Chisoo's heart beat faster. Several times he had noticed the same expression on Kuchon's face and, each time, his heart would beat faster.

'You grew up at a monastery?' he had asked in a low voice.

Only then did Kuchon seem to recognize him.

'Pardon?'

'When you were small you lived at a monastery?'

Kuchon's lips turned white and then they moved: 'That's not so.'

'Do you have a father?'

This time he shook his head and looked Chisoo straight in the eye. His expression was not that of a servant, nor was his manner.

'Your face seems familiar. Who does it remind me of?'

He was pressing hard. At once Kuchon's eyes had changed into those of a savage wolf. If he bared his teeth, he would doubtless be a beast. It was only for an instant. A firm and heavy mask fell over his face and it had become quite expressionless. After Kuchon had run off with his wife Chisoo could easily have sent a party after them if he had wanted to. Why did he not do it? He could not understand it himself, nor could he appreciate that it was due to some mysterious emotion, not hate nor vengeance, but a desire for the real truth combined with the feeling that he had to repress this strong impulse to investigate.

After spending the day in his room in a state of torpor, deep in the night, when there was no sign of anyone around, as if the whole place were dead, Chisoo would slip out of the gate like a bat and roam the village below. At dawn when the big bell of the monastery

410

tolled, like a hymn of heavenly praise that penetrated the depths of one's soul, or the cry of the dead in hell — ringing through the mountains and the trees and up to the sky as darkness receded, he would return to his room, soaked with night dew.

After staying three nights, avoiding another meeting with Ugwan to the last, he told Soodong to be ready to set off. At the moment of departure he went to Ugwan to say farewell. The monk silently followed them to the gate and, leaning on his stick, stared at Chisoo's receding back. From the direction of the temple came the leisurely sound of wooden gongs and the chanting of scripture.

Chapter Thirty-Six

AT a village below the mountain, where about a dozen thatched huts huddled together, they left the mules and supplies not immediately needed – food and ammunition that they planned to fetch when necessary – and went further into the hills. They spent the night in a fire-field farmer's hut and the next day set off again to make their way through the deeper part of the mountains. Chisoo carried one of the guns from Seoul and wore an ammunition belt, while Kang *posoo*, as well as a gun and ammunition belt, had a game bag at his waist. Soodong followed with bags of powder and shot and a pack of food on his back.

They went through a dale covered with azaleas and wild magnolias, their trunks as thick as the span of one's arms, and pushed on through a belt of shrubbery. It was virgin forest and the dense growth of bamboo blocked out the sky. It would have been the place for a hermit's cell, with the sound of the wind rustling in the trees, and now and again the noise of water tumbling down the valley. The hunter, leading the way, often gave warnings to those behind but, though he called loudly, his voice was instantly lost in the sounds of the mountain. Over what span of time had the fallen leaves been piling up, layer after layer? – they seemed to be floating on them for, though their feet sunk into the decaying pile, unlike a sandy beach, there was no firm resistance at the bottom. All the air around was charged with damp that rose from the valley – from the thick moss on every rock, from decaying stumps of trees and from the leaves, their reflected greenness giving out flashes of light as if in a shower of rain, some still and some stirring, and from the bamboos underfoot. Flying creatures flapped noisily from branch to branch, calling sharply as if to warn of approaching humans. Small animals ran to hide in thickets or under rocks. As they left the valley further behind, the sound of water grew fainter.

Kang *posoo* was a hunter, a hunter in his very bones. He had looked as though he would never get over his infatuation with Guinyo but, like a drop of mercury that scatters when touched and the next moment resumes its natural shape, his distracted mind was now focused on the one purpose of the chase and the bitter-sweet image of Guinyo dispersed like a mist. All his senses were now concentrated on the tracks of animals, their scent and the rumpled traces they had left on piles of fallen leaves. An expert hunter, he was now in an unusual state of excitement. A noted marksman, he never missed with the matchlock, which kicked severely when the trigger was pulled, making one's shoulder ache. Certainly, in that situation, precision of aim had been the first necessity, for the range was so short and the bullet so slow that, unless you pierced some vital organ of the quarry, your own life was at stake. This man, who had shot numberless animals with his matchlock, had left it in store at the village and stood now with the new-style gun, so it was natural for him to be excited. After all the time spent in practice with Chisoo on Dangsan he knew its capabilities and was accustomed to handling it, but had not yet drawn blood.

As they passed a face of rock, Chisoo saw a baby deer and was about to shoot it for a test.

'Please, don't!'

At the hunter's strong tone, he stopped motionless and looked up at him.

'A tiny thing like that – what are you going to do with it?'

'. . .'.

'If you are going to shoot, aim at a big one. Don't they say "Early in the evening a tiger is only after pretty maids, while at dawn, even a rat or a dog will do?" Our hunting is still only in its early stage.'

With a faint trace of a smile, Chisoo lowered his gun.

'A gun shouldn't be used thoughtlessly. When you fire a shot you must think that you are exchanging it for a life. It's the same with animals, they have a right to live . . . killing a young one will make the mountain god angry.'

It was spoken in a tone of admonition. Away from the hills, he had stuttered in awe of Chisoo's authority, or had been too infatuated to answer questions. Now, back there, he was completely changed. There was no sign of timidity in his words or actions.

(Look at him! He's frightened of no one!)

To Soodong his fearless way of speaking seemed insolent, but he liked his words about how an animal should be allowed its full life and felt a curious affection for this thickheaded and uncouth man. Chisoo did not speak but next time they passed a deer in a thicket, he did not shoot even though it was not a young one. The hunter, walking in front, talked away regardless of whether he could be heard or not. It was the story of a bear that he had had his eye on for two years or more.

The day passed without any gain. Chisoo seemed indifferent throughout. They were still some distance from the fire-field far-mer's place they were making for so, at the hunter's suggestion, they went into the empty hut of a wood carver. After supper, prepared by Soodong, there was nothing for the three of them to do but to sit round facing each other. As if suddenly feeling uncomfortable, Kang *posoo* took out the still unused rifle and point-lessly polished the barrel and examined it. In the light of the resin flame, his face, with its bushy whiskers, gleamed red. Chisoo sat with his eyes closed, one knee folded, and leaning back slightly against the pile of baggage. He was obviously very tired but seemed to have forgotten it as he sank deep in thought. Soodong sat upright with folded knees in readiness for any word from his master.

'Kang *posoo*,' called Chisoo his eyes still closed.

'Yes, sir?'

'How many fire-field farmers do you think there are?'

'It is hard to say. How can a man like me know such things?'

'Why not? – Pyongsan said that in the hills you'd know even the ants that crawl past.'

Perhaps because of the chilly mountain air, his lips looked dark.

'In a way, he's right, as I'm always wandering round the mountain.'

'. . .'

'But it's only the animals I am interested in and I don't take much notice of the people.'

'. . .'

414

'Besides, those fire-field farmers – naturally they don't settle down in one place.'

'Why not?'

'They are wanderers like myself, I suppose.'

Kang *posoo* stared at the resin flame for a moment and added, 'They burn off the scrub and grow millet or maize for a year or two – then the soil is used up and they set off to look for another plot.'

'Yes, I know.'

Sitting on his knees, Soodong struggled to shake off the sleepiness that came over him.

'Not only the land – they are people whose situation doesn't allow them to live in the world, so naturally they move about to escape the eyes of others.'

'What kind of people are they?'

'Some have horrible diseases – there must be lots of lepers here. Empty huts are safe for them, and there will also be criminals, won't there?'

'What kind of crimes?'

Chisoo's eye-lids fluttered slightly.

'There would be all sorts. Debtors turned out of their houses by the bailiffs; and traitors' families; sons of the gentry who have been crossed off the family tree; and a fair number of the Dong Hak in hiding.'

'I suppose so.'

'In the olden days, they say, there were lots of Catholics – people of the Western Learning. In one way or other, they are those who can't live in the broad light of day. There will be escaped slaves, or those who have carried off another man's wife. There are all kinds of sinners and here, deep in the hills, the law is far away.'

Soodong, who had been nodding off, opened his eyes as the hunter's last words slipped into his dwindling consciousness. After glowering at him, he examined Chisoo's face with scared eyes. He was vaguely smiling as the light of the resin lamp slid down the side of his face and the sharp edge of his nose. He called in a low voice, 'Kang *posoo*.'

'Yes, sir?'

As he replied he acknowledged his slip of the tongue with a belated 'Oh, dear!' His eyes, like Soodong's also became frightened. He had little to do with the affairs of the world and it was rare for anyone to tell him these tales – even if someone whispered them into his ear, it would go in one and out the other. As for the affair at the Choi house, he did belatedly remember it, because of his lengthy stay there.

'In future, as far as possible, make sure that we don't have to sleep in empty huts.'

'Yes, certainly.'

He blindly agreed but added, 'Even so, after chasing something, it may well be . . .'.

'There is no need to rush about. We don't have to shoot things to sell . . . Soodong!'

'Yes, sir?'

'Put some wood on the fire.'

'Yes, sir.'

He put some dry pine branches on the embers and revived the dying fire. As the flame rose, the lamp seemed to pale and the inside of the wood carver's hut was brightly lit.

'Kang *posoo*!'

'Yes, sir?'

'Have you ever shot a tiger?'

'Of course.'

'How many?'

'Two or three.'

'M'm . . . they say a hunter once caught a tiger in our bamboo grove.'

'In the grove?'

'So I've heard . . . I don't know if it's true . . . It seems it had come down after a deer.'

Remembering the story told him by an elderly servant, long since dead, he smiled to himself. A deer – it was connected with a tragic event, but he smiled. He could not really feel the truth of a story concerning his father, whose face he had never seen. Nor could he believe that he had died as the punishment for eating the flesh of a deer after a ceremony at a monastery. The story was

416

usually passed on leaving out the bit about the tiger, but when he was a child an old servant whose name even he could not remember had told him and, whenever it recurred, strangely, it made him smile. On that night when the two dogs howled so madly, the truth was that a tiger had come down after the deer. So, in fact, the dogs must have fought the tiger before they caught the deer. But for some mysterious reason the tiger had remained in the grove and a famous hunter had been engaged to kill it. According to the servant, after the shot had been heard, no sound came from the grove, so he stealthily crept in to see what had happened. He found the huntsman floundering around waving the gun, as if he was rowing a boat, and a great tiger fallen nearby. The old man said that too great a fright had sent him out of his mind. He went up to him but he just went on rowing with his gun.

'You need strong nerves to shoot a tiger, don't you?' said Chisoo.

'That's true. You need more than ordinary courage or you'd just pass out at the sight of its fiery eyes.'

'I have no inclination to chase a tiger, Kang *posoo*.'

'Right, sir.'

'Always make sure that we reach a farmer's hut before sunset.'

The hunter agreed, but added, 'Well, if you find the sleeping too uncomfortable, I can fix you up at a mountain lodge where I often stay – but it would mean that we couldn't go very far. Hunting means that, if you have your eye on a certain animal, you follow it for several days and nights . . .'

'Anyone knows that!'

He spoke forcefully and his lips trembled.

'Did I suggest that we should stay in one place and just go round about it?'

'. . .'

'Wherever we go, there will be farmers' huts, won't there, whether they are occupied by lepers or robbers.'

'. . .'

'Chasing animals is not the first priority.'

'. . .'

'I am looking for a man!'

'Yes, I will arrange things accordingly, sir.'

417

The slow-witted hunter could not guess what it was all about and, cowed by Chisoo's manner, he spoke in confusion. Unconsciously, Soodong poked fiercely at the fire. Sparks flew up, making him dodge, and then he felt Chisoo's stare. But the master was not staring at him.

(Chance . . . Am I waiting for chance? I am hoping to meet him by chance in some hut . . .)

His eyes turned towards the hunter. He laughed to himself and then openly. Kang *posoo* looked at him wide-eyed.

'Yes, I'll do that. If you want me to find someone . . .'.

Then stopping short, he stood the gun in a corner and stared blankly at Chisoo.

(If only I could, I'd like just to go back. And then put it off to next year. Wasting time like a lazy servant . . .)

He again laughed to himself. What he could not tolerate was any damage to his dignity. By whatever means, he had to bring the matter to a conclusion. As for the method, there were easier ways. He could have sent men out in all directions to bring them back, or first investigate their whereabouts and then set out. So why had he come here just to wander vaguely in the hills? Was it that he feared an outburst of rage and a merciless punishment that would set the whole village abuzz? All he needed was to convince himself that he had restored his injured dignity, that sense of his own absolute authority . . . but he had to admit that his passionate deter-mination to throw everything into it was losing ground. On the other hand, that desperate struggle not to clear things up with Ugwan had been because of his fear of decisively abandoning the task. It would remain a painful task until the final conclusion. To bring it to a close was his duty. On a battlefield, you can't run away. Even if you have no fervent love for your country, there is no other way but to rush at the enemy – that is the only possible concept, a chronic disease called 'the ideal'. The almost tangible pattern of the probable truth concerning Lady Yoon and Kuchon, Ugwan and Kim Gae-joo, Dr Mun, Wolsun *ne*, Bawoo and his wife – because of these facts, he was now chasing Kuchon, but in which direction it would drive him was an emotional matter that he himself could not decide. Avoiding the certain confirmation, he had left Yon-goksa, but had he acquired the proof, would his desire to punish Kuchon have been stronger, or would he have abandoned it? He could not be sure even of that.

Soodong went out of the hut with a sack. A strong gust of chilly mountain air hit him and made him shudder. Perhaps because it was high ground, the stars seemed to twinkle from somewhere very close, or rather to shudder, like Soodong. From far away, in the direction of the rock face, came the cry of an animal. Perhaps a mountain goat being chased by a beast of prey? He fancied that it could be the cry of Kuchon. He swept up some fallen leaves and crammed them into the sack.

(Out of all of them, why did he have to pick on me to come here? How can I bear to see Kuchon killed? God forbid!)

After filling the sack with leaves, he stood blankly for a long time before he went back to the hut. Chisoo still leaned back as before. The hunter, now relaxed, stared at him blankly.

(It really beats me. He's not mad, but why does he keep bursting into senseless laughter?)

'Move over, please!'

Soodong pushed the hunter aside and spread out the dry leaves to prepare a bed for Chisoo. He brought over a wooden pillow, probably left behind by the wood carver, and covered it with the leaves, taking great care. Chisoo lay down, and Kang *posoo*, though only leaning back against the baggage, was asleep in no time, breathing heavily. After a while, Chisoo's breathing also became regular. He must be asleep, thought Soodong, and he took down the resin light and threw it on the fire. Flames shot up and died again. Crouched by the fire, he could not sleep. The drowsiness that had shamelessly clung to him before was dispersed, and he rather felt the inside of his head becoming clear as if it had been dowsed in cold water. The cries of wild beasts still came from outside and also the incessant sound of the wind as it drove the fallen leaves.

(How forlorn it is, as if the whole world was dead!)

Suddenly he felt sobs rising.

(Really desolate!)

It must have been four or five years or more since his wife, Booni, provided by his master's house, had died in an epidemic.

(Come to think of it, I feel sorry for the master. A woman came into the family and . . .)

After his wife's death he had loved Kuchon who, wherever he may have come from, had turned up at the gate of the house, like a younger brother, or a son. Or rather he had admired him, in the way one does a superior.

(He has something about him different from the rest of us.)

This belief was so deeply rooted that, even after Kuchon had sinned and run away, it did not change. The only one he could not forgive was the mistress of the *byoldang*. His thoughts about her were merciless.

(A woman came into the house . . . women are wicked creatures, anyway. When you think about her daughter and her mother-in-law, widowed young and ageing alone – what a wicked woman she is! While the master is alive and well . . . it's because of her wagging tail that Kuchon fell.)

When he thought of how, because of this woman, Kuchon was about to be killed, he was even more indignant.

(The wickedest of creatures . . .)

As the night deepened, the wind fell. 'Ba-a-ow, ba-a-ow.'

Somewhere very close, a deer called. For such a gentle and mild animal it was a very loud cry.

'Ba-a-ow, ba-a-ow.'

The next day, with the hunter's consent, Chisoo shot a deer. At the spot where it fell, Kang *posoo* took out a knife and slit its heart. The three of them drank from the flow of fresh blood as a substitute for lunch. Soodong took the deer on his back and, by the time they reached a nearby fire-field farmer's hut, the sun was already setting. In the yard, while the hunter was cutting up the dead animal, Soodong brought a basin of water for Chisoo to wash. As he stood up after washing, he let out a shriek. A large centipede was crawling by his foot. Soodong ran with a stick and hit it. Kang *posoo* carried on without paying any attention, as if it was nothing.

The farmer's wife said with a smile, 'Another one will follow.'

'Another one?'

Chisoo's face was white.

'They are a pair, so the other one is sure to come looking for it.'

He gave her a quick, glowering glance.

'It's the principle of Ying and Yang,' put in the hunter as he filleted the meat.

'Fool – why is he so tactless?' thought Soodong as he mentally clicked his tongue. Before long, as expected, another centipede exactly the same size as the dead one appeared.

'Look! Just as I said.'

The woman laughed. Chisoo felt a bitter taste in his mouth. He hated centipedes. He was probably more frightened of them than of tigers. All through the night he dreamt of being chased by one.

Chapter Thirty-Seven

IT was much more than a case of 'Same bed, different dreams'. Sometimes in the water mill, or on the grass or behind a rock, and more frequently in the Fertility Shrine, Guinyo and Chilsung, burning with different expectations and ambitions, continued a physical relationship that was as infertile as barren land. These respective ambitions and expectations not only denied all human love but would not allow even the lust which might naturally accompany such an affair. They acted only for a purpose – it was mortification for the attainment of an end that transcended all instinct. It was an ugly and inhuman affair – in this respect, the woman was even stronger and more thorough than the man. These heartless assignations which took place deep in the night were kept entirely secret, thanks to watertight plans and instructions from Pyongsan. Whether or not a child was conceived seemed like some great gamble with the gods. If a son were born, the three of them would raise a toast to victory. If it were a girl, Chilsung would be dropped out of a new plot by Pyongsan and Guinyo. The shrine of the Fertility Spirits buried deep in the woods of Dangsan solemnly kept watch over the night and, inside, the child Buddha, with smiling face, looked down on these ardent deeds of supplication. The bleak autumn wind whispered past the eaves of the shrine, the leaves rustled as they rubbed together, a nightingale cried like an elderly spinster and an owl like the ghost of an old bachelor, while the figure of the Buddha – was it no more than a lump of metal melted by a craftsman and mindlessly poured into a mould? – never spoke but only smiled.

'I say – Guinyo.'

Squashed beneath his chest she did not reply.

'I mean "Ondal" . . .'.

'. . .'.

'What about if he doesn't come back after a month and then

two months – there'll be trouble, won't there? If you become pregnant during this time, they'll be suspicious, because they will count up the months, won't they?'

'Ondal' was Pyongsan's code-name for Chisoo. She burst out shrilly, 'You don't have to worry about that. Do you think he won't be back in time for the harvest festival?' and added, in a voice that was lower but full of contempt. 'It's none of your business.'

'What? Oh, really? If I don't worry about it, who will?'

'It's hardly anything to do with you.'

'Hardly anything to do with me? A child's born – and the father has hardly anything to do with it?'

He pressed on her hard, and she responded with laughter that was like a groan.

'Don't count your chickens before they are hatched. Even if there was baby . . . and, as there isn't, what do you mean, "father"?'

'That may be so, but, I reckon it will come – so I might as well think about what needs to be thought about.'

'You're filled with greed right up to your neck . . .'.

Having released each other, they parted like enemies. Guinyo went down the mountain first. As if following her receding figure, as she descended with her outer skirt over her head, came the successive hoots of an owl. When he reached the spring Chilsung fell on his knees to drink and, as he rose, he saw Pyongsan, who had been on guard, strolling down towards the village, his hands thrust into his waist-band.

'Bloody hell! That cat! It's the seed that counts – what does the soil matter?'

After Chilsung, wiping the drops from his lips with his fist, had also gone down, the moon, a piece missing, hung faintly above the roof of the shrine.

'Do they think it will all happen just as they wish?' – Was the little Buddha saying something like this to himself?

In Bongsoon *ne*'s room at the Choi house, Haman *dek* and Yimi *ne* were helping her with her sewing. Another fortnight and it would be *Chusok*, the Harvest Moon. She could not manage all the servants' clothes by herself so she had called in Haman *dek* and Yimi *ne*, known in the village for their agile fingers. In the previous

423

year, also, they had come in to help. With her painstaking nature, Haman *dek* enjoyed sewing and, though not as skilful as Bongsoon *ne*, she could run up clothes good enough for people such as Kim *subang*, Guinyo or Samwol. Yimi *ne* was a fast worker who could cut and sew servants' clothes with ease, though her stitches were a little coarse.

'Whatever you say, I prefer jobs where you can stand up. Sitting down to sew makes my hips ache.'

'It's all a matter of getting used to it,' said Haman *dek* as she pulled her needle off the thread, pinned it in the hem of her jacket and raised the wick of the lamp.

'Kim *subang*'s wife was saying how she dreaded it and wasn't I fed up with it? – but I find, if I'm working, I don't notice the time.'

Bongsoon's mother measured the width of a chest as she spoke.

'It's your fate, I guess. You have the knack as perfect as an apple straight off the tree,' said Yimi *ne*.

'If you didn't like it, your skill wouldn't have grown like that, would it?'

'When I was young, I was proud of my skill and didn't notice how late it was getting, but as I grow older, I keep thinking of the sad past . . . Still, as soon as I pick up my work I can forget about it, so work is my treasure.'

'That's true. They say, of all sorrows, living by yourself is the saddest.'

'What's the use of talking about it? If a child becomes ill, there's no one to share your worry . . .'.

'They say that Bongsoon's father so much wanted to have a child.'

'It's just my luck. For a short while I thought that at last I was living as well as others. Now it seems like a dream . . .'.

Haman *dek* just listened to the conversation between the two of them. Bongsoon's mother started to tell the story of her life with an indifferent expression, as if she was talking about someone else.

'I was married when I was sixteen and went into my husband's house. He was only eleven. And he was full of mischief. In summer he went after loach in the stream, making a mud-cake of his clothes; in winter he slid on his bottom all day on the ice so that the seat of his trousers was worn out, or he'd fly his kite day after day,

424

cutting his finger on the string just about every time. When this happened he'd come home and say, "You, damn girl, I've cut my finger because of you!" and pull my hair by the roots. But I put up with it all and never once spoke back, as he was my so-called husband. As I went on like this, he soon fell in love with someone else and went astray – it is true, though, that he was above me. Bongsoon has taken after him in every way.'

'Yes, I'm not just saying this – I really mean it – when she's bigger, so many matchmakers will be lining up for her that the dog's throat will be hoarse from barking.'

'Well, for that, we'll have to wait and see . . .'.

'So what happened next?'

Yimi *ne*, who found it unbearable to work in silence and liked to talk, urged her to go on.

'Just then the rebellion came and, whatever he knew about it, he had to be in the forefront. Our house was in chaos and he himself became a wanted man – even in that state he managed to take a *kiseng* with him when he ran off.'

'He must have been no end of a playboy – to take a woman with him even when he would be put to death if he was caught.'

'Apparently it was the girl who insisted on following him. Some-how he wandered round for more than ten years and then, whatever wind blew – when I think about it, it must have been to drop the seed for Bongsoon – he came back. Since our place was all in confusion, I had come here through knowing someone who put in a word for me and he just turned up one day. He was over thirty and I was thirty-five. So I resigned and we went back to our native place. He was not a wicked man by nature. And, probably because he'd been through so much himself, he took great care of me, saying that he would never again allow me to suffer any hardship . . .'.

'This time you caught the wind, as they say.'

'I was beginning to think the time had come for me to have a decent life. Besides I was pregnant.'

'So it was the Fertility Spirits that drew you together!'

'How pleased he was! He'd say, "Look, be careful. I'll do every-thing, you just keep still." He trembled with the fear that I might have a miscarriage. He wouldn't let me go out at night in case I had a fall.'

'After all that, you'd never have any more regrets or wants. I wish I could have had such happiness, even if it was for only one day and I had to die the next,' said Yimi *ne*.

While she fluttered, Haman *dek* still wordlessly stitched away.

'That's what they all said. They said I'd blossomed out in blessings. At night, in spite of my protest, he'd say "Let me stroke your tummy to feel how big it's grown" – you can understand it, can't you? He was over thirty, and still no child. He was making such a fuss that it made me nervous – what if it was a girl? I asked him, "What'll you do if it's a daughter?" and he said, "What does it matter whether it's a girl or a boy?" But I was still worried – it had to be a boy. As I kept harping on it, he used to say, "Even if it's a girl, just deliver it safely and I'll be dancing." '

Bongsoon *ne* seemed to be sunk in her own thoughts of the past rather than talking about it to Yimi *ne*. 'From the first signs of pregnancy, we had a hard time to make ends meet. He tried to go into trade, which he didn't know anything about. When I was about six months gone, he rushed off to Seoul on business, saying that he ought to be back home for the month of my delivery – who could have known that it would be the last of him? He was waylaid by bandits and . . .'.

Haman *dek* opened her mouth for the first time,

'That's it – the world doesn't go the way we want it to.'

'We'd been together less than a year after the reunion. I gave birth to our Bongsoon in the middle of wailing before his tablet. The man who'd said he'd dance when she came was nowhere to be seen and, as an elderly neighbour cut the umbilical cord, she wept and I did, too. Was it because he had to go so quickly that he'd given me so much love? After driving a nail into my heart, that heartless and inconsiderate man who used to arrange my shoes on the shoe-stone in case I missed a step and harmed the baby . . . when the first meal after the delivery was brought in, it wouldn't go down my throat. Really, if it hadn't been for that little bundle of blood, I'd have followed him. As I came back to this place with Bongsoon in a swaddling cloth in my arms, I couldn't see for tears . . . still, we are tough. As time passes, you are hungry and you eat, tired and you sleep, and the day when you can forget comes . . .'.

'What else can you do? You have to go on living.'

'That's right. I must carry on until Bongsoon is off my hands. Other people of my age already have daughters-in-law or sons-in-law . . . The time will soon pass . . .'.

As the night deepened and one after the other the lights went out in the rooms, Haman *dek* and Yimi *ne* left off and, lighting their steps with an old lantern, went down the slope. After they had gone, Bongsoon *ne* went on sewing without stopping, listening to the sounds of the night.

'Is it the wind?'

She turned her head.

'It's strange. Recently, every day just at this time . . .'.

She put the needle in her lapel, lit a latern and silently opened the door to go out. As she turned into the backyard, a shadow flickered.

'Who's that?'

'. . .'.

'Who is it?'

'Who do you think it is?'

It was the low voice of Guinyo. She lifted the lantern, and saw her face. She blinked once or twice in the light.

'Guinyo?'

'Yes. Did you think it was a burglar?'

'Every night, about this time, I hear someone, so tonight I decided to go out and see.'

Guinyo's face, like a mask, did not move. She shot a glance at Bongsoon *ne* from her deepsunk eyes.

'I can't sleep.'

Her face was still like a mask and only her lips moved.

'Why not? If a grown-up girl like you can't sleep, it must be a serious illness.'

'H'm, so is that why you're not asleep, because you're sick?'

Bongsoon *ne* was silenced.

'The Harvest Festival's getting near and it makes me think of my mother. When I think about her spirit, not getting so much as a bowl of rice and water, just wandering around . . . I can't sleep.'

This was what she said but her face, still rigid like a mask, was strange. Bongsoon *ne* felt scared.

'Do you really have such thoughts?'

She lowered the lantern to keep Guinyo's face out of sight.

'You mean that I wasn't born of a mother?'

'It's a hard thing to fulfil one's duties. You mustn't be resentful, you have to follow your fate.'

Bongsoon *ne* herself did not know why she was talking like this.

'What a queer thing to say!'

'It's rather . . .'.

'Do you think I am resentful of someone?'

Bongsoon *ne* was at a loss. It had happened often enough and always in similar circumstances. Nevertheless, overcome by her feelings, she spoke up rashly again, 'I don't know why, but there's something that gives me a queer feeling. You mustn't blame others. You mustn't blame others for your fate . . .'.

'This is crazy. I just popped out for a bit of fresh air. What's wrong with that?'

'It's not that there's anything wrong with it . . . it's just that, as I look at you it seems to me that you have some kind of grievance . . . no, I don't mean that . . . it's more that you seem to be hardhearted.'

Unlike other times, Guinyo did not bother to take the quarrel any further. With a swing of her skirt, she turned her back and disappeared to her room.

Bongsoon *ne* also went back the way she had come swinging the lantern. She could not think why on earth she had said such things to Guinyo. Perhaps it had been because of those words about how she thought of the spirit just wandering around, not getting so much as a bowl of rice and water. It was so plainly a lie made up on the spot. It was not, of course, that she had been touched by it, but just that she was frightened of Guinyo. Her big, deepset eyes with their dark pupils were frightening in the lamplight. In those pupils, some tenacious purpose flickered like the slithering of a snake. Or was it just because it was night?

428

'Look at her, she's kicked off the quilt – she's going to catch a cold.'

In her room again, Bongsoon *ne* pulled the cover back over the child and blankly looked at its face. The floor was hot and there was the brazier as well. Her cheeks were as red as cherries. Strands of hair stuck to her forehead and she gave off a faint sour smell of sweat.

'As pretty as a picture! Though I shouldn't be like this about my own child – but when she's grown up I bet the dog at the gate really will be hoarse from barking at the people coming to ask for her hand!'

She smiled to herself. Bongsoon kicked off the quilt again.

'If her father had lived, how he would have adored her! Like a treasure of gold or jade, he'd have held her on his palm to admire her . . . Still, that's her sad fate . . .'.

She picked up her sewing and took the needle from her lapel.

When he came down from Dangsan, Pyongsan went straight home. Haman *dek* had returned from helping with the sewing at the Choi house and was about to set up the loom in the small room when she heard him. She blew out the lamp. He entered the main room, took off his clothes and got into bed. After a while he fell into a deep sleep and dreamed he was sitting on top of a pile of gold.

'Do you think it will all happen just as you wish?'

If the little Buddha had appeared in Pyongsan's dream to tease him like this, it would have been better, but while his miscalculation was infinitely pitiable, the Buddha must be rather mischievous. While they doggedly climbed perilous slopes in the hope of grasping the five-coloured rainbow, instead of giving them a hint of the disasters and pitfalls ahead of them, did he not beckon them on with, 'A little further, just a little further?'

Putting aside the question of what may happen in the next world, no doubt the hellish struggle taking place in this one is a spectacle worth seeing.

'I don't associate with sinners.'

'I have no connection whatsoever with the murderer.'

'I was merely an onlooker.'

429

With complacent face, he may mumble to himself like this. They say that long ago God, the ruler of earth and sky, sent his beloved son into the world to let him share the sufferings of humanity. Sakamuni prophesied that the Maitreya will come to save mankind and then there will be a happy world where the ground is paved with gold and food and clothes appear when needed, where pleasure is boundless and, even at the age of five hundred, men and women will marry. But while we wait for fifty millions of years, the Maitreya, it seems, is just a spectator. If that is the case, the world is a stage on which the good and the bad play out their roles according to a fixed plan and mankind are merely performers. Anyway, Pyongsan now dreamed of sitting on a pile of gold: the question is, by whom was he being deceived?

Chapter Thirty-Eight

A S the muzzle of the gun followed the profile of a figure moving between the branches, Soodong shouted, 'Kuchon!' Following the shout, the report of a gun shook the hills. The figure jumped up, somersaulted away and, as if in an extension of its rolling, tumbled over a rock and ran off.

'Catch him!' roared Chisoo.

Kang *posoo* ran. Running with him, Soodong caught him by the belt, 'Kang *posoo*, Kang *posoo*, listen to me . . .'. he gasped, 'Please let him go . . .'.

The hunter's pace slackened.

'What are you doing, you two?' shouted Chisoo, fallen far behind, as he ran after them.

'Faster than a ghost! Where could he have gone so quickly?'

The hunter spoke awkwardly as he clambered over a rock. Knowing in which direction Kuchon had gone, he circled round, pushing aside the bushes. If he was going to catch him, flying through the hills like a phantom, he would have to hurry. Chisoo and Soodong, no mountaineers, would not have caught him even if they had wings.

After some wandering, they found a grass hut set low under a hill. There were signs that someone had been there a little earlier but it was now empty and a woman's shoe lay where it had dropped, upside down. It was plain that Kuchon, carrying her on his back, had run away. Chisoo kept firing at the empty hut.

'Birds of a feather . . .'. spat Chisoo as he glowered at Soodong, who trembled like an aspen, his face the colour of grass.

Where they had first spotted Kuchon there lay some arrowroot and a patched cotton sack filled with wild grapes. This incident occurred when they had been in the mountains for about fifteen days. For the next two days Chisoo set Kang *posoo* and Soodong in

431

front of him and thoroughly searched the mountainside, almost without rest, but they had no further glimpse of their quarry.

'It's raining.'

In his sleep Soodong thought it was the sound of a shower but, waking up, realized it was water tumbling down the valley. If he was asleep, he always mistook the sound of water for rain. Milky morning light filtered into the hut. Chisoo lay on his side, sleeping as if dead and the hunter on his back with his bewhiskered mouth open, breathing harshly through uneven teeth and occasionally smacking his lips.

'Another day.'

Soodong sat up and shook dry leaves from his clothes. Where the fire had been the night before the ashes still preserved the shape of the pieces of wood. He put a handful of leaves on them and lit them with his flint. He put more wood on it and watched the flames grow. Gradually warmth spread through the hut. The ceaseless, repetitive sound of tumbling water added to the early morning desolation of the mountains.

Soodong cleaved the dawn mist as he left the hut. Chilly air that cut the flesh like a razor struck his throat. A pair of elk, which, unlike deer, rarely go about alone, passed by hidden among the trees. Grasping supple branches of azalea and treading mossy stones, he went down to a small stream divided from a larger one. The wild vines that wound themselves roung the shrubs were soaked blackish with dew. The silvery backs of the azalea leaves were also covered with drops of moisture. Leaves turned yellow by the autumn were more conspicuous and the light in the woods before sunrise was clear and predominantly bluish.

Soodong, who had been looking down at the stream, lifted his head and turned towards the peaks of the eastern mountains. They rose, range after range, while above them clouds, scattered like thin ice, turned a faint pink that grew deeper moment by moment, giving each peak a slightly different hue. The deepened colour of the clouds turned to crimson and the sky became a sea of fire. The solemn and splendid rite of sunrise was about to begin. Soodong, however, was not absorbed in this majestic and dazzling spectacle.

(The day after tomorrow will be the Harvest Moon but I don't know whether he's given a thought to going home. How can they offer the sacrifice without the head of the family? And what about visiting the graves . . . ?)

Everything seemed to point to Chisoo spending the festival season in the hills.

(I can't breathe. It chokes me. I'd rather my throat was blocked up once and for all.)

He looked at the vine that had wound itself round and round a pine tree. Clinging tightly and increasing in thickness, it was like the skin of an ancient animal and as repulsive as a snake as it twisted itself ever more tightly round the tree.

(The master – why does he just ignore me? Does he leave it for now, so as to punish me more severely when we are back home? Didn't he say 'Birds of a feather flock together'? Naturally, he would. He's letting my guts dry up minute by minute.)

It was plain that he had let Kuchon escape, not by mistake, but on purpose – so it was natural to expect punishment, yet strangely there was no sign of any action. Apart from spitting out that one phrase, 'Birds of a feather . . .' there was not even a trace of anger on his face. It wasn't because he was wholly absorbed in seeking Kuchon. If he had wanted to punish Soodong, he could have done so before he went to sleep, with his perverse temperament, just killed him as a servant who had betrayed him. In some ways Chisoo even seemed to have forgiven him for what he had done. In other ways, he looked as if he had forgotten the incident completely. The more it looked that way, the more fearful Soodong became. He also felt a terrible sense of guilt. Even if the master magnanimously forgave him, he would not be able to forgive himself. He felt such uncontrollable pity and respect for Kuchon that he could not guarantee that in similar circumstances he would not again betray Chisoo, though his servant's sense of loyalty to his master, deeply ingrained in his bones, was quite unchanged.

When he came back to the hut after washing his face, the hunter, wherever he might be, was not to be seen. Chisoo had risen and sat as comfortably as if he was in his own study. Soodong made his morning greeting and began to prepare breakfast when Chisoo called him.

'Yes, sir.'

The tip of his small nose was red as he snuffled.

'What day is it today?'

'The twelfth.'

'It's nearly the Harvest Moon.'

'Yes, sir.'

Soodong, who had been cautiously studying his face, lowered his eyes. Chisoo said nothing more.

(Isn't he going to go back? Still, how can he avoid it?)

Outside, he put rice and water into an earthenware pot. As he snapped dry pine branches to burn, he noticed vine stalks curled round them. Twisted and intertwined they had wound themselves round the branch like a cobweb as if to illustrate the fierce persistence of the life-force.

(It was nearly a year before he set off after Kuchon. All that time he never showed any sign. So, even if he treats me just as usual, it doesn't prove anything. There's no doubt about it. As soon as we are back in the village, he'll have . . . he'll hang me on a tree . . .)

At Kim *jinsa*'s house many years ago, when the grandmother of the present young widow had been young and Soodong only an urchin with a runny nose, he had witnessed the summary execution of a young man from the village for trespassing at night near the room occupied by the young lady of a gentleman's house. He had been hanged on a tree on Dangsan. Dangling upside down, he swung to and fro like a ball on the end of a string each time he was struck by the club. He cried and cried, protesting his innocence until finally he bit his tongue and died. Though it did not often result in death, private punishment within the village, by hanging the culprit on a tree and beating him according to his crime was a common practice. As he sat alone in the empty mountain hut without the hunter or Soodong, Chisoo did not move, as if he was intently studying an unfamiliar side of himself. How should one compare his persistence with that of the wild vine? Perhaps one could say that, while Guinyo's persistence was like that of the vine, his resembled more the will of the pine tree which, despite the winding vine, still stretches upwards and gives no ground.

All things in heaven and on earth must have a beginning and an end – that is the very precondition of life; they say every new birth means a new inscription on a grave stone; in life's progress towards death, persistence is its rhythm, its progress and its fruition, and neither plants nor birds, beasts nor insects can be excepted from this rule. For humans, death must be a little more ceremonious, so the dead are buried deep underground, or sometimes, according to custom, put to sea in a little boat for their heavenward journey. At the same time, they can be eaten by fish, like any animal, or be torn by wild beasts or become food for crows. With this multifarious death ahead of him, man is born to futility, yet how grand is the pattern of his persistence, for he has put on robes and developed language to make up the fabulous drama of culture and civilization. One show, perhaps with two faces – tragedy and comedy back to back – the daily routine of a comedian with hidden tears, and a tragic actor suppressing his laughter, following one another towards the grave. It was like that with Guinyo and Pyongsan, and with Chisoo also, setting out after Kuchon; the reason for his persistence lay in the need to deal with immorality and avenge the damage to a gentleman's dignity – was he a tragic actor suppressing his laughter? Even if you should insist that this persistence was quite apart from his own instincts and had little to do with his own passions and desires, being in accordance with the customary rules of his environment, complicated by the laws of 'cause and effect', – and that in carrying it out he was no more than a puppet, it appears, nevertheless, to be a kind of persistence. Even though it was not accompanied by any clear awareness or sense of mission – as with followers of the Dong Hak or Catholicism, or believers in the fundamental goodness or badness of human nature, or of revolutionaries who would overthrow the country and seize the seats of power to save mankind – habit and custom have a long history, so that, though Choi Chisoo's conscious intention was not strong, in the end it proved harder to erase than a clear awareness or a sense of mission. An old stain, even though faint, is hard to remove.

For the two days since Kuchon had been spotted Chisoo had appeared to be lively, strong and energetic. He who had lived like stagnant water in a pond, doing no more than come and go between garden house and *sarang*, withdrawn and with no one to talk to, inert and prone to illness, now sweated till his clothes were soaked, his skin taut, his face pink with excitement. His eyes, reflecting the sun, sparkled like jewels, looking wise and even beautiful – there was no sign of anxiety in his appearance, nor did he look bored. No cold smile rose to his face. There was the beauty of burning life and a rapture that comes from forgetting the sense of time. He had until then been rather more miserable than he should have been because of his inborn temperament. Under the whale's-back roof, enclosed by ring after ring of walls, in the middle of sleepless nights, he had been crazy in his loneliness, brandishing his fist in the air. As he now considered leaving the woods after two hard days, the stagnant illusions of madness were returning and spread through his veins like an evil potion.

(You, devil, there's no point in keeping your eye on me, because I won't take any notice of you.) (Ha, ha, ha . . . master, I'm not doing anything, am I? I'm just keeping still. I don't see why I should be repugnant to you. What do I do wrong? Go on dancing freely. Thinking about me – that's what makes you ill.)

(Devil! Don't press on my neck. Don't twirl round me like a ghost. Let go of me! I'm giddy. My head weighs a ton. Will I dance to your tune? Do you mean me to fall for a woman or buy a job with bags of gold? Be a soldier and carry a gun in the Army of Justice? Or be charitable and earn a monument? Stop it, I won't be cheated by you. Wait for the dawn. When dawn comes . . .)

(Even when dawn breaks and the sun shines on that pomegranate tree, there is nowhere for me to go, is there? There's no other thing for me to do but sit here like this. A million aeons may pass but I will remain unchangeable because I am immortal. You can't cut me with steel, nor burn me with flame nor freeze me with ice – I am indestructible and immortal. Do you understand? I am the hours of the day, time itself – do you understand?)

(I know, I know! You are time. Did you say you were immortal? – That's right. But now I am eating you up, don't you agree? Minute by minute, I am eating you up, don't you agree? Let's stop quarrelling – you breathe in your way and I in mine – you are you and I am I.)

(It is unbearable – so why don't you listen to me? Just try and

436

read. Through the words of a wise man, you might just be rid of your desperate hunger.)

(Ha! Ha! Ha! . . .)

(Even a burnt out lump of charcoal glows red and hot when it's rekindled – haven't you seen it? Samachon, born as a man, having lost his origin, licked time, treasuring it the way you lick a lump of salt. Though they say time is as short as a spring dream, for him it must have been useful and comforting. If you don't care for that, become another Yonsangun. Just crunch it and eat it up like a melon. Just roll about in a great harvest field.)

(Stop! Stop! Stop talking nonsense. To tell the truth, I am time, and time is me. Can't you hear? I am in you and you are in me.)

Those truly futile times, times of mad visions and words in the middle of the night under the whale's back-like roof, were now returning to attack him mercilessly. As he planned to go home, the illusions came, each holding the tail of the one before – monsters from whom he had long been free now spread out before him and gloated. Though it had not been a glorious battlefield in which, as a great general commanding an army of ten thousand, he had shouted war cries as he surged forward, but only the chasing of a poor servant who gathered food in the wilds, the two days since the sighting of Kuchon had been tense and now the woods produced sounds even more oppressively boring than before. Time had gone limp.

When breakfast was nearly ready Kang *posoo* returned, his face flushed. With a quick glance towards the hut, Soodong said, 'Where have you been?'

'Hah, really!' he said breathlessly, 'A tiger as big as a hill!'

'A tiger?'

'Yes, a tiger!'

'Where?'

'I don't mean that I have seen it – only its tracks. I went towards the spring to wash. There was a smell, the sickly smell of blood – a strong whiff of it. So I searched around. It had caught a mountain goat, savaged its innards and eaten them. It must have happened at dawn. The cunning creature had dragged it into a bush to eat, intending to come back and have some more. You could see from its tracks that it was unusually big. So I took my rifle and went after it. I thought it couldn't have gone far, but could I find it? Anyway, it can't be far away and I'm sure it will return at night to finish the leftovers, so I've come back.'

'It's no time to be thinking of hunting animals.'

'But it's a tiger, isn't it? A tiger!'

He was in a state of excitement: 'Do you think it's easy to find one? When a hunter sees a tiger, it's the same as if a herb collector spots a ginseng as big as a baby – it really is!'

'The master won't give way. You can try, but the day after tomorrow – it's *Chusok* – only the day after tomorrow.'

While they were eating, the hunter brought up the subject of the tiger. As Soodong had predicted, Chisoo showed no interest.

'I can tell just from its spoor, that it's as big as a hill – it's no ordinary one. It's sure to come back at night. Wait for it to return, just one shot and then . . .'.

But there was still no response.

After breakfast, Chisoo, as usual, showed no sign of leaving and it was past midday before he broke his silent meditation to speak of going down. At these words, the hunter was confounded. Blinking his big eyes, he seemed to be anxious as to what kind of instructions he would receive. Such things as tiger hunting had already left his mind. Chisoo said nothing about whether he was to go down with them or to stay in the hills and meet them again after the festival. All he said was, 'Don't breathe a word about what happened on that hill.'

The hunter was getting ready to leave even more quickly than Soodong. He was like a child frightened that they might by some chance go off and leave him behind. No such words as 'What do you want me to do, sir?' left his lips.

From the beginning of the descent Chisoo's expression began gradually to change. His face seemed to gather into wrinkles. His glossy lips became dry and chafed. He dropped into a stooping posture that made you think of an old mule trotting along beneath an ash-coloured sky from which fell white, powdery snow. Kang *posoo* walked in front, his tense eyes sparkling. He could not be sure that when they reached the foot of the mountain he might not be told to stay behind. If that happened he would never see Guinyo again. For him the Choi house, once as stifling as a cage, was now as sweet as a dream, and the court of the servants' quarters with the well circled by Guinyo's feet was a place for which he yearned with trembling heart.

Soodong followed Chisoo, sweating to keep up. He was worn out from worry, apart from the load on his back, and his body had never been strong. They collected the mules and the packs left in the village and reached Curae before sunset, calling at the house of Yom *subang*, steward of the Choi land in that district.

'Master, what brings you here?'

On seeing Choi Chisoo, he started as if lightning had struck out of a blue sky. He was so confused that, without offering him a place to sit, he left him standing blankly and ran into his room to make a fuss over putting on his hat and changing his clothes, while the women of the house stood wide-eyed, wondering what it was all about.

'Why can't you put out the mat?'

Yom *subang* glowered at his son and called to the servant, 'Go and clean the *sarang* and light the fire at once.'

'Really! Soidol, you light the fire and, my dear, you put out the mat in the hall.'

His wife calmly gave orders.

As Yom *subang*, hurriedly tying the ribbons on his outer coat, came towards him, Soodong explained that they were on the way back from a hunting trip and, as it was getting late, they had come for the night. When he went up on to the verandah Chisoo accepted greetings from the steward but said not a word about farming matters. Yom *subang* had seen Choi Chisoo only twice at the house and then he had only offered new year greetings and come out again. He had heard from others of his finicky temperament, but now, as Chisoo's melancholy eyes blankly stared at him, he felt unable to sit at ease. Just then a servant reported that the *sarang* was tidy and Yom *subang*, having settled Chisoo there, hurried breathlessly round the house, giving orders such as to kill a chicken or soak the rice, in order to escape.

It was a thatched house, but roomy. The thick pillars and large courtyard showed that he was fairly well off. After the huts of the fire-field farmers, his spacious *sarang* was like a palace but, thinking only of the grand style of the Choi house, he kept apologizing for its 'shabbiness' and even kept repeating it to Soodong, who was giving the asses the fodder he had asked for.

Having got as far as Gurae, Kang *posoo*, now at ease, said almost arrogantly, 'Never mind. In the woods we slept curled up in mud huts. Compared to that this is a great palace.'

A girl of about fourteen or fifteen came up with a smile carrying a large folding screen on her head.

'Father, I've brought back our screen.'

Yom *subang* frowned as he said, 'They should have returned it as soon as they'd finished with it, the idiots.'

Presumably it was to be put up in the room where Chisoo was to sleep. Whatever it was that made her so happy, the girl, swinging her buttocks and the maroon ribbons at the end of her plaits, went on into the house.

Soodong, who had been staring at her from behind turned white. He had momentarily felt a strange impulse. He was ashamed at feeling like that at the sight of a child so young and was surprised by such an unrestrained urge – he had never been like that. He recalled Samsoo's words after accompanying Pyongsan to the mountain last year, of the murderous lust he had felt at the sight of a woman sleeping in a hut and that on the way back Pyongsan had paid for him to have a woman, which had been so enjoyable. At the time he had heard it, Soodong had abused him, calling him a dirty rascal. When he had married the now-dead Booni, though older, she had been small of build and short. Perhaps it was because he was reminded of her that he felt this desire for Yom *subang*'s daughter. Was it a time to think of such things? – the day before their return to the village, and with his mind desperate and ill at ease. Once there, he could not guess what would become of him. In such circumstances, to feel a wicked urge, and for such a young girl! He leaned weakly against the tree to which the donkey was tied. Yom *subang* hurriedly ran inside, while out in the fields the after-glow receded and all was gradually buried in darkness.

'Kang *posoo*.'

'What?'

'At *Chusok* you must go to your ancestors' graves.'

'You have to have some ancestors first.'

'Every child has parents. It's different for people like me who are tied to someone else's family . . .'.

'Sure, I must have been dropped by someone but when I was old enough to understand they said the old hag at the wine shop had picked me up from somewhere. So how should I know where I came from? The name of Kang, too, when I come to think of it, was hers.'

'Whoever brought you up are your parents, aren't they?'

'Don't say that. If she had lived any longer, I'd probably have died.'

'She treated you badly?'

'I survived thanks to meeting a widower, a hunter, but I've no idea where he died. He went out hunting one day and not a word has been heard of him since – probably he was eaten by a wild animal. At the time, I was so sad that for several days I searched the woods looking for him . . . that's how I became a hunter myself.'

That night Soodong lay down but he could not sleep. Once back in the village, he had no idea what would become of him. Chisoo, smiling, might order the servants to carry out a private punishment. The strange thing was that the more frightened and desperate he felt, the stronger the pain of physical desire. Just before the festival, the moon was so bright. On the paper door the shadows of persimmon leaves danced. It was like the beckoning of a woman's hand, like the flapping of her skirt or the ruffling of her hair.

'Ah! It's unbearable. Probably I am doomed to die. Otherwise, how is it possible for me to obsessed in this way? That rascal Samsoo said he nearly committed a murder. He was right. I could do it myself. I cursed him, calling him an animal, but human beings are bound to. Ah! how bright the moon is! It's so bright, it's driving me mad.'

He sat up.

'Why can't you sleep?'

Kang *posoo*, whom he had thought to be asleep, spoke up. Soodong was startled and a little embarrassed.

441

'Why are you mumbling to yourself like that?'

'Oh, it's nothing.'

'Doesn't the moon drive you mad, it's so bright.'

'What?'

Soodong, thinking he had been overheard, felt sweat on his spine.

'Really, I'm going mad, Soodong.'

'. . .'.

'A man with no parents or brothers, I must have someone to lean on, but . . .'.

He let out a deep sigh.

'At my age, I must be crazy. What is it like, to be married?'

'Are you asking me – don't you know?'

'Just two people in the same bed – is that all?'

'I suppose so.'

'No. It can't be that. There's no shortage of women in the world. It's fixing yourself in one direction – how can I put it? It's staking your whole life . . . what's the word for it?'

Soodong stared at the hunter's whiskery face in amazement.

From afar came the first cock-crow.

Chapter Thirty-Nine

WITH the Harvest Festival over, the fields from which the grain had been gathered looked forlorn. Only in the hillside paddies dependent directly on rain did patches of uncut rice remain. Like insects swarming on a withered leaf, flocks of sparrows gathered over these paddies, where the scanty crop did not promise much to thresh and garner, and feasted at ease. Here and there the yellowing leaves of mooli or cabbage caught the eye like stains on the grey expanse of fields. Before the ground froze they also would have to be gathered, either for the market, or to make *kimchi* for the winter, but the cold was not yet imminent. The stooks of rice still basked in warm sunshine.

'What boundless greed – to shake off the last grain of millet as well!'

'It's shocking. It's like sucking the blood of a flea. How long has he been a landlord? As they say "Seeing the big fish leap, the little fish leap too." It's so childish.'

Kim *hunjang* and Suh *subang* were indignant over the story of a new landowner in the next village who rented out some acres of riceland nearby and, saying the rice payment was short, had taken away from Tajul even the grains from his millet stalks.

'Well, they say "A man with ninety-nine sacks will rob a man with one to make it a hundred," but even so . . .'

' "Evil times, evil customs." People have become so mean, the country is bound to go down.'

'That shows you don't understand, sir,' said Suh *subang*.

Remembering Kim *hunjang*'s contemptuous attitude towards his close relationship with his wife, saying "Evil times, evil customs," and "low-class things" and so on, he went on sulkily, 'It's not that the world has changed: it has been like this from the beginning. Even the noble house of Choi – everyone knows how they accumulated their wealth – taking someone's land for a handful of barley

443

after a bad harvest, and so multiplying it again and again. If you see it like that, how can you think that it's all suddenly gone wrong?'

'Huh, really! So the world's going well – is that it?'

'It's not that it's going specially well – it's always been the same.'

'It's shameful, just shameful! The country is perishing but the leaders can think of nothing but their own interests and the people can barely survive. Who will stand up to stop the enemy?'

'When even the king himself can't do anything, do you think you can put it right by worrying about it? That must be why your hair keeps getting whiter.'

'You are wicked! That's what I mean when I say, "Evil times, evil customs" – when the lower orders don't even respect a gentleman . . .'.

He stopped to knock out his pipe on the stake to which the ox was tethered. Talking with people like Junku or Dr Mun he stuck strictly to the manners of a gentleman and, even when roused to a heated argument, never lost his composure, and could rise to greatness, but in his dealings with ordinary people he became a little ridiculous. His feelings of joy, anger, sorrow or pleasure showed so instantly on his face that he seemed whimsical. Perhaps this unrestrained frankness was because he felt closer to the common people than to the gentry. With Yoon Bo or Suh *subang* he would volunteer opinions on this and that and end up by raising his voice in anger, but when he met them next time he would start chatting with them just as before. On their side, neither Yoon Bo nor Suh *subang* were in the least afraid of his temper and never took to heart the gross insults that he sometimes poured out upon them.

'In the old days people at least knew how to behave according to their rank but now, gentlemen or commoners, they are all in a mess. "The road is there but you can't walk it; the sun's up but it's dark as a cave". "No one knows where to stand." – it's deplorable.'

'What can you do about it? We have to just live out our days. "Even if the sky falls in, there'll still be a crack to crawl through", as they say.'

'Huh, that's just what I mean . . . "pearls before swine" . . .'.

While this was being said Suh *subang* had one eye on something else.

444

'Where's he off to?'

Tajul was coming along with a bundle under his arm.

'Where are you going?' asked Suh *subang*.

He first bowed quickly to Kim *hunjang* and then said to Suh *subang*, 'Where do you think? To the town.'

'To the town?'

'Yes. I might as well try being a servant at the inn.'

He puckered his blotchy face.

'Money, money . . . without it you are nothing but a scarecrow. With it, even if you are a cripple, girls will do anything you want them to.'

So he had once said and now, having lost his last grains of millet, he was leaving the village.

'Even one less mouth to feed makes it easier. Besides, I must earn something so that I can help the family out with a bit of barley gruel.'

'That's true.'

Kim *hunjang* was silent.

'Off you go then. As they say, "As long as you are still breathing there won't be any cobwebs in your throat." '

'It's all right. I'm used to this kind of thing.'

'You'd better go, then.'

'Yes.'

Tajul bowed again to Kim *hunjang*, twitched his face, sniffed and shuffled away down the road. The teacher's pipe hit the stake again. Twice, three times, and then he took out his tobacco pouch.

Chilsung's and Yongi's vegetable plots ran side by side with a low bank between them. With a hemp cloth over her head and drawn halfway down her brow, Yimi *ne* was pulling mooli and Yongi cabbage to take to market. Well manured, the mooli in her plot had gone as deep into the ground as they could and then risen above it, looking most tempting. They pulled at their respective vegetables, following the furrows, and, as the piles of mooli and cabbages grew, the distance between them shortened until they were separated only by the low bank across which they could talk without raising their voices.

'Isn't Kangchong *dek* feeling well?'

445

Yimi *ne*, dying for the chance, began the conversation.

'I've no idea.'

He threw a newly-plucked cabbage on to the pile and did not bother so much as to glance at her.

'Pulling up cabbages is a woman's job. She ought to be ashamed of herself.'

' . . .'

'She's very lucky.'

' . . .'

She stopped work and stared at this heartless man who didn't even bother to look at her.

'What big roots those cabbages have'

She tried again to attract his attention.

'What's the use of big roots when they've got no hearts?'

'It looks as if they've had no manure. Or is it because the leaves are tough and they're full of greenfly? It's true, when they have big roots the hearts are usually poor.'

' "A useless calf grows a horn on its buttock," as they say. Isn't it the same with people?'

Whether the sarcasm was intended for her or Kangchong *dek*, she interpreted it to suit herself as a fault in the latter and rolled with laughter.

'Still, they say "The useless paddy becomes a memorial field." '

He closed his mouth and only his hands moved.

'Last spring . . .' she changed the subject, 'when I was pregnant, I was dying to eat some cabbage roots. As if someone had hidden them and was refusing to give me any, I was ready to cry. It's a funny thing – how you always want something that can't be had.'

' . . .'

'For a month and a half I couldn't eat and I was on my knees. With so much work to be done. I don't think there's anyone in the world as heartless as our Yimi's dad. He gobbled up a bowl of rice at every meal as fast as a crab hides its eyes, and didn't care in the least whether his nearest and dearest was dead or alive. If he hadn't said anything, it wouldn't have been so bad but he used to say that it was not because of the child but because my belly was full that I

446

wasn't eating. Even if he wasn't serious, how can anyone say such things? When I look at those roots, it reminds me of those days.'

Yongi briskly cut off several cabbage roots with his sickle.

'Here you are. Have as many as you want.'

He threw them across to her as if to shut her chattering mouth.

'I didn't mean I wanted them now. I was just telling you about it – about how stupid he is.'

Nevertheless, she could not hide her pleasure and she picked them all up to put aside. As if to draw closer, she said, 'Even with white rice to eat and silk to wear, they say, you can't live without love.'

She was frankly opening up and boldly advancing but he showed no interest at all.

'Even if you're beggars, if you love one another, you can live, can't you? Burning your heart out for another woman is bad enough, it's true, but even that depends on how you handle it, doesn't it? Whatever a man does out of sight, if, when he comes in, he cares about his wife and treats her kindly, that's enough, isn't it? He's full of greed up to his arsehole. The only thing he notices if his rice is short – he wouldn't notice it if his wife or his kids fell dead beside him. As I live longer and grow older, I feel sad about it. It seems so ridiculous and I get resentful.'

Knowing what Chilsung was like, Yongi did not think her words were empty, nor was he unsympathetic, but whatever women might say among themselves, he could not approve of her talking about her husband's faults to another man.

'If I was in Kangchong *dek*'s position, I wouldn't mind even if I had to carry you around on my back. She makes such a fuss, but you never beat her or swear at her – I'm shy about saying this to your face, but I think you are a gentleman – a real gentleman. If you were like my husband, her bones would have been broken long ago. He's the sort of man who keeps on slapping your cheek with a wooden spoon if you as much as spill a few grains of barley – he was like that from the day we were married. It's only because I work myself to the bone that we manage without too much trouble – you'd think he'd have learned something from all the hard times on his travels, but I suppose you can't change your nature.'

447

Yongi spat out angrily, 'That's your particular fate, isn't it?' and tried to get ahead of her by quickening his pace but she was determined to keep up. In her haste, mooli roots broke off. There wasn't likely to be such a quiet chance again. Whatever she may have been thinking, she took the cloth off her head and wiped her face and hands. Then she chose a smooth skinned white mooli. She scraped it with her sickle, cut it lengthwise and with a smile went over the ridge to Yongi.

'Here . . .'.

He did not look pleased.

'It's so juicy. Try it. You must be thirsty, and it makes a little snack.'

It was a supplication. Her heart was in her eyes. Yongi stared blankly at her, without a word as he held it by the tail, took it to his full lips and bit into it with a crunch. Goose-flesh appeared on his dark sad face, which never lost what his wife called the 'love-sick look'. The mooli was cold to his teeth. Chilsung had become an observer of the scene.

'Having a good time, eh? You surprise me.'

Yongi's face changed colour.

'What do you mean?'

'You think I'm jealous, don't you?'

'Don't talk like an animal.'

'What's the difference? When you are stuck together, you're just like animals, aren't you?'

His face white, Yongi gave a hollow laugh.

'Even the lowest people, when they're sober, don't talk like that. For a man with children . . . I hope they don't turn out like you.'

'Huh!'

'Shut your big mouth and go and give her a hand – it's getting dark.'

'What do I keep a woman for – to boil and eat?'

'You get more and more like a certain person – I suppose it's because you are always following him around. Follow his example and you'll end up with a beggar's bowl – and not even a family tree to help you.'

'As they say "There are times when the sun shines even into a

448

rat hole." There's no law to say that I must carry manure buckets all my life.'

Chilsung, who would once have been the first to pull up the mooli and take them to market, looked as if he had slept through the day. His eyes were puffy and Yongi felt sick at the sight of him as he stood vacantly with his hands in his waistband. Since beginning his dealings with Guinyo, his character had deteriorated and coarsened. Yimi *ne* had quickly gone back to the mooli plot to carry on working. She was not embarrassed or concerned about how her husband felt. Chilsung, though he spoke sarcastically as if he had witnessed a scene of adultery, as he said earlier, was not really jealous. As wife and mother of his children, she was not important to him, being no more than a strong and useful worker. Even in bed, when he desired her body, it was no different from his dealings with whores in his days as a pedlar. It was not only with his wife that he was like this. It was the same with Guinyo and indeed would be with whoever became his woman. There were not many in the village who worked as hard as Yimi *ne*, and no one as pretty and full of vigour after giving birth to three children.

For the first time Yongi felt compassion for her but, as if afraid of tempting an evil spirit, he threw away the mooli. Then he fetched his A-frame from among the furrows, propped it up and hurriedly piled it with cabbages.

Seeing Yongi loading his cabbages, Yimi *ne*, in a natural tone and without a blush, said to her husband, 'I say, stop talking rubbish and, as you're here, you might as well carry some mooli.'

'What would you have done if I wasn't here?'

'No help for it – I'd have had to go on till I finished, even if it was midnight . . . The ground's going to freeze any time – we can't just leave it.'

'If that was your idea, you might as well carry on till midnight. I'm going to have an easy time thanks to my wife's work.'

'H'm, so there are those who work and those who eat? If you've got eyes, look and see what other people are doing. While Kangchong *dek* has a nap, her husband works all day with no lunch . . . I give you smart kids and this is all I get.'

449

She gave a laugh as if to turn all that had happened so far into a joke.

'It's because you wag your tail that he even forgets to eat, you bitch.'

This time Yongi went on working without a further word.

'Stop that silly nonsense. It's bad enough to have no comfort from your husband without having to hear groundless talk.'

'Give comfort to a loose woman and that's the end of it.'

In the west the sun was sinking. Sparrows that had been huddling together on a stack of straw as if they were chilly flew off to the bamboo grove by the river to prepare for sleep. Along the road, which had been quite empty of passers-by, came a young monk walking quickly. The sun went down, its lingering light turning the river red. At the gate of the Choi house the young monk explained his purpose and Dori ran across the untidy yard to the inner quarters.

'Ma'am.'

'. . . .'

'There's a monk here from Yon-goksa.'

'A monk? Which one?'

Her voice sounded impatient.

'A young one.'

'Has he brought a letter?'

'Yes, so he says.'

'Call Samwol.'

Samwol ran up and was told to bring the letter and show the visitor where to sleep. Lady Yoon picked up a bunch of keys from the floor, put them on top of her writing desk and then into a drawer. As if still restless, she took a jacket off the hook and made an unnecessary change of clothes.

'Ma'am, here it is.'

Samwol gave her an envelope and was about to light the lamp when Lady Yoon said, 'You can go.'

She left off and hastily retreated. Lady Yoon sat as she was, holding the letter. It was getting dark in the room. As she finally took it out she realized how dark it was and stopped to light the lamp. Her hands were trembling.

450

Concerning Hwani. It has been agonizing to have no definite news, but last night he walked in of his own accord, looking exhausted. I wept at the great mercy Buddha bestows on insignificant humanity. I have moved them both to a temporary hiding place and will work out a plan for the future, so please don't worry.

Blessing,
Ugwan

She could not sleep. In the morning, despite passing a wakeful night, her eyes were bright and looked soft and peaceful. It was the face of a thankful patient who miraculously begins to heal after a long illness. Late in the morning Chisoo came in as if he knew the import of the letter. As soon as he had come back from the mountain he had collapsed into bed, unable to get up for several days, but four days ago he had risen and the day before he had been to see Jang-am *sonseng*, who was still sick. Chisoo looked almost the same as usual. As he entered her room her face also had its customary stiffness. Feeling as always the insurmountable barrier between them, mother and son talked a little about Jang-am's illness, and unable to find any other subject fell into a heavy silence. He no longer waged a campaign of investigation and she did not try to detect his feelings. Both were aware of a lull in their war of nerves. Eventually he brought up his intention of going hunting again in a few day's time.

'You are not well enough, so why do you have to do it?'

He smiled mysteriously and came up with a quite irrelevant reply.

'Jang-am was saying that you live in a world of fantasy even more than I do, and then he smiled and added that it was no easy thing to do in times like these – he was rebuking me I suppose.'

He stood up as if forced to by his own words. She felt a kind of hatred which, through all the numberless battles of nerves they had fought, she had never felt before.

(That's right – chase after him! Hwani will never fall into your hands!)

After he had gone, she spread out her own bedding, lay down

451

and fell into a deep dreamless sleep. A short rest after crossing a perilous ridge? The eyes that had sparkled with a clear gentle light were closed, as shutters were drawn over her mind – the peaceful mind of a short while before. The broad forehead with its innumerable lines, and the withered cheeks – it was a desolate and empty face. Just as she woke from her nap Bongsoon *ne* came in with a newly made *jogori* for her.

'Does Sohi still worry about her mother?'

Bongsoon *ne* was embarrassed by the question. For several months she seemed to have completely forgotten her grand-daughter, which had made Bongsoon *ne* sad.

'Yes, ma'am . . .'.

' . . .'

'Just lately, she seems to have suddenly got worse. She had been playing happily until then . . .'.

'How can she ever forget? There are too many heartless mothers in the world.'

Her voice was scornful, but relaxed and she went on, 'It's all due to their sins. Any woman who has a child is a sinner.'

Bongsoon *ne* lowered her head without speaking.

'Wolsun's mother . . .'.

'Yes, Ma'am?'

'I mean her daughter – Wolsun. I suppose she still carries on her trade?'

It was a question quite out of the blue.

'Well . . .'.

Bongsoon *ne* blushed more as if she had been rebuked than from confusion.

'Isn't she still running the tavern?'

'Well, she has such bad luck, I'm afraid. She seems to have gone off somewhere. I am too ashamed to face your ladyship . . . she has such a gentle nature, but it seems as though no one has control over their fate . . .'.

She broke off. She had not been thinking of the *byoldang* mistress, but Lady Yoon might misunderstand.

'If she's taken after her mother, she would have a gentle nature.'

452

'I think she's bound to have a hard life, as she's not grasping and she's too good-natured.'

'Her mother too – she had no greed.'

'. . .'.

'I would like to see her.'

'Wherever she's gone, no one seems to know.'

'She will come back – sometime or other. If she does or if you find out where she's gone, let me know.'

'Yes, ma'am.'

Bongsoon *ne* seemed to be thinking, 'She's not her usual superior self, I wonder why?', but her expression was grateful.

'I owe something to her mother . . . she would not take what was due to her.'

When Bongsoon *ne* had gone and she was alone, she mumbled to herself.

(If she's like her mother, she's bound to be good and gentle.)

> . . . . *The great mansion*
> *Rises high in the sky.*
> *In the world beyond – a human being!*
> *See what the five jailors are doing!*
> *They tie a cord round the dead one's neck,*
> *And bring him before the King,*
> *The King sitting on the throne.*
> *The Judge holds papers in his hand,*
> *And speaks to the deceased:*
> *You, in that world,*
> *What good deeds have you done*
> *To be brought here? . . .*

She could still hear Wolsun *ne* singing the incantation as she presided at the rite of the Ten Kings in the Requiem. The sorceress, brandishing her trident with seven bells, flicking open her seventy-ribbed fan – in her flower-decked hat and her robes she had been handsome and tall. She rose very clearly before Lady Yoon's eyes.

(Be patient, lady. Trust me. The calamity will pass.)

Wolsun had been born late and her mother had been more than ten years older than Lady Yoon.

(Sins committed in this world must be washed away in this world before you go. If you become a sin-bearing spirit, you will bring evil on your descendants and the house of Choi. If you take your own life and die an unnatural death, the gates won't open until your time is up, you see.).

Wolsun *ne* had long arms. As she raised them, trident in the right hand, bells and fan in the left, and circled the courtyard, people held their breath, awed by her authority. At such times, whoever they were, they would be compelled to believe in her power. Of the many shamans in the area she was the only true sorceress, and, among amateurs who could not manage big rites, the great professional. In spite of that, she had always been poor, sometimes even going short of clothes and food, but she had never refused to go anywhere to hold rites as long as food for the altar was provided, nor had she, on her own behalf, ever expressed any regrets at her low status as a shaman. Only for the sake of her daughter, Wolsun, had she felt sorrow or compassion.

(I did it because I was moved to. Take it back and say no more. If I took it, I'd be spiritually punished.)

As a reward for delivering the oracle concerning Lady Yoon, Dr Mun had sent Bawoo with some gold trinkets, but she had refused to take them. After Chisoo's grandmother died and the running of the household passed to her, Lady Yoon had tried to help her but she had never taken anything. When Bawoo came with Lady Yoon's wish to pay her she had rebuked him and said, 'The water is pure and clear but if I take this, it will be muddied. After cheating the spirit, how can I take money or grain?'

Only when a rite was requested by the Choi house, and she had carried it out with devotion, would she take payment, so Lady Yoon had to hold frequent rites in order to provide her with fees. People would say, 'Last autumn she did several rites, so why does she look so poorly – as if she hadn't taken a mouthful of gruel in three days?'

'It's because she's so reckless.'

'When she has money and grain is plentiful, she should store some up for the winter. Instead she goes on living from hand to mouth, as if she could still do rites when she's old and bent.'

'There's a story that she's got a young man. Don't you remember seeing her with black eyes last time? They say she went to see him and got beaten.'

'That's nonsense. It's easy to gossip about others. Her black eyes would have been because she likes wine and fell over on the way home. She's not one to be hit. The pity is that a shaman is despised and that she was born as a woman. If she'd been a man she'd have been a real gallant.'

An object of scandal and pity to the village women, she had always been poor and fond of wine. It was because of this that, after her daughter had gone away to a far off place, one night, on her way back to her tumble-down cottage, she had fallen over by the brook and died. They said it was because she had got drunk on an empty stomach.

Lady Yoon rose and left the room. As she went into the *byoldang* courtyard she saw Sohi chattering as she played with Bongsoon by the pond. Unaware of her presence, Soodong passing by in the backyard, leant against the wall and let out a weary sigh. His eyes were deep sunk and his face a sickly colour.

Chapter Forty

IT was not that Kang *posoo* was treated badly at the Choi house, but unmistakably a hanger-on, he could not help feeling awkward. Even though everyone understood that he was a lonely man with no home or family of his own, spending the festival in someone else's house made him feel confused and unhappy. Until then, he had passed it casually in a fire-field farmer's hut or a familiar tavern, eating the millet cakes that were offered, with no idea of how lonely and desolate it could be.

In the village the children went about in bright clothes and the grown-ups attended the family graves with food in wooden basins or willow hampers. At the Choi house, also, maids and servants, all in new clothes, ate and drank as much as they wanted – indeed, Soodong had several times asked him to join them. Alone amidst all this jubilation, looking at his dirty clothes, he had felt a pain in the ridge of his nose. Bongsoon *ne* was truly sorry for him, but she could not entirely be blamed as it had been such a busy time immediately before the festival, with the whole house in an uproar. She had had no time to make clothes for him and, as an outsider, she had never expected him to reappear in the trail of Chisoo. He had said, 'It's all right. Don't worry. I'm all right,' but insensitive as he might be, he could not help being concerned with what others thought of him. He had felt this particularly with Guinyo, and had tried, as far as possible, to keep out of her sight. The fact was that the day before the festival, that is the day after their arrival on the thirteenth – there had been no time before – he went to the town and bought a length of silk for a lady's *jogori*. Innocent as he was, it never occurred to him to think about his own clothes. In the evening, he ran after her just as she turned the corner into the backyard, and held out the tightly folded silk.

'What's this?'

'Stuff for a *jogori* – it's not much for *Chusok*, but . . .'

456

When she asked, 'Why give it to me?' he had nothing to say except, 'Take it quickly. Someone might see.'

'You really are funny. Why should I?'

Looking round quickly in case someone was coming, he was nervous. Suddenly he was angry.

'So you won't have it?'

'How can I when I don't know why?'

'All right, then. I'll burn it.'

He was about to thrust it into an outside fireplace.

'What temper! Let me have it then.'

He immediately broke into a broad smile and, repenting of his anger, he said, 'It may not be good enough for you . . . I don't know anything about these things.'

'Compared to a pair of gold rings – it's only blood in a bird's leg.'

She pouted. The object she had obtained from him had proved quite ineffective. He vigorously rubbed his whiskers with his hands.

'Well, about them . . . though I've sold them and they're gone, I'll certainly do something about it . . .'.

She giggled, 'Like stealing them back?'

'Don't talk like that. I can get them for you. Of course I can. It's not just words. I've only got to catch one bear . . . better than that, I saw an enormous tiger in the hills this time. Catch that, and you'll see! You've no idea how much a hunter can earn.'

She did not believe him. Still giggling, she hid the wrinkled *jogori* material in the folds of her skirt and stealthily turned to go.

After spending *Chusok* dispirited and cringing, he still felt awkward about staying on in the house and could not help studying people's expressions. It was natural as, since the day they had returned, Chisoo had taken ill and never once showed his face. There was no promise of going to the hills again and, with no firm injuction to stay, he could not help feeling like a patch of oil floating on the water. During the day he usually went to the tavern to pass the time in chatting and, when he came back to his room at night, his ears cocked in the direction of where Guinyo was, he passed sleepless nights. That was how, though entirely ignorant of what

457

was going on, he came to notice that she often went out in the night, crossing Kim *subang*'s vegetable plot.

(What does she go out for? Is she in love with some other man?)

It seemed very likely. In his anguish he went to the tavern and gulped down wine. When bored, Pyongsan would tease him, saying, 'Kang *posoo*, what are you sitting here for instead of being out in the woods catching wild beasts?'

Blinking his bloodshot eyes, he would say, 'I'm in love with this place and I can't leave.'

Pyongsan would then make some nonsensical remark – 'Fallen in love with this place eh? H'm, I've been a bit suspicious – it's the hostess, Yongsan *dek*, isn't it? But, man, you're not going to let your woman work in a drinking house, and live like a *kiseng*'s husband, playing around and eating free, are you?'

Then the woman would scream at him, 'You are mad, and not the only time. I have a husband with eyes as bright as a lamp – if you don't want your limbs broken, you'd better keep your mouth shut.'

'Didn't we just hear it? Didn't he say he was in love with this place?'

'People don't pay up and I'm already boiling with anger without you provoking me too.'

'Look, Kang *posoo*, it's simple – you just do as I tell you. Even the daughter-in-law of a certain distinguished family, where honour is worshipped like an ancestral tablet, ran off with a servant. This husband of Yongsan *dek*'s – he's only a man she happened to meet in passing. You just carry her off to Chiri mountain and that's the end of it. Even if, like someone else, he chases after you as a hunter of adulterers, he's no match for you. And you – Yongsan *dek*, that chap who comes night and day to take the money you earn by selling wine, you'd better kick him out straight away. As for Kang *posoo*, he's not a servant tied to someone's house nor a peasant watching the sky and eating barley gruel, he's the famous hunter, known to the whole world, even to the kids. When he kills a tiger, do you know how much the skin is worth? Or a bear, how much it's liver fetches? He's not to be compared with servants or peasants

– do you understand? A man of forty, in his prime, isn't he? Besides his heart, of all things, his heart is as pure as jade.'

As he recited the very words that the hunter had once poured out with his fists clenched on their way back together from the town, Pyongsan chuckled.

'Stop talking nonsense,' said Kang *posoo* as he gulped down some wine, a weak smile rising to his lean face.

'What I meant was the hills and rivers round here that I love – who said anything about her?'

'Huh! However much you love them, you can't sleep with them in your arms, can you?'

' "If you love your wife, even the stakes round her house look lovely," they say.'

The hostess also seemed to be concerned about the change in the hunter.

'It's true, he is a sick man. He's completely changed. A simple man, when his mind flows in one direction, he's in real trouble.'

'Don't say anything. Don't. No one knows my trouble. Damn it! It's like trying to catch the shadow of a tree on a moonlit night – that damned girl's heart . . .'.

'What? A girl?' asked Pyongsan.

The hunter, wide-eyed, said no more.

(Is he?)

A stranger came in and the hostess greeted him.

'It's quite chilly,' he said as he folded the corners of his coat and sat down.

'There'll be a frost, I reckon.'

Kang *posoo* was set firmly and did not want to budge but Pyongsan just managed to coax him out. 'I don't want to go yet. The sun is still up – what will I do just sitting there like a wounded tiger?'

'Who's telling you to go there? Stop talking nonsense now.'

As they strolled side by side, Pyongsan said insinuatingly, 'Are you going back to the hills? Has Chisoo said anything about it?'

'I've no idea. He will go, sooner or later, I suppose.'

'Even so, you shouldn't waste time like this, putting aside all your own business.'

459

'That's true. Sometimes I think I ought to go, but love – it's beyond your own control.'

'Don't be like that. Tell me all about it and I might be able to help you. Who have you set your heart on?'

'Well, it's . . .'.

'Come on, speak up.'

'Well, it's . . .'.

'Huh, really!'

As if he had made up his mind, Kang *posoo* said, 'It's that girl at the Choi house – that Guinyo.'

'Ah, that won't do, you know.'

Pyongsan's heart missed a beat.

'Why not?'

'I bet her eyes are fixed on something very high.'

'High? how high? She's only a servant – how high can she go?'

He shouted as if he was maddened.

'I know what to do. I'll have a word with the master and ask for her instead of money. Don't despise me! You just wait and see! There's no law that says Kang *posoo* can't marry a virgin!'

He sounded as if he was ready to attack Pyongsan.

'Huh, just try it, and see what happens,' he scoffed, but as he did so he realized that things were becoming tricky.

On the next day he went to the servants' quarters, pretending he had come to see the hunter. In fact, he didn't go there but looked around until he caught Guinyo's eye from a distance. Drawing close from behind after she had gone to the well and was pretending to wash her hands, he whispered a warning, 'Watch out at night. Last night I saw Kang *posoo* following you and I just managed to drag him off to the tavern.'

What had happened was that after leaving the tavern and having a row with Pyongsan, the hunter had gone home and during the night had followed Guinyo and been seen from a distance by Pyongsan who was on guard.

'Where are you off to?'

His arm tucked in his sleeves, Pyongsan had stepped in front of him. Hiding his embarrassment, the hunter had said, 'Nowhere in particular.'

460

'Let's go and have a drink. Earlier, I talked a lot of nonsense, knowing well enough how you feel. Who knows? Some good idea might come up.'

Wheedling, he had pushed the reluctant hunter from behind and dragged him along to the tavern. They had awakened the hostess, who had just fallen asleep.

'You're driving me mad! It's sending me off my head. Do you think this is your own sitting room? What do you come here for at this time of night, keeping people from their sleep?'

'What difference does it make whether it's night or day if there's customers? Don't fuss. Maybe it's the middle of the night outside, but isn't that just the best time for a tavern?'

'Do you think I keep prostitutes?'

'Don't make such a fuss. I'm going to help your sales, so what is there to grumble about?'

Kang *posoo*, who had been staring around blankly, remembered Soodong's words that evening that in a few days time they would be setting off again for the hills. Pushing Pyongsan aside, he was about to go out again.

'Damn it! Where do you think you are going?'

Pyongsan grabbed him and sat him down. After hastily swallowing a cup of wine, he resolutely stood up again.

'Look, man, where do you think you are going? Have you got some treasure hidden away? Is another pair of gold rings going to appear?'

It was meant to be a kind of threat. Pyongsan, thinking that it would be best eventually to get him out of the village, clung to him each time he tried to stand up. At last Kang *posoo*, waving his arms, challenged him,

'It's my body, Mr Kim, not yours! With my body, I go where I like – why hang on to me like this?'

The hostess, who had sold them wine only because she could not refuse the hunter, came in on his side and said, 'You'd better stop your bad deeds. If you're bored, you can go and wrestle with a goblin – why do you keep bothering an innocent man to death?'

After bickering for a while, Pyongsan, worried about what was happening on Dangsan and thinking that Kang *posoo* could not

461

possibly know about it, stood up to go. To keep the briskly walking hunter in sight, he followed from a distance. As if such a thing as Pyongsan's existence was not even in his thoughts, he walked up the hill by the Choi house and looked into the darkness. His arms rose and dropped again in a gesture of helplessness while he stood as if transfixed. After a time, he walked down to a tree by the wall of the *sarang* and flung himself down beneath it. By this time Guinyo was already home. After Pyongsan had been to tell her about what had happened on the previous night, Guinyo waited for the darkness and, more cautiously than ever before, looked round as she came out across Kim *subang*'s vegetable plot. But the hunter had already gone out and was waiting close to a tree, his eyes as wide as an owl's. The thought that he would have to leave in a few days' time gave him reckless courage. As she slipped by as silently as a shadow, he grabbed her by the scruff of the neck, giving her no chance to speak. She choked the scream inside her throat. She realized who it was. Twisting her body, she faced him and tried to thrust him away with her fists. His chest was as firm as a rock.

'Where are you going?'

'. . . .'

'Where are you going?'

'. . . .'

'Come with me!'

In a biting voice she said, 'I'm going to offer my prayers!'

'That's a lie.'

She said sharply, 'Lie or not, it's all no use. It's spoilt now, so I might as well go back. Why do you follow me round like bad luck?'

'Come with me.'

'I won't.'

'That, or both of us will die.'

'Let me go before I scream.'

'I'm afraid of nothing.'

'Don't you know what will happen to you if you do something like this? Don't you know you'll be beaten to death?'

'Scream then!'

He grabbed her wrists.

462

'Ouch!'

In fact, she was not in a position to shout. She felt as if the bones of her hand were cracking but she endured it. She was the one who was more afraid of waking others. The hunter dragged her along by the wrist. Determined not to go, she put up a desperate resistance but she was no match for his strength.

'Where are you going?'

'. . .'

If they went towards Dangsan, she thought, they would meet Pyongsan. He had told her that he had run into the hunter the night before. If they met again, she realized, it would be dangerous. As she was being dragged along, she turned him towards the back of the garden house, away from the direction where Pyongsan would be on watch. As for Kang *posoo*, he walked on blindly, regardless of whether there was a path or not – anywhere would do as long as it was away from the house with no one around. After passing the backyard of the garden house they pushed through a secluded clump of bushes. When they had gone quite a way she slumped as if she was falling.

'G – Guinyo!'

Unlike his former confident self, he was trembling.

Waned to less than half, the moon hung frozen in the sky. From a distance came the sound of water.

'Guinyo.'

Not knowing what to do with her, he was still trembling like an aspen.

'What do you want?'

'Come and live with me.'

'There's no chance of that.'

'I can't wait any longer. We are leaving for the hills very soon.'

'I haven't the slightest intention of living with you. If this comes out, there will be big trouble. I'm not in the position to marry you. I can't tell you why now, but you'll know when the time comes . . . If this comes out, you'll lose your life.'

(Do you know who I am? I am the woman waiting on the master of the Choi house. If you treat me as an ordinary servant, you'll be in trouble. I'm the woman who will have a child to carry on the

463

family line and you won't be able to lift your eyes to look on my face.)

She did not, of course, think exactly like this, but she was obviously speaking with some such intent and with the implication that, looking back some day, he would understand what she had meant.

'To save regrets for the future, I'll treat what has happened tonight as if it never occurred – understand that. If anything happens now, even if you had ten lives it wouldn't be enough.'

However, these words had the opposite effect of driving him into a frenzy.

'I don't care if I die!'

He thought she had been on her way to meet another man. It was not new, but it roused jealousy enough to burst his heart.

'I don't care if I die!'

As he shouted he rushed at her and knocked her over on to a pile of dry leaves.

'Kang *posoo*! Wait a minute.'

'No!'

'I'll do what you tell me to, but wait just a minute.'

She pushed back his sturdy body.

'I'll do what you say. How can I escape here in the middle of the woods? I've thought of something, so wait a minute and listen.'

It sounded reasonable. She had resisted but, after all, she had gone with him, while on his side, also, he was not thinking only of satisfying his desire. As he let her go, he went on panting like an ox that had carried a heavy load for several miles. Guinyo sat up, drawing in her knees and resting her hand on them.

'Let me think . . .'.

As if laying stones one on top of the other to build a dam, she reflected on the whole situation from beginning to end. Her thoughts revolved rapidly and energetically. Her body was in any case spoilt. She had no husband for whom to keep chaste. Whether by Chilsung, Kang *posoo*, or anyone else, all she wanted was a male child. Things had certainly become rather complicated but there was no way out of it. He was threatening her with life or death – what else could she do?

(Would it be better to find some excuse to throw Chilsung over? That's hardly possible — it's gone too far. How will I face Kang *posoo* in the future? When he sees me settled as the mother of the precious only son of the Choi family, surely he'll never think of giving it out that he dragged me up here and raped me? He would be easier to handle than Chilsung. He's thick in the head and doesn't notice things . . . well, things will sort themselves out when the time comes.)

Her thoughts turned quickly. Come to think of it, it was admittedly her fault for not showing him clearly whether she liked him or not. At first, she had felt trapped because of the shameful object, and then she had thought it fun to see him fretting over her. Chilsung, who thought only of his own gain, or Choi Chisoo who never gave her as much as a glance, even Pyongsan — how they had all hurt her lofty pride. That she was a woman confident in her own appearance made it all the more unbearable. In this situation, Kang *posoo* clumsily hanging around, even though she was not interested in him, had been a slight source of comfort.

'All right then.'

As these words fell from her mouth he began to tremble again.

'Seeing how it is, there's no choice. You're not likely to let me just go away.'

She spoke in the manner of a gambler.

'But I must warn you. If this becomes known, it'll be the end of you.'

With no thought of the circumstances or the consequences, he just nodded. He was so ecstatic at being accepted that he felt as if he was floating in the air and his blood boiled to a point that made him shiver. Not knowing what to do now that he had this precious treasure in his hand, he whimpered like a puppy, feeling as awed as if he was faced with a Buddha, the spirit, a mountain god, and his shyness was like that of an innocent bridegroom on the first night of his wedding. As he laid his jacket over the dry leaves and held her body in his arms, it was a scene of tearful and touching purity. Having already experienced a man, she had expected him to be as shameless as Chilsung. It was rather on her side that there was no

465

shyness, an attitude of total abandonment. She realized how different he was from Chilsung.

'Come and live with me! – come!'

She heard his voice as if in a dream. Though the mountain breeze was chilly, their bodies were sweating. Waned to less than half, the frozen moon still hung above. Leaves fluttered down from the trees, while those still on the branches rustled. Guinyo had just begun to learn the secret of sleeping with a man, the pleasure of it.

Looking up at the waning moon, she murmured to herself, 'Why did I hate it so much? With that Chilsung it was so horrible I nearly vomited. Perhaps that's why I didn't become pregnant?'

As they were parting she said, pretending she was angry, 'Well, then, go and stay the night at the tavern.'

'You'll catch cold,' he said as he followed her.

'What do you keep following me for? That way, please go round that way!'

'All right, but don't catch cold . . .'.

Two days later, Chisoo, whatever may have been in his mind, instead of punishing Soodong, took him again, with Kang *posoo*, to set off for the hills.

Chapter Forty-One

LYING on her back, Bongsoon tried banging the floor with her heels. It didn't make her feel any better – she was lonely and bored. The low ceiling was cheerless, like a low, dull sky. She thought it would be nice if it would split open and the sun appear, clouds dance, and the yellow birds that flitted about in the hills fly in, or a white kite come floating by.

'I hate you, Bongsoon, I hate you, do you hear? Silly girl, go away! Candlestick! Skeleton!'

A little while before Sohi, holding Samwol's hand, had screamed at her like this as she stamped and waved her fist – how unfair of her! Kilsang, too, was hateful as he stood by with a knowing smile on his face. All she had said to Sohi was, 'Your head is a gnome's head.'

'What's a gnome?'

Bongsoon, bringing her fists on to her own smooth forehead, had said, 'Like this, a forehead sticking out like this is a gnome's head – that's what they say.'

That had seemed to upset her.

'You're a candlestick! Are you listening? A candlestick! A skeleton! Gad–dongi's mother said so. A candlestick! A skeleton!'

Not only Sohi, but Samwol had also scolded her.

(Me too – I only said what I heard Gad–dongi's mother say . . .)

But she had kept that to herself. She kicked the floor again with her small stockinged feet sticking out from the end of her pantaloons.

'Look here, can't you get up?'

Her mother scolded her without slackening her work. Whether it was due to the sun moving to the west, or winter on its way, the paper panel on the door had a bluish tinge.

Kim *subang*'s wife noisily rattled her jaws as she opened the door and put her face in: 'It's getting quite chilly.'

'It is. They say there's already been a frost.'

Again Bongsoon *ne* did not pause as she replied. As she entered the room Mrs Kim tore a strip of paper from the loose edge on the door, took some tightly wrapped tobacco from her waist band, rolled it in the paper and licked the edge.

'The way it goes, it will suddenly get cold and then we'll have all the bother of the pickling to do . . .'.

Mumbling away, she picked up a coal with the fire tongs and lit her cigarette. Her wrists were as skinny as twigs. Bongsoon, lying on her side glared at her through her folded arms. As she exhaled the smoke, Mrs Kim said, 'Take it easy. Has someone died and got to be laid out? What's the hurry?'

'If you put things off, there's no end to it. It's better to get it finished first and then have a rest.'

'Anyway, it's your hands you're using, not your mouth.'

In other words, she wanted someone to talk to.

'What's happened?'

'Listen. As a woman with a son-in-law and a grandchild, is it right for him to hit me? Am I to be thrashed by my own husband at my age?'

'You must have done something wrong, Mrs Kim.'

'You people always blame me without even knowing what happened.'

'That's because Kim *subang* is so good.'

Kim *subang*'s wife sucked on her cigarette.

'Suppose it was my fault. Suppose I was being silly. Am I to be beaten at my age?'

Even so, her face showed no real sign of anger.

'Last night – whether a spider pissed or an ant stung me, my back was itching like anything, so I asked him to scratch it . . .'

Bongsoon *ne* smiled wryly.

'It's nothing to laugh about.'

'A shy man like him would have gone rigid.'

'Lying down with his back to me, he wouldn't budge. If that had been all, I wouldn't have minded, but, by chance, my foot must have touched his. And do you know what he did? He kicked it away, hard. So, I sat up. I lit the lamp and I had it out with him.

"What's wrong with my foot? – it's as smooth as an egg! Am I a leper? The three children I've had – were they got by a monk from Chiri Mountain?" I let him have it.'

It did not look as though her story would soon come to an end. Bongsoon had been glowering at her till the whites of her eyes showed, but she was carried away by her own rhetoric and the girl could only stare at the ceiling. It was yellowed and covered in fly spots that looked like crawling insects. Narrowing and then widening her eyes, she stared at them hard, wondering if they really were insects. The black dots seemed to be moving. The harder she focused on them the more she was convinced that they were insects, her eyes smarting and tears forming. She remembered when she had been on the ferry going to town, feeling that the boat was still and it was the water that was moving. It had seemed as though the bamboo clump by the river was moving too, and the thatched roofs, the hills, and the clouds – they were all speeding past. It was a similar illusion by which, alternately narrowing and opening her eyes, enduring the smarting, she stared fixedly at the fly spots that she had decided were insects.

'Has your spine gone solid? Aren't you going to get up?'

Bongsoon *ne* slapped her daughter's leg with her measuring stick.

'Ouch!'

Interrupted in the middle of her tale, Mrs Kim said, 'Let her be. All kids are the same . . .' She was ready to go on, 'Even so, how could he . . .' when suddenly Bongsoon sat up, and bringing her knees against Mrs Kim's said, 'Why did you call me a skeleton?'

'What?'

'Why am I a candlestick?'

'What are you talking about?'

'You said the young Miss had a forehead like a gnome and then you said I was a skeleton. I'll tell her it was you that said it.'

When she understood what Bongsoon meant, she shook with laughter.

'It's because you're so thin – that's why. Ha ha ha! . . . that's why you are so angry, I see . . . ha ha ha!'

Bongsoon's mother gently smiled.

'You eat day and night and have nothing better to do than make

469

fun of other people. Who goes "ho, ho, ho, ha ha ha–ing" about? "Putting your own shame behind you and others" out in front.'

Bongsoon gave a lively imitation of Gad–dongi with his mouth hanging open and dribbling.

'What a sharp tongue that little bitch has!'

'Why do you swear at me? Did you bring me up?'

'Stop it, you naughty girl. Is that the way to speak to a grown-up?' scolded her mother.

'I don't know.' Kim *subang*'s wife was not angry and only smiled but, as if she had lost interest in her tale, she said, 'I'd better be going. I'm frightened of Bongsoon.'

When she had gone, Bongsoon *ne* said, 'She only does it from affection. You mustn't speak to grown-ups like that.'

She did not scold her any further. Bongsoon sat huddled up with her face still sulky and stared at her mother as she worked. By now she was not just bored but felt a surge of anger. She did not hate anyone in particular nor was she much bothered by words such as 'candlestick' or 'skeleton'. She was just angry. She felt that, if only she had wings and could freely fly away, her anger would be relieved.

'Mum.'

'What is it now?'

'At the New Year, you'll let me go and see the Masked Players again, won't you?'

' . . .'

'Mum? Like we did last year. I'll go with Kilsang again this time.'

' . . .'

'Auntie Wolsun will put us right in the front row.'

'Don't talk nonsense . . . isn't this collar a bit too low?'

Whilst pressing it with the little iron, Bongsoon *ne* stopped to measure it with the stick.

'An ample three inches. That should be right, so why does it look too low?' she murmured to herself.

'Mother!'

' . . .'

'So you are not going to let us go – is that what you mean?'

'They say if you talk about what you are going to do tomorrow, the scarecrow laughs.'

'How can a scarecrow laugh?'

She lashed out with her foot and kicked the scissors away.

'Will it be New Year the day after next? What's the hurry? You're putting me off my work.'

'Just say that you'll let us go and it'll be all right.'

'. . .'

'When we went last time, Auntie Wolsun made soup for us and bought us nut brittle and fetched us a brazier . . . the soup was lovely – better than we have at home . . .'.

(If only she was still there . . . come to think of it, it was because of these children that the whole thing went wrong. That's why that woman Kangchong *dek* wants to eat me up whenever she sets her eyes on me. Besides, where could Wolsun have gone? I thought she might come back at harvest to cut the grass on her mother's grave . . . Maybe she's having a hard time.)

'Mummy.'

'. . . .'

'Mother!'

'I told you you're putting me off, stop it now!'

'Bother.'

Fixing the lining of a *jogori*, Bongsoon *ne*'s hands flew. She slipped a needle-full of gathers down the thread, spreading them out like a fan, made a knot, and cut the thread with her teeth.

(You'd expect her to come back. She'd have no difficulty in feeding herself. Her ladyship sounded as if she would help her out, too. She'd do better to come back than be hard up in a strange place and, to put it bluntly, what does it really matter if she lives in the same house with Kangchong *dek*? It's gone that far anyway. A poor farmer with two wives – it may look bad to some people – but you can't help it if it's your fate. Then eventually, if a child comes, looking after it . . . tut tut tut . . . whatever they say, she couldn't have gone off with another man. With a ginseng trader from Kangwon province, they say, but did anyone actually see her going? How could she be so unlucky. All alone in the world . . .)

Her daughter, too, was mumbling to herself. (With powder on her face and in a silk dress, how pretty she was! As pretty as the *byoldang* mistress . . . she sang well . . . yes, beautifully.)

471

'What was that?'

'The masked players, Mum. You've never seen them, have you?'

'Day and night, just go on about them and no doubt rice will appear by itself, and clothes too.'

'Some day, when I'm grown up, I'm going to be a singer too, with a silk dress and powder on my face.'

'What?'

Bongsoon *ne* looked up. Her daughter's eyes were misty and dreaming.

'Some day when I'm grown up . . .'.

'You idiot! Say that again and I'll scorch your mouth with this iron.'

'Why? What's wrong?'

'What a bright future! What a future for your mother, too, who's put all her hopes in you!'

'Why? What's wrong with it?'

To aggravate her, Bongsoon became argumentative. Her mother, who had been assertive, became confused and could say no more. She was not only speechless but also embarrassed. She could see how glamorous and beautiful the players must have seemed to the children, with their powdered faces and silk dresses, lit by the flames of the wood fire. How could she tell her daughter that they were women who for the asking, would sell themselves indiscriminately to gamblers, servants or pedlars?

Bongsoon *ne* thought of any entertainers, whether they were dancers, actors, or singers, as women who sold their bodies. Usually it was so, but masked players and their male singers had been through a long and exhaustive apprenticeship, following strict rules, so that they were mature, with a stubborn pride in their profession, and quite different from the troupes without rules or masters who drifted from village to village, providing motley shows. These people combined shaman rites with selling sex, so the main emphasis was on the women. They had a husband called a *gosa* who looked after his wife, paid a proportion of the money she earned by prostitution to the *mogap*, the manager of the troupe, and lived on the remainder – in other words, a man who ate by hiring out his wife. In this way, a female dancer was a low-class woman not much different from an ordinary prostitute.

There had been one such player with the name of Chaesun who had put all contemporary singers to shame. She became renowned not only among the dissolute gentry, but as the favourite of the Regent, Taewon Gun, who was very fond of musical drama. Bongsoon *ne* probably would not have known of such cases, but even if she had, she would definitely have preferred her daughter to be a peasant's wife, living in perpetual hardship, rather than have her become an entertainer.

'With a silk dress and powder on my face . . .'.

Bongsoon could be uncommonly malicious. She mumbled on to annoy her mother who, unable to stand it any longer, dealt her a blow on the head.

'Out you go, at once!'

So, it ended in tears. As if she had been waiting for the chance, she went out crying. As she stitched the lining into a jacket, Bongsoon *ne* mumbled to herself, 'Damn it, it was all my fault. By sending them to that show for no particular reason. I must have woken up a sleeping tiger. It's all because of those masks of Kilsang's.'

She started as a thought occurred to her. Wondering if Bongsoon was still by the door and had noticed her, she quickly glanced that way. Certainly her face had changed colour.

'I suppose the blood from her mother's side is also a part of her . . . From the time she was born . . .'. Her eyes blurred so that she could not see her sewing clearly.

Her grandfather had come from a place called Woonbong. Along with Gurae and Soonchang, Woonbong, especially, had produced many giants of the musical drama. The best known of all the popular singers, renowned as the second founder of the opera and the king of song, the arrogant and capricious Song Seung-rok, had also been a native of Woonbong. Apart from him, there had been his brother, Song Kwang-rok, and his son, Song Wooryong, and Yang Hakchon who were the great stars of the eastern region. Bongsoon *ne*'s grandfather had also been at one time a well-known player but he had come to rather a sad end. All that remained in her memory was of a graceless and shabby old man who, after a stroke, had lost the use of one arm. But she still remembered the many stories he had told her. Sitting out on a sunny spot on the verandah, probably bored to tears by the long days, he had often told these tales to his little granddaughter, his sunken lips trembling.

'Long ago, there was a famous singer called Kwon Samduk. He was not a commoner but the son of a country gentleman, you see. From his childhood, instead of studying as was expected of him, he was mad about opera and his parents were always telling him to give it up. Just think about it! It is not the right thing for a gentleman to do, is it? Even so, he wouldn't listen to them. It was such a disgrace to the family, that all the relatives were gathered together to discuss it, and they decided to kill him. Willing to die, he put the sack over his head, ready to be killed and asked one last favour. He wanted to sing once more before he died. His death was decided so how could they deny him this last favour? They stood round him and listened as he sang underneath the sack and it completely melted their hearts. It was a sea of tears all around. They were so moved that the relatives had another discussion. This time they decided just to cross him off the family tree and turn him out. Truly he was a great man, a real hero. He'd rather throw away his life than give up music – it's easy to say but . . . That's how he became the world's greatest singer.'

Besides this her grandfather had told her of the complicated love affair between the bad tempered and arrogant Song Hong-rok and Maengryol, a no less ill-tempered and high spirited *kiseng*, or the story of how Yom Kae-dal who, naked and hungry, had tied his topknot with a string to the ceiling to keep his head straight as he practised until in the end he became a great singer.

'Huh, you think great singers are just born, don't you? In no way. You have to go to places renowned for their scenery – and sweat blood for ten or twenty years. Even then some people fail to achieve it – it shows that it's no ordinary task. You only get there by wearing away your bones and draining your blood. One famous singer was practising with his arms round a column, circling it, in full blast, when he heard his throat burst and fainted, thinking he had been struck by lightning. It's no ordinary matter, you see, to become a great singer.'

The old man had died while Bongsoon *ne* was still a child. Her own father, regretting the way that his father had had to give up half way through ill health, without achieving his aim, often had tear-filled eyes. Though he had not entered the profession himself, he had seemed to be more gifted than her grandfather. Bongsoon *ne* had often listened to him as he cleared his throat and sang and she could still hear that clear voice ringing in her ears:

> *All rivers go east to the sea;*
> *When will they ever flow back to the West?*
> *The sun setting behind Mount Woosan,*
> *The tears of Lord Jae-Kyong,*
> *The sound of the autumn wind,*
> *The sorrow of Woo-Jae of the Han dynasty.*
> *Nightingale with notes like drops of blood,*
> *Do not pour out your clotted sorrow.*
> *Do you also mourn the soul*
> *That will not come back in a thousand years?*

Turned out of the room, Bongsoon saw Kilsang coming in the distance and began to sniffle afresh, though her tears had dried.

'What are you crying like that for?'

'Why, what's it got to do with you?'

'All right, cry! Cry as much as you like.'

He hurried past. If he had said a few words, she would have stopped crying, she thought, but he had just gone by. How heartless and hateful!

She would have gone on a little longer but could not force the tears. She went to the stable. With two of the mules gone to the hills it was almost empty. The one left behind gazed at her with blank eyes. She squatted down in front of the stable. The slightly bitter smell of it came to her. The donkey blinked its beady eyes. Its coat was darker and more shiny than in the summer. It extended its tongue, whitish, and bluish, yet also pinkish, and gathered the hay into its mouth. Bongsoon looked eagerly into its big nostrils.

The animal put out its tongue again, gathered the dry grass into its mouth and champed it with a sound like turning mill stones.

(How I hate that tongue of his! What's it like? It's nasty!)

She jumped round in her squatting position. For some reason the whole place seemed to be quiet. Not a sound, as if all the people of the great house had abandoned it, taking their bundles with them.

(Gannan *halmum* – she's dead!)

Before her eyes rose the wizened face of the old lady. As she opened her eyes wide, it disappeared. After a while, it came back like the face of someone floating under the water. Hair like the roots of onions covered her face, and liquid oozed from ulcers and her eyes, and she gasped for breath with her toothless mouth half open. It scared her. When she had been alive, Bongsoon had got on with her well enough but now she was unbearably frightened of her. She remembered Kilsang's account of Hell.

'Do you know what the underworlds are like? There are eight of them, called the Hells of the Eight Fires. In Deung-hwal, the sinners become enemies and bite each other until only their bones are left. Then the jailors come with iron hammers to crush them into powder and cut them like meat. If you died there once, that would be enough, but it only needs the wind to blow and they revive and start biting each other again. They live like that for five hundred years, and it's the place where people who committed murders in this world go. The next one is Heuk-seung. It's a place where you live for a thousand years and they chop you up with an axe and take off your flesh by lashing you with red-hot iron chains.'

Because he had been brought up in a monastery, he had plenty of information about hell: how a sinner was put in a mortar and pounded with the pestle; how beasts such as lions, tigers, wolves or eagles, all made of iron, came in packs and ate up the culprits right to the marrow of their bones, or they were pierced with iron skewers and roasted until their intestines burst and so on. To shake off the horror, Bongsoon looked up towards the eaves. The swallows that had come with the spring had now gone and their nest was empty.

'Swallow! Swallow! Swallow from the south,' she called dispiritedly, but they had already gone south and could not come. She sprang up and ran out of the house. With her mind still full of fears about Gannan *halmum* and about hell, she thought.

(Why should I go to the young Miss? Pooh, I won't go. Kilsang is only a boy – let him go and play with her. I won't go. Samwol can wipe her nose and wash her face, not me, pooh!)

The river at the foot of the hill, reflecting the early winter sun, gleamed white. The cloudless sky looked high, infinitely high. Children played on the threshing ground and the ferry, loaded with horses and people, steered towards the centre of the river. She was thinking of going down to the village but it occurred to her that Kilsang might be at the garden house. She turned her steps in that direction. When she looked down at it from the top of the stone steps, there was no sign of him by the fireplace either. Instead she saw Dochul *ne* standing conspicuously in front of the pavilion.

'Dochul *ne*!'

As if pleased to see somebody, she called and then ran up to her and, with arms akimbo, said, 'What are you doing?'

'Who? Me?'

Standing and glaring straight at the sun, she smiled broadly showing her teeth.

'I've come to the middle gate to receive the message.'

'What message?'

'Damn it, have you sent your ears off to be married? What a dreadful world – dreadful! What an awful world – awful! I've offered five hundred sacks of rice to Buddha and hung lanterns in every valley and prayed for a thousand, ten thousand years of happiness, but Buddha's gone blind, the Divine General's gone blind, the Guardian Spirit's gone blind and the reverend ancestors have gone blind all of them – blind!'

Suddenly she clapped her hands and shouted, 'See the soldiers coming like swarms of bees! Are you saying that my son is the head of the Dong Hak? That's ridiculous! Look here, Master, Master of the Court, my son's gone to Seoul. He's gone to take the state exams. Sure, it's true! I swear it's true! Do you know Lee Mong-ryong, the Inspector General Incognito? That's my son, as precious as a golden branch with leaves of jade. I begot him after offering a hundred days' prayers to the Wood God at the Western Hill – do you hear me? Look here, young master, take me with you – you can't leave me behind and just go off on your own.'

Bongsoon cackled with laughter.

'How long is the night! Autumn night and the boundless sky, and the long, long nights. How I miss my lover's face! His face like jade, his presence like the moon, the more I think of him, the more I long to see him. The East wind blows warm and the thoughts of my love blow for me. Welcome is the spring wind, and the flower opening to it like the smiling face of my love. I want to see him as I see that flower . . .'.

After going on like this for a time, she began to float about in a dance. All her teeth showed as she kept breaking into broad smiles and continued to dance. Probably some brigand, hawker or boorish traveller had assaulted her somewhere on the road on the previous night, for the lower parts of her clothes were torn and flapped wildly, revealing her bruised thighs as she danced. In no time the last weak rays of the sun had hidden their tails and in the west a red afterglow rode the sky. The gatherers of firewood, chattering, came down from the hill.

Chapter Forty-Two

THE relationship between Yongi and Chilsung, recently weakening, became even more distant after the incident at the cabbage-picking. Not only was there bad feeling but it was rare for them to see each other in the village. It was the quiet season between the end of work in the fields and preparations for winter, so that, if they had wanted to share a cup of wine, it could easily have been done, but Yongi, after finding Wolsun's shop nailed up, rarely went to town or to the tavern in the village. In fact, he hardly saw anyone, let alone Chilsung. He spent the day stuck in his shed, weaving sacks and straw shoes or tending his tools. He threw himself into his work, afraid of the times when his hands were still and he sat blankly. He was a man who had not only deserted his village friends but had departed even further from his wife. She used to weep, or force herself into the small room where he slept, or go round the village like a mad woman picking a quarrel with anyone, but now she had hardened into stone, as he had, and turned as cold. She did not speak, nor was she seen around the village, but stayed in the inner room, sometimes sewing patches on socks and occasionally at the loom. There were rare times, very rare, when she wept, plucking out her hair by handfuls. Just once she had gone out to the jar stand and smashed one of the jars. When she cried and plucked out her hair he would come and stand by her blankly.

Coldly cut off from each other, they had both changed, though one thing was unchanged in Kangchong *dek*, her hatred of Yimi *ne*. It was a jealousy that burned like fire. Whenever they met, her eyes lit up as in her heart she tore her into shreds.

'Really, that woman goes out of her mind, and not just once or twice. Have I killed her father? Am I a deadly enemy who's dug up her ancestor's graves? She's wasting away like a stick because she can't eat me up.'

Yimi *ne* would deride her to others with false laughter, perhaps savouring a hidden delight, but she avoided any direct confrontation. The other women, taking her side, would laugh and say, 'Yimi *ne*, you must get a shaman to remove the curse. You can't go on like this – you are next-door neighbours and not likely to stop seeing each other.'

She became even more indifferent to the care of the house, but it was cleaner and tidier, perhaps making it even chillier. When he had nothing to do, Yongi would fetch the carving knife from the kitchen and sharpen it on the whetstone. He would tidy again the already tidy shed and continuously boil fodder so that there was never a time when the bucket was empty and the ox hungry. It was the happiest and most comfortable member of the household, with plump flesh and a smooth and shining coat. He often went into the woods with his A-frame flung over his shoulder. Once there, he would let himself go. He would gather up fallen leaves, light them and endlessly stare at the river. How long would he have to go on like this? – sometimes he raised the question with himself. As a man, why can't you forget a woman who has left you? – he was even angry with himself. Often he wished that there was no river or road in the village – then he would stop wondering if she was on the ferry or plodding up the track. Whenever he caught sight of the ferry, or the road lined with tall willows, his heart trembled and, when he did not see her, he wished he was blind. When the sun slowly dropped in the west and the birds flew to their nests, he came home carrying his empty A-frame.

'They say you can change suddenly one morning, but can you imagine anyone changing the way that Yi *subang* has? If your husband was going to change like that, you'd offer him a bag of money and beg him to go astray, wouldn't you? He looks after every detail and keeps the place spick-and-span and she never has to lift a finger. Thanks to her husband, she's having such a good time – she must be happy, mustn't she?'

'That's right. She's the one that failed even to produce a child, but she overflows with blessings, and they say she just lies down night and day. He's good looking and with a fine figure – that's more than enough blessing to expect in a husband, but she can lie down on her back and food goes into her mouth – what farmer's wife was ever as lucky as she is?'

They were fully aware of the situation and were only being sarcastic but one of them, taking it seriously, opened her mouth to say, 'What's the use of having the house spick-and-span? What's the use of good looks and a fine figure? They're living under the same roof as strangers. If you don't feel like food, you can leave it for later, but if you don't like a person – well, they say, if there's someone you hate, you just can't live in this world. Even if you go round carrying a beggars' bowl . . .'.

The others pretended to be innocent and went on saying, 'Quite right,' 'True,' until they broke into a roar of laughter. Kangchong *dek* took no notice of what was going on among those outside and kept her mouth firmly shut even when she met a neighbour at the well. After drawing the water, she flew off without a word of greeting and eventually she chose to go at night when no one was about. A new rumour spread through the village. Some one had seen her plucking the grass on the top of her mother-in-law's grave, and someone else saw her sitting all alone by the stream in the middle of the night muttering to herself, and it was said that she was possessed by the spirit of Wolsun's mother.

The eighth day of the eleventh lunar month was the anniversary of the death of Yongi's mother. As he set off to market with a sack over his shoulder to buy the sacrificial food, Kangchong *dek*, sitting on a straw mat in the yard, was polishing brass bowls ready for the rite.

The wind from the river was bitter. Probably the cold weather was coming early. The breeze was charged with sand. He rubbed his eyes with the end of his sleeve as he walked. It was his first trip to the market since he had seen Wolsun's nailed-up shop some months before. On the embankment children were flying kites. In a clear blue sky where the wind had brushed away all the clouds, a white kite soared up and up. Riding smoothly on the wind and pulling the string off the reel as it went higher and higher. To the sounds of the unrolling string, reinforced with pottery powder and resin, tough as wire, the wind and the rising waves, the children stood with their eyes entirely fixed on the white kite. As he went

481

down the slope to the landing stage, Hanjo, with his fishing rod fixed to the boat, was bailing water from the bottom and he called, 'Hallo, Yongi, on your way to market?'

'Yes. Are they biting?' he asked as he went nearer.

'Not really, I'm too busy getting the water out of this rotten boat. Why do we never see you nowadays?'

Without answering the question, he said, 'It's my mother's anniversary tomorrow.'

'Ah! really, she'll eat well, as it's the day after the market.'

Yongi looked towards the river to see it the boat was coming.

'If you have the money, it doesn't matter whether it's market day or not. You can always get things from somewhere.'

'What are you going to do about meat?'

'At least I ought to have some salted fish.'

'Buy some from me.'

'You're crazy! Whoever heard of using freshwater fish for a sacrifice?'

Hanjo chuckled. Yongi took out his pipe and filled it.

'This autumn, brother Yoon Bo hasn't come back. I wonder if anything has happened to him?' said Hanjo.

'I don't know . . .'.

'If he doesn't come back for the New Year, there must be some serious reason.'

'What could happen to him?'

'If something has, I'd like to know the date, so that I can offer a sacrifice.'

'Don't be silly. People don't die so easily.'

'You never know. If it's your fate to die, you're as helpless as a fly. I heard from a traveller that, outside, things are hopeless. The palace guards are all monsters with yellow hair and blue eyes and the real truth is the king is really no more than a hostage – that's what he said. And he said that the country will soon be ruined and they will take it over. When things are as unsettled as that, Yoon Bo, with his past record, can't be safe, can he?'

'. . .'.

'He may have rushed to join the Army of Justice and be taking

482

an active part . . . if he had just been quietly working at someone's house, he would have been back in the autumn, wouldn't he?'

'That's true. With a man like him – you never know.'

'Kim *hunjang* was saying the same thing. At the time of the Dong Hak he used to abuse him, saying he was a traitor, but these days he is full of praise for him. He said that, in spite of it all, he is a man of sense, so he must have enlisted in the Army of Justice and, as he has a strong sense of filial duty, if he did not come to trim his parents' graves, he must be working for the country even though he is a commoner. Come to think of it, Kim *hunjang* himself looks as though he is dying to do something active himself . . .'

Hanjo laughed. As he was about to enter the market, Yongi's eyes naturally turned to Wolsun's shop and his legs stood like stakes unable to move. The house, left to decay, reminded him of Dochul *ne*, who had lost her soul. It was only a few months – how could it have changed so much just because nobody lived in it? It was only natural that the roof of a deserted cottage would not be rethatched. All around were golden roofs cosily recovered and ready for the winter but hers was grey and one corner had fallen in, so that it looked as if there would be holes in it before the summer.

'I'll re-thatch it! I'll do it quickly and change the whole thing before the cold weather comes!'

This sudden idea gave him great comfort.

'If I run out of the straw, I can ask Dooman's father to lend me some – that'll do it!'

He felt as if she was close. The shabby house made him think of her body. To put a new thatch on it would be like clothing her. Amidst all his tearing sorrow, he felt a warm satisfaction. He managed to walk on. 'Heartless woman!'

The market was slack. With autumn gone and winter just begun, it would be deserted until the big days before the New Year. The chanting of the beggar troupe lacked vigour as did the cries of the hawker off to Seoul to find his son and his wares looked old, worn and soiled, and seemed to be trembling before the onslaught of early cold. Only the tavern teemed. The traders, hoping to warm themselves with a bowl of cabbage soup and a cup of wine, came and went without ceasing.

483

'They say "Old monks freeze in the flower-wind of February," but this is only the beginning of winter – why is it so cold?'

'It's like people – wine mixed with water or water in the wine is no good. If it's going to be cold, it might as well be really cold – then you feel better.'

'Come off it. Have you eaten a big ginseng root or something?'

Like every other year, he put all the materials for the sacrifice in his sack. For the last items, the incense and candle, he stopped in front of a general store. He had taken the parcel from the shopkeeper and was about to pay when someone tugged at his sleeve and he heard a lisping voice say, 'You're no stranger to me.'

He turned to see. An old woman with a hamper of goods on display smiled at him, her toothless mouth hanging open.

'Oh, hallo.'

'You remember me?'

'Yes.'

His eyelids lowered as his face stiffened.

'I haven't seen you for a long time – so you have settled down then?'

She was much more kind and dignified than she had been before.

'What's happened to your face?'

She clicked her tongue. He said goodbye and had turned to go when she asked, 'Did you see that girl called Wolsun?'

The words hit him in the back.

'Where would I see her?'

'Mm . . . So you never saw her? I did, once.'

'What did you say?'

He turned like a flash.

'It was a few months ago now.'

'Where? Where did you see her?'

'Here, in the market. I told her about you.'

'. . . .'

'She wept so much her tears kept falling like rain. I said to her "Listen to me, if you can't get over your love for him, why don't you go and live with him?" She didn't say anything but just kept crying. I asked her where she had gone to. She said it wasn't too

484

far away, but she had now decided to go somewhere a long way off, so she had just come to have a last look.'

'. . .'.

'She said she'd come in the hope of meeting someone from the village with news of you and hadn't seen anyone, but I had told her something. So she gave me three pence and said goodbye and went off. She looks such a gentle thing.'

'Where did she say she was going?'

'She didn't say. She only said it was far far away – really far. She was crying so much, it made me cry too.

As when a light is extinguished, the spark went out of his eyes.

'Goodbye then, granny.'

He left in a hurry. The trader, who had stood blankly not knowing what was going on between the two of them jumped up and shouted, 'Hey, look here! Are you going to go off without paying for the candle?'

'I'm sorry. I forgot . . .'.

He came back and undid his purse. As he sorted out the money his hands were trembling. When he had come home and put down the sack with the shopping in it, he was restless. One moment he walked up and down the courtyard and the next he went to the shed and got all his tools ready, only to put them back again – he was like a man out of his mind.

Kangchong *dek* soaked some rice for cake and moved about busy in the kitchen. In previous years she had invited neighbours to help, and while they worked indulged herself more in chattering, cackling with laughter, but this year she worked alone, coming and going like a shadow, and seemed to be putting more care into it than ever before. In the night he could not sleep a wink. His wife, perhaps because she had been moving about all day, seemed to be fast asleep. About midnight, unable to stand it any longer, he got up, put on some clothes and opened the door. At the same moment Kangchong *dek*, whom he had thought to be asleep in the inner room, kicked the door open and came out.

'Where are you off to?'

'To get some fresh air.'

'On a cold night like this?'

'I'm choking. It's driving me mad.'

'You can't! I know where you're going.'

'What's it got to do with you where I go?'

'I know all about it! You're off to see that bitch, Yimi *ne*!'

'What?'

'Don't you know the saying "A woman's resentment can bring frost in summer?" Do you think I'll die before I've seen you hanged on a tree?' Her voice was as eerie as if it rang out from deep underground, an infinite depth. Yongi laughed out loud. Her words did not make him angry. He stepped out of the room, lit a lamp and went into the shed with it. He hung it on a post there and went round behind it to return with a stack of rice straw. Then, squatting on the ground and pulling out a few strands, he began to weave a thatch. Clad only in her underclothes, she stood quietly watching him with folded arms. He took a handful of straw, wove it in, and took another. Under the lamplight his torso moved back and forward following his hands, but his closed lips never once opened.

Kangchong *dek* watching and Yongi working were like two trees sprung from the ground and, when they moved, like trees riding on the wind. Dry leaves from bundles of twigs piled in the yard rolled and rustled. She began to shiver. Her body gradually contracted. Her slight form, small feet, and long thin neck all shrank. The bitter wind filtering mercilessly into her flesh through the legs of her bloomers and the ends of her sleeves.

At last he spoke.

'Go back to your room. I'm not going anywhere.'

As if she had been waiting for that, she went back with a sound of crunching steps. After a while came the sound of her door shutting.

On the following night husband and wife, after performing ablutions, laid out the sacrificial table. It was covered with rice paper on which the dishes were arranged – a handsome offering. After setting out the name tablet of the deceased, Yongi dressed in the proper robe, offered incense, prostrated himself twice, and knelt down. His wife, dressed in white, poured wine into a cup and offered it to him. He took it in both hands and sprinkled it three times on a dish of sand and straw to call down the spirit, and gave it back to her. While she placed it on the table and bowed, he again prostrated himself twice. A prayer was read, a second cup offered to the spirit, and he made the last prostration. After filling the cup with wine, she removed the lid of the rice bowl and stuck a spoon and chopsticks into it. They lay face down before the sacrificial table for a long time. Her small shoulders heaved. Although she made no sound, she was weeping with her whole body. On the table the candles flickered. As if dawn was still far off, though the first cock had crowed, the village lay silent in the dark.

(Mother, mother, when you were alive, you told me to live with her, teaching her as we went along . . . I haven't even a child. What must I do with myself?)

Forgetting to burn the tablet and the prayer paper, or remove the things used for the ritual, they sat at opposite ends of the table and stared at each other with blank eyes. The incense had burnt out, and only the scent still hung in the air. In the sky the stars were countless and clear. She set out for the village with a large wooden bowl on her head to distribute the food from the sacrifice. Dogs barked, Dooman's being the first.

'*Songnim!* Dooman *ne songnim!*'

She shook the gate and the dog barked madly.

'Who is it?'

Dooman *ne*'s voice was drunken with sleep. A light was lit in the room. As she pushed the gate open and went into the yard, the dog, after a sniff, stopped barking and followed her in. Dooman *ne* opened the door and stepped out on to the verandah.

'You've done the sacrifice?'

'Yes.'

She put down the bowl. Dooman *ne* fetched bowls from her kitchen. After breaking a piece off the corner of the rice cake and throwing it away, she took another piece and tasted it.

'It's good.'

Disturbed by the noise outside, Yongman crawled out, calling 'Mummy.'

487

Dooman *ne* smiled. Shy, the child curled his tongue and made a crying sound.

'Shush! You'll wake up the others.'

She tilted the soup bowl and let him drink some and then gave him a piece of cake.

'You've done very well, all by yourself. I thought it was about the time for your sacrifice but, as you didn't say anything, I couldn't go and help. Have you been crying? Your eyes are all swollen.'

'I was sad, so I cried a bit.'

'You shouldn't have. Don't be too sad – it's just life, isn't it?'

Then she whispered so as not to wake up the other children as she pushed the food into the room.

'Look, here, Dooman's dad, wake up and try some of the memorial food.'

Kangchong *dek* was about to go when Dooman *ne* called, 'Listen, how many houses have you been to so far?'

'Yours is the first.'

'It will be a long time before you finish.'

'I suppose so.'

'It's bitterly cold – you'll be frozen stiff.'

'. . . .'

'By the way – I hope you don't mind me saying this – you won't miss out Yimi *ne*, will you?'

'. . . .'

'However you may have fallen out with her, you must never be unkind with food.'

'. . . .'

' "Neighbours are cousins," as they say. You can't finish with her in a day, can you? I think you've got some exaggerated ideas . . .'.

'. . . .'

'She has a husband with eyes as bright as a lamp, and children too. How can a woman like that even dream of such a thing? Forget about it.'

Kangchong *dek* turned away angrily. She went into Pyongsan's yard next. At the sound of someone moving, the door of the small room clanged open.

'I've brought you some of the memorial food.'

488

Haman *dek* smiled as she put the lamp out by the door. Her face was terribly emaciated and, despite the bitter night air, her forehead was moist with sweat. 'I am ashamed of myself just sitting here and receiving it.'

'You don't look well.'

'I'm always the same.'

When she had delivered the food all round the village she finally went into the yard of Yimi *ne*'s. It was growing lighter. As she emptied the bowls, Yimi *ne* tried to make conversation about this and that as a gesture of good-will, but Kangchong *dek* never once opened her mouth until she had piled up all the empty bowls in her basket and turned to go.

'Damned bitch! If she was going to be like that, why did she bother to bring it at all? I wouldn't be surprised if she'd put poison in it.'

Yimi *ne* spat, but nevertheless she cut off a corner of the cake and stuffed her mouth until her cheeks bulged.

Chapter Forty-Three

AFTER breakfast had been cooked more wood was put into
the stove under the hot floor and a brazier brought in as
well, so that the room was hot and stuffy. Roundish bags
of seed such as maize, millet, and sorghum dangled from the beam
across the ceiling, and from a pile of soya bean blocks fermenting
at the warm end of the room came a smell that stung the nose.
Haman *dek*, who had been cutting out a dress from a roll of silk,
drew in her breath and finally broke into shallow coughs. From her
throat came the sound of bubbling phlegm. As she cut off a thread
with her teeth, Dooman *ne* said, 'Songnim, you're just obstinate.'

'If I wasn't, how would I . . .'.

Breaking off in the middle of the sentence, she again coughed
painfully. Dooman *ne* opened the door and put her head out.

'Listen, girl, isn't your grandmother calling?'

Suni was pounding barley.

'Pardon, mother?'

'I think Grandma wants to go to the toilet. Go and see.'

Suni put down the pestle and quickly went to the old woman's
room. Dooman *ne* shut the door and, as she picked up her work,
she said, 'Don't be like that – go to the town and let the chemist
take your pulse for once.'

'. . .'.

'Above all, you must stay alive. Even if the whole land is yours,
if you're not alive to see it, it's no use. What's the good of going
on weaving if you're spitting blood?'

'Who told you that – Yamu *ne*?'

'Yes. You brought up blood and fainted away, she says. Just as
well she was there or it'd have been terrible, wouldn't it?'

'I told her not to tell anyone, but she has a light tongue.'

'It's not that. When she saw me going to ask you for help, she
told me you wouldn't be able to – she told me because she was

490

worried about you. As they say, "Neighbours are cousins." We must know how you are, mustn't we? If we don't, it's our fault.'

'. . .'.

'I was going to get some help from the next village, but when I saw you weaving . . .'.

'I owe you so much for your kindness, yet when you have a big occasion, instead of making a contribution, I get paid – I can't look you in the face.'

'Don't say such a thing. Don't worry about that, but just this once, don't think of the money as for the family, but use it to buy some medicine for yourself.'

'When we hardly manage to eat, how can I think about medicine . . . She's bigger round the chest than you'd think to look at her . . .'.

Checking the chest size of Suni's jacket, she evaded Dooman *ne*'s suggestion.

'It's because her breasts are already formed.'

'Well, she's fifteen, so it's about time they were. It's just the right age to marry her off.'

'It'll be a great relief when it's all over. As it's the first time, I don't know how to go about it, and I'm afraid of making a fool of myself.'

'It depends on how you do it. There's no need for it to be burdensome. Anyway, there's plenty of time.'

'That's true . . . the other thing is that, though we don't have the shrine here, we're still in mourning for my auntie of the Choi house – it doesn't seem quite right to have a marriage.'

'Legally speaking, she adopted your son, Yongman but I wonder if that makes her a relative . . . but yours is not a family that needs to worry too much about decorum – you can do whatever suits you.'

'That' true, I suppose. But I think even lower-class families ought to behave correctly.'

Her suggestion that her family did not need to worry about decorum was disagreeable to Dooman *ne*.

(She is likeable in every way except that, even in the state she is

491

in, she can't get out of the habit of looking down on ordinary people.)

She went on, 'Anyway, time flows like a river. It seems only the other day that I married and came here . . . whatever happens, I'd hate to hear anyone say we'd brought her up badly – that's what worries me.'

'Yes, from the way they are going about the preparations, it looks as though her future mother-in-law is no ordinary person.'

'That's right. As they say, "Plant big beans and you get big beans, plant small beans, you get small ones." Not only her, but the whole tradition of the family seems to be in that way.'

'I hear they are quite well off.'

'Yes. They run the market boat and things like that, so they must be pretty comfortable.'

'Your daughter has a nice nature, so she should be happy.'

'You have to wait and see, don't you?'

'That's true. On the wedding day everyone thinks they'll be happy. You have to wait and see.'

As she snipped, Haman *dek* went on, 'When I was married, everyone said I'd done well.'

Instead of sighing, she smiled brightly and, even though she was sweating, she moved up to the warm end of the room.

'Because you were marrying into a higher class, I suppose.'

'For him, too, you could say the world hadn't been kind. If it had, would he have married into the middle class?'

'. . .'

' "You can live off good families," as they say – when you're young you live off the mother's family, after marriage the wife's and when you're old the in-laws.' Isn't that what they say?'

'Speaking of dowries, you brought a big one, didn't you?'

'Well . . . wife's property – it's nothing much really.'

'Even so, if it's managed well . . .' '

'It was only blood in a bird's leg – not worth mentioning.'

'We never had our own land until we got this one patch, though strictly speaking it's not ours but a sacrificial paddy for my auntie – if only you have your own land, what is there to worry about?'

'It's no use talking like that. A gentleman like him – would he dig the soil like a common peasant?'

'If there was no choice about it, what else could he do?'

Dooman *ne*'s tone was sharp and anger rose to Haman *dek*'s face. 'He's not the sort to be forced.'

'Of course, it would be hard for him to do work he's not accustomed to, but it's because of his excessive drinking and his bad habits that you have all this hardship.'

'Is it because he doesn't know how to that he doesn't work? You don't understand. Maybe he drinks a lot, but a python that's failed to become a dragon will flounder in the water . . . how can he but grieve for being born at the wrong time?'

Tears rose to her eyes.

'*Songnim*, please don't mind me saying this – I am saying it because I feel so sorry for you. The saying goes, "Don't even look at the tree you can't climb." Will he attain high office or anything at this stage? Look at Kim *hunjang*. He works on his farm just like the others, but nobody ever regards him as less than a gentleman. If the whole country is yours and you loose your eyes, what's the use of it? You grind your bones with work and, if anything happens to you, what then?'

'One's life depends on Heaven. One must not forget a wife's duty to serve her husband. However ill one may be, it would never do for a woman of good family to go out and get medicine for herself.'

After making a pronouncement that left no room for argument, she pursed her lips. Her heart-shaped face could not look more chilly while her hands, calloused and swollen jointed from hard work, trembled as if with suppressed anger. Dooman *ne*, who by nature hated to say anything unkind, regretted her pointless speech. 'She's pathetic,' she thought spitefully, yet, on the other hand, she admired her for her virtue.

(How sad she must be. She has to earn money from the low-class people she despises. She has this one fault of showing off about the gentry but, no doubt, there are plenty of things to learn from her, and what a good example she sets. Whatever they say, her husband is her god.)

493

Dooman *ne* put down her work and went out. 'Suni, what about supper? Put in another handful of rice and make it soft.'

'Yes, mother.'

'Have you given Granny her gruel?'

'Yes.'

Dooman *ne* came in again with a wooden tray.

'*Songnim*, stop now and try some of this.'

'What is it?'

She spoke as if she also was trying hard to smother ruffled feelings though her voice was not even.

'Cabbage roots, boiled and rolled in soya powder. They're quite nice.'

'You've still got some left?'

'I hid them away in a jar. Then this morning I steamed them on top of the rice but the kids – because they're growing, I suppose – were mad to have them.' They both put their work aside and ate the cabbage roots. They were tender, fragrant and slightly bitter on the tip of the tongue. As they ate, bean powder was left round their mouths.

'It seems as though the cold is coming early this year.'

That's because your mind is rushing ahead now that you've fixed the day for the wedding.'

'That's probably it . . .'.

As she spoke, the loud voice of Magdal *ne* was heard in the yard, 'It's cold! – But here the top end of the room will be nice and warm.'

There was the sound of footsteps crunching on the ground, frozen hard by the cold wind. An embarrassed look came on Dooman *ne*'s face. The door clanged open and a voice said, 'Can I come in and warm my bottom – the frozen bottom of a poor widow?'

When she saw Haman *dek*, Magdal *ne* stopped in embarrassment.

'Oh dear!'

(Am I sinner with my nose cut off – why shouldn't I go in?)

She closed the door with a bang and, folding her arms, squatted down beside Dooman *ne*. Haman *dek* stopped eating and wiped the bean powder from round her mouth. She drew out her handkerchief and neatly wiped her fingers, and, without giving Magdal *ne* a glance, picked up her work.

'Have some more.'

'I have had plenty, thank you.'

'Magdal *ne*, would you like some of these?'

Dooman *ne* pushed the tray in front of her.

'How do you still have precious things like this?' She quickly picked one up and took a bite.

'I hear you've fixed the date for the wedding.'

'Mm.'

After a quick glance at Haman *dek*, Magdal *ne* said, 'With no family and no learning . . .'.

'Don't be silly . . .'.

Dooman *ne* gave her a wink, as if to cut her short.

'. . . I can't help with the important work, can I? But if there's any odd job, let me do it.'

'It's still early. We have plenty of time — there's nothing that's needed urgently.'

'Why did you fix it so late? Won't it be quite cold by then?'

'I know. When they were fixing it, they realized there was a family sacrifice due and so on, so it had to be after the month was out — I think that's how it came to be fixed like that.'

'It would've been nice to have had it in the autumn.'

'I agree with you.'

Haman *dek* continued her work without once raising her head.

'I hear that by their family tradition they are mean and make people work hard — Suni is going to have a tough time.'

'That's how you become mature.'

Even so, Dooman *ne* did not look pleased at the comment.

'I went to Hwasim-li yesterday, *Songnim*.'

'What for?'

'There was supposed to be a big exorcism, so I went to see it.'

'You have a good time.'

'It was a youngster from the town. Apart from her face, it wasn't worth watching — the spirits didn't come up.'

'A novice is no good — though they may be nice looking.'

'It's the same with a *kiseng*. It's the music and the dancing that

495

matters, not their looks. This one was useless – just useless. She kept fiddling with her hat string and had no idea how to do the chants.'

'Mother! Quick, there's trouble! Mother!'

Suni was shouting from outside the gate. Dooman *ne* opened the door and put her head out, 'What's the matter?'

'Gobok's mother – there's trouble!'

Haman *dek*'s face turned white as she put down her work.

'You have to say what it is, first.'

'We – I – I was drawing water when Gobok threw a stone at Bongsoon, and she's b – bleeding! She's bleeding to death!'

Magdal *ne* and Dooman *ne* stood up at once. Haman *dek*, as if turned to stone, could not move.

'It must be bad.'

Dooman *ne* went out first. As she followed her out, Magdal *ne* shouted, 'At last it's happened. What did I say? I've always said he shouldn't be allowed in the village . . . father and son – like butchers! What do they take people for, eh?' Inwardly she was probably thinking 'Well done!'

Haman *dek*'s small eyes, as lifeless as painted black spots, looked once at the ceiling, once at the door, swept across the floor and back to her work, and she started sewing again as if nothing had happened. She became totally absorbed in her work, as if nothing at all had occurred and she had been born into the world only for this.

After Suni, who seemed to fly along the embankment, waddled the plump Dooman *ne* and Magdal *ne* with her arms still folded. At the deserted threshing ground only Sohi's shrill voice rang out, 'You wicked boy! You wicked boy!'

She had taken off one of her embroidered shoes and was beating Gobok on the knees, while he stood as if turned to stone. His face had gone the colour of ashes. Dooman *ne* picked up Bongsoon, who had fallen over, her face smeared with blood. Suni gabbled breathlessly, 'I was drawing w- w- water wh – when the boys started shouting that Bongsoon was k – k – killed and ran off, and when I came to see there was b – b – blood . . .'

'That's enough. Run and get some water.'

She ran off at once to the well and Gobok, who had stood like a statue while Sohi hit him on the legs with her shoe, suddenly began to cry and ran off like an arrow. Sohi fell over as he broke away and also burst into tears.

'Mum – water!'

Suni held out the bowl. Dooman *ne* took a mouthful and squirted it over Bongsoon's face. At the second attempt, she came round.

'Bongsoon, look dear!'

'Uh – uh – '

'Bongsoon! Can you see me?'

Following her mother, Suni shouted,

'Bongsoon! Can you see me?'

'Um . . . m'

'She's alive! Bongsoon!'

Suni shouted again. Sohi was screaming loudly enough to pierce their ear drums as she flailed her legs.

'Suni, look after the young Miss. Put her on your back.'

After washing most of the blood off her face with the water, Dooman *ne* wiped it with the corner of her skirt.

'Looks like a nosebleed.'

Magdal *ne* peered at her.

'I say! – it's her forehead that's cut. Tut, tut . . . It won't do for a girl to have a scar on her face.'

'It's only a small cut. When it's healed up it won't show.'

Dooman *ne* spoke as if to emphasize her hope that it would not be serious. Bongsoon smothered her sobs as she continued to cry, her lips twitching. The urchins who had run away gradually began to sneak back with cautious glances.

'You rascals! You shouldn't be allowed to stay in the village. You can't hang about like this – going round in a gang instead of behaving yourselves, taking after that dog-butcher. Naughty boys, you ought to be hung up on the tree and thrashed till you wet your pants!'

Magdal *ne* brandished her fists as she shouted while Suni tried hard to force Sohi, still screaming her head off, to get on to her back.

'We didn't do it.'

497

'It's because she called him a low-bred bastard that he hit her!'

'It's because he called her Kilsang's girl.'

'No, it's because he tried to touch her, saying, "Have you got any tits yet?" '

'Ha ha ha ha . . .'.

The children broke into a chorus of laughter.

'That's what the world's coming to – kids with the tops of their heads still soft . . . ugh! little pigs! . . .'. Dooman *ne* gave a hollow laugh.

'It's not that! He was caught stealing the potatoes at Kim *subang*'s and thrashed. So he took it out on Bongsoon.'

'Naughty boys! Come here the lot of you! Those who steal, those who hit people, and those who say dirty things – I'll grab you all and break your legs!'

As Magdal *ne* chased them brandishing her fists, they scuttled away in all directions.

'I didn't hit Bongsoon!'

'I didn't steal any potatoes!'

'I didn't say dirty things.'

Each made his excuse as he ran. Dooman *ne*, carrying Bongsoon in her arms, and Suni, with Sohi on her back and the shoes in her hands, walked along the embankment towards the Choi house.

'To her mother Bongsoon is as precious as gold and jade – it'll break her heart. I hope it won't leave a scar on her forehead . . . a girl must never have a mark on her face . . .'.

Dooman *ne* mumbled to herself as she walked with the setting sun directly in front of them. On Suni's back, Sohi still cried. When they were nearly at the gate Bongsoon began to wriggle as if ashamed of being carried and said, 'Let me down – I'll walk.'

When Dooman *ne* went in again, she found Haman *dek* still sewing as if nothing had happened, with literally not a hair out of place. As she came into the room her shoulders heaved once but her hands did not stop working.

'I think she fainted. Her nose was bleeding.'

Only then did Haman *dek* let go of the sewing and lift her eyes to Dooman *ne*. Sweat appeared on her face as if her pores had all at once opened and her lips trembled. She almost smiled and then her eyes filled with tears.

'I didn't think she would quite be dead.'

Seeing Haman *dek* relax seemed to make Dooman *ne* suddenly angry.

'There was a terrible row at the *Champan*'s house. Bongsoon *ne* was crying and sighing and saying, if it had been just a nosebleed it wouldn't have mattered but her forehead was cut, and what could she do about it? If it had been on the cheek, she wouldn't have minded so much, but right in the middle of her forehead – how will she marry and so on? She is right, you know. If a girl has a scar on her forehead, they say it's unlucky, don't they? It will be hard to marry her – she couldn't help feeling bad about it – she doesn't have any other children but only this one whom she's brought up like a precious jewel. The young Miss as well – she must have been shocked – her head was boiling hot.'

Haman *dek* dried her tears and picked up her sewing again without a word.

'*Songnim*, you are so unfortunate. God seems to be unfair.'

Gobok did not go home that night, nor was he back on the night after. On the third day at about lunch time, he sneaked into the yard, his eyes sunken and looking like a beggar. He was about to climb over the half-door into the kitchen but started at the sound of someone moving and pressed himself against the mud wall by the back door. The bundle of dry cabbage leaves hanging on the wall rustled in the wind and brushed his face. He stretched his neck to peer into the kitchen. Out of the corner of his eye he saw Hanbok fill a bowl from the water jar and take a drink. Relieved, he smiled and lightly kicked on the sill of the door. Hanbok glanced roung holding the bowl. When he saw his brother, he walked around, not knowing what to do, and then with the bowl still in his hand, he took a look round the front yard and crept up to the back door.

'Brother!'

'Is she at home?'

'Mm.'

'Where?'

'In the small room.'

'There's no sound of weaving.'

'She's just sitting there.'

'I'm dying of hunger – get me something to eat.'

'You haven't had anything?'

'Not a thing. Quick, give me something.'

Hanbok stealthily crept back to the iron cauldron and struggled to lift the heavy lid. He turned to Gobok with a disappointed look and shook his head, 'There's only a bowl of rice for father.'

'Give it to me then. I'm dying of hunger, damn it!'

After looking round the kitchen, Hanbok noticed a basket with some boiled barley in it. Signalling to his brother to go and wait in the backyard, he put some into a bowl which, along with some leftover soup and a spoon, he put out on the door sill, climbed over and carried them over one by one to Gobok, who was waiting in the backyard. He gobbled them down like a madman.

'Where did you sleep?'

'In the hills.'

He had thought that Bongsoon was dead. That was why he had been unable to come down to the village and had slept two nights in the woods. He had been so hungry that he had picked up acorns and crunched them and dug the ground until his nails were worn down to get the roots of plants, but it had hardly diminished his hunger. Hunger and cold were driving him mad and, unable to bear it any longer, he had come down and met some children. Relieved at the news that Bongsoon had not died, he had gone home but he was still scared of his mother.

'What is she doing?' he asked again when his hunger was reduced.

'She isn't doing anything.'

'Why?'

'. . .'

His young eyes were accusing.

'M – M – Mother!'

Suddenly Gobok fell back with a cry. She had come up from behind and grabbed him by the front of his jacket. 'Mother! Forgive me! I will never, never again . . . forgive me just this once!'

'. . .'

He was dragged along by the scruff of his neck. Hanbok followed them crying.

'Hanbok, you go out and play.'

When she had dragged him into the room she bolted the door from inside.

'M – M – Mother! I will never, never again . . .'.

'Listen to me, Gobok.'

'Yes, mother.'

'However I think about it, it's not your fault, it's mine.'

She spoke quietly.

'I've – I've been naughty.'

'The only way is for you and me to die together. If you die, you may be born again as a good boy, and I may be a happier woman.'

'Mother!'

'Come on, you and I will hang together on one line and die. Do you understand?'

From inside came the sound of Gobok crying loudly while outside the trembling Hanbok beat on the door with his fists.

'Mother, don't die! Mother!'

Gobok, who was kicking wildly inside, shouted, 'Hanbok, go and get father!'

He ran barefoot in the direction of the tavern.

'Father! Father!'

Chapter Forty-Four

THERE had been a continuous drizzle of late winter rain but now it had ceased. When he got off the ferry, Dr Mun took the path to the village without mule or servant. The temperature was not yet freezing and under the midday sun the road was muddy. Some young fuel gatherers had flung down their A-frames and were making a fire on the embankment. The grass should have been damp but it had been dried, perhaps, by the breeze and the fire seemed to be burning slowly. The smoke changed its direction with the wind.

Dochul *ne*, her ragged clothes hanging in shreds, walked along the path between the paddies, clattering her wooden clogs. Dr Mun stopped for a moment as he blankly watched her pass. Probably there had been a sacrifice at someone's house, as she had a piece of rice cake in her palm from which she took bites as she went. A thin dog padded after her. From her hanging garments one strip had slipped down and swept the path like a snake at the heels of her clogs. The thin dog that followed, eyes fixed on the piece of cake in her palm, trod on the bobbing strip of cloth and rolled over but picked itself up and continued to follow her with dribbling mouth and wagging tail. After she had gone some distance, she shouted something, threw away what was left of the cake and ran off like an arrow. The starving dog, so happy that he waved his tail enough to break, took possession of the piece of cake. To the persimmon tree, from which the frost-bitten fruit had all been taken, and without even a single leaf, came a magpie which cawed as if to announce the coming of a welcome guest and flew away.

At Kim *hunjang*'s gate, the doctor called, 'Is anyone in?' and lightly coughed. Immediately the teacher himself appeared.

'Good heavens, what brings you here?' The doctor looked at him, as if puzzled.

'I had a message that you were ill.'

He gave a wry smile.

'To tell you the truth, the patient is somewhere else. I'm afraid you'll have to go there with me.'

'Where?'

'It's Kim *jinsa*'s daughter-in-law . . .'

He spoke hesitantly as he walked in front, waving his walking stick. He looked unusually sad. When they reached the house, he coughed several times to announce their arrival. A faint movement was heard from within. He opened the gate and went into the yard.

'I say, the doctor's here.' And to the doctor, 'Please come in.'

Kim *hunjang* told him that he would wait in the *sarang* and retreated. How long since it had last been heated? The floor was like ice. Awkwardly squatting, he filled and lit his pipe and as he put it in his mouth, he looked round. The earthen base showed through where part of the floor covering had rotted during the summer and a bitter wind came mercilessly through tears in the paper door.

(Of all the miserable things you can think of, childlessness is the worst. How can a family line end like this . . . As the last survivor what must I do? It's exasperating. Another year comes to an end with nothing done.)

After the harvest he had gone to Hamyang where he had some relatives. Once again it had been a fruitless journey. The only gain was the information that there was somewhere a certain Kim who, without his parents, wandered around, a man of nearly thirty, and less than a fifth cousin. Apparently he was not a great man but kind hearted, poor, and as yet unmarried.

(During the next year I must by all means find him . . . if I close my eyes without being able to appoint anyone to continue the sacrifices, how can I face my ancestors in the afterworld? Even at the cost of losing the house and selling the land . . .)

Puffing out tobacco smoke, he was sunk deep in thought. When he heard the doctor coming out he sprang up and left the *sarang*. He had no heart to ask him into the freezing room. He did not inquire about the patient but thanked him for his services and walked down the muddy road in front of him, waving his stick as before.

When they reached his house he said, 'Won't you have some lunch? – though there's not much to offer you.'

He was fully aware that, if the doctor went to the Choi house, he would be given a sumptuous feast. But he believed in behaving correctly and it was up to the doctor whether or not he accepted his sincere offer. Knowing this, the doctor said, 'Yes, please. I would be very grateful.'

While they were waiting, they sat facing each other in the *sarang* and Kim *hunjang* said, as if he had just remembered, 'Did you send some medicine to the wife of Kim Pyongsan?'

Without answering, the doctor gave a knowing smile.

'You were wasting your time.'

'I know. He sent it back.'

'If it had been for himself, he wouldn't have been so arrogant.'

'Probably not.'

'How did you know she was ill?'

'Don't you remember? I went there recently.'

'Oh, yes. Because of that son of Pyongsan and the young Miss and the seamstress' daughter.'

'That's right. The young Miss had convulsions. I also happened to see the wife of Gannan *halmum*'s nephew.'

'You mean Yi Pangi's wife?'

'That's right. She told me about Pyongsan's wife. From what she said I gathered it was tuberculosis.'

'Oh, what a shame.'

The teacher, who had been waiting patiently for the doctor to say something about Kim *jinsa*'s daughter-in-law, felt his heart miss a beat even at the mention of someone else's illness.

'I don't know much about her but I gather she is gentle and . . .'.

'That is quite right. She is an exemplary woman. Though she is of lower status, she must have learned from good families – she is really much too good for that rascal. I rather admired the kind concern of Gannan *halmum*'s niece, Dooman *ne*, and I realized how serious the illness was, so I couldn't just leave it at that – that's why I sent some medicine, but that miserable man . . . huh, really!'

'It probably started from worry.'

'If she's just left like that, she won't last long.'

'By the way, what is wrong with Kim *jinsa*'s daughter-in-law . . .?'
Unable to put it off any longer, he brought up the subject.
'I'm not sure. There is nothing definitely wrong but it seems to me that she has had some kind of shock.'
'Shock?'
'She wouldn't answer my questions . . . anyway, we'll have to wait a bit and see what happens. It's not too serious.'
'. . .?'.
'Don't worry. No one can avoid occasional illnesses.'
Then the table came in. Two bowls of plain boiled barley without a grain of rice, soyabean soup, kimchi and some soya sauce – that was all there was on the little table.
'Let's start.'
'I shall enjoy this.'
They began to eat without talking. Kim *hunjang* had a good appetite at any time while for the doctor, though the barley did not go down smoothly, he emptied his bowl with no hesitation. It was his way of repaying the teacher's good will.
After the table had been taken out, Kim *hunjang*'s face showed great contentment as he took a mouthful of rice tea.
'As I mentioned just now, Kim Pyongsan's son is no ordinary troublemaker. As the phrase goes, "Swallows and sparrows can't produce a peacock." He has thieving habits. Only a few days ago, the village people had a meeting at the hall to discuss him, with various opinions on what to do, but we can't really turn him out. It seems that the mother had decided to kill herself and had put a rope round her own neck and her son's when the father, as he's called, ran up and, instead of admonishing his son for his bad behaviour, thrashed his already half-dead wife until she was unconscious.'
'I heard about that.'
'If your son was going to be like that, you'd be better off without one, wouldn't you? But when I think about my own family situation, I am in serious trouble.'
'. . .'.
'It occurred to me while I was waiting for you in the *jinsa*'s *sarang* that nothing is as miserable as childlessness. Even if you can't have

a talented son to carry on the scholarly traditions of the family, you ought to have at least one to look after the family graves. As I looked at that dilapidated room, it made me shudder.'

'Yes – when you see the state of those two, both widowed young . . .'.

'They still breathe so you can say they are alive, but really they are like living corpses. They ought to go out more and mix with people but they seem to regard themselves as sinners – it is pitiable indeed. I know it is important to keep up appearances, but we weren't born just for the sake of appearances.'

'How can you just call it "appearances"? It's the way of human duty.'

'It may sound disagreeable to you, Mr Kim, but what originally were duties have not been kept up as duties. They have become a matter of appearances. It is all vanity. I often think that the common people do their duties more sincerely than the gentry. What's the good of a pile of ceremonial offerings? A bowl of clean water offered with tears of affectionate remembrance would be worth more. I think it has always been the common people who have kept the spirit of the original customs. Look at those who favour the Japanese, cut off their hair and change their clothes to the western style – aren't they all from the gentry? They want to use foreign power to dominate their own people, even to attack them – how do appearances come in there? Well, I seem to have digressed.'

Kim *hunjang*, who had been frowning severely, said with a wry smile, 'You seem to have a rather cross-eyed view of the world.'

'I'd say yours is equally cross-eyed.'

The doctor laughed.

'By the way, I hear that in Seoul something called the "The People's Congress" or the "Congress of Officials and People" has been formed. What's it all about? They say that all sorts of people from high-ranking officers to women and children, and even butchers, gather together to discuss things – is it true?'

'I think so. You know that man called Suh Jai-pil who ran off to America at the time of the Gapsin incident? (A conflict in 1884 between the progressive Independence Party and the conservative government.) He has returned and formed something called the

Independence Club. It seems as though it's their doing. On the other hand there's a faction called "The Royalists" that the third minister Cho Byong-shik scratched together from market pedlars. He realized that if the People's Congress flourished the monarchy would be endangered, and, besides that, the king himself dislikes the progressive party, so he let loose a mob of Royalists to smash them up. It's incredible the way the world is going.'

'Yes, it's extraordinary, indeed. On the one side they call in women, children and even butchers, while on the other side pedlars – it certainly is the age of the lower orders.'

'I wouldn't say that it's their age but rather that they've become the prey of the half-educated and the power seekers.'

After this pointless contest of wits Dr Mun got up to leave the teacher's study on the pretext of the short span of the winter sun. When he had reached the top of the sloping road to the Choi house, he saw the back of Guinyo, who was walking up towards the garden house with an armful of fire wood.

After making a fire in the external fireplace at the back of the house, she listened for a sound from outside. Because of the high bank behind, on which the pavilion stood, the backyard of the garden house was like an empty alleyway. After a while Pyongsan made a silent appearance. They whispered in low tones.

'Whatever happens, he will be back for the New Year, won't he?'

'I suppose so, but if by any chance, he is delayed . . .'.

As she spoke, she spat, which was a sign of pregnancy.

'It would be perfect if he could be frozen to death, or become a meal for a tiger in the forests, heh! heh! heh! . . .'.

'Eat your cake lying down and the crumbs get in your eyes, as they say.'

'Whatever happens, produce a son, just one.'

'How nice that would be.'

'If it's destined to be a success, even if you go wrong, it turns right, you see. From the way everything is going in our favour . . .'.

Whenever she may have come, Dochul *ne* was looking down on them from the top of the high wall, her bottom jutting out above them. Continuing to spit Guinyo said, 'It was lucky he came back at *Chusok*.'

As she said this she recalled the bushy bearded face of Kang *posoo*. (Whether it's his or not only the fertility spirits know.)

'As things have gone this far, we must plan the next step, but don't tell that bastard Chilsung yet.'

'You're the one who should be careful. Ugh! . . . him . . . the father.'

'Why? Is it bad stock?'

'Couldn't be worse.'

'Anyway, I spoke to him when I saw him this afternoon.'

'What did you say?'

'That he'd better not meet you while Chisoo is away. Sooner or later he's got to know, but somehow I don't feel quite happy about him.'

'. . .'.

'That he's there with his goggling eyes on us is what worries me . . .'

Their eyes met. They could each read in the other's a murderous intent. Guinyo turned hers down and spilled her thin snake-like smile.

'That's it, then. Let me hold your hand.'

With a roguish smile he took her hand, smooth and slightly sticky as if it was exuding oil.

'What's this for?'

'Don't be silly. Are you a prudish virgin? From now until Chisoo comes back I can have a good time with you. You are not likely to give birth to a child resembling me – are you, eh?'

'Are you mad?'

'For you too. You've got the taste of having a man by now – your body will fret and you won't be able to sleep.'

Whatever was in her mind she did not shout at him. After a while she said in a low voice, 'In a way you're right, but only if we can strike the right bargain – my body is ruined now, anyway.'

He knew what she meant – that it was to do with the murderous intention shown earlier on.

'Why should we two strike the wrong bargain? We are both in

the same boat – in other words, I'm the oarsman and you're the passenger. To reach our journey's end without meeting any storms, the oarsman must use his brains, mustn't he? We are together for life or death so we ought to be one in mind and body.'

With a repulsive smile he was about to put a hand on her breasts when Dochul *ne*, who had been looking down on them from the edge of the wall with her bottom sticking out over the edge and her mouth hanging open, broke into cackling laughter. Their faces instantly turned the colour of ash.

'Bloody bitch! It's taken ten years off my life!'

Pyongsan lifted his face to Dochul *ne* and poured out abuse as he stroked his chest.

'I know all about it. Ha! Ha! Ha! . . .'.

Though they knew well enough that it was but the chatter of a mad woman, they both seemed to feel a chill.

'You'd better go then.'

She poked him in the ribs.

Dochul *ne* continued to cackle. As if plastered with resin, her hair was stiff and hard and, as she smiled down, her face, with her stiff hair falling round it, looked like that of a devil glaring down on his prey in the pit.

'The daughter-in-law of a good family, you go for adultery, eh? What a naughty girl. I know all about you two. Of course I do. A poor woman widowed young, and, after staying chaste for ten years, she climbed over the fence and ran off with a crop-headed monk, leaving her child behind like rice in a gourd bowl – how could she do such a thing? Mad woman! – possessed! How can a dead child come back?'

'Damn! What blighted luck! That bitch – I'll . . .'.

Breaking off, Pyongsan turned to go out of the backyard and disappeared into the woods. Guinyo, after pushing the wood in the fireplace further under the *ondol* floor, walked down the slope with Dochul *ne*'s mutterings ringing in her ears.

'You rogue! You ought to be chopped to death with an axe! You ought to be made to rot in an adder's den! I see, it's you two, the bitch and the bastard who racked my son's legs! Goboo Paiksan Mountain . . .'.

Guinyo turned and said, 'I pray that this winter you may go out somewhere and freeze to death, you mad thing!'

In Kim *subang*'s vegetable plot there was still some spinach, frozen and reddish. She was passing it when his wife called breathlessly, 'Guinyo! Guinyo!'

'What do you want?'

She turned round unenthusiastically.

'Come here and look at this!'

'What is it?'

'Huh, really, it's not going to hurt you.'

Guinyo retraced her steps. Clad only in her thinly quilted underclothes, Kim *subang*'s wife stared out, her torso thrust out of the door which had been flung open.

'I am doing you a service. Unscrew your face, can't you?'

'Face or no face, put your skirt on for heaven's sake. There are menfolk all around.'

'What will they do to an old woman?'

'If her ladyship sees you, what will she say?'

'I'm stifling . . . come up here a minute.'

'Whatever for?'

'Ah, I'm going to give you something nice.'

She stepped into the room.

'What are you doing? Where have you been?'

'To the garden house.'

'Whatever for?'

'To make an extra fire.'

'Why? The master is not here.'

'He's away, but the room might get mouldy in this damp weather.'

'You should have asked Kilsang to do it.'

'Well, I didn't have much else to do, so . . .'.

'I was feeling peckish, so I've made some marrow pudding . . .'.

'Marrow pudding?'

Guinyo's eyes flashed for a moment and then she opened the door and spat out of it. Kim *subang*'s wife took a china basin from underneath a blanket at the warm end of the room.

'This year the dried marrows are as sweet as honey. So I cooked them with some red beans and rice – it melts in your mouth.'

There was a sound of swallowing in Guinyo's throat.

'As a matter of fact I haven't been able to eat recently – my stomach must have been upset or something . . .'

'Wait a minute. I'll get some spoons and bowls from the kitchen.'

She wrapped a skirt round her waist and straw shoes on her bare feet and went to the kitchen. Guinyo, her appetite whetted, opened the lid of the bowl, dipped her finger into the marrow pudding and licked it. Mrs Kim returned, her skirt flapping. She put a small bowl of boiled, dressed spinach down on the floor and another bowl with a spoon, into which she generously scooped some of the pudding and pushed it towards Guinyo.

'Frost-bitten spinach, it's really tasty. Try some.'

Without needing any encouragement, Guinyo devoured the pudding as if she was famished. She emptied the bowl in a flash and said, 'I feel life coming back to me now.'

'Sweet, isn't it?'

'Yes, it's lovely.'

If there was anything praiseworthy about Kim *subang*'s wife, it was her cooking. She was also fond of sharing it with others and, when she did, she was freehanded and gave out generous portions. On the other hand, the recipient had to put up with listening to her long and tiresome stories which had neither head nor tail. Whenever she got hold of anyone she would stuff their mouths with everything she could find, as if they were starving, and then hold on to them while she chattered away regardless of whether the sun was setting or rising.

'You've never heard anything like it before. Listen to me, Guinyo. My in-laws, I mean the mother-in-law of my elder daughter . . .'.

'Never mind that. Are you talking about the ghost that ate up the seed grain one by one again?'

'Huh, really, why do you all treat me like this whenever I try to say something? After she'd been home in the autumn, I did my best to give her things to take back – I gave her sesame seeds, as much as two measures, glutinous rice, glutinous millet, ming beans and aduki beans . . .'.

She crooked a finger for each item.

'I packed them all into small and big bags. If I had to depend on the master's house for such things, there'd be no chance, would there? Luckily we have some land of our own, so there I was, an old woman who has even seen a grandchild, practically living outside to work all through the summer – that's how I was able to do so much. As they say, "A married daughter is an outsider." Even if I'd sent her back empty-handed, there was nothing they could do. They are legally married – could they turn her out? But do you know what the mother-in-law said to her? "Child, can you live on sesame seeds, with no clothes?" – that's what she said.'

'Who told you that?'

'Nami had to go with her to carry the bundles, big and small, you see. As she had the baby on her back, she couldn't carry much herself. There was a lot of trouble after the marriage. Apparently they were saying, "What's so great about being a farmer?" and "Really, from our side, they are beneath us." They meant that Gaddongi's father was originally a serf. Nobody forced them to marry beneath themselves! They are finding fault with this and that, probably because we don't send them enough. Well, I never learnt to weave, so I can't help it.'

Chapter Forty-Five

AFTER returning to Chiri Mountain, Chisoo wandered for a month or more, leaving no corner untrodden, but he could not find Kuchon. Hwani (Kuchon) who had once gritted his teeth and sworn never to turn to the Master, Ugwan, had finally gone to Yon-goksa to seek the old monk who, in secular terms, was his uncle.

A lonely pine sprung from a seed dropped by the wind on a mountain wall to sprout and perilously to grow, seeing only sun and moon rise, in turn, and set again behind the screen of the peaks that enfold it, can have no idea of the wide world beyond the ridge line, upon which sun and moon also rise and set. As a boy, Hwani had been like that lonely seed fallen on the rock, that single pine tree perilously growing on the face of the mountain. From birth he had grown up to echoes of the forest changing with the seasons: the distant movements of animals, the wing-beat of birds, the scents of plants and wild flowers, the beckoning rainbow in the sky – he had sweated, slept and dreamed in the following of these pure essences. His awareness of a world beyond the mountains, on which sun and moon also rose and set, began one summer day when, following through forest paths a man who had come to find him at the monastery, he came out of the hills and reached an inn. He learned that this man who scrutinized him with such sharp and sparkling eyes was his father. He commanded great hosts of Dong Hak rebels and the boy, following him like his shadow, took part in the uprising, witnessed the bitter end of the fighting and lost his father in the execution yard.

The several hundred miles of the escape route had been a long and thorny path across close-packed mountain ranges. He realized now not only that the sun and moon were different when they shone in the forest surrounded by a screen of mountains from what they were outside, but also that the mountains were the country of the moon, cool and calm, while outside was that of the burning sun – the one a desolate peace like an illusion and the other a reality in which the body writhed in agony.

'Don't resent it. It is the same for all living creatures. Accept it and the pain will turn to pleasure' thus had Ugwan once advised him.

He could run in the hills faster than others on a flat road. He knew the skills of concealment and could catch the scent of the chase as well as any mountain animal, but to be endlessly pursued made one short of breath. He had to run faster than the hunter and with no respite. Even so, he did not have the courage to leave the mountains and go amongst ordinary people. It may be that his birth and upbringing and the disasters that followed had already formed in him the habit of sad wandering, and it may be also that there was a lonesome restlessness already in his blood that made it impossible for him to settle in one place. That seemingly orderly and peaceful village had never been the right place for him to set foot in. On flat land, like a fish out of water, his mountain feet lost their strength and the wisdom of concealment was wasted. Even though he had to go round like a squirrel on a wheel, he could not bring himself to leave the mountains.

Alone, he would rather have fallen and died by some brook or in a gap between rocks than seek the Master, Ugwan, but his companion, filled with fear, was in a state that bordered on hysteria. Even when not asleep, she was delirious, saw phantoms or would run to the edge of a cliff. Hwani, seeing before him the respite offered by death, and an almost ecstatic vision of the end, also found himself screaming in delirium. Treading ground hardened by the bitter wind, followed by the cries of an owl, holding the sick woman's burning hand, he came to stand before Ugwan.

'Save us!'

In the patch of light from the stone lantern, Ugwan looked like a tower. He stood with his back to the dark wood. Penetrating rays of light came from his eyes as he remained motionless. To Hwani, his body seemed to grow bigger and bigger until the whole of it could not be seen, while that of the woman seemed to become smaller and smaller, until the burning hand held in his was all of her, and perhaps in the end even that might turn into froth and disappear – such was his illusion. He bent his knees and knelt on the ground.

'Please save this woman.'

The old monk turned and beckoned. The ends of his robes flapped in the wind as he walked in front of them.

Chisoo realized that Kuchon must have found a safe hiding place.

'No, thank you. I cannot imagine anyone about to die an unnatural death who would depend on me for prayers.'

He remembered Ugwan's words. It was not unexpected, but it seemed strange that only now had he come to realize it. Just before *Chusok*, when he had left the mountain, he had known that he was loosening the reins of the chase and it had crossed his mind then that he was allowing them a breathing space and the chance to find a refuge, nor was it hard to imagine that during his month's absence from the mountain Ugwan might have reached out to rescue them.

Why did he go back there then? Was he again just trusting in chance? He was not a man to be afraid of what others thought, nor with a pious mind towards his ancestors. That being so, it cannot be said that the duty to offer wine to the spirits of his forebears at the harvest season had been an irresistible reason for returning. Apart from that, why was he staying on now in the forests where the snow was beginning to pile up, knowing that the couple must have gone to some safe hiding place?

After they had been in the hills for well over ten days, Dori brought up a supply of clothes and provisions with a message from Lady Yoon that, as they might be snowed up and it would be very cold in the woods, she thought they should come home. Chisoo said nothing about going back and did not even think of it. This vague and unpredictable master was a riddle to Soodong, a riddle of terrible force, that might at any time explode, and he was filled with trepidation as he waited on him each day. Frightful imaginings constantly clung to him, driving him to the verge of madness. He was not timid like Kim *subang*, but he had a nervous temperament. Chisoo had overturned his expectations for not only had he never punished him in any way after their return, but had never shown even the slightest sign of rebuking him for his intention to let

Kuchon escape. It was odd, too, that on this occasion, putting aside physically stronger servants, he had once again ordered Soodong to go with him. While he suffered from being unable to leave the side of this puzzling master, he was also scared of the mountains, these snowbound, desolate mountains. Chisoo and the hills – perhaps he was scared of the hills because of Chisoo, and scared of Chisoo because of the hills, desolate in the snow. It seemed that this fear was something quite different from the fear of a merciless punishment that might be inflicted at any time for the wrong he had done. Of course, there were times when he shuddered, gripped by the illusion that Chisoo's ferocious energy would surge up and the rifle be aimed at his heart, as it had been once at Kuchon's, leaving him to be pushed to the bottom of some snow-covered ravine, but most of the time he could not understand the cause of the fear that would rise like mist from the bottom of his heart. Sometimes he felt as if he was wandering alone through some back-alley of hell and at other times the whole world, emptied even of birds, seemed to be sunk in red mud in which he floundered alone, or he seemed to be standing amongst fearsome cast-iron guards with spears and swords, hundreds and thousands of them; or the naked body of the girl he had seen at Yom *subang*'s house at Gurae clung to him in the shape of a centipede he had killed with a stick at the fire-field farmer's hut.

When he collected himself he saw all around him hills, and the snow that thickly covered the pine trees scattering on the wind, and the unchanging sight of Chisoo, that riddle of a man, steadily walking. Was it perhaps a mental disturbance caused by his long period of abstinence, or the effect of extreme loneliness? It can also happen among animals or birds that they became ill and die from loneliness, which is quite different from the breeding instinct. There are tales of deep affection between birds and fish which seem to indicate how terrible a disease loneliness must be. Of course, Soodong never thought of himself as ill, even less that loneliness could be the cause of it. In other words, it was a kind of neurosis. After losing his wife, the presence of Kuchon, turning up at the Choi house had meant a great deal to him and his love for him, as if he were a brother or a father, must have given him endless comfort. Consequently the sense of emptiness from the loss of Kuchon must have been a greater sorrow than he himself could realize. The best explanation might be, however, that his failure to maintain the role of a loyal servant which until then he had upheld as his moral principle, caused a mental chaos, pushing the loneliness stagnating at the bottom of his heart into a state beyond control.

As well as Chisoo and the snow-covered hills, there was something else he was afraid of – the women in the fire-field farmers' huts who spread out their mattresses every evening.

(Kang *posoo*, please, please, tie up my hands and feet!)

Several times he had had to gag his mouth to stop a scream bursting from him in the middle of the night. When morning came, he was exhausted and came out as if from a tiger's mouth to totter along behind the party.

(I'm sure these damned mountains will eat me up!)

He thought that the mountains wept – it certainly seemed that they cried, or laughed aloud.

Chisoo had once asked, 'Why are you looking so awful?'

'He doesn't seem to be able to sleep,' said Kang *posoo* on his behalf.

Chisoo smiled gently. In the midst of all this, Soodong was quite certain that Kuchon was no longer in these woods.

'Ah, was it them? – a young couple? When I saw a woman like a fairy princess and a tall handsome man drinking at the spring, I knew they must have some special reason.'

'Let me think . . . yes, I remember. It was about sunset. They came in to ask for some food – they didn't look like low-class people, probably about twenty-four or five?'

Arrived in the hills for the second time, they heard this kind of talk here and there, but as time passed all that came was, 'I don't know. I haven't seen anyone like that.'

'It's winter and the paths are blocked. He's not a hunter, and particularly with a woman following him – no, I can't see any point in going on with the search.'

There was no longer anyone who said they had seen them. Even Kang *posoo* mumbled to himself, 'If he hasn't got out, he must be dead – it's no use looking any more . . .'.

517

Soodong did not believe that he could be dead. Meanwhile, though they had shot nothing big, they had bagged enough to save them from boredom. Kang *posoo* often talked about the big tiger he could not catch. He seemed to be much more self-possessed and confident than he had been in the autumn.

(Now she has given her body to me where else can she go? I will ask the master's consent and take her to live with me. I'll work myself to death for her, and we'll have a good life. When you are born you come paired with somebody, so why shouldn't I have my partner? She talks the way she does because she's tied to someone else's house, but certainly it would be better for her – it would be a blessing not to have to please anyone else.)

He continually thought like this, but never talked about her, as he remembered the pledge of secrecy she had demanded. Only in obtaining Choi Chisoo's consent would this promise have to be broken. In this way, he was as thick-headed and obstinate as a bear. In the early afternoon Soodong went down to the village at the foot of the mountain to fetch provisions and clothes that had been sent from home and, as it was a cloudy day, Chisoo and Kang *posoo* rested in the hut.

(I can't put it off for ever, can I?)

Strengthening his determination, he gave Chisoo a glance to sense his mood. As he leaned back against the luggage, he seemed to be asleep and then he opened his eyes. He kept on opening and closing them. With a fire burning, it was not cold in the hut. Kang *posoo* wet his lips.

'Master!'

Chisoo's eyes slowly turned to him.

'I want to speak to you about something . . .'.

'. . .'.

'I – I have something to tell you.'

'. . .'.

He began to tremble. Suddenly Chisoo seemed to look as hard as a rock.

'I . . .'.

Chisoo did not encourage him to speak: the ice-cold eyes just stared at him.

'I mean, Guinyo.'

'Guinyo?'

'Yes, sir.'

'. . .'.

'I mean at my age . . . you may say it's shameless, but it doesn't matter for a man . . . I mean I am still in my prime . . .'.

His face, turned purple, twitched as he stuck out his tongue to wet his lips again.

'I've served you all this time without any agreement. At first I wasn't going to do it even if you'd offered me a million pieces of gold let alone the usual earnings of autumn and winter. I was enchanted by the rifle brought by that gentleman from Seoul, that was why . . .'.

He was in the process of putting his case calmly when he saw Chisoo's eyes and felt sweat trickling down his spine.

'For me, there's nothing else I want: Master, please let me have Guinyo.'

Shutting his eyes tightly he wiped his face with his sleeve. Looking away, Chisoo muttered, as if to himself, 'So it's Guinyo you want?'

'Yes, sir, please. If only you will give her to me, all my life I will do whatever you tell me. Tell me to catch a tiger, and I'll go and catch it . . . tell me to catch a bear . . .'.

'Or a man?'

'Pardon?'

'Would you also catch a man?'

'Yes, well . . .'.

Choi Chisoo closed his lips.

'You mean the runaway Kuchon?'

'. . .'.

'You want me to kill him with my own hands?'

'No.'

'Just to find him?'

'Don't worry about it any more.'

'Sir?'

Chisoo closed his eyes and his face seemed to say that he did not want to hear any more. For the hunter all went dark before him.

In this growing darkness the words of Guinyo repeatedly demanding a pledge of secrecy touched his heart for the first time like the point of a knife.

On the following day the wind was bitter but the weather was fine and the sun shone brightly. The party set off to hunt. As animals tend to come down lower in the winter, it is not a bad time for hunting. Bear hibernate, but as an unexpected bounty you might be lucky enough to discover one asleep. Soodong, who had passed the night undisturbed by hallucinations, seemed livelier than usual but Kang *posoo* was unsteady on his feet. Chisoo, in snow boots with a cartridge belt round his waist, walked in front, carrying his gun. He now had the air of an experienced hunter.

Kang *posoo*!'

'. . . .'

'What's wrong with you? Aren't you well?' asked Soodong, but again there was no answer, only a twitch of his beard-encrusted mouth. They walked on, the hunter treading in Chisoo's footprints and Soodong in the hunter's. In the gorges the frozen streams were as white as if water from rinsing rice had been thrown over them and the rocky cliffs showing through the snow were like an ink painting. No noise except the wind and, as if oblivious of why or where they were going, the three men walked on, hearing only the sound of their own steps. Snow fell from the branches of trees and, now and then, lumps dropped on to their shoulders. Under it the mountain seemed to be sleeping or even dead, yet they felt as though at any moment it might raise its great body and give forth a howl that would shake heaven and earth. In the far distance was Candle Peak, also clad in white, and glistening in the winter sun. They were not on the upper slopes, so the way was not too difficult.

'You live in a world of fantasy even more than I do – a fairy tale. It's not easy in times such as these.'

Chisoo remembered the words of his mentor, Jang-am *sonseng*.

(This is truly a life of fantasy, Master. A hunter who refuses to be tied to anyone else even for a thousand pieces of gold – and it seems this fairy-tale hero has been bewitched by a female. It is all very well for him to be a madman or a hero. But what about me, who can't be a hunter in the hills, nor a man in the village, nor a scholar in his study, can't be the head of a family, even though he has the deeds to a thousand acres, can't be a son to his mother, a father to his child, or a husband when he had a wife – what can a man like this do? Join the Progressive Party? Or the Conservatives? Lead my servants as a general of the Army of Justice? If I can't be a fairy-tale hero, I ought at least to be a madman, but what is there for me to go mad about? Even so, I can't forget all these hum-drum things ... even in these lonely woods, I can't forget that I am someone's son, but why do I feel so strongly that there are no Spirits? Tell me, Master, why is it that, when I take one step out of this mountain, filled with the awesome cries of life, into the world of men, I can't see myself as human? I seem to be a lamp that wants oil, a book covered in mould, a pillar riddled with woodworm, one to whom people seem to be just objects. Is it because I hate them? No, I have been only pretending to hate them. Would you say that neither spirit nor life is real, only an eternal and indestructible time that mocks the spirit yet takes pity on life? The hunter who once despised a thousand pieces of gold must have encountered the Spirit in the woods. When he begged for the girl he must have come to know life. Is he not a fortunate young horse to whom time has given blinkers? If you knew the meaning of time, would you be willing to depart from the world? I can't believe that you would. Now in front of my eyes, there are more grey trees and green pines to be seen than snow. Look! over there, a deer is running!)

He released the safety catch on his gun. The deer flickered among the bare trees. It was a powerful runner and went up towards the ridge of the hill. Although Kang *posoo* had also released the safety catch on his gun and given chase, the animal did not run straight ahead but in a zig zag. There was no need to hurry as, once over the ridge, it would pause to look round. They went up to the crest but stayed on this side of it and kept out of sight as they peeped over. It had gone some distance, though not quite out of range, and was looking round. As they shifted their position to clear the trees that obstructed them, for some reason or other the deer started running again. At other times an oath would have come from the hunter's mouth, but now there was only silence between them, like deep earth sealed under the crust of the earth.

Chisoo shook himself as he stood up and looked back down the hill they had climbed. He seemed to have lost interest in the chase. He saw Soodong slowly crawling up. Kang *posoo*, oblivious of Chisoo standing up and the deer escaping over the ridge, stared at a hill that lay across his field of vision. Chisoo's face in the hut the night before, and Guinyo's face staring straight at him, alternated before his eyes so fast that they blurred his sight.

'Aah . . .'. He bit off a rising moan. An enormous boar, as big as a small ox had stepped into his line of vision.

(Mm . . .)

Guinyo's face, Chisoo's face, and a beast as big as a house, entangled into a ball of fire and revolved before his eyes. A shot echoed through the hills. The echoes continued as the wounded boar turned and ran towards the top of the hill, showing curved fangs like spears. Chisoo, casually standing by, fell flat on the ground. It all happened in an instant, a disaster in the flicker of an eyelid. The boar had disappeared leaving a trail of blood and as he flew to the spot where the scream had come from, Kang *posoo* saw blood spurting like a fountain from Soodong's torn trousers. The hunter groaned.

(How could I, how could I . . .?)

Chapter Forty-Six

CHISOO and Kang *posoo* put Soodong's blood-covered body on the ass – as he was wrapped in sacking and his cotton-padded jacket, the blood did not show, but he looked like a corpse – and at the beginning of the eleventh lunar month they came back to the village. At every house the villagers stood by their gates to watch the donkeys and the people going past. Even the children, who had been flying kites on the embankment wound in the strings and picking them up, ran towards them. The crows, dipping their sleek tails, scattered over the barley fields now white with frost, rose all at once. They skimmed river, hills and sky and interweaved and circled with dismal and eerie cries.

For a while the village buzzed. Here and there women gathered in groups and busily jabbered. In the tavern also words came and went between men from the village and passers-by. Some said Soodong was dead, others said not. He had been bitten by a tiger, or he had been wounded by Chisoo's rifle. His head had been cracked or his bowels burst – and then, of course, there followed the story of Kuchon and the *byoldang* mistress.

Rumours spread to the neighbouring villages and then further. Messages went to far-off places, one after another, that he was dead, that he was not dead, that he had been bitten by a tiger and shot by a gun, in the course of which the victim had changed from Soodong to Chisoo. Kuchon and the *byoldang* lady became the subject of convincing rumours. It reached the ears of Yi Dong-jin in the town. Here it had grown into the tale that Choi Chisoo had been shot and killed by Dong Hak rebels in Chiri mountain, or by Japanese soldiers chasing the Dong Hak. Dong-jin did not believe any of this as he was sure that, if there had been a real disaster, he would have been told, and he had not bothered even to ask Dr Mun for the truth, but after he had been to see the sick Jang-am *sonseng* in Hwasim-li, as he left the courtyard where a lonely plum tree stood, he had turned his mule to the north. When he approached the *sarang*, peaceful as if all were asleep, at the Choi *Champan* house, he called, 'Sog-woon (Chisoo's pen name), are you there?'

There was in his voice something solemn, as of deep and heavy gloom, like a ship with its anchor dropped. Chisoo received him with downcast eyes. As he entered the room shaking his broad shoulders, he said, 'There's not really been a death in the family, has there?'

In contrast to his heavy tone he broke into a mischievous smile.

'So you've come to pay your respects to the dead, is that it?'

'That's it.'

He pulled back the ends of his coat as he sat down, and rested his hands on his knees. Bluish veins stood out on them from the cold, and where the hat string had touched his cheekbones goose-flesh showed. The well polished surface of the brazier reflected like a mirror and the coals glowed like pomegranates as if they had just been replaced.

'As they say, "No one calls when the Premier dies, but they do if his dog does".'

'What are you talking about? There can't be a dog in your house. Do you mean to say a foal has died or something?'

Chisoo seemed pitifully weak and his eyes dim, as if the light had gone out of them.

'Mm. It might be as well to pay your respects early,' he scoffed, and then added, 'When lightning strikes, are you scared?'

It seemed a totally irrelevant question.

'What?'

'A pitch dark night with rain pouring down, lightning flashing and thunder that sounds as if the sky is falling, and you are alone in the middle of it all – would you be scared?'

'Huh, what nonsense . . .'.

'In fact, it's not. Just answer me.'

'Of course I would – who wouldn't be? They say that at such times everyone feels the same.'

'That's right. But why?'

'Why? Because we might be hit by it.'

'Might be hit? In other words, you want a long life.'

'Of course. Who doesn't? Stop talking rubbish.'

Dong-jin's voice became heavy, as it had been earlier, and a look of irritation rose to his face.

'What do you want a long life for?'

'Don't be silly. That's the way we used to talk before we had learned the Seven Books of Wisdom. You'll soon be forty – why be so childish?'

Chisoo took no notice and went on, 'When I was small, I once watched an ant building its house. There it was carrying the earth out of its hole in its mouth. The soil was being piled up round the entrance like a castle. For the little ant, it was indeed a great fortress. Then he dragged up a dry leaf to stop the soil from falling, put some more soil on top, and then another leaf, and so on. There's another thing I saw recently in the hills. A rabbit went by, so just for fun I chased it. It went into a blind corner and I thought that was the end of the chase, but it disappeared like magic. Seeing that I was nonplussed, the hunter who was following me grinned and told me it had gone into a pile of stones. He must be crazy, I thought. The pile had no gap big enough for a rabbit to squeeze into, yet he was telling me it was in there. When I looked at it closely, I saw a bit of fur stuck on the edge of a tiny hole. I moved the stones, quite a few of them, not believing his words – and there were a pair of red eyes. "What do you want to catch a rabbit for? We shouldn't kill anything unless we have to". I was touched by his words so I gave it up, but that hole, you see, that tiny hole, I mean . . .'.

As he faltered his face looked like that of an imbecile. His eyes were more and more losing their lustre. Dong-jin shook his head from side to side as he stared at him in distress. His chest where it showed through the front of his loose open jacket was bony and bluish white in contrast to his face, still burnt dark from the mountain air. Light returned to his eyes. He was like a man awakening from a doze. At the same moment he smirked. It was the expression of an intelligent and crafty animal.

'So, you called at Hwasim-li?' he said, as if suddenly remembering.

'Mm . . .'.

'Is he any better?'

'How can you expect him to be? He has been fighting back long enough. As Dr Mun says, he can defeat even illness with his obstinacy – but how long can it last? He's nothing but skin and bones, and it was painful to see him, but even so he remembered you. I didn't tell him the rumour about your going to Chiri mountain and getting shot.'

'What are you talking about?'

'Why, about you.'

'Me?'

' "Bitten by a tiger and died," "Done in by Japanese soldiers", and what else was it – oh yes, "Shot by the remnants of the Dong Hak." The rumours were dreadful but, thanks to that, you should live long.'

(It was a popular belief that to be falsely reported dead added to one's life.)

Chisoo chuckled. He did up his jacket and, after chuckling on for a while, said, 'I thought I had long since become a corpse, but now it's died again. Ha Ha Ha . . . from the way things are going the news of my death will be like a daily routine so when I really do die, maybe you won't come at all. Ha Ha Ha . . .'.

Dong-jin's face slightly changed colour.

'That could be possible.'

'By the way, the rumour was not entirely groundless.'

'You mean you did nearly die?'

'I did. And Soodong died and came to life again. A boar had its revenge. It seemed to have a clearer idea of what to do than we have.'

'Certainly better than some of the helpless gentry of our country, then.'

Dong-jin, knowing what Chisoo meant by 'a clearer idea of what to do' and also knowing the nature of his desire for revenge, spoke with intent to hurt him, indirectly.

'Still a beast is only a beast after all. He got the wrong chap, not the one who'd shot him. Soodong's leg was done for. A little bit further over and he wouldn't have survived at all.'

'So beast hunts man! Thanks to those damned new-style guns, it seemed that man-hunting was the fashion, and now even the beasts do it too – isn't it wonderul!'

Yi Dong-jin gave him a sideways glance.

(There is no doubt about you being one of the gentry. But you are not a scholar. Your family, from the time they settled here, never were real scholars. I have always been embarrassed by the sight of that relative of yours, with the name of Cho, who put on narrow trousers, cropped his topknot, and tried to be clever – as shallow as a plate. And you, chasing an adulterer with a gun over your shoulder – what a sight! Neither his name nor that of the faithless woman have to be entered on the family tree – so what does it matter?)

Choi Chisoo knew what was in his mind.

'Why? Are you jealous? I'll lend you my gun, shall I? and you can have a go too.'

'That's very tempting. You should have made the offer sooner. While you are about it, you can let me have the other one as well. Though for hunting animals, strictly speaking, it should be a bow, shouldn't it?'

'Both the rifles – so you are going to clear the Japs out of the land completely – is that it?'

'Huh, so you're telling me to follow the example of Kim Ok-kyun? That is possible only when you are sitting right at the top.'

'You mean two are not enough? If so, shall I put you in touch with that gentleman in Seoul?'

'Yes, do. My head will be cut off and that enlightened gentleman who has been looking up for a crumb to fall from the jaws of the Japs will get a good post.'

'When Yoo In-suk, the leader of the Army of Justice, fought the Japanese troops at Choongjoo, do you know what the range of their muskets was? – barely one hundredth of that of the rifles. During the fight they ran out of ammunition and I heard that the group under Ahn Seung-woo went on fighting with stones. Besides, the modern guns are not affected by wet weather. They say that Kim Paik-sun, a man from a humble family, did ten times as much

527

as their leader, but the new guns will do a hundred times as much as a musket.'

They were both aware of the pointless nature of their argument until Yi Dong-jin came out with, 'Are you going to join us, then?'

His tone had changed. Chisoo did not seem surprised. He stared at him piercingly, and asked, 'So, you are leaving!'

'. . .'.

'Going off like that – what will you do?'

Dong-jin was silent for a long time. Resting his fists on his knees, he twiddled his thumbs. They could hear Kilsang panting as he ran up with an armful of firewood. After a while he muttered, 'If I don't, what else can I do?'

'Of course, you know best.'

'Actually I've come to say goodbye.'

'If you must, nothing can stop you. Where will you go?'

'To Seoul first and stay there for a while, as I have people to meet and some business to attend to. Then I will probably have to cross the river.'

'The river? Which river?'

'The last one to the north – what else?'

'On the Russian side or the Chinese? that's what I mean.'

He had asked because he knew that Yi Dong-jin was second cousin to Yi So-ung, who belonged to the pro-Russian faction under Yi Bom-jin and had, in January two years before, raised a troop of the Army of Justice in Kangwon province.

'Once out of the country, it will depend on the circumstances.'

He avoided any further explanation.

'Whether you cross the river or the sea, it makes no difference – they are all the same kind of hungry wolves.'

'I suppose so.'

'At one time, when that fool of a king moved into the Russian consulate, those who fawned on them seemed to have a good time, but now Japan has recovered it's strength and it's aiming to share the spoil. You have made a big decision, and I hope your journey won't be in vain.'

'Don't be silly. Do you think I have some ambition to eat up the country?'

'In that case, for whom are you going away? In this village, there's a madman called Kim *hunjang* who's perpetually howling for revenge on those who killed the queen – are you one of those?'

'Chisoo!'

'Well, go on.'

'You must get out of this habit of mocking people. If you want to make fun of everything in this world, there is nothing that can't be made to look silly. If you are going to be like that, you might as well have never been born. I agree that Kim *hunjang* who doesn't know what's really happening, chatters in a stuffy way and certainly he's pitiable. But he has more real feelings than you do.'

'It's just that you are telling stories and I am speaking the truth. I have a question – please settle my doubts – your reason for crossing the river – is it for the sake of the people? Or the king?'

His thin lips growing even thinner he gave a wicked smile. Yi Dong-jin countered it with a wry one as he said, 'It would be hard to say for the people – or for the king.'

'. . .'

'If you insist on an answer, perhaps I could say, for the sake of these hills and rivers of ours?'

'You do it to get your name on the roll of fame – why else? You've always treasured those words "a man of honour".'

'There is certainly something in what you say.'

Dong-jin chuckled.

'When the country is falling, what's the use of a loyal subject?'

'The heart-rending sight of a falling blossom is a thing of beauty.'

At this piece of rhetoric the two of them joined in a loud guffaw. The wine table was brought in and, as they sat facing each other, they drank as if to fill up the emptiness that followed that outburst of hollow laughter.

'Knowledge is a kind of disease.'

'. . .'

'Listen to me. In a case like yours, Chisoo, it is even worse – an incurable, chronic disease. Come to think about it, our teacher Jang-am must have been somehow lacking in scholastic virtue. It seems that he has produced only colts with horns on their buttocks.'

Dong-jin's face grew pink with wine. As he stared at the cup into which Chisoo was pouring some more, he muttered, 'Sometimes I envy the common people.'

'That's easy enough. Take off your robes, that's all you have to do. Shave your head and you're a monk; take up a knife and go into the slaughterhouse, and you're a butcher.'

'Shut up. Can we take all the beliefs that have been hammered into our bones for hundreds of years and hang them on a tree? There are hundreds and thousands of little roots in our mind so that, if you cut off this one, that one sprouts, cut that one down, and another one shoots out – that is the state that this country is in, very much like a gentleman's head. That's what I mean by saying that I envy the simplicity of the common people – when they know one thing, they think that is all there is to know. For the gentry, there are too many appearances they have to keep up. They look round this way and that, and glance upwards and downwards, and while they are doing this all the time, they are, in reality, neither one thing or the other – that's what they are like, you see. Also for them, all the bits of reading they've done, that is another trouble. How free and easy to be a commoner or a simple man who can set off with a pitchfork or a hoe! They are quick, cunning and courageous in the way that animals are in the face of an enemy. They may not know The Three Bonds and The Five Moral Duties, but they feel in their hearts what is right and what is wrong, when to stop and what to reject.'

'What rubbish. It's like bemoaning the death of a caterpillar.'

'Oh, you're hopeless.'

'You may say that the gentry are rotten and only stuffed with conventions but, thanks to these damnable conventions they don't quite fall to the level of animals! If one has to fall anyway, it's better to become a beast rather than a commoner. Animals are better. To survive, at least they will fight on their own and shed their own blood, but the mob needs numbers. Only when they are swept along in a crowd will they brandish knives or pitchforks or what have you, and gloat with their silly gobs agape over the taste of blood. Cowardly creatures like that, what do they know about "rights" and "wrongs"? Brave and quick with feeling hearts, indeed! Huh, if there was any man who could stand up by himself to face the gentry and say that he, too, has rights as a human being, I would give him a hundred acres of land.'

'What if I say there are such men? Anything carried to extremes becomes narrow. I was not saying that all the common people are like that any more than all the scholars are men of principle. In the disorderly world of the present time, if there are intelligent people who may not know a thousand theories but are clear about one principle and can wholeheartedly perform a definite deed, they may be more desirable than learned people whose brains are blackened with useless letters – that is what I meant.

'To take one example – Kim Paik-sun, a commoner who led the Vanguard of the Army of Justice. As you mentioned just now, he fought ten times as well as the leaders with a scholarly background. The reason why he was so much better than they were was that he concentrated on one thing, and the reason why Ahn Sung-woo failed to send him reinforcements was because he tried to decide things with his mind rather than from his heart. When Kim Paik-sun returned, defeated because of his failure to send them, he couldn't control his anger and he drew his sword and threatened Ahn, for which general Uiam dealt with him by the strictest martial law. That is another example of it – it was not because of his straightforward nature, it was more the result of his being a scholar and an intellectual. They were desperately in need of men to fight, yet a leader who was worth ten Confucian generals was put to death like a dog.'

Uiam (Yoo Insok), a man from Kangwon Province, was an outstanding Confucian scholar who had maintained the traditional virtues and never coveted high office, a man of strict principles and honourable poverty. He was chosen to lead the Army of Justice which rose to avenge the assassination of the queen in 1895 and to resist the enforcement of short hair, and he gathered and consolidated his fellow scholars all over the country by writing and distributing manifestos against the 'Enlightenment' and 'New Laws.' He violently purged local officials and fought the Japanese troops. This Yoo Insok executed Kim Paik-sun according to martial law without even granting him his last wish to see his aged mother, because, as leader of the vanguard, he had drawn his sword at Ahn Sungwoo, unable to control his anger when the well fought battle had been lost from the failure to send reinforcements. His death contributed to their defeat at the battle fought at Hwang-gang, Choongjoo.

Yi Dong-jin was referring to this and Choi Chisoo could make no answer.

'So if Kim Paik-sun had lived, he would now be able to claim a hundred acres – what a shame.'

Dong-jin chuckled and emptied his cup. He went on, 'Whatever their background, many strong pillars have been felled. Not only Chon Bongjun, but that Kim whatever his name was who swept through here – he was quite a worthy character.'

At the words 'Kim whatever his name is' Chisoo's eyes burned and the muscles beneath them quivered.

After staying the night, Yi Dong-jin took his leave – exactly as usual. It was a parting, with the prospect of one of them going beyond the river for good, but neither of them mentioned it. Dong-jin went down the slope on his donkey, the end of his coat flapping in the wind. As they neared the ferry, he asked the servant who led the animal, 'What's going on over there?'

'Looks like a marriage party, sir.'

It was obvious enough even without the answer. The palanquin was already on the ferry and the groom on horseback could also be seen. He stood by as such things as chests of drawers, boxes and the wicker hamper containing the gift of silk were put on board. It was the wedding of Suni. The boatman, in high spirits, was giving instructions in a loud voice as to where to put things, while her father, in brand-new clothes and shoes, with a horsehair hat on his head, stood looking as if he was angry. Her young brothers Dooman and Yongman, obviously escorting her to her new home, had smart new clothes and smirked at the envious urchins that gathered round.

Surrounded by the village women, Dooman *ne* wiped away her tears.

'Because the bride is so good, even in the cold of the eleventh month it's like a spring day when the snow melts – it's lovely,' said Magadal *ne*, speaking loudly as if to make sure the bridegroom heard it as well.

'The river's as smooth as a mirror, like the bride's way ahead,' added Yamu *ne*, 'What else could you expect for the daughter of such a family?'

'It was blowing so hard until yesterday, and the day had been fixed so there was nothing we could do about it. I was so worried in the night that I couldn't sleep. But now the weather's improved, I don't feel so sad.'

Wiping away her tears, Dooman *ne* smiled wryly.

Even on a happy occasion like this, though it was not their own affair, cold war raged beween Kangchong *dek* and Yimi *ne*, who had come out with their arms folded across their chests. Every time Yimi *ne*'s eyes turned towards Yongi, who stood among the men, looking across the river with a blank expression, Kangchong *dek*'s eyes lit up and she shamelessly moved in front of her to block her view. Then, on Yimi *ne*'s side, as if purposely to set Kangchong *dek*'s heart burning, she changed her position as she looked at Yongi with smiling eyes.

'We had better go by road,' said Yi Dong-jin, not wishing to travel with the wedding party. The servant, looking a little put out, turned the mule round.

The day after his departure, two packloads left for the town from the Choi house. They stopped at Yi Dong-jin's gate.

Chapter Forty-Seven

SOODONG, whose survival had been thought doubtful because of the heavy loss of blood, revived a little after a few days of delirium but, according to Dr Mun, he was likely to be permanently disabled. That incident in the wood had seemed to happen in an instant, as in a dream, and in the aftermath of the turmoil Kang *posoo* had followed the party back to the house dazed and stumbling. Once there he was as out of place as a puppy at a house of mourning. All he could do was to sit huddled in the servants' quarters and sigh deeply as he cocked his ears for any sound from outside.

As Choi Chisoo had said nothing, nor the hunter himself, no one knew how Soodong had come to be attacked by the boar, but he assumed that all the servants knew that it was because he had missed it. When they reached the house, Soodong had been in a coma, and the hunter in a state of extreme agitation would shudder as he imagined all the servants brandishing clubs and rushing upon him to beat him to death. The fact that he, the famous hunter, had for the first time missed his target was an even bigger shock than the injury to Soodong. Even after the victim began to improve, he could neither see the incident in perspective nor decide what he should do with himself in the future. The steely silence of Choi Chisoo, when he had begged for Guinyo in the hut, had severely squashed him; the icy face of Chisoo and the smiling face of Guinyo alternating before his eyes as he lay on the ridge of the hill, and then the sudden appearance of a great wild boar with fangs like spears, and the bloodied body of Soodong with white lips and closed eyes – it all seemed to have happened in a dream. Everything was vague and misty and he felt as though he was wrapped in a sea of cloud. Despite it all, Guinyo's face continued to grow ever clearer before his eyes and, however he tried, he could not shake it off.

'Now it's all gone wrong – completely.'

534

As he realized that all his dreams and hopes for her had been shattered, he beat his breast and mumbled to himself in a pitiable whisper, 'Yes, I missed – how could I? Me – the famous hunter.'

Even as he muttered away, he still longed to see her, but she never appeared before him. Sometimes he glimpsed her in the distance, but in the next moment she had disappeared like smoke – truly, he thought, like smoke. There had been several close encounters, but each time she had run off before he had the chance to open his mouth.

(She must have been strictly ordered by the master, otherwise, how could she be like this?)

(Silly girl – no doubt it's because I didn't shoot straight – well, in that case, I will lay down my gun . . . I will give it up.)

From his crouching position he watched the light on the paper door and sensed that it was early afternoon. He thought several times of going to the tavern, but he could not bring himself to move.

'Kang *posoo*, what on earth are you doing there?' – the indignant voice of Samsoo heard in the darkness the night before was lodged in his mind, and he could not leave the room. It had been in the middle of the night. On his way to the privy, his steps had taken him in quite the wrong direction. He saw in front of a room two pairs of white shoes side by side – dainty little shoes. He could hear fallen leaves rustling in the *byoldang* courtyard. From the room the sound of breathing seeped out – the breathing of Samwol and Guinyo. His legs fixed like two stakes, he could not move. Had it snowed and piled up round his ankles, he would not have moved. Had it deepened, burying his knees and on up to his neck, probably he still would not have shifted. He stood in a dream, carried away in fantasy – he could hear Guinyo breathing against his chest; he actually held her in his arms; he was stroking her hair as he murmured over and over again, 'You are my other half, my pre-destined love' completely in the grip of his illusion he stood as if transfixed.

'Kang *posoo*, what on earth are you doing there?'

He raised his dreamy eyes. There was nothing but darkness. The woman in his arms had disappeared, and apart from the weight of his own body on his motionless legs, all was dark.

'Huh, really, Kang *posoo*!'

It was Samsoo's voice.

'What are you up to! Where do you think you're standing?'

'Mm . . .'.

'You've gone mad!'

Samsoo dragged him by the arms. As if coming round, he said, 'Ah!'

'Are you mad? There will be big trouble, you know – standing like that in front of a room where girls are sleeping!'

'Nothing, really. I just . . .'.

He laughed miserably.

'Getting on in age . . . if you want a woman, you'd better go down to the tavern. Do you want to die – standing there like that? You have brought back a man half dead, and is that all you can do – standing with your mouth watering at the thought of a woman?'

It was a just accusation and, even if it had not been, with no defence, what could he say?

'Damn it. Even people like us are not likely to have them. An old thing like a mountain thief from nowhere – you've got a nerve! You must be quite shameless.'

With these words of abuse Samsoo had gone. The more he thought about this event of the previous evening the more he blushed.

'Kang *posoo*!'

'Yes!'

Sitting crouched, he spun round as if clutching air. The door opened from outside and Kim *subang* peered in. The hunter's heart missed a beat. He jumped up in confusion. Kim *subang* entered the room. Of small build, he looked up at the hunched Kang *posoo* as if standing on his toes.

'Sit down,' he said as he sat down himself.

The hunter sat. His face had gone white.

'I have some instructions from the master . . .'.

'. . .'.

536

'He said to tell you that he will see to it, so you can go back to the hills and wait.'

'Pardon?'

'He said that you would know what he meant.'

Kim *subang* now and again glanced with scared eyes at the hunter's evil-looking face — it did indeed seem evil to him.

'Yes, I understand.'

He thought that what had happened last night must have reached Chisoo's ears.

'I understand.'

He picked up the small sack left at the far end of the room and from the wall took the matchlock gun that had accompanied him for so long.

'He also told me to give you some money to keep you going in the meanwhile. How much should I give you?'

Kim *subang*, scared of the gun, moved back as he said this.

'Well, I didn't do it for money. A hunter won't starve as long as he's got a gun.' At the start he had been crazy about the new gun, but now he did not have the slightest desire to possess one.

'Even so, you ought to take something, though I've no idea of what the master's intentions are.'

'If you insist, give me just the travelling expenses.' As he said this his eyes filled with tears. He quickly lowered his face so that Kim *subang* would not see them. When he brought some money out to the gate for him the steward said, 'There is no need to take leave of the master. He has a visitor.'

Even if he had not been told, the hunter had had no intention of going to bid farewell to Chisoo. As he trudged down the slope he thought.

(All I have done has been for nothing. Even if I did miss — there is this difference between their world and ours. They are different — the worlds of the gentry and those of the people.)

For the first time in his life resentment was sown in his heart. He had not bothered to think carefully what Chisoo might have meant by saying he would 'see to it.'

(It is because I am a simpleton that I am so upset. I should have known that gentlemen are the sort who peel the skin off the lower

537

class. I see now what the people who hide in the hills mean. I can understand why the Dong Hak grind their teeth at the mention of the gentry. We are all born as men – even though there is a difference between the upper class and the lower, and even though it can be said that Soodong was injured because of me, we are people who rode the hills together and ate from the same pot all that time. Doesn't he have the least fellow feeling?)

All his resentment sprang from being unable to have Guinyo. He had already suspected in the hills that Chisoo would not let her go, and it was this thought that had spoiled his aim and left an ineradicable stain on his reputation as a great hunter: a man had been wounded and through all this he now trudged down the road with a bit of money for the journey – he saw himself as no better than a tramp begging at the gate and, when his thoughts reached this point, his original instinct to be tied to no one rose up in unbearable rage. The river breeze was more bitter to his heart than on his skin. It was a day he was never to forget. As he went down from the village, urchins skating on the ice in the paddies saw him and ran up with strange cries.

'Kang *posoo*?'

'. . .'

'Soodong's belly was blown up! It's true!'

It was not a question, but an outcry.

'Kang *posoo*! Bushy beard Kang *posoo!*'

'. . .'

'Soodong was really shot!' they chanted in a monotone. It was like the chorus of frogs in the summer paddies. He silently walked on.

'Dumb Kang *posoo!*'

'Bushy beard Kang *posoo!*'

'Prickless Kang *posoo!*'

He did not chase them but they ran off with noisy cries.

'They say that Kang *posoo* hasn't got one!'

They were croaking like the offspring of devils. He who had been known even to children as a mighty hunter had come down to being the object of their mockery. The first time he had passed this way after bringing Soodong home, they had asked with concern. He had not been able to say a word in reply. Known as a mighty hunter, he thought, how can I tell them about how I missed? Besides, the shock had been so great that he was not quite himself. The next time he passed they had asked him again, and the next time, and again. In this way, he had soon become the object of their ridicule.

'Kang *posoo* hasn't got one, they say.'

'Dumb Kang *posoo*!'

'Bushy-beard Kang *posoo*!'

Again they sang in chorus like frogs.

'Stop it, you rascals!'

Suh *subang*, who had come off the ferry and was on his way to the village, saw their cruel teasing and scolded them, but, as if trusting in their numbers and the distance, they took no notice of his glare.

'Bushy-beard Kang *posoo*! Idiot Kang *posoo*! Dumb Kang *posoo*!'

'Little rats!'

Suh *subang* put down his bottle of oil by the roadside to pick up a stone and throw it at them. They scurried away towards the threshing ground, their cries growing fainter.

'The world must be turning upside down – the kids trying to get on top. But where are you off to, Kang *posoo*? I see you've got your bundle.'

With a hand, bent and stiff with cold, he wiped the beard round his mouth, wet with his own breath.

'I'd better go back to the hills.'

'You mean you're leaving?'

'Yes.'

'How's Soodong?'

'They say he'll be crippled . . . but he won't lose his life.'

'What can you do in the hills at this time of year? It would be better to go when the worst of the cold is over.'

'. . .'

'The kids are trying to eat up the grown-ups.'

'Well, goodbye, then. I am going this way.'

When he had parted from Suh *subang*, he went to the tavern.

'Where are you off to with your bundle and gun?' asked the hostess.

After looking down at his bag with the money in it and his gun as if they were unfamiliar he gathered strength and said, 'Where do you think? To the hills of course.'

He sat before the counter.

'I can see you've had enough.'

'Enough to make me sick.'

As she ladled cabbage soup into a bowl, she gave him a quick glance. The room was hazy with steam. A drop hung on the tip of his purple nose. It was about to fall when he sniffed in and said, 'Give me some wine then.'

'Because some one was injured, it's the end of your work there, and he's giving up hunting, is that it?'

'It's come to an end. If there's a beginning, there has to be an end.'

He rubbed his face with his large hands.

'You must have been well paid. This time, don't just waste it, but get yourself married – eh?'

She spoke persuasively as she briskly wiped the table and put the bowl of soup before him. As she laid out a spoon, she said again, 'Pull yourself together and get married, do you hear me? At the age of forty, it's high time you thought about looking after yourself. Don't you agree, Kang *posoo*?'

He noisily sucked up the soup and gulped down the wine she poured out. He put down the cup, and put into his mouth a piece of kimchi, which he crunched noisily.

'Get married? Well, I've probably got enough to pay for today's wine . . .'

'According to Pyongsan, you should have had a fair sum of money.'

'A gentleman doesn't understand another gentleman, you see. It's only the lower classes who understand a gentleman.'

'What do you mean?'

'. . .'

'You mean you didn't get anything?'

'Why do you worry about me, Yongsan *dek*?'

540

'We've known each other long enough – how can I help it?'

'. . .'

'In a way, you can understand it. When someone is badly hurt how can they spare any thought for other things? But you could have stayed on in a warm room until the New Year was over.'

'The New Year's for people with wives and kids. For the likes of me, a rootless tree, what does the perishing festival mean? It's like an egg to a dog's feet.'

He gave a hollow laugh.

At this moment a man entered saying,

'Ah! I've come back 'cos I was dying to see you, Yongsan *dek*. I've been round the eight provinces, every corner of the land, but your wine still tastes the best!'

It was Yoon Bo. His pockmarked face, bluish as if bruised all over, showed yellow teeth as he broke into a smile.

'My goodness! It's the pockmarked plumber! You're not dead but alive and kicking, then?'

'How could I die? Never married, wouldn't I become a bachelor ghost?'

He put down his tool sack.

'Gosh, that's right! Just when I'm in the middle of advising this other bachelor of forty. Oh, dear, so there's two of you – two bachelor ghosts together. I'd better call a shaman to exorcise you if I'm to be safe. It really is a special occasion!'

She was in a happy mood and gabbled on as she threw off the heavy lid of the iron cauldron.

'Who's this? Isn't it Kang *posoo*?'

Yoon Bo bent forward at the waist and, feigning the expression of a idiot, thrust his face over the hunter's shoulder brushing his whiskers. Turning slowly he looked at Yoon Bo. It was no longer the good-natured, slightly idiotic looking face of the old days.

'It's a long time since I saw you,' said Kang *posoo*.

'You look as though you haven't had a mouthful of millet gruel in three days. Why do you look so weak? Whatever it is, we ought to wet our throats first.'

He sat down next to the hunter. Probably he had been handling fish, for he smelt of the river shore. She served both these monstrous men with wine and, while doing so, on behalf of Kang *posoo*, she told the other briefly what had happened to him. Unlike his earlier affectionate manner on recognizing him, Yoon Bo, as he listened to her tale, kept a cold expression on his face throughout.

'So it seems like all his labour was lost.'

She poured more wine into Yoon Bo's empty cup. Without putting in a word, the hunter had listened as if to someone else's story.

'The way you keep on talking about it makes me feel queer. It's like feeling "Happy even if your house is burning down because it kills the bugs." Better not say any more about it. But what I want to know is why did the boar go for Soodong in particular? What could a servant like that do wrong?'

'. . . .'

'Kang *posoo*, tell me why?' he repeated.

'Bad marksmanship' was the blunt reply.

'Bad markmanship? Who by?'

'Who do you think? By me.'

'Ha, ha, that's is extraordinary. So you've been punished by the mountain spirit! A pine caterpillar dies if it eats oak leaves. You took up your gun to follow that gentleman, for the sake of a few cursed pennies from his evil store. I didn't know you were like that. What a state for a mighty hunter!'

He chuckled loudly.

'Even if it was dirty money, if only he had it, he could at least get married, couldn't he?' said the hostess, trying to help by coming in on his side.

'What's the use of getting married? It's better for you or me to wander to and fro to the end of our days, and not be tied down. Seeing the way the world goes – they say there's trouble coming – real trouble – what is the point of taking on any more useless burdens?'

'There's to be trouble?'

Her eyes opened wide.

'So they say.'

'If there's to be trouble, what should people like us do?'

'If we knew the answer to that we would be in heaven, not

542

hanging round here. They say the Dong Hak rebellion was nothing to what is coming.'

'Oh, dear! Do you mean it's already started?'

'The sort of troubles where governors have to run away in their socks are everyday affairs, but according to what the learned people say – I've heard them say it myself – in the end the Westerners and the Japs will come into collision.'

'If they do, they can sort it out between themselves – what's it got to do with us?'

'You idiot. You run a wine shop at a fork and you don't even understand that? Just think about it. They are dying to eat up this land of ours and gulp it all down – where do you think they are going to face each other?'

'You mean that they are going to kick up the trouble in our country?'

'That's right. As the saying goes, "When the whales fight the shrimps get squashed." That's it exactly. Once fighting breaks out, the rifles and cannons used against the Dong Hak will be nothing to compare with it – they say they'll use weapons where one shot is enough to knock a hill down. Besides, the Westerners and the Japs will crawl up from every side, swarming like ants. That will be the end of it all.'

'So, what should we do? We ought to roast some beans and flee to the hills, oughtn't we?'

'You don't want to die then?'

'Who does?'

'Then you ought to go with Kang *posoo*.'

'Why do you all keep teasing me like that? It's not funny.'

'Don't worry. Even after the Choi household have all gone it won't be too late. You can see from the way he goes off hunting with the servants that it's peaceful enough here. Yongsan *dek*, what have you got to worry about? From your sales you must have a bit of money put by.'

'If I had any savings, would I carry on with this job? Anyway, this is going to keep me awake at night.'

She smiled but her eyes were charged with fear. For some time the hunter seemed to have been asleep, leaning back against the wall, but he was not really sleeping. He was reflecting on the night when he had loved Guinyo among the shrubs, in the same way as he had been dreaming the night before while standing like a stake in front of the room where she and Samwol slept. The others thought he was asleep.

'Has anything special happened in the village?' asked Yoon Bo as he ate the soup with rice in it that had been put before him.

'Haven't you been there yet?'

'I was longing for a drink.'

'Dooman's family – they've married off their daughter to Jang *subang* – do you know him? – the man who runs the market boat.'

'Um. He used to be the watchman at a warehouse.'

'Whether or not he used to be a watchman, he owns the market boat now and they say he's pretty well off. When you look at Dooman *ne*'s, they don't have all that much, so everybody says she's marrying well – they also say she received some quite handsome presents. And that scoundrel, Kim Pyongsan – they say his wife is near to death. If you spit blood you're not expected to live for long, are you? Dr Mun felt sorry for her and apparently sent her some medicine, but he sent it back – in the state he is in, trying to keep up his rotten dignity. If you had ten mouths, it wouldn't be enough to laugh at him.'

'What about Yongi?'

'There's too much to tell. The village has been full of it. You know how he was in love with that girl Wolsun, the shaman's daughter? Then when she went off with another man . . .'.

'Another man? What man? Why, I met her in Jinjoo . . .'.

'Did you really?'

Yoon Bo smacked his lips with distaste.

'Anyway, Yi *subang* nearly died of it. He's been ill.'

'He's crazy.'

'As the old saying goes "Shoes must fit your feet!" They are not gentry. As ordinary people, they needn't have made it all so difficult from the beginning.'

'He's stupid. Why couldn't he have both of them in the house?'

'Kangchong *dek* goes too far. Apparently she went and thrashed her like a dog.'

'They say if a man is smart enough, he can keep ten women – he should have seen that that didn't happen.'

'By nature he is so patient . . . nowadays he doesn't let her come near him and they use separate rooms – so they say. She went around crazy for a while, but she seems to have quietened down a bit now.'

Yoon Bo laughed loudly.

'He is a coward,' he said, when at that moment, Yongi himself came in.

'*Hyongnim!*'

'Speaking of the devil . . . Let me have a look at you!'

He had been calling him things like 'coward' and 'crazy' but his eyes were gently smiling.

'Somebody said they'd seen you coming, so here I am. Let's go to our place.'

'No I won't – not to your place.'

'Why not?'

'I hear you're sleeping in separate rooms. Will she want to cook supper for me?'

He blushed.

'We were all worried about you. Come on.'

'Didn't I say "no"?'

'You'll stay here, then, will you?'

Even so, Yoon Bo was grateful for Yongi's goodness in coming to look for him as soon as he knew he was back and, as he glanced at him out of the corner of his eyes, his lips broke into a smile.

'Do as Yi *subang* tells you. He does it because he cares about you.'

The hostess who had been sitting abashed since Yoon Bo had mentioned the separate rooms, in case Yongi was angry with her for telling tales, put in a word of advice.

'I don't know.'

Feigning defeat, he got up. They followed each other out so that only the hunter remained, lying on the floor like a forgotten piece of luggage.

Chapter Forty-Eight

WITH the approach of the New Year the Choi household was busy on all sides. The area round the kitchen, especially, seethed with activity. Guinyo and Samwol, as they had to attend the *sarang* and the inner room as well as look after Sohi in the *byoldang*, though Bongsoon was with her, were unable to assist with the work in the yard. Kim *subang*'s wife, Nami, Yochi *ne*, all the servants and even some extra women called in from the village, under the direction of the cook, Yoni *ne*, had been busy now for several days. The largest steamer set on a huge iron cauldron constantly turned out steamed rice, some for wine and some for toffee, so that each according to its kind, wine now fermented, and toffee in porcelain containers, lay on the cool floor. More rice for honey biscuits and cookies was carefully dried, and there was the constant arrival of things such as raw or dried fish from the town. From the storeroom came dried persimmons, dates, chestnuts, pinenuts, walnuts and ginko nuts, while dry pieces of gourd and marrow prepared in the autumn were brought out to be candied. By the well were two baskets piled high with ginger roots.

Yoni *ne*, sleeves rolled up, whirled her red arms as she washed sesame seed. The quantity was greater than even that of the rice that would be used for cake in an ordinary farmer's home.

In one corner they were slicing fish to be fried, while on a straw mat in the sunny yard of the servants' quarters, other women gossiped as they polished brass bowls for the sacrificial food. Wherever you turned there were piles of food, and at your feet, work to be done. The village women thought of their children at home as they looked at the abundant food. There were probably some of them outside, sucking their fingers as they peered over the wall hoping their mothers would bring out at least a lump of rice. Before they had set off in the morning they had firmly told the children not to follow them, and if the little ones still persisted, had picked

546

up a stone from the side of the path, and threatened them saying, 'Naughty – if you don't go home . . .', so they did not expect them to be there by the gate. Consequently they frowned at Yimi, who whimpered as she clutched her mother's skirt. Yimi *ne* told her to go home, but they were empty words. She picked up some rice just out of the steamer, blew on it as she held it on her palm, made it into a lump and gave it to the child, and now and again, watching the other's reactions, she gave her chestnuts or dates.

Kim *subang's* wife, preparing meat for the skewer, clicked her tongue and said, 'She's spoiling that brat. Why does she have to bring it with her when she comes to work?' but at such times Yimi *ne* pretended to be deaf. Meanwhile Bongsoon *ne* was busy sorting out the New Year clothes, the making of which had kept her up for several nights. This time, though Yimi *ne* and Dooman *ne* had helped her, with no Haman *dek*, progress had been slow, but somehow or other all was done but for a few collars or ribbons. Dooman *ne*, saying her mother-in-law's illness had taken a doubtful turn, had gone home as soon as the sewing was over, but Yimi *ne* had stayed on to join the hired helpers on the outside work. Because of the child, she received some sharp looks, but she was quick with her hands and brisk and lively in dealing with work whether inside or outside.

It was the last day of the last month, New Year's eve, which was, for the children, 'Magpie New Year'. Sohi, wearing a multi-coloured 'magpie' jacket underneath a 'magpie' coat, hopped about in the *byoldang* courtyard with Bongsoon, also in a 'magpie' jacket. She still had not forgotten her mother, but seemed to be enjoying the Magpie New Year's Day. On Bongsoon's forehead was a scar. It was not likely to mar her pretty face, but it would have been better without it. On New Year's eve, lamps burn all night in every room. Crouching at the front of the store room, Dori, having brought out all the lamps there were, was filling each one up to the brim with oil. In the yard of the servants' quarters the pounding involved in making *duk* had been loud since the morning.

'*Aiya hoit!*'
'*Daiya hoit!*'

Strong voices chanted in time with the pounding of the glutinous rice.

'That will do! My poor back! From now on only the ones who want to eat the *duk* will beat it.'

Samsoo stepped back as he dipped his club in water.

'What a fuss to make! If I see you eating any, I'll split your mouth,' said Kim *subang*'s wife, who lent over the tub sprinkling water on the lump of glutinous rice and turning it over, as she gave him a sidelong glance. Gad-dongi, dribbling, stared at his mother. Yongpari stepped forward with a smile. He spat on his palm and picked up the club.

'Let me have a go.'

The women, sitting in a row on a straw mat, patted the rice cakes into shape and rolled them in soya powder tasting a little to test for lumps. Kim *subang*, neatly dressed, sat with Suh *subang* in the best room of the servants' quarters and trimmed chestnuts while his companion snipped at a dried octopus leg, more than a yard in length, to make the shape of a phoenix. Guinyo, carrying a small table of food, lowered it in front of the door of Chisoo's room and called, 'The table is here, sir.'

'Lunch, is it?'

'Yes, sir.'

No more was said, and she quietly slid the door open and took it in. Chisoo looked her up and down, and a curious smile rose to his lips. He then fixed his eyes on the area round her waist. It was by nature on the broad side and, in any case, it was too early for any change to be visible, but his stare was piercing. After coming out she stood for some time in the yard before returning to the kitchen. It was thick with smoke and steam, and a smell of oil assaulted her nostrils. Frying was in full swing.

'Why doesn't Kangchong *dek* even show her nose?' asked Yochi *ne*.

'What difference would it make if she did? She's so slatternly . . .,' said Yimi *ne*, derisively.

Having no ears for these exchanges, Guinyo stood absently with folded arms and then filled a bowl with rice tea and went out.

'Here is the tea, sir.'

548

As before, she quietly slid open the door, entered with the bowl held in both hands, and put it down on the table. Chisoo picked it up.

'Shall I take the table out, sir?'

There was no answer. When he had finished the tea he suddenly said, 'Bitch!'

'Sir?'

'Bitch! Have you got yourself pregnant yet?'

Recollection of the occasion when she had gabbled prayers to all the spirits in the Fertility Shrine had kindled his cruelty. To her, pregnant beyond all doubt, the words came out the blue. Her face turned white.

'Wha..what do you mean . . . ?'

'You are a wicked woman . . . As they say, "a newborn puppy doesn't know enough to be afraid of a tiger." '

'. . .'.

'In view of what you've done, I can't just ignore it, but Kang *posoo* has said something to me and for that reason I am forgiving you.'

'Sir?'

She seemed to be gradually, very gradually, regaining her composure.

'Would you like to go to the hills, burn the fields, and live there?'

'I don't understand you, sir?'

She challenged him boldly. She had quickly grasped that his questions referred only to her relationship with the hunter and had nothing to do with their plot.

'I will give you papers to free you from serfdom.'

It was not really a question of giving her papers or not, as serfdom remained only as a matter of custom, having been officially abolished four or five years before.

'I don't understand what you mean, sir.'

For the first time she raised her face, her big eyes shining faintly as she looked straight at him. His expression, in contrast to when he had roared at her as a bitch, was pleasantly amused.

'You are to be Kang *posoo*'s wife – that's what I mean. I am going to give you to him instead of the rifle.'

His smile instantly disappeared as he stared at the change in her expression. As if suddenly filled with blood, her red eyes, far from avoiding his, gave them a frightening challenge.

'That is not fair.'

Her voice was strong, as if pushed up from her stomach.

'Wouldn't it be better than being a servant?'

'No, thank you!'

'Why?'

'I don't want to.'

'I have promised to grant his request.'

'An old creature like that – it must have been his dying wish.'

'For a man to want a woman is just the principle of *Yin* and *Yang* . . .'

He stopped short and his eyes lit up. His face became strangely twisted and his lips trembled. He roared, 'Tell them to light a fire in the garden house.'

She stood up calmly and, with equal calm, took out the table.

She found Kilsang and told him to make a fire in the garden house and then went behind the storeroom, where no one was about, and squatted down with folded arms. From this shady spot, on which the sun never shone all through the year, rose a chill enough to freeze her stomach. Her whole body trembled, not only from the cold. Her face was flushed, which was rare for her, and her cheeks were ablaze.

(What must I do? To cut him up and eat him wouldn't be enough for that enemy. I can't wait, I can't wait another minute!)

She ground her teeth.

(Whatever happens, I can't put it off until after dark!)

There was no need to worry about how much he knew of the relationship between Kang *posoo* and herself. Before he could go to his mother and say, 'I have decided to give Guinyo to Kang *posoo*,' she would have to bury that mouth of his in the darkness. Once he had said, 'I have decided to give Guinyo to Kang *posoo*,' it was all over. Their hopes would collapse like a castle of sand and the child inside her would be but a useless lump of blood, an object to be thrown away in the woods. Since the day he had returned with Soodong on the back of the donkey and greeted his mother in the midst of the general confusion, mother and son had had no further meeting. There was thus no reason to think that he had told her that he meant to give her to the hunter – it was not too late. At this point a horrible sound issued forth from between her teeth: the face of the devil, the smile of the devil, the rapture of the devil, the incarnation of revenge.

(Could I live with Kang *posoo*? Go and live by burning fields?)

Now it was not ambition; it was revenge. Long before, when Sohi had spat on her, she had first sharpened the knife of vengeance. Now there would be no hesitation in striking with it. They had already decided to kill him, and she would not have been reluctant in any case. Now, stronger than the dream of riches, even of measureless riches, was the wrath of a woman scorned. It was not that she had been in love with him, but that the resentment of a servant trampled on burnt more fiercely than the ambition to be wealthy.

(That bastard has never respected me as much as the dirt under his finger nails!)

Hers was the kind of simple pride that differentiates between silk and rags. She had given her body to the beast-like Kang *posoo* and slept with worthless Chilsung, yet still she had hoped to appeal to Chisoo – was it love? or vanity? or just persistence? For Guinyo, who had performed ritual ablutions and prayed to Buddha before committing a deed that increased the burden of karma, everything started from outside. Nobility, desire, or love had their origins externally. As long as the outside was fresh and fragrant, the inside did not matter – the inner garbage that she alone knew did not release its odour. Thus she was not a woman who had known loneliness or awoken in the night to think of death, nor did she fear Buddha. She hurried across the vegetable patch and up towards the garden house. She went round to the back where Kilsang, having lit the fire, sat sprawled in front of it busily whittling away with his pocket knife.

'Kilsang!'

Absorbed in his carving, he started and sprang up. He still had the knife in his hand but the piece of wood rolled away on the ground.

'Goodness! You gave me a shock.'

'You must take a message.'

'Where to?'

'The master will be coming up here soon. You know Kim Pyongsan, Gobok's father?'

'Yes.'

'Go and tell him to come here. It's the master's orders.'

As he was about to go, she added, 'Tell him I sent you, and he's to come direct to this place as the master will soon be here. I will look after the fire while you're gone. Run along now.'

He ran off down the hill.

(What shall I do if he is not there?)

She hurriedly took out some of the burning wood and put it in the other fireplace under a small room attached to the one used by Chisoo when he came there. It had a back door and a fireplace below it. As it had not been used for some time, the fire was not easy to start. Her eyes running with tears, she managed to get it going and anxiously went round to the front. To her relief, she saw Pyongsan coming with Kilsang, his round body rolling and arms swinging. She went back to the fireplace and sat down. When she heard him reach the front of the house, she gave a loud cough. Then she called, 'Kilsang,' and he came round.

'Hurry up with another load of fire wood.'

'I thought I'd brought enough.'

'No, it isn't. As the side room was damp, I put some there too. We must make it nice and hot before the master comes or he'll strike like a thunderbolt. Why didn't you lay a fire for that room? It's New Year's Eve so there has to be a fire in every room.'

He ran off again and when Pyongsan saw that he had gone, he hurried round to the back.

'This is serious.'

'What's happened?'

He came close.

'Don't say anything, but just listen – before Kilsang is back again. That bastard told me today to go off with Kang *posoo*.'

'Really?'

'Don't speak – just listen. He hasn't seen his mother since he

552

greeted her on the day he came back from the hills, so he couldn't have told her he was going to give me to the hunter. However, now it's urgent. If she has the slightest idea of what he is intending to do, it's all up. Just a minute – please listen. So, before he can tell her, we've got to take the plunge once and for all. He ordered the fire to be lit, so he's going to come here to sleep. I suppose it's because it's so noisy in the house that he intends to come up here. Get yourself ready and wait at the shrine. I'll keep my eye open and slip out at the right moment.'

She finished it all in one breath and glared at him, as if to put pressure on him with her tremendous and frightening determination. His face stiffened and the upper lip over his crooked tooth fluttered as if he was going to say something but, before he could open his mouth, she went on, 'Now, go and stand at the front. When you see Kilsang coming, pretend you've been waiting and say something like, "Never mind, I'll go and see him myself," and go down. On your way down just call in at his room to say "hallo" so that Kilsang doesn't suspect anything. It will save all sorts of gossip in the future. Go on, then.'

She pushed him away. It might seem a reckless way of rushing to a conclusion, but for such a short space of time it was a remarkable plan. As he had been told, Pyongsan was hanging about in front of the house when Kilsang came up with an armful of firewood.

'Did he say he was coming?'

'I'm not sure. If he said he would, he will I suppose.'

'Well, there's no need for me to wait here. I might as well go down there.'

When he reached the *sarang*, Pyongsan chatted about this and that, in a way that was neither greeting nor gossip, to Chisoo, who had no reason to be pleased with him, and then went away with an indecisive air. Chisoo wondered what could have brought him, but he did not bother himself with it, knowing that, as it was New Year the next day, he might have come to ask some favour and then decided against it and gone off again.

In the darkness of New Year's Eve, Pyongsan waited a long time for Guinyo to appear. He was shivering.

(What a terrible creature she is! And why doesn't she come?)

He stamped his frozen feet. He was strongly tempted to light a small fire, but had to endure without.

(It's too cold to do anything.)

Momentarily he felt ready to throw over the whole scheme. Not only the cold, but he felt fear rise shuddering from the bottom of his heart. But when she appeared in front of the Fertility Spirits Shrine, he was the first to speak: 'Is he in the garden house?'

'He's sleeping there now. Here, drink this first.'

She thrust a porcelain flagon into his hands. It was wine which she had brought to protect him from the cold and embolden his heart.

'Mm . . .'.

He took the bottle and gulped it down. As he handed it back he said, 'That's better!'

'Are you all right?'

'What do you mean?'

'You're trembling.'

'That's just the cold. It will all be finished tonight. Then the world will be ours . . .'.

He spoke as if to cheer himself up.

'How will you do it?'

'I know what to do. You can just sit back and watch.'

He hadn't the courage to explain to her his methods of murder.

'That bastard! I hate to think I won't see him die.'

'Once he's dead, that's all there is to it.'

He began to tremble again.

'By the way – I nearly forgot. I'd better warn you just in case the question arises later. If you are asked why you wanted to see Chisoo this afternoon, say something about advising him to inquire into the whereabouts of Kuchon, and make sure you don't slip up.'

Then she added that he had better get on with it soon, as Chisoo was likely to come down early to offer the sacrifices.

He had another drink from the bottle. A pitch dark New Year's Eve, with lights twinkling in the village. When she came down to the house with the empty bottle she did not go to sleep but went to the yard in the servants' quarters, walked up and down for a while, and then went into the kitchen to join those who were preparing food and chattering. Pyongsan groped his way over the steps leading to the garden house and went towards Chisoo's room, treading silently. Not even a shadow – it was just the right kind of night. He listened for sounds from inside the room. Steady breathing could be heard. He must be fast asleep. He pulled at the door handle. It was locked on the inside. He applied a palmful of saliva to the door, wet the paper and made a hole through which he unclasped the ring. The door opened and then shut. How long had it taken? A long time passed.

A sound of choking . . . A low voice, the sound of legs thumping up and down, a low gasp for breath, again the flailing of legs, a sound of writhing, more noises . . . the sound stopped. Time passed. Sounds of gasping and squeezing of breath were heard. They grew louder. There was a hiss as air came through gritted teeth; the door opened, and a figure leapt out. It landed on the ground. In front of it rose another in black. The latter shook with giggles.

'Who . . . who's . . . who's that?'

But his voice would not come out. Pyongsan seemed to be crawling for a moment and then he rose and went out of the yard of the garden house. His original plan had been to make off through the woods to avoid the village but, having forgotten about that, he ran towards it like a mad man. The village was all awake. It was not until he had reached the road in front of his own house that he came to his senses. A light showed in the small room but there was no sound of weaving, no sound of movement at all. He crept into the large room but came out again, kicking the door, and ran back to the small one. He opened the door and went in. Haman *dek* was bent over the loom. After staring at her blankly he barked, 'What the hell are you doing with the light on!'

His fists were tightly clenched and his plump body shook.

'I said what the hell are you doing with the light on!'

She lifted her face. It was a miserable face distorted with pain.

'Why don't you stand up?'

'Ah – h!'

She shuddered.

'Oh! What an awful dream! – I've had an evil dream.'

His fists flew.

'I'll split your mouth! Go to bed, you idiot!'

He grabbed her by the neck and dragged her away from the loom.

'What is the matter with you?'

'Umn! I must kill . . .'.

'What is the matter with you, dear?'

He knocked her down. Her body was nothing but bones, like a dry winter tree from which the leaves have fallen. He pounded it with his fists, tugged her hair at the roots, kicked her and then screamed as he indulged his lust. He did not stop there. He repeatedly moaned and assaulted her, turning her body, now like a corpse, this way and that. He was in fact repeatedly discharging, as if vomiting from fear.

After he had run away, the dark thing in front of the garden house, which was in fact Dochul *ne*, giggled on and then began weakly to cry.

'What was wrong with my son for the wicked bitch to run away on her wedding night? Where shall I find her and bring her back? May the High God look down on him. Guardian Spirit, look down upon him. When my son makes a glorious homecoming wearing the badge of honour there will be musicians – three stringed instruments and six percussion, in every village, monuments of praise, even Choon-hyang will be dazed.'

The mad woman mumbled on endlessly before she rose to her feet.

'My goodness, what bitter weather, like pepper. We've got the room for the newly wed. The bride and the bridegroom will be frozen stiff. I must light a fire. I'll light a fire – it'll be adding to my good deeds.'

As if she was not in the least hindered by the darkness, she ran down the slope like an arrow and into Kim *subang*'s vegetable plot. The house was empty, as the whole family had gone within the walls of the Choi house to work through the night.

Only a kerosene lamp on a pillar shone over the yard. Entering it, she took the lamp off the hook. The breeze whistled through the bamboo grove. The loose paper around the door frame fluttered. As she walked up to the garden house, fine frozen snow crackled down. She walked to and fro in the yard ceaselessly muttering, 'I beseech thee . . . I beseech thee – may my prayer be granted,' and then went up the steps to the pavilion. She entered it, still mumbling, 'May my prayer be granted . . . may my prayer be granted,' and went on, as with firm steps she walked round and round the wooden floor, 'May my prayer be granted . . . may my prayer be granted. Oh, dear, I must light a fire, lest my son be frozen stiff.'

Leaving the lamp on the wooden floor, she ran down the slope again like an arrow. In Kim *subang*'s yard she picked up a bundle of dried pine branches. It had needed a strong man, straining his knees, to tie them up, but she put it on her head as effortlessly as he might have done, and walked up to the pavilion, beating the air with one arm while the other balanced the bundle, and put it down on the floor. She repeated this three or four times, piling up the dry branches on the floor.

'Well, that will be enough to make the room nice and warm . . .'.

Burning fuel from the kerosene lamp that had overturned when she threw on the last bundle of branches spread slowly towards the pile. Meanwhile the granular snow had ceased and it was lightening in the east, urging on the solemn sunrise of New Year's Day. Flames crackled as they consumed the pine branches. The whole pavilion was lit up. Dochul *ne* floated in a dance and, still dancing, went down to the yard of the garden house.

'I beseech thee, may my prayer be granted!'

In the courtyard covered with granular snow she lightly bowed again and again. With dawn, the unsleeping village seemed to grow even more lively and active. It was from there that the burning pavilion was first noticed.

'Fire! Fire!' someone called, and it echoed here and there. 'Fire! Fire!'

In a matter of seconds people surged out from the village and the house. They ran up the slope each with a stick. When she saw them coming Dochul *ne* ran off towards the pavilion, shouting that the soldiers were coming to take her son.

Kim *subang* ran first to the garden house.

'Master! Master!'

Tiles came flying from the pavilion.

'Master!'

He burst into the room.

'Master!'

He dragged out the body. It was only after he had dragged it out that he realized that Chisoo was dead.

'The Master – the Master – the Master has passed away!'

A scream spread through the crowd.

'The Master has passed away – '

'Get hold of that bitch!'

'The master is dead!'

'Catch that bitch!'

Fire, death, buckets of water and sticks – in a moment Dangsan was pandemonium. The sun rose. As it rose it bestowed a solemn New Year blessing on earth and heaven. River, sky, and land, all were beautiful and made new.

Dochul *ne* was burnt to death along with the fallen pavilion. Choi Chisoo, last male survivor of his family, strangled by a length of hemp cord, had bidden farewell to the world.

Chapter Forty-Nine

THE lone shadow of one who has lost the others in a desert – or could she be likened to a blind snake crawling into a patch of reeds? Yet Lady Yoon's self-control was astonishing and magnificent. There was not the slightest change in her appearance: her tall straight body now wrapped for mourning in plain white cotton skirt and *jogori*. Her lips were split and blood-stained but her eyes shone brightly and all her words and movements were clear cut.

Originally from Yongchon, no one knew just when the Choi family had first established themselves in this village on a hill that overlooked the river, but for more than a hundred years they had lorded it over the area through the power of scholarship and property, largely built up and preserved by the hands of strong women. And now a great crowd assembled for the funeral of the last male descendant. As chief mourner – a little girl. Pyongsan was also amongst the crowd. To Kim *hunjang*, whom in the past he had always ignored, he bowed politely and said, 'What a strange thing to happen!'

Kim *hunjang* was about to shake his head solemnly, sigh, and say 'Truly, a strange affair,' but, noticing that Pyongsan's hat was askew and that his tiny eyes seemed to be full of wine, he smacked his lips and turned aside. The eyes of the rejected Pyongsan busily searched those of others until they reached the face of Guinyo. This time the lumps of flesh beaneath his eyes trembled violently. Amongst the many mourning servants, her appearance of sorrow was distinctive.

(How many men will that bitch eat up?)

As if starved for conversation, he grabbed hold of Suh *subang* and hastily said, 'What a strange thing!'

In fact it was far more than a strange thing. For the people of the village and for all those who had rushed to join them from near and far because of ties of one kind or another with the Choi family, it was a staggering blow, almost as if God had been murdered. There was no space in their minds to inquire into the cause of this unexpected disaster or to chatter with curiosity. A little more time would be needed for that. Whatever the circumstances they were practical creatures, bound by habit. In a land which, apart from a few items of culture from the North, had been completely shut off, all its necessities, spiritual or material, had to be supplied from within itself. It was probably for this reason that the political system of the Yi dynasty in the Korean peninsular had sustained itself so firmly through five hundred years. This was an unprecedented length of time during which, one might say, the regime had become as hardened as was possible, and also old and exhausted. In such a society, any change is slow, so that, whatever a person's occupation, there is usually little change in their circumstances, rather like the way that they take out their well-worn tools according to the season and then put them away again. This applied particularly to the farmers who, apart from being sensitive and fretful over the changes in the seasons, were faithful servants of the existing order as they clung to the life of the soil, which, apart from natural disasters, never changed. If the seasons were kind, and the extortion by government officials moderate, if the autumn harvest was enough to last until the barley came in spring, if only they could keep the *ondol* floor warm, and had enough cotton to pad their clothes, they were bound to be conscientious in carrying out the obligatory rites, rather like traders well trained in commercial etiquette.

They offered thanks to god, to the king, to guardian spirits, and to their ancestors. To say that the farmers were realistic could mean a certain humility in recognizing their own status. Perhaps it was just because of this meekness in accepting their social position that they had been so shocked by the death of Chisoo. It was, indeed, as if God himself had been murdered. Of course, they had never seen God and, if it came to that, they had never seen the king either, nor had they any idea of what a guardian spirit or their ancestors looked like. They might have seen, when young, ancestors of up to three or four generations, but certainly they had not seen them since their death. The only way in which they sensed God was in sky, sun and moon, starlight or cloud, the river and all the massive things, or mysterious, or dangerous things that existed in nature. They felt the presence of the king in the six-sided cudgel brandished by the police, and in the grand procession of the local governor; the guardian spirits in the shaman's exorcism; ancestors in the tablets. God was one who had created all things and, specially significant to farmers in that the four seasons obeyed his will, and he governed the human affairs of birth and death. As for the king, he was the father of the country, who owned its land and to whom were due the duties of military service and compulsory labour, who received the taxes and dispensed the law. The guardian spirits, and all other spirits and ancestors, were those who protected the family. As they acknowledged the power of these beings to send good or evil, pain or comfort, it was natural for them to offer thanksgiving when they had full stomachs and enough to wear – only in that way could they be assured of successors in the family line. While the give-and-take relationship with these invisible beings was rather a matter of habit, and taken for granted, the Choi house had been for them a reality more clearly and closely visible. Like themselves, the masters of the family had two eyes and a mouth, and took three meals a day, people they could see before their eyes, to whom they were bound, and to whom they offered thanks. The owner of the whole country, the king, was far away but, as land-owners who received tribute from their many tenants, the Choi family were near. For the peasants, whose life depended on his land, the master, Choi Chisoo, in the fortress-like tiled house that rose high on top of the hill, waited on by many servants, had been, regardless of much gossip, the symbol of an absolute authority. Just as they recognized God as ruler of the earth, so they recognized the wealth of the house which gathered in ten thousand sacks of rice. Though affected by this wealth and power, they did not concern themselves with how the wealth had been accumulated or the power consolidated, for they knew of no other life beyond its boundaries. As long as the harvest was not so bad that they starved or went naked, and the extortion grew no worse, such questions had no reality for them.

'Of all the sad things in the world, nothing is like hunger.'

The misery of hunger. A hand like a fern shoot gleaning barley; a husband leaving the village with his wife on a hand cart, her eyes hidden in a face swollen from starvation; brothers fighting at the table over a piece of salted fish – even conditions as harsh as this were not seen in relation to the abundant acres of the Choi family. The fields were the property of the house, and so were the ears of grain that grew on them. While they lived on such a precarious margin, the farmers disliked any form of change. People such as the wandering carpenter Yoon Bo, or Chilsung with his past as a migrant pedlar, who had tasted life in other regions might occasionally deplore the unfairness of the world or make caustic comments on the acts of wickedness by which the Choi family had accumulated their wealth, but they paid no more attention to these scathing words than to the chanting of a mendicant monk outside the gates of someone else's house. A wise statesman with a comprehension of this precarious balance would have made it his first priority to keep the peasants pleasantly asleep, and through the generations the great women of the Choi family might be said to have performed a similar task. Anyway, this had been the peoples' attitude towards the house. Accordingly, they had shown little interest in their master while he was alive, but with his death it was very different.

'At the time of that terrible famine, perhaps because he was out of his mind after starving and starving, father asked for some meat – at a time when the river was dried up and the bed cracked, so that there was not even a bit of fish to offer him, let alone meat. At that time, we couldn't give him as much as a bowl of gruel – even now, when I think of it, it breaks my heart – and because of getting the children married, he was pushed aside – how will I ever be able to put a piece of meat in my own mouth again?'

It was common enough for sons to beat their breasts at their father's funeral with such words, and someone, knocking out his pipe against the wall, would reply, 'Well, it's a good funeral. He's lived his full life. He was ready to go.'

When someone's son was drowned in the river they would say, 'You'll have another one. "Better without brats" as they say. After all, the monks live without them.'

They watched unmoved as the mother screamed, asking to be

taken as well, or the father ran, as if mad, to the burial hill behind with a hoe in his hand. Not only the onlookers, but those who had lost children, parents, or even a husband needed quickly to forget the parting, and indeed they did. Worry about lack of rain, or worry that the banks of the river would burst from too much of it, watching the sky to catch the right moment for sowing, drawing water for dry paddies, day and night, they had no choice but to bury in forgetfulness their sorrowful partings.

'Of all the miseries of the world, nothing is worse than hunger.'

For them, both sorrows and pleasures were simple, but the disaster to the Choi household could not be simple: there seemed no obvious reason why it should be a more sorrowful occasion than their own family losses, yet the women wept till their skirts were soaked while the men, speechless, snuffled. They cried at the sight of the unweeping Lady Yoon and of little Sohi as chief mourner in the same way that spectators at the folk-drama of the Dutiful Daughter Shim Chong burst into tears at the climax when she throws herself into the sea. That was it – it was not their kind of death – it was more that they were crying over the fate of characters larger than life from an ancient tale.

After the funeral was over, they had expected a rite to appease the spirit of one who had died an unnatural death, and on that occasion too the women's skirts would be soaked, but their expectations were not fulfilled. The family held no further events. The disordered New Year festival passed, and the poles with grain for a good harvest set up at the full moon, fifteen days later, were replaced by Granny Yongdung's water pole.

It was now the second month of the lunar year. The breath of spring was felt on the earth, and the bamboo grove by the river took on a softer hue. Food from offerings was unobtrusively shared among the villagers as they prayed for another bountiful year.

'*Songnim*, why is it so cold? The wind is so strong you can hardly open your eyes.'

Yimi *ne*, with blue lips entered Dooman *ne*'s room. Dooman *ne*, mending a sock, said, 'Yes, this year Granny must be coming down with her daughter-in-law as well. It's unusually strong. Sit down here.'

She pulled up one corner of the quilt that covered the warm end of the floor.

'Whether they're people or spirits, I suppose, they must hate their daughters-in-law just the same.'

'Maybe . . . it depends who it is. Our mother wasn't like that. Now she's gone, I miss her like anything.'

'Yes, she was really blessed. She saw her granddaughter married and departed without any regrets.'

'That's true. Still, I wish she could have lived a bit longer . . . Even though she had to sit propped up against the wall, it was a great comfort to have her . . .'

'Just as well she went. It was well timed.'

As her body began to thaw after the cold outside, Yimi *ne's* cheeks grew crimson.

'Isn't it cold! Are you at home, *songnim?*'

It was Magdal *ne.*

'Come in.'

She looked at Yimi *ne* and chuckled.

'So you're here, Yimi *ne.* I know why.'

'You know? What do you know?'

As she thrust her legs deep under the quilt Magdal *ne* said, 'I've heard about your great fight with Kangchong *dek.* I can understand why her eyes lit up, though. I suffer from jealousy myself – how can she help it?'

'What is there for her to be upset about?'

'You look like a gourd flower, or a peach blossom – how can anyone help being jealous? And such lovely skin . . . Really, you're too pretty for a farmer's wife.'

'Don't flatter me.'

As she lowered her eyes, she could not but be pleased.

'Why should I flatter you? I know I won't get anything out of you. I don't even know when your birthday is. I've had some of everyone else's birthday cake but I've never had even a bowl of cabbage soup from you.'

'Don't exaggerate so. It's only in winter that my face looks all right. As soon as work starts in the fields . . .'.

She tactfully avoided an embarrassing subject by turning the conversation back to her face.

Magdal *ne*, smirking, said, 'Don't talk about it. This face of mine is just the same in summer or winter. Unless I rub it against the bark of a tree to peel the skin off. Damn it, what do you need a pretty face for if you've already got a man? Lend it to me, and I'll see if I can get one.'

Dooman *ne* frowned: 'Don't be so disgusting, Magdal *ne* – that's the trouble with you.'

'*Songnim*, don't say that. It's not the same with a full stomach as it is with an empty one. You've got everything, so you've no right to talk.'

'By the way, *Songnim*.'

'Why? What are you going to say next?'

'I mean the Choi house – the gentleman who's died – apparently the fortune teller in the town is going round saying that he didn't die a natural death.'

'That's nothing new – everyone knows.'

'I don't mean that. He says that, if Soodong had died, it wouldn't have happened. In other words, he was taken instead of Soodong – anyway, Soodong, who was supposed to be dying, seems to be getting better, little by little.'

'That's a lot of nonsense.'

'According to him, it's all because they neglected the shamans. When Wolsun *ne* was alive, they used to have rites every month, and now they've stopped altogether, so the spirits thought nothing of swopping two lives – that's what people are saying. It seems to stand to reason.'

'Don't be silly. He talks like that because they don't give him anything, so his belly aches. If everything is decided by your former existence, how can it be swopped with someone else's?'

'You can't just say that. The former life can't be all that different from this one, can it? There must be times when things don't go quite according to plan.'

As if such things did not interest her, Yimi *ne* turned the conversation.

'Listen to me, *songnim* – you know at the time of the funeral.'

'What funeral are you talking about?'

'The Choi funeral. Did you notice Guinyo?'

'Why?'

'Did she look her natural self?'

'Well, I don't know.'

'She looked about to die herself, didn't she? – out of her wits, as if she was mad?'

'She did look very sad.'

'Who didn't? Everyone cried.'

'Come to think of it – I have heard that she goes to the grave every day to weep, but I didn't pay any attention to it.'

'Do you think that he could have loved her?'

'You can never tell with men and women. What's the use of talking about it now?'

Dooman *ne* casually dismissed the subject.

Magdal *ne*, who had been patiently listening without interrupting, abruptly put in, 'I heard an extraordinary thing.'

'What was it?'

Yimi *ne* quickly took her up.

'There will be trouble if it leaks out.'

'Why should it leak out?'

'It's just a rumour – I might have to eat my words.'

'To this day I've never caused any trouble through gossiping.'

'There's a rumour that Guinyo is pregnant, though, of course, you can't be sure until you've checked the pulse of what's under her skirt.'

'Really? Fancy that. So it's the master's child – is that what it comes to?'

'It can't be,' scoffed Dooman *ne*.

'If that is so, if – if it is – if it is – if she has a son – oh! – really! *Songnim*, it's amazing – an inheritance of a thousand acres . . .'.

Yimi *ne* was gasping for breath, but Dooman *ne* said confidently, 'It isn't possible.'

That night Yimi *ne*, waiting for her husband who, recently, had done nothing but go out drinking, fell asleep with her nipple still in her child's mouth.

It was shortly before midnight when he came in drunk and gave her a kick. She sat up angrily and gathered her hair.

'No doubt it's a good life going round drinking, but why kick me? Kicking somebody when they're asleep!'

'Because you're like this, nothing ever comes right. Why can't you stay awake to welcome me home? You've never done that once. Nothing's ever come right since I met you.'

'You'd make a cow laugh!'

He kicked her again.

'You bring bad luck. I can't understand why everything goes wrong. As they say "Ten years' study all in vain."'

'Hm. You've been cleaned out in some gambling den. Even if it's the end of the world, you're not going to take any grain, I'm warning you.'

'Gambling den? Do you think I worry about a place like that where a few miserly pennies roll about? Don't talk about that sort of chicken feed! You unlucky bitch!'

'I can't stand hearing that any more. Just tell me why I'm unlucky. Have I ever taken anything away from the house? Even one spoon? – if anything, I've added to it. What's ever been missing? What did I ever take away to be called "unlucky?" You've been drinking but your mind is clear, so you feel a bit ashamed of yourself. If you want to cover your embarrassment, do it sensibly.'

Her last words had a touch of coquetry. It was a long time since they had slept together. With Chilsung also, it had been with such a thought that he had kicked her, so that even while they had been quarrelling, abusing and hating each other like enemies, their feelings of desire were in harmony.

'Bloody woman! If you want it you ought to begin by holding me and stroking me and so on, not by kicking up a row.'

'Look who's talking! If you were thinking about it, why couldn't you come in and gently lie down beside me instead of kicking me around?'

'Damn woman. How charming you are!'

As she rubbed her back against him and he was gently turning towards her, she said in a nasal voice, 'Shut up. Magdal *ne* wanted to borrow my face.'

'What?'

'If she could borrow my face, she said, she would go man-hunting. She said it was like a gourd flower, or a peach blossom. And that's not all – I am too pretty for a farmer's wife.'

'That woman must be cross-eyed. It's not that hard to find a man. It looks as though I'll have to go and satisfy her needs.'

'Hm, do you want to see a certain woman die?'

'I wouldn't blink an eyelid. Do you think I'd be worried if you died? There's plenty of girls about. I'd have a new one.'

'What? Who said anything about me dying? I meant I'd kill her!'

She scratched him. It could be called a love-fight, or a prelude to making love. They chuckled as their bodies mingled – it belonged entirely to the animal world. In this sense Yimi *ne* and Chilsung could be seen as well-matched adversaries. They had a persistent energy of life and fertility, and pleasure for them was something like a vigorous appetite, a greed that made you push one more spoonful of rice into your mouth. Their violent sexual activity was without care or protectiveness, like hand to hand fighting. When the storm was over they lay speechless and exhausted as if dead.

From outside came the first cock crow.

'Listen!'

'What?'

'I heard something strange today?'

'What was that?'

'About Guinyo.'

'What?'

His voice rose high.

'Guinyo at the Choi House, I mean . . .'.

'So?'

'She's pregnant or something.'

'Really?'

He sprang out of bed and sat down.

'What are you getting up for?'

'I must get dressed. Can it be true?'

'Magdal *ne* said she'd heard it from somewhere, though it's not certain. But if she's pregnant, it must be the child of the gentleman that's died, mustn't it?'

568

He held his breath. He could not move.

'Why don't you finish dressing?'

Without replying to this, he said, 'Did you really hear that?'

'Yes, of course, but she was trembling with fear and telling me not to breath a word of it to anyone, as it is not certain. Fancy, if it really happens like that, if it turns out to be true, what luck for her. Whoever had such a fortune fall into their lap? Who could ever dream of it?'

Suddenly he burst into laughter.

'What's the matter, dear!'

'Oh! ha! ha! ha! . . . oh! ha! ha! ha! . . .'.

As if possessed he continued to roar with laughter.

'Hey! Have you gone mad?'

She raised her half-naked body.

'Look, stop it!'

Having managed to control his laughter, he said, 'It's funny, it really is funny.'

'What's so funny?'

'It's like pushing hard when someone else is giving birth. The life of a millionaire is glimmering before your eyes – only . . .'.

He spoke as if his tongue was twisted as he tried to suppress the happiness that was driving him out of his mind.

'Oh, dear! I thought you'd gone mad.'

'It's you that's mad, not me!' As he spoke he threw himself at her once more.

Chapter Fifty

STRAIGHT after breakfast Chilsung went down to the village but, after coming and going several times between Pyongsan's house and the tavern, he still had not met him. He guessed that he must have gone to the town. It was very difficult to quieten his anxious, trembling heart. He mumbled again the words he had already said to himself many times, 'If it's true, the top place is as good as mine already!'

He wasn't at all hungry, but he could not go on aimlessly walking between the house and the tavern waiting for someone who was not there, so he went home and was given lunch in the dark room. While he hastily consumed a bowl of boiled barley dumped in rice tea, the children, sitting before him each with a lump of barley in his bowl, eyed each other's portions and grumbled that theirs was smaller.

'Bloody kids! Eat it up quick.'

He glared at them but they continuously whimpered and fretted while the baby, just over a year old, crawled round and tried to pull the soup bowl off the table. Yimi *ne* dragged the infant away and smacked its bottom. The little one cried and the bigger ones still whimpered but the mound of barley in her bowl was steadily diminishing.

'Bloody hell! Why can't you suckle the brat while you eat?' he shouted but he was far from being angry. On the contrary, he was feeling like a bridegroom on horseback, his mind floating high in the boundless heavens. But this joyful mood – so happy that he felt an impulse to bite someone – was not due to love for Yimi *ne*, so he tried to be angry. Glaring at him she roughly grabbed the child, popped her nipple into its mouth, and put a large spoonful of bean-paste soup into her own.

Irritated, perhaps, by the sight of Yimi *ne* relishing her food while he had no appetite, he sat back from the table and mumbled,

'Bloody hell! With all these little devils hanging on to me, when am I ever going to straighten up and live decently? Working twelve months of the year till my back aches, to feed a woman with a belly as big as a cow.'

But again, he did not really mean it.

'H'm, why don't you find a woman who would eat off a saucer and just sit in the house? I can't work without eating.'

He picked up the short pipe that rolled on the floor, tucked it into his waist band and went out. Yimi *ne*, noticing the cabbage soup and barley unexpectedly left over, tipped them into her own bowl and went on eating, opening the door a little to peep out. Chilsung, hanging about in the yard, blew his nose with the hand on which the missing joint showed and rubbed it on his clothes.

'I say!' she called, but he took no notice. 'Look here! Yimi's dad!'

'. . .'

'Have you got cotton wool in your ears? Look here, Yimi's dad!'

'Damn it. What is it now!

'It seems to be thawing today. Why don't you take some manure down to the barley field?'

'I don't know anything about it.'

'What's that? You don't know anything about it? Do you mean you expect me to carry it down bit by bit on my own head?'

'Why not? If you want to, nobody will stop you.'

As he said this, he chuckled and, after chuckling, he raised his chin and looked up at the sky. He fancied that, through the air, an endless succession of carts of rice were racing towards his house. Yimi *ne* opened the door wide and put out her head.

'Say that once again – what you just said. I can't believe it . . . do you think that the people in this village are all blind?'

'Why? Is it a disgrace for a woman to carry manure? If they want to complain, let them. None of them will be doing anything to fill up that cow's stomach of yours. I've never heard of anyone who stopped fermenting bean paste because of the maggots.'

'So I should just keep a good-for-nothing husband to boil and eat?'

'Hmm, let them wait until my barn is full of treasure. Then what fault will they find? They'll all come up to me and rub their hands like flies. Who will be counting my faults then? The shade will be sunny, and the sunny patch in the shade – that day is coming.'

'How nice for you! You must have had a dream about a house with a barn like that.'

'They say, "Any other kind of fault can be concealed but not adultery." '

He turned and laughed, showing a row of healthy teeth fit to chew up a whole ox.

Yimi *ne* blushed as she glared at him.

'Why? Is it an empty accusation? Or does your conscience prick you? I have known long since that you go around wagging your tail.'

After circling the yard a few times, he wriggled one shoulder, made as if to move, and then slowly turned and left the house.

(You know what it's like when you're rich – who will despise me? People are all the same – glad to see the rich man, even if he comes to take something away, and sorry to see the poor one, even if he brings them something. The time is coming when I will make a noise and live in style.)

When he reached the tavern, he saw Pyongsan among the customers. As soon as the hostess saw Chilsung she said, 'Has your tail caught fire? What have you been coming and going for ever since early morning?'

He gave Pyongsan a meaningful look and pushed his way through to him, but Pyongsan pretended not to see him.

'Now things have ended like that, it looks as though the mother's side will have to take over.'

Yoon Bo's great voice rang out.

'Maybe, but there could be a posthumous adoption,' said a stranger.

Dooman's dad, rarely seen, was among them, sitting almost back-to-back with Pyongsan, but saying nothing.

'A posthumous adoption? There has to be a relative. The seed has dried up in that family – where would they find one?'

'If a family's fortunes are declining, there's nothing you can do. There's an old saying, "Money, money, if you are going to go, go quietly," but that damned money won't go without vengeance. When a household falls it's the people who get hurt first.'

'It's still too early to say,' put in Dooman's dad unexpectedly.

The stranger looked at him and blinked.

He went on, 'The late master didn't manage the estate himself and her ladyship is quite capable. There's no reason at all to think that it will be shaken.'

Pyongsan was picking his teeth while Chilsung, watching his expression, was attentive to the talk. Yoon Bo said teasingly, 'Hm, will she live for ever? An old woman of over fifty – who knows when she will go?'

'If it comes to that, with death there's no old or young. You can't say that young ones won't die, or that old ones will.'

Dooman's dad spoke angrily.

'Now then, don't get overheated. If you get too hot while you're drinking you'll fall over backwards.'

'When you see someone else doing well, it makes your belly ache, and, if they fail, you're happy. That's not the way to earn a blessing.'

'That's right – when I think of you getting those acres of paddy, it makes me gnash my teeth so much I can't sleep at night.'

Yoon Bo grinned as he provoked him.

'I don't take their side because I was given a few acres of land. There's a way to behave – and that's not it – that's all I'm trying to say.'

'You're the sort of chap who would try to roast beans by a flash of lightning and it's no use trying to argue with you. But listen to me, man, you only live once, so relax and try to enjoy yourself a little. It's praiseworthy for someone like you to concern yourself about others, but the way you live is what the learned call *Cho-song ja-ok* – "Wife your fortress and children your prison." '

'Wandering round as a beggar, you've picked up a few learned phrases, I see.'

'Well, as you're not a gentleman, nor a scholar, and not a general in the Army of Justice nor a member of the Dong Hak either, maybe it's all right even if you do live *Cho-song ja-ok*, but it will lessen your life, it will make it shorter. Even with work there has

573

to be a limit. I don't mean being idle, or stealing and gambling. Even a meal, if you eat it all at once, will choke you, and likewise with work, if you try to do it all at once, you break down – the way you go, Yi Pangi, you'll soon be a traveller on the river of Hades, leaving your wife and the kids all dressed in silk. Look at you – just a bag of bones.'

Pyongsan, after picking his teeth, kept on just sucking in air and blowing it out noisily. Chilsung, with a cup of wine before him, persistently followed Pyongsan's eyes as he slowly sipped it but the other never once gave him a chance to meet them.

'My stomach's bad, so I can't drink,' Pyongsan mumbled to himself, though no one had offered to buy him one.

(Let's see, what's going to happen now? Even if she is pregnant – supposing it is true and not an empty rumour – now, as Choi Chisoo is dead, I can't imagine what's going to happen next. From the look of that gentleman, there doesn't seem to be any sign of good tidings. So does it mean all my efforts have been in vain? Now that Choi Chisoo, 'Ondal', is dead, the father of the child . . . there has to be a father . . . in that case . . .)

Chilsung, who had been floating on the clouds, had now dashed his forehead on a great rock of doubt.

(Let me see. There is a catch somewhere and it's not simple. Let's see. That disappointed expression on his ugly face possibly means that the whole thing has gone wrong. Let's see. But all that we planned – how can he give it up so easily? Let's see. What's going to happen to the child in Guinyo's belly? Am I going to be regarded as its father? Oh, my god! It can't be, can it? That will never do. As for whose child it is, Chisoo also had relations with her so there's no reason why I should be landed with it. In that case, it will have to be the Choi family who take it over . . . then . . . let's see.)

While he struggled with all his mind and strength to sort it out, Pyongsan stood up and wiped his mouth with a plump hand like a woman's. Yoon Bo, the stranger, and Dooman's father were still talking, but their words no longer entered his ears. After Pyongsan had disappeared he fidgeted on for a while and then quietly got up and left. From behind, Pyongsan looked even fatter than before, but his clothes were shabby and seemed poorer than ever. Chilsung quickened his steps and came near but he did not look round. He seemed to be doing it on purpose.

'Excuse me.'

'. . .'.

'Kim *sengwon*!'

He had no choice but to call, though he always felt awkward about using this title. Naturally his words tailed off. Pyongsan, twisting his neck and thrusting out his protruding lips further, turned to glare to him. It was a face to make one shudder.

'What do you want?'

He raised his voice as if speaking to a servant.

'. . . ?'

Pyongsan clicked his tongue.

'It's about something I've heard . . . I wanted to ask you about it.'

Pyongsan's eyes momentarily brightened and then calmed. Dejected, Chilsung said, 'Have I done something wrong? You weren't like this before.'

'You haven't done anything wrong,' he said, resuming his steps.

'It didn't used to be like this between the two of us. What's the matter?'

' "The two of us", indeed!'

'Well, I mean . . .'.

'When a commoner treats a gentleman with less respect than a doormat, I have to give him a lesson. Am I your drinking companion? What do you mean "the two of us"?'

'That . . . that's not right. Was I the one who first asked you to be a friend?'

As he thought about it, he grew angry.

'Did I ever ask you to gamble with me? Or to be a partner? What do you mean "less respect than a door mat?" '

'. . . '.

'I've had some thoughts that made me want to see you. I'm not just hanging round you for nothing. When you start something, you have to see it through to the end, so I want to know about the end – that's all. Now the man is dead, what's going to happen? I've heard enough rumours.'

At this, Pyongsan turned his face away. Before those turned eyes appeared the Choi House and Dangsan. And the place where the pavilion had stood. Resignedly he brought his gaze back to the road ahead.

'I hear that Guinyo is pregnant.'

'What?'

For the first time he showed surprise and stopped in his tracks.

'That's what I've heard – that she's pregnant.'

'It's the first I've heard of it.'

He made an extravagant gesture of surprise.

'Really?'

'Why should I lie to you?'

'Didn't she tell you?'

'Did she tell you, then? She should feel closer to you than to me.'

He looked at Pyongsan, filled with doubt. The latter went on, 'I haven't seen a sign of her lately. It's a complete surprise. I thought you two were hand in glove – and keeping me out of it. Is she really pregnant?'

At this, Chilsung completely lost confidence.

'I don't know – it's a rumour.'

Not only had his confidence gone but it was an enormous disappointment. It occurred to him that the whole story of the pregnancy might be false.

'Come to think of it, that bitch Guinyo must have been trifling with both of us. From the look of her I guess ten men wouldn't be enough for her – I only hope that there won't be any trouble to come from this.'

'So, you also planted some seeds?'

'Aye, aye.'

Pyongsan waved his arm.

'Isn't that what they call "Brothers sharing the same pillow"? I'm so ashamed of it . . .'.

He repeated, 'I do hope there won't be any trouble,' and with this he left and disappeared. 'This story doesn't make sense.'

He spat at the side of the road.

'It's not a story that will end today. Let's wait and see. Anyway, at the worst, I haven't lost anything.'

Even so, his mood was one of anger and irritation, as if he had suffered some great loss and he felt as though he needed somewhere to vent his anger before his mind could settle.

'Are you there, Yongi?' he called, as he went into the gate of Yongi's house.

'Huh!' scoffed Yongi. 'I thought it was human, but it's that two-legged animal.'

He was chopping pine branches with an adze and making them into bundles.

'I thought you must be crippled, but I see you've crawled out – what are you up to?' replied Chilsung as he leaned against the wooden mortar.

'The winter's over – what do you need firewood for?'

'Winter comes again. After your first birthday you have another one, don't you?'

'You're going to prosper, I can see.'

'Of course – why not?'

'Why are you so quarrelsome? Did I pray for you not to prosper?'

'I can't regard you as a decent man, so I'm not very pleased to see you – that's all.'

'Huh, really.'

Since the incident in the mooli field when he had said a few things in a coarse way, Yongi, offended, had avoided him.

'Your wife must have an easy time,' mumbled Chilsung, as if to himself, subdued by Yongi's disdainful manner.

'What wind brings you here?' asked Yongi, who had stopped working and, sitting on the bundle of wood, took out his pipe and began to fill it.

'I'm fed up with everything.'

'So you're becoming human.'

'Shut up and give me some tobacco.'

He took out his pipe. Yongi put a little into his palm and lit his own pipe. For some time they gazed at the sky, where threads of cloud floated by, and puffed at their pipes.

'Yongi, you are as mad as anyone.'

'. . . .'

577

'Did you think that if you put a new thatch on the roof of that empty tavern, she would come back?'

'. . .'.

'You can never understand them. As for me, the very mention of a woman makes me sick. They're wicked, crafty creatures.'

He thought of the alley-cat-like Guinyo and, at the thought of her, his mind, which had quietened, began to bubble again.

(Huh! do they think I'll just quietly go away? They're going to be in trouble if they think I'm a blind man with open eyes. There must be some dirty scheme. For quite a long time now Kim Pyongsan has been avoiding me.)

'Yongi!'

'. . .'.

'I was at the tavern earlier on and I saw Yoon Bo and Yi Pangi and others. They were all talking about the Choi House.'

'. . .'.

'The family is ended, so it's going to perish – how can they avoid it?'

'Why should it? Just because someone wants it to?'

'But, as they were saying at the tavern, if a house is to fall, the people usually get hurt first. And what a dreadful way to be killed.'

'It was strange, wasn't it?'

'Very strange.'

As he agreed, he studied Yongi's expression.

'Dochul *ne* has no reason to harm him.'

'She's a mad thing, so it could have been her, if her sick mind boiled over . . .'.

'In all her life she never hurt anyone.'

Full of suspicion, Yongi stared at him and feeling uneasy, his face stiffened.

'But she killed herself after starting the fire.'

'It may be because I was thinking like that, but she appeared to me in a dream.'

'How?'

'She was dancing and saying, "Why should I want to kill anyone?" '

'It's because that was the way you were thinking.'

578

'Even so, it's strange – a mad woman getting hold of a hemp cord. If she carried it around with the intention of killing the master, she wouldn't have been mad, would she?'

'Well, then, what do you suggest?'

'That's why I say it's strange. The Master had a fierce temperament, that's true, but he didn't do anything to make anyone hate him and, though people say things about him, he was a good man.'

His eyes filled with tears.

'I knew him so well.'

'If it wasn't Dochul *ne* . . . they say that he did hit her once.'

'He wasn't the only one, was he? You've hit her too, haven't you? And the kids were hitting her all the time.'

'Well . . . .that's true, but . . .'.

Yongi again looked at him with eyes full of suspicion. Avoiding them, he mumbled, 'Well, could it have been Kuchon?'

'Did he come on wings? It couldn't have been.'

Yongi closed his mouth. He showed his doubts so strongly that Chilsung felt a strange sensation as though he himself was under suspicion. This, added to his connection with Guinyo and Pyongsan, was enough to fill him with terror. He hurriedly left Yongi's house in a way to make him worthy of suspicion but, by the time he was home, he had come to a great understanding. All his questions were suddenly resolved. It gave him such a shock that he felt as if he was about to vomit blood. For him, it had been a great revelation, and a sensation of happiness spread through his system as he felt the reality of it, not a dream, but something solid beneath his feet.

(That's right! Dead men cannot talk. A hemp cord is no common thing, not like straw.)

The days seemed to have become longer. Chilsung wrung out his thought as he walked along the embankment in the early dusk. Dooman's father, who had still been in the tavern a short while before, was leading his ox homewards. Kim *hunjang*, who had probably been to Kim *jinsa*'s house, could be seen coming down the road carrying a long pipe and swinging his arm. It was already the end of the second lunar month and from now on the farmers would be busier.

579

He went straight to Pyongsan's and through the open gate directly into the courtyard. It seemed that no supper was cooking, as there were no sounds from the kitchen, only the noise of weaving from the small room.

'Is Kim *sengwon* at home?'

There was no answer. He called more loudly, 'Kim *sengwon!*'

The door of the small room opened and Haman *dek* put out her emaciated face.

'Who is it?'

'It's me, Ma'am, Chilsung.'

'What do you want?'

'Is Kim *sengwon* in?'

'He has not come back yet.'

'He left the tavern with me earlier on.'

'He has not come home.'

The sight of Haman *dek* with the light behind her was eerie, so he hastily turned away.

(Has he gone back to the tavern?)

Unlike when he left, he ran towards it, breathing hard. There was Pyongsan. The other customers had scattered and gone and he sat by himself, desolate and lonely, gazing down at the cup of wine before him.

'Goodness gracious, is your tail on fire? Since the morning, you've been running backwards and forwards – what's the matter with you?'

As before, the hostess was sarcastic, but he turned a deaf ear. He had run there breathlessly, but he smiled in a leisurely manner, and said, 'So you're back here again?'

'Yes,' said the hostess, 'it really is a rare sight. Is he meditating on the truth? Or is he going to become a Buddha? He has set one cup of wine before him and he has been sitting like that all this time.'

She gave him a sidelong glance as she wiped the table and put the cups, spoons and chopsticks into the washing-up bowl.

'Looking for me?'

He lifted bleary eyes towards Chilsung.

'Not particularly, but I've nothing else to do and I was feeling a bit bored.'

'It's good – being bored.'

'Pardon?'

'It's not bad to be bored,' said Pyongsan, as he broke into a guffaw.

'What do you mean?'

'I only said it because I'm bored too.'

The hostess went out, taking the bowl to throw away the dirty water.

'Kim *sengwon*!'

Chilsung edged closer. 'I mean, the hempen cord – not just a straw rope but a hempen one.'

Chilsung observed him out of the corners of his eyes. The backs of his hands were trembling. His knees were slightly jerking too.

'It's strange – where could that cord have come from? – the dead don't speak, but the living can.'

His hands, which he had intertwined to repress their trembling, were smoothly released and one hand went to the wine cup and grasped it firmly.

'As long as you can stuff that mouth of yours with meat all through the year – that's all that matters to you, isn't it?'

'Well, that may be.'

'Don't worry. Silver, gold, and all precious things will be clinking before your eyes.'

'Well, that may be.'

'You'll have a golden ring for that broken finger of yours.'

'Don't tease me.'

Pyongsan laughed loudly. There were daggers in his smiling eyes, but Chilsung followed suit and laughed also. He laughed with pleasure and with wonder.

'I guess he's gone mad. He's been sitting there all this time with a face as fierce as a leopard – now what's all this about? The house is going to float away.'

To the hostess' remark, Chilsung replied swaggeringly, 'Bring some wine. Fill up his cup, too, to the brim, and let's have a plate of fresh octopus!'

'What kind of devil's game is this?' she said.
'I guess he really has gone mad!'
Pyongsan just kept on roaring with laughter.

Chapter Fifty-One

PEOPLE thought that as not only the victim, but the killer also, was in the other world, the whole incident was closed. Neither villagers nor servants had any doubt that it had been the work of Dochul *ne*.

Apart from Yongi, there were only two others who did not think that she could have been the murderer or that the matter was ended. One of them was Lady Yoon and the other was Bongsoon *ne*. As with Yongi, Lady Yoon's suspicion started with the cord. To have prepared a hempen cord for the murder – was it likely that a mad woman could have thought out such a careful plan? At first Hwani rose before her eyes, because it was possible that they had pre-empted Chisoo, who would have continued to pursue them until he had brought the matter to an end. However, since obtaining a letter from Ugwan to confirm that Hwani had not moved one step from his hiding place, she could dismiss this horrible vision. The next person to come to her mind was Kang *posoo*. Though she had no idea of what dealings or promises there had been between them, she had learned from Kim *subang* that he had been given nothing more than his travelling expenses when he left. However, after she had heard in detail how on New Year's Eve, in a fire-field farmer's hut in the mountains, he had gulped down wine and wept, she could not but abandon her suspicions.

'Who can it be, then? Who has done it?'

In the middle of the night she would mumble to herself as she stared into the darkness.

'What a wicked mother I am – what must I do, this sinful mother?'

Tears came to her eyes and ran down her cheeks. She had lost the one who had constantly been applying the lash, for Chisoo in his lifetime had been not so much a son as a jailor. She had wanted it to be that way and she herself had created the situation. Now she could not think of it without horror. A pitiful jailor who had gnawed and gnawed away at the passing of time until, able to bear it no longer, he had finally been crushed by it – perhaps he could be likened to an emaciated sacrificial animal offered on an altar raised to expiate her sin? Wasn't it because she had been shaking her head in rejection of forgiveness that he could not lay down the whip and, as a starving sacrificial animal, had to gnaw away at time before the altar to the very end? Ever since that day when, on her return from the monastery, he had come running to her overcome with joy and calling 'mother!', she had brushed him aside, she had not been a wife to her late husband nor a mother to his son. At the deepest level of her consciousness there was something else as well as the despondency caused by the conventional stigma of being an unchaste woman and therefore disqualified as wife or mother, the heart-piercing despair of a mother who has cast away her own child. In the one case she had been disqualified as a mother and in the other she had herself given up her maternal rights, but in either case it could be seen only as an abandonment. An abandonment, but it did not end there – it was also an accumulation of sin, a burden, the weight of which she had to bear. It was heavy enough to make her sink to the ground. As she felt the weight pressing on either side, her back would bend and her ankles sink into the earth. It seemed as though, if she moved at all, she would break into pieces, yet for more than twenty years she had borne it stoically. In silence she had wept bitter tears for the child, born of her flesh, but abandoned without once sucking her breast, and watched Chisoo change, through a lonely childhood and a twisted youth, and on into an adulthood squashed by apathy, a wasted life. And now one of her burdens had fallen to the ground, and the other hung upside down in mid air while she stood beneath it, yet it was not because the balance had broken that she was crushed.

Digging deeper into her consciousness, one might have found an area that was poisoned by a sinful passion. For a period of more than twenty years, a man had lived there. The tragedy of that man had left a gossamer web as strong as flax. That man who had perished like dew at the place of execution – it was because she had lived with the tragedy of that man that she had rejected forgive-

584

ness and welcomed the bruising flagellation by her son. As the incident had not ended as a mere unexpected disaster, she did not blame fate. Within her, wishing to remain unforgiven forever, was coiled this tenacious and frightening egoism of love.

'Wicked mother that I am, sinful mother, what must I do?'

Even if it had meant deceit, even if it had meant piling pain upon pain, she should have been a mother to Chisoo – now belatedly she had come to realize this. It was not because the weight on the balance had shifted that she had been broken in pieces – it was because of regret. She could not think of Chisoo as her chastiser without horror – it had not been a simple case of losing one's son. Mokyon, the disciple of Sakyamuni, was said to have questioned him about the law, to save his mother from torture, but he had, by her, been made his mother's torturer. She realized that she had been an evil mother, worse than Mokyon's. She began to develop the strange habit of secretly scrutinizing the faces of the servants. Even Kim *subang*, stiff with loyalty and incapable of change, was examined by eyes that were dark and full of suspicion.

Though she spared the girls, she would now and again summon the servants for no reason at all and stare piercingly into their eyes, making them extremely embarrassed. Sometimes, she would suddenly appear in Kim *subang*'s quarters and look all around them, something she had never done before. The discipline of the house, so tightly kept for so long, was about to collapse. Her mask-like face was suffused with venom and the servants lived in trepidation. As the days went by the venom that issued from her grew stronger, charging the air with such gravity and terror that the servants, as if under a spell, could find no way of escape and each one would fall into the illusion that he was the one who had killed Chisoo. Bongsoon *ne* came also to believe, in a rather different way, that it had not been the work of Dochul *ne*.

While Lady Yoon's suspicions groped here and there, without any focus, she directed her attention on one spot and kept it under close scrutiny. Though there was no definite proof, she trusted an intuition that pointed to Guinyo. What supported this was not so much the way Guinyo had hated Sohi, resented the master, or sighed over her plight as a servant, but what she had seen on one particular night. She could not forget her face reflected in the lamp light. It remained at the back of her mind as if it had been the visage of an evil spirit.

'No one in the world is really wicked. According to their circumstances, they turn out bad or good. If you are comfortably off, why should you envy others? Isn't that so? If you've starved for three days, unless you are a very remarkable person, you will easily do wrong.'

Bongsoon *ne* would talk like this to Samwol and Samwol would reply in her own way, 'Would everyone steal just because they were hungry? Even if his guts were twisted, an honest man wouldn't climb over his neighbour's wall, would he?'

Then Kim *subang*'s wife would put in, 'It all depends on your nature. Some are born to be whores and some are born to be thieves.'

Bongsoon *ne* would still insist, 'I don't agree with you there. Does a good person never have any bad thoughts? They would already be Buddhas. Everyone has evil impulses every day. Bad people, too, have at least one good thought a day and feel afraid of their sins.'

She had always spoken like this but, to Guinyo, she could not extend the trust that she would have granted to anyone else. It was not that this ordinary good-natured woman had any great reasoning powers or keenness of judgement: it was simply intuition and instinct, like the way in which an animal can feel the presence of an enemy. Once the notion had come to her, it stuck persistently. Thanks to the unexpected entrance of Dochul *ne*, the secret of Chisoo's death had been completely buried and Guinyo, regarding this fortune as the grace of the deity that protected her, could wait with untroubled mind for the baby in her womb to grow. Now, in the second stage of her scheme, her enthusiastic acting to earn Lady Yoon's approval had reached its height, and Bongsoon *ne* was watching her two different faces. One face, covered with a confident smile, glimpsed through a crack in the door, and the other, when she looked grief stricken and hardly able to stand – while observing these two faces Bongsoon *ne* came one day, to realize that she was pregnant.

(Undoubtedly there's something in it!)

While keeping an eye on Guinyo, she took even greater care of Sohi. She stayed in the *byoldang* sewing all day, watching over her and alert for the approach of Guinyo.

'Bongsoon *ne*.'

'Yes, Miss.'

'So, what happened to Shim Chong?'

'After offering to the temple three hundred sacks of rice that were bought with her body and praying that her father's eyes would be opened, she jumped – "plonk" – into the blue sea.'

'Oh, poor thing!'

'So the king of heaven, moved by her great filial devotion, revived her.'

'What's "revive"?'

'It means that she was brought back to live again in this world.'

'Mm . . .'.

'After she threw herself into the sea, she was taken to the palace of the dragon king. There she found her mother, Mrs Kwak, you see?'

Sohi's eyes sparkled.

'Oh dear!'

Bongsoon *ne* instantly realized her mistake as the child drew close and put a hand on her knee as she looked up at her.

'If I go to the dragon king's palace, will I be able to see my mother?'

'Well, not really. It's only a story. As they say, "Tales are all lies and only songs are true." '

She tried to go back quickly to the main story but Sohi, showing no interest, was already biting her finger and ready to start whimpering.

'The dragon king in the palace put Shim Chong in the middle of a lotus flower and sent it up to the surface of the water. It was the most beautiful flower in the world. A boatman was just passing by. When he saw it . . .'.

'I won't listen. I don't like it . . .'

She thrashed her legs but she did not cry. Affected by the heavy

587

atmosphere of the house since Chisoo's death, she seemed to try hard to control herself and be careful.

When it was dark and she had put her to sleep, Bongsoon *ne* opened the door to refill the brazier. She had to hold back a scream. Lady Yoon sat blankly at the edge of the verandah. As she did not even look round, Bongsoon *ne* was confused, unable to go out or to shut the door again, when Lady Yoon called her.

'Yes, Ma'am.'

'I can't get up. Will you give me a hand.'

'Yes, Ma'am.'

She stepped down quickly on to the shoe stone and grasped her arm as if in awe. As she stood up, Lady Yoon let go of Bongsoon *ne*'s hand. She tried to walk by herself. She wobbled.

'Ma'am.'

Bongsoon *ne* put her hand out once more to support her.

'I don't know what's going to happen to me.'

'. . . .'

'Bongsoon *ne*.'

'Yes, ma'am.'

'How much longer do you think I'm going to live?'

'You must live for a long, long time. The young Miss . . .'

Bongsoon *ne*, choking, could not go on.

'You mean Sohi?'

'The young Miss – who can she rely on . . . isn't she all alone in the world?'

'Poor child.'

'You must try and get over it.'

'Get over it? How can I until I find out who did it? I must find out.'

She lifted her head and looked into Bongsoon *ne*'s face.

'But . . .'.

'Bongsoon *ne*, you would know.'

'. . . .'

'It was not that mad woman.'

'Ma'am?'

'You know that, don't you?'

Bongsoon *ne* supported her back to her room and tried to make

588

her lie down on the mattress but she firmly shook herself free, sat up and stared at her vacantly.

'Do you understand what I mean?'

'Yes, Ma'am.'

'Then tell me who it was.'

She spoke almost in a whisper without taking her eyes from Bongsoon *ne*'s face.

'How could I . . .'.

'You mean you don't know?'

Bongsoon *ne*'s face twisted. Beads of sweat appeared on her forehead.

'You mean you think it was that mad woman?'

'. . .'.

'Please tell me.'

'. . .'.

'It's someone in this house. The hand that wove that hempen cord is in this house. Bongsoon *ne*, please lift the millstone from my heart.'

She began to weep. It seemed as though she was being torn in pieces. She looked the most pitiable woman in all the world. Bongsoon *ne* began to cry as well.

'Ma'am.'

Bongsoon *ne*'s eyes, when she had wiped away her tears, looked as if they were frozen, yet, they seemed also to be feverishly shimmering. She had made up her mind. For her, it meant putting her life at risk. More than that, for, if it had meant putting only her own life at risk, she might well have made up her mind before.

'I should interrogate Guinyo.'

'What did you say?' Her eyes opened wide, as if to pierce the darkness.

'Her body looks strange – I am sure she is pregnant . . .'.

'Pregnant?'

As she mumbled the word, her eyes returned to their dimness and she collapsed into tears again.

'If you question her, something else might crop up.'

Drops of sweat fell from Bongsoon *ne*'s forehead. Her lips were as white as paper.

(I may be accusing an innocent person . . . an innocent person.)

Back in the *byoldang*, she pulled the quilt over her head and shuddered all night as if in a fever. In the morning, with half lowered eyes, Lady Yoon watched Guinyo as she removed the bowl of water from the room.

(Yes, she's pregnant.)

In regard to this she felt tolerant. It was not so much generosity as that she had no room in her mind to concern herself with it. Nor was there space to recall that once she herself had had a secret pregnancy.

When the sun had set and supper was over, she summoned the girl. As if aware of the reason, Guinyo did not raise her head from the beginning. The flap on the front of her jacket was slightly raised and her breast appeared to be swollen. The line of her shoulders was thinner than usual, the characteristic slender outline of a pregnant woman.

'Don't you feel uncomfortable?'

'. . .'

'Answer me.'

'Ma'am?'

'You are with child, aren't you?'

'Mm, Ma'am.'

'Tell me the truth.'

Big tears fell from her eyes and dropped continuously on the clasped hands that rested on her knees.

'Don't start crying. Just tell me the truth.'

She threw herself down in front of Lady Yoon and cried loudly, 'Please kill me!'

'Who is the father?'

'Please kill me!'

Lady Yoon looked calmly at the weeping figure.

(What has her pregnancy got to do with it?)

Before her eyes rose Bongsoon *ne*'s face, drained of blood, her lips like paper.

'Who is the father? If you tell me that I'll set you up as a pair.'

She wept even more loudly. Lady Yoon resumed her silence as she watched the weeping servant.

'Is it a man you couldn't marry?'

'Yes, Ma'am.'

'Why? Is he already married?'

'No, Ma'am. It's someone who is no longer in this world.'

'. . . .'

'Ma'am, the Master . . .'.

'What?'

'Please kill me. The child..the child's father is our late Master.'

'What!'

Lady Yoon sprang up.

'That's it!'

She gave a shrill cry.

'What – what must I do, Ma'am?'

'That's it!'

Again the shrill cry rang out. Guinyo lifted her eyes to look at her. It was an ashen face, the face of a dead woman, over which there spread a smile.

'Samwol! Is anyone there?'

Samwol came running.

'Tell Kim *subang* to come here.'

He came running. His face also had a strange look.

'Come up here.'

'Yes, ma'am.'

He came up on to the verandah.

'Come into the room.'

He trembled as he stepped into it.

'Take this woman out.'

'Yes, Ma'am.'

'Ma'am!' screamed Guinyo.

'Take her out and lock her up in the storeroom.'

Confused, he grabbed her shoulder. Shaking her body she screamed, 'How dare you!'

'Be quick!' ordered Lady Yoon.

'Out you go.'

'Don't lay your hands on me! I'll bite my tongue and kill myself.'

Lady Yoon ordered Samwol, restlessly pacing the courtyard, to go and fetch Dori. Dori came. Under her merciless orders, the two men almost twisted Guinyo's arms out of joint to make her stand up.

'Madam! You can't do this!'

When she had been dragged as far as the verandah, she turned to look at Lady Yoon and screamed, 'Madam! Why are you treating me like this?'

'Wicked girl! Don't you know your own wickedness? You ought to be beaten to death with iron hammers. Get on with it!'

She was dragged down to the courtyard.

'I carry the heir of the Choi family within me. What have I done to deserve this?'

Kim *subang's* eyes widened and Dori flinched. Lady Yoon stepped down into the yard and followed them to the storeroom. Guinyo seemed on the verge of madness and screamed continuously. Kim *subang* and Dori pushed her into the room and closed the door.

'Lock her up.'

The click of the great padlock mingled with her screams. Lady Yoon took the key. Locked in the storeroom for three days and nights, she was not allowed even a drop of water. Only when her miserable voice, which had been appealing for water night and day, was silenced did Lady Yoon come at dawn with a lantern and, after making Kim *subang* open the door, she went in. Famished and thirsty, Guinyo gathered her last drop of energy to make a protest. With the lantern in her hand, Lady Yoon stood over her like a messenger of death.

'Bitch! You killed my son!'

A faint smile appeared on Guinyo's face.

'Didn't you know that he was unable to have a child?'

Guinyo fell forward. This time a faint smile appeared on Lady Yoon's face.

'It wouldn't be right for you to die by yourself, would it? Who was your partner? Who's the father?'

'. . .'.

'Do you want to wet your throat before you speak?'

She moaned.

'Wa – water, wa..'

She tore at her throat as she repeated the word.

'All right, you shall have some water. Now, speak. Who was your partner?'

Lady Yoon nodded to Kim *subang* to fetch some water. He brought it in a gourd bowl. As he handed it over to his mistress his jowls were trembling.

'Here's some water. Before you drink it, speak. Who was your partner? Who is the father?'

'Chi – Chil – Chilsung . . .'.

Lady Yoon threw the water over her face. She struck out her tongue to lick madly at it as it ran down.

Lady Yoon struck her on the face with her hand. She fell forward and lay flat, only her head raised like that of an adder with eyes that gazed piercingly. Her face looked like a skull with it's prominent nose and deeply sunken eyes aflame with evil and hatred.

'Give her some water. And some food as well.'

As she gave the order, Lady Yoon was trembling violently. When the water and food were brought in Guinyo still lay on her stomach on the floor and, raising only her head, like a snake, she put it into the bowl and sucked the water. The door was locked and Lady Yoon again took the key. Still in front of the room she called Dori.

'Go to Chilsung's and fetch the rogue. Tell him that Guinyo wants him and avoid any disturbance.'

To Kim *subang* she said, 'Let Bogi and Samsoo wait by the gate and, when he comes, lock him up in the storeroom. He must be tied up. Make sure he doesn't escape.'

Chilsung was brought in without even Yimi *ne* knowing. Realizing that the whole thing had gone wrong, and having had no part in the actual murder, without great persuasion, he readily confessed to his plotting with Pyongsan, his suspicions about the hempen cord, and as a result of that his guarantee of a share in the future.

'I haven't done anything wrong. Apart from being asked to supply some seed and letting them have it – I don't know a thing about it. It was only after the whole thing was over that I realized . . . Apart from lending the seed . . .'

Pyongsan, when brought in, bellowed loudly from the beginning. He did not seem to realize that by making such a row he was digging his own grave. It was a kind of convulsive fit.

'What's it got to do with me? They did it between them. It's nothing to do with me. It's the first I've heard of it. May God be my witness! My family fortunes have declined but we are a family of military rank! Ah! I know nothing about it!'

Saliva spattered from between his crooked teeth. While being dragged along, he had fallen down a bank into a field and blood oozed from cuts on his face, and his thick cotton coat, soaked in muddy water, had lost its tape so that it was half undone.

The news spread through the village.

'Huh! They say, "Even the grower doesn't know when a gourd is rotting inside." For a servant girl, she went wrong in a big way, didn't she?'

'She's got some guts? How could she dream of such a thing?'

'From the start it was like jumping on to a fire with gunpowder on your back – trying to foist a child on a man who's impotent.'

Guinyo, half dead, realized that there was no way out and resigned herself to silence. Chilsung, feeling that his sin was no more than the lending of seed – compared to that terrible murder, what did adultery with a servant girl matter? – did no more than blabber,

'Bloody hell, I was so unlucky! Damned unlucky I was . . .'

It was Pyongsan who continued to shout and throw fits to the very end. Tightening again and again fists now swollen beyond their usual plumpness, he repeated over and over, as if inexhaustible, his protests at a titled gentleman being insulted in this way, for that in itself was an eternal injustice, making him ashamed to face his ancestors and passing on a grievance to his descendants, in view of which Lady Yoon must judge with heavenly wisdom and release him from this shameful association with the sins of a maidservant and a common rascal.

On the day when the accused were taken to the courthouse in the town, people gathered even from other places, with oiled paper covers on their hats, as they walked through the early spring rain to see the faces of the criminals who had been involved in this bizarre assassination.

Chapter Fifty-Two

ON the day when Guinyo and the two men were taken off to the courthouse rain continued to fall through the night. It was the thin rain that hurries along the spring. Towards dawn its gentle sound ceased and, as busy cockcrows announced the coming of day, the village began to appear little by little through the damp mist. In the unfenced yard of Pyongsan's house a dead apricot tree that had been left in place of a fence also showed up dark and sombre.

'*Hyong*! Brother – mother . . .!'

'Help! Mother!'

Gobok and his brother called and cried. Haman *dek* had hanged herself. Hearing the uproar, neighbour Yamu *ne* was the first to arrive. As she called loudly to the others, menfolk ran down the muddy road. The corpse, dangling from the black decaying tree, had been soaked by the rain. Regardless of the noise made by the chattering crowd, crows, drawn by the smell of death, cawed as they perched on the tops of roofs and the ends of the tangled branches of the tree by the village pavilion.

'The nastiest creature in the world! He ought to be stoned to death.'

With bloodshot eyes, the men were ready to have torn Pyongsan to pieces if he had been there.

Still covered in misty rain, the edge of the river looked whitish. Loggers in rain capes floated their rafts downstream towards the estuary through the mist and it also covered the middle slopes of the mountains so that only the peaks dimly showed their faces.

'Hah! a virtuous woman! A virtuous woman has appeared!'

Bong-gi, who had run, holding up the legs of his trousers as he went, as if to see a shaman perform in the market place, jabbered away excitedly like the crows on the roofs. Bluish circles round his eyes made him look like an owl, but the eyes were those of a crow whose mouth waters at the sight of a funeral feast. He had had the cheek to say, 'You might as well set light to your finger and hope to go up in the air as hope to collect a debt from me,' but, owing money to Chilsung, who was just as tough as he was, always made him feel uncomfortable. Luckily for him, Chilsung had been taken to the courthouse the day before and this had greatly pleased him. His eyes flashed as he slyly kept watch on the cord that hung round the neck of Haman *dek*.

'Undoubtedly she is a virtuous woman. Yes, truly . . . but what's a virtuous woman to a murderer? – it's a case of "pearls before swine." '

He, no doubt, thought it witty, but none of the excited crowd paid any attention to this tasteless remark. They milled about with no idea of what to do. Pushing them aside, Yoon Bo stepped forward.

'Why do you all think it's such a jolly sight to gather round and stare at? Yongpari, come here! Don't just stand there like an idiot.'

At his shout, the beanpole-like Yongpari stepped forward, his face looking even longer than usual. His tight lips twitched as if about to open. Yoon Bo and Yongpari held up and cut the straw cord, squelchy from the rain, and lowered the dead body wrapped in its outer skirt.

'What a shame! She was so clever and well-mannered . . .'.

Dooman *ne* wept as she followed the corpse to the house.

'That's true, she was so good at everything and with such good taste . . .'

Suh *subang*'s elderly wife also dabbed her eyes. While the crowd followed the body and gathered round outside the door of the room, Bong-gi kicked off his straw shoes and went up the tree like a monkey. When he had untied the cord that had been round her neck, neatly wound it up and put it on his wrist, he grabbed the branches and snapped them off. At the sound of the snapping a few women turned their heads with looks of disapproval, but only for a moment. In no time, they were rushing together under the tree. Even young men like Bawoo and Buddol threw themselves into it. Crowded together, they busily snapped the branches and collected them. In a moment the tree became a bare stump.

Kangchong *dek* absent-mindedly stood and watched the spectacle. Suh *subang*, after hesitating, cast a quick glance at his wife, who was standing face to face with Dooman *ne* squeezing tears. He furtively picked up a branch that had fallen to the ground and slipped it up his sleeve, no doubt thinking of his wife who suffered regularly from stomach worms. As he looked up at the now naked trunk, Bong-gi, in high spirits, said, 'It's supposed to be good for everything and especially for epileptics.'

'What if the tree's dead? Will it still work?'

One of the women expressed a doubt. Bong-gi gave a fleeting smile. They had scrambled for the branches in the belief that the tree, having received the dead person's spirit, would have curative powers, but now had come a doubt as to whether the spirit could enter dead wood. It was a belief that had come down from ancient times that a cord or straw rope from which someone had hanged was the most potent cure for illness. As the one who had got hold of it before anyone else, Bong-gi could not but have the greatest satisfaction.

'The little rat!' spat Hanjo and cursed him under his breath.

'Take these home. Be careful with them,' said Bong-gi as he handed over the precious cord and branches to his pretty daughter. As they came to feel ashamed of the way that, after the death of a familiar neighbour, they had greedily rushed about so as not to miss gathering something that was not after all the elixir of life or even pennies from heaven, the womenfolk began to chatter. They spoke of how they were sorry for her and of what an exemplary woman she had been. They seemed to feel that, after a little praise, the angry spirit might forgive their heartlessness.

Magdal *ne*, waving her branch like the baton of a commanding officer, raised her voice: 'She was matched with the wrong man. As its turned out, she might have done better to be on her own like I am. There's nothing to regret in being a widow. That creature, who deserves to have his tongue stretched a thousand yards . . .'.

'He is going to have it stretched anyway,' cut in the hostess of the tavern.

'Pulling out his tongue is not enough. He ought to be hacked to pieces. How can anyone that's supposed to be human behave like that? What have I been saying all this time? Over and over again I've said that he ought to be turned out of the village but nobody would take any notice. If they had listened to me sooner, the Choi family wouldn't have had this horrible disaster. Mind you, in one way or another, Gobok's mother was bound to die sooner or later. She's been bringing up blood night and day, but she is still stuck to the loom like a spider. If you don't eat and don't sleep, the strongest person can't survive, can they?'

When he came out of the house after laying out the corpse, Yoon Bo looked up at the apricot tree reduced to a lonely trunk.

'Ha! Ha! What good people! What generous hearts! Don't they try so hard to live a long life! Ha, ha!'

There were plenty of people swarming round but the poverty of the family was beyond description and, without a single relative, the house in mourning was infinitely desolate. It seemed that there were a few distant relatives in the vicinity but they had lived cut off from one another. It was unlikely that people who had always shared a mutual indifference would now come forward to take part in a funeral at the house of a murderer. Even if they had wanted to send a message, the village people had no way of knowing where or to whom to send it. It was the same with Gobok's mother's home at Haman. To go there and back would take several days, there was really no one to send and, besides, if they were too shamed to come to collect the corpse, nothing could be done. In the end, it had to be dealt with by the village. Haman *dek* rested at last in a coffin hurriedly hammered together by Yoon Bo, in front of which crouched the two brothers in their usual rags. Exhausted with crying, Hanbok was nodding off, his navel, mottled with dirt, showing above his trousers. Each time he woke, he cried again as he remembered and his body trembled convulsively. Gobok, his head hung low, looked up furtively from under his narrow brow, wrinkled like an old man's, his eyelids puffy like those of his father's. Now and again he jabbed his dozing younger brother with his elbow, causing him to shake and start crying loudly again.

When she had seen the village people running along the muddy road shouting that Haman *dek* had hanged herself, Yimi *ne* was thrown into confusion, running first to the shed and then to the

598

bundles of straw in the yard. Eventually she ran into the house and fastened the door.

'What shall I do? What shall I do?'

As she walked up and down inside she felt as though the villagers would come rushing up to demand that she also must put a rope round her neck. The children, scared by her behaviour, huddled in a corner and looked up at her. The youngest was sprawled on the floor asleep.

'Is it a dream? Is it real?'

She beat her chest and tugged at her hair, then she wept. As she wandered about in the room, she rubbed her eyes to look again and again at the soiled wicker trunk, the chest of drawers, the seed bags and the dusty lamp, but just because they all kept their accustomed places was no guarantee that Chilsung would walk in as usual. On the previous day, with her own eyes, she had seen him dragged off to the courthouse. Of all crimes, it was murder, the murder of the master of the Choi house by a peasant. To believe that it was slander or to hope that he would be cleared of it – these were empty hopes, with chances of less than ten thousand to one.

'Where can I go? Where can I take these little ones and live?'

She wept and beat the floor. At this noise, her youngest awoke and, as he cried, the other two, huddled in the corner, also burst into tears.

'May his neck be broken, the fool! How could he be a murderer? We're as good as dead. It's death for all of us!'

After the rain had cleared, the sun shone with unusual brilliance. The fresh green of the watercress plots caught the eye and the sunlight played on the water running in the ditches. The sun soon hid itself and the wind began to rise. By now there was nothing much to be seen at the house of mourning. The several young men who had been helping to prepare the corpse, make the coffin, or get ready for the funeral were eating some red-bean porridge brought in by Dooman *ne*. The children, who had been watching them from a distance, mouths watering, lost hope as the bowls were emptied, and ran off. As they went down the squelchy village road, they stopped by the gate of Yimi *ne*'s yard. They gathered in front of it and peeped inside. One of them picked up a stone and threw it. Then another one did the same and they all picked up stones and threw them. Some fell on the verandah, some on the jar stand, and some hit the door.

'Murderer!'

'Thief!'

'Mangled hand!'

They chanted loudly. Yimi *ne*, her hair dishevelled, threw open the door and ran out. They stopped throwing things and stared at her with eyes full of curiosity. Her face was purple with swollen veins. She glared at them with flashing eyes but they did not run away. She did not open her mouth either. It seemed as though a long time passed like this.

'This bloody life! This bloody life!'

Suddenly she ran to the shed and came out with a long hoe.

'Will I take all this with me when I go? Will I take this with me when I die?'

She began to smash the sauce jars. The children began to push into the yard to get a better view. They were not the only spectators. Soon, grown-ups had entered as well. No one tried to stop her and no one tried to comfort her. As if their mouths were sealed, children and adults alike stood and watched her smash up her household belongings. The soya sauce jar was broken. Black liquid gushed out.

'Aren't you afraid of heaven!'

For the first time someone shouted.

'Afraid of heaven?' she cried, foaming at the mouth and twisting her body, 'Afraid of heaven? Why? Am I a murderer?'

She stood undaunted facing the surrounding crowd.

'What kind of law is this? What has my husband done for those bastard officers to drag him off like a dog? Everyone knows the great power of the Choi house but they can't put this crime on to an innocent man! Heaven knows, earth knows and the spirits know that he's innocent! Just you wait and see! Wait and see, I say! He will be cleared and released! Heaven knows, earth knows – he'll be cleared. Now I know what's in your hearts! I know what you're really like! What neighbours!'

She came to a stop and looked around her. Twenty or thirty

pairs of eyes stared at her coldly. Children and adults alike, they did nothing but stare at her face, which had gone a deep shade of red.

'As the saying goes, "Even if your mouth is twisted, speak straight!" Is my husband the sort of man who'd kill someone? His only sin is that he lent his seed, that's all! That most evil bitch in all the world, that bitch who eats men alive, it's her and that devil Pyongsan between them that have done it! It's a thousand times, ten-thousand times wrong – why should my husband be unjustly blamed? It's that bitch, that bitch that wound herself round him like a water snake – even if I pulled her liver out and ate it, it wouldn't be enough! Listen to me, all of you! What man would ever refuse a woman? They wouldn't say "no" to ten women. When that bitch, as sly as a thousand-year-old fox, offered him her body, who would be so daft as to say no? If there's a man as daft as that anywhere, I'd like to polish my eyes and have a good look at him! Do you hear, I'd like to polish my eyes and have a good look at him!'

'. . . .'

'Have I said anything wrong? Isn't it all true? Why don't you say something? Not a word from you! If I'm right, say so, or if I'm wrong! I ought to go and hang myself like Gobok's mother – is that what you want? Even though I'm innocent, I'm to go and hang myself on a tree – is that what you want? I see! You are ready to bury me when I'm dead. You've come here to watch me dying?'

'. . . .'

'So, you feel sorry about the death of a murderer's wife, but not for the wife of an innocent man who has been taken away on a false charge? What good neighbours! What good neighbours you are!'

She fell to the ground in a faint.

The next morning Chilsung's little cottage was left empty and in disorder. Yimi *ne* had taken the children and gone. The news of her midnight flight soon spread through the village. People had swarmed round Haman *dek*'s house the day before but now it was almost deserted and looked even more desolate. The villagers feared the eyes of the Choi house. In fact, Samsoo had gone there in the evening and caused a disturbance. It was not that he would have been encouraged by any member of the household, but rather his own way of looking down on people weaker than himself. When the vigorous Yongpari set off with the coffin on his A-frame, he was followed only by a few young men with hoes and spades, and there was hardly anyone to see her off on her last journey. A few people watched from a distance as the coffin came out but from fear of Yoon Bo's sarcasm they quickly disappeared into their houses. Already their concern was focused on who would get the land that had been tilled by Chilsung.

As they walked up the shaded hillside, Yoon Bo asked, 'Is it heavy? Are you tired?'

'It's all right,' said Yongpari briefly but, as the road became even steeper, he bent further under the weight.

'I don't know what I've got to do with dead bodies but, counting only the ones that I've laid out myself, there's been over ten,' said Yoon Bo as he looked up at the clouds that floated over the ridge of the mountains.

Yongi and Hanjo walked in silence, and a little behind, Suh *subang* followed them and then, much further back, Gobok and Hanbok.

Yoon Bo slipped past Yongpari and walked ahead. Across the steep northern face of the hill the wind whistled noisily. Between the branches of the thin dry pines, remarkable only for their height, shone a blue sky that seemed to have no connection with the shady spot where they were. On the poor pebbly ground rolled little pine cones smaller than chestnuts. Here and there clumps of azalea doggedly trying to push out buds caught the eye.

'It's fairly flat here. I don't think we need to look any further,' said Yoon Bo as he tapped with his hoe a space that looked barely big enough for a grave. Yongpari leaned on his stick as he lowered the legs of his A-frame. He released his shoulders from it, propped it up with the stick and wiped his forehead.

'I wonder if the ground has thawed,' said Hanjo, as he stood by the coffin.

'I don't know. It's a bit on the shady side, isn't it?'

Yoon Bo dug his toes into the gravel.

'There's so many pebbles.'

602

'We can't be too fussy. It's the best we can do.'

Suh *subang* came up short of breath and added in a whining tone, 'I'll have to just watch I'm afraid – I can't help with the work.'

'Help me with the right position, then,' said Yoon Bo.

'Which way should the head go?'

'I'm not a diviner but let's see.'

He pointed his walking stick in the air to work out the directions. 'This is north-west. That's it, put the head towards that side.'

The faces of Gobok and Hanbok were shiny with tears that had dried like glue. Hanbok's upper lip was red as a cat's where his nose had been running.

'H'm, that fellow Yi Pangi,' Yoon Bo mumbled as he struck with his hand hoe. Yongi was silent as they dug the ground together.

'He seems to have had an almighty row with his wife over her sending us that porridge. That'll be it. That's why there's been no sign of her today.'

'They're afraid of what the Choi house might think – that'll be why,' said Suh *subang* as he filled his pipe.

'As I say, he's the sort of chap who would roast beans from a flash of lightning. It's no good trying to be too smart.'

'Well, it's loyalty, isn't it? Not only has he had a piece of sacrificial paddy but his ancestors have eaten off them for generations.'

'That's not loyalty. Bowing and scraping because of a bit of land, is that what you call loyalty? It's a mentality that will keep him an underling all his life. I know very well that he's not malicious or wicked. But as a man he's as shallow as the bottom of a dish, no depth – that's what I mean. Still, he's been lucky with his wife.'

'Hell, it's nothing but pebbles,' grumbled Hanjo, who had been digging.

They took turns and dug deeper until soft yellow soil appeared. Yoon Bo picked up a handful and examined it.

'Maybe this is a propitious site for a grave. The soil's like pure gold – look at it!'

But no one showed any interest in the subject. Even for the speaker himself, they were just words. When you thought about the two brothers with both parents gone, branded as the offspring of a criminal, their future as bleak as the poor soil of this northern slope, what nonsense it was to talk about 'a propitious site'.

Suh *subang*, who had stood by steadily smoking, said, 'You never know. A good grave plot is like a child-shaped ginseng root – it can't be obtained by human power.'

'H'm, what's the use of food to those who've already died of hunger or a blanket to those who've frozen to death?' said Hanjo sardonically as he wiped his brow.

'Well, there's a story. Long long ago, while fleeing from a disaster, a mother died and her two sons buried her roughly at the side of the road. At the end of their struggles they were successful and amassed great riches but they had one continuing worry – the thought of how they had left their poor mother buried at the road-side. So one day they set off together. They groped after their early memories and, as they say, "Devotion can move Heaven," for eventually they found the spot. As money was no object, they paid an enormous fee to bring along a famous geomancer who selected the best spot and they set about moving the body. When the gravedigger dug it up and lifted the lid, a cloud of steam rose like a winter fog. At this the geomancer cried, "Oh dear!" and ordered the gravedigger to put the lid back quickly – this had been itself the very best spot.'

Yongpari swallowed as he said, 'So what happened?'

'As the grave had been opened, the power had all evaporated. After that they failed completely. They say they were reduced to beggary overnight.'

When they had lowered the coffin and built up the dome of earth over the grave, a little sunshine crept through the tall thin pines. All the time the work was in progress the two boys had stood fixed to the spot. Their faces were black with cold and their frozen fingers bent like the claws of a crab. Yoon Bo dusted the soil from his hands as he stood back. Rising to his feet, Suh *subang* made a little speech of thanks: 'Well done, lads. I'm very grateful. Yongpari, you too – carrying a corpse about on an A-frame in broad daylight.'

'If it had been one of my own family, I couldn't have done such a thing – not take a coffin on an A-frame in broad daylight,' said Yongpari with a wry smile.

'That's what I mean.'

Yongpari and Hanjo were resting their bottoms on a rock. Yoon Bo, filling his pipe, called, 'Gobok!'

The boy, still standing stiffly in his place, glanced up at him.

'Do you know what day it is today? It's the seventeenth. So the day of your mother's death was the sixteenth of February and this is her grave. You'll remember that, won't you?'

At that moment Gobok, who had been standing stiffly all this time, suddenly started to run. Like a bull with head lowered and horns aimed at the target, he ran and butted the trunk of a pine tree. He butted it again and again and broke into a wail that shook the mountain.

'*Hyong*! Brother!' shouted Hanbok as he stamped his feet, but his voice, frozen by the cold, was stifled. Tears streamed down his cheeks. Yongi ran over and seized Gobok. Blood flowed from his forehead where it had been pierced by the gnarled tree.

Yoon Bo collected his tools and started down without a word, as if in anger. The others fell in behind. The boys, too, had nothing else to do but to follow the grown-ups. By the time they were back in the village the sun was sinking fast in the west.

Chapter Fifty-Three

THE curious thing was that Pyongsan did not seem to lose weight. In the purgatory-like jail, where the only food was a lump of boiled millet and his body was torn and bruised all over from daily interrogations, his weight did not go down. This is not to say that he was looking well. Like the body of a drowned man brought up out of the water, his flesh was so swollen that it reminded one of a globefish. Compared to Chilsung, who was nothing but skin and bone, as if ready to die at any moment, he looked even worse. His inability to lose weight seemed to be due to some natural tendency or, if not, some kind of disease. Not only did he look like a clown or laughing stock, but he also behaved like one – perhaps that was how he prolonged his life a little.

'You, rascal, why can't you make a straightforward confession?'

'I will, your honour!'

He looked up to heaven and then down to earth. His gestures were always exactly the same. Then he would loudly smack his lips and begin a so-called straightforward confession before the head of the court: 'I was born a gentleman, the rightful heir of an officer's family, and, though our fortunes have declined, I am not the man to abandon the honour of a gentleman and conspire with a low-class servant girl. Moreover, as the woman has made clear, and as you, my lord, have established, I never had intercourse with her. Also, in committing such an atrocious crime, secrecy, absolute secrecy, would have been essential, so is it likely that I would disclose it to that rascal and ask him to be my accomplice? In the unlikely circumstance that I did covet the wealth of the Choi house and intended to harm them, it would have been natural for me to have intercourse with the girl myself and sow my own seed, but as it is as clear as can be that this was not the case, how can I be guilty? Even a small child could understand that, so I appeal to you, sir, to release me, and, as I have said over and over again, I was born a gentleman, the rightful heir of an officer's family, though our fortunes have declined . . .'.

The judge and the other officials who shared the bench held back their laughter as they listened to his dignified statements.

'Yes, I see. Just tell me, then, whether or not the rogue Chilsung was involved in the plot?'

Carried away by his own eloquence, he said, 'No, sir, he only lent the seed.'

Then with an 'Oh, dear!' to himself, he hurriedly stuck out his tongue to wet his pig-like protruding lips.

'You rascal!'

'I didn't mean that, my lord. I know nothing about it.'

'Thrash him until the truth comes out!'

'Yes, sir.'

The torturer dragged him to the frame and tied him down.

'My lord, it's unfair! I am as innocent as a babe!'

After the first stroke he would say, 'My lord! Have I betrayed my country? What is my crime?'

But before the fifth stroke had passed, 'I admit I did it! I . . . him . . . I did it with a hemp cord . . . r . . . r . . . round his neck.'

Then when he was taken off the frame and brought before the judge he would begin again, 'I was born a gentleman, the rightful heir of an officer's family, though our fortunes have declined . . .'

It was truly a scene from a farce.

'Crazy idiot.'

The judge bit back his laughter while the officials enjoyed the spectacle of Pyongsan, swollen like a globefish.

On the other hand, when Guinyo was interrogated, faced with the two men, she spoke in a clear, ringing voice and never once denied her crime. She told it all without hiding anything. Only when she stated that Chilsung was also involved in the plot, did she depart from the truth.

'When you had secret intercourse, were you just committing adultery or were you also involved in the murder?'

'We were involved in the murder, sir.'

'That – that bitch deserves to be struck dead!'

Chilsung tied up with a rope, would jump up and run towards

her and, with his foot encased in a worn straw shoe, give her a kick on the bottom. Each time this happened, the officer who held the rope was pulled along with him. Guinyo gave him a sidelong glance as a chilly smile spread over her face.

(Bastard! I'll drag you down with me. Do you think I will go by myself and leave you alive after you trampled on my pure body just for greed? No chance, no chance at all!)

'You bitch. The most wicked woman in the whole world! You cru . . . cru . . . cruel . . . Are – aren't you afraid of heaven?'

He jumped up and down until, exhausted, he clenched his teeth and fell in a faint. However much he was tortured, he never admitted to having any part in the plot. Through torture, distress and hatred he became as emaciated as the bark of a tree, as though the flame of his life might at any moment be extinguished, but his hatred of Guinyo and his desire for revenge seemed to keep him going. His front teeth were all broken and gone.

Pyongsan and Chilsung were in due course executed. With no one to take away their bodies, they rotted in a desolate field, the prey of stray dogs and crows. Because of her pregnant condition, Guinyo's execution was postponed until after she had been delivered.

· Meanwhile, early in January, Kang *posoo*, having left Chiri Mountain and gone in the direction of Kangwon Province, lost his usual self-control and hunted rather ruthlessly. Doubt about his skill after his failure with the boar, and his inconsolable love for Guinyo – to forget these pains, he had gone wild. In this way, on one occasion, he felled a doe, and when he seized it, saw that it was with young. From that moment he came to his senses and, in so doing decided to go back to Chiri Mountain. All the way back he was troubled by the thought of the pregnant doe. He had never forgotten a story told by the hunter who brought him up. It had remained as a kind of moral precept that he had strictly observed and now, for the first time he had broken it. He could not deny that he had known the doe was pregnant. It was not that he had realized it only after killing it but rather that, having done it, he was reminded of the teaching and repented. The story was as follows. A hunter, on his way, came upon a deer. Seeing him, the animal did not run away. As he aimed his gun without hesitating it looked at him with sad eyes, raised its front legs and waved. It seemed to be a gesture that appealed for mercy. Curious, the man examined it carefully and saw that it was in the process of giving birth. Nevertheless, the greedy hunter fired and killed it. He slung it over his shoulder and was on his way home in high spirits when he saw another deer standing blankly in the vegetable plot in front of his house. Thinking to himself what a lucky day it was, he felled this one as well. Very pleased with himself he called to his wife as he entered the house. What was the matter? Another deer stood upright in the yard. He quickly reloaded his gun with powder and killed it. It turned out that the creature that looked like a deer had been his wife and the other in the yard his child.

When he reached Sanchong, Kang *posoo* met at a tavern a fire-field farmer whom he recognised.

'You must have made quite a lot of money, Kang *posoo*.'

'Nothing to speak of.'

He waved his hand in the air, but in fact, he had collected quite a heavy load of goods that could immediately be changed into money if put out on market day, including the skin of the pregnant doe. As he drank with the farmer and chatted about this and that, he finally came to hear the story of the terrible murder at the Choi *champan* house. Though it actually happened before he had left for Kangwon Province, news from the outside world was slow to reach the hills, so that it was not only fresh to him but a very great shock.

'Wh – wh – what? Is it true?'

He sprang up, nearly overturning the table. He went as far as the vicinity of the Sangae-sa, where he stayed the night, and, catching the ferry from Hwagae in the morning, he reached the town the same day. He passed the night in an inn without a wink of sleep and the next day, by selling about half of his goods, he was able to raise a considerable sum of money and set off to see the jailor. Though there was no way he could save her life, he had made up his mind to look after her until her last day. It was late in the night when he went to see her with food that he had collected.

'Who is it that wants to see me?'

Her clear ringing voice was heard from within the dark jail.

'Me. Me – it's me, Kang *posoo*.'

As his eyes became accustomed to the dark, he saw her whitish face through the barred window. It seemed that, as a serious offender, she was held in shackles.

'Kang *posoo*, – why did you come?'

'Heartless girl!'

He grabbed the bars and shook them with his leathery hands as he swallowed his sobs.

'H'm!'

'How could you do such a thing? Weren't you afraid of Heaven?'

'Shut up. What's the use of talking like that to someone who's about to die?'

'You heartless woman. What's money? – to do a thing like that!'

'Whether you die one way or the other, death is all the same.'

Kang *posoo* visited her again the next evening. He bribed the jailor and brought her some more food. Until his money ran out, he came to see her every night. She did not seem to be pleased to see him, nor grateful. But he offered her his pure heart.

(I have run out of money. What can I do?)

In the innermost room of the tavern, he sighed. As he was a familiar figure and known as a man who would pay his debts, there was no difficulty about his staying on, but without money he could not take care of Guinyo. To go back to the hills to hunt and earn more was out of the question in such an urgent situation. As soon as the child was born she would die. There was not much time left before the expected time of birth. His helpless looking whiskered face grew shabbier. Whoever the father might be, he intended to bring up the child himself. For that, no small sum of money would be needed, but for the moment to look after her was the more urgent task.

Spring had come. Without his noticing them, the peach blossoms outside the tavern fence were already falling. The weeping willows that had looked like a lime-coloured mist in the distance were now a clear shade of green. The voices of children, chattering as they passed the tavern, echoed high and clear. Without a word about going or coming back, he left the tavern. He caught the ferry. The helmsman had heard rumours about him and, smiling broadly, tried to tease him by asking why his face was in such a state but the hunter just stood with his eyes fixed on the far off hills that bordered the river. In the village, the work in the fields was at its height. People and oxen alike were out working in the warm sunshine of late spring. To avoid meeting anyone, he kept off the road and hurried on between fields where the owners were not about. Along the paths between the plots, the weeds grew rank and buzzed with insects. When he came to the top of the rise on which the Choi house stood, instead of going to the servants' gate, he went round the wall of the *sarang* to Kim *subang*'s vegetable plot, where plump hens pecked at the lettuces. He stopped and quietly peered into the yard. Beyond the kitchen door flickered the end of Mrs Kim's skirt. He saw that she was hopping backwards and forwards over the threshold with a bottle on her head. It was a flagon with a long slender neck. She held it with both hands as she continued to hop back and forth over the threshold, mumbling, 'Mr Vinegar, come, live with me as I have no man. Mr Vinegar, Mr Vinegar, come, live with me as I have no man.'

Then she would lower the bottle and loudly kiss it. Even this spectacle did not make him smile as he furtively approached her.

'Mrs Kim.'

'My goodness, who is it? Why, it's Kang *posoo*!'

'Yes.'

'The vinegar is about to die, so I'm trying to revive it with an incantation, 'Mr Vinegar, Mr Vinegar, come, live with me as I have no man.'

She kissed it once more as she took it away to the jar stand where she put it down and came back.

'They say that one night's stay is enough to establish a lasting relationship . . . '.

She began, in a tone that suggested a lengthy rebuke.

'From last summer you followed our master, eating from the same pot . . . How could you behave like that? Thousands of people came from all over the place to weep at his funeral and you didn't show even the tip of your nose.'

'I didn't know about it. I'd gone away to Kangwon *do*.'

'Kangwon? From what I've heard, you are always hanging around in the town after that wicked woman in the jail.'

'. . .'

'As they say, "Save an animal and it rewards you, but save a man and you get cursed." '

His eyes flashed.

'Here, we are all shaking with anger at not being able to tear her to pieces . . . it's just as well her ladyship doesn't know what you are up to or you wouldn't be able to set foot in the village.'

At this moment Kim *subang* appeared. The hunter's face became tense.

'It's a long time since I saw you.'

He spoke first.

'It is, indeed.'

Kim *subang* did not look pleased either. It seemed as though he also had heard about his staying in the town because of Guinyo.

'I want to have a word with you.'

'What is it then?'

'Can we go outside for a minute?'

He looked even more displeased, but he was incapable of being callous, and followed him out. As he came out, Kang *posoo* noticed for the first time that the pavilion on Dangsan had gone. His fixed expression grew even stiffer. He stood for a while as if he had lost his tongue.

'If you've got something to say, speak up.'

'Well, it's about . . .'.

He stopped and began again,

'I have come here shamelessly . . .'.

'. . .'

'It's partly due to fate, and no doubt I was blind, but when the Master was still alive . . . that is while we were in the hills – instead of any wages, or rifle, I asked him for Guinyo.'

'What?'

'He didn't say anything at the time. Then we came back with Soodong in that state. I was feeling ashamed so I just went away. As I was given only my expenses when I left, I felt bad about it . . .'.

Unlike his usual self, he spoke calmly and with logic.

'As you will understand, Mr Kim, if I had been busy hunting all through the summer until the winter – not that I want to argue about that, especially when I think about what that stupid woman has done. However, whether it's because I am blind or because love is an awful thing, she hasn't got much longer to live.'

Tears came to his eyes. All that he said was new to Kim *subang*. At last, he seemed to understand what Choi Chisoo had meant when he had said that he would know what to do.

(Had the master intended to give her to Kang *posoo*?)

Being sensitive and kindly, he was sorry about the hunter's unhappy state and felt something pierce his own heart.

'Besides, who's going to look after the child when it comes? What crime has that little thing committed? You can't just throw away a baby, can you?'

(It's true that he was sent away with nothing more than his travelling expenses. Even a common servant gets paid when he has done a job, and he is a famous hunter. He did not want to come, and had to be forced into it . . . now that I know, I can see that it was natural for him to be put out. Don't I know what a good man he is?)

'I swore never to stand again before this gate. I realized that there was a distance of a thousand miles between the world of the aristocrats and that of the lower classes. What made me come back after all is the girl, that sinful and heartless girl . . . during her last days to provide at least some water and rice . . . who is there in the whole world to care about her? I could tear her to pieces, but a man's love . . . this love is an awful thing.'

Kang *posoo* was about to cry.

'I see. I understand. Don't say another word – just wait here. When I think about how her ladyship feels, I daren't open my mouth, but . . .'.

He quickly disappeared into the inner quarters. The hunter flung himself down on the ground. He saw nothing before his eyes except the vision of a boar running towards him baring its spear-like white fangs. How long had it been? Suddenly it seemed to be getting dark all around. When he opened his eyes, he saw that passing

613

clouds were covering the sun, white clouds like clusters of cotton wool.

'Kang *posoo*,' called Kim *subang*.

He looked round. Dori came with a sack which he put down in front of him and hurried away without a word of greeting. Kim *subang*'s face was bleached. Even his lips were white.

'On my own account, I requested three hundred *yang* which her ladyship has granted. To begin with I've brought one hundred. Take this for now and go. You can come back and collect the other two hundred another day. You'd better leave at once.'

He pointed to the sack of a hundred *yang* put down at his feet.

'Thank you . . . Thank you.'

'Hurry up and go!'

His lips were still white. The hunter returned to the town that day and, bribing the jailor with a few coins, met Guinyo in the evening. She treated him as coldly as before, as if for her he did not exist. As he continued to see her every few days, she began to behave hysterically towards him. These hysterics grew worse and developed into violence and ravings.

'What's this? Do you expect me to eat these rotten mouldy persimmons? Your eyes must've gone wrong! Pull them out if they can't tell rotten persimmons and let the dogs eat them.'

She threw them at his face as he pressed it against the bars of the jail.

'You look like a brigand from the hills and you want to be a philanderer – for an old thing, what cheek and how shameless! I can't stand the sight of you, so for heaven's sake don't show yourself here in front of me again! Ah, I'm going crazy! My guts are turning over!'

She would rave like this and then at the next moment chatter about such whims as having some steamed cake, or wanting some spring-onion pancakes. Then he would hurry off to get the things for which she craved. Even then she would find fault with him and pour out abuse. She screamed as she wept, telling him to fall into a ditch and die on the way, as she beat her breast. But the more she did so, the more he felt comforted on his way, as if he had taken half of her pain upon himself. It might be that on the day

614

when her life ended his also would come to an end. That is not to say that they would die together, but rather that after her death his life could not go on the same but would have to change its form.

Now they were together. One inside the prison and the other outside, their hands beyond each other's reach, separated by the stern power of the law – so near and yet so infinitely far – feeling each other's presence only by sight, and yet he had never before felt her so close to him as he did now. Even when he had laid her down on the pile of fallen leaves, she had been a most distant being. The question of whether or not she liked him no longer had any meaning. It did not concern him whether she was a cursed demon or a blessed angel. All that mattered was that she was there, and that he was there as the only one who cared about her.

The day of delivery seemed to be drawing near. Often he wondered whether the child in her womb was his own, but such thoughts disappeared at once like bubbles. The birth of the child meant her death – birth for one was death for the other. Her death was, for him, an overflowing flood, a flood of red, muddy water that he was powerless to stop.

He had given up wine but took to drinking a cup or two again. The departure of spring and the coming of summer were for him unbearable. Day by day the amount he drank increased. As her ferocity grew, so did his drinking, though not on its former scale, partly because his body was weakened and partly because he had to be careful about money. He was using the further two hundred *yang* that Dori had brought from the Choi house on a donkey last market day, which he had left in the keeping of the tavern. When he had used it all he would indeed be in trouble. As he drank, he looked out on a world that seemed to be turning just as usual. As always the traders popped in and out. Among those who loosened the strings of their soiled purses or did them up again, were familiar faces and unfamiliar. If there were bachelors of twenty, there were also men with white hair. He saw some peasants from Pyongsa-ri quarrelling as they passed the tavern. They seemed to have forgotten the tumultuous and terrible affair at the Choi house. They seemed also to have completely forgotten that a female servant still lay in jail, her life barely preserved because of her expected child. All they talked about was the weather and the barley harvest or the mating of cows and pigs. The traders, as traders will, just waited to see how much grain or money they could get out of the peasants. To get more out of them, they could not but hope for a good season. Some were concerned with national affairs. They argued about whether or not the king had taken poison and whether there would be a state funeral. If there were, everyone would need white hempen hats, so the losers would be the makers of ordinary hats. Thus the hat-makers worried lest there be a state funeral, while the pedlars complained that, because of brigands using the name of the Dong Hak, the hill-paths were dangerous, and poor scholars lamented that learning had lost its usefulness while pack loads of bribes to buy posts or promotions still went up to Seoul.

'With money, a commoner becomes a gentleman. It's no use at all holding up a family tree if you've got no money. Yes, when a commoner becomes a gentleman and goes to live somewhere else, that makes sense, but I can't stand it when a man who's clearly lost his wealth still keeps putting on the airs of a gentleman.'

'Documents everywhere are in confusion,' said an educated man.

Kang *posoo* left the tavern for a few days to travel through the hills and, when he had arranged for a wet nurse, he returned.

(As I haven't seen her for several days, she must have missed me.)

He went there taking some steamed cake and dried fish from the market.

'Guinyo,' he called in a low voice.

He called again but there was no answer.

'It's me. Kang *posoo*.'

A voice was heard, 'Huh, he's come back. I thought he'd dropped dead somewhere.'

He let out a sigh of relief.

'I've brought you something to eat. Come and get it.'

She could be heard dragging herself nearer. She stretched her hand through the bars.

'I'll just push it through. Put your hand back.'

He was about to push the parcel lengthwise through the bars.

'Kang *posoo*, your hand.'

'What?'

He drew back in astonishment.

'Give me your hand.'

She still held out her own through the bars. Scared, he trembled as he held her small hand in his. Such a tiny hand, it seemed as though it would break in his grip.

'You've gone thin – very thin.'

'Your hands are like leather.'

Her voice was soft and low.

'Here – you must be hungry.'

He was going to push the parcel through when, on her own accord, she grabbed hold of his hand.

'Kang *posoo*, I have been wicked – forgive me.'

'As long as you know, it's all right.'

'The reason I was so rude to you was because I was sorry. I wish I could live with you and dig the soil . . . to be your wife, give birth to your child . . .'.

She began to sob. When he came out, he pushed his head against the wall and cried like a wild creature. In the sky the stars shone. The Plough was clear and sparkling.

Just after the middle of May, in the prison, she gave birth to a son. She died without hating the world. Kang *posoo* disappeared, carrying in his arms the little bundle of blood that she had borne. He never appeared again to anyone who had known him, nor was there anyone who could claim to have seen him. No one knew what became of him.